Classroom Companion: Business

The Classroom Companion series in Business features foundational and introductory books aimed at students to learn the core concepts, fundamental methods, theories and tools of the subject. The books offer a firm foundation for students preparing to move towards advanced learning. Each book follows a clear didactic structure and presents easy adoption opportunities for lecturers.

Dirk Klimkeit • Pengji Wang • Huiping Zhang

# International Management in Service Firms

## Environments, Strategies and Operations

Springer

Dirk Klimkeit
Baden-Wuerttemberg Cooperative State University (DHBW)
Stuttgart, Germany

Huiping Zhang
James Cook University Singapore
Singapore, Singapore

Pengji Wang
James Cook University Singapore
Singapore, Singapore

ISSN 2662-2866 ISSN 2662-2874 (electronic)
Classroom Companion: Business
ISBN 978-3-031-50344-3 ISBN 978-3-031-50345-0 (eBook)
https://doi.org/10.1007/978-3-031-50345-0



This Springer imprint is published by the registered company Springer Nature Switzerland AG
The registered company address is: Gewerbestrasse 11, 6330 Cham, Switzerland

Paper in this product is recyclable.

# Preface

Service firms increasingly dominate the world economy, making up about two-thirds of global value creation. Indeed, many of the biggest multinational firms are service firms. Services account for two-thirds of global foreign direct investment. At the same time, the international management of service firms exhibits many specific features different from manufacturing firms. Nevertheless, until now, there is no English-language textbook focusing on the specifics of international management in service firms. This textbook aims to address this gap with its focus on service firms' internationalization and international management.

## What Is Special About This Textbook?

The book starts with a brief outline of the specifics of service firms and their role in the global economy, followed by an overview of the international environment that faces service firms. Besides the internationalization process, it then characterizes the multinational service firm and its strategies and organization. Unlike most texts on international services, the book goes beyond internationalization and addresses the ongoing management of service firms. In addition to functions such as global service marketing, financial management, and human resource management, it contains chapters on topics not usually found in international business (IB) textbooks:

- Global account management
- Global service delivery management
- International project management
- International corporate governance
- Managing distributed virtual teams
- Offshore shared services and business process outsourcing
- International change management

Discussions of ethics and the corporate social responsibility of multinational service firms, as well as managing services across cultures, complement these chapters.

Each chapter starts with an opening case study that raises students' attention to key issues of the upcoming chapter with real-world examples. Chapters wrap up with closing case studies that illustrate further ideas from the chapter. This is complemented with case study questions, illustrations, a chapter summary, and revision questions. Definitions are highlighted in boxes throughout the text. Many chapters contain additional embedded case studies for illustration.

For the first time, this book brings together insights from the fragmented literature on the subject in an accessible textbook. The work additionally benefits from insights from our own research. Since we have also been teaching the topics we write about here for many years, this helped us make them appealing to a student audience. As a Euro-Asian author team based in Germany and Singapore, we aim to provide a global perspective, bringing together the East and the West. We include

case studies from around the world. Drawing on our specific areas of specialization, we have divided the work in such a way that each of us took the lead for several of the chapters as follows:
- Dirk Klimkeit: ► 1 (with Pengji Wang), ► 3, 4, 6, 8, 9, 10, 11, 14, 15, 17, 18
- Pengji Wang: ► 1 (with Dirk Klimkeit), ► 2, 7, 12, 13
- Huiping Zhang: ► 5, 16

## Aims and Objectives

- To provide an accessible and interesting textbook for students that brings together knowledge on international management in service firms, integrating research insights, cases, and examples of practical application
- To prepare students for international careers in the dominant sector of the world economy
- To provide a truly global perspective with an author team combining the West and the East
- To provide a text in international management of service firms that will be as applicable and valuable for small- and medium-sized enterprises as it is for large international corporations

## Target Audience

While the book has a focus on service firms, we deliberately designed it in such a way that it can be used as well in general courses on international business. It contains most of what one would expect from an IB textbook and more, plus the specifics of service firms. We believe the book can be valuable for:
- Undergraduate and postgraduate students in study programs on International Business, International Management, Service Management, or Service Marketing
- Students enrolled in respective specializations/majors or elective modules of General Management courses and others that cover Service Management or International Management
- Those enrolled in management education courses
- Managers involved with international service management, from CEOs to country managers
- Entrepreneurs who are interested in starting international service businesses

**Dirk Klimkeit**
Stuttgart, Germany

**Pengji Wang**
Singapore, Singapore

**Huiping Zhang**
Singapore, Singapore

# Acknowledgments

We thank Matthias Mohr at DHBW Stuttgart for a friendly review of ► Chaps. 5 and 16. We thank our editors Jialin Yan and Yvonne Schwark-Reiber at Springer Nature for their support.

We hope you enjoy this textbook.

**Dirk Klimkeit**
Stuttgart, Germany

**Pengji Wang**
Singapore, Singapore

**Huiping Zhang**
Singapore, Singapore

# Contents

# III The Ongoing Management of Multinational Service Firms

# List of Case Studies

# The International Environment for Service Firms

Contents

# Introduction: Services in International Business

Contents




D. Klimkeit et al., *International Management in Service Firms*, Classroom Companion: Business,
https://doi.org/10.1007/978-3-031-50345-0_1

**Learning Outcomes**

After completing this chapter, you should be able to:

- Define services
- Describe distinctive characteristics of services
- Distinguish different types of services
- Outline the concept of the service triangle

## Introduction

This short chapter aims to set the scene for the book by introducing some key terms and concepts relevant to the international management of service firms. It defines services and their unique characteristics. Different types of services are distinguished. Concepts relevant to the international provision of services, especially the service triangle, are introduced.

Flixbus. (Image by Konrad Krajewski from Pixabay)

## Opening Case: Flixbus: We Know Nothing About Buses!

The office of Jochen Engert, co-founder of Flixbus, contains several yoga balls and surfboards. Outside his office, a slide allows employees to reach their offices one floor below quickly. Flixbus, a major operator of coaches in Europe, likes to see itself as an IT startup, and its management claims, "We know nothing about buses!" (Economist, 2015).

Flixbus started in 2013 as one of 13 companies that took advantage of the liberalization of the German coach market. Until 2012, to protect the state-owned rail company, Deutsche Bahn, coaches running within Germany on routes longer than 50 km were not allowed for decades. Of the initial 13 companies, Flixbus is one of the few who survived and now has a more than 90% market share. This came about as Flixbus acquired one by one its main competitors who were struggling to be profitable in this initially very competitive market. First, Flixbus merged with its main competitor Meinfernbus in 2016. However, it soon turned out it was really a takeover of Meinfernbus by the smaller Flixbus. Only the green color of Meinfernbus and the slogan "Go green!" of Meinfernbus were retained, as the management of Flixbus believed that this slogan was unbeatable. Flixbus designed the new branding to be "internationally clear and consistent" (Fockenbrock, 2016a), which already demonstrated Flixbus' aspirations beyond the borders of Germany. Indeed, André Schwämmlein announced following the merger with Meinfernbus, "Together, we make Europe green!" (Fockenbrock & Koenen, 2016). In 2016 Flixbus took over competitor Postbus, and the last major competitor, Deutsche Bahn, gave up its coach service. Flixbus occupied all feasible routes and drove competitors out with aggressive pricing.

Outside of Germany, Flixbus acquired the Continental European operations of Scottish competitor Megabus. Megabus continued to operate as a subcontractor to Flixbus. Flixbus expanded to Italy, France, and Scandinavia. In France, it benefited from a similar market liberalization as in Germany. Beyond meeting basic safety standards, authorities required no license anymore to operate a coach service. In Poland, Flixbus entered a cooperation with market leader Polskibus. In Austria, the network of Hellö coaches of rail operator ÖBB was taken over and integrated into the network of Flixbus. The arguably most striking market entry of Flixbus is its latest one: In 2021, Flixbus took over the iconic Greyhound buses of the United States that were almost synonymous with coach travel in the United States. Before, Flixbus was active on the US West Coast, but now taking over 1200 buses, drivers, and the Greyhound brand, they suddenly became number one in the US coach market. Besides, Flixbus has already entered the Brazilian and Turkish markets. In Turkey, they had successfully taken over coach operator Kamil Koc, which convinced investors that they could also lead the Greyhound acquisition to success. Through the Greyhound takeover, Flixbus now also operates in Canada and Mexico.

The basis for Flixbus' success in these competitive markets can be seen in various reasons: Following an "asset light" strategy, Flixbus generally does not own the buses or employ the drivers but draws on subcontractors. Sometimes, Flixbus convinces hotels to own the buses, as they can bring them guests. Flixbus itself focuses on its IT-driven marketing and booking platform. This explains the surprising opening statement that the company understands nothing of buses. Once the platform is set up, it can be scaled quickly at virtually no cost. In the United States, while taking over the assets of Greyhound is a departure from its asset-light strategy, Flixbus intends the acquisition to bring Greyhound onto Flixbus' booking platform, using it as a lever. After some initial investment, the platform allows Flixbus to make profits quickly. As stated by commentator Jens Koenen:

> "Flixbus is shaking up the US market with intelligent technology" (Koenen, 2021b, p 27).

Success can be further attributed to its private investors who were patient enough to wait until 2016 for Flixbus to become profitable, while the shareholders of the often publicly listed competitors were losing patience more quickly. Flixbus also undertakes significant efforts to have high utilization of its buses of at least 60%.

Flixbus is also taking on the challenge of reducing emissions to fight climate change. In 2018, it launched its first fully electric bus, charged with renewable energy from Greenpeace Energy. In 2019, Flixbus partnered with Uber to connect customers' first and last mile from their homes to the Flixbus coach station and from the destination station to their final destination. Customers can use an app to book an Uber ride with the Flixbus ticket.

Flixbus is also facing challenges, however. Since March 2020, the COVID-19 (coronavirus disease-2019) pandemic has hit the bus operator hard. For an extended period, it suspended the operation of buses in Germany, Poland, and the United Kingdom. In other countries, some routes partly continued to be served. In 2021, it slowly opened some routes again, observing the development closely to open up further or restrict operations depending on government regulations. The management believes that COVID-19 delayed its global expansion by 1 or 1.5 years. Connected to losses German railway operator Deutsche Bahn incurred due to COVID-19, the German government planned to provide 5.5 billion Euro fresh equity to Deutsche Bahn. Flixmobility, the parent of Flixbus, which also operates trains in Germany under the brand Flixtrain, filed a complaint to the European Commission about the move, stating that capital support to Deutsche Bahn distorts competition and should be provided to the entire sector.

After years of rapid growth, Flixbus realized it needed to professionalize its management. In 2016, the former head of finance of Air Berlin, Arnd Schwierholz, joined the management team. For the first time, an external manager joined the leadership. As Schwierholz stated: "Flixbus is on the way to becoming an internationally recognized company" (Fockenbrock & Koenen, 2016, p 20).

**Questions**

1. Why is it beneficial for Flixbus to extend its platform to Greyhound buses?
2. Why does Flixbus emphasize internationally consistent branding, and why have they nevertheless retained the Greyhound name?
3. Why is it significant for Flixbus as a service firm to have high utilization as a target?
4. Why has the COVID-19 pandemic hit bus operators like Flixbus particularly hard?
5. Why can the fact that Flixbus uses subcontractors pose a potential challenge?
6. Why can the partnership with Uber be particularly important in some cities?

Sources: (dpa, 2018; Economist, 2015, 2018; Fockenbrock, 2016a, 2016b, 2016c, 2020, 2021; Fockenbrock & Koenen, 2016; Handelsblatt, 2019; Koenen, 2021a, 2021b; Siebenhaar & Fockenbrock, 2017).

## Service Firms in the World Economy

Walmart, Amazon, UnitedHealth Group, Berkshire Hathaway, Ping An Insurance, Alphabet (Google), Industrial and Commercial Bank of China, Microsoft, Allianz, AXA, Deutsche Telekom—some of the largest firms of the world in terms of revenue are service firms (Fortune, 2021). Whether you think of financial services, wholesale and retail, internet services, e-commerce, IT services including software, logistics and transportation, telecommunication, accounting, and legal services—today's world economy is unthinkable without service firms. Some of them provide service directly to consumers. In contrast, others provide services such as financing, insurance, logistics and transportation, or wholesale to manufacturing firms, enabling them to sell their products to customers globally. The added value created by services has been growing steadily and today makes up two-thirds of global GDP, and about half of the world population is employed in the service sector (Blagoeva et al., 2020). At the same time, deriving from the unique characteristics of services that will be addressed below, managing a service firm across a range of countries is, in many ways, different from managing the international operations of a manufacturing firm. This chapter will shed some light on this, and the remainder of this book will spell out in more detail how to manage a service firm across borders.

## What Are Services?

*Services* are multifaceted and difficult to grasp, hence the multitude of definitions in the literature. Bordoloi et al. (2019, p. 4) found that most definitions have two defining characteristics of services in common. Unlike manufactured goods, they cannot be touched (they are "intangible"), and they are typically produced at the same time as they are consumed by customers (production and consumption are "simultaneous").

**Services**

*Services* are "economic activities performed by one party to another. Often time-based, these performances bring about desired results to recipients, objects, or other assets. In exchange for money, time, and effort, service customers expect value from access to labor, skills, expertise, goods, facilities, networks, and systems. However, they do not normally take ownership of the physical elements involved" (Wirtz & Lovelock, 2018, p. 14).

This definition contains several essential elements. The fact that the receiver of a service does not acquire ownership is a key element: When you rent a car, stay in a hotel, or use a mobile connection for your mobile phone, you do not become an owner of the car, the hotel room, or the telecommunication infrastructure you use. In these examples, you pay for the temporary right to use these assets. In many cases, the "things" you obtain use rights to are less material: They could involve the knowledge, skills, and expertise of a tax consultant, lawyer, physical therapist, or hairdresser. The use rights obtained are typically restricted to a timeframe, such as one or several days for a rental car or a hotel room. Generally, the service provider conducts some performance for the customer rather than to convey a good. This can be in the literal sense of a theater or musical performance or in less literal senses, such as providing legal advice or cutting hair. Another aspect of the above definition worth noting is that the customer typically needs to provide "money, time, and effort" himself or herself. Someone using the services of a lawyer needs to not only pay significant fees but also take time to explain the problem to which advice is sought and provide relevant documents that the lawyer needs as input. Finally, the service can be provided to the customer himself or herself, such as the haircut mentioned above, or to objects of the customer, such as a car repair or the transport of a parcel, or to assets, such as the financial assets that a bank increases by paying interest on the deposits of its customers. A customer of Flixbus obtains the right to sit on a bus for a specific duration to be transported from A to B. The driver performs the service of transportation. The customer contributes by arriving at the bus stop on time, getting on and off the bus, and behaving orderly during the ride.

## Distinctive Characteristics of Services

Now that we have a basic understanding of what defines a service, let us take a closer look at the specific traits that characterize services. A review of the literature shows that the following six characteristics can be identified: customer participation, simultaneity, perishability, intangibility, heterogeneity, and non-transferrable ownership (see ◘ Fig. 1.1). Some authors list all six characteristics (Bordoloi et al., 2019, pp. 13–16; Grönroos, 2015, pp. 49–51), while others list a subset. Lovelock and Yip (1996) reject the characteristics traditionally used and suggest a set of eight alternative characteristics: the output is a performance instead of an object; customer involvement in production; people as part of the service experience; likely quality control problems; complex for customers to evaluate; lack of inventories; greater importance of time; and electronic channels available for distribution. While they are helpful in emphasizing the process character of services, by the end of the day, they can all be mapped onto the six characteristics we outline here. For example, their "likely quality problems" maps onto "heterogeneity," and their "performance, not an object" maps onto "intangibility." The literature mentions customer participation, simultaneity, and intangibility most frequently, so we start by outlining those.

**Customer Participation**: Several practical consequences for managing services derive from the customer being present in the service process to a certain degree. Moreover, the customer typically also plays an active role in creating the service he or she receives. Think of a customer at a hairdresser who needs to explain how his or her hair should be done and then sit still or move as requested by the hairdresser.

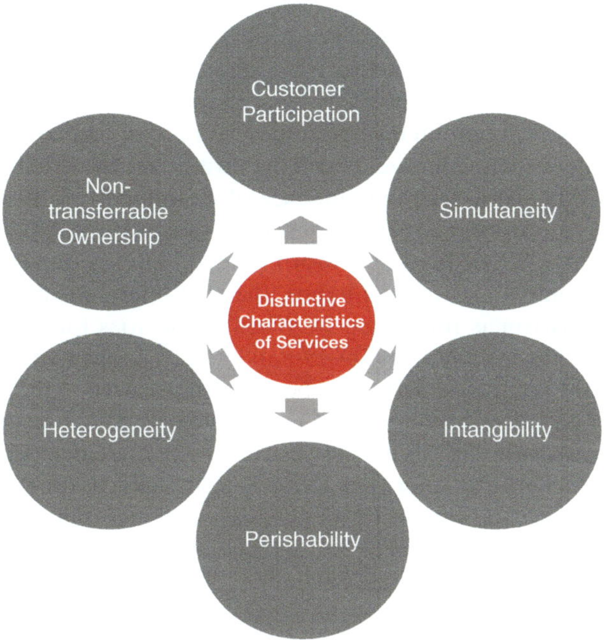


**Fig. 1.1** Distinctive characteristics of services. (Own diagram)

In professional services, customers must provide relevant information to a tax consultant or lawyer for the right advice or tax return. Therefore, customers often become co-producers, influencing the service process and its outcome (Grönroos, 2015, p. 50). This can pose challenges for the service provider if the customer does not participate appropriately as needed for efficient and effective service delivery. This can significantly impact the quality of the service and, therefore, customer satisfaction (Zeithaml & Bitner, 2003, p. 354). Suppose the information provided by the customer to the tax consultant is incomplete or inaccurate. In that case, the tax return may not be favorable, leading to inquiries from the tax authorities or even legal action. Customers of Flixbus returning late after a break can cause delays. Increasingly, customers are expected to conduct self-service, making the process effective and efficient for the firm and affordable and flexible for the customer. Consider self-check-in at airports, online banking, and self-assembly at IKEA as examples (Scherer et al., 2009) or Flixbus customers buying their tickets online. By expanding its efficient online platform to Greyhound, Flixbus expects efficiency gains. The level of customer participation varies, though, as will be outlined in detail in later chapters. Compare the attendance of a concert (low participation, simply requiring the presence of the customer) to a long-term consulting project, where the customer needs to be much more involved and actively co-create the service product (Zeithaml & Bitner, 2003, pp. 353–354).

**Simultaneity**: Since services are performances and the customer is involved in them in some form, for most services, the production and consumption of the service cannot be separated ("inseparability") but happen simultaneously. A haircut, advice from a consultant, a restaurant meal, or a concert is consumed at the same time by the customer as the service provider produces them. This is connected to the fact that most services are performances or processes rather than goods, as outlined above. While this applies to most services, technology has increasingly enabled some services to be provided separately from consumption (Erramilli, 1990). For example, a computed tomography (CT) scan can be transmitted electronically to someone who analyzes it and then transmits the results to the hospital where the scan was taken. One consequence of simultaneity is that most services cannot be stored for later sale to customers once they want to buy them (Bordoloi et al., 2019, p. 14). A hairdresser cannot produce haircuts in advance and store them before customers arrive. At Flixbus, the customer consumes the transport service while the driver is producing it. When authorities put contact reduction measures in place during the COVID-19 pandemic, Flixbus had to shut down its services in several countries. This was because the service could not be offered unless the driver and all customers were to be physically present on the bus together.

**Intangibility**: As outlined above, services can be perceived as a performance or an outcome of interaction rather than as a physical good. In other words, they are generally "intangible" and cannot be touched. This implies that a service cannot be sold on a second-hand market once provided and consumed. For the customer, this means that services cannot be inspected, unlike goods in a supermarket. Customers cannot touch, smell, or look at the service before buying it. Services are mostly so-called "experience goods" or "credence goods." Experience goods can only be evaluated once one has experienced them, e.g., a meal in a restaurant, while credence goods cannot be evaluated entirely even after experiencing them. For example, consider the services of a lawyer. Customers have to believe they fit their needs and are performed in their best interest. This sets services apart from "search goods," like a car that can be tested before the purchase (Segal-Horn & Faulkner, 2010, p. 287). A bus ride is an experience good as well. So, an internationally consistent name or a well-established brand, like Greyhound in North America, can instill confidence in potential customers contemplating a bus ride on a Flixbus in the absence of search qualities.

**Perishability**: A seat on an airplane that remains empty on a given flight cannot be sold again after the plane has taken off. Nor can a bed in a hotel that remains vacant on a given night be sold again once the night is over. From a service management perspective, the same seat on the next flight or the same bed on the following night is not the same anymore. The potential revenue lost from the vacancy cannot be recovered. So, services are "perishable." This creates problems for service providers as they have to hold a specific capacity ready if customers do turn up but cannot be sure it will be used. The problem here is variation in customer demand that cannot be fully predicted. Therefore, service providers employ several mechanisms, such as smoothing demand, adjusting service capacity to demand, or allowing customers to wait for free capacity (Bordoloi et al., 2019, pp. 14–15). In other words, service firms need to engage in *capacity management* to align demand and capacity (Ingwald et al., 2009). This is why Flixbus pursues the target of high utilization on its buses.

**Heterogeneity**: Services are performed by people interacting with the customer, called "the service encounter" or "the moment of truth." In this encounter, service quality is judged by the customer. Because services are provided by people, they are difficult to standardize. Different people have different abilities and skills, but also motivations. Even the same service provider may have good and bad days for various reasons. A guest in the same restaurant on 2 days may receive quite a different service from different servers or even the same server who serves that table on that day. Frequently, frontline staff in contact with customers are quite junior and low in rank. However, they are the ones who leave a lasting—good or bad—impression on the customer (Segal-Horn & Faulkner, 2010, pp. 287–288). A gruff driver on a Flixbus ride can dampen the experience of the ride. This can lead to quality control problems for service firms (Lovelock & Yip, 1996). Since Flixbus uses subcontractors for the bus rides, this can pose particular challenges. Another reason for the heterogeneity of services is the involvement of customers, outlined above. For most services, customers need to play a part in the service's production, and the behavior and ability of customers cannot be standardized. Hence, the outcome is bound to show variation in quality (Ingwald et al., 2009). If the customer keeps moving randomly on the seat of a hairdresser, the hairdresser may accidentally create a hairdo that was not intended.

**Non-Transferrable Ownership**: A guest staying at a hotel room does not acquire ownership of that room. A music lover attending a concert does not acquire ownership of the concert. Instead, customers obtain the right to temporarily use something or access skills, expertise, facilities, or networks, usually for a defined period (Wirtz & Lovelock, 2018, pp. 12–13). Wirtz and Lovelock, who particularly emphasize this *non-transferrable ownership* as a key characteristic of services, distinguish the following temporary use rights: labor, skills, and expertise rental such as car repair; rental of goods services such as renting a boat; renting a space and facility, such as a seat in an airplane; obtaining access to shared facilities, such as a theme park; getting access to networks and systems, such as in telecommunications; and so on (Wirtz & Lovelock, 2018, p. 13). Frequently, this implies that the location of these assets to which use rights are granted plays an important role, such as the location of a hotel, a theme park, or the place where a rental car can be picked up. This is why Flixbus started cooperating with Uber to enable customers to reach its bus terminals, which are located far from the center in some cities. For networks, such as in telecommunication, availability, ideally, 24 h, 7 days a week, is essential (Bordoloi et al., 2019, p. 16).

While these characteristics have been mainly outlined separately, there are connections. For example, the participation of customers impacts the heterogeneity of service quality. In later chapters, especially ► Chap. 8 on the multinational service firm, we will outline what impact these characteristics have on the international management of service firms.

## Types of Services

Services are very multifaceted and diverse. Not all of the characteristics outlined above apply equally to all service firms. Making broad-brush statements about all services would not be appropriate. Nor would it contribute to our understanding to treat each service industry separately. Therefore, it is helpful to distinguish different *types* of services, which could have important implications for the differences in their international management. Scholars have developed typologies of service industries. The typology initially developed by Lovelock and Yip (1996) and then elaborated by Wirtz and Lovelock (2018) is particularly helpful for this book. This is because it lends itself particularly well to distinguishing different approaches for the international management of service firms. Therefore, several scholars use their typology to discuss various aspects of the international management of service firms.

Wirtz and Lovelock distinguish services by two criteria: (a) to what extent are the actions performed by service providers *tangible*, and (b) to what extent are services *directed at people themselves or their possessions*, which also impacts the need for the physical presence of the customer. They distinguish people-processing, possession-processing, mental stimulus-processing, and information-processing services (Wirtz & Lovelock, 2018, pp. 15–16) (see ◘ Fig. 1.2).

**People Processing**: People seek services directed at themselves, whether transportation, food and beverage, accommodation, or similar. Tangible actions are performed on people's bodies. To receive these services, customers must enter where the service is provided (or the service provider sometimes comes to them).

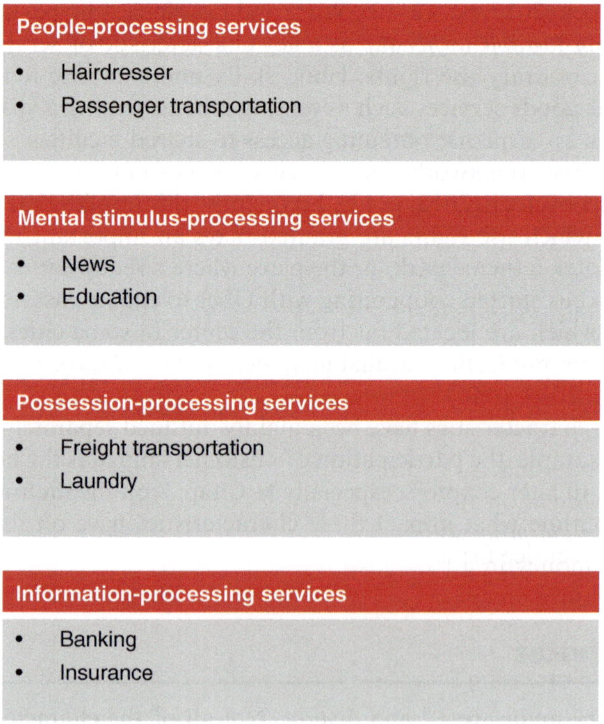


◘ **Fig. 1.2** Four broad categories of services—examples. (Drawing on content from: Wirtz & Lovelock, 2018, p. 16; Dolski & Hermann, 2004, pp. 92, 99–100)

Customers need to be physically present, and active cooperation by the customer is required, as in the example of the hairdresser. The location of the service facility plays a vital role so that it is convenient for the customer. Flixbus is a case in point of *people-processing services.*

**People-Processing Services**

*People-processing services* are directed at customers themselves physically.

**Possession Processing**: Customers also seek services for some physical possession, such as cleaning their laundry, repairing their car, or transporting a parcel. In this case, production and consumption do not necessarily happen simultaneously. In *people-processing services,* customers tend to be less involved, for example, dropping and collecting laundry for cleaning, maybe making the cleaner aware of stains that need special attention.

**Possession-Processing Services**

*Possession-processing services* are directed at physical possessions of customers.

**Mental Stimulus Processing**: This type includes services like professional advice, education, and information. It requires some active presence of the customer to benefit from the service. However, using technology, the place of production can be separate, such as in online education courses or when a customer streams a recorded piece of music from the living room sofa. In *mental stimulus-processing services*, consumption is frequently possible after production, as for music or films on CD, DVD, or streaming.

**Mental Stimulus-Processing Services**

*Mental stimulus-processing services* are directed at the mind of customers.

**Information Processing**: Tax consultants, lawyers, market researchers or bankers, and modern information and communications technology (ICT) can process information. *Information-processing services* are directed at intangible assets of the customer, such as money in a bank account. Information is very intangible but can take a more tangible form in documents of some format.

**Information-Processing Services**

*Information-processing services* are directed at intangible assets of customers.

Another relevant distinction for the international management of services is between hard and soft services or between a service's hard and soft elements. Many services today contain some combination of hard and soft elements (Erramilli, 1990; Segal-Horn & Faulkner, 2010, p. 294).

**Hard Services**: *Hard services* or service elements are tangible. Think of the furniture and decoration of a restaurant and the food and drinks. They can be managed to some extent, like manufactured goods. For example, the restaurant's decoration will happen well ahead of the arrival of guests, so production is quite separate from consumption. This applies to the booking platform and buses at Flixbus.

**Hard Services**

*Hard services* are tangible.

**Soft Services**: *Soft services* or service elements are intangible. In the restaurant example, think of the ambiance, maybe music running in the background, or how the servers approach the guests and interact with them. Soft services or elements of services display the typical management challenges that come with the largely intangible characteristics of many services. The interaction between waiter and guest requires the physical presence of the guest in the restaurant, and production and consumption are simultaneous. At Flixbus, the behavior of the driver toward the guests belongs here.

**Soft Services**

*Soft services* are intangible.

One more typology of services is important for understanding how the requirements for international management differ between different types of service firms: **business services**, also called business-to-business (B2B) services, versus **consumer services**, also called business-to-consumer (B2C) services.

**Consumer Services**: *Consumer services* are services offered to households/individual consumers. Various examples of consumer service are around us, such as lodging services provided by hotel companies, personal insurance, rail travel, education, health care, recreation, catering, tourism, finance, entertainment, and home maintenance. Consumer services differ from customer services. The latter entails the support and advice provided by the company to those who buy or use its products, such as an after-sales service you obtain after you purchase and own a washing machine. The former does not entail owning the hotel building when you purchase the hotel service for 2 days.

**Consumer Services**

*Consumer services* are those offered to households/individual consumers.

**Business Services**: *Business services* are those ultimately used by business firms and other productive enterprises, including activities concerned with handling tangible products, such as machinery repair or catering, and providing intangible expertise, like accountancy or consultancy services (Roberts, 1999). Business services have distinctive characteristics that differentiate them from consumer services (Cooper & Jackson, 1988). Business services typically entail a more rational buying process, longer-term relationships, greater product complexity, larger amounts of money exchanged, and greater use of group decision-making. Business services also involve the design of customized service mixes unique to particular organizations, which requires a greater level of customer participation. For instance, when a client engages a business service company to provide machine repair service, the contract usually lasts several years. Multiple departments, such as the production, finance, and purchase units, will be involved in a group decision in choosing the service provider. When providing the actual repair service to the client, the client needs to participate deeply in the trouble-shooting process, to help the service company understand the unique problems they encounter and, sometimes, to co-develop the solution.

**Business Services**

*Business services* are those services "used ultimately by business firms and other productive enterprises," "including activities concerned with handling tangible products, such as machinery repair or catering, and providing intangible expertise, like accountancy or consultancy services" (Roberts, 1999, p. 69).

**Professional Service Firms (PSFs)**: These provide one subtype of business services that merits special attention. Think of accounting firms, law firms, consulting firms, advertising agencies, architects' offices, investment banks, or physician practices. PSFs are very knowledge-intensive, and many PSFs have a low capital intensity and a professionalized workforce. Knowledge intensity means that the production of services depends on a substantial body of complex knowledge embodied in the staff. Frontline employees of PSFs are intellectually skilled and highly educated, typically exhibiting an academic degree and often a professional certification. This implies that these highly qualified employees sought after in the labor market have high bargaining power and a tendency for autonomy, i.e., resent interference in how they go about their work. This also implies that clients' difficulty in assessing the quality of professional services is particularly pronounced. Remember the example of legal services outlined in the section on intangibility. Low capital intensity means that the service production typically does not require significant physical assets such as machines and equipment. A professionalized workforce relies on staff—professionals—who share a particular knowledge base, say legal or accounting knowledge. A profession, as represented by a body such as the chamber of public accountants in a country, regulates access to the profession, for example, by requiring specific exams or certificates before one is allowed to practice. This is regularly the case for accountants, tax consultants, lawyers, or doctors. Further, it exhibits a professional ethic, such as doctors are bound to work in the best interest of patients or accountants in the interest of investors and the general public. Not all PSFs exhibit all three distinctive characteristics. In fact, all three characteristics only apply to those that von Nordenflycht labels "Classic PSFs": accounting firms, law firms, and offices of architects. Other types of PSFs share knowledge intensity but have either higher capital intensity (e.g., hospitals), not a professionalized workforce as defined above (e.g., consulting firms and advertising firms), or are neither low in capital intensity nor have a professionalized workforce (e.g., biotech firms or R&D labs) (von Nordenflycht, 2010). Empson et al. (2015) extend and refine von Nordenflycht's definition by emphasizing that—in varying degrees—PSFs customize their services to solve their clients' problems, allow much autonomy to their staff, and that core staff recognize each other as members of a profession.

**Professional Service Firms**

In *professional service firms*, service depends on a substantial body of complex knowledge embodied in the staff as a core asset of the firm. Frontline employees of PSFs are intellectually skilled and highly educated. In varying degrees, staff of PSFs recognize each other as members of a profession, apply their knowledge to customize solutions to their clients, and enjoy much autonomy.

Regarding the international management of service firms, PSFs are very specific and interesting; consequently, there is much research on managing them internationally. Further, scholars see them as an extreme form of knowledge-intensive firms that become increasingly relevant in the knowledge economy or knowledge-based economy (von Nordenflycht, 2010). Finally, consider the examples of PSF industries outlined above, such as the so-called "Big Four" accounting firms. They are among the largest firms in the world in terms of the number of global employees and locations and play a vital role in the global economy (Klimkeit & Reihlen, 2016). Therefore, in several chapters, we will discuss how the theme of the respective chapter applies specifically to PSFs.

## The Service Triangle

You may have noticed in what we outlined above, especially the section on heterogeneity, how important employees, especially frontline staff, are to a service business. The staff that provides the service to the customer is the "face" of the service firm toward its customers. Service quality, as perceived by the customer, depends much

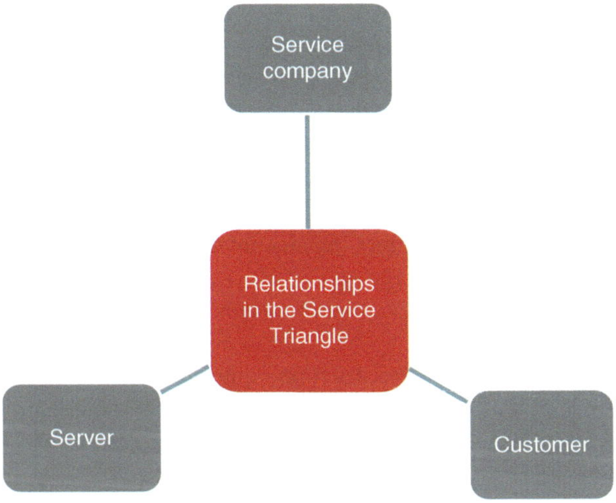


**Fig. 1.3** Relationships in the service triangle. (Redrawn from Heskett, 1986, p. 69)

on the frontline staff. So, in services, there is not just a dyadic relationship between the firm and its customers but a triangle consisting of the service firm, its customers, and its "servers" (frontline employees; see Fig. 1.3). A service firm needs to carefully manage all three relationships in this triangle in order to be competitive. Heskett found that many service firms have failed due to mismanagement of the triangle (Heskett, 1986, pp. 68–70). The strength of the three relationships will vary from case to case. Sometimes, the strongest relationship will be between the server and the customer. Think of a management consulting or law firm where highly qualified and competent consultants or lawyers will establish strong relationships with their customers, who end up feeling more attached to the individual server than to the service firm that employs them. The consequence can be that when the server leaves to set up an independent practice, customers may follow and be lost to the service firm. To prevent this, such service firms need to strengthen both the bonding of the server and the customer to the firm. For example, the firm can make its collective capabilities more visible to the client. At the same time, the firm may increase incentives, compensation, and career opportunities for its key staff to retain it (Heskett, 1986, pp. 68–70). For a service firm to succeed internationally, it must find the right balance between the relationships in the triangle to effectively manage its services across borders (Segal-Horn & Faulkner, 2010, p. 294).

**Servitization**

Nowadays, "pure goods" and "pure services" are diminishing in number. Most "products" sit at a point along this goods–services spectrum, with goods/services characteristics overlapping one another at specific points. One trend contributing to such overlapping is the phenomenon of *servitization*. Servitization is the phenomenon of companies that previously saw themselves as "pure manufacturers," increas-

1

ingly "adding services components to tangible products" or "bundling services with the goods they produce and sell" (Del Javan & Touri, 2012). According to Baines et al. (2017), the definition of servitization has coalesced as "a process of building revenue streams for manufacturers from services." (Baines et al. 2017, p 257) distinguish three levels of services that manufacturers can offer:

- Base services—goods and spare parts.
- Intermediates services—product repairs, maintenance, overhauls, helpdesks, training, condition monitoring.
- Advanced services—customer support agreements, outcome contracts.

Caterpillar, the world's largest construction equipment manufacturer, provides an excellent example of a company transforming from pure manufacturing to servitization. See the closing case below.

## Review Questions

1. Define and explain the concept of services.
2. Briefly outline the role that services play in the world economy.
3. Explain the distinctive characteristics of services.
4. Why is it important to distinguish different types of services?
5. Explain the four types of services distinguished by Wirtz and Lovelock.
6. Outline the difference between hard and soft services.
7. Distinguish between hard and soft elements of the service of a hotel.
8. Explain the difference between consumer services and business services.
9. What characterizes professional service firms? Why can it be very interesting to look at them more closely? Why can it be challenging for PSFs to manage their employees?
10. Why is it important in services to consider a company, customer, and server triangle?
11. Apply the concept of the service triangle to a company of your choice: how would you characterize the three elements and their relationship? What are the implications?
12. Critically discuss the six characteristics of services outlined here! Why would there be authors who reject them?

## Closing Case: Servitization of Caterpillar—From Selling Products to Selling Service

The Caterpillar Tractor Company was formed in 1925, and its first manufacturing plant was in East Peoria. In 1951, the company opened its first overseas manufacturing facility in the United Kingdom. Caterpillar manufactures more than 300 machines, attachments, power systems, and parts. Product offerings include articulated trucks, backhoe loaders, dozers, engines, excavators, generators, motor graders, skid steer loaders, and wheel loaders.

Caterpillar manufactures its products and components in 110 facilities world-

Construction machine. (Image by H. Peter from Pixabay)

wide, with 51 plants located in the United States and 59 overseas plants in Australia, Belgium, Brazil, Canada, China, Czech Republic, England, France, Germany, Hungary, India, Indonesia, Italy, Japan, Mexico, the Netherlands, Northern Ireland, Poland, Russia, Singapore, South Africa, and Sweden.

Caterpillar products are distributed to end-users in 193 countries through its worldwide network of 160 dealers. Caterpillar's dealers are independently owned and operated businesses with exclusive geographical territories. Dealers provide sales, maintenance and repair services, rental equipment, and parts distribution (AGA Parts Catalog). With its global operation, in 2021, 62% of the sales and revenue are generated outside of the United States.

Besides the products, services are key components contributing to Caterpillar's customer satisfaction and revenue. Caterpillar's machines are often integral to their user's operations. Downtime can mean inconvenience and financial losses. Therefore, services provided through its dealer network aim to deliver whatever customers need to ensure uptime-data, advisory support, or full-time fleet management. Such services are important in enabling customers to operate their fleets as efficiently and effectively as possible.

As a result, Caterpillar took on its servitization journey. To understand its servitization model, let us look at one example. In the past, Caterpillar might sell a large bulldozer to a construction company through a financing company. The construction company provided fuel and lubricants for the bulldozer throughout its useful life. During this time, the bulldozer was used and serviced directly by the construction company, with replacement parts provided by Caterpillar when something broke. With the servitization model, Caterpillar offers usage-based services for their products. The construction company pays Caterpillar when they use the machine. Caterpillar receives this revenue stream in exchange for providing access to the asset, maintaining its performance, and ensuring its uptime. Such services can deliver gross margins two to three times that of selling the commodity product alone.

Such a servitization model has become a core part of the competitive strategy to allow Caterpillar to focus on services and stay ahead of the competition from third-party providers and manufacturers. Statistics show that such a business model increases sales and profits. The advantage was even more pronounced during the economic crisis when Caterpillar proactively provided equipment financing services for small and medium-sized enterprises with tight cash flow to help them improve performance and income. In this way, its customers experience the value of Caterpillar's services, which enhances customer loyalty and helps establish long-term relationships with customers. Jim Umpleby, the Caterpillar chairman and CEO, commented,

> "When market demand is high for new equipment, services tend to be 30% of our machine, energy and transportation sales," he said, "During down markets, that percentage moves closer to 40%" (Doyle, 2019).

To implement the servitization model, Caterpillar leveraged its global dealers to manage customer relationships, service equipment, and provide parts. By 2005, dealers offered Customer Support Agreements (CSAs) in various forms for years. In 2005, Caterpillar's CEO launched "Vision 2020," its 15-year enterprise strategy for growth. A vital aspect of the strategy was to work closely with its dealer network to "be the global benchmark in delivering integrated business solutions to customers" (Advanced Services Group, 2023 p. 2). Caterpillar and its dealers had to become less product-focused and more customer outcome-focused to deliver a high standard of solutions.

Caterpillar has servitized by providing five overarching areas of services aimed at machine health, optimization, and maintenance. These areas are:

1. **Technology and Solutions**, which entails employing advanced technologies to provide a service-oriented Product-Service System (PSS) by optimizing vehicle performance through productivity and efficiency enhancements as well as remote access possibilities.
2. **Financing and Insurance**, which operates under the brand Cat Financial and provides an integration-oriented PSS by offering businesses various options for financing and insurance when purchasing Caterpillar products.
3. **Safety and Efficiency Education**, which are services aimed at educating customers to facilitate better use of Caterpillar products and promote safety around the surrounding working environment, categorized as a product-oriented PSS.
4. **Maintenance and Support**, which is a comprehensive list of services aimed at helping the customer—including everything from delivery of equipment to ensuring the availability and functionality of the customer's equipment through spare parts provision, manuals, and fleet man-

agement—thereby establishing integrated PSSs.

5. Various combinations of the above areas through **comprehensive customer support agreements** (CSAs).

With its strategy, Caterpillar expands its service offerings through flexible product purchasing terms and service-integrated product solutions. These leverage digital capabilities to track performance and outcomes. For instance, Caterpillar products with telematics and the internet of things (IoT) feature advanced connected equipment services. Caterpillar launched the Cat Product Link program in 2019. The program involves the equipment manufacturer remotely capturing data on the buyer's equipment usage. Caterpillar then uses the data to provide customized after-sales services, such as maintenance support, to which the buyer must subscribe.

When leveraging global dealers to implement the servitization model, Caterpillar found issues such as disappointing contract renewal rates and unreliable delivery. These led to doubts about their ability to generate profits. Caterpillar realized that services needed to be much more standardized among its dealers, for instance, what was included in the service offering, the description and marketing of services, delivery systems, and key performance indicators (KPIs). As the manufacturer whose name was on the product, it needed to lead this standardization exercise across its dealer network.

In the past decade, Caterpillar adopted technologies, such as telematics, to achieve consistency to a great extent across all dealers. For example, customers can receive monthly reports measuring the health and utilization of Caterpillar equipment. Asset Tracking monitors the location and deployment of assets and hours in use in real-time across multiple sites. Fleet Benchmarking Report compares equipment performance over time to identify early maintenance concerns and operational inefficiencies. Condition Monitoring Advisors at the dealership use real-time data to identify potential problems, notify the customer, advise on actions, and recommend ways to drive down long-term operating costs gradually.

According to Bob De Lange, group president of services, distribution, and digital, Caterpillar estimates that 95% of the service opportunity comes after a machine has accumulated 5000 hours. In 2019, Caterpillar set a 10-year aspirational target to double its parts and service revenues to $28 billion from $14 billion in 2016.

**Questions**

1. How do the characteristics of the services provided by Caterpillar make it necessary to leverage global dealers to provide services?
2. How do you categorize the services offered by Caterpillar using different classification schemes?
3. How does digitalization facilitate Caterpillar's servitization process?

Sources: Advanced Services Group, 2023; AGA Parts, 2023; Baines et al., 2017; Caterpillar, 2022, 2023; Del Javan & Touri, 2012; Doyle, 2019; Magneteg & Parkosidis, 2019; Riggle, 2015.

1

**Summary**

This chapter:

- Provides and explains a definition of services
- Outlines distinctive characteristics of services
  - *Customer participation*, describing the involvement of customers in service provision
  - *Simultaneity* of the production and consumption of services
  - *Intangibility* of services that can be perceived as a performance rather than a good
  - *Perishability* of services due to the need to provide capacity that may not be fully used
  - *Heterogeneity* of services due to their performance by people and the involvement of customers
  - *Non-transferrable ownership* of services as customers only obtain usage rights
- Distinguishes different types of services, especially
  - *People-processing, possession-processing, mental stimulus-processing, and information-processing services*
  - *Hard services and soft services*
  - *Business services and consumer services*
  - *Professional services* as a subcategory of business services
- Explained the *services triangle* that consists of the company, the server, and the customer, where the company needs to manage all relationships well

## References


Advanced Services Group. (2023). *Servitization case study: Caterpillar and its dealerships*. https://www.advancedservicesgroup.co.uk/wp-content/uploads/Caterpillar-Case-Study.pdf

AGA Parts. (2023). *Caterpillar equipment parts*. https://www.aga-parts.com/caterpillar/

Baines, T., Ziaee Bigdeli, A., Bustinza, O. F., Shi, V. G., Baldwin, J., & Ridgway, K. (2017). Servitization: Revisiting the state-of-the-art and research priorities. *International Journal of Operations & Production Management, 37*(2), 256–278.

Blagoeva, D. H., Jensen, P. D. Ø., & Merchant, H. (2020). Services in international business studies: A replication and extension of Merchant and Gaur (2008). *Management International Review (MIR), 60*(3), 427–457.

Bordoloi, S. K., Fitzsimmons, J. A., & Fitzsimmons, M. J. (2019). *Service management: Operations, strategy, information technology* (9th ed.). McGraw-Hill Education.

Caterpillar. (2022). *Caterpillar fact sheet*. https://s7d2.scene7.com/is/content/Caterpillar/CM20220311-3557f-0e839?_ga=2.268910962.2066052495.1675138965–852975693.1674822925

Caterpillar. (2023). *Caterpillar*. https://www.caterpillar.com/

Cooper, P. D., & Jackson, R. W. (1988). Applying a services marketing orientation to the industrial services sector. *Journal of Services Marketing*, 2(4), 67–70.

Del Javan, A., & Touri, S. H. (2012). *Servitization: Challenges, classification and categorization*. LAP LAMBERT Academic Publishing.

Dolski, J., & Hermanns, A. (2004). Internationalisierungsstrategien von Dienstleistungsunternehmen. In M. A. Gardini & H. D. Dahlhoff (Eds.), *Management internationaler Dienstleistungen: Kontext - Konzepte - Erfahrungen* (1st ed., pp. 85–110). Gabler.

Doyle, M. (2019). *How Cat intends to double its parts and service sales by 2026*. https://www.equipmentworld.com/big-iron-dealer/article/14971083/cat-plans-to-double-2016-parts-and-service-revenue-in-2026
dpa. (2018, October 25). *Flixbus startet ersten Elektro-Fernbus* (p. 206). Handelsblatt.
Economist. (2015, October 22). Revolution on wheels: The options for passengers are multiplying
Economist. (2018, May 10). How Flixbus conquered the European coach market: America is its next target
Empson, L., Muzio, D., Broschak, J. P., & Hinings, B. (2015). Researching professional service firms: An introduction and overview. In L. Empson, D. Muzio, J. P. Broschak, & B. Hinings (Eds.), *The Oxford handbook of professional service firms* (pp. 1–22). Oxford University Press.
Erramilli, M. K. (1990). Entry mode choice in service industries. *International Marketing Review, 7*(5), 50–62.
Fockenbrock, D. (2016a, February 5). *Flixbus + Mein Fernbus = Flixbus* (p. 25). Handelsblatt.
Fockenbrock, D. (2016b, June 30). *Flixbus verdrängt Preisbrecher Megabus* (p. 124). Handelsblatt.
Fockenbrock, D. (2016c, September 16). *Die Bahn kapituliert vor Flixbus* (p. 180). Handelsblatt.
Fockenbrock, D. (2020, December 21). *Klage gegen Staatshilfen für die Bahn* (p. 247). Handelsblatt.
Fockenbrock, D. (2021, March 18). *Flixbus geht vorsichtig wieder an den Start* (p. 54). Handelsblatt.
Fockenbrock, D., & Koenen, J. (2016, September 7). *Flixbus wird erwachsen* (p. 173). Handelsblatt.
Fortune. (2021). *Global 500*. https://fortune.com/global500/
Grönroos, C. (2015). *Service management and marketing: Managing the service profit logic* (4th ed.). Wiley.
Handelsblatt. (2019, March 22). *Flixbus kooperiert mit Uber* (p. 58). Handelsblatt.
Heskett, J. L. (1986). *Managing in the service economy*. Harvard Business School Press.
Ingwald, J., Nott, A., & Holzmüller, H. H. (2009). Koordination im internationalen Dienstleistungsmanagement: Herausforderungen und Gestaltungsansätze. In D. Holtbrügge, H. H. Holzmüller, & F. Wangenheim (Eds.), *Management internationaler Dienstleistungen mit 3K: Konfiguration—Koordination—Kundenintegration* (pp. 29–56). Gabler.
Klimkeit, D., & Reihlen, M. (2016). Local responses to global integration in transnational professional service firms. *Journal of Professions & Organization, 3*(1), 39–61.
Koenen, J. (2021a, October 22). *Flixbus kauft Greyhound*. Handelsblatt.
Koenen, J. (2021b, October 22). *Flixbus und Sixt: Eroberung in Windeseile* (p. 205). Handelsblatt.
Lovelock, C. H., & Yip, G. S. (1996). Developing global strategies for service businesses. *California Management Review, 38*(2), 64–86.
Magneteg, E., & Parkosidis, M. (2019). *Servitization in manufacturing firms: Exploring possible relations between the product-service systems offered by highly servitized manufacturing firms and the market environments in which they operate*. https://lup.lub.lu.se/luur/download?func=downloadFile&recordOId=8981845&fileOId=8981852
Riggle, C. (2015). *Manufacturers boost profits with servitization and IoT*. https://www.linkedin.com/pulse/manufacturers-boost-profits-servitization-iot-charles-riggle/
Roberts, J. (1999). The internationalisation of business service firms: A stages approach. *Service Industries Journal, 19*(4), 68–88.
Scherer, A., Zimmer, M., & von Wangenheim, F. (2009). Kundenintegration bei internationalen Dienstleistungen: Theoretische Einordnung, Motive und Herausforderungen. In D. Holtbrügge, H. H. Holzmüller, & F. Wangenheim (Eds.), *Management internationaler Dienstleistungen mit 3K: Konfiguration—Koordination—Kundenintegration* (pp. 57–80). Gabler.
Segal-Horn, S., & Faulkner, D. (2010). *Understanding global strategy*. Cengage Learning EMEA.
Siebenhaar, H.-P., & Fockenbrock, D. (2017, May 23). *ÖBB verkauft an Flixbus* (p. 99). Handelsblatt.
von Nordenflycht, A. (2010). What is a professional service firm? Towards a theory and taxonomy of knowledge intensive firms. *Academy of Management Review, 35*(1), 155–174.
Wirtz, J., & Lovelock, C. H. (2018). *Essentials of services marketing* (3rd ed.). Pearson.
Zeithaml, V. A., & Bitner, M. J. (2003). *Services marketing: Integrating customer focus across the firm* (33rd ed.). McGraw-Hill Irwin.

## Further Reading

Empson, L., Muzio, D., Broschak, J., & Hinings, B. (2015). *The Oxford handbook of professional service firms*. Oxford University Press.

Johnston, R., Shulver, M., Slack, N., & Clark, G. (2020). *Service operations management: Improving service delivery*. Pearson.

# International Service Business and Globalization

Contents




D. Klimkeit et al., *International Management in Service Firms*, Classroom Companion: Business,
https://doi.org/10.1007/978-3-031-50345-0_2

**Learning Outcomes**

After completing this chapter, you should be able to:

- Describe the globalization of the service market and service production
- Identify the drivers of globalization
- Discuss globalization's benefits to customers and businesses
- Outline the cost of globalization

## Introduction

This chapter will address the globalization of service markets—its origins, drivers, and effects on service businesses. It distinguishes the globalization of service markets from the globalization of the production of services. It is capped off with a critical discussion on the effects of globalization on people and societies.

American Express cards, image by Republica from Pixabay

## Opening Case: American Express' Service Globalization

Founded in 1850, American Express started as a freight forwarding and mail service company. A few years later, the company expanded into the financial services industry by offering a money order component. It launched its first charge cards in the 1950s and has become one of the best-known credit card companies worldwide. Besides credit card services, American Express also offers other digital products. American Express divides its operations into three large segments:

- Global Consumer Services Group (GCSG)
- Global Commercial Services (GCS)
- Global Merchant and Network Services (GMNS)

American Express makes most of its money through transactions on its merchant network. The company offers consumers great rewards programs, with cashback, flights, hotels, and even amusement park admissions available for swiping their American Express cards at participating merchants worldwide. In turn, American Express earns the discount revenue from transactions occurring at partner merchants.

The company's merchant fees are a lot higher than those offered by Mastercard and Visa. Many merchants willingly accept the high merchant fees because the average American Express cardholder is relatively wealthy and buys more goods and services. Hence it is worth the increased fees to get said customers.

With its global reach, American Express connects millions of customers and businesses worldwide. In 2021, American Express issued 121.7 million cards. In 2022, over 66 million businesses were involved. According to a recent Amex Trendex survey, 70% of Millennial and Gen Z Card Members said they plan to use their American Express for the majority of their purchases when traveling internationally.

In addition, American Express is one of the pioneers of offshoring its back-office operations. American Express partnered with companies from India and the Philippines to take care of its customer service. In terms of Information Technology (IT) service, American Express contracted with IT companies in India, such as Infosys Ltd. and Tata Consultancy Services, for the needed application development, system maintenance, and technical support.

With its effort on a global scale, American Express delivered $36.1 billion in revenue and $3.1 billion in net income in 2020. In its 2020 annual report, American Express indicated that it had focused on four strategic initiatives over the prior year: expanding its leadership in the premium consumer area, growing its commercial payments segment, improving its global integrated network, and continuing to focus on its digital offerings.

**Questions**

1. What drove American Express' internationalization?
2. Did American Express achieve economies of scale? How did it achieve it?

Sources: American Express Website (n.d.); Knowledge at Wharton (2002); Sheth (2022)

## The Globalization of Service Markets and Production

Referring to the definition given by the Organization for Economic Cooperation and Development (OECD), the term "globalization" has been widely used to describe the increasing internationalization of financial markets and markets for goods and services. Globalization refers to a dynamic and multidimensional process of economic integration whereby national resources become more and more internationally mobile while national economies become increasingly interdependent (OECD, 2005). We can experience such globalization everywhere. When a consumer in Germany purchases a pair of NIKE shoes manufactured in Vietnam, there is no doubt that globalization of the product market is involved. But have you noticed? When a US tourist eats in a restaurant while traveling in Thailand or when a Chinese company receives an online course provided by an Australian training company, consumers and companies have been involved in some globalization of services.

**Globalization**

The term "*globalization*" has been widely used to describe the increasing internationalization of financial markets and markets for goods and services. *Globalization* refers to a dynamic and multidimensional process of economic integration whereby national resources become more and more internationally mobile while national economies become increasingly interdependent.

Cross-border service transactions have a long history of facilitating trade in tangible goods, for example, transporting and repairing tangible goods. However, many services are intangible and perishable and require simultaneous production and consumption. As a result, service activity was predominantly confined to local and domestic markets before the 1980s. A more detailed review of the trade of service is in ► Chap. 3.

Service was included in the Uruguay round of the General Agreement on Tariffs and Trade (GATT) negotiations in 1986 and the General Agreement on Trade in Services (GATS) in 1995. Since then, the globalization of the service market has sped up. ► Chapter 6 will give more details on the development of international service trade negotiations.

In 2020, services accounted for an average share of 22.1% of the world's total trade, compared to a share of 19.6% in 2011. The increase in the market share of services confirms that services are a growing part of globalization (Eurostat, 2023).

## Globalization of Service Markets

### Causes of Service Market Globalization

Globalization of service markets arises because of the convergence of buyer preferences in markets around the world. This trend occurs in many service categories, including consumer and business services, for instance.

> **Convergence**
>
> *Convergence* refers to the phenomenon that consumers allocate an increasingly similar proportion of their budget or income to similar items across countries over time (Ozturk & Cavusgil, 2019).

Various reasons have been identified to lead to convergence.

- Economically, the global convergence trend results from increased purchasing power (Ter Hofstede et al., 2002). Since 2003, when the number of poor and vulnerable people in the world reached a historical peak of 4.4 billion people, the middle class has been growing fast, especially in Asia. By 2030, another 700 million people are expected to join the global middle class, making it more than half of the world's total population (Wallach, 2022). The growing middle class worldwide is increasingly more connected, possesses considerable purchasing power, and represents a new dominant socioeconomic category for consumers. The rise of the new middle class is significant, particularly in populous emerging markets including China and India, as they have the resources and hunger for consumption (Fioratti, 2006) and strive for better lifestyles. They generate a sense of social belonging to the global consumption culture and consumer cosmopolitanism and show the tendency to imitate the consumption habits of middle-class consumers in developed markets. This has generated large-scale first-time buyers for goods and services associated with high-class status (Song & Cui, 2009).
- Technology facilitates convergence in many areas. In economics, the diffusion of technology gives emerging countries the impetus to grow faster than rich countries, enabling convergence of incomes (Lee, 2013; Rassekh, 1998). Similarly, technological advances such as improved internet infrastructure, higher patent applications and grants, and higher investments in telecommunications provide resources for consumers to connect with each other across borders. Such technological developments increase consumer connectivity, spread ideas faster, and facilitate emulation of each other's spending behavior.
- Regional integration is a major political factor affecting consumption behavior. Regional integration refers to the growing economic interdependence that results when two or more countries within a geographic region form an alliance to reduce trade barriers (Cavusgil et al., 2014). Regional integration yields formations such as regional blocs (e.g., North American Free Trade Agreement

[NAFTA], Association of Southeast Asian Nations [ASEAN], Mercosur, and the European Union [EU]). These blocs have helped productivity increase across countries (Sheth, 2011). Through such formations, cross-border consumers increasingly have access to products and services from other member countries. Over time, regional blocs create a homogenizing environment due to similarities in policies, legal systems, business practices, and social norms (Malhotra et al., 1998). This harmonization process will eventually lead to increasing similarity of consumer spending habits. As a result, mass consumption societies similar to each other in their consumption behavior rise, contributing to the emergence of convergence of consumer spending.

**Interesting Facts**

There are many definitions of the middle class. Some define the group earning between $10 and $100 per person per day (e.g., Mondiale, 2007; Kharas, 2010). Middle class is also defined as people with an income between 75 and 125% of the median income level in a country (Birdsall, 2010, p. 162; Birdsall et al., 2000). The terms "middle income" and "middle class" are often used interchangeably. This is especially true among economists who typically define the middle class in terms of income or consumption. But being middle class can connote more than income, be it a college education, white-collar work, economic security, owning a home, or having certain social and political values. "Class" could also be a state of mind, that is, it could be a matter of self-identification. The interplay among these many factors is examined in studies by Hout (2008) and Savage et al. (2013), among others.

## What Services Have Been Traded Globally?

When looking into the types of traded services, World Trade Report 2019 shows that the top five types of traded services globally are distribution, financial services, telecommunication/computer services/audiovisual services, transport, and tourism services.

Given the crucial role that wholesalers and retailers play in connecting producers and consumers worldwide and ensuring consumers' access to various goods at competitive prices, distribution services are the most extensively traded globally, with US$ 2634 billion, accounting for 19.9% of total services trade in 2017.

The financial sector is the backbone of the economy. Its essential functions are to enable international transactions and facilitate the smooth exchange of goods and services between countries. Financial services hence are the second largest traded services globally, with US$ 2463 billion, accounting for 18.6% of total services trade in 2017.

Computer services and related activities (IT services) have recorded remarkable growth from 2005 to 2017. IT services expanded by 11% annually and were resilient during the financial crisis due to steady demand for new software and mounting cybersecurity concerns. On-demand music and video streaming, such as through online platforms, has turned audiovisuals into the most dynamic segment in recent years.

Transport plays a vital role in today's economy and society and significantly impacts growth and employment. The transport services market consists of sales of services that transport goods and people from one location to another for a fee. The transport services market's main types are air transport, general transport, pipeline transport, rail transport, transit and ground passenger transport, truck transport, warehousing and storage, and water transport. Given its importance in facilitating the movement of goods and people, the traded transport services accounted for 11.8% of the total service trade in 2017. Overall, around half of the world trade in transport services is driven by trade in goods, including both goods that directly reach consumers and those used as inputs in production processes. As freight shipping rates fluctuate according to global demand, the transport sector tends to be relatively vulnerable.

Another sector that has experienced fast growth is tourism, owing to the rise of low-cost airlines and the multiplication of direct routes. In 2017, world trade in tourism reached US$ 1029 billion, almost doubling its 2005 value. Foreign travelers' expenditure during stays abroad enters the tourism service value chain via the hospitality sector, transport, retail, entertainment, and cultural activities. Tourism indirectly contributes to developing other sectors, such as conference and events management or communications. It also drives the construction of infrastructure and accommodation.

Lastly, a range of services is taking baby steps in international trade, such as educational, health, or environmental services. These services account for a negligible share of world trade but are rising.

**Research Task**

Do your own research to understand more information about service trade at ► http://i-tip.wto.org/services/Search.aspx.

## Where Are the Global Service Markets?

At the regional level, the EU was the world's largest trader of services: Its exports were valued at €1027 billion, and its imports were valued at €894 billion in 2021. Based on 2020 data for world trade in services, the EU accounted for more than one-quarter of global exports (25.9%) and global imports (26.2%). For comparison, the shares of the United States were 17.6% for exports and 12.0% for imports.

In addition, data also suggest that developing economies' share of world services trade has grown by more than 10 percentage points since 2005, reaching 25% of world services exports and 34.4% of world services imports in 2017 (WTO, 2019). This is particularly the case for China and India. China accounted for 8.1% of service export and 11.1% of service import in 2021, up from 5.6% and 7.1%, respectively, in 2011. India accounted for 5.8% of service export and 3.5% of service import, up from 3.8% and 2.2%, respectively, in 2011 (Eurostat, 2023). However, the least-developed countries accounted for 0.3% of world services exports and 0.9% of world services imports in 2017 (WTO, 2019).

## Globalization of Service Production

Other than the service market, the production of services is also globalized.

> **Globalization of Production**
>
> *Globalization of production* refers to the dispersal of production activities to locations that help a company achieve its cost-minimization or quality-maximization objectives for a good or service. This includes sourcing key production inputs (such as raw materials) and the international outsourcing of services (Wild et al., 2016).

### Reconfigure Service Value Chains Globally

Since the early 1990s, new technologies and market liberalization (particularly telecommunications and finance) have made it possible to break down the service value chain and geographically separate service production and consumption. The "production" process of certain services allows for dispersion similar to that of goods. Delivering software, for instance, involves many discrete steps like developing codes, testing, maintenance, and training and education, most of which can be performed remotely. This enables countries with IT talents to join services global value chains (GVCs) just as they join goods GVCs. Publishing services provide another excellent example of this globalization of service production. An edited book may be commissioned from an editor in one country, produced from a collection of chapters from authors scattered across several countries, copyedited in another country, and typeset and printed in yet another. In those examples, service players can reconfigure their operations worldwide, procuring the service components and processes from around the world to receive the best prices, rates, talents, and services.

### Offshoring

Global service production is closely associated with the phenomenon of "offshoring." The offshored services can be delivered in an internal mode (setting up a subsidiary in another country, such as a shared service center) or an external mode (outsourcing the service to another company in another country) (Pisani and Ricart, 2016).

**Offshoring**

*Offshoring* refers to a domestic company sourcing products or services from a foreign-based company, either a subsidiary of the local firm (captive or international in-sourcing) or an independent service provider (offshore outsourcing).

- A range of services can be offshored. For instance, a US company offshores its IT and IT-enabled services in India, such as software development services. It can also offshore some business process services, such as call center services, in the Philippines. The company may also offshore higher-value-added knowledge-intensive services, such as its research and development (R&D) centers, in Germany and China to develop the technology or new products for the regional market. In professional services, banking and IT services lead the way and have established global delivery models that combine proximity to local customers and operational industrialization. For example, in 2002, HSBC diverted 15,000 telephone queries a week from British small business customers to be handled at an HSBC call center in Hyderabad, India. This was because staff in India were often well educated but only received 20–25% of what their British counterparts earned. In addition, HSBC also offshored thousands of cheques, direct debits, and other paperwork to Guangzhou in China (Sunderland, 2002). According to a report published in 2022 by Precedence Research, the global business process outsourcing market was estimated at US$ 268.21 billion in 2021 and is expected to surpass around US$ 576.98 billion by 2030, poised to grow at a compound annual growth rate (CAGR) of 8.9% during the forecast period 2022–2030 (Precedence Research, 2022). A detailed discussion on the configuration of the value chain and offshoring is in ► Chap. 10.

## Who Are the Service Producers?

Large advanced economies have traditionally dominated service exports. Indeed, in global rankings of services exports, the United States, the UK, and Germany continue to be the leaders. However, further down the rankings of the world's largest services exporters, there is a shift in global economic power from the West to the East. As reported by Kupelian (2020), the United States, the UK, and Germany occupied the top three spots, accounting for around one-third of the global market share in 2005. But this is gradually changing, as there has been a steady erosion of advanced economies' share of world service exports since 2005. In 2018, China became the world's fifth largest services exporter, overtaking the Netherlands, Spain, and Italy. Meanwhile, India has overtaken Japan and held the 8th spot in the global rankings of service exporters in 2018, up from just 14th in 2005.

## Drivers of Globalization

Many types of drivers are suggested for manufacturing firms' globalization. The most relevant ones for service globalization include the following.

### Global Customers Driven by Common Customer Needs

Industries with common customer needs and tastes across countries offer more opportunities for globalization. Large corporate customers, when becoming global, often seek to standardize and simplify the array of services they consume. For instance, firms may seek to minimize the number of auditors they use worldwide, using the "Big Four" accounting firms that can apply a consistent worldwide approach (within the context of national rules within each country of operation). Corporate banking, insurance, business logistics, and management consulting are further examples (Lovelock & Yip, 1996).

Among individual consumers, globalization also leads to convergence, as discussed in ► Sect.2.3. As income increases for the middle class in the world, affluent, educated, and cosmopolitan customers tend to share similar purchasing power. With higher purchasing power, people, irrespective of nationality, tend to enjoy similar educational levels, academic and cultural backgrounds, and access to information. As these cultural and social dimensions begin to resemble each other in many countries, the group of individual global customers rises, whose desire for material possessions, ways of spending leisure time, and aspirations for the future become increasingly similar (Kotabe & Helsen, 2022). For instance, when purchasing goods and services on their travels, individuals demand unified characteristics such as ubiquity, timeliness, convenience, safety, and so on. These unified characteristics thus create opportunities for travel-related services globally, ranging from transportation to credit, communication, hospitality, and emergency support. For instance, global customers seeking airline services look for aircraft to be maintained properly in the same way everywhere. A New Zealander who breaks her leg in Pamplona needs medical treatment on the spot. The American executive has lost his traveler's cheques in Shanghai and needs reimbursement there, not back home in Indiana later. In the opening case, the internationalization of American Express is made possible by affluent global customers who demand high-quality goods and services globally.

It must be accepted that standardized services may not meet the needs of many customers worldwide. However, the nature of service delivery makes both standardization and customization equally feasible. A standardized core service can be augmented (and differentiated) by embedding nationally customized supplementary service elements. For instance, an international resort chain can integrate Balinese dancing in Indonesia into its Club Med vacations. An international airline can use local cabin crews as service providers to overcome the foreignness of a standardized service.

## Favorable Logistics



"Customer involvement in production" makes logistics more salient in service globalization. In some possession-processing services (such as repair services), customers are willing to transport their possessions to another location for better service. In most people-processing services, the need for convenience prevents concentration. Some people-processing services have succeeded similarly in having customers come to them. One example is the London hospitals that maintain a flourishing business among wealthy Middle-Eastern patients (Lovelock & Yip, 1996).

Logistics is seldom a barrier to globalization for information-based services. Using electronic channels to deliver services allows providers to concentrate production in locations with specific expertise and offer cost savings or other meaningful advantages. For instance, banks in the Cayman Islands are not conveniently located from a purely geographic standpoint. Still, money can be shipped there electronically to take advantage of the tax benefits conferred by offshore funds status (Lovelock & Yip, 1996).

## The Spillover Effect from Goods Exports

There are spillover effects between goods and services exports. For example, businesses are selling goods (e.g., jet engines) embedded with services (e.g., maintenance service contracts for jet engines) as a source of additional revenue without the extra costs associated with finding new clients and markets (a model termed "servitization") (Peng, 2020). As illustrated in the closing case in ► Chap. 1, *Servitization of Caterpillar—From Selling Products to Selling Services*, the manufacturer servitized their business, i.e., by providing ongoing leasing, repair, and maintenance, instead of simply selling machines or equipment. Such a servitization model necessitates the service to be exported globally. As uncertainty in the global merchandise trade sector continues, we expect to see more of this spillover effect into services trade.

## Liberalization of World Trade

International barriers to services trade are deeply intertwined with national regulatory, investment, and immigration policies and can comprise things such as restrictions on foreign direct investment (FDI), restrictions on the recognition of professional qualifications, residency/local presence obligations, and limitations on the scope of activities that can be undertaken by foreigners. Although lagging behind good trade liberalization, the liberalization of service trade has made some progress in recent decades.

At the global level, the General Agreement on Trade in Services (GATS) introduced in 1995 is the most prominent instrument to liberalize trade

(Chaudhary, 2016). Under the framework, most trade liberalization was identified in air transport services, commercial banking, computer services, and aviation (OECD, 2021). For example, an agreement on freeing trade in telecommunications was finally reached by the World Trade Organization (WTO) in 1997, although many countries retain limitations on their areas of compliance (Bronckers & Larouche, 1997).

Some liberalization efforts are also made at the regional level. For instance, as part of the Single European Market initiative, the 2006 Services Directive aimed at facilitating the cross-border provision of services within the EU, covering services representing some 45% of EU GDP (Ebeke et al., 2019). Manila Action Plan for APEC (MAPA) included several important items in services trade liberalization, for instance, the adoption of sets of APEC (Asia-Pacific Economic Cooperation) principles to develop open markets for energy services and telecommunications (APEC Secretariat, 1997).

Government authorities have privatized services such as utilities (water, electricity), telecommunications, and mail delivery, and taken steps to lift restrictions targeting foreign service firms (Nestor & Mahboobi, 2000). The Philippines, for example, opened up its telecommunications and airlines to foreign companies (Venzon, 2022).

In fact, the OECD Services Trade Restrictiveness Index (STRI) provides a snapshot of services regulatory regimes to help businesses understand the status of service trade liberalization of the countries. Such service trade liberalization measures reduce regulatory barriers to the provision of services across borders (trade) and the establishment of a firm in another country (FDI), simplify administrative procedures, and foster cooperation between countries, thus facilitating service firms to explore new markets and exploit low-cost resources on a global scale.

Nevertheless, the *liberalization of service trade* is considerably more complex than the liberalization of trade in goods (Sauve & Mattoo, 2003), and restrictions on trade in services generally remain more significant than those on manufactured goods. The following box provides some information about the OECD Services Tarde Restrictiveness Index, a tool businesses could use to understand countries' service trade restrictions.

**Interesting Fact**

Launched in 2014 and updated annually, the OECD Services Trade Restrictiveness Index (Digital STRI) is a tool that provides information on regulations affecting trade in services in 22 sectors across all OECD member countries and Brazil, the People's Republic of China, India, Indonesia, Kazakhstan, Malaysia, Peru, Singapore, South Africa, Thailand, and Vietnam. These countries and sectors represent over 80% of global trade in services. More information about this database can be found at ► https://www.oecd.org/trade/topics/services-trade/

## Digitalization



The advancement of information technology and digitalization has sped up the globalization of services in various ways. Digital technologies significantly bring down the costs of searching for, matching, tracking, and verifying information (Goldfarb & Tucker, 2019), thus reducing information and transaction costs in trade. Correspondingly, digitalization allows firms to reach larger numbers of digitally connected customers across the globe. For instance, in the travel industry, operators such as Expedia and Booking are positioning themselves as direct competitors to travel agencies and hotel operators to capture customers worldwide. Another example is online labor platforms being developed to connect freelance service providers with clients worldwide. Individuals can offer their services across borders more flexibly through online freelance marketplaces using web collaboration software and video conferencing. Occupations such as software development, creative design and multimedia, sales and marketing support, and professional services are the most likely to be offered online (Kässi & Lehdonvirta, 2018). Workers operate more like entrepreneurs in a global marketplace. In many economies, the wages earned through such platforms exceed the averages for local companies (Lund & Manyika, 2016).

Digitalization also transforms professional services. The number of virtual law firms and freelance management consultants on digital platforms is growing. With no physical offices to run, they have lower operating costs, and clients can benefit from reduced fees (WTO, 2019).

Digitalization facilitates the outsourcing of activities for easier scaling of production. A company may gain significant economies of scale by centralizing "value chain activities" globally to benefit from favorable labor costs or exchange rates. For instance, a company can consolidate supplementary services (e.g., reservations) or back-office functions (e.g., accounting) in just one or a few countries. This will be discussed more in ► Sect. 2.5, *Economies of Scale in Services*.

Digitalization also creates new services trade, often replacing goods trade. Digital technologies are blurring the distinction between trade in goods and services while increasing the importance of data flows and intellectual property (Strange & Zucchella, 2017). For example, Apple has established itself in music distribution, with an 80% market share in online music. This has broken the traditional industry rule forcing consumers to buy an entire album to acquire a single song (Sen, 2010). Another example in business service is 3D printing, which fosters trade-in software design rather than final products. Web-based portals now enable users to buy and download 3D data files for home fabrication; parts for generators, pumps, or valves; and others (WTO, 2019). IoT applications are also being integrated into services to enable remote monitoring and central feedback systems and offer other services (Oracle, n.d.). These factors are expected to drive the services market going forward.

## Overall Assessment of Drivers

Most globalization drivers apply to all services, but their impact varies by service type and industry. This conclusion highlights the importance of systematically evaluating globalization drivers for individual sectors rather than taking generalized views that service businesses can be more (or less) easily globalized than manufacturing businesses.

## Economies of Scale in Services

Much of the historical pattern of competition in services occurred within domestic market boundaries as a result of the small-scale, fragmented structure of service industries and their culture-specific patterns of demand and consumption (Wild et al., 2016). In addition, many services are perishable and require customer involvement in production, challenging the tenet of standardization or concentrating production. They hence have exhibited minimum efficient scale at low levels.

Globalization increases competition and pressure on firms to become more cost-efficient to be able to offer competitive prices. Companies, therefore, look for economies of scale and scope to reduce their cost. In recent decades, thanks to the new development in the service industry and technological advancement, service companies can pursue economies of scale and scope on a global scale.

**Global Scale Economies**

*Global scale economies* apply when a firm increases the scale by supplying to the worldwide market to achieve the optimum scale and reduce the average costs. Any asset that yields economies of scale can also be the basis for *economies of scope* if it provides input into two or more processes, that is, when the cost of producing two outputs jointly is less than the cost of producing each output separately (Teece, 1982).

First, service industries are increasingly concentrated via merger and acquisition activities. This has been observed in hotel chains, accountants and management consultancy firms, airlines, telecommunications, software, information services, and financial service. Many sectors now resemble oligopolies (as in international catering and contract cleaning services), although small local firms coexist as local providers in most markets. Increased concentration has generated the potential for economies of scale and scope in production, distribution, marketing, and management (Segal-Horn & Faulkner, 2010). For example, the service company could stock input through bulk orders, as the Fast-food chains take advantage of bulk orders. The distribution cost could also be lowered. As an airline gets bigger, for instance, the overhead cost per passenger carried declines as the fixed cost is spread over more passengers. In terms of marketing, advertising MNCs (multinational corporations) such as Interpublic or WPP derive economies of scale from bulk purchasing of media time and space, as well as the internal transfer of market and design data in managing global campaigns for clients (Segal-Horn & Faulkner, 2010).

Second, just as automakers invest in the latest manufacturing processes, service companies can also have high capital asset structures and high fixed costs when bringing in new technology, largely IT-related. The high-cost facilities will be shared to produce services in multiple markets. Google, for instance, has invested in six data centers in the United States, three in Europe (Ireland, Belgium, Finland), and four in the rest of the world (Chile, Hong Kong, Singapore, Taiwan) (Google Cloud, n.d.). In Singapore, with the construction of three data centers in 2011, 2015, and 2020, respectively, Google's long-term investment in Singapore data centers reached $850 million (Benton, 2020). Google uses these large data centers to provide services to 330 million people in South East Asia. The services combine large drives, computer nodes organized in aisles of racks, internal and external networking, environmental controls (mainly cooling and humidification control), and operational software (especially as concerns load balancing and fault tolerance). In our opening case, American Express also captures the economies of scale by spreading the fixed cost across a larger market. The fixed cost of building and maintaining a global payments network is enormous, yet the marginal costs of running additional transactions over the web are negligible.

In addition, the proprietary know-how and specialized indivisible assets generated by the capital-intensive assets become a common input into two or more products, thus creating economies of scale and scope. For example, American Express uses its information systems to set and monitor service standards for fast response times for card inquiries or to provide additional services such as "free" travel arrangements or theatre bookings for cardholders. Airlines use sophisticated software to maximize yield from higher-revenue seats on all flights, a major contribution to profitability in a service business with high fixed costs. Database management and the opportunities it provides for mining detailed customer information and profiling give the potential for retail chains and financial services, for example, selling travel insurance to an airline passenger booking a flight to go on holiday. It allows them to target cross-selling of additional products, which is a classic economy of scope (Segal-Horn & Faulkner, 2010).

Third, service firms increasingly concentrate on selected activities in a few locations to serve multiple markets. To do this, service companies usually have to standardize production processes rather than through physical concentration and concentrate the upper stream rather than the downstream stage of the value chain (Lovelock & Yip, 1996). Service production and delivery systems can be divided into "front office" and "back office." The former is the portion encountered by customers, while the latter is part of the service factory that can have low contact with and hence be located remotely from the customers. In the opening case, American Express consolidated its financial transaction recording process in two financial shared servicing hub locations to achieve low average cost and 24/7 coverage. This is an example of concentrating the selected parts of its value chains, particularly the back-office activities through offshoring.

*Service-to-product model*: In most services businesses, getting more business means hiring more people. This makes it difficult for most service businesses to achieve economies of scale. Companies such as Microsoft have adopted a service-to-product model. In such a model, businesses begin their lives by providing customized services and eventually draw on their accumulated expertise to deliver packaged solutions that stand independently. The packaged solution can be used or consumed by the customer largely without seller support. The following case illustrates this.

**Microsoft's Journey from Services to Products**

In 1975, Gates and Allen built software operating systems for companies such as Ricoh, Texas Instruments, and others, all of which marketed their then-new-fangled personal computers (PCs) at the beginning of the PC age. These early PCs could not do much without operating systems. So Gates and Allen's services business was doing well. At times, they received up to $180,000 up-front, which Gates recalled as "incredible." However, Gates and Allen often encountered delivery challenges because delivering services takes time.

In 1980, IBM hired Gates and Allen's company, Microsoft, to build the operating system for its new IBM "personal computer." Microsoft delivered PC-DOS to IBM.

Having seen that the operating systems they had been building for the clients were remarkably similar, Gates and Allen decided to do something different. They structured the contract with IBM to permit Microsoft to provide a copycat DOS for future IBM PC copycats. MS-DOS was born.

Thus, Microsoft could *profit from licensing MS-DOS to companies that offered computers more or less compatible with the IBM PC.*

Gates and Allen no longer had to spend weeks and months writing code for another operating system for new PC entrants like Compaq. They simply licensed a product that could be shipped in a shrink-wrapped box or downloaded digitally. As PC penetration grew, Microsoft began developing additional software products—Word, Excel, and more—that also came in shrink-wrapped boxes and could be supplied to any PC maker running on DOS.

Microsoft had successfully transformed its services into stand-alone products that could be sold to multiple customers without requiring additional time or hand-holding from Gates or Allen.Source: Mullins (n.d.)

The pursuit of economies of scale and scope benefits the demand side. Economies of scope in service firms can lower transaction costs and search costs for customers. For instance, consumers are now able to compare prices and quality on comparison websites. They can also directly book a hotel or buy insurance in any country at a lower cost, thanks to the service company's investment in its own website, which undercuts all brokerage services (known as "disintermediation") such as travel agents, insurance brokers, or investment analysts. However, when a service company attempts to deliver multiple services through a single service delivery channel, there might be some unintended negative consequences. For example, you may have booked a quiet hotel room while only finding on arrival that many other guests are groups of business delegates using the hotel's conference facilities. That is a potential economy of scope for the business that has negative consequences for the customer (Segal-Horn & Faulkner, 2010).

## The Biggest Service Firms Around the World

The pursuit of economies of scale and scope due to globalization led to strong growth of multinational enterprises (MNEs) (Holtbrügge & Welge, 2015), also in the service sector. From the 2000s, the number of employees working in the service sectors surpassed those in the industry and agriculture sectors. As in ◘ Fig. 2.1, about half of the employment opportunities have been provided by service companies since 2015. We can also find the importance of service companies by looking at the 100 largest companies in the world by market capitalization in 2022. Numerous companies in communication services, financial services, and information technology services, such as Alphabet, ► Amazon.com, Berkshire Hathaway, UnitedHealth, Tencent Holdings, and Visa, stand out in the Top 100 largest company list.

This has led to a situation where the largest Service MNEs have become very powerful, also in interaction with governments in countries where they are present or contemplating setting up a presence (Holtbrügge & Welge, 2015). Take a look at the following ◘ Table 2.1 showing the 20 biggest economic units of the world in 2013. What do you notice? Yes, some MNEs are so big in annual turnover that they

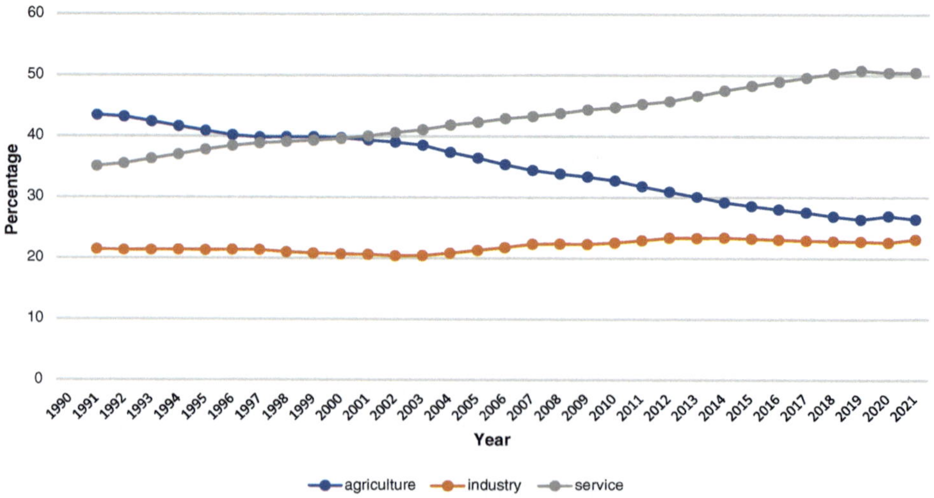


◘ **Fig. 2.1** Percentage of employment in agriculture, industry, and service sectors. (Source: Author's own figure. Data extracted from The World Bank open data, ► https://data.worldbank.org/ [The World Bank, 2023a, 2023b, 2023c])

**Table 2.1** Top 20 companies in the world 2022 by market capitalization (USD). Source: Author's own table based on the information extracted from FinanceCharts (2023)

| # | Name | Country | Sector | Market capitalization |
|---|---|---|---|---|
| 1 | Apple | United States | Information Technology | $2.098T |
| 2 | **Microsoft** | United States | Information Technology | $1.78T |
| 3 | **Alphabet** | United States | Communication Services | $1.158T |
| 4 | ► Amazon.com | United States | Consumer Discretionary | $869.691B |
| 5 | **Berkshire Hathaway** | United States | Financials | $675.613B |
| 6 | **UnitedHealth Group** | United States | Health Care | $496.429B |
| 7 | Johnson & Johnson | United States | Health Care | $464.018B |
| 8 | Exxon Mobil | United States | Energy | $447.576B |
| 9 | **Tencent Holdings** | China | Communication Services | $436.533B |
| 10 | **Visa** | United States | Information Technology | $424.357B |
| 11 | Tesla | United States | Consumer Discretionary | $388.877B |
| 12 | **Walmart** | United States | Consumer Staples | $387.719B |
| 13 | **JPMorgan Chase & Co** | United States | Financials | $385.071B |
| 14 | Taiwan Semiconductor | Taiwan | Information Technology | $384.083B |
| 15 | NVIDIA | United States | Information Technology | $374.068B |
| 16 | Eli Lilly and Co | United States | Health Care | $363.163B |
| 17 | Procter & Gamble | United States | Consumer Staples | $361.663B |
| 18 | LVMH Moet Hennessy Louis Vuitton | France | Consumer Discretionary | $360.065B |
| 19 | Chevron | United States | Energy | $343.027B |
| 20 | **Mastercard** | United States | Information Technology | $330.358B |

are "bigger" than many countries in terms of their GDP. Can you imagine the negotiation power of such companies toward host governments? As an example, consider the case of Amazon, which had planned to set up a second global headquarters in the United States in 2017. Due to its strong growth, Amazon's headquarters in Seattle was getting too small, so the group looked to set up a second one in the United States where they would invest US$5 billion and create 50,000 jobs. Cities were asked to enter a competition. In total, 238 locations across the

United States submit a bid, rolling out the red carpet for Amazon. New York City illuminated the Empire State Building in Amazon orange. New Jersey offered US$7 billion in tax breaks and subsidies. Amazon's conditions included subsidies and that there needs to be an airport with a direct flight to Seattle. Amazon selected a shortlist of 30 cities that were allowed to send representatives to Seattle and pitch personally to Amazon boss Jeff Bezos. All of this occurred under strong time pressure.

## The Benefits of Globalization

### Benefits of Globalization to Consumers

Putting aside the possible benefits of globalization for individual economies and the world economy as a whole, globalization also provides potential benefits or advantages for individual consumers and companies. Consumers benefit from globalization in a range of ways:

- In general, globalization decreases the cost of manufacturing. This means that companies can offer goods at a lower price to consumers. The average cost of goods is a key aspect that contributes to increases in the standard of living.
- Globalization allows consumers to access a broader range of products. No individual country could produce the sheer variety of goods that can be produced globally. Through globalization, consumers in one country can access goods and services that they would never otherwise have access to. In some cases, this may contribute to improved health by enabling a more varied and healthier diet; in others, it is blamed for increases in unhealthy food consumption and diabetes (Effects of Economic Globalizaiton, n.d.).
- Higher quality. As each nation concentrates on its own specialty industries, there is far less "re-inventing the wheel." For example, every country does not need to waste its scarce resources producing its own version of the smartphone when one can be imported from a country that specializes in this product.

### Benefits of Globalization to Businesses

Companies also get benefits from globalization. Levitt advocated for the homogenization of markets, which implies the need for globally standardized products/services rather than customized ones (Levitt, 1983), thus forming the globalization of the market. Corporations sell standardized products or services in the same way everywhere—autos, agricultural commodities and equipment, industrial and commercial construction, banking and insurance services, transport, and telecommunications, to mention some of the obvious (Levitt, 1983). Companies thus benefit in a range of ways:

- It reduces marketing costs. Companies that sell global products/services can reduce costs by standardizing certain marketing activities and achieving economies of scale and scope. This point has been discussed in more detail in ► Sect. 2.5.
- It creates new market opportunities. A company selling a global product/service can explore opportunities abroad if the home market is small or saturated. When the global producer offers lower costs internationally, its patronage expands exponentially. It not only reaches into distant markets but also attracts customers who previously held to local preferences and now capitulate to the attractions of lower prices. The standardization strategy not only responds to worldwide homogenized markets but also expands those markets with aggressive low pricing (Levitt, 1983).
- Companies are able to reach a broader range of suppliers at a lower cost. An international enterprise can increase its overall profitability by outsourcing certain functions, such as payroll and HR (Human Resource), to countries where this can be provided at a lower cost. But globalization does not just mean outsourcing: Setting up separate legal entities (such as foreign subsidiaries) and branches or using Global Professional Employer Organization (PEO) solutions can be effective mechanisms for setting up a more cost-effective business location (Wild et al., 2016).
- Companies can access lower-cost workers and technical expertise. Globalization gives all nations access to a wider labor pool. Companies in developing nations with a shortage of knowledge workers might, for example, "import" labor to kickstart their business. Companies in wealthier nations, on the other hand, might outsource low-skill work to developing nations with a lower cost of living to reduce the cost of goods sold and pass those savings on to the customers (Stobierski, 2021).
- It helps in spreading risks. Individual countries are vulnerable to economic events and fluctuations specific to that country. An advantage of globalization and expanding into multiple countries is that an enterprise can spread this risk and ensure they do not place "all their eggs in the same basket."

## The Cost of Globalization

Not everything about globalization is beneficial. Various concerns have been raised regarding the globalization of services.

There is a widespread view that services offshoring could cause significant job losses, particularly in developed countries. When HSBC offshored the call center and paperwork services to India and China, 1500 jobs were lost to "natural wastage" in the UK from 1998 to 2002 (Sunderland, 2002). One study suggests that almost 30% of US jobs are susceptible to offshoring because technological progress allows firms to disentangle service delivery from service consumption and exploit labor cost differences between advanced and developing economies (Blinder, 2009a, 2009b).

Service offshoring is also argued to cause lower wages in developed nations. When a manufacturing job is lost in a wealthy nation, the new job (if it is found) pays less than the previous one. Some evidence shows that a displaced manufacturing worker, especially an older one, receives lower pay in a subsequent job. Workers in developed countries like the United States face pay-cut demands from employers who threaten to export jobs (Couch & Placzek, 2010; Couch et al., 2011; Deelen et al., 2018). This has created a culture of fear among many middle-class workers who have little leverage in this global game, decreasing employee loyalty and morale, and job security.

Critics charge that globalization and international outsourcing exploit workers in low-wage nations. In trade debates, multinational corporations are often cast as villains exploiting low-wage workers in low-wage countries with weaker labor laws. For instance, prisoners and child workers are used to working in inhumane conditions. Safety standards are ignored to produce cheap goods (Collins, 2015). Many multinational firms outsource their subcontractors to produce goods or services. Some subcontractors, such as Foxconn and Formosa, are themselves large and multinational. But many subcontractors—especially in complex and long supply chains—are small, geographically dispersed, and focused on minimizing costs. It is difficult even for well-intentioned firms and sophisticated rights advocates in such locations to monitor and respect for labor standards (Mosley, 2016). This will be given more discussion in ► Chap. 11.

Another debate about globalization is whether it deepens inequality around the world. Economists usually stand by the belief that globalization made the world more integrated. The improvement in development that happened over the past 200 years has been very supportive for developing countries, making both poverty and inequality fall over the past two decades for the first time in 150 years: "a decline of people in absolute poverty, fall from 31% of the world's population to 20%" (Held & McGrew, 2016, p. 441). This is further extended, as "between 1981 and 2001 the percentage of rural people living on less than $1 a day decreased from 79 to 27% in China, 63 to 42% in India, and 55 to 11% in Indonesia" (Bardhan, 2006). Providing such data, one could conclude that globalization has strongly contributed to improving the economic and living situation in developing countries. However, critics believe that globalization widens the gap in average incomes between rich and poor nations. Globalization, according to Luke Martell, is "the integration of poor countries into a world economy of open competition" (Martell, 2017, p. 148). While supporters of globalization view the process as equalizing, democratizing, and expanding the horizons of the poor, anti-globalists see this process as a producer of inequality, maintaining that inequality is not the same as poverty, as inequality can rise while poverty can reduce. The World Inequality Report (2022) shows that at a global level, the average income for an adult is $23,380 (when adjusted for Purchasing Power Parity or PPP). However, the report explains that this conceals wide disparities between and within countries. The richest 10% of the global population currently take home 52% of the income. The poorest half of the global population earns just 8%. Critics mainly attribute such inequality to globalization in three ways, illustrated in the following box.

**Why Does Globalization Lead to Inequality?**

First, the *Green Revolution* between 1950 and the late 1960s invoked a boom in agricultural production and pushed demand for more in developing countries. This meant something different for poor Africans than that for rich corporations. It indeed increased production, but at the same time, it rejected small farmers who could not afford the high-tech inputs and went bankrupt or disappeared (George, 2013).

Second, in the 1980s and 1990s, developing countries opened and liberalized their markets by creating reforms, reducing tariff barriers, privatizing their economies, and, after time, opening up capital markets. On the one hand, the companies of rich countries benefited from it because of the easing of tariffs (Martell, 2017). On the other hand, this created a situation where organizations and rich countries provided financial support to poor countries to stimulate development (Martell, 2017), which led to poor, negative growth, a dramatic increase in external debt, a decrease in exports, and, in the end, doubled poverty.

Third, service trade benefits the high-skilled workers more than the low-

A beggar on the street; Critics accuse globalization of having increased inequality, image by Mihail Menshov from Pixabay

skilled workers, thus creating greater inequality in both developing and developed economies. In developing countries, highly skilled workers in trade-intensive services jobs (e.g., Information Technology in India) benefit more from service export than those less skillful workers in agriculture or manufacturing industries. In contrast, in developed economies, service imports (through offshoring to other countries), such as bookkeeping and calling centers, adversely affect relatively less skilled workers, while services exports, such as marketing or consulting, positively affect those skilled workers (Görg et al., 2011).

The next concern is related to the brain drain from some countries, particularly developing countries (Zhatkanbaeva et al., 2012). In 2002, an article in *The Economist* addressed the topic of "brain drain," asking whether developing countries gain or lose when "their brightest talent goes abroad" (Outward bound, 2002). Zhatkanbaeva et al. (2012) suggest that 15–20% of university graduates leave the country of Kazakhstan in search of the opportunity for self-realization. A report from the World Bank (2002a, 2002b) has expressed similar concern at the rapidly increasing rates of emigration of knowledge workers from developing countries; this could result in the emergence of a global knowledge divide, which will inevitably delay economic growth in the developing countries.

Many critics have also pointed out that globalization negatively affects the environment (Song et al., 2020). For example, the massive development of transport that has been the basis of globalization is responsible for serious environmental problems such as excessive use of fossil fuels, contributing to greenhouse gas emissions, global warming, or air pollution (Farooq et al., 2019). Globalization also contributes to deforestation and the degradation of animal habitats (Zhang et al., 2022). A 2010 World Trade Organization report found that trade liberalization increases deforestation, which is responsible for roughly 12% of global $CO_2$ emissions (Robalino & Herrera, 2010). Henders et al. (2015) showed that between 2000 and 2011, the production of beef, soy, palm oil, and wood products in just 7 countries was responsible for 3.8 million hectares of forest loss annually, leading to 1.6 billion tons of $CO_2$ emissions per year.

Lastly, with McDonald's, Starbucks, Facebook, and Hollywood movies expanding globally, people around the world eat the same foods, watch the same movies, read information from all over the world, and embrace different cultures. Such high exposure to foreign cultures, on the one hand, helps improve our awareness of different societies. On the other hand, anti-globalists argue that globalization eradicates cultural differences and destroys the rich diversity of cultures. In Japan, for instance, industrialization and technology have led to declining traditions in their culture, such as arts, social practices, and artisanship (Rutten, 2021). Many languages are on the verge of becoming extinct due to the development of globalization. There are around 7000 spoken languages in the world. About 71% of those spoken are estimated to be in danger in a few years, and half of those are even losing their value in the world because they are not used for any purpose. Languages are under threat when under 1000 people can speak them (Held & Anthony, 2016).

**Review Questions**

1. Discuss the drivers of service globalization.
2. How do service companies achieve economies of scale and scope?
3. Service sectors are the most important employers in today's world. Does service globalization help or hurt the world's poor?

## Closing Case: Zoom's Boom

It was on April 9, 2020. Eric Yuan, the founder and chief executive officer (CEO) of teleconferencing software company Zoom, got up each morning after 3 or 4 h of sleep and nervously checked the previous day's capacity numbers to ensure the servers were not overwhelmed by traffic. Then he slogged through videoconference calls from his Bay Area home. "It is too many Zoom meetings," he said via Zoom. "I hate that."

Headquartered in San Jose, Zoom built a research and development team in China, where personnel costs were less expensive than in many other jurisdictions. Zoom disclosed in its IPO (Initial Public Offering) prospectus in 2019 that most of its product development personnel are based in China. Zoom employs over 500 people across multiple R&D centers in China, accounting for roughly 30% of its total workforce and 70% of its non-US-based employees. Zoom spent $33 million on R&D, or just 10% of total revenue, which was a much smaller share than other business software makers. For example, Atlassian's development cost

The Zoom app on a smartphone, image by Biljana Jovanovic from Pixabay

accounted for over 40% of its revenue, while smaller companies like Zendesk and Hubspot spent over 20% of their revenues on R&D.

A few months ago, in 2019, Yuan's company was merely a fast-growing success story in the communication service sector. In 2020, the Pandemic hit the world. Suddenly, Zoom became a critical infrastructure. Zoom was appealing, in part, because it was a neutral platform. It was not tethered to Apple, like FaceTime, or Google or Microsoft, like Hangouts and Skype. Anyone, even someone without an account, could join a meeting, from any device, just by clicking a link in a text or email. Hosts could record video and audio and generate transcripts, and it was easy for people to screen-share.

As billions of people worldwide had to observe social distancing to control the coronavirus, those lucky enough to still have jobs were trying to work them from home. To do so, they turned to remote collaboration tools. Messaging platforms such as Slack and videoconferencing software like Cisco Webex, Microsoft Teams, and, especially, Zoom had seen explosions in traffic.

"Every day is a record," Yuan said. Zoom's daily users were ten million in December 2019, then numbered 200 million in mid-2020. The company's share price had climbed 72% in the same period—doubling from early February to late March 2020—even as markets and the global economy had plummeted.

Zoom's new traffic was not just from workplace conference calls. Its simple interface—users enter a meeting with one click—has made it perfect for millions of people who want to maintain at least a diluted form of human contact. Schools and colleges taught classes on Zoom; Alcoholics Anonymous groups used it to hold meetings; people went to Zoom family reunions and happy hours, and trivia nights. They dated, talked to therapists, and celebrated birthdays. For many, Zoom has become not just a way to socialize but the social fabric itself.

Since then, it has been a dead sprint to cope with the bombing demand. When you are in a Zoom meeting, the app adjusts bandwidth so that one participant's poor signal does not degrade another user's experience. Zoom does this by linking each participant to the closest of the 17 data centers it rents worldwide; if one center is overloaded, it sends traffic to the next closest. To keep up with its new audience, the company has added two data centers, and it has been buying more of the cloud storage capacity it uses for surge protection. Zoom relies heavily on Amazon Web Services Inc., as well as on Oracle Corp., for cloud computing. So far, these efforts have paid off: There have been complaints of poor call quality, and Zoom's website was briefly down for maintenance, but the platform has bent, not broken, under the new demands.

While many new users were not paying for the service, some have sprung for Zoom's paid tiers, and some corporate clients had upgraded when they sent their workforces home. On April 1, 2020, AllianceBernstein analyst Zane Chrane said the Pandemic could generate "a few hundred million" in additional revenue.

In 2022, the Pandemic seemed to end soon globally. As firms throttled back on mandatory home working, many analysts have pondered whether Zoom Communications would begin a downward trajectory. But its first-quarter total revenue in 2022 went up 12% year on year, with the number of customers rising by 46%.

The 3-month period that ended on April 30, 2022, saw the core conferencing solution complemented with the launch of Zoom Contact Center, Zoom Whiteboard and Zoom IQ for Sales, a conversation intelligence service for sales professionals, and Zoom Events and Webinar functionalities such as Backstage and Webinar session branding. These offerings were designed to put engagement at the center of the experience and transform how users work, connect, and collaborate. The company said the products demonstrated its focus on enhancing the customer experience and promoting hybrid work.

In February 2023, Zoom announced its plan to lay off around 15% of its staff—roughly 1300 people—as part of a wider restructuring to eliminate duplicative roles. Yuan's base salary for the last financial year was $301,731, though his total compensation was reportedly closer to $1.1 million. Other executive staff would also take a 20% pay cut and lose bonuses. CEO Eric Yuan wrote in a message to staff:

> As the world transitions to life post-pandemic, we are seeing that people and businesses continue to rely on Zoom. But the uncertainty of the global economy, and its effect on our customers, means we need to take a hard—yet important—look inward to reset ourselves so we can weather the economic environment, deliver for our customers and achieve Zoom's long-term vision. (A Message from Eric Yuan, CEO of Zoom, 2023)

**Questions**

1. What drives Zoom's global growth during the Pandemic?
2. How did Zoom achieve economies of scale and scope?
3. Do you think Zoom can maintain its global growth after the Pandemic?

Source: A Message from Eric Yuan, CEO of Zoom (2023); Bennett and Grant (2020); Kim (2019); O'Halloran (2022)

**Summary**

This chapter

- Identified the reasons and types of services traded globally and the regional development of the service market.
- Explained that the globalization of service production is made possible by service companies' efforts in reconfiguring service value chains globally.
- Discussed the drivers of service globalization, including global customers driven by common needs, favorable logistics, spillover effect from goods exports, and digitalization.
- Outlined how service companies achieve global economies of scale and scope.
- Introduced service companies as the most important employers globally.
- Assessed the benefits and costs of service globalization.

## References




A Message from Eric Yuan, CEO of Zoom. (2023, February 7). Retrieved from https://blog.zoom.-us/a-message-from-eric-yuan-ceo-of-zoom/.

American Express Website. (n.d.). Retrieved from https://about.americanexpress.com/newsroom/press-releases/news-details/2022/Spend-with-Amex-Card-Acceptance-More-than-Doubles-Globally-/defa.

APEC Secretariat. (1997). *The impact of trade liberalization in APEC.* . Retrieved from https://www.apec.org/docs/default-source/Publications/1997/11/The-Impact-of-Trade-Liberalization-in-APEC-1997/97_ec_impacttradelib.pdf.

Bardhan, P. (2006). *Does globalization help or hurt the world's poor? Overview/globalization and poverty.* [Online] Scientific American. Retrieved from https://www.scientificamerican.com/article/does-globalization-help-o-2006-04/.

Bennett, D., & Grant, N. (2020, April 9). *Zoom goes from conferencing app to the pandemic's social network.* Retrieved from https://www.bloomberg.com/news/features/2020-04-09/zoom-goes-from-conferencing-app-to-the-pandemic-s-social-network.

Benton, D. (2020, May 17). *Google takes Singapore data centre spending to $850 million with third data centre.* Retrieved from https://constructiondigital.com/digital-construction/google-takes-singapore-data-centre-spending-to-dollar850-million-with-third-data-centre.

Birdsall, N. (2010). The (indispensable) middle class in developing countries. In *Equity and growth in a globalizing world* (p. 157).

Birdsall, N., Graham, C., & Pettinato, S. (2000). *Stuck in tunnel: Is globalization muddling the middle?.*

Blinder, A. S. (2009a). How many USS jobs might be offshorable? *World Economics, 10*(2), 41.

Blinder, A. S. (2009b). How many US jobs might be offshorable? *World Economics, 10*(2), 41.

Bronckers, M. C., & Larouche, P. (1997). Telecommunications services and the World Trade Organization. *Journal of World Trade, 31*, 5.

Cavusgil, S. T., Knight, G., & Riesenberger, J. R. (2014). *International business: The new realities.* Pearson Education Limited.

Chaudhary, P. (2016). *Retail marketing in the modern age.* SAGE Publishing India.

Collins, M. (2015). *The pros and cons of globalization.* https://www.forbes.com/sites/mikecollins/2015/05/06/the-pros-and-cons-of-globalization/?sh=6daf54ddccce.

Couch, K. A., Jolly, N. A., & Placzek, D. W. (2011). Earnings losses of displaced workers and the business cycle: An analysis with administrative data. *Economics Letters, 111*(1), 16–19.

Couch, K. A., & Placzek, D. W. (2010). Earnings losses of displaced workers revisited. *American Economic Review., 100*(1), 572–589.

Deelen, A., de Graaf-Zijl, M., & van den Berge, W. (2018). Labour market effects of job displacement for prime-age and older workers. *IZA Journal of Labor Economics, 7*, 1–30.

Ebeke, M. C. H., Frie, J. M., & Rabier, L. (2019). *Deepening the EU's single market for services.* International Monetary Fund.

Effects of Economic Globalizaiton, n.d. *National Geographic.* Retrieved from https://education.nationalgeographic.org/resource/effects-economic-globalization/.

Eurostat. (2023, July 5). *World trade in services.* Retrieved from https://ec.europa.eu/eurostat/statistics-explained/index.php?title=World_trade_in_services#International_trade_in_services_.E2.80.93_overview.

Farooq, M. U., Shahzad, U., Sarwar, S., & ZaiJun, L. (2019). The impact of carbon emission and Forest activities on health outcomes: Empirical evidence from China. *Environmental Science and Pollution Research, 26*(13), 12894–12906.

FinanceCharts. (2023). *Biggest companies in the world by market cap for 2023.* Retrieved from https://www.financecharts.com/screener/biggest.

Fioratti, A. C. (2006). The low income consumer: A growth opportunity. Research paper. ESOMAR-European Society for Opinion and Market Research.

George, S. (2013). *Whose crisis, whose future?* Wiley.

Goldfarb, A., & Tucker, C. (2019). Digital economics. *Journal of Economic Literature, 57*(1), 3–43.

Google Cloud. Retrieved from https://cloud.google.com/about/locations.

Görg, H., Geishecker, I., & Krieger-Boden, C. (2011). Services offshoring increases wage inequality. VOX: CEPR's Policy Portal. Retrieved from https://cepr.org/voxeu/columns/services-offshoring-increases-wage-inequality.

Held, D., & Anthony, A. (2016). *The global transformations reader* (pp. 440–480). Polity Press.

Held, D., & McGrew, A. (2016). *The global transformations reader*. Cambridge: Polity Press.

Henders, S., Persson, U. M., & Kastner, T. (2015). Trading forests: Land-use change and carbon emissions embodied in production and exports of forest-risk commodities. *Environmental Research Letters, 10*(12), 125012.

Holtbrügge, D., & Welge, M. K. (2015). *Internationales Management: Theorie, Funktionen, Fallstudien*. Schäffer Poeschl.

Hout, M. (2008). How class works in popular conception: Most Americans identify with the class their income, occupation, and education implies for them. In *Social class: How does it work?* (pp. 25–64). Russell Sage Foundation.

Kässi, O., & Lehdonvirta, V. (2018). Online labour index: Measuring the online gig economy for policy and research. *Technological Forecasting and Social Change, 137*, 241–248.

Kharas, H. (2010). *The emerging middle class in developing countries*. Retrieved from https://www.oecd.org/dev/44457738.pdf.

Kim, E. (2019, May 26). *Zoom, one of the most anticipated tech IPOs of the year, has one key profit driver: Engineers in China*. Retrieved from https://www.cnbc.com/2019/03/26/zoom-key-profit-driver-ahead-of-ipo-engineers-in-china.html.

Knowledge at Wharton. (2002, December 18). *What works, what doesn't: Lessons from two companies that outsource back-office tasks*. Retrieved from https://knowledge.wharton.upenn.edu/article/what-works-what-doesnt-lessons-from-two-companies-thatoutsource-back-office-tasks/.

Kotabe, M. M., & Helsen, K. (2022). *Global marketing management*. Wiley.

Kupelian, B. (2020). *Will "slowbalisation" snowball into the global services trade?* Retrieved from https://www.pwc.com/sg/en/publications/assets/global-economic-watch-032020.pdf.

Lee, K. (2013). *Schumpeterian analysis of economic catch-up: Knowledge, path-creation, and the middle-income trap*. Cambridge University Press.

Levitt, T. (1983). The globalization of markets. The McKinsey Quarterly. Retrieved from https://edisciplinas.usp.br/pluginfile.php/4180851/mod_resource/content/1/Levitt%20Globalization%20Markets.pdf.

Lovelock, C. H., & Yip, G. S. (1996). Developing global strategies for service businesses. *California Management Review, 38*(2), 64–86.

Lund, S., & Manyika, J. (2016). *How digital trade is transforming globalisation*. International Centre for Trade and Sustainable Development (ICTSD).

Malhotra, N. K., Agarwal, J., & Baalbaki, I. (1998). Heterogeneity of regional trading blocs and global marketing strategies: A multicultural perspective. *International Marketing Review, 15*(6), 476–506.

Martell, L. (2017). *The sociology of globalization* (2nd ed.).

Mondiale, B. (2007). *Global economic prospects: managing the next wave of globalization*. Retrieved from https://www.worldbank.org/content/dam/Worldbank/GEP/GEParchives/GEP2007/381400GEP2007.pdf.

Mosley, L. (2016, September 15). *Does globalization hurt poor workers? It's complicated*. Retrieved from https://www.washingtonpost.com/news/in-theory/wp/2016/09/15/does-globalization-hurt-poor-workers-its-complicated/.

Mullins, J. n.d. *Microsoft's secret to scaling services businesses*. Retrieved from https://blog.growthinstitute.com/funding/service-to-product.

Nestor, S., & Mahboobi, L. (2000). Privatisation of public utilities: The OECD experience. In *Privatization, competition and regulation* (pp. 13–49).

O'Halloran, J. (2022). *Zoom boom continues as it delivers billion-dollar first quarter*. Retrieved from https://www.computerweekly.com/news/252520664/Zoom-boom-continues-as-it-delivers-billion-dollar-first-quarterult.aspx

OECD. (2005). *OECD handbook on economic globalisation indicators*. Retrieved from https://www.oecd.org/sti/ind/34964971.pdf.

OECD. (2021, February 1). Services trade liberalised in 2021, showing significant decrease in volume and effects of new measures, OECD says. Retrieved from https://www.oecd.org/newsroom/services-trade-liberalised-in-2021-showing-significant-decrease-in-volume-and-effects-of-new-measures.htm.

Oracle. (n.d.). Retrieved from https://www.oracle.com/internet-of-things/what-is-iot/.

Outward Bound. (2002, September 26). *The Economist*. Retrieved from https://www.economist.com/special-report/2002/09/26/outward-bound.

Ozturk, A., & Cavusgil, S. T. (2019). Global convergence of consumer spending: Conceptualization and propositions. *International Business Review, 28*(2), 294–304. issn:0969-5931.

Peng, S. Y. (2020). A new trade regime for the servitization of manufacturing: Rethinking the goods-services dichotomy. *Journal of World Trade, 54*(5), 669.

Precedence Research. (2022). *Business process outsourcing market size, share 2022-2030*. Retrieved from https://www.precedenceresearch.com/business-process-outsourcing-market.

Rassekh, F. (1998). The convergence hypothesis: History, theory, and evidence. *Open Economies Review, 9*, 85–105.

Robalino, J., & Herrera L. D. (2010). *Trade and deforestation: What have we found?* Retrieved from https://www.wto.org/english/res_e/publications_e/wtr10_robalino_herrera_e.htm.

Rutten, E. (2021, March 29). Does globalization threaten our cultural identity? Retrieved from https://www.linkedin.com/pulse/does-globalization-threaten-our-cultural-identity-eva-rutten-/.

Sauve, P., & Mattoo, A. (Eds.). (2003). *Domestic regulation and service trade liberalization*. World Bank Publications.

Savage, M., Devine, F., Cunningham, N., Taylor, M., Li, Y., Hjellbrekke, J., et al. (2013). A new model of social class? Findings from the BBC's Great British Class Survey experiment. *Sociology, 47*(2), 219–250.

Segal-Horn, S., & Faulkner, D. (2010). *Understating global strategy*. South-Western South Western.

Sen, A. (2010). Music in the digital age: Musicians and fans around the world. *Global Media Journal, 9*(16), 1–24.

Sheth, J. (2011). Impact of emerging markets on marketing: Rethinking existing perspectives and practices. *Journal of Marketing, 75*(4), 166–182.

Sheth, N. (2022, August 18). *How does American Express make money?* Retrieved from https://finty.com/us/business-models/american-express/.

Song, K., & Cui, A. (2009). Understanding China's middle class. China Business Review, 1–7.

Song, M., Zhao, X., & Shang, Y. (2020). The impact of low-carbon city construction on ecological efficiency: Empirical evidence from quasi-natural experiments. *Resources, Conservation and Recycling, 157*, 104777. https://doi.org/10.1016/j.resconrec.2020.104777

Stobierski, T. (2021, April 1). 6 pros and cons of globalization in business to consider. Harvard Business School Online. Retrieved from https://online.hbs.edu/blog/post/pros-and-cons-of-globalization.

Strange, R., & Zucchella, A. (2017). Industry 4.0, global value chains and international business. *Multinational Business Review, 25*(3), 174–184.

Sunderland, R. (2002, August 5). *HSBC banks on Indian call centers*. Retrieved from https://www.standard.co.uk/hp/front/hsbc-banks-on-indian-call-centres-6342026.html.

Teece, D. J. (1982). Towards an economic theory of the multiproduct firm. *Journal of Economic Behavior & Organization, 3*(1), 39–63.

Ter Hofstede, F., Wedel, M., & Steenkamp, J.-B. E. (2002). Identifying spatial segments in international markets. *Marketing Science, 21*(2), 160–177.

The World Bank. (2023a). *Employment in services (% of total employment) (modeled ILO estimate)*. Retrieved from https://data.worldbank.org/indicator/SL.SRV.EMPL.ZS.

The World Bank. (2023b). *Employment in agriculture (% of total employment) (modeled ILO estimate)*. Retrieved from https://data.worldbank.org/indicator/SL.AGR.EMPL.ZS.

The World Bank. (2023c). *Employment in industry (% of total employment) (modeled ILO estimate)*. Retrieved from https://data.worldbank.org/indicator/SL.IND.EMPL.ZS.

Venzon, C. (2022, March 22). *Philippines allows foreigners to own telcos, airlines and railways*. Retrieved from https://asia.nikkei.com/Economy/Philippines-allows-foreigners-to-own-telcos-airlines-and-railways.

Wallach, O. (2022, February 3). *The world's growing middle class (2020–2030)*. Retrieved from https://elements.visualcapitalist.com/the-worlds-growing-middle-class-2020-2030/.
Wild, J., Wild, K., & Han, J. (2016). *International business: The challenges of globalization* (Vol. 8). Pearson.
World Bank. (2002a). *Constructing knowledge societies: New challenges for tertiary education*. Author.
World Bank. (2002b). *Global economics prospects and the developing countries*. Retrieved from https://thedocs.worldbank.org/en/doc/4aa0b654ecdbaf8302d5901aaada3fbf-0350012021/related/Global-Economic-Prospects-2002.pdf.
World Inequality Report. (2022). Retrieved from https://wir2022.wid.world/executive-summary/.
WTO. (2019). *World trade report 2019: The future of services trade*. Retrieved from https://www.wto.org/english/res_e/booksp_e/00_wtr19_e.pdf.
Zhang, L., Xu, M., Chen, H., Li, Y., & Chen, S. (2022). Globalization, green economy and environmental challenges: State of the art review for practical implications. *Frontiers in Environmental Science*, 199.
Zhatkanbaeva, A., Zhatkanbaeva, J., & Zhatkanbaev, E. (2012). The impact of globalization on "brain drain" in developing countries. *Procedia-Social and Behavioral Sciences, 47*, 1490–1494.

## Further Reading

### About Offshoring

Pisani, N., & Ricart, J. E. (2016). Offshoring of services: A review of the literature and organizing framework. *Management International Review, 56*, 385–424.
Niccolò, Pisani Joan Enric, Ricart (2016) Offshoring of Services: A Review of the Literature and Organizing Framework Management International Review 56(3) 385–424 10.1007/s11575-015-0270-7

# Development of International Trade and Investment in Services

Contents




D. Klimkeit et al., *International Management in Service Firms*, Classroom Companion: Business,
https://doi.org/10.1007/978-3-031-50345-0_3

**Learning Outcomes**

After completing this chapter, you should be able to:

- Outline the historical development of international trade
- Explain the role of services in international trade
- Distinguish trade from foreign direct investment and different modes of services supply
- Describe patterns of trade and investment in services today
- Explain the regional character of many (service) multinationals

## Introduction

This chapter outlines the development of international trade and investment, focusing on services. It starts with a brief historical overview of the development of international trade and the vital role that services play. It distinguishes and defines trade and foreign direct investment (FDI) and the specific modes of service supply used by the World Trade Organization (WTO). Then, today's patterns of trade and investment in services are described. The regional character of many (service) multinationals is pointed out.

Hindu temple in Bangalore. (Image by Bishnu Sarangi from Pixabay)

3

### Opening Case: The Indian Service Industry: More Than Call Centers

In his first meeting with Softbank boss Masayoshi Son in 2014, India's prime minister Narendra Modi did not know what to expect of him. Son promised to invest US$5 billion in India. Seven years later, Softbank's investment in India is not at 5, but 14 billion US$, and further investments of US$5–10 billion are announced in technology startups. Son is not the only investor: Venture capitalists are betting on India. Investors see the greatest potential in India in fintech—firms based on digital business models offering services in the financial services sector. In 2020, Razorpay, a payment services firm, became a unicorn—a startup firm valued at more than US$1 billion. In 2021, even 35 Indian startups became unicorns. Another payment service provider, Paytm, was listed on the stock exchange—with the biggest initial public offering (IPO) in India ever.

At the beginning of the 1990s, cautious liberalization of India's foreign trade induced a substantial inflow of foreign direct investment (FDI). In the mid-1990s, American firms like Motorola, HP, and IBM began inviting highly qualified computer experts from India to the United States. As government authorities started to handle the granting of visas more restrictively, companies shifted parts of their development activities to India. Especially Bangalore attracted investment as the first city to open a software technology park in 1991. The necessary infrastructure was implemented, like satellite lines, air-conditioned offices, and an independent electricity supply. Leading information technology (IT) services and consulting firms opened offices in Bangalore, including Accenture, Capgemini, IBM, Oracle, SAP, and Novell. Also, Infosys and Wipro, two of the biggest Indian IT service firms, have their headquarters in Bangalore. Traditionally, these firms offered software development, customer service in call centers, and business processes outsourcing (BPO) of functions like accounting, IT, or HR (human resource). The population of Bangalore increased fourfold, and Western-style restaurants, boutiques, and shopping malls sprang up next to Hindu temples. However, the transportation infrastructure was inadequate, and power outages could be an issue. So, companies installed their own diesel generators and offered bus services to bring their employees to the office.

In India, services made up almost 50% of GDP (gross domestic product), up from just 30% in 1970. India is the second-largest exporter of IT services after the European Union (EU). Exports from the IT services industry exceeded US$52 billion in 2017; 13% of this was generated by deploying IT experts abroad. What has been driving the growth of India's information and communications technology (ICT) services sector is a combination of low wages, broad availability of sufficiently skilled workers, proficiency in English, and the establishment of software technology parks. In 2014, ICT services contributed 9.5% to India's GDP, and exported services accounted for more than 10% of employment in the services sector. Today, the ICT sector employs about five million people in India. Among them, 1.2 million work for the biggest three firms—Wipro, TCS, and Infosys. Increasingly, IT firms are extending their services to areas like product development, including the internet of things, cloud services, analytics, and artificial intelligence. Also, more creative services are offered, such as designing a new Walmart supermarket. In 2018, TCS, India's biggest firm, acquired a London-based digital design studio.

The Coronavirus Disease-2019 (COVID-19) pandemic gave another boost to the Indian ICT services sector. COVID-19 pushed digitization in many ways, such as enabling home office work and digital tracing apps. Indian IT professionals developed much of the software behind this. The drive to cloud IT provided many opportunities for Indian ICT firms helping with the migration into the cloud, cybersecurity, and analytics running on top of cloud services. The mentioned factors enabled at the same time remote work. This allows Indian IT consultants to take over core white-collar jobs from Western firms at a much lower cost. However, some Western firms are reconsidering the desirability of remote work and virtual collaboration. Also, high-value work at the core of a firm's business requires constant communication, continuity, and confidentiality—necessitating proximity. Some BPO providers in India report staff turnover rates of 100% per annum. Salaries in India are also rising fast, between 20 and 30% in 2021, due to intense competition over qualified professionals. Besides businesses in the West, Western governments are becoming wary of the shift of white-collar jobs to India. Visas for Indians are more challenging to obtain, and authorities restrict cross-border data flow. Therefore, Indian IT service providers have established offices in the West, where their primary customers are based. Infosys and TCS now operate in 40 countries. Infosys had 25,000 staff in the United States in 2022 and planned to add 10,000 further in the following years.

In 2022, Softbank boss Masayoshi Son planned to invest another US$5–10 billion in India. At an online conference in December 2021, he stated:

> I believe in India's future. I believe in the passion of young entrepreneurs in India. India will be great. The country has a bright future (Peer & Dörner, 2021, p. 14).

Questions

1. How can the trade in services from India also facilitate international business in the world?
2. Why is the export of services like the ones offered by Indian ICT service firms less straightforward to define than the export of a car?
3. Which ways of delivering services to customers abroad can you distinguish in this case study?
4. Why are Indian ICT service firms increasingly opening offices in the West, employing local staff?

Sources: Economist (2019, 2022a); Holtbrügge and Welge (2015, pp. 19–20); Peer and Dörner (2021); WTO (2019a).

## A Short History of International Trade and the Role of Services

» Cross-border Trade in Services is Not New! (Jackson, 2021, p. 7)

3

The above citation from Sarita Jackson summarizes it well: Services have been traded across borders for millennia and have played a key role in enabling the trade of goods. In fact, trade in goods would not be possible without services. Think of the transportation and warehousing of goods, which is a service, as well as the facilitation of payments and financing of trade, which is a service as well. Service firms have established a transportation and communication infrastructure for international business. Add to this the insurance of traded goods, the accounting for traded and warehoused goods, and the auditing of that accounting, which are services, and it becomes clear that services have played a key role in trade for a long time.

## The Development of International Trade

Before looking at the role of services trade in more detail, let us briefly examine the history of cross-border trade more generally. Given the scope of this chapter, it cannot be complete in any way but give you an idea of how international trade developed. For further reading, see the recommended sources at the end of this chapter. Please note that partly, when referring to historical states, names of today's countries in that location will be used to facilitate your geographic orientation.

As early as 3500–3200 BC, Sumerians set up trading posts across the Near East, importing copper and other goods. In 2250–2100 BC, trade links with India were established. By 2100–2000 BC, there was lively trading between India and the Near East, using Dilmun (Bahrain) as an intermediate. By 2600 BC, a growing trade system had been established in the Eastern Mediterranean, including Ebla, Egypt, the Aegean, Anatolia, Sumer, and the Gulf and Indus Valley. In the Indus Valley, a civilization emerged that built cities in 2600 BC. In 2000–1500 BC, enterprises grew in Assyria and Babylon. Assyrian merchants based in Iraq established trading colonies in Turkey. In 1500–500 BC, the Phoenicians traded across the Red Sea, then invested in trade establishments in Israel, Syria, and Anatolia. At its peak, in 800–600 BC, a trading network stretched from Babylon to Spain, and Phoenicians established colonies in Spain, Tunisia, Cyprus, Egypt, and Italy. The ancient Greeks set up trading colonies in Tunisia, Spain, Cyprus, Egypt, and Italy. Consequently, 331–100 BC saw the height of Greek trade, driven by their entrepreneurial spirit and commercial and financial know-how. During this Hellenic period, India and China integrated into this trading system, eventually reaching from Scotland to Shandong, China (Moore & Lewis, 2009, pp. 21–205).

In 200–250 BC, there was extensive trade between Iran and India. Around 110 BC, Chinese rulers contacted Parthian intermediaries to establish trade with the Near East. By 100 BC, the Silk Road enabled the trade of precious goods between Syria and China. The Greeks and Phoenicians traded with India, and China was now entering this trading system. Under the Romans, European markets were included in this trade as well. The Parthians helped to bring China into this trade with the Mediterranean world. In 14–37 AD, Chinese traders were even present in Rome with a silk bazaar they had established. By 44 BC, empires from China to Spain were connected by trade. Romans further developed the role in this trade they had inherited from the Hellenistic era. Goods traded along the Silk Road included pearls from the Persian Gulf or Sri Lanka, Mediterranean or Red Sea coral, and amber from the Baltic coast. Also, gold, silver, horses, and items made of glass were traded eastwards. Chinese traders brought silk, iron, lacquer, bamboo objects, and cast metal goods (Moore & Lewis, 2009, pp. 179–105). The Silk Road was not just one road but a network of trade routes embodying connectivity between Europe and Asia. Routes changed over time, depending on local conditions. Besides commercial exchange, also cultural, religious, scientific, and technological exchanges took place. Exchanges along the Silk Road continued for 2000 years until around 1750 AD when Russia conquered large parts of Central Asia (Barisitz, 2017, pp. 10–11).

In Asia, between 200 BC and 200 AD, trade from Northwest India across the Gobi desert into China took place, also spreading Buddhism. By 1523, well-established trade routes ran from India to Sumatra, Indonesia. In Africa, Berbers from North Africa traded across the Sahara (Foreman-Peck, 1998, pp. 14–15). Carthaginian trade routes went as far as Ghana and Nigeria (Moore & Lewis, 2009, p. 151).

After establishing European colonies in the Americas, tobacco and potatoes were traded to Europe for horses and firearms. Spanish colonists were interested in gold and silver. By the seventeenth century, European traders traveled the Indian Ocean and beyond. By the eighteenth century, goods from Asia, such as textiles, coffee, tea, sugar, and chocolate, were sought-after in European high society. The Dutch, British, French, and Danish established companies that would trade with Southeast Asia (then called the "East Indies"). A big part of the production of colonial goods in the Americas was produced by slaves from West Africa that were sold by African kings and chiefs to European slave traders, who brought them to the Americas. Only in the nineteenth century was the slave trade forbidden (Foreman-Peck, 1998, pp. 16–17).

In the nineteenth century, advancements in technology and infrastructure propelled trade. The spread of the railway lowered the cost of transportation. The Suez Canal created an advantage for steamships on the route to India. The telegraph facilitated communication across continents. Japan, which had remained relatively isolated until 1858, started to get involved in international trade much more. Between the two world wars, a period of de-globalization set in, however. Currency movements created trade barriers, and the 1930s saw the debt crisis (Foreman-Peck, 1998, pp. 20–23).

After the Second World War, economic development took different routes in developed Western market economies than in countries that became part of the socialist block led by the Soviet Union. Socialist planned economies affiliated with Russia, especially in Central and Eastern Europe, introduced a state monopoly on foreign trade. Trade between members was initially confined to goods that could not be produced in-country in sufficient quality and quantity. In 1949 the Council for Mutual Economic Assistance (Comecon) was founded, including Cuba, Mongolia, and Vietnam, besides Central and Eastern European countries. This led to the specialization of member countries on specific goods, which increased trade between them. After the reforms initiated by Mikhail Gorbachev and the collapse of socialist regimes in Central and Eastern Europe, Comecon was dissolved in 1991. Most former members transformed into market economies and integrated into the world economy. Consequently, the division of the world economy into two blocks was superseded by a multipolar world economy with several regional centers that became more globally integrated (Holtbrügge & Welge, 2015, pp. 5–6).

In market economies, international trade and investment recovered after the Second World War. Especially, US multinationals grew rapidly by FDI, making up 85% of FDI between 1945 and 1965. Also, British and Dutch FDI was significant. FDI from Germany and Japan remained comparatively low as firms preferred to export than invest abroad. In terms of target countries, by 1980, almost two-thirds of FDI went to Western Europe, the United States, and Canada. While before the Second World War, most FDI was in natural resources, by the end of the 1970s, manufacturing made up 52% of accumulated world FDI. Regarding services FDI, new professional business services, hotels, restaurants, and fast food played a significant role. Under the General Agreement on Tariffs and Trade (GATT), to be treated in more detail in later chapters, tariffs that hampered international trade were reduced, significantly propelling global trade. The foundation of trade blocks, such as the European Economic Community, which eventually became the European Union, reduced trade barriers, however, only for members (Jones, 1996, pp. 46–52).

The 1980s saw the fastest growth of FDI since the late nineteenth century. Western Europe returned to being the largest source of FDI, especially the UK. In the meantime, since the 1970s, Japanese FDI had also surged, reaching 13% of global FDI by 1993. This led to the establishment of the so-called "triad" of the United States, Europe, and Japan, which accounted for four out of five FDI investments in the 1990s. South and Southeast Asia became a more important host of FDI, particularly Singapore, Hong Kong, China, Malaysia, Thailand, and Taiwan. By the 1990s, services accounted for half of the total world stock of FDI, especially in trade-related activities and financial services. Many developing countries engaged in export-led growth and more active participation in the world economy. China's turn toward more market-based economic policies in the 1980s opened opportunities for international trade and investment (Jones, 1996, pp. 52–57). At the beginning of the twenty-first century, the world economy exhibited its highest degree of integration in history. Especially the establishment of the World Trade Organization (WTO) as a successor to GATT contributed to reducing tariffs, combatting dumping, and improving intellectual property protection. In 2013, 97.1% of world trade was conducted between WTO members (Holtbrügge & Welge, 2015, pp. 8–9). Privatization and deregulation in many parts of the world provided new opportunities, especially in telecommunications, aviation, tourism, and financial

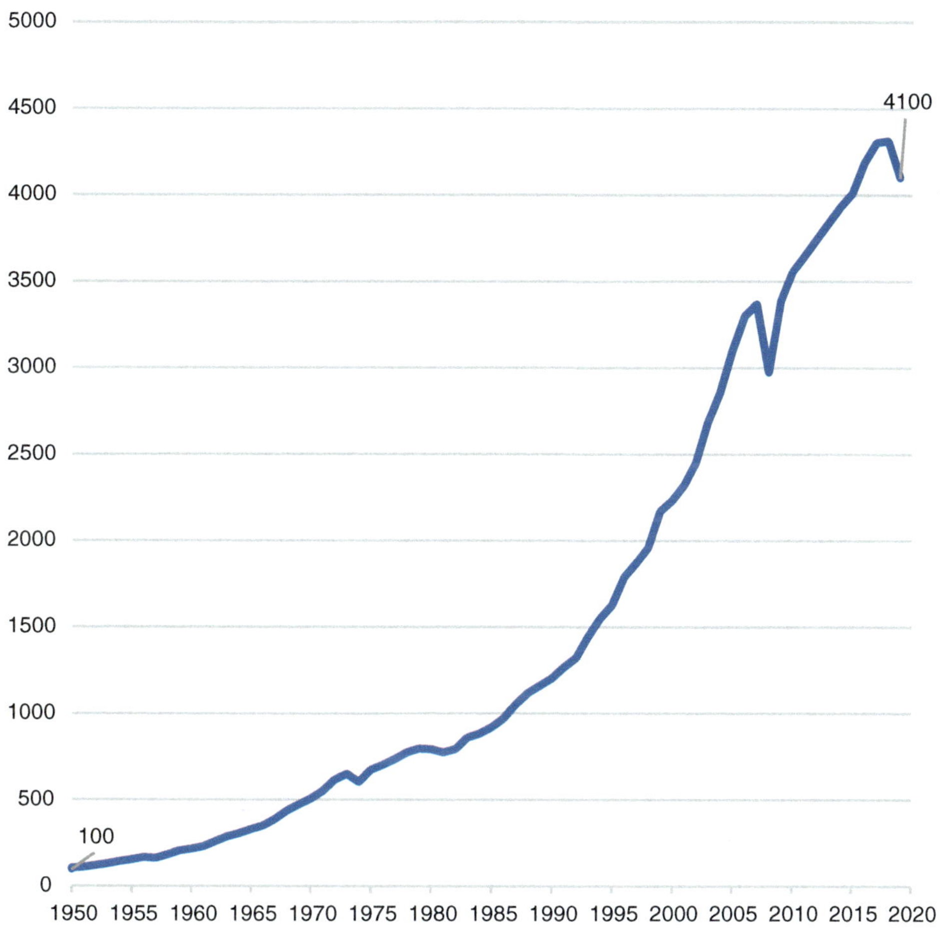


**Fig. 3.1** Evolution of world trade 1950–2020; Volume index 1950 = 100. (Source: WTO, 2023)

services. While trade in the nineteenth century focused on natural resources and manufacturing, the services sector has increasingly become the leading sector in the world economy (Jones, 1996, pp. 57–59). In 2008, subprime mortgage failings in the United States, particularly the failure of Lehman Brothers bank, triggered the global financial crisis. From there, it quickly spread to financial markets around the world. Global trade in goods drastically fell in the second half of 2008. Despite economic stimulus packages by governments, in 2009, trade in goods dropped by 23% compared with 2008, the most significant decline in over 50 years. Trade in commercial services declined by 12%. In the second half of 2009, trade recovered, faster in emerging markets in Asia than in developed markets (WTO, 2009, p. 3; 2010, pp. 4–6). Figure 3.1 shows the evolution of world trade from 1950 to 2020. At the end of this chapter, we will continue this short trade history with recent developments since the financial crisis.

## The Role of Services in Enabling Trade



As the opening quotation highlights, the trade in services is not new. It goes back to ancient times, especially in enabling the trade of goods. We will look here especially at the role of transportation and logistics services, and finance and insurance services.

Transportation services facilitate the transportation of goods. Maritime transport has already evolved in ancient times. Around 3000 BC, shipping enabled the transport of goods throughout Africa, the Middle East, and Asia. Along the Silk Road, traders used to transport by land. Between the fifteenth and seventeenth centuries, the Dutch, Portuguese, and Spanish relied on land and water transport to reach Asia. Since the thirteenth century, China has relied on shipping to trade with other parts of Asia, the Middle East, and Africa. Britain relied heavily on maritime transport to bring goods to and from America and the Caribbean. The use of steam power made shipping faster and more reliable. The steam engine also powered trains in Britain by the early nineteenth century, lowering transport costs and enabling land transport across longer distances (Jackson, 2021, pp. 8–10). From the 1880s, Japanese shipping companies developed international shipping routes, setting up offices in major European and US ports. German shipping companies acquired their own docks in New York (Jones, 1996, p. 151). Eventually, after the Second World War, airplanes could increasingly transport goods fast across long distances. With the US airline industry deregulation in 1977, private freight carriers like UPS and FedEx developed. Freight forwarding came up as a related service industry. Forwarders arrange for end-to-end shipping across several modes of transport and take care of all the paperwork, tracking of shipping, and negotiations with subcontracted transport firms. Thomas Meadows and Company Limited can be traced to be the origin of modern freight forwarding. Starting in 1836, Meadows drew on his network of carriers to assist merchants with transportation and paperwork. Due to the industrial revolution in the eighteenth and nineteenth centuries, there was a growing need to transport manufactured goods safely to customers, especially between Europe and America, increasing the demand for freight forwarding service firms (Jackson, 2021, pp. 8–12).

Finance and insurance services address the need of merchants to pay for goods and to ensure any losses that might occur, for example, during maritime transportation, are covered. Historically, trade in goods often took the form of barter. That is, traders exchanged goods for other goods. In the thirteenth century, the bill of exchange was introduced: a written order issued by the vendor to the buyer, requiring the buyer to pay a stipulated amount at a fixed point in time. Banks offered specific forms of financing for importers and exporters, particularly since international trade reemerged after the Second World War (Jackson, 2021, pp. 12–13). In the 1830s, the first multinational banks comparable to today's appeared when British banks set up offices abroad in Canada, Australia, and Southeast Asia to finance foreign trade and foreign exchange services. By 1914, the Yokohama Specie Bank of Japan had 20 foreign offices. Citibank of the United States had opened 100 foreign offices by 1930. Thereby it was faster to internationalize than most US manufacturing firms (Jones, 1996, pp. 152–153). Already in ancient times, merchants in Rome, Greece, and Babylon gave specific loans to traders that did not have to be repaid if the goods were lost during transport. During the mid-fourteenth century in Italy, underwriters started to offer insurance for goods transported by sea. They then extended their services to other parts of Europe and America. By the sixteenth century, marine insurance firms such as Lloyd's grew in Spain, the Netherlands, Britain, and France, and by the late eighteenth century, in the United States to provide insurance for American exports. Today, e-commerce firms like Amazon rely on the internet, digitalization, and automation to ensure fast, efficient, and flexible delivery of goods. Financial service firms like PayPal developed digital payment options to facilitate e-commerce (Jackson, 2021, pp. 12–16). In this context, the ICT service firms in India introduced in the opening case have played an essential role in enabling international business. They often played a key role as IT systems and software (co-)developers, enabling digital communication, collaboration, and information exchange across geographic locations.

## Development of Trade and Investment in Services

Besides facilitating trade in goods, service firms later expanded their role in enabling international business more generally (Jones, 1996, p. 147). Since the second half of the twentieth century, service firms increasingly provided services to consumers abroad.

In addition to the transportation infrastructure built by engineering service firms, the telecommunication infrastructure put in place by telecommunication service firms play an important role in the development of international business. Imagine the importance for international business of the first transatlantic cable in 1866 that enabled telephone connections between America and Europe (Holtbrügge & Welge, 2015, pp. 2–3). In the late nineteenth century, telecommunications attracted foreign investment. Initially, American firms took interests in European telecommunications. Later, European telecommunications firms invested in Latin America and other regions. By the end of the 1920s, the International Telephone and Telegraph Corporation (ITT) already had 100,000 employees outside of the United States in Europe, Latin America, and Asia-Pacific (Jones, 1996, p. 158).

Audit firms also play an essential role in international business. Imagine a British merchant setting up a trade establishment and warehouse in the United States. Then he or she would want to ensure that what goes into, is stocked, and leaves the warehouse is appropriately accounted for, as well as the sales, costs, and profits made in the new world. The merchant would also want to know that an independent third party, an auditor, has checked these accounts. In the 1890s, British accounting firms Deloitte and Price Waterhouse opened offices in the United States. By 1975, Price Waterhouse had offices in 76 countries. Similarly, the merchant would need legal advice in all the countries where he or she set up trade establishments to deal with local laws in the respective countries. So, law firms typically, as a first step, set up networks with local partner law firms in the countries where their customers do business to serve them there as well. To successfully market and sell his or her products, the merchant would further want to draw on the expertise and capabilities of an advertising agency in those countries where he or she offers goods for sale. US advertising firms have been the first to internationalize. Even before the First World War, they opened offices in Europe and expanded between the wars, such as J.W. Thompson (JWT). In the 1920s, JWT agreed with GM to open an office wherever GM had operations. Once established, they moved on to develop a local client base. After 1945, US multinational enterprises (MNEs) developed a preference to appoint one advertising agency for their global advertising. However, since the 1980s, advertising agencies from other countries like Britain and Japan have challenged US dominance (Jones, 1996, pp. 72–73, 160, 173–174).

In the twentieth century, especially after 1950, service firms increasingly offered consumer services internationally, particularly in hotels, restaurants, travel, and passenger transportation. The American pioneer Pan American Airways expanded its network to Latin America and began to offer transatlantic flights. From the 1970s, the airline industry was increasingly deregulated, further facilitating the spread of airlines abroad. After the Second World War, hotel groups expanded abroad, notably from the United States, Britain, and France. They operated as hotel chains, facilitating international expansion into developed and newly industrialized countries like Singapore, Hong Kong, and Thailand. In addition, fast-food restaurants have grown internationally since the 1960s. In 1967, McDonald's opened its first restaurant outside of the United States in Canada, and in the 1970s, it expanded on a large scale. By the 1990s, McDonald's operated more than 2500 restaurants in 50 countries. Service firms in the retail business started international expansion even earlier. For example, F.W. Woolworth started investing abroad in the nineteenth century. In the 1960s, Safeway Stores from Canada opened outlets in the UK, Germany, and Australia. In the 1970s, niche firms like IKEA expanded rapidly across the world. The international expansion of service firms has played an essential role in shaping people's lifestyles around the world. For example, multinational retailers spread modern marketing concepts worldwide. Fast-food restaurants and hotels brought the Western lifestyle to many people globally. Multinational service firms spread technologies abroad and played an important role in including formerly peripheral parts of the world into the global economy (Jones, 1996, pp. 162–180).

## Trade and Investment and Modes of Services Supply

In what was outlined above, the terms "export" and "investment" or "foreign investment" have been repeatedly used. Let us look more closely at what they mean precisely and how to distinguish them.

## Export

When thinking of manufactured goods, it is easy to imagine what an export is. If Volkswagen produces a car in Germany and then ships it to France to sell to customers there, it exports that car. In services, it is less straightforward what an export would mean.

> **Export**
>
> *Exporting* is the sale of products produced by a firm in one country to customers that reside in another country (Daniels et al., 2021, p. 396).

This fits the Volkswagen example perfectly well. Now, what about service exports? When an office of architects based in one country builds an opera house in another, they export their architectural services to that country. When consulting firms send consultants abroad to advise on a merger & acquisition (M&A) transaction in another country, they export that service. When an advertising agency creates an advertising campaign for a customer in another country, even if they physically remain in their office and communicate electronically with the customer, they export their service to the customer abroad. What about a coffee shop chain like The Coffee Bean & Tea Leaf, founded in Los Angeles, United States, setting up a coffee shop in another country? Is this an export by this service operation? In the international business literature, this would typically not be considered an export but something else: *Foreign Direct Investment* (FDI).

## Foreign Direct Investment

When a firm establishes facilities in another country, this is called FDI.

> **Foreign Direct Investment (FDI)**
>
> We speak of *FDI*, "when a firm invests directly in facilities to produce or market a good or service in a foreign country" (Hill, 2021, p. 232).

In the example mentioned, by setting up a coffee shop abroad, The Coffee Bean & Tea Leaf would invest directly in facilities to produce a service in another country. It would procure premises and put furniture, coffee machines, and other things in place to produce its coffee shop service there. Someone who buys shares of a company based in another country would conduct a foreign investment, but not FDI, as he or she would not directly invest in facilities to produce or market a good or service himself or herself. FDI comes in several forms. Frequently, companies enter foreign markets by buying an existing firm, called an acquisition. In other cases, as in the Coffee Bean example above, firms establish their own operations abroad without acquiring an existing firm, called a greenfield investment. In still other cases, firms join forces with a local firm, setting up a joint venture co-owned and operated by both firms. ► Chapter 7 will discuss these and other options in more detail, so we will not investigate this further here.

Coffee shop; Setting up a wholly owned coffee shop abroad involves FDI. (Image by Pexels from Pixabay)

## Modes of Service Supply

Let us take a closer look at the international delivery of services. The World Trade Organization (WTO) defined different types of service delivery that are very helpful for understanding the various ways services can be provided across borders. WTO distinguishes four types of delivering services internationally, so-called "modes of supply" (see also ◘ Fig. 3.2), depending on the geographic presence of the supplier and consumer of the service (WTO, 2013):

Mode one: *Cross-border trade*: services supplied from the country of the service provider to customers in another country

Mode two: *Consumption abroad*: services supplied in the country of the service provider to consumers coming from another country

Mode three: *Commercial presence*: services supplied by a service provider from one country through a commercial presence in another country

Mode four: *Presence of natural persons*: services supplied through the presence of a natural person, such as an employee of a service firm, from one country in another country

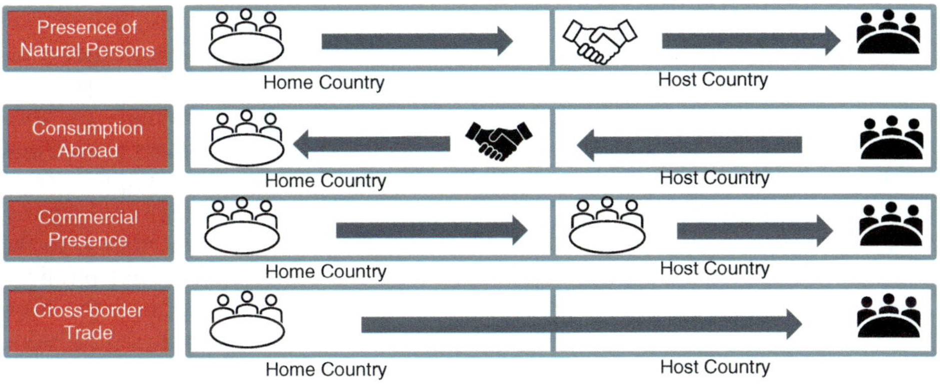


**Fig. 3.2** Modes of service supply. (Own diagram, based on content from WTO, 2013, p. 3)

Let us go through them from the bottom up. Remember the example of a consulting firm sending a team of consultants to another country to advise on an M&A transaction. The consultants would spend a certain amount of time, say several weeks to months, in the customer's country and then return home once the project has been completed. This would be mode four, the presence of natural persons. The consultant could also be a self-employed independent consultant. The same applies to the office of architects that would send architects to oversee the construction of the opera house. As you may remember, this was the initial mode of service supply from India when Indian IT experts were invited to the United States by American firms.

Suppose the consulting firm or the office of architects repeatedly has projects for customers in a given country abroad. At one point, they might decide that sending professionals abroad, again and again, is not the most efficient way of providing the service. So, they might decide to set up an office in that country. It would hire professionals to operate out of this office permanently. In this case, the firms would establish a commercial presence—mode three, according to WTO. Other examples could include hotel chains setting up a hotel abroad or restaurant chains setting up a restaurant in another country. The example of The Coffee Bean & Tea Leaf would also fit here. In the opening case, Indian ICT firms increasingly use this mode to address political concerns and benefit from proximity to their customers.

The service provider does not always have to be present in the customer's country. Think of tourists traveling to a country like Thailand, staying at local hotels, dining in local restaurants, or making day trips conducted by a local tour guide. They would engage in consumption abroad, mode two, according to WTO. The same would apply to students spending a year abroad at a university in the UK or patients from the Near East traveling to Germany for medical treatment. In all these cases, the customer travels to the service provider's country to establish personal contact, which is necessary for most services due to the simultaneity of production and consumption.

Given today's possibilities afforded by modern information and communications technology, in some cases, services can be provided with neither service provider nor customer moving away from their regular location. Think of a market research agency whose staff conduct the research from their desk and then electronically provides the final report to the customer abroad. Likewise, the plans of an architect can be sent by email. Software developers in India can make the software code they developed available to customers in the United States via a cloud platform. Staff in a call center in the Philippines can answer service requests from customers in Australia. Arguably, given the geographic and often temporal separation of production and consumption, this mode shares some similarities with the trade in goods. However, the transfer of the outcome is electronic, not physical, and therefore still intangible. As you have seen in the opening case, this is the dominant mode of service delivery by Indian service firms whose staff, based in India, provides services remotely to customers abroad.

If you relate the four modes of supply to the distinction made above between export and FDI, you may have noticed a difference between mode three (commercial presence) and the other modes of supply. While modes one, two, and four represent exports, mode three usually implies FDI. A commercial presence typically involves direct investment in facilities to produce and market a service in a foreign country. This can be confusing as WTO uses the four modes of supply in conjunction with the term “services trade.” The term “trade,” though, is frequently associated with “exporting” or “importing,” as in the frequently used expression “trade and investment” (for example, UNCTAD, 2022), where “trade” relates to export/import, while “investment” relates to FDI. So, in this book, we avoid using the term “trade” in direct relation to the four modes of service supply and instead imply export/import transactions when we speak of trade, as in the first sections of this chapter.

## Trade in Services Today

Today, trade in services can be seen as the most dynamic sector of world trade. A key enabler has been technology. Enabled by information and communications technology, trade in services has grown three times as much as trade in goods since 2011. Forecasts expect services trade to make up 40% of global trade by 2040 (WTO, 2019a). The following two sections draw on a services-focused publication by WTO with data from 2017, which is somewhat dated. However, it provides a good presentation of the situation before the COVID-19 pandemic, which has enormously distorted the more recent data due to its profound effect on many service industries. The following section will then review the impact of COVID-19 with more recent data.

## Modes of Supply

Now, let us look more closely at the patterns of services trade today. If we look at how services are supplied to customers in terms of the modes of supply (see ◘ Fig. 3.3), we can see that establishing a commercial presence is by far the domi-

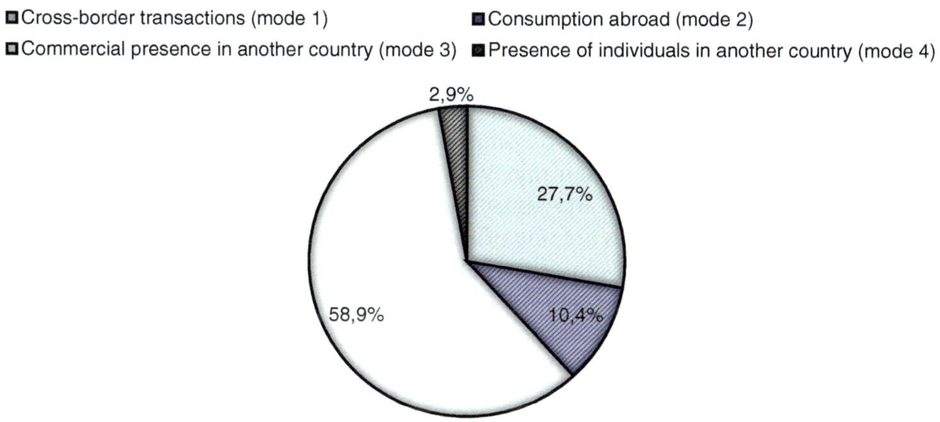


**Fig. 3.3** World trade in commercial services by mode of supply, 2017, WTO estimates. Note: World trade is calculated as the average of world exports and world imports. (Own diagram based on: WTO, 2019a, p. 24)

nant mode, making up 58.9% in 2017, according to WTO estimates. Given the distinctive characteristics of services, it is not surprising that most service firms want to be permanently present where their customers are. Half of the service firms that supply via this mode are financial services and distribution services. The cross-border supply of services makes up the second most important mode of supply. This applies to a broad range of service industries, like professional and other business services, transportation and distribution, and communication and computer services. Consumption abroad makes up 10.4% of services supplied across borders, with tourism accounting for 60%. The presence of natural persons is negligible, constituting only 2.9% of services supplied to customers abroad (WTO, 2019a, pp. 22–25).

## Service Industries

Next, let us investigate the most important service industries that are supplied internationally. Distribution services (19.9%) and financial services (18.6%) are the most supplied services internationally. As outlined in previous sections in this chapter, services play a crucial role in international trade, and wholesale and retail are key service industries in this context. The same applies to financial services that finance and insure international trade. Moreover, in times of e-commerce and e-banking, the role of cross-border supply has increased in this sector. Distribution makes efficient transportation necessary. Also, the transportation of people has increased. Tourism as a service industry plays a special role as well as the most inclusive trade sector in the sense that it exhibits the broadest participation of countries from all levels of development. From 2005 to 2017, the value of tourism almost doubled. Construction is another service industry where international supply has grown significantly by 7% from 2005 to 2017, with China being the biggest exporter of construction services. This is primarily due to the "Belt and Road" initiative launched in 2013 by the Chinese government, which led to infrastructure construction in Africa and other developing parts of the world (WTO, 2019a, pp. 25–31).

The export of information and communications technology (ICT) services has more than doubled in this timeframe, with the EU being the largest exporter, followed by India. India has become a prominent exporter of ICT services. Intellectual property (IP)-related services are one of the most dynamic segments of the services trade. You might wonder what IP-related services comprise. Think of Netflix, Amazon Prime Video, Disney + (video streaming), or Spotify (music streaming). They are IP traders that offer access to copyrighted software, audiovisuals, books, or broadcasting of live performances. As advertising has increasingly used digital channels, the display of online ads also belongs to this category. Think of online ads by internet giants like Google (Alphabet) or Facebook (Meta). In the reported timeframe, US cross-border advertising exports have almost increased fourfold. As the economy globalizes, services provided by accounting and law firms expanded by 8% in the reported period, to be precise, both by commercial presence and increasingly virtually and, therefore, by cross-border supply (WTO, 2019a, pp. 25–31).

Education is also a service expanding internationally. In 2017, over five million students were studying at a university abroad. Traditionally, the United States, UK, and Australia have attracted international students. India, China, and Malaysia increasingly emerge as destinations for international students. If you remember the four modes of supply, you will not be surprised that this segment typically happens via consumption abroad. Increasingly, though, cross-border supply plays a role as courses can be taught online. Finally, health services have grown by 11% between 2005 and 2017. Healthcare providers from developed countries provided 72% of these by establishing healthcare facilities in other countries; 22% of cases attracted patients from abroad, making it another growing segment drawing on consumption abroad. As patients from developing countries travel to developed countries for more reliable health care, there is also a movement of patients from developed countries in the other direction. They consume more affordable health-related services in developing or emerging economies, such as dental care or aesthetic treatments (WTO, 2019a, 25–31).

## Countries

The following ◘ Fig. 3.4 from WTO provides an excellent visual representation of the relative importance of countries in services trade pre-COVID-19. It displays the size of trade in commercial services (defined by WTO as all service categories except government services) (WTO, 2019b, p. 87).

It contains two quite different insights: On the one hand, services trade is somewhat concentrated. The top ten trading countries make up 53% of services trade, most of which are developed countries. On the other hand, compared to trade in goods, emerging economies play a more prominent role. Services trade is more

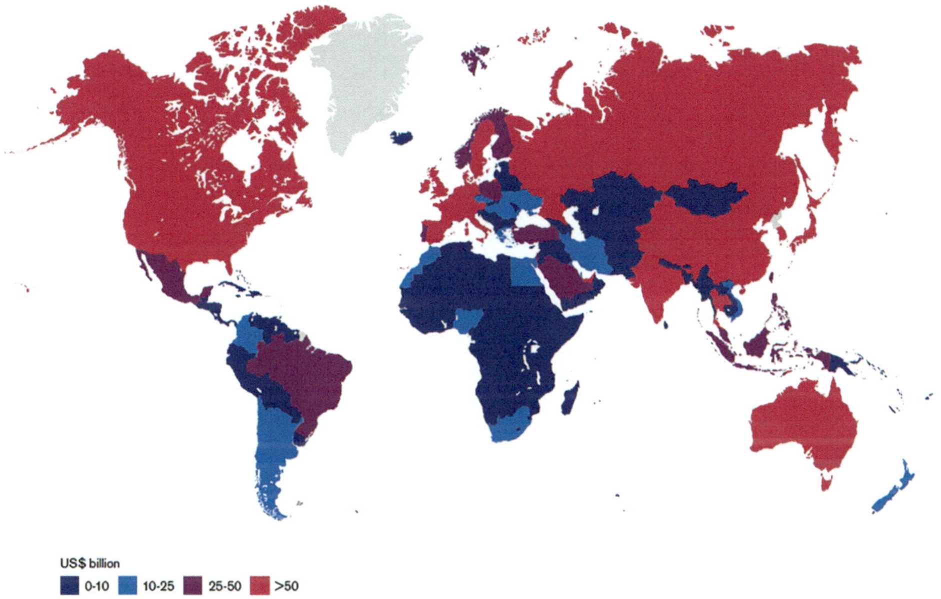


**Fig. 3.4** Economies by size of trade in commercial services, 2018, WTO-UNCTAD-ITC estimates. (Source: WTO, 2019a, p. 15)

inclusive than the trade in goods. The map shows countries like China, India, Russia, and Thailand as important traders. According to the most recent data from 2020, Turkey, the Philippines, Brazil, Romania, the Czech Republic, Hungary, Malaysia, and Vietnam are among the top 40 traders in commercial services (WTO, 2021, p. 60). The 2020 data, however, show the impact of COVID-19. For example, Thailand has dropped from the 19th to the 30th spot on the list. Certainly, the effect of the shutdown of tourism can be witnessed here, among other factors that might play a role.

Table 3.1 details the top exporters and importers of services. As can be seen in the table, the United States is by far the leading exporter of services, followed by the UK and Germany. China and India are the leading emerging economies in service exports. The top ten exporters are also the ten biggest importers of services. However, some differences in the ranking and value can be detected. The United States exports significantly more (US$684 billion) services than it exports (US$432 billion), in contrast to goods trade, where the United States has a trade deficit (US$1432 billion exports vs. US$2408 billion imports). This is interesting given that former US president Donald Trump repeatedly denounced the US trade deficit and undertook protectionist measures to reduce it, neglecting the US trade surplus in services (Müller, 2016). In contrast, Germany, frequently criticized for its long-running trade surplus (Economist, 2017), when looking at services, imports slightly more (US$307 billion) than it exports (US$305 billion) (WTO, 2021, pp. 58, 60).

**Table 3.1** Leading exporters and importers in commercial services, 2020, in US$, in billion (own table based on data from WTO, 2021, p. 60)

| Exporters | Value | Importers | Value |
|---|---|---|---|
| United States of America | 684 | United States of America | 436 |
| United Kingdom | 339 | China | 378 |
| Germany | 305 | Germany | 307 |
| China | 278 | Ireland | 296 |
| Ireland | 262 | France | 232 |
| France | 245 | United Kingdom | 201 |
| India | 203 | Japan | 183 |
| Singapore | 187 | Singapore | 172 |
| Netherlands | 186 | Netherlands | 169 |
| Japan | 156 | India | 153 |

## COVID-19

As you can imagine, COVID-19 has seriously affected service trade. Many service industries have been less resilient than manufacturing industries. Especially transport, hospitality, and tourism, as well as cultural and recreational services, have been severely affected by the restriction on movement and contact that many governments put in place. While trade in goods declined by 8% in 2020, trade in services lost 21%. In 2020, trade in travel decreased by 63%. International transportation sales fell by 20%. Telecommunications, computer, and information services exports rose by 10% instead, as many institutions switched to home office and virtual communication to maintain their operations. Especially in the United States, the export of cloud-based services grew by 25%. Geographically, in all regions, services trade was hit by the pandemic. Countries relying strongly on tourism were hit particularly hard, as in the case of Thailand mentioned above (UNCTAD, 2021a, 2021b; WTO, 2021).

## The Regional Service Multinationals

Walmart, the biggest company in the world by sales, Carrefour, and Tesco: Many of you will have seen supermarkets operated by these retailing giants outside their home countries, the United States, France, and the UK, respectively. Nevertheless, they are not as global as you might think regarding the geographic spread of their revenues.

## Regional Trade

▣ Table 3.2 shows the origin and destination of trade in goods between different regions of the world.

The table reads as in the following example: Companies from North America sold 15.2% of their goods in Europe according to a WTO report published in 2015 (unfortunately, more recent editions no longer show this table). What do you notice? Many regions, especially North America, South and Central America, Europe, and Asia, trade the largest chunk of their exports within their home region. Especially in North America, Europe, and Asia, most goods exported are sold to customers within the home region (WTO, 2015). In retail services in 2009, Walmart made 76% of its sales in the United States alone, French retailer Carrefour 69% in Europe, and British supermarket Tesco 87% in Europe (Rugman & Collinson, 2012, p. 84). These are examples of insights generated by Rugman and Verbeke, who reviewed the Fortune Global 500 list of the largest MNEs in the world. Focusing on North America, Europe, and Asia, the so-called "triad," where most MNEs have their home base, they defined a criterion for when firms can be really called "global." According to this definition, only firms making at least 20% of their sales in each region of the triad and at the same time not making more than 50% of their sales in their home region are labeled as genuinely global. Enough data were available for this analysis for 365 of the 500 MNEs. According to this definition, only 9 of these 365 (2.5%) of the world's largest firms were genuinely global. Most firms instead focused on their home region, making more than 50% of their sales in their home region, or were bi-regional, making at least 20% in one more region outside their home region (Rugman & Verbeke, 2004). This was a striking finding running counter to our intuitive perception that the biggest 500 firms in the world must be very global. One can certainly argue that focusing on the geographic distribution of sales across the triad is an imperfect indicator of the degree of globalization of MNEs. Nevertheless, it indicates the success of MNEs outside of their home region in other regions where significant competitors have their home base (Rosa et al., 2020). A later study that investigated the spread of assets of MNEs across the triad in addition to sales came to a similar conclusion (Rugman & Verbeke, 2008).

More recently, Rosa et al. (2020) wanted to find out if the pattern identified by Rugman and Verbeke, drawing on data from 2002, still holds today. Using the 2017 Fortune Global 500 list, they applied the same methodology and criteria as the original study. The results confirmed the original findings. Most Fortune Global 500 firms (more than 90%) were still not global, according to Rugman and Verbeke's definition. However, the number of global firms increased from 9 (2.5%) in the original study to 36 (9.3%) in the recent study. So, the globalization of Fortune Global 500 companies has increased, but the majority are still primarily oriented toward their home region.

**Table 3.2** Inter- and intraregional merchandise trade, 2014 (own table based on data from WTO, 2015, p. 41)

| Origin | Destination | | | | | | | |
|---|---|---|---|---|---|---|---|---|
| | North America | South and Central America | Europe | CIS countries | Africa | Near East | Asia | World |
| Share of regional trade flows in total goods exports of each region (percentages) | | | | | | | | |
| **World** | **17.3** | **4.0** | **36.7** | **2.8** | **3.5** | **4.2** | **29.7** | **100.0** |
| North America | 50.2 | 8.6 | 15.2 | 0.7 | 1.7 | 3.2 | 20.2 | 100.0 |
| South and Central America | 24.8 | 25.8 | 16.4 | 1.4 | 2.5 | 2.4 | 24.5 | 100.0 |
| Europe | 7.9 | 1.7 | 68.5 | 3.2 | 3.3 | 3.4 | 10.8 | 100.0 |
| Community of Independent States (CIS) | 3.9 | 0.9 | 52.4 | 17.8 | 2.1 | 3.1 | 18.2 | 100.0 |
| Africa | 7.0 | 5.1 | 36.2 | 0.4 | 17.7 | 3.3 | 27.3 | 100.0 |
| Near East | 7.7 | 0.8 | 11.5 | 0.5 | 2.8 | 8.8 | 53.9 | 100.0 |
| Asia | 18.0 | 3.1 | 15.2 | 2.1 | 3.5 | 5.1 | 52.3 | 100.0 |

## Service MNEs

Does this finding apply to service firms the same way as to manufacturing firms? The re-study of 2008 by Rugman on Verbeke focused on service firms. The authors found that in service firms, the percentage of sales in their home region is even higher at 84% compared to 66% for manufacturing firms. The same holds for the firms' assets, such as offices or IT infrastructure service firms have 84% of their assets in their home region compared to 70% of manufacturing firms (Rugman & Verbeke, 2008). A look at the data from the recent study by Rosa et al. shows a similar picture: While the authors themselves do not categorize firms into industry sectors, one would only classify a few of the 36 MNEs identified as "global" as service firms: IBM (IT services), Trafigura (commodity trading), Mizuho (Banking), Schlumberger (oil-related services), Avnet (electronics wholesale), Arrow Electronics (electronics wholesale), and Swiss Re (insurance).

To put this in perspective: A service firm that originates, for example, in one country in Europe and does business in a dozen other countries in Europe, plus some activities in other parts of the world, is still very international, even if not "global" according to the specific definition of Rugman and Verbeke. So, the studies outlined above show that success in other parts of the world can be difficult. Therefore, many firms prefer to focus the bulk of their business in their home region and have comparatively less business in more remote parts of the world. Nevertheless, as the statistics in services trade quoted in the previous chapter demonstrate, international trade in services has grown a lot. It does make up a significant and increasing segment of world trade.

## Trends in Foreign Direct Investment in Services

Like in international trade, foreign direct investment was also severely impacted by COVID-19 as investors reassessed their investment projects. FDI flows to developing countries receded less than investment flows to developed countries in 2020. More than half of global FDI in the first year of the pandemic was in developing countries in Asia. Accordingly, FDI from developing countries fell to a record low (UNCTAD, 2021c, p. 2). In the second year of the COVID-19 in 2021, FDI bounced back by 64%. This was partly due to the significant stimulus packages by governments across the world but also to pent-up demand from 2020 and low financing costs. While in 2020, FDI decreased more strongly than international trade, in 2021, it accelerated faster. However, still in 2022, China implemented lockdowns to curb COVID-19 outbreaks in areas that play a major role in global value chains, adversely impacting investment activity. Besides COVID-19, the war in Ukraine caused a food, energy, and financial crisis far beyond Ukraine, leading to rising prices and escalating debt. This is a further reminder of how unexpected events can suddenly depress trade and investment (UNCTAD, 2022, pp. 2–5).

3

## The Largest Recipients of FDI

Let us look at the geographic patterns of FDI: Who are the primary providers and recipients of FDI? ◘ Figure 3.5 shows the 20 largest recipients of FDI in 2020 and 2021. The United States remained the largest recipient of FDI in 2021, and more generally, FDI flows to developed countries reached their pre-pandemic level, at about half of FDI inflows. At the same time, FDI to developing countries reached the highest level ever due to the economic upswing in Asia, Latin America, and Africa. Indeed, the table shows a diverse mix of recipients in developed countries like Canada, Germany, Israel, and the UK and developing countries like China, Brazil, India, and Mexico (UNCTAD, 2022, p. 9).

## The Largest Providers of FDI

Now, let us look at the primary providers of FDI (see ◘ Fig. 3.6). Developed countries' share in FDI outflows rose to three-quarters of the global total in 2021. Like being the major recipient, the United States was again the largest provider of FDI as well. The table shows the dominance of developed countries, with Germany, Japan, the UK, and Canada being in further top spots. Nevertheless, developing countries also play a significant role as investors, led by China as the fourth largest investor overall. Further, Saudi Arabia, Brazil, United Arab Emirates, and Thailand also appear in the top 20 providers of FDI (UNCTAD, 2022, p. 21).

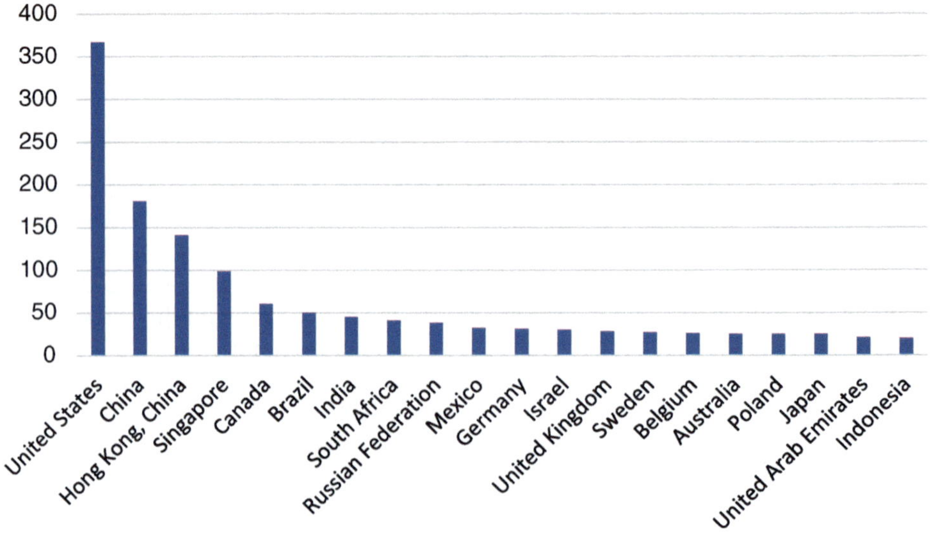


◘ **Fig. 3.5** FDI inflows 2021 (in US$, in billion): top 20 host economies. (Own diagram based on data from UNCTAD, 2022, p. 9)

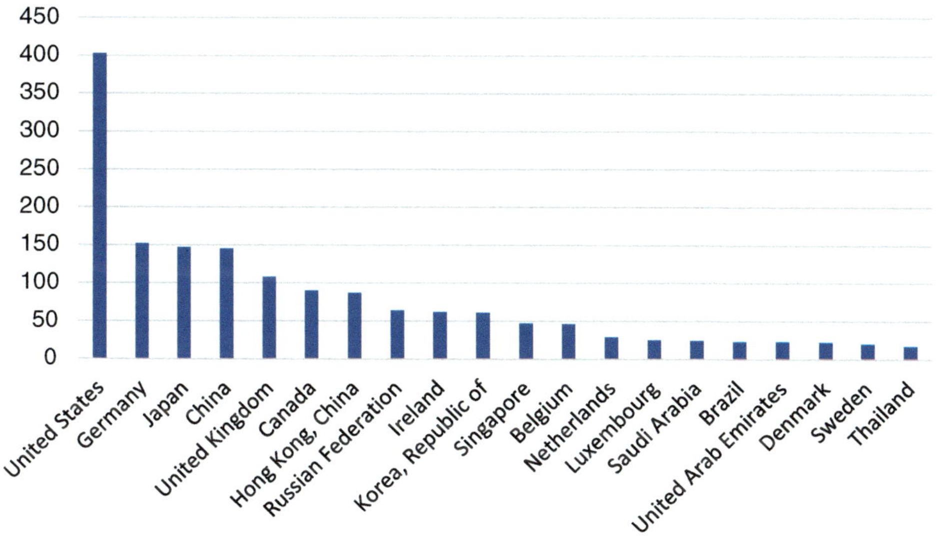


**Fig. 3.6** FDI outflows 2021 (in US$, in billion): top 20 home economies. (Based on data from UNCTAD, 2022, p. 21)

## FDI in Services

Now, what role do service firms play in foreign direct investment? Put shortly: a very significant one. In 2021, both greenfield and M&A investments surpassed manufacturing investments in value. Greenfield investments totaled US$350 billion for services versus US$297 billion for manufacturing investments. Service industries that saw the highest total value in greenfield investment were information and communications technology (ICT, US$104 billion), construction (US$49 billion), and transportation and storage (US$33 billion). Due to the strong growth in global demand for digital infrastructure in the context of COVID-19, greenfield investments in ICT grew, with Amazon being the most significant single investor. In M&A, the lead of services investments (US$461 billion) over manufacturing investments (US$239 billion) is even more pronounced. Indeed, M&A investments in the services sector rose to one of the highest levels recorded. ICT (US$136.3 billion) was the most significant service sector, and even the biggest sector overall, receiving M&A investments. Investments in finance and insurance (US$72 billion), trade investments (US$63 billion), and transportation and storage investments (US$53 billion) followed (UNCTAD, 2022, p. 21).

## De-globalization or Slowbalization?

We reported in this chapter on the enormous growth of international trade and investment in the second half of the twentieth century. Our short history of international trade and investment would not be complete, though, without addressing the apparent slowing down and even partial reversal of globalization that can be observed since the global financial crisis in 2008/2009.

Since 2008, global FDI and trade have been stagnating or shrinking in relation to global GDP. Trade fell from 61% of global GDP to 58% of GDP between 2008 and 2018, while FDI decreased from 3.5% of global GDP to 1.3% (Economist, 2019). Observers speak of a new era called "slowbalization" (D'Urbino, 2019). Interestingly, some service industries withstood this trend. For example, the number of cross-border parcels sent increased the same as international airfare. The volume of data crossing borders has increased 64 times in the same period, not least due to platforms streaming audiovisual content like YouTube (Economist, 2019). There are several causes of slowbalization. The expansion of international trade was partly driven by falling transport prices, which have ceased to fall further. Following the financial crisis, banks became more critical of international investment projects when financing them. As will become more apparent in later chapters of this book, doing business in foreign markets is not always easy. Many companies have failed in their international ventures and therefore became more reluctant to invest further in them. The rate of return from international ventures dropped from 10% in 2006–2007 to 6% in 2017 (Economist, 2019). Emerging markets can increasingly make their own inputs for manufactured goods and rely less on imports. So, factories in China can, for example, now make most components needed for the iPhone themselves rather than only assemble imported components as in the past. All of these factors are compounded by a rising trend of protectionism. The Trump administration in the United States imposed high import tariffs on many goods from China. The Chinese government retaliated likewise, damaging trade of other countries that do business with China and the United States. While the Chinese government has repeatedly taken action against foreign firms, not giving them a level playing field with domestic firms, the Trump administration took action against Chinese firms like Huawei (Economist, 2019). Western MNEs like Daimler, GSK, and Starbucks have been publicly accused of unfair business practices by Chinese Government authorities—accusations that observers considered questionable (Daniels et al., 2019, pp. 102–104). In 2023, the Chinese government asked state-owned enterprises not to grant audit contracts anymore to the "Big Four" audit firms from the United States. The government gives data privacy as a reason, but industry insiders fear that China wants to exclude Western audit firms from significant parts of the audit market in China (Fröndhoff, 2023). Chinese firms are obliged to collaborate with the Chinese security forces if need be. So out of fear of espionage via Huawei components in the US mobile phone infrastructure, the Trump administration prohibited US telecommunications firms from using them in their mobile networks (see the opening case in ► Chap. 6).

Since the above-cited article that popularized the term "slowbalization" was published in *The Economist* in 2019, COVID-19 and the war in Ukraine further disrupted international trade and investment. It became apparent that global supply chains optimized for efficiency by procuring every component in the least expensive place could be disrupted; the component thus can suddenly become very expensive. During the Ukraine war, Russia reduced gas deliveries to retaliate against sanctions imposed on it; this made governments and businesses aware of the risk of dependence on autocratic and unpredictable states. Like many countries depending on Russian gas, the world economy depends on many goods and resources from China (Economist, 2022b). The onset of the COVID-19 pandemic in 2020 has shown that many countries depended on medical supplies like face masks, medical devices, and medicine no longer produced in-country. As a response, several governments across the world restricted exports of critical medical supplies to at least keep those available in-country from leaving the country (Fuest, 2020).

As a response, businesses put in place precautionary measures to increase their resilience. What creates risks is not global supply chains per se but the dependence on individual suppliers, customers, and locations. Therefore, companies diversify their supply chain to have suppliers that can replace each other. To the extent that this happens, it will deepen globalization (Fuest, 2020). Furthermore, companies have created large stocks to protect against supply disruptions. For the biggest 3000 firms in the world, inventories have risen from 6% in 2016 to 9% in 2022 (Economist, 2022b). Moreover, companies trade more with firms in their region. The share of inputs sourced from one's region has increased in Asia, Europe, and North America. FDI, therefore, became more regional. For example, in 2008, a third of supplies in Asia came from other countries in Asia, while a decade later, the share rose to half (Economist, 2019). Some firms like Tesla conduct vertical integration by coming to own supplies from nickel mines to chip design. The new shape of globalization is prioritizing security over efficiency.

The problem is that a reasonable security strategy for critical supplies can turn into protectionism. If multinational enterprises duplicate a quarter of their activities to become less dependent on individual suppliers, the extra costs will exceed 2% of global GDP (Economist, 2022b). Keeping stocks of critical goods like medical supplies can make sense. Producing essential supplies in one's region can also be reasonable. However, some level of international diversification can still be the best protection against the supply risks of MNEs. The same strategy helps avoid an over-reliance on individual countries for MNEs sales. During the European currency crisis of 2009–2013, German car makers benefited from selling cars not only in Europe but worldwide (Fuest, 2020). As a result, businesses need to find a new balance between security and efficiency (Economist, 2022b). Governments may require businesses to diversify supply chains in areas dominated by unreliable autocracies instead of resorting to protectionism.

Witnessing the current trend, it should be noted that there have been phases of more and less globalization in history. So, slowbalization is not unprecedented and is likely to be followed by a phase of renewed acceleration of global trade and investment (Economist, 2019).

## Review Questions

1. Define exporting and FDI and explain the difference between them.
2. Explain the four modes of service supply.
3. Provide examples of the four modes not mentioned in the text.
4. Outline the key periods in the history of international trade and investment.
5. Explain why services play an essential role in facilitating the trade of goods.

6. What characterizes trade in services today regarding key players, modes of supply, and major service industries traded?
7. What characterizes today's pattern of FDI in terms of major providers and recipients?
8. Imagine a service firm in an industry of your choice. Discuss what the firm should do to cope with today's challenges addressed in the context of slowbalization.
9. Critically discuss the concept of slowbalization: Do you agree that globalization will accelerate again? Are stock-keeping and diversification good recipes for dealing with it? Should governments foster local production of critical supplies? How should one balance security and efficiency? Should one avoid business with countries with unpredictable autocratic regimes?

**Closing Case: Fintechs in Africa Expanding Across the Continent**

Flashing billboards advertising Kuda, a digital bank, can be seen everywhere in Lagos, Nigeria's economic capital. Signs of Paga, a mobile payment firm, are seen at thousands of corner shops. In a continent often associated with poverty, famines, draughts, violence, and political instability, fintech firms providing internet-based financial services are not the first thing that would come to mind. Nevertheless, recent years have seen a surge in fintechs, many of which have received significant financial investments from outside Africa. Stripe, the most valuable fintech in the West, acquired Nigerian digital payment firm Paystack. VISA has taken a 20% interest in Interswitch, a payment processor. In 2021, four African fintechs became unicorns—startup firms valued over US$1 billion: OPay, which received funding from Japanese Softbank; Senegal-based Wave, running a mobile money network; Chipper Cash, offering peer-to-peer payments; and Flutterwave, which simplifies payments for businesses.

Conditions in Africa encourage fintech: By 2025, there will be 1.5 billion people in Africa, and most of them grew up in the internet era. Like more than half of Nigeria, many African people do not have a bank account. Nigeria has 200 million people and a young and entrepreneurial population, where 95% of transactions are still done in cash. Traditional money remittances by banks are very expensive, and bank loans are difficult to obtain for people who engage in informal work. So, across Africa, unbanked people turn to fintechs. In Côte d'Ivoire, 95% of school tuition fees are paid by mobile money. OPay was once a ride-hailing app but now offers interest-free credit that is easier to get for informal workers than traditional bank loans. Chipper Cash lets Nigerians in Britain send money home instantly, potentially revolutionizing remittances in Africa. Nigeria saw two-thirds of investments in fintech in 2021.

There are challenges as well, however. Electricity and the internet are unreliable, and erratic regulation makes running a fintech difficult. So fintechs expand across the border to other countries in Africa. Indeed, some see Nigeria as a launchpad for their continental aspi-

African with a smartphone. (Image by Emilian Danaila from Pixabay)

rations. Wave from Senegal entered Côte d'Ivoire in 2021 and now operates in four African countries. Bamboo is expanding into Ghana and contemplating entering Kenya. Flutterwave, Africa's largest unicorn, now operates in 33 countries. Facilitating this is the African Continental Free Trade Area, signed in 2018 and ratified by 38 countries. In 2021, it launched the Pan-African Payment and Settlement system. This should facilitate cross-country operations and encourages international investors to back African fintechs with international aspirations. Nevertheless, some observers are cautious and warn of a hype that may not last. Foreign investors may underestimate the difficulty of entering African markets, each with its own regulation of the fintech sector.

3

**Questions**

1. Which mode of international supply would seem appropriate for African fintech firms expanding abroad?
2. Why do African fintechs focus on other African countries for their expansion?
3. Discuss if the African market can boost a "slowbalizing" world economy.

Sources: Economist (2021a, 2021b).

## Summary

This chapter:

- Provided a brief overview of the history of trade and foreign direct investment generally and specifically regarding services as well as the role of services in facilitating the trade in goods.
- Distinguished *exporting* as a form of trade from *foreign direct investment (FDI)*:
  - *Exporting*: "The sale of products produced by a firm in one country to customers that reside in another country"
  - *FDI*: "When a firm invests directly in facilities to produce or market a good or service in a foreign country"
- Distinguished four *modes of service supply*:
  - *Mode one: Cross-border trade: services supplied from the country of the service provider to a customer in another country*
  - *Mode two: Consumption abroad: services supplied in the country of the service provider to consumers coming from another country*
  - *Mode three: Commercial presence: services supplied by a service provider from one country through a commercial presence in another country*
  - *Mode four: Presence of natural persons: services supplied through the presence of a natural person from one country in another country*
- Described patterns of both trade and investment in services today.
- Outlined the primarily regional character of most multinational enterprises.
- Discussed the concept of "slowbalization" of global trade and investment happening today.

## References

Barisitz, S. (2017). *Central Asia and the silk road: Economic rise and decline over several millennia*. Springer.

D'Urbino, L. (2019, January 24). Slowbalization: The steam has gone out of globalization. *Economist*.

Daniels, J. D., Radebaugh, L. H., & Sullivan, D. P. (2019). *International business: Environments & operations* (16th ed.). Pearson.

Daniels, J. D., Radebaugh, L. H., Sullivan, D. P., & Click, R. W. (2021). *International business: Environments & operations* (17th ed.). Pearson.

Economist. (2017, February 11). Germany's current-account surplus is a problem. *Economist*.

Economist. (2019, January 24). Globalization has faltered: It is now being reshaped. *Economist*.

Economist. (2021a, July 31). *Fintech is booming despite a weak economy. Can that last?*.
Economist. (2021b, November 6). *Africa's fintech firms vie for domination.*
Economist. (2022a, April 2). The next wave of outsourcing: A half-a-trillion-dollar bet on revolutionizing white-collar work. *Economist.*
Economist. (2022b, July 18). *The tricky restructuring of global supply chains: Why too much resilience is dangerous.*
Foreman-Peck, J. S. (Ed.). (1998). *Historical foundations of globalization*. Edward Elgar.
Fröndhoff, B. (2023). Strafe für Deloitte in China. *Handelsblatt, 62*, 27.
Fuest, C. (2020). Corona verändert die Globalisierung, aber beendet sie nicht. *Handelsblatt*, 2020(133), 48.
Hill, C. W. L. (2021). *International business: Competing in the global marketplace* (13th ed.). McGraw-Hill Education.
Holtbrügge, D., & Welge, M. K. (2015). *Internationales management: Theorien, funktionen, fallstudien* (6th ed.). Schäffer-Poeschel.
Jackson, S. D. (2021). *International trade in services: Effective practice and policy*. Routledge.
Jones, G. (1996). *The evolution of international business: An introduction*. Routledge.
Moore, K., & Lewis, D. C. (2009). *The origins of globalization*. Routledge.
Müller, H.-C. (2016). Abenteuerlicher protektionismus. *Handelsblatt, 2016*(220), 24.
Peer, M., & Dörner, A. (2021). Indien: Investoren wetten auf den nächsten großen Asien-Deal. *The Hand, 2021*(250), 14–15.
Rosa, B., Gugler, P., & Verbeke, A. (2020). Regional and global strategies of MNEs: Revisiting Rugman & Verbeke (2004). *Journal of International Business Studies, 51*, 1045–1053.
Rugman, A., & Collinson, S. (2012). International business. Pearson.
Rugman, A., & Verbeke, A. (2004). A perspective on regional and global strategies of multinational enterprises. *Journal of International Business Studies, 35*(1), 3–12.
Rugman, A., & Verbeke, A. (2008). A new perspective on the regional and global strategies of multinational services firms. *Management International Review (MIR), 48*(4), 397–411.
UNCTAD. (2021a). *UNCTAD handbook of statistics 2021: Fact Sheet #5: Total trade in services.* Retrieved from https://unctad.org/system/files/official-document/tdstat46_FS05_en.pdf.
UNCTAD. (2021b). *UNCTAD handbook of statistics 2021: Fact Sheet #6: Trade in services by category*. Retrieved from https://unctad.org/system/files/official-document/tdstat46_FS06_en.pdf.
UNCTAD. (2021c). *World investment report 2021: Investing in sustainable recovery*. Retrieved from https://unctad.org/system/files/official-document/wir2021_en.pdf.
UNCTAD. (2022). *World investment report 2022: International tax reforms and sustainable investment*. Retrieved from https://unctad.org/system/files/official-document/wir2022_en.pdf.
WTO. (2009). *International trade statistics 2009*. Retrieved from https://www.wto.org/english/res_e/statis_e/its2009_e/its2009_e.pdf.
WTO. (2010). *International trade statistics 2010*. Retrieved from https://www.wto.org/english/res_e/statis_e/its2010_e/its2010_e.pdf.
WTO. (2013). *The general agreement on trade in services: An introduction*. Retrieved from https://www.wto.org/english/tratop_e/serv_e/gsintr_e.pdf.
WTO. (2015). *International trade statistics 2015*. Retrieved from https://www.wto.org/english/res_e/statis_e/its2015_e/its15_toc_e.htm.
WTO. (2019a). *World trade report 2019: The future of services trade*. Retrieved from https://www.wto.org/english/res_e/booksp_e/00_wtr19_e.pdf.
WTO. (2019b). *World trade statistical review* 2019. Retrieved from https://www.wto.org/english/res_e/statis_e/wts2019_e/wts2019_e.pdf.
WTO. (2021). *World trade statistical review* 2021. Retrieved from https://www.wto.org/english/res_e/statis_e/wts2021_e/wts21_toc_e.htm.
WTO. (2023). *Evolution of trade under the WTO: Handy statistics*. Retrieved from https://www.wto.org/english/res_e/statis_e/trade_evolution_e/evolution_trade_wto_e.htm.

3

## Further Reading

The annual World Investment Report by the United Nations Conference on Trade and Development (UNCTAD) provides up-to-date information on Foreign Direct Investment (FDI, https://worldinvestmentreport.unctad.org/).

The annual World Trade Report (https://www.wto.org/english/res_e/reser_e/wtr_e.htm) and the annual World Trade Statistics Review (https://www.wto.org/english/res_e/statis_e/wts_e.htm) of the World Trade Organization (WTO) provide reliable information on the state of international trade in goods and services.

WTO has set up a gateway page bundling all information on trade in services (https://www.wto.org/english/tratop_e/serv_e/serv_e.htm), also outlining the four modes of international service supply.

# National Differences in the Environment of Service Firms

Contents




D. Klimkeit et al., *International Management in Service Firms*, Classroom Companion: Business,
https://doi.org/10.1007/978-3-031-50345-0_4

### Learning Outcomes

After completing this chapter, you should be able to:

- Distinguish different political systems and identify political risks
- Distinguish different legal systems and legal risks
- Explain the concept of the rule of law
- Distinguish different types of economic systems
- Explain key indicators of economic potential and development



## Introduction

This chapter outlines the international environment where service firms do international business, focusing on the political, legal, and economic environment. The cultural environment will be addressed in ► Chap. 18. The chapter will introduce different political systems and the risks they can imply for companies doing business in a country. Then, different legal systems and risks will be outlined, as well as the concept of the rule of law and its distribution in the world. Finally, the chapter will distinguish different economic systems and outline indicators for measuring economic potential and performance. Based on this, the role of the BRICS (Brazil, Russia, India, China, and South Africa) and other emerging markets in the world economy will be addressed. Throughout, specific opportunities and risks for service firms are addressed.

Vkusno i tochka. (Image by Mos.ru, CC BY 4.0, ► https://commons.wikimedia.org/w/index.php?curid=119255857)

## Opening Case: Foreign Businesses in Russia and the War in Ukraine

On March 29, 2022, Andrij Melnyk, ambassador of Ukraine to Germany, posted on Twitter: "Quadratisch, Praktisch, Blut" (square, practical, blood), replacing "gut" (good) in the slogan of chocolate producer Ritter Sport. The background was that Ritter Sport refused to withdraw from Russia in response to the invasion of Ukraine by Russian troops earlier in 2022. Following Ritter Sport's decision, activists called for a boycott of the popular square-shaped chocolate bars. The company explained its decision to remain in Russia, where it makes 10% of its sales, by pointing out that many of its suppliers, farmers in Africa and Latin America, would lose their livelihoods if it decided to shut down their operations in Russia. Many other companies who at least initially decided to continue operations in Russia were met with much public criticism. Nestle eventually relented to public pressure and decided to only continue with essentials such as food for babies and hospitals and would also donate profits made in Russia to charity.

Many companies with operations in Russia were put in a difficult situation following the Russian aggression in Ukraine. Manufacturing firms with production sites in Russia worry about losing their assets when they retreat from the country. Many service firms in banking, insurance, telecommunications, information technology (IT) services, retail, and hospitality face complex considerations, too. Deutsche Bank has transferred several hundred of its 1500 IT experts from its technology center in Moscow to Berlin. Through this, they reduce the risk of losing the know-how of their experts if—due to rising tensions between Russia and the West—they cannot continue to operate their technology center in Russia. In the centers in Moscow and St. Petersburg, software for Deutsche Bank is being developed and maintained. This risk exists due to sanctions by Western governments against Russia and measures taken by the Russian government against Western firms. Likewise, Deutsche Telekom brought 2000 people, Russian staff members and their families, into hotels in Antalya, Turkey, pending a decision on a final destination. Between March and May 2022, German authorities issued 1850 work permits for Russians. The reasoning at Deutsche Telekom is that the knowledge of their staff in Russia is so valuable that it is preferable to transfer them to another country than to build their department from scratch. Deutsche Bank tried to keep its preparations as secret as possible as Russian authorities put foreign firms planning to shut down their operations massively under pressure. There were indicators that the Russian government would block the sale of foreign banks. Subsidiaries of foreign banks in Russia might be put under control by state-owned banks. Several firms, like Italian Unicredit bank, were planning a sale with a repurchase option in case the situation improves.

Many firms like German Insurance giant Allianz have not entirely given up their business in Russia but significantly reduced it. Allianz has sold most of its business in Russia to a Russian insurance firm, Zetta Insurance, retaining 49.9% of the shares. As the firm states, this ensures continuity for customers and staff. Other insurance firms withdrew from Russia. Zurich Insurance sold its business to 11 staff members, who continue operations under a different brand. Visa and Mastercard suspended their operations in Russia; however, they hesitated as it might damage ordinary Russians. Especially it might make it difficult for Russians who want to leave Vladimir Putin's regime to pay for tickets out of the country.

Software giant SAP eventually decided to shut down its operations completely. Initially, the firm only decided to stop entering into new business. However, public criticism grew stronger. On Twitter, Ukrainian Digital Minister Mychaljo Fedorow provocatively asked how long SAP wants to continue helping Russia to kill children, followed by a blood-splashed logo of SAP. Internally, 1700 staff of SAP demanded in an open letter to the management to discontinue all business in Russia.

In comparison, Metro, owner of retailers such as Saturn and Media Markt, decided to remain in Russia. The firm argues they need to ensure the supply of the population with groceries and have responsibility for their local management and staff in Russia. Also, a quarter of the retail properties owned by Metro are located in Russia. Finally, the withdrawal of McDonald's has symbolic properties. When the first McDonald's restaurant opened at Moscow's Pushkin Square in January 1990, still during Soviet times, long queues formed as people were eager to get a taste of freedom. It represented the fall of the iron curtain. Now, the firm sold its 850 fast-food restaurants operated by 65,000 staff to a local investor who is no longer allowed to use the name and logo. By selling its operations, McDonald's wants to preempt expropriation. McDonald's boss Chris Kempczinski stated that the loyalty and engagement of their staff and suppliers did not make it easy to decide to leave. Still, he added:

> However, we have an obligation to our global community and must adhere to our values (Handelsblatt, 2022c, p. 22, translated from German).

German business and finance newspaper *Handelsblatt* identified four problems for firms who want to shut down operations in Russia: worries about their local management, contractual obligations, the threat of expropriation, and dismissal of employees (Handelsblatt, 2022b). Russian parliament discussed a law that would make local managers of foreign companies who shut down operations liable to prosecution. They would risk spending up to 10 years in a penitentiary camp. As stated by a manager from a company in the automotive industry:

> We do not know in the event of a withdrawal whether the Secret Service will come by then (Handelsblatt, 2022b, p. 14, translated from German).

Frequently, companies have contractual obligations for service and maintenance toward their customers that need to be fulfilled. Exiting contracts would be tricky, as there is a risk of claims for damages and contractual penalties. SAP is a case in point: Their contracts with business customers for their software products have a long duration. Frankfurt-based Airport operator Fraport has a 25% share in St. Petersburg airport. Contractually, a sale before 2025 is not allowed. Companies that produce goods for daily needs or of strategic importance can be placed under fiduciary administration. To preempt this, DIY retailer Obi has given away their 27 stores in Russia for free to an investor, who is no longer allowed to use the brand name. Obi made 5% of its total revenues with 4900 staff in Russia. German companies have 280,000 employees in Russia. Stefan Hartung, boss of Bosch, who has 3500 staff in Russia, states:

> This is not only about the business point of view, but first and foremost about our caring duty (Handelsblatt, 2022b, p. 15, translated from German).

Deutsche Telekom continues to pay salaries to local staff, also to preempt expropriation.

According to a blog post on its website, Ritter Sport, remaining in Russia, claims to donate all revenues made in Russia, their second most important market after Germany, to charity. The firm pointed to its responsibility to its employees and their families. It stopped all further investments and publicity in Russia while continuing to sell chocolate to the Russian population (Ritter Sport, 2022).

**Questions**

1. How are the challenges foreign businesses in Russia face related to its political system?
2. How does the state of the rule of law in Russia impact the situation of foreign businesses?
3. How does the political and legal situation in a foreign firm's home country play a role?
4. How are the challenges of service firms in Russia different from manufacturing firms?

Sources: Economist (2022d, 2022f); Handelsblatt (2022a, 2022b, 2022c); Müller (2022); Osman (2022); Schier (2022); Schwarz and Müller (2022).

## The Political Environment

As service firms do business across different countries in the world, it becomes evident that decisions by political authorities, such as movement control orders due to the Coronavirus Disease-2019 (COVID-19) pandemic, can seriously affect the viability and profitability of businesses. As most services traditionally depend on direct contact between the service providers and customers, they are particularly vulnerable to restrictions experienced due to COVID-19. While many democratic governments significantly reduced or even abandoned restrictions in 2022 as the situation stabilized, in China still in 2022, whole cities were blocked off and put under quarantine as soon as a few cases of COVID-19 appeared (Economist, 2022e). This, among other reasons, is one pointer toward different political systems and a government's accountability to the population it implies. Also, the war in Ukraine, which led many employees of Western service firms to leave the country, demonstrates the role of political risks, in this case, catastrophic risk by warfare, impacting all businesses in a country.

## Political Systems

Given the potential challenges and risks businesses face in various countries, managers analyze the country's political situation when they contemplate doing business. The first approach to examine the impact of politics on service businesses is to distinguish different *political systems*.



**Political System**

A *political system* consists of the structural elements and dynamics of the government of a country that comprise both the political institutions and rules and norms that govern political activity (based on Daniels et al., 2021, p. 105).

As the definition outlines, in a political system, there are structural elements, such as different levels of government (federal, state, municipal), different players (government, parliament, political parties), and rules and norms for how the government comes into office. The latter includes whether elections occur in certain intervals and how laws come into force.

A key concept used to distinguish different political systems is *democracy*. The political system in some countries is considered democratic, while in others, it is considered non-democratic. Unfortunately, it is not straightforward to classify countries into these two boxes. Consider North Korea: The country is called "The Democratic People's Republic of Korea." Is it a democratic system? In Cuba, a much greater proportion of the population vote in elections than in the United States. Is Cuba more democratic than the United States? Democracy has become a label that almost every country wants to associate itself with, regardless of the political reality. Representatives of hardly any political system would call their system non-democratic. In theory, in a democracy, all citizens of a country would directly and actively participate in making political decisions. In practice, most citizens do not have the time and interest to participate actively in every law passed. Instead, we see *representative democracies* where citizens elect people who represent them, for example, in parliament, and make political decisions on their behalf. However, if only a part of the (adult) population is allowed to vote—as in Kuwait—or there is only one candidate from the unitary party per district to elect without alternatives—as in Cuba—most observers would not consider such a system as very democratic. Further, one would expect that candidates elected once would not stay in power indefinitely but that elections take place regularly and that if representatives lose in an election, they would voluntarily cede office to their elected successors. Finally, in a democracy, one would expect that citizens and media enjoy some right to express their opinion openly, even if it opposes the government in place (Danziger & Smith, 2016, pp. 168–171).

**Democracy**

Governance by leaders whose authority is based on a limited mandate from a universal electorate that selects among genuine alternatives and has some rights to political participation and opposition (Danziger & Smith, 2016, p. 171).

Danziger and Smith have chosen the modest expression "some rights" to account for the fact that some democracies ("liberal democracies") provide extensive political and civil liberties to their citizens, while in others, they are more restricted ("illiberal democracies").

Now, how are systems that are not democratic to be referred to and characterized? Several terms are used here: dictatorship, autocracy, totalitarian regime. Most frequently, political scientists apply the term "*authoritarian regime.*"

**Authoritarian Regime**

The political actions and decisions of the ruler are not constrained, while the political rights and freedoms of citizens are significantly limited (Danziger & Smith, 2016, p. 173).

In authoritarian regimes, citizens' abilities to participate in the political process are very restricted unless they are organized by the regime, such as mass rallies. Media are not free, and the regime in power restricts the availability of political information. Citizens are not allowed to question the regime's policies (Danziger & Smith, 2016, pp. 173–174).

As might have transpired from the above, countries do not simply fall into either of the two boxes—democracy or authoritarianism. For example, some democracies are more liberal by allowing more freedom of expression and free media independent of the government, while this is more restricted in illiberal democracies. Therefore, we must see democracy as a continuum with full democracy on one end and total authoritarianism on the other end. Most countries' political systems would fall somewhere between the two ends of the continuum. So, democracy is not a matter of "either–or" but a matter of "more or less."

The Economist Intelligence Unit (EIU) uses this idea of a continuum to rate political systems worldwide by specific criteria and calculate a score, placing them on such a continuum. They rate each country on five criteria: the electoral process and pluralism, civil liberties, the functioning of government, political participation, and political culture. The average of the five scores constitutes an overall democracy score for a country. The EIU then categorizes countries into four regimes: full democracies, flawed democracies, hybrid regimes, and authoritarian regimes. In *full democracies*, political freedoms and civil liberties are respected. This is underpinned by a democratic political culture. Media are diverse and independent of the government. The judicial system is also independent of the government. There are effective checks and balances on the power of the government. Democracy and government function well. Conversely, *in authoritarian regimes*, pluralism does not or hardly exist. Formal institutions of democracy have little real substance. Elections are not free and fair. Civil liberties are strongly limited. Media are controlled by the government. The judiciary is not independent of government, and freedom of expression is not guaranteed. *Flawed democracies* are distinguished from full democracies by an underdeveloped political culture or low levels of participation by citizens in political processes. There might be some limitations to the freedom and diversity of media. The government may not be functioning fully effectively. *Hybrid regimes* have characteristics that place them between flawed democracies and authoritarian regimes. Overall, 37.1% of the world's population (citizens of 59 countries) live in authoritarian regimes, while only 6.4% of the world population live in full democracies (21 countries). Also, one can see regional patterns. Western Europe and North America have 13 full democracies, while Eastern Europe, North Africa, and the Middle East have none, and Sub-Saharan Africa has only one. Instead, there are 23 authoritarian regimes in Sub-Saharan Africa and 17 in the Middle East and North Africa (Economist Intelligence Unit, 2022). See ◘ Table 4.1 for a list of selected countries from the Economist Democracy Index.

The development of democracy has been a history of ups and downs. Between 1974 and 1990, about 30 more countries turned to democracy, doubling the number of democratic countries. This was labeled the "third wave of democracy" by political scientist Samuel Huntington (1991). The first wave took place in the nine-

◘ **Table 4.1** Selected countries from the Economist Democracy Index 2021

| Rank | Country |
|---|---|
| 1 | Norway |
| 2 | New Zealand |
| 3 | Finland |
| 4 | Sweden |
| 5 | Iceland |
| … | |
| 162= | Syria |
| 162= | Central African Republic |
| 163 | Democratic Republic of Congo |
| 164 | North Korea |
| 165 | Myanmar |
| 166 | Afghanistan |

Source: Based on data from Economist Intelligence Unit (2022, pp. 12–16)

teenth century, while the triumph of the Allies in the Second World War initiated the second wave until 1962. Huntington sees several reasons for this turn toward democracy: legitimacy problems of regimes due to economic failure, the turn of the Catholic church against authoritarianism, a growing middle class, and a snowballing effect with earlier transitions providing a model for other countries. Under the impression of the collapse of authoritarian communist systems in 1989, Francis Fukuyama even famously declared "The End of History" with the universal spread of Western-style liberal democracy across the world (Fukuyama, 1992). In practice, Fukuyama has been proven wrong. Huntington was closer to the truth by predicting that following the third wave of democracy, a third wave of de-democratization might follow. This is indeed what one can witness in recent years. A growing skepticism of the value of democracy can be observed across the world. Going back to the 1950s, modernization theory holds that socioeconomic conditions, such as industrialization, urbanization, wealth, and education, foster democracy in a country. To sustain democracy, a government needs legitimacy, typically through continuous economic growth. In a more recent study, Wucherpfenning and Deutsch generally find empirical support for this theory. However, they state that the exact connection between the various factors and their causality is unclear. The authors conclude: "For democracy to be stable, it must come from within since it is the socio-economic conditions which create and maintain an environment for stable and enduring democracies" (Wucherpfenning & Deutsch, 2009, p. 7). In practice, the Economist Intelligence Unit has witnessed in its Democracy Index a decline in democracy across the world for many years. Since the launch of the Democracy Index in 2006, one can observe a receding of democracy, with a declining or stagnating total index score in 108 out of the 167 countries monitored. For example, in Russia, democracy declined consistently in the Democracy Index year after year, from 5.02 in 2016 to 2.94 in 2018. However, the retreat of democracy is not universal. Most of the 59 countries whose scores improved are located in emerging economy regions (Economist Intelligence Unit, 2022).

Now the question is: What follows from this for businesses? The most relevant question to managers is: Is there a relationship between democracy and the civil liberties it brings for citizens and the freedom of companies to go about their business largely undisturbed by government interventions and without political risks to the viability and profitability of their business? While the relationship is not an exact 1:1 relationship in that more democracy always equals more economic freedom, increasingly, the two are interrelated, as European think tank Breugel has found. Democracy and a market economy can support each other. There are market-oriented authoritarian countries, such as in East and Southeast Asia and the Gulf. However, most high-income countries today have both democracy and a market economy. In the long run, there is no example of a stable democracy without a market economy. Data show that the correlation between political and economic freedom is not very strong, but it exists. In countries with an authoritarian trend, such as Russia, market economic reforms were also stopped or reversed. As the situation outlined in the opening case shows, Western businesses in Russia and their managers are under threat of arbitrary penalties and nationalization. In countries such as Georgia after 2003 and Ukraine after 2014, progress in democratization enabled market economic reforms. Democracy can foster freedom of businesses as in a market economy in several ways: Having a system of political checks and balances as in a liberal democracy limits the abuse of power by governments. A liberal democracy increases transparency, limiting opportunities for corruption and guaranteeing property rights. The rotation of political leadership, as is typical of democracies, reduces the abuse of power. The civil liberties of democracy support economic freedom (Dabrowski, 2018).



## Political Risks

As outlined above, political systems come with *political risks* for companies that conduct business in a country. While political risks frequently affect all firms in a country, foreign companies are more often the target of adverse government interventions.

**Political Risk**

*Political risk* refers to the threat that decisions or events in a country will negatively affect the profitability and sustainability of an investment (Daniels et al., 2021, p. 117).

One can classify political risks usefully into four categories: *systemic*, *procedural*, *distributive*, and *catastrophic* political risk (Daniels et al., 2021, pp. 118–119).

**Systemic Political Risk:** Frequently, policies impact more or less all companies in a given country. For example, a newly elected government may significantly increase taxes for businesses, impose strict environmental protection rules, or change labor laws in ways that make laying off employees difficult. Sometimes, populist governments that come into office decide to nationalize sectors of the economy they see as dominated by foreign multinational enterprises (MNEs). Frequently, one could observe this in Latin America in countries like Venezuela or Bolivia, where especially the energy sector became the target of expropriation (Economist, 2006).

**Procedural Risk:** In several especially developing and emerging countries, the political situation can make doing business difficult. It may appear like sand in the gears of the business. Corruption is a case in point. If officials regularly require extra payment to provide public services they should be providing for free, it increases the cost of doing business and lowers profitability.

**Distributive Risk:** Often, governments, especially in emerging markets, wonder if they cannot take a larger share of the profits that foreign-owned multinational enterprises make in their country. So, they institute policies that successively expropriate MNEs, for example, through taxation or regulation of the repatriation of profits.

**Catastrophic Risk:** Pandemics like the COVID-19 pandemic and its consequences and the war in Ukraine are recent examples of catastrophic risks. They devastate the business environment in a country for all businesses. They can comprise civil unrest, war, coup d'états, and similar catastrophic events.

The question is how companies can deal with these political risks to protect their business. Here we need to distinguish between businesses that contemplate investing in a country and businesses that are already active in a country. Before venturing into a country, managers analyze the political risk, starting by analyzing the type of political system and level of democratic freedom. To address systemic risk, managers need to be aware not just of the current government's policies but also of upcoming elections and political programs of opposition parties that might constitute the next government. For example, many did not take it seriously when Evo Morales in Bolivia proclaimed in his electoral campaign that he would nationalize energy companies if he became president. They believed he would moderate his position once in power. Instead, once president, he did exactly what he had announced, and foreign-owned businesses lost much money (Economist, 2006).

Once in the country, companies facing procedural risk monitor the situation closely, being mindful of contacts with government officials and having clear policies on matters such as corruption. Companies carefully consider how much exposure they want regarding systemic and distributive political risk. In other words, how much money do they want to invest in a country that might be lost? Today, increasingly regarding China, companies pursue a "China plus" strategy: In addition to facilities in China, they set up a twin facility in another country in Asia, such as Malaysia, Vietnam, or Indonesia. Suppose rising tensions with China make pursuing operations in China difficult or impossible. In that case, they can switch entirely to the backup operation in another country without completely disrupting the business (Peer, 2021). While this is a safeguard for an extreme scenario, as long as companies are still active in a country with an authoritarian regime, they make it a point to maintain good relationships with the government to reduce the risk of becoming a target of adverse measures. Entering a joint venture with a local firm can also be an option, as, typically, governments would be more reluctant to damage a firm co-owned by a local company than a purely foreign firm. Further, companies maintain contact with local lawyers. Lawyers specializing in business relations between their home and host countries can be helpful intermediaries.

## Politics and Service Firms

Service firms are also affected by a country's political system and political risks but in different ways due to their characteristics. Several service industries are regulated by governments. Think of banking, insurance, telecommunications, airlines, and others (Dahringer, 1991). Especially following the 2008/2009 financial crisis, the regulation of banks increased in many countries (Chidlow et al., 2019). As firms expand abroad, they must deal with different regulations in each country, making international expansion cumbersome. For example, to practice as a chartered public accountant (CPA) in the United States, one needs a degree from a recognized US business school and pass a national exam (Dahringer, 1991).

The characteristic of the *intangibility* of many services and the related distinction between soft and hard services made in the introductory chapter helps analyze the effect of political risk on service firms. Due to the intangibility of their assets, many service firms are relatively less affected by political risks, such as nationalization (systemic/distributive risk), or catastrophic risk, such as warfare. This is because they have fewer tangible assets in a country that could be seized or damaged. This holds especially true for firms offering predominantly soft services, such as most professional services. These risks are higher for service firmswith a large proportion of hard services as hotel chains, operators of theme parks, or restaurant chains (Chidlow et al., 2019). This makes leaving Russia due to the war in Ukraine relatively easier for many service firms than for manufacturing firms that leave factories and machinery behind. Nevertheless, as can be seen in the case of the war in Ukraine, catastrophic risks such as warfare can also make providing soft services difficult, if not impossible, when the life and physical integrity of staff in a country is in danger. So, some service firms have moved their staff from their offices in Ukraine to Poland, Germany, or other countries to continue operations. This is only possible for services that do not require a physical presence in the customer's country.

Some services are more difficult for governments to regulate, such as those provided by the presence of natural persons who cross the border (Chidlow et al., 2019). Lorry drivers from Eastern Europe driving to Western European countries are an example that the European Union attempts to regulate (Schlautmann, 2018). Similarly, digital services (cross-border supply) are more difficult to regulate by governments. In the opening case, the aggressive critique of SAP as they did not leave the Russian market shows that political risks can affect the reputation of service firms and the trust of their customers and employees. Therefore, service firms need to demonstrate that they satisfy the needs of the societies in which they are active to obtain the goodwill of the community and government. Further, they need to build relationships with government authorities and—if they can—use their business power to move government action toward them to a supportive mode (Chidlow et al., 2019). The lobbying the "Big Four" audit firms conduct to avert stricter regulation of their industry is a case in point (Quack & Schüßler, 2015).

**Regulation of Professional Service Firms (PSFs):** So, let us take a closer look at the regulation of professional service firms. The regulation of professional services such as auditing or law varies between countries. In some countries, such as the United States and the United Kingdom, regulation is left mainly to self-regulation by professional associations. In Continental Europe, the state plays a more active role in regulation. The "bargain" in countries with self-regulation is that as long as the profession ensures that they serve the public interest, they are allowed to regulate things like admission, education, and standards themselves. This includes screening foreign professionals wanting to practice, as in the case of CPAs mentioned above. Large PSFs, such as the Big Four audit firms, have actively lobbied for deregulation to expand their activities more easily across borders. Following the

Enron scandal in 2001, where auditor Arthur Anderson helped cover up the fraud at the energy-trading firm, regulators in the United States and most other countries introduced stricter regulations for audit firms. For example, many countries demanded that audit firms auditing a company's financial statements are not allowed to provide significant consulting services to the same company to avoid a conflict of interest. Since then, governments have been taking a more active role in monitoring PSFs. Therefore, PSFs engaging in international activities face various licensing and training requirements and procedures. Their purpose is to protect customers and ensure the trustworthiness of PSFs. Especially larger PSFs are under increased scrutiny where their operations are seen to endanger the public interest (Quack & Schüßler, 2015).

## The Legal Environment

When a company enters a new country market, it would expect procedures for setting up its business to be transparent, easy to navigate, and not overly burdensome and lengthy. When they enter contracts with suppliers and customers, they would expect that when their business partners do not honor their contractual obligations, they can take them to court and that the court will rule within a short period and in their favor. All these things and more are regulated by the *legal system* in a country.

**Legal System**

The *legal system* is the mechanism for developing, stipulating, interpreting, and enforcing the laws in a formal jurisdiction (Daniels et al., 2021, p. 121).

When laws are transparent and enforced consistently and efficiently, companies are more confident investing in a country. If not, they would reconsider their contemplated investment unless the market opportunities are so significant that they would be willing to take a certain level of legal risk.

## Legal Systems

As you may assume, legal systems across the world differ in many ways. Based on tradition and custom, different types of legal systems have emerged. They can be classified as *common law*, *civil law*, *theocratic law*, and *mixed systems* (Daniels et al., 2021, p. 123; JuriGlobe Research Group, 2022). See ◘ Fig. 4.1 for a summary of the four types.

**Common Law:** Common law exists in the United Kingdom and countries with a British heritage, such as the United States, Canada, Australia, New Zealand, and India. In these countries, laws passed by legislators tend to be somewhat broad,

| Common Law | Civil Law |
| --- | --- |
| • Courts interpret and specify legislation<br>• Role of precedents<br>• UK, US, Canada, Australia, India | • Based on detailed laws by legislators<br>• Courts settle disputes<br>• 150 countries, e.g., Germany, France |
| **Theocratic Law** | **Mixed Systems** |
| • Based on religious foundations<br>• Religious leaders interpret religious texts<br>• Saudi Arabia, Iran | • Combination of elements<br>• Often includes elements of theocratic law<br>• Pakistan, Indonesia |

**Fig. 4.1** Types of legal systems. (Own diagram, drawing on content from Daniels et al., 2021, p. 123, and JuriGlobe Research Group, 2022)

leaving more room for interpretation by courts, which stipulate what a particular law means in practice for a given situation. This court ruling then becomes a precedent that must be considered for future court rulings. So, judges, when addressing a court case, before considering the law, also consider custom, general legal principles, and precedents. By considering precedents, law grows from the bottom up through a series of court rulings, all based on preceding court rulings.

**Civil Law:** In civil law countries, laws passed by legislators are codified in more detail. Precedence is given to the written law developed by legislators. Preceding court rulings play a lesser role than in common law countries. Courts come into play to rule in disputes between different parties. Civil law is the most widespread type of law and can be found in about 150 countries, such as Mexico, Chile, Germany, France, Russia, Kuwait, and Thailand.

**Theocratic Law:** Theocratic law is based on religious systems of belief. Religious leaders play a crucial role in interpreting key religious texts. The most relevant theocratic law today is Islamic law, shari'a, based on the Koran, decisions and sayings of the prophet Mohamed, texts from Islamic scholars, and the consensus of legal communities in a given country. It is mainly found in the Near and Middle East (for example, Saudi Arabia).

**Mixed Systems:** As the name says, mixed systems combine elements of the above three systems. Frequently, either common law or civil law is combined with elements of theocratic law. This is the case, for example, in Indonesia, where based on Dutch colonial heritage, a civil law system is combined with elements of Islamic law. Likewise, Pakistan, starting from the British colonial heritage of common law, has also integrated elements of Islamic law.

Indonesia; Indonesian law combines civil law with Islamic law. (Image by Iqbal Nuril Anwar from Pixabay)

## Legal Systems and Professional Service Firms

While generally, legal systems apply to and impact all types of firms the same, they have a particular impact on professional service firms especially law firms. The English common law system, emphasizing interpretation and precedent, provided an attractive basis for lawyers to develop and expand their services. So, the English legal profession sought to benefit by extending its mandate to generate new business for itself. Historically, lawyers in common law countries like the United Kingdom and the United States have become more entrepreneurial than their counterparts in civil law countries. For example, lawyers became involved in constructing financial instruments. In contrast, in Germany, a civil law country, lawyers historically remained more conservative in their business development as detailed civil law provides fewer opportunities for lawyers to develop entrepreneurial approaches (Morgan & Quack, 2006). Likewise, contract lawyers in common law countries have more work and can generate more revenues because contracts tend to be very detailed, including all potential contingencies. In civil law countries, contracts tend to be shorter as detailed laws cover many potential problems. Notaries, though, play a more significant role in civil law countries as contracts need to be adequately notarized or registered to be valid. In contrast, in common law countries, proof of agreement is sufficient to enforce a contract (Cavusgil et al., 2020, p. 192).

## The Rule of Law

When companies enter a country, they would want to be able to find out precisely which rules apply to them and know that they are fairly and consistently applied, regardless of the national origin of a company or connections to government officials. They would want to know that the rules in place are, by and large, also adhered to by their business partners. In countries where this is the case, the *rule of law* exists.

> **Rule of law**
>
> *Rule of law* refers to a legal system in which rules are clear, publicly disclosed, fairly enforced, and widely respected by individuals, organizations, and the government (Cavusgil et al., 2020, p. 191).

The rule of law is a hallmark of democracy, so there is a connection to the type of political system. In a democracy, it is more likely to find the rule of law. Fair enforcement implies that all members of society are treated the same in front of a court, including public officials and government members. If public officials, such as policepersons, act in a way not in line with the law, they can be brought to justice. The rule of law allows businesses to thrive as managers confidently invest in a country and enter contracts with business partners. In its absence, companies face many uncertainties. In countries with authoritarian regimes, the governing group, such as a unitary party, is often seen as above the law. Government interferes with court proceedings to suppress dissent and reward loyalty. The World Bank regularly identifies the rule of law in countries and territories worldwide and posts it on its "Worldwide Governance Indicators" website. ◘ Table 4.2 shows select countries, ranked in percentiles by the rule of law, with 100 as the most robust rule of law and 0 as the lowest. As can be seen, there is quite a strong correlation between the rule of law and the level of development. Countries with the most robust rule of law (top 10%) are developed countries like Finland, Norway, New Zealand, Singapore, Switzerland, Netherlands, Canada, Australia, Germany, and Japan. Countries in the bottom 10% are less developed, such as Venezuela, Somalia, Afghanistan, Democratic Republic of Congo, Eritrea, and Tajikistan. Russia has a very low rule of law at the 22.6%. This can be seen in the opening case in how foreign businesses in Russia face great legal uncertainty when they contemplate leaving the country (World Bank, 2022c).

## Legal Risks

Legal requirements and procedures for companies impact how easy it is to do business in a country. Doing business is difficult if registering a new business takes long and is very bureaucratic or if court proceedings are expensive, not transparent, and

**Table 4.2** Distribution of Rule of Law, 2020: selected countries from World Governance Indicators website

| Country/territory | Rank | Country/territory | Rank |
|---|---|---|---|
| Finland | 100.00 | Saudi Arabia | 60.10 |
| Canada | 92.79 | Thailand | 57.69 |
| Australia | 92.31 | India | 54.33 |
| Germany | 91.35 | China | 52.88 |
| Japan | 90.87 | South Africa | 49.52 |
| United Kingdom | 89.90 | Egypt, Arab Rep. | 39.90 |
| United States | 88.46 | Kenya | 31.25 |
| Korea, Rep. | 84.62 | Mexico | 26.92 |
| United Arab Emirates | 79.33 | Russian Federation | 22.60 |
| Poland | 69.23 | Venezuela, RB | 0.00 |

Note: Reflects perceptions of the extent to which agents have confidence in and abide by the rules of society; data are gathered from survey institutes, think tanks, non-governmental organizations, international organizations, and private sector firms
Source: Own table based on data from World Bank (2022c)

lengthy. From 2004 to 2020, the World Bank reported annually on how easy it is to do business in 190 countries. Cost, requirements, and procedures for things like starting a business, dealing with construction permits, employing staff, registering property, enforcing contracts, and closing a business were monitored and rated. After data irregularities were reported, the World Bank paused the report in 2020. A new methodology was under development at the time of writing. In the following, we report select findings from the corrected data for 2020 (World Bank, 2021).

**Starting a Business:** In some countries, starting a new business is easy and swift. In others, it is bureaucratic, costly, and takes a long time. In Georgia, starting a business takes only one step and is completed within 1 day. It costs just 2% of the income per capita (100 GEL [Georgian lari], about US$35). In comparison, in Venezuela, it takes 20 steps to register a new business, and the procedure takes 230 days. One step, registration at the Social Security Institute, already takes 130 days. Obtaining an industrial or commercial license takes 50 days. The cost for the various registrations amounts to 212% of the income per capita in Venezuela.

**Enforcing Contracts:** When an amicable agreement between business partners is impossible, one might have to take the other party to court. In some countries, this takes a long time and costs a lot, and the procedure is far from transparent and trustworthy. In South Korea, resolving a commercial dispute through a first-instance court takes, on average, 290 days. The court proceedings cost 12.7% of the value of the claim. On a scale from 0 (worst) to 18 (best), the World Bank ranks the quality of the judicial process as 14.5. For this, the World Bank rates items such as court structure and proceedings, case management, and court automation. In Bangladesh, the same court case would take 1442 days, costing 66.8% of the claim value. The quality of the judicial process is rated as 7.5.



**Resolving Insolvency:** Managers entering a country may not have closing the business down due to insolvency at the front of their minds. Nevertheless, investigating how insolvency is dealt with in a country can be an important element of how easy or hard it is to do business. In Japan, bankruptcy proceedings take 6–7 months and cost 4.5% of the estate. Most likely, insolvency will lead to a reorganization of the firm, which can then continue to operate. In Ecuador, bankruptcy proceedings would take more than 5 years and cost 18% of the estate. Typically, the result would be that the business will not be able to continue operations, and its assets would be sold piecemeal.

Starting a business, entering and enforcing contracts, and closing a business constitute ongoing operational concerns that can constitute risks. For example, think of a company that expects a sizeable outstanding payment from a customer that does not come. If the court proceeding that would force the customer to pay takes too long, the company might go bankrupt in the meantime. Likewise, if starting a business is expensive, bureaucratic, and lengthy, the company might similarly run into financial issues before it even starts operations in a country. There are several other ways in which a country's legal environment impacts businesses, for instance, which products they can offer and how they can sell to customers in a country, constituting additional legal risks. From discussions of risks by Cavusgil et al. (2020, pp. 197–199) and Daniels et al. (2021, pp. 129–131), we highlight some areas particularly relevant for many service firms:

**Foreign Investment Laws:** Most countries restrict how foreign companies can enter the country. Sometimes, some sectors of the economy are closed to foreign direct investment (FDI) from foreign firms to protect local businesses, culture, and security. The Indian government has a range of restrictions for foreign firms wanting to set up retail businesses, such as requiring sourcing at least 30% of the value from local sources. In Russia, data collected need to be processed and stored locally (Daniels et al., 2021, pp. 128–130). In China, in many sectors, such as telecommunications, firms must enter joint ventures with local firms and cannot set up a wholly owned operation. This is to retain control of these industries while ensuring the transfer of know-how, capital, and technology to local firms. In telecommunications, in the United States, the government banned Chinese firm Huawei from obtaining contracts for telecommunications equipment due to fears of espionage (Economist, 2019a).

**Laws on Income Repatriation:** Normally, multinational enterprises want to transfer at least parts of profits from foreign operations back to the parent country. Some governments, however, restrict such repatriation of profits. This is typically done by governments of countries with challenges in their foreign trade balance or a weak currency experiencing undesired exchange rate devaluations. This was repeatedly the case in Argentina, especially during the presidency of Christina

Kirchner, who attempted to stabilize the exchange rate of the Argentinian peso against the dollar like this (Economist, 2021).

**Internet and E-commerce Regulation:** Regulation in e-commerce and Internet-based business models is the most dynamic area in legal systems and continues to evolve. In China, for example, for a long time, consumer-privacy protection was weak until 2021, when the Chinese government introduced sweeping measures to improve consumer privacy (Gusbeth, 2021).

**Intellectual Property Protection:** In many countries, protecting intellectual property (IP) is a challenge. Intellectual property (IP) can consist of literary or artistic works, patents, trademarks, designs, inventions, logos, names, images, blueprints, and similar intangible objects of high value that provide a competitive advantage to their owners. Given the intangible nature of most services, intellectual property plays a particular role in services. As you will remember, some service firms like Netflix or Spotify base their business model on intellectual property trading. When vaccines against COVID-19 became available in 2021, widespread discussions broke out about whether to lift patent protection for the vaccines to enable faster production of vaccines. Others argued that protecting IP gives pharmaceutical firms the incentive to develop vaccines. A company's IP is protected by an *Intellectual Property Right* (IPR).

**International Property Rights**

*Intellectual property rights* are the rights given to persons over the creations of their minds. They usually give the creator an exclusive right over the use of his/her creation for a certain period of time (WTO, 2022).

An IPR allows the innovating firm to decide how to use the IP, for example, the innovation. A challenge is that an IPR granted by one country does not necessarily hold in other countries. For example, a US patent creates an IPR only in the United States. A second challenge is the enforcement of IPRs. While most governments claim to protect IPRs, counterfeiting goods is widespread, especially in developing countries where the rule of law is not very strong (Daniels et al., 2021, p. 131). The World Trade Organization (WTO) administers the Trade-Related Aspects of Intellectual Property Rights (TRIPS) agreement that provides minimum standards for protecting intellectual property (WTO, 2022).

**Legal Jurisdiction:** When companies from different countries do business with each other, it is not obvious whether the law of the country of the vendor or the customer will apply in case of a lawsuit. Intuitively, both sides would often prefer a court in their home country to be in charge as they might expect preferential treatment. Generally, as part of contractual freedom, both parties can choose which jurisdiction to apply. Especially when doing business in countries with weak rule of law, MNEs often prefer their contract with a local firm to be subject to their home jurisdiction (Enders, 2021).

## Legal Risks Arising from the Home-Country Legal Environment

Companies not only face legal risks in host countries. There can also be legal risks originating in their home countries. One reason for this is that some countries apply a principle called *extraterritoriality*.

4

**Extraterritoriality**

*Extraterritoriality* refers to "states [...] applying or seeking to apply their laws and regulations to persons or conduct outside national borders" (International Chamber of Commerce, 2006, p. 1).

Governments pass laws with applicability outside their territory to combat crime, terrorism, corruption, cartels, and other things it considers undesirable. However, it can have adverse effects on international trade and investment. In addition, to comply with legal regulations in host countries where companies do business when extraterritorial regulations from their home countries apply, they also need to be considered. This can make international business more complicated than it already is and create conflicting or overlapping legal requirements for businesses. It increases companies' legal risk (International Chamber of Commerce, 2006).

The US Patriot Act of 2001 allows the US government to seize funds held by a non-US bank in the United States if a customer account abroad is subject to forfeiture proceedings under the US money laundering regime. In France, a law prohibits the exhibition of Nazi propaganda and the sale of Nazi memorabilia. Based on this, a French court required Yahoo to remove such goods from websites accessible in France, including the US website, as it is also accessible in France. This also highlights the challenges of cross-border e-commerce. Sometimes, rules on corporate governance can apply extraterritorially, such as the comprehensive listing rules of the US stock exchange. Foreign firms listing their shares in the United States to access the attractive US capital market must comply with these listing requirements even if they do not have business in the United States. In addition, merger review authorities can have a far-reaching impact. For example, in 2001, the European Commission blocked a proposed merger between GE and Honeywell, two US firms, even though the US regulator had approved it (International Chamber of Commerce, 2006).

Bribery of government officials is widespread in developing countries to facilitate obtaining public contracts. Public officials demand bribes for various reasons, including low salaries, the broad authority given to them by the state, low accountability, and societal attitudes (Scott et al., 2002). However, since 1977, US firms have been prohibited from paying bribes to foreign government officials to obtain or retain business under the Foreign Corrupt Practices Act (FCPA). As the official definition reads:

» In general, the FCPA prohibits offering to pay, paying, promising to pay, or authorizing the payment of money or anything of value to a foreign official in order to influence any act or decision of the foreign official in his or her official capacity or to secure any other improper advantage in order to obtain or retain business (U.S. Department of Justice & Securities & Exchange Commission, 2020, p. 9).

Violations of the FCPA can lead to civil and criminal penalties, sanctions, and remedies, including fines and imprisonment (U.S. Department of Justice & Securities & Exchange Commission, 2020).

As outlined in the opening case, Western companies that want to continue their operation in Russia might get into conflict with their home governments, which prohibit business with Russia in certain sectors due to the Russian invasion of Ukraine.

## The Economic Environment

Companies also analyze the economic environment in a country before deciding if, how, and when to do business in that country. The World Bank regularly publishes data for 189 member countries plus 28 other economies, adding up to 217 territories for which economic statistical data are available (World Bank, 2022a). As resources are scarce, most companies will not do business in all 217 economic territories but choose attractive ones that do not exhibit too high risk compared to expected returns. Companies analyze primarily two elements of a country's economic environment: (a) the type of economic system, and (b) the level of economic development, performance, and potential.

## Types of Economic Systems

Before doing business with a country, managers want to know how the government regulates markets, how much economic freedom companies enjoy, how resources are allocated, how prices are determined, and how goods and services are traded across borders. As a first approach, it is beneficial to classify the world's complex variety of economic systems into *types of economic systems*.

**Economic System**

An *economic system* organizes the production, distribution, and consumption of goods and services (Daniels et al., 2021, p. 151).

Traditionally, three types are distinguished: the market economy, the command economy, and the mixed economy. Today, one must add state capitalism as a fourth type. The types of economic systems are summarized in ◘ Fig. 4.2.

| Market Economy | Centrally Planned Economy | Mixed Market Economy | State Capitalism |
|---|---|---|---|
| • Most resources privately owned<br>• Invisible hand of the market<br>• US, Hong Kong, Switzerland | • Most resources owned by the government<br>• Visible hand of the state<br>• Central planning<br>• North Korea | • Private and government-owned resources<br>• Balance between economic efficiency and social justice<br>• Japan, Sweden, Germany, France | • Market-economy system for growth<br>• Strong unideological state intervention<br>• Building national champions and industries<br>• China, Russia |



**Fig. 4.2** Types of economic systems. (Own diagram based on content from Daniels et al., 2021, pp. 150–154)

**Market Economy:** In a market economy, individual companies and consumers make most economic decisions. A market economy is based on the idea of capitalism that there are private property rights that convey the owner of these rights profits as a return for initiatives, investments, and risks taken. Resources are allocated via a market mechanism where consumers make choices about the goods and services they buy, and companies respond accordingly. This is because they can profit most by providing what consumers want. Therefore, economists speak of the "invisible hand of the market," which coordinates demand and supply without a government making decisions. In this type of economic system, governments do not get involved in the market process much. The government provides certain public goods such as transportation infrastructure, public security, a judicial system, and an education system. The state protects property rights and ensures competition is maintained and remains fair. Sometimes this "pure" form of the market economy is also referred to as a "free market economy," "liberal market economy," or "neoliberal market economy" to distinguish it from other forms of market-based economies subsumed below under the label "mixed market economy." Traditionally, this can be found primarily in the United States, Hong Kong, and the United Kingdom (Daniels et al., 2021, pp. 151–152).

**Centrally Planned Economy:** Sometimes, it is called a "command economy." We use the term *centrally planned economy* due to the role of central planning by the state. During the Cold War, this has historically been the counterpart to the market economy. Based on the ideology of communism, the state owns all economic resources and controls all economic activity. The state determines which goods are to be produced in which quantity at which price. Therefore, resource allocation is determined centrally according to government priorities. As practice has shown historically, in this system, the government struggles to plan correctly according to the needs of the consumers and allocate resources efficiently. Productivity has proven to be low, and such systems have not been able to improve the population's living standards significantly. While in the past, the Soviet Union and its allies in Central and Eastern Europe and China followed this model, today, mainly North Korea still applies such a system (Daniels et al., 2021, pp. 152–153).

**Mixed Market Economy:** Many economies exhibit characteristics of both "pure" systems outlined above and are therefore commonly referred to as "mixed systems." Typically, though, they are closer to a market economy than to a centrally planned economy, so we call them a *mixed market economy*. Ownership of economic resources in these systems is primarily private, and resource allocation is typically market driven. As in the market economy, consumers make choices that drive companies to allocate resources accordingly. However, the state intervenes more than in the market economy, for example, in areas like regulations on labor law and environmental protection. It owns some resources, such as state-owned enterprises in key sectors. Frequently, this system is based on the philosophy of socialism or social democracy, as it is frequently referred to in Europe. The idea is to ensure fairness, protect weaker members of society and redistribute some income to them, prevent the abuse of market power, and eventually ensure peace and stability in society. In some countries, some of these systems are referred to by titles like "social market economy," as in Germany. France, Germany, Sweden, Brazil, Japan, South Korea, and India can be classified as mixed market economies (Daniels et al., 2021, pp. 153–154).

**State Capitalism:** In recent years, a fourth system needs to be added to the list that has received growing attention worldwide. State capitalism can typically be found in countries that have traditionally followed the communist model of the centrally planned economy and have then, in the early 1990s, introduced a more market-driven system. However, in these countries labeled state capitalist, the state retains a much more substantial role in the economy than in market or mixed market economies. Unlike centrally planned economies, state capitalist systems do not follow an ideology like communism but aim to strengthen the government's authority by fostering economic development. In countries like China and Russia, the number of state-owned enterprises is higher than in mixed economies. The state takes a more active role in managing foreign trade. As in China, the state may decide on industry sectors on which it wants to focus development. For example, automotive, aerospace, pharma, semiconductors, robotics, and communications are in focus in China. What is more, the state builds what is called "national champions." These companies are selected as authorities see them as having the potential to become global market leaders. The government then actively supports them by providing tax breaks or low-cost loans and sometimes merging companies to achieve a critical size that enables them to become global market leaders. The latter happened in China, where authorities created national champions through mergers in the rail carriage industry and the aerospace industry. Especially this latter aspect distinguishes state capitalism from the market economy and mixed systems, where the state would not typically build national champions actively as this would be seen as an inappropriate intervention in market competition. In state capitalist systems, governments create barriers to trade and investment to foster local industry development. In China, the government requires foreign investors in many industries to enter a joint venture with a local firm and transfer their know-how and technology to the local partner to foster their development actively. Countries following this model are, in particular, China and Russia, the two largest ones, and others, such as Vietnam and Saudi Arabia (Daniels et al., 2021, pp. 150–151).

We want to add that in the realm of economic systems that tend to be mainly market-based (market economy and especially mixed market economy), there is a great variety of sub-types labeled as "*varieties of capitalism*" by some authors. Each nation has developed unique institutions that shape its specific type of market economy. For example, the system that reigned in Germany for more than 50 years since the end of the Second World War is labeled "organized capitalism" by Barry Clark. Sweden has instead maintained a "welfare capitalism" system during most of the twentieth century. Britain oscillated between "neoliberal" and "welfare" forms of market economy, as did France. The system that operated in Japan from the end of the Second World War until 1990 is labeled "planned capitalism" (Clark, 2015).



The enormous economic success of the "Chinese model" has lifted many millions of people out of poverty within a relatively short time. Therefore, many regimes in developing countries, especially those politically leaning toward authoritarianism, closely observe the further development of state capitalism in China, taking it as a potential template for their own economic model and an alternative to the more market-based models outlined above. The global financial crisis of 2008–2009, where the fault is often seen in the market economic system of the United States, further fostered a turn away from the market economy (Bremmer, 2009). The financial crisis inspired economist Anatole Kaletsky's book *Capitalism 4.0*. He claims that the capitalist market economy has shown to be flexible and adaptable since its inception about 200 years ago. Due to several historical events and streams of thought, the capitalist market economy went through several waves of more and less state intervention in the economy. The 20 years from 1979 until 2009 had been characterized by Ronald Reagan's (in the United States) and Margaret Thatcher's (in the United Kingdom) belief that markets as free from state intervention as possible would lead to the best economic results. The financial crisis led to a new capitalism 4.0 where the state would play a more prominent role, for example, by implementing regulation in the financial services sector. Effectively, Kaletsky argues for a mixed economy where the market and state go hand in hand instead of seeing the two as contradictions (Kaletsky, 2010).

## Economic Systems and Professional Services

Whether a country has a relatively free or "liberal" market economy or a "non-liberal" mixed market economy impacts the role professional service firms can play. In liberal market economies, relationships between economic actors, such as companies and their suppliers or companies and their employees, are individualized and based on contracts. Conflicts are taken to court and eventually resolved by litigation. In "non-liberal" mixed market economies, either the state (as in France or Japan) or interest associations (as in Germany or Austria) play a role in coordination and conflict resolution. For example, in Germany, the association of employers and trade unions negotiate pay raises and other aspects of employment relationships. In liberal market economies, the more fragmented and individual contract-based relationships give rise to privately organized intermediary services that help bridge information gaps and resolve problems of uncertainty in areas like compliance and contracting. This is reflected, for example, in the more prominent role that law firms as service intermediaries can play in liberal market economies. In non-liberal mixed market economies, the state and associations play a more active role, leaving a lesser role for service intermediaries. One could say that in a liberal market economy, private service intermediaries fill a gap left by less organized and coordinated economic actors (Morgan & Quack, 2006).

## Economic Development, Performance, and Potential

Besides determining the type of economic system of a country, managers analyze the level of economic development, performance, and potential of an economy. A first approximation can be the level of development according to common typologies. The level of development can be perceived as a comprehensive indicator as it is typically based on a range of different indicators of a country. There are, however, different classifications based on different criteria. The most basic categorization would be between developed and developing countries. The question is where to draw the line between them. Some countries, say the United States or Mali, would be easy to classify as developed and developing, but what about Malaysia or Russia? A categorization with more than just two categories seems more appropriate to capture the diversity of development levels. Nielsen (2013) compared different classifications of international organizations like the World Bank, International Monetary Fund (IMF), United Nations Conference on Trade and Development (UNCTAD), and the WTO. We believe categorizing into *developed*, *emerging*, and *developing markets* can summarize the different approaches well. This resembles the classification of the International Monetary Fund (IMF) into "Advanced Countries," "Emerging Market and Middle-Income Countries," and "Low-Income Developing Countries." According to the IMF, 14% of the world's population lives in advanced countries, generating 42% of the global gross domestic product (GDP); 66% live in emerging markets, accounting for 53% of global GDP; while 20% of the world population lives in low-income developing countries, generating less than 5% of global GDP. These figures already show well the differences in economic development. The IMF lists members of the Eurozone, the United States, Japan, Canada, and others among the advanced countries. Examples of emerging markets, according to the IMF, are Malaysia, Indonesia, Argentina, Brazil, Turkey, Montenegro, and South Africa. The IMF lists Burkina Faso, Mali, Afghanistan, Haiti, and Cambodia among the low-income developing countries (IMF, 2022). Now, what further characterizes developed, emerging, and developing countries?

**Developed Economies:** Developed economies enjoy good infrastructure, high income levels, and advanced technologies. Typically, residents have a high level of education, well-developed healthcare systems, availability of healthy nutrition, and a broad range of goods and services. The average income per person is high at an average of US$47,904 in high-income countries in 2021 (World Bank, 2022b).

Traditionally, developed countries focused on manufacturing, therefore also the frequently used category of *industrialized countries.* Then, they diversified into services, with the service sector now making a significant part of their income. In developed countries, employees with a high level of education earn high salaries in an increasingly data- and technology-driven economy. Partly due to the offshoring of industrial jobs to emerging markets, there is a high level of unemployment or underemployment. Salaries are stagnating. Economic growth is low compared to emerging or many developing countries (Daniels et al., 2021, pp. 140–141).



**Developing Economies:** Developing economies comprise about 120 countries in Africa, Latin America, the Middle East, and Asia. Typically, they exhibit an underdeveloped infrastructure, weak government institutions, political instability, corruption, cronyism, high crime rates, trade barriers, and inefficient capital markets. National income per capita is low, with, on average, US$722 in low-income countries and US$2485 in lower-middle-income countries in 2021 (World Bank, 2022b). The education level of workers is frequently low, and unemployment is widespread. The agricultural sector plays a significant role in employment. Health and life expectancy are low. Poverty is widespread (Daniels et al., 2021, p. 141).

**Emerging Economies:** Emerging economies are also called "newly industrializing countries" (NICs) due to their relatively recent industrialization compared to developed countries. Typically, deregulation, privatization, and liberalization have made these countries attractive for foreign investment and encouraged entrepreneurial initiatives within these countries. This leads to strong economic growth, productivity, and rising incomes. Accordingly, emerging economies have a growing middle class. According to the World Bank, the average income of upper-middle-income countries in 2021 is US$10,363. Growth is driven by still relatively low-cost resources, high productivity, increasing consumption by the growing middle class, and business-friendly economic policies (Daniels et al., 2021, pp. 142–144). Since emerging economies play a crucial role in today's international business, we will discuss them in more detail.

Cavusgil and Kardes see the growing middle class as the most significant aspect of emerging markets. The middle class is characterized by having at least 30% of its total income available for discretionary purchases, that is, the income left after paying for necessities such as food, clothing, shelter, and taxes. Members of the middle class can spend money on improving their homes, technical gadgets, and other things. This has created a new market for foreign companies in emerging markets (Cavusgil & Kardes, 2013). The middle class in emerging markets constitutes a new bourgeoisie of 2.5 billion people. Its members are open-minded and tend to favor democracy and free markets (Economist, 2009). However, there are still many challenges facing businesses in emerging markets. One of them is rising wages. Since low wages have been a key reason foreign businesses set up operations in emerging markets, the fact that wages in many emerging markets rise fast must be a concern. For example, between 2001 and 2015, wages rose by 12% per year in China. Therefore, increasingly companies are automating production in China. At the same time, companies move to lower-cost regions within China. However, Chinese workers are increasingly vocal about their rights, leading to many strikes and conflicts. This led to the rise of Southeast Asia with a large pool of labor at low cost and mostly market-friendly policies. While an average factory worker in China earns US$27.5 per day, it is US$8.60 in Indonesia and US$6.70 in Vietnam. However, infrastructure is less developed in these countries than in China (Economist, 2015).

India is a case in point. On July 1, 2012, the world's most extensive power outage occurred across Northern India, affecting over 600 million people. Since then, the power supply has improved significantly, doubling between 2007 and 2017, and is now much more reliable. Roads were often in bad shape, and the railway was often single-track, causing delays, and narrow gauge, limiting transport capacity. However, improvements have happened. India's prime minister made it a point to build bridges and tunnels to improve the rail infrastructure. Rapid transit systems have been implemented in several cities. Air traffic has grown significantly. Work on high-speed train lines has started. Progress on the road network, especially in the mountainous north, is still slow (Economist, 2017b). Bureaucracy is a further challenge in many emerging markets. Remember the differences in the ease of starting a business outlined in the first part of this chapter. Setting up a business in a country like the Philippines can take 16 steps. An entrepreneur must make 20 different tax and contribution payments and visit multiple agencies in person. Out of the top 20 countries for ease of doing business, according to the World Bank, 18 are developed high-income countries, and only two are from emerging markets. The World Bank identifies a clear association between business-friendly administrations and wealth: Countries with cumbersome bureaucracy tend to be less developed (World Bank, 2018).

Finally, we want to reemphasize the challenge of protecting intellectual property rights (IPR). In many emerging markets, the protection of IPR is not strong, causing legal risks for investing companies. An interesting example from the service sector is retail knockoffs. Retail knockoffs mimic the offering of brands like Starbucks, McDonald's, or 7–11, which has been observed especially in China, Cambodia, and Vietnam. Knockoff retailers copy a retailer's branding design, including the logo, decoration, furniture, signs, and menu offerings. Since knockoff retailers only resemble the original brand's outlets, they are not illegal. However, they threaten the exclusivity of a brand and confuse consumers (Rosenbaum et al., 2016). Illegal retail knockoffs do exist as well, however. In 2015, a fake German drugstore chain DM outlet appeared in a shopping mall in China. The logo, tagline, decoration, and product offering looked like genuine shops in Germany. This shop was neither opened by DM nor had anyone obtained a franchise to open a DM outlet in China. The background is that many Chinese when they come to Germany like to buy products like milk powder at DM because Chinese milk powder for babies has earned a bad reputation due to scandals of contaminated milk powder. So, an entrepreneurial businessperson in China believed offering a seeming DM shop in China was a good idea. In the meantime, the shop has been closed (Hielscher & Fehr, 2015).

## Economic Development and Opportunities for Service Firms



A country's economic development level particularly impacts the extent of business opportunities for service firms. Put simply, the more developed a country is, the more services are consumed. In developing countries, most people are preoccupied with obtaining food, shelter, clothing, and similar basic goods. The more developed an economy is, and the more disposable income people have, the more they develop a preference for investing in their education and health. Further, people spend money on leisure, travel, and other personal services (Jackson, 2021, p. 24). Therefore, the service sector has become the leading sector in developed countries. Accordingly, sometimes developed countries are also labeled as "post-industrial" societies. In these, quality of life becomes the primary concern rather than the number of goods owned. Recreation plays an increasing role besides health and education. People orient their spending on making memorable experiences, such as through entertainment and tourism (Bordoloi et al., 2019, pp. 3–11).

This does not mean, though, that there are no business opportunities for service firms in developing countries. Remember the case of innovative payment services that fintech startups offer across several African countries in the previous chapter. In India, Animall, a new online cattle-trading platform, makes trading cows and buffaloes cheaper, easier, and more efficient. Rather than travel to a cattle fair and pay much money to an intermediary, farmers can find cattle sold close to their residence on the platform, including veterinary information, detailed pictures, and videos, all verified by a service provider's team. Animall claims to have made one million sales between 2019 and 2022 (Economist, 2022g). The term "base of the pyramid" (BOP) has been coined for business opportunities in developing countries. The world's low-income population, earning US$8 a day or less, constitutes the *base of the pyramid* (BOP) regarding income levels. As of 2009, when the *World Economic Forum* published a study on the BOP, 3.7 billion people were considered to be largely excluded from formal markets. However, they comprise an income of US$2.3 trillion, which has increased fast. These people provide a largely untapped customer group and growth potential for businesses. Traditionally, the BOP has remained below the radar of businesses. To tap into this potential, companies must develop innovative business models addressing the specific needs of these customers and set prices to match their budgets. One way of doing this, particularly relevant to this book, is to shift from selling goods to granting access, which is a service. The Grameen phone in Bangladesh is an example of a phone shared by several people in a poor neighborhood who rent access to a shared mobile phone rather than buy one (World Economic Forum, 2009, 5–6;14).

## Indicators of Economic Performance and Potential

While the classifications of countries outlined above give a first approximation of a country's economic performance and potential, companies also draw on more specific indicators.

**Gross National Income (GNI):** The GNI comprises personal consumption, investments, government spending, and the net export of goods and services. It addresses the worldwide income generated by persons and businesses residing in a country.

**Gross National Income (GNI)**

*Gross National Income* (*GNI*) [...] measures the value of all production in the domestic economy together with the income that a country receives from other countries in the form of profits, interest, and dividends, less the same sort of payment it has made to others (Daniels et al., 2021, p. 155).

The value of a smartphone made by Samsung, a company from South Korea, in Japan would count toward the GNI of South Korea. In some countries like Ireland, subsidiaries of foreign multinational enterprises can play a significant role. Since the profits repatriated to their home country do not count toward the GNI of Ireland, one underestimates the performance of the Irish economy using GNI as a measure (Daniels et al., 2021, p. 155).

**Gross Domestic Product (GDP):** The GDP takes the territory of a country as a reference rather than the resident population.

**Gross Domestic Product**

*Gross domestic product (GDP)* is the total market value of all goods and services produced by workers and capital within a nation's borders (Daniels et al., 2021, p. 155).

So, any good or service made within a country, whether by domestic or foreign companies, counts toward the GDP of that country. You may have heard the term GDP more frequently than GNI; indeed, GDP is the most frequently used measure of economic activity. Returning to the Samsung example, a smartphone made by Samsung in Japan does not count toward the GDP of Korea. It counts toward Japan's GDP. By measuring only national production, it facilitates cross-country comparisons (Daniels et al., 2021, p. 155). See ◘ Fig. 4.3 for the 12 biggest economies by GDP. Due to the economic disruption caused by the COVID-19 pandemic, we use data from 2019 in this section.

**GDP Growth:** Now, GDP or GNI only provide a part of the picture companies are interested in when assessing a country's economy. The GDP of a country like the United States may be big, but how is it changing? Is it growing, stagnating, or shrinking? Investing in a country with a fast-growing GDP can mean the company's revenues could grow fast along with the overall *GDP growth*. Growing revenues in a shrinking economy is more difficult. In other words, if the cake is getting bigger all the time, getting a sizeable piece is easier than if the cake remains the

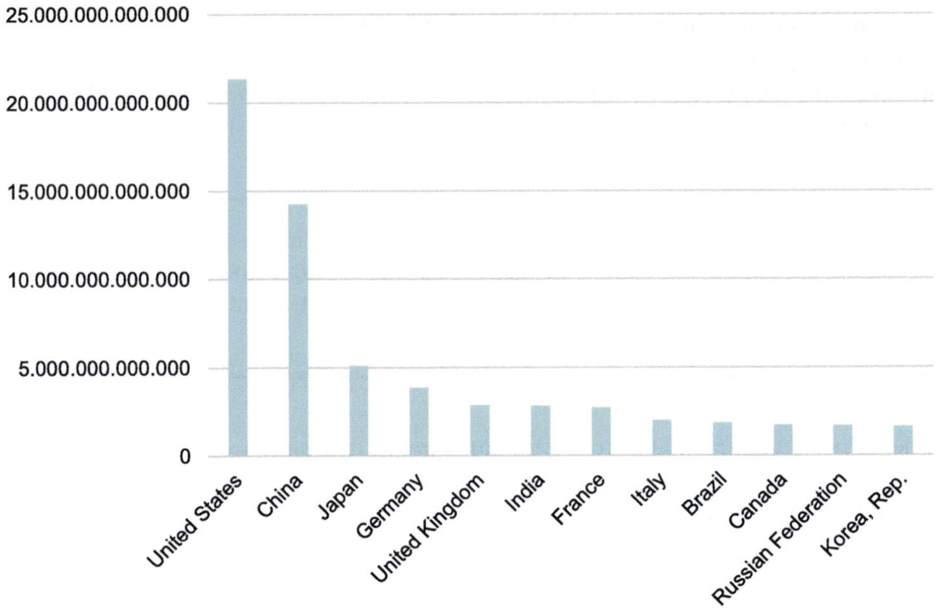


**Fig. 4.3** The 12 largest economies by GDP, 2019, in current US$, World Bank national accounts data, and OECD (Organization for Economic Cooperation and Development) National Accounts data files. (Own diagram based on data from World Bank, 2023a)

same or is getting smaller. So, companies also consider the growth of GDP in addition to absolute GDP. Typically, developing and emerging economies grow faster than developed countries. This can be seen in Fig. 4.4, which shows countries with higher annual % GDP growth in darker shades. For example, the annual growth rate of India's GDP has been between approximately 4% and 10% in most years over the past four decades (World Bank, 2022b).

**GNI per Capita:** Finally, companies would want to understand a country's wealth level. So they put the absolute GNI of a country in relation to the number of people residing there. For example, Indonesia may be ranked 16 in the world in terms of its absolute GNI of US$1097 billion in 2019. However, given its large population of more than 270 million, its *GNI* per capita of US$4050 only puts it on the margin between lower-middle-income and upper-middle-income countries, according to the World Bank. So, Indonesia, though it is a large economy in the world, is not a very wealthy country (World Bank, 2022b). Figure 4.5 shows GNI per capita in 2019.

As can be seen by the darker-shaded countries on the map, it is mainly developed countries that have a high GNI per capita. The picture is almost the inverse of Fig. 4.4. While developing countries tend to have higher growth rates than developed ones, GNI per capita is higher in developed countries. GNI per capita is a commonly used indicator of a country's wealth or development level. This becomes clearer by looking at the figures for the top 20 countries by GNI per capita in Table 4.3.

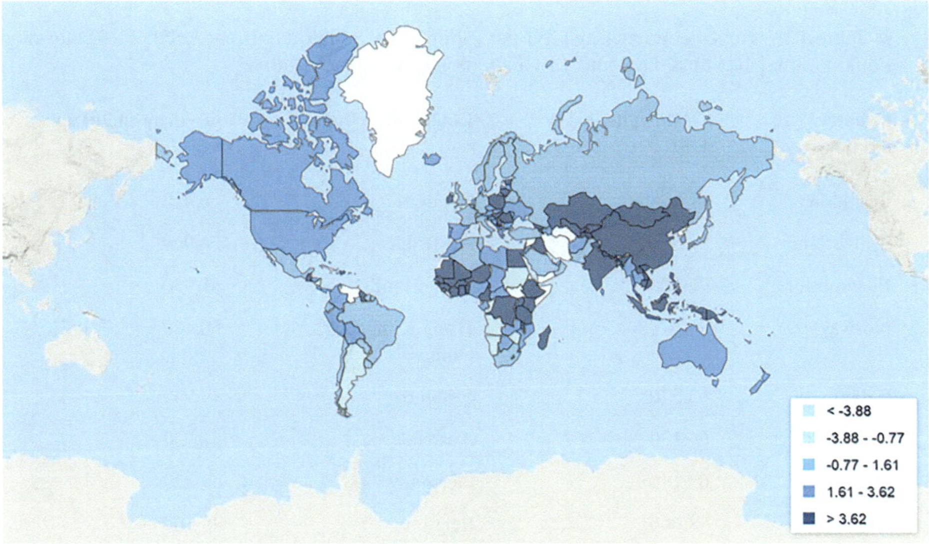


**Fig. 4.4** GDP growth (annual %) 2019, World Bank national accounts data, and OECD National Accounts data files. (Source: World Bank, 2023b)

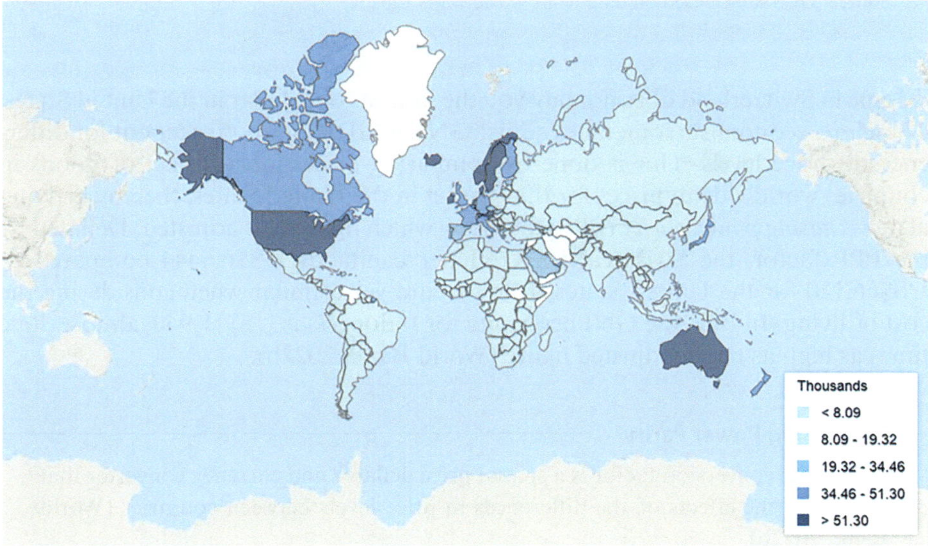


**Fig. 4.5** GNI per capita, Atlas method (current US$), 2019, World Bank national accounts data, and OECD National Accounts data files. (Source: World Bank, 2023c)

**Purchasing Power Parity (PPP):** Looking at the table of GNI per capita, it seems that the Swiss, earning US$84,260 per capita in 2019, are much wealthier than US Americans, who earn US$65,970. However, the prices for goods and services in Switzerland are much higher than in the United States. So, one dollar of

**Table 4.3** Top 20 countries by GNI per capita, Atlas method (current US$), 2019, World Bank national accounts data, and OECD National Accounts data files

| Country/ territory | GNI/capita 2019, US$ | Country/territory | GNI/capita 2019, US$ |
|---|---|---|---|
| Bermuda | 117,280 | Sweden | 56,420 |
| Switzerland | 84,250 | Australia | 54,900 |
| Luxembourg | 77,500 | Netherlands | 51,930 |
| Norway | 81,670 | Hong Kong SAR, China | 50,480 |
| Ireland | 63,570 | Finland | 49,940 |
| United States | 66,130 | Austria | 51,020 |
| Denmark | 63,140 | Germany | 49,220 |
| Singapore | 58,060 | Belgium | 48,100 |
| Iceland | 72,950 | Israel | 44,070 |
| Qatar | 61,720 | Canada | 46,540 |

Source: Own table based on data from World Bank (2023c)

4

income in Switzerland does not buy you the same as one dollar in the United States. Therefore, economists sometimes adjust GNI or GDP figures to account for differences in price levels. This is done by comparing prices for a basket of goods in countries worldwide to prices for that basket in the United States, thereby arriving at a *purchasing power parity* (PPP) factor by which figures are adjusted. Deflated by the PPP factor, the Swiss earn a GNI per capita of US$69,444 compared to US$66,120 for the United States—the two are very similar when considering the cost of living. In PPP, the GNI per capita for Indonesia is US$11,940, almost three times as high as the unadjusted figure (World Bank, 2022b).

**Purchasing Power Parity**

[The] *PPP* conversion factor is a spatial price deflator and currency converter that eliminates the effects of the differences in price levels between countries (World Bank, 2022b).

**The Informal Economy:** Government authorities worldwide collect data on their countries' economic performance. The problem is that in any country, some part of the economic activity is not recorded. Think of street vendors in developing countries, factory workers paid in cash, cleaners that clean private homes without registration, and illicit activities like drug trafficking. They go under governments' radar and do not appear in official statistics. A recent study estimates this informal or shadow economy to account for more than US$10 trillion annually and 23% of global GDP in 2016 (Kearney, n.d.). While informal economies exist everywhere, the informal sector is much larger in developing and emerging markets than in developed economies. The share of the economy taken up by informal activities ranges from 18.3% in developed countries to 89.8% in developing countries (OECD/ILO, 2019, p. 27).

## The BRICS and Other Emerging Market Groupings

Looking at the 12 biggest countries by GDP in 2019 in ◘ Fig. 4.3, one can notice that four emerging markets—China, India, Brazil, and Russia—show up that had not been among the world's largest economies in previous times. These are the so-called BRIC, named after the initials of Brazil, Russia, India, and China. In 2001, a study by Jim O'Neill of Goldman Sachs coined the term BRIC and predicted the growing importance these countries would have in the world economy in the following decade and beyond (Goldman Sachs, 2001). In 2006, Wilson and Purushothaman predicted that by 2040 the combined GDP of the BRIC would be bigger than that of the G6 (the United States, Japan, Germany, the United Kingdom, France, and Italy). Further, among the G6, only the United States and Japan would still be among the biggest six economies of the world. The authors summarized that by 2050, the list of the ten biggest economies could look quite different from what it was in 2006 (Wilson & Purushothaman, 2006). ◘ Figure 4.6 shows details of their predictions, adding Canada to make the G7 as we know them today. It shows at which point the authors believe which of the BRIC would overtake which developed country in terms of GDP. Look at the prediction in

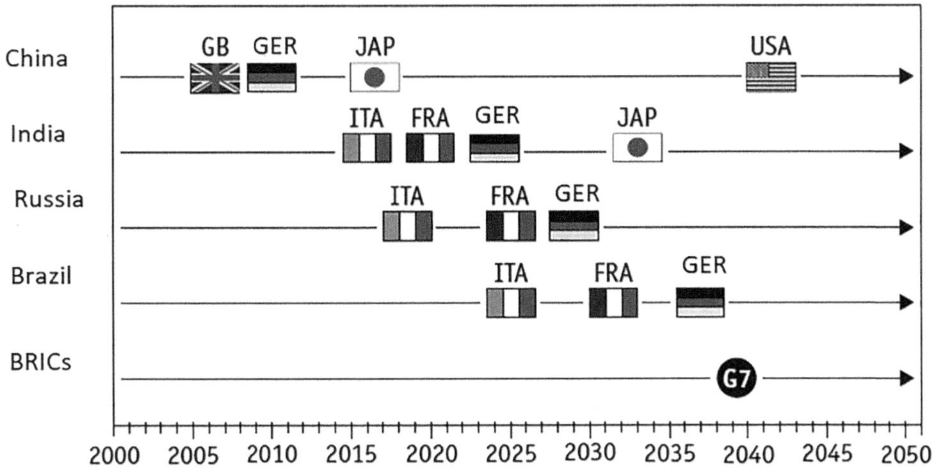


◘ **Fig. 4.6** Points in time at which the BRICS' GDP should be greater than that of the G7. (Source: Adapted from Holtbrügge & Welge, 2015, p. 9; permission obtained)

◘ Fig. 4.6 below and the current situation as of 2019 in ◘ Fig. 4.3. To what extent was their prediction correct as of 2019? Interestingly, much of the prediction was indeed correct. The Chinese economy has become bigger than the United Kingdom, Germany, and Japan. India's economy has taken over the Italian and French economies by GDP. Brazil, predicted to have a bigger economy than Italy by 2025, is only closely behind (US$1873 billion) Italy (US$2011) as of 2019, making a takeover by 2025 seems feasible. Only Russia is lagging behind predictions of overtaking Italy by 2019, while in reality, it trailed behind Brazil and Canada at US$1693 billion in 2019.

In November 2021, exactly 20 years after Jim O'Neill's famous prediction, the German business daily *Handelsblatt* took stock of the state of the BRICS (Brazil, Russia, India, China, and South Africa): Especially the rise of China was indeed true. For Russia and Brazil, O'Neill was overoptimistic. O'Neill still believes today that before 2040, BRICS will be bigger than the G7, though mainly because of China. The fact is that in 2000, the BRIC made up 7.7% of global GDP. In 2021, they made up a quarter, a jump one would not have seen as possible 20 years ago. The G7's share of world GDP has shrunk from 65 to 45% since 2001. Today, O'Neill points to other countries instead of Russia and Brazil: Especially Indonesia and Vietnam play important roles in the future global economy. The BRIC states formed a formal association in 2009, and in 2011 South Africa joined to form the BRICS. However, Brazil and Russia play in a second league in this group. Wealth in natural resources made Brazil and Russia sluggish, a phenomenon that economists call the resource curse. They have lost touch with technological developments and must diversify their economy. Unlike China and India, poverty has increased in Brazil and Russia for 6 years. However, the demand for technologies and resources that can brake climate change could lead to a re-industrialization in Brazil and Russia. So O'Neill's prediction could still hold after all (Busch & Münchrath, 2021).

In 2005, Goldman Sachs introduced the label "Next 11" (N-11) to raise awareness of the next group of emerging markets after the BRIC that could rival the G7 developed countries one day. They include Bangladesh, Egypt, Indonesia, Iran, Korea, Mexico, Nigeria, Pakistan, Philippines, Turkey, and Vietnam. The rationale for selecting those was a good recent performance and promising economic reforms. Especially Mexico and Korea, and, to a lesser degree, Turkey and Vietnam, were seen to have the potential and conditions to rival the G7 and the BRICS. In addition, Nigeria and Indonesia were seen to have the size to become potentially important in the world economy if they can deliver long-term growth. The economies of Korea and Mexico were projected to be bigger by GDP than Canada's by 2025. Given the 2019 GDP data, this appears feasible for Korea but overoptimistic for Mexico. By 2050, of the G7, only the United States, Japan, Germany, and the United Kingdom would remain in the top ten countries by GDP, the remaining six places taken by the BRICS plus Mexico and Indonesia (Goldman Sachs, 2007).

**? Review Questions**

1. Define and explain the concept of "political systems."
2. Explain the differences between democracy and authoritarianism and the idea of a continuum between these two poles.

3. Explain the different types of political risks and how companies can deal with them.
4. Discuss how service firms specifically are affected by political systems.
5. Define and explain the concept of "legal systems" and the different types of legal systems.
6. Define and explain the concept of the "rule of law."
7. Explain different legal risks for companies generally and the impact of legal systems on professional service firms.
8. Define and explain the concept of "economic systems" and the different types of economic systems.
9. Discuss the impact of different economic systems on professional service firms.
10. Explain what characterizes developed, developing, and emerging economies.
11. Define and explain indicators of economic performance and potential.
12. Explain why purchase price parity is sometimes applied to these indicators.
13. Research how easy it is to do business in a country of your choice, drawing especially on items outlined in the section on legal risks.
14. Discuss your point of view on the respective risk of doing business in democratic versus authoritarian systems: Can businesses hedge the risks of doing business in authoritarian regimes sufficiently? Can there be specific risks of doing business in democratic regimes?

## Closing Case: Argentina—The Pendulum Swing-Back Toward Peronism

On October 19, 2021, the Argentinian government issued a decree fixing the price of 1432 products, from cheese to shaving cream. An 881-page annex sets out the maximum price for each product in minute detail. The reason was an unexpected price rise of 3.5% in the previous month and important upcoming mid-term elections. Still, the government lost the mid-term elections, losing many parliamentary seats. The conclusion drawn by Christina Kirchner, the left-wing populist acting Vice-President: The government had intervened too little in the economy.

In 1914, Argentina ranked among the ten wealthiest countries in the world before Germany, France, and Italy. At that time, it seemed the land of opportunity, attracting millions of migrants, mainly from Europe. Harrod's of England had opened its first emporium overseas in Buenos Aires. In 1998, it was closed. Today, the country's standing in the world is far from what it was 100 years ago. While its population remains wealthier than many other Latin Americans, its GDP per capita trails neighboring Uruguay and Chile. A series of military coups from 1930 to 1976 is a political symptom of decline. Now close to 40 years after the end of the dictatorship, democracy has not led to economic stability. Many reasons are to blame for the county's decline: the First World War and the following depression, the military coup of 1930, and the rise of Juan Domingo Peron, who, together with his wife Eva ("Evita"), led the country on a populist trajectory. Argentina relied on exporting largely unprocessed agricultural products and resources for a long

4

Puerto Madero, Buenos Aires. (Image by Claudio Bianchi from Pixabay)

time and to some extent until today. When other countries opened for trade after the Second World War, Argentina became more closed, substituting imports. As evidenced by the many military coups, state institutions remained weak. Presidents like Christina Kirchner attempted to tinker with the Constitution to enable another term in office. Property rights are insecure. In 2012, the government nationalized Spanish firm Repsol's stake in Argentinian oil company YPS. Since the times of Peron, who inspired most presidents who followed, called "Peronists," interventions of governments in the economy have created perverse effects. Under Ms. Kirchner, heavy taxes were imposed on wheat exports as this was one of the few sectors of the economy doing fine, which led to a lack of agricultural investments. So, Argentina fell from being the fourth-largest exporter of wheat in 2006 to being only the tenth-largest in 2013. There have been phases of economic liberalization and deregulation, but time and again, politicians have been tempted to use subsidies and giveaways to win voters for the next election.

To fund populist subsidies and give-aways, governments printed money to fund their budget deficit, in 2021 at 4% of GDP. This led to high inflation rates, sometimes up to 50%. Hence the current government implements price controls. However, this creates artificial stability with side effects: The economy has seen almost no growth since 2008. Argentinians are getting poorer as inflation has climbed faster than salaries for most of the past 10 years. Those who can afford to send their money abroad to protect it from devaluation do so. To hide the high inflation rate, the government of Christina Kirchner, in 2012, removed the independence of Argentina's statistical office, which henceforth published low inflation rates. This led *The Economist* and the International Monetary Fund to stop publishing data provided by the Argentine statistical office, qualifying it as inaccurate. *The Economist* explained the move in an article entitled "Do not lie to me, Argentina" (Economist, 2012). As much of Argentina's foreign debt was denominated in foreign currencies, especially US dollars, the Kirchner government was keen on maintaining the exchange rate. It imposed a whole barrage of measures preventing the conversion of Argentine pesos to dollars. This made foreign travel for citizens and international business for companies difficult. The government also reinforced the substitution of foreign-made goods for local goods. Frustration about all of these and other interventionist measures led to the election of business-minded Mauricio Macri, the first president not referring to himself as Peronist, as president of Argentina in 2015.

Macri pursued several reforms. He reduced subsidies on energy and transport to alleviate the budget deficit. He lifted the controls on currency exchange. A deal with foreign creditors was struck to end the long isolation of Argentina and regain access to international capital markets. The government reinstalled the independence of the statistical office. While lifting currency controls led to an expected devaluation of the peso, which had been maintained at an artificially high level before, economic reforms began to work. Growth recovered, inflation fell, and the poverty rate fell. Argentina became head of the G20 group of countries and hosted the G20 summit in Buenos Aires in 2018 to honor Macri's reforms. In mid-term parliamentary elections in 2017, the majority of Macri's party Cambiemos was strengthened. However, in 2018, problems came up. Macri's approach to bring down the budget deficit only gradually so as not to endanger success in the mid-term elections meant that Argentina still had to finance a sizeable deficit. Observers found he was doing the right thing but was too slow to reform the country.

As interest rates were increased by the central bank of the United States, making investments in emerging markets like Argentina appear riskier in relation to the interest rates offered in the United States, investors became alarmed by the still-high budget deficit in Argentina. This forced the government to look to the International Monetary Fund (IMF) for help, requiring strict austerity measures, which fostered a recession. This was compounded by a severe drought that cut Argentinian farm exports, driving up the country's current account deficit. In December 2017, the government decided to loosen its inflation target, raising questions about Argentina's credibility. In August 2019, Macri lost parliamentary elections to the party of Alberto Fernández and his vice candidate Ms. Kirchner. Capital markets reacted in shock at the prospect of another left-wing government in Argentina. Two months later, a presidential election was due that would, according to opinion polls, bring Ms. Kirchner back to power as Vice President for Mr. Fernandez. The value of the peso crashed, driving up inflation by 50%. By October 2019, when indeed Fernandez and Kirchner won the presidential elections, the economic outcome of Macri's presidency was dismal. The economy had shrunk by 4%, prices had increased by 250%, and real wages had fallen by 15% in the past 15 months. Many had high hopes for Mauricio Macri's presidency. The reformist government failed due to a mix of fundamental problems in the country, political mistakes, and disadvantageous external circumstances. As *The Economist* summarized, Macri's advisors had failed to perceive the sentiment on the streets of Argentina. Populist governments, *The Economist* goes on, are better at explaining away economic deficiencies than technocratic governments like Macri's (Economist, 2019b).

There are also conflicts over the right economic policy within the Fernandez/Kirchner government between Vice President Ms. Kirchner, who pushes for aggressive state intervention, and President Fernandez, who advocates a more moderate policy. When economy minister Martin Guzmán took steps to cut the fiscal deficit and engaged in talks with the IMF to renegotiate debt, Ms. Kirchner showed her anger. She requested that the government reduces imports to remedy dollar shortages. In protest, Mr. Guzmán and industry minister Matías Kulfas resigned. On August 22, the federal prosecutor accused Ms. Kirchner of having provided inflated public works contracts to a friend during her presidency. The loss to the state is said to be US$1 billion. Already before, she had been investigated in 11 cases of suspected corruption, bribery, and money laundering and had tried to get the prosecutor removed from the case. On November 19, 2023, Javier Milei, a radical libertarian, won the presidential elections against the Peronist candidate Sergio Massa. It will be interesting to see how this pendulum swing-back to more business-friendly economic policies will work out.

**Questions**

1. Which type of economic system exists in Argentina? What does the case of Argentina tell us about this type?
2. To what extent is Argentina a typical emerging market?
3. Discuss the effect of democracy in a country like Argentina from the point of view of foreign investors.

Sources: Economist (2014a, 2014b, 2017a, 2017c, 2019b, 2021, 2022a, 2022b, 2022c).

## Summary

This chapter:

- Introduced the economic environment
  - Explained the concept of *political systems*, defined as "the structural elements and dynamics of government of a country that comprise both the political institutions and rules and norms that govern political activity"
  - Distinguished between *democracy* and *authoritarianism*
  - Outlined how countries in the world fall on a continuum between these two endpoints as *full democracies*, *flawed democracies*, *hybrid regimes*, and *authoritarian regimes*
  - Discussed *political risks* as "the threat that decisions or events in a country will negatively affect the profitability and sustainability of an investment"
  - Distinguished *systemic*, *procedural*, *distributive*, and *catastrophic* political risks
  - Discussed how companies can deal with political risks
  - Outlined the consequences of political systems for service firms

- Introduced the legal environment
  - Defined legal systems as "the mechanism for developing, stipulating, interpreting, and enforcing the laws in a formal jurisdiction"
  - Distinguished types of political systems: common law, civil law, theocratic law, and mixed systems
  - Explained the consequences of legal systems for professional service firms
  - Defined rule of law as "a legal system in which rules are clear, publicly disclosed, fairly enforced, and widely respected by individuals, organizations, and the government"
  - Outlined various *legal risks* for businesses
- Introduced the economic environment
  - Introduced *types of economic systems* as "An economic system organizes the production, distribution, and consumption of goods and services": *market economy*, *centrally planned economy*, *mixed market economy*, and *state capitalism*
  - Discussed the impact of types of economic systems on professional service firms
  - Distinguished *developed economies*, *developing economies*, and *emerging economies*
  - Discussed opportunities for service firms that follow from the development level of an economy
  - Introduced *indicators of economic performance and potential*: GNI, GDP, GDP growth, GNI per capita
  - Explained the role of the BRICS and other emerging markets in the world economy

## References

Bordoloi, S. K., Fitzsimmons, J. A., & Fitzsimmons, M. J. (2019). *Service management: Operations, strategy, information technology (Ninth Edition, international student edition)*. McGraw-Hill Education.

Bremmer, I. (2009). State capitalism and the crisis. *McKinsey quarterly*, 1–6.

Busch, A., & Münchrath, J. (2021). BRIC: Zwischen Vision und Hybris. *The Hand, 2021*(232), 14–16.

Cavusgil, S. T., & Kardes, I. (2013). Defining and measuring the middle class in emerging markets: The GSU-CIBER Middle Class Scorecard. *ESOMAR Research World, 1*, 46–49.

Cavusgil, S. T., Knight, G., & Riesenberger, J. R. (2020). *International business: The new realities* (5th ed.). Pearson.

Chidlow, A., Ghauri, P. N., & Hadjikhani, A. (2019). Internationalization of service firms and their interactions with socio-political actors. *Management International Review, 59*, 499–514.

Clark, B. (2015). *The evolution of economic systems: Varieties of capitalism in the global economy*. Oxford University Press.

Dabrowski, M. (2018). Are economic and political freedoms interrelated? *Breugel.* Retrieved from https://www.bruegel.org/blog-post/are-economic-and-political-freedoms-interrelated.

Dahringer, L. D. (1991). Marketing services internationally: Barriers and management strategies. *Journal of Services Marketing, 5*(3), 5–17.

Daniels, J. D., Radebaugh, L. H., Sullivan, D. P., & Click, R. W. (2021). *International business: Environments & operations* (17th ed.). Pearson.

Danziger, J. N., & Smith, C. A. (2016). *Understanding the political world: A comparative introduction to political science* (12th ed.). Pearson Education.
Economist. (2006, May 4). *Bolivia: Now it's the people's gas.*
Economist. (2009, February 12). Two billion more bourgeois: The middle class in emerging markets. *Economist.*
Economist. (2012, February 25). *Don't lie to me, Argentina.*
Economist. (2014a, February 15). *The parable of Argentina: There are lessons for many governments from one country's 100 years of decline.*
Economist. (2014b, February 17). *A century of decline: One hundred years ago Argentina was the future. What went wrong?.*
Economist. (2015, March 12). *The future of factory Asia: A tightening grip.*
Economist. (2017a, May 27). *Argentina's new, honest inflation statistics.*
Economist. (2017b, July 27). *India's once-shoddy transport infrastructure is getting much better.*
Economist. (2017c, October 21). *Breaking the spell of Peronism: Mauricio Macri's government deserves an endorsement in the mid-term congressional election.*
Economist. (2019a, May 16). Donald Trump gets tough on Huawei. *Economist.*
Economist. (2019b, August 24). *Argentina's crisis shows the limits of technocracy: What went wrong for Mauricio Macri.*
Economist. (2021, October 30). *Argentina's government has fixed the price of 1,432 products.*
Economist. (2022a). *Argentina's economy minister resigns because of political infighting.*
Economist. (2022b). *Argentina's vice-president could face 12 years in prison.*
Economist. (2022c, January 29). *The IMF cannot solve Argentina's dysfunction.*
Economist. (2022d, March 12). Amid Russia's war, America Inc reckons with the promise and peril of foreign markets. *The Economist.*
Economist. (2022e, April 16). *China: Locked down, fed up: The way Chinese think about covid-19 is changing.*
Economist. (2022f, April 16). *The Russia remainers: Companies fear consumer boycotts.*
Economist. (2022g, April 21). *Moo with the times: Indian cows (and buffaloes) are going online.*
Economist Intelligence Unit. (2022). *Democracy index 2021: The China challenge.*
Enders, T. (2021). *Gründzüge des internationalen Wirtschaftsrechts* (3rd ed.). Vahlen.
Fukuyama, F. (1992). *The end of history and the last man.* Free Press.
Goldman Sachs. (2001). *Global Economics Paper No: 66: Building Better Economic BRICs.* Retrieved from https://www.goldmansachs.com/insights/archive/archive-pdfs/build-better-brics.pdf.
Goldman Sachs. (2007). *BRICs and beyond.* Retrieved from https://www.goldmansachs.com/insights/archive/BRICs-and-Beyond.html.
Gusbeth, S. (2021). Regulierungspolitik: China macht viel richtig. *The Hand, 2021*(164), 26.
Handelsblatt. (2022a). Softwarekonzern: SAP zieht sich vollständig aus Russland zurück. *The Hand, 2022*(76).
Handelsblatt. (2022b). Ukraine-Krieg: Die vielen Tücken des Rückzugs. *The Hand, 2022*(76).
Handelsblatt. (2022c). Fast Food: McDonald's verlässt Russland. *The Hand, 2022*(95).
Hielscher, H., & Fehr, M. (2015, September 10). *Chinesen kopieren dm-Filiale: WirtschaftsWoche liegt Foto vor. WirtschaftsWoche.* Retrieved from https://www.wiwo.de/unternehmen/handel/dm-drogeriemarkt-chinesen-kopieren-dm-filiale-wirtschaftswoche-liegt-foto-vor/12303130.html.
Holtbrügge, D., & Welge, M. K. (2015). *Internationales management: Theorien, funktionen, fallstudien* (6th ed.). Schäffer-Poeschel.
Huntington, S. P. (1991). Democracy's Third Wave. *Journal of Democracy, 2*(2), 12–34.
IMF. (2022). *World Economic Outlook April 2022: War sets back the global recovery.* Retrieved from https://www.imf.org/en/Publications/WEO/Issues/2022/04/19/world-economic-outlook-april-2022
International Chamber of Commerce. (2006). *Extraterritoriality and business: Policy statement.* Retrieved from https://iccwbo.org/publication/extraterritoriality-and-business/.
Jackson, S. D. (2021). *International trade in services: Effective practice and policy.* Routledge.
JuriGlobe Research Group. (2022). *Juriglobe.* Retrieved from https://www.juriglobe.ca/index-en.html.

Kaletsky, A. (2010). *Capitalism 4.0: The birth of a new economy in the aftermath of crisis*. Public Affairs.
Kearney. (n.d.). *Digital payments and the global informal economy*. Retrieved from https://www.kearney.com/financial-services/digital-payments-and-the-global-informal-economy?utm_medium=pr&utm_source=prnewswire&utm_campaign=2018AmericasDigitalPayments.
Morgan, G., & Quack, S. (2006). The internationalisation of professional service firms: Global convergance, national path-depencency or cross-border hybidisation? In R. Greenwood & R. Suddaby (Eds.), *Professional service firms*. Elsevier.
Müller, A. (2022). Großhandel: Metro sieht sich in einer "Dilemmasituation". *The Hand, 2022*(93).
Nielsen, L. (2013). How to classify countries based on their level of development. *Social Indicators Research, 114*(3), 1087–1107.
OECD/ILO. (2019). *Tackling vulnerability in the informal economy*. https://doi.org/10.1787/939b7bcd-en.
Osman, Y. (2022). Verlagerung von IT-Fachkräften: Von Moskau nach Berlin. *Handelsblatt*, 2022(108).
Peer, M. (2021). China-Konkurrenz sieht Chancen. *Handelsblatt, 2021*(213), 17.
Quack, S., & Schüßler, E. (2015). Dynamics of regulation of professional service firms: National and transnational developments. In L. Empson, D. Muzio, J. Broschak, & B. Hinings (Eds.), *The Oxford handbook of professional service firms* (pp. 48–70). Oxford University Press.
Ritter Sport. (2022). *Unser statement*. Retrieved from https://www.ritter-sport.de/blog/page/4/.
Rosenbaum, M. S., Cheng, M., & Wong, I. A. (2016). Retail knockoffs: Consumer acceptance and rejection of inauthentic retailers. *Journal of Business Research, 69*(7), 2448–2455.
Schier, S. (2022). Versicherer: Allianz verkauft Mehrheit an Russland-Geschäft. *Handelsblatt*, 2022(108).
Schlautmann, C. (2018). 'Germany first' mit Nebenwirkungen. *Handelsblatt*, 2018, 30.
Schwarz, D., & Müller, M. (2022). Auslandsbanken: Schwieriger Rückzug. *Handelsblatt*, 2022(142).
Scott, J., Gilliard, D., & Scott, R. (2002). Eliminating bribery as a transnational marketing strategy. *International Journal of Commerce and Management, 12*(1), 1–17.
U.S. Department of Justice & Securities & Exchange Commission. (2020). *A resource guide to the U.S. Foreign Corrupt Practices Act*. Retrieved from https://www.justice.gov/criminal-fraud/fcpa-resource-guide.
Wilson, D., & Purushothaman, R. (2006). Dreaming with BRICs: The path to 2050. In S. C. Jain (Ed.), *Emerging economies and the transformation of international business: Brazil, Russia, India and China (BRICs)* (pp. 3–45). Edward Elgar Publishing.
World Bank. (2018). *Doing business 2018: Reforming to create jobs*. Retrieved from https://archive.doingbusiness.org/en/reports/global-reports/doing-business-2018.
World Bank. (2021). *Doing business archive*. Retrieved from https://archive.doingbusiness.org/en/doingbusiness.
World Bank. (2022a). *How does the World Bank classify countries?* Retrieved from https://datahelpdesk.worldbank.org/knowledgebase/articles/378834-how-does-the-world-bank-classify-countries.
World Bank. (2022b). *World Bank Open Data*. Retrieved from https://data.worldbank.org/.
World Bank. (2022c). *World Governance Indicators*. Retrieved from https://info.worldbank.org/governance/wgi/.
World Bank. (2023a). *Data: GDP (current US$)*. Retrieved from https://data.worldbank.org/indicator/NY.GDP.MKTP.CD.
World Bank. (2023b). *Data: GDP growth (annual %)*. Retrieved from https://data.worldbank.org/indicator/NY.GDP.MKTP.KD.ZG.
World Bank. (2023c). *Data: GNI per capita, Atlas method (current US$)*. Retrieved from https://data.worldbank.org/indicator/NY.GNP.PCAP.CD.
World Economic Forum. (2009). *The next billions: Unleashing business potential in untapped markets*. Retrieved from https://www.weforum.org/reports/next-billions-unleashing-business-potential-untapped-markets.
WTO. (2022). *TRIPS – Trade-related aspects of intellectual property rights*. Retrieved from https://www.wto.org/english/tratop_e/trips_e/trips_e.htm.

Wucherpfenning, J., & Deutsch, F. (2009). Modernization and democracy: Theories and evidence revisited. *Living Reviews in Democracy*, 1–7.

## Further Reading

Danziger, J. N., & Smith, C. A. (2015). Understanding the political world: A comparative introduction to political science, Pearson provide an overview of political systems worldwide.

The JuriGlobe website provides information on legal systems and how countries can be classified. Retrieved from http://www.juriglobe.ca/index.php.

The most recent version of the Democracy Index can be downloaded from the Economist Intelligence Unit's website when completing contact details. Retrieved from https://www.eiu.com/n/.

The World Bank collects detailed data on the business environment in various countries. The methodology was under revision at the time of writing. Retrieved from https://www.worldbank.org/en/programs/business-enabling-environment.

The World Bank provides comprehensive economic indicators for countries worldwide on its website. Retrieved from https://data.worldbank.org/.

Todaro, M. P., & Smith, S. C. (2020). Economic development, Pearson provide an overview of economic systems across the world.

# The International Monetary and Financial Environment

## Contents




D. Klimkeit et al., *International Management in Service Firms*, Classroom Companion: Business,
https://doi.org/10.1007/978-3-031-50345-0_5

**Learning Outcomes**

After completing this chapter, you should be able to:

- Understand the institutional structure of the foreign exchange market and stages of the international monetary system
- Outline different approaches to forecasting exchange rates
- Distinguish different types of foreign exchange exposures
- Comprehend various financing tools in the global debt and equity markets



## Introduction

This chapter focuses on the global monetary and financial market faced by multinational service companies. It introduces the stages of the international monetary system that each exhibits different characteristics and describes the structure, participants, and various types of trade within the current system. Different approaches to forecasting future exchange rates are presented to outline the critical determinants of exchange rates, which can assist in forming strategies to hedge foreign exchange risk. Three main types of foreign exchange exposures faced by multinationals are introduced. They require different risk management strategies due to their respective attributes. We also outline various tools for multinational service companies seeking global capital. Last, trends and challenges of the international monetary and financial market are summarized.

Skyscraper, image by Jason Goh from Pixabay

## Opening Case: Sea Group: How Does a Singaporean Firm Raise Capital Globally?

Sea Group is a technology conglomerate headquartered in Singapore. It was established in 2009 by Forrest Li. Initially founded as Garena, the company rebranded itself as Sea after securing funding worth US$550 million in May 2017.

Sea has grown extremely fast over the last decade. It now operates with three arms providing unparalleled digital services: (i) Shopee, the e-commerce arm of Sea. It was first launched in 2015 and has become one of the largest e-commerce platforms in Southeast Asia, with 16 million monthly visitors in Q4 2021. Thanks to the COVID-19 pandemic, Shopee has expanded aggressively worldwide. Outside of its core markets in Southeast Asia and Taiwan, Shopee marked its entry into Latin America in 2019 when it launched a localized site in Brazil, followed by Mexico, Chile, and Colombia in 2021. Within Europe, it introduced a marketplace in Poland in September 2021, followed by launches in Spain and France in the next 2 months. In other parts of Asia, Shopee launched in India in November 2021 and started its operations in South Korea in the same year to help local merchants reach customers in markets where Shopee operates. (ii) Garena is the digital entertainment arm of Sea. Garena distributes game titles on Garena+, an online and social platform since 2012 for people to discover, download, and play online games in various countries across Southeast Asia and the world. In 2017, Garena developed Free Fire, an online action–adventure game that became one of the top 10 most-downloaded games of 2021. (iii) SeaMoney, the digital payments and financial services arm. Its offerings include mobile wallet services, payment processing, credit offerings, and related digital financial services and products. These are available in seven markets across Southeast Asia and Taiwan under various brands, including ShopeePay, SPayLater, and other brands. Active users across SeaMoney products and services reached 53 million as of Q2 of 2022.

Before going public in 2017, the primary investor of Sea was Tencent Holdings Ltd., the Chinese social media giant, which owned around 40% of Sea before the listing. At that time, venture capital from around the globe was pouring into Southeast Asia and backing various tech companies competing in the region's large and rapidly expanding e-commerce sector. As a result, Sea was among the first to be listed in the US stock exchange. In September 2014, Sea filed with the Securities and Exchange Commission (SEC) of the United States, seeking to raise US$1 billion through an initial public offering (IPO) of American depositary shares. The underwriters include Goldman Sachs, Morgan Stanley, and Credit Suisse. Sea managed to raise US$884 million when it was listed in the New York Stock Exchange under "SE" in October 20, 2017. The share ended the day solid despite some initial uncertainties. Trading opened at US$16.25, and the price dropped below the US$15 mark in the morning. It rallied in the afternoon and closed at US$16.26, up 8.4% from its list price of US$15. Since then, the share price of Sea has soared and reached above US$360 in October 2021, resulting in a market capitalization of about US$ 200 billion. However, its share price kept decreasing after that and dropped to around US$65 by the end of August 2022.

Sea also raised capital through debt and several post-IPO equity offerings to support its business expansion and other general corporate purposes, including potential strategic investments and acquisitions. For instance, in September 2021, Sea raised about US$6 billion in an equity and convertible bond sale (US$3.5 billion through equity offering and US$2.5 billion through convertible bonds), making it Southeast Asia's largest fundraising. According to the balance sheet reported for Q2 2022, Sea had liabilities of US$6.74 billion due within 12 months and liabilities of US$5.29 billion due beyond 12 months. While the high leverage (a large portion of financing via debt) seemed to increase its distress risk, Sea had US$8.1 billion in cash and receivables due within 12 months.

**Questions**

1. Why did Sea go for IPO on the New York Stock Exchange instead of the Singapore Exchange?
2. What are the pros and cons of debt and equity financing for Sea?

Sources: (Macro Trends, n.d.; SeaMoney, n.d.; BusinessWire, 2022; Chia, 2017; Guild, 2022; Hirschmann, 2022; Koetsier, 2021; Mulia, 2022; Murdoch, 2021; Russell, 2017a, 2017b; SEC, 2017; Statista, 2022; Yahoo Finance, 2022).



## The Foreign Exchange Market and the International Monetary System

*International* finance differs in several dimensions from purely domestic finance, one of which is the foreign exchange risk faced by multinational enterprises (MNEs). Traditionally, purely domestic companies with suppliers, production, and customers in the local market in a fixed exchange rate regime are not, or less, directly exposed to foreign exchange risk. Alternatively, MNEs may face limited foreign exchange exposures when their local currencies are pegged to common international currencies. For instance, Danish companies have little foreign exchange exposure within Europe because of the Danish krone's close peg to the euro. More broadly, however, in the era of globalization and international trade, almost every business is or will be exposed to foreign currency risk. To understand this type of risk, suppose emerging markets such as Brazil, Russia, India, and China (BRIC) are the major export markets for your company in the United States. In 2012, the Brazilian real, Russian ruble, and Indian rupee weakened the most among developing-nation currencies, and the Chinese yuan had depreciated more than in any other period since its 1994 devaluation. Your company would face a difficult situation since the price of your services in these currencies would rise and hence the revenue from these markets was very likely to drop. Nowadays, corporations operate in an environment with volatile exchange rates, which may impede their competitiveness in the marketplace. Therefore, managers of MNEs need to understand the determinants of exchange rates and, more broadly, how the international monetary system works.

## Stages of the International Monetary System

The international monetary system defines the overall financial environment in which MNEs and international investors operate. Kumar defines the international monetary system as:

**International Monetary System**

The international monetary system refers to the operating system of the financial environment, which consists of financial institutions, multinational corporations, and investors. The international monetary system provides the institutional framework for determining the rules and procedures for international payments, determination of exchange rates, and movement of capital. (Kumar, 2014, pp. 125–164)

Over the last two centuries, the international monetary system has evolved with several distinct stages. ◘ Table 5.1 presents each stage's name, period, and main characteristics. Currently, most currencies in the world are pegged to the dominant currencies, particularly the US dollar and the euro, or baskets of currencies such as the Special Drawing Right (SDR).

The International Monetary Fund (IMF) has played a vital role in the international monetary system. Seeking to avoid the mistakes that led to the Depression and World War II, representatives of 44 Allied nations met in July 1944 to establish the IMF for a new economic order built on global cooperation. They set up a system of exchange rates linked to the US dollar to be supervised by the IMF, and they give the IMF three critical missions: promoting international monetary cooperation, supporting the expansion of trade and economic growth, and discouraging policies that would harm prosperity (IMF, n.d.-b). Presently, its membership embraces 190 countries. The IMF's main resources come from the money its member countries pay as their capital subscription (quotas), which are based broadly on the countries' relative positions in the world economy (IMF, n.d.-a). In addition, the IMF nurtures global financial stability by (1) monitoring the economic and financial policies of member countries and providing them with policy advice, an activity known as *surveillance*; (2) providing financial support to countries hit by crises to create breathing room as they implement policies that restore economic stability and growth; and (3) offering capacity development (e.g., technical assistance and training), which can help member countries to improve tax collection, bolster public finances, and modernize their monetary and exchange rate policies IMF (n.d.-c). Over the years, the IMF has helped its member countries tackle economic crises and thus stabilized the international monetary system.

5

**Table 5.1** Stages and characteristics of the international monetary system, own table, based on content from Eun, Resnick, & Chuluun (2020, pp. 33–38)

| Name | Time period | Main characteristics |
|---|---|---|
| Bimetallism | Before 1875 | • Both gold and silver were used as international means payment.<br>• The exchange rates among currencies were determined by either their gold or silver contents. |
| Classical gold standard | 1875–1914 | • Gold alone is assured of unrestricted coinage, two-way convertible with national currencies at a stable ratio and freely exported or imported.<br>• The exchange rates among currencies were determined by their gold contents. |
| Interwar period | 1915–1944 | • The gold standard was abandoned by many countries due to economic and political instabilities.<br>• No coherent international monetary system prevailed.<br>• The US dollar emerged as the dominant world currency. |
| Bretton Woods system | 1945–1972 | • A US dollar-based gold-exchange standard.<br>• The US dollar was the only currency that was fully convertible to gold with a ratio of US$35 per ounce. Other countries established a par value in relation to the US dollar.<br>• Special drawing rights (SDRs) created by the International Monetary Fund (IMF) supplemented gold and the US dollar for international payments. |
| Flexible exchange rate regime | Since 1973 | • Gold was officially abandoned as an international reserve asset.<br>• Flexible exchange rates were accepted and central banks could intervene in the exchange market to stabilize their currencies.<br>• Exchange rates became much more volatile than before. |

## Exchange Rate Arrangements

Back in 2009, the IMF classified the exchange rate arrangements of its member countries into 10 categories based on their actual, de facto arrangements, analyzed by IMF staff, instead of their officially announced, de jure arrangements (IMF, 2022, p. 1). The details of these exchange rate classifications are summarized in ◘ Table 5.2. Over the past two decades, many developing countries have shifted away from *fixed* exchange rate regimes, in which the value of the domestic currency is pegged to one or more foreign currencies, and moved toward more *flexible* exchange rate regimes where the market supply and demand of a currency determine its external value. This shift seems to have served several countries well during rapid economic growth, driven by the twin forces of globalization and liberalization of markets and trade. However, as several currency crises, including the Asian

**Table 5.2** Classification of exchange rate arrangements, own table, based on content from IMF (2022, pp. 1–12)

| Type | Categories | Main characteristics | Examples |
|---|---|---|---|
| Hard pegs | Exchange arrangement with no separate legal tender | • The complete surrender of the monetary authorities' control over domestic monetary policy.<br>• The currency of another country circulates as the sole legal tender (formal dollarization). | Ecuador, El Salvador, Panama |
| | Currency board arrangement | • Based on an explicit legislative commitment to exchange domestic currency for a specified foreign currency at a fixed exchange rate.<br>• Domestic currency is fully backed by foreign assets. | Hong Kong, Bulgaria, Brunei |
| Soft pegs | Conventional pegged arrangement | • The country formally pegs its currency at a fixed rate to another currency or a basket of currencies.<br>• The country authorities stand ready to maintain the fixed parity through direct or indirect intervention.<br>• The exchange rate may fluctuate within narrow margins of less than ±1% around a central rate. | Jordan, Saudi Arabia, Morocco |
| | Pegged exchange rate within horizontal bands | • The value of the currency is maintained within certain margins of fluctuation of at least ±1% around a fixed central rate, or the margin between the maximum and minimum value of the exchange rate exceeds 2%. | Tonga |
| | Stabilized arrangement | • The spot market exchange rate remains within a margin of 2% for 6 months or more and is not floating.<br>• The required margin of stability can be met either with respect to a single currency or a basket of currencies. | Indonesia, Singapore, Lebanon |
| | Crawling peg | • The currency is adjusted in small amounts at a fixed rate or in response to changes in selected quantitative indicators, such as past inflation differentials vis-à-vis major trading partners. | Honduras, Nicaragua |

(continued)

**Table 5.2** (continued)

| Type | Categories | Main characteristics | Examples |
|---|---|---|---|
| | Crawl-like arrangement | • The exchange rate remains within a narrow margin of 2% relative to a statistically identified trend for 6 months or more, and the exchange rate arrangement is not considered as floating. | China, Iran, Serbia |
| Floating regimes (market determined rates) | Floating | • The exchange rate is largely market determined, without an ascertainable path.<br>• Foreign exchange market intervention may be either direct or indirect, but policies targeting a specific level of the exchange rate are incompatible with floating. | Brazil, South Korea, India, Thailand |
| | Free floating | • Intervention occurs only exceptionally and aims to address disorderly market conditions. | Australia, Canada, Japan, the United Kingdom, the United States, the euro zone |
| Residual | Other managed arrangement | • The exchange rate arrangement does not meet the criteria for any of the other categories. | Algeria, Cambodia, Sudan |



currency crisis in 1997, have dramatically demonstrated, globalization can amplify the costs of inappropriate policies. Moreover, the challenges facing countries may change over time, suggesting a need to adapt exchange rate policy to the evolving circumstances (Caramazza & Aziz, 1998).

In Europe, many countries realized the necessity of having stable exchange rates for promoting trade and economic integration within the region several decades ago. Among other arrangements, the European Monetary System (EMS) was launched in 1979 with the principal objective of establishing a zone of monetary stability in Europe. The European Currency Unit (ECU) was one of the main instruments of the EMS, which is a "basket" currency constructed as a weighted average of the currencies of member countries of the European Union (EU), with the weights being each currency's relative GNP and share in intra-EU trade. The EMS also paved the way for the eventual European Monetary Union. In January 1, 1999, 11 of 15 EU countries adopted a common currency, the euro, voluntarily abandoning their monetary sovereignty. Since then, several other countries have joined the eurozone. Currently, the euro is the official currency in 19 out of 27 EU member countries. However, EU members such as Poland and Sweden have not adopted the euro because the necessary conditions have not been met. In addition, Denmark kept its former currency, the krone, even after becoming a member of the EU.

## The Foreign Exchange Market

The Bank for International Settlements (BIS), established in 1930, conducts a survey of currency trading activity, the BIS Triennial Central Bank Survey, every 3 years since 1986. This survey is the most comprehensive source of information on the size and structure of the global foreign exchange market. The most recent one, conducted in April 2019, estimated the daily global net turnover in the foreign exchange market to be US$6.6 trillion per day. The United Kingdom (London) continues to be the world's most active foreign exchange market, followed by the United States, Hong Kong SAR, Singapore, and Japan, which facilitated 79% of all foreign exchange trading in April 2019. Mainland China recorded a significant rise in trading activity, making it the eighth-largest foreign exchange trading center in 2019 (up from 13th in April 2016). The currency composition of trading over the last two decades is shown in ◘ Fig. 5.1. Being the dominant currency over years, the US dollar has been involved on one side of more than 80% of all trades. The following two currencies, the euro and the Japanese yen, have been used in 30% and 20% of all currency trading, respectively. Notably, the Chinese yuan has been increasingly used in international trade. This is a natural consequence of China's unprecedented economic growth over the last three decades and fewer barriers to global capital flows. In addition, the IMF included the Chinese yuan as one of the constituent currencies of the SDR in 2016, further stimulating the usage of the currency in international trade and investment.

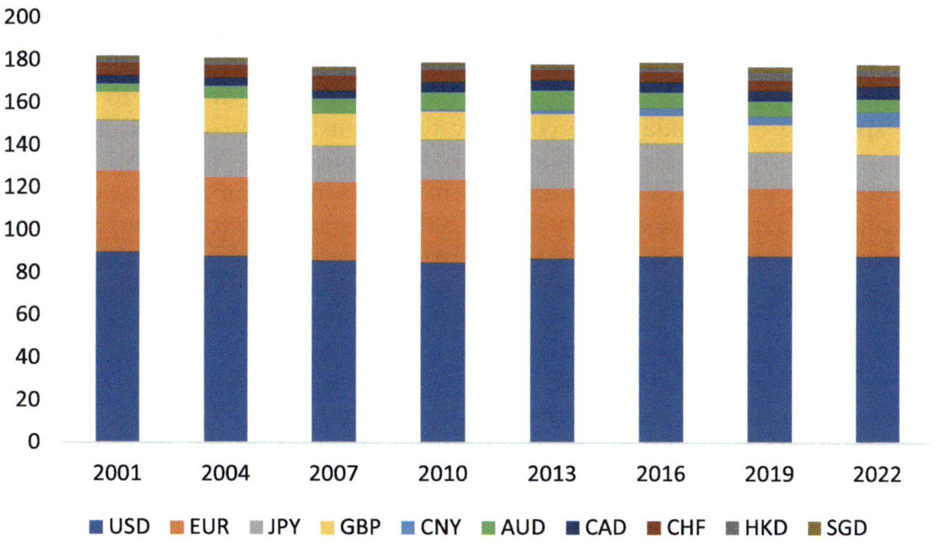


◘ **Fig. 5.1** Turnover of main currencies over time, in percentage, source: (BIS, n.d.-c)

Participants in the foreign exchange markets can be grouped into five broad categories:

1. Bank and nonbank foreign exchange dealers, who function as market makers and profit from buying foreign exchange at a bid price and reselling it at a slightly higher ask or offer price.
2. Individuals and firms (e.g., multinational corporations, importers and exporters, international portfolio investors, and tourists) conducting commercial or investment transactions.
3. Speculators, who seek profit from exchange rate changes, and arbitragers, who profit from simultaneous exchange rate differences in different markets.
4. Central banks and treasuries, which intervene the foreign exchange market through the country's foreign exchange reserve to influence the value of their currency to benefit the interests of their citizens.
5. Foreign exchange brokers, agents facilitating trading among dealers at a small commission.



In the past, foreign exchange markets were characterized by a two-tier structure: the interbank or wholesale market and the client or retail market. Over the past decade, however, electronic platforms and the development of complex trading algorithms have shifted this market to a single-tier structure and made the market accessible to traders of all kinds and sizes.

There are three basic types of transactions in the foreign exchange market: (1) A *spot* transaction, which refers to the purchase or sale of foreign exchange with delivery and payment taking place almost instantaneously (usually within two business days for large-size transactions). It is the fastest way to exchange currencies, and knowing the prevailing (spot) exchange rate is crucial for this type of transaction. For example, a German company must pay US$1 million to its US supplier on Wednesday. Therefore, it could enter a spot transaction with a bank on Monday to buy US$1 million and sell the corresponding amount of euro based on the spot rate on Monday. The company then transfers euros to the bank and receives US$ from it, after which it can pay its supplier in the United States. (2) A *forward* transaction, which requires the delivery at some specified future date of a specified amount of one currency for a specified amount of another currency. The exchange rate applied is called the forward exchange rate, established at the time of the agreement. Each forward transaction has a specified maturity date when payment and delivery are required. For instance, a Japanese customer will need to pay €2 million to the German company in the previous example in 6 months. To lock in the exchange rate, the Japanese firm could sign a six-month forward contract with a bank to buy €2 million with a forward rate of yen 140/€. The delivery and payment of this contract are to be made within 6 months from the time of the agreement. If, at the time of the transaction date with the German company, the market exchange rate increases to yen 145/€, the Japanese company benefits by locking in the rate of yen 140/€ (i.e., save 5 yen per one euro). (3) A *swap* transaction, which is the simultaneous purchase and sale of a given amount of foreign currencies at an initial date, then exchanging the amounts at a predetermined rate and maturity. There are several types of swap transactions, including spot-against-forward and forward-forward swaps.

## Foreign Exchange Rate Determination and Forecasting

Foreign exchange risk is the most common form of market price risk managed by treasurers, which is one of several groups of risks that businesses must manage within their enterprise risk management framework. To address the foreign exchange risk, one needs to understand the *determinants* of the exchange rate between currencies. However, identifying these determinants is an important yet difficult question to answer. It is crucial because MNEs have a variety of foreign-currency-denominated payables, receivables, credit purchases, and credit sales, exposing them to exchange rate risks. On the one hand, risk sometimes signifies opportunities, and therefore some MNEs choose to bear these foreign exchange risks due to the high volatility in currency markets in the last couple of years. On the other hand, many MNEs decide to hedge against these potential losses. Financial management of these companies involves financing and investments across countries whose values are affected by exchange rates. More accurate predictions of exchange rate movements will result in more accurate cash flow predictions and better company decision-making. However, forecasting future exchange rates is difficult since there have been many theories and empirical findings in this area. Still, no one seems to work consistently better than others in predicting future exchange rates.

A good starting point in understanding the determinants of exchange rates is Rudiger Dornbusch's tripartite categorization of exchange rate theory (Dornbusch, 1980, pp. 144–172), in which he summarized the determinants into three views: the relative price of monies, goods, or bonds. Eiteman et al. (2016a, p. 262) formalize this opinion and organize the theoretical determinants of the exchange rate into the following three primary schools of thought.

## International Parity Conditions

These economic theories link exchange rates, price levels (inflation), and interest rates. As the oldest and most widely accepted theory, the purchasing power parity (PPP) approach is built based on the law of one price. It states that the ratio of domestic prices to foreign prices determines the long-term equilibrium exchange rate (Eiteman et al., 2016a, p. 263). Several indexes have been constructed based on the PPP theory to understand the undervaluation or overvaluation of currencies. For example, the "Big Mac Index," created by The Economist in 1986, proposed to use the Big Mac sold worldwide as a tool to understand whether the market value of a currency is close to its "theoretical" value implied by Big Macs in this currency. In addition, based on the PPP, some new theories have been developed (with the relevant determinants of exchange rates shown in brackets): absolute PPP (price indices), relative PPP (relative inflation rates), the international Fisher effect (comparable interest rates), and interest rate parity (forward exchange rates).

Let us focus on the international Fisher effect as an example to understand how interest rates can affect long-term exchange rates. This theory extends the Fisher effect hypothesized by American economist Irving Fisher. It states that the spot exchange rates should change equally but in the opposite direction to the difference in interest rates between two currencies. For the exchange rate between the US dollar and the euro, this theory implies:

$$\frac{S_0 - S_1}{S_1} = \frac{i_{\delta} - i_{\varepsilon}}{1 + i_{\varepsilon}} \approx i_{\delta} - i_{\varepsilon}$$



where $S_0$ is the current spot exchange rate quoted as euro per one US dollar, and $S_1$ is the (predicted) spot exchange rate at the end of the period. $i_{\$}$ and $i_{€}$ stand for the expected nominal interest rates in the United States and the eurozone, respectively. For example, suppose the current spot rate is €0.98/US\$, and we expect the interest rates to be 6% and 4% in the United States and the eurozone, respectively, in the next year. In that case, the value of the US dollar relative to the euro will drop approximately by 2%, and the future spot exchange rate implied by the international Fisher effect is €0.96/US\$.

## Asset or Financial Markets

This approach suggests that exchange rates are adjusted to international transactions in the financial market. It assumes perfect capital mobility, meaning capital flows can move freely between countries without significant transaction costs or capital controls. Shifts in the supply and demand for various financial assets (e.g., stocks, bonds, real estate, rare wines, and so on) determine exchange rates. Monetary and fiscal policy changes also alter exchange rates because they change the risks and expected returns of financial assets (Eiteman et al., 2016a, p. 264).

To understand the link between asset returns and exchange rates, let us use the one-year deposits in the eurozone and Japan as a simple example. The interest rate on the euro is 5% per year and on the yen is 3% per year. The spot exchange rate is ¥140/€. To compare the two deposits, one must calculate their returns based on the same currency. Suppose we assume the exchange rate remains the same over the next year. In that case, the euro deposit is more attractive to international investors since it has a higher return (5%) than the yen deposit (3%). In this case, the demand for the euro deposit is high, pushing the euro price relative to the yen. On the other hand, if the exchange rate is expected to drop next year, the higher return on the euro deposit will be eroded by the euro's depreciation. For instance, with an expected spot exchange rate of ¥137.33/€ at the end of the year, the value of the yen deposit is 140*1.03/137.33 = €1.05, the same 5% return in euro as the euro deposit. This is when the market is in equilibrium (no type of deposit is in excess demand or excess supply), and investors are indifferent to the two deposits. If the expected spot return is below the equilibrium rate of ¥137.33/€, the yen deposit offers a higher return in euro than the euro deposit, and hence the price of the yen will be pushed high relative to the euro.

Indeed, international investors do not consider the return on assets the sole factor for their investment decisions. Among other factors, they care about at least two main characteristics of an asset. The first one is risk, which is the volatility of return. In the above example, the euro return of the yen deposit is variable or risky because it depends on the actual spot exchange rate at the end of the year. The second one is liquidity, which measures how easily an asset can be purchased or sold quickly without affecting the asset price. Assets such as bonds and stocks are more liquid than others such as real estate, whose sale usually requires time and the services of brokers and inspectors. All else equal, investors prefer to hold assets with the highest expected (real) rate of returns and dislike risky and illiquid assets. In more detail, we illustrate the classical portfolio theory showing the link between expected return and different types of risk (systematic versus idiosyncratic risks) in ► Chap. 16 of the book.

## Balance of Payments

The balance of payments (BOP) systematically classifies a country's trades with other nations. It includes them into two sub-accounts: the current account (import and export of goods and services and unilateral foreign aid transfers) and the capital or financial account (foreign direct investments, portfolio investments, and other types of investments). The third sub-account is the reserve account which includes the reserve assets such as gold, foreign currencies, SDRs, and reserve positions in the IMF. Allowing minor errors and omissions, the BOP must balance; that is, the sum of the values of the three sub-accounts must be zero. As a theory on exchange rate determination, the BOP approach argues that the equilibrium exchange rate is established when the net inflow (outflow) of foreign exchange arising from current account activities matches the net outflow (inflow) of foreign exchange of the capital account (Eiteman et al., 2016a, pp. 263–264).

Based on the BOP approach, the currency of a country with a trade surplus (e.g., it exports more goods or services than it imports) will increase in value (appreciation) because of the high demand for its goods or services and hence this currency. Theoretically, the higher currency value makes its goods, services, and products more expensive and will reduce foreign demand but will also stimulate imports since the foreign prices are now lower. This is expected to balance the trade surplus and bring currency rates back to equilibrium. To prevent a high appreciation of its currency, the central bank will use its currency to buy more reserve assets, so it will experience an increase in its foreign reserves. The whole process reverses when a country has a trade deficit (e.g., it imports more goods and services than it exports).

## Technical Analysis

Unlike *fundamental* analysis, such as the three approaches mentioned above, which focus on fundamental relationships between economic variables and exchange rates, *technical* analysis is a currency forecasting technique that uses historical prices or trends. Proponents of technical analysis believe that all market-driven prices, including exchange rates, follow trends, which may be analyzed to predict price movement in the future. Put differently, technical analysts assume that studying past price behavior provides insights into future price movements. There are various types of technical analysis. For instance, mechanical rules are a type of technical analysis where a set of rules is adopted to help make the analytical process more disciplined. Resistance levels (local peaks) and support levels (local troughs) are identified to understand future price movements. Technical analysts generally suggest buying a currency when it rises more than a given percentage above its support level and selling it when it falls more than a given percentage below its resistance level.



Practitioners almost universally use technical analysis in formulating short-term exchange-rate expectations. Nonetheless, many economists consider it implausible or far-fetched. For instance, Malkiel (2007, p. 117) analogizes it to "alchemy." On the other hand, the popularity of technical analysis among practitioners could be attributed to the inadequacy of economic theories in predicting exchange rates. Decades of theoretical and empirical studies suggest that exchange rates do adhere to the fundamental principles in the long run. Still, various random events and institutional frictions do cause currency values to deviate significantly from their fundamental values in the short term. Therefore, to predict exchange rates more accurately, one may combine the two approaches and needs to consider the forecast period as well as the regimes of the forecasted currency (i.e., fixed rate or floating rate).

## Foreign Exchange Exposure

Hekman defines foreign exchange exposure or risk as:

**Foreign Exchange Exposure**

The foreign exchange risk of any particular investment or project depends on both the variability of the exchange rate forecast and the specific sensitivity of the project's or investment's current value to changes in forecasts. In turn, the investment-specific sensitivity is determined by such factors as the physical location of the investment, the structure of its revenues and costs, the industrial structure of the markets in which it operates, and management's response to changing forecasts. This investment-specific sensitivity to changes in exchange rate forecasts is foreign exchange exposure. (Hekman, 1985, p. 84)

This exposure is a common risk faced by MNEs, which frequently engage in financial transactions or maintain financial statements in a currency other than where they are headquartered. For example, a company based in Australia that does business in India has account receivables and other operations in the Indian rupee but

Mixed currencies, image by PublicDomainPictures from Pixabay

reports its financial statements in the Australian dollar and thus is exposed to foreign exchange risk. An essential duty of the financial manager in these firms is to measure the effect of foreign exchange exposure and manage it to maximize the firm's value.

To measure the impact of exchange rate movements on an MNE, we need to identify the types of foreign exchange exposure the firm faces and the amount of risk it encounters. It is conventional to classify foreign exchange exposures into three types (Eiteman et al., 2016b, pp. 294–295):

## Transaction Exposure

It measures changes in the value of outstanding financial transactions (e.g., receivables or payables) incurred before a shift in exchange rates but not due to be settled until after the exchange rates change. It deals with changes in cash flows resulting from existing contractual obligations: how the amount of money a firm owes in foreign currency and expects to receive in foreign currency changes due to exchange rate fluctuations. For example, a UK-based company sells service on an open account to an Australian buyer for A$500,000, which will be paid in 90 days. The British firm expects to exchange the A$500,000 for £294,118 with a current exchange rate of A$1.70/£ when payment is received. Transaction exposure will occur because the actual pound value of the A$500,000 may not be the expected £294,118 after the A$500,000 are exchanged for pounds. If the exchange rate becomes A$1.75/£ 9 months later, the British firm will receive only £285,714, which is £8404 less than the anticipated amount. Another example of transaction exposure arises when a company borrows or invests, denominating the amount in a foreign currency. In the previous example, let us assume the British firm borrows A$10 million from an Australian bank for 5 years. With an exchange rate of A$1.70/£, the loan is worth £5,882,353. If the exchange rate drops to A$1.60/£ 5 years later, the loan is due with the cost of repayment of the principal at £6,250,000. The British company will suffer a significant foreign exchange loss in this case.



## Operating Exposure

It measures changes in the present value of a firm resulting from changes in future operating cash flows caused by unexpected changes in exchange rates. It focuses on the impact of unforeseen changes in exchange rates because anticipated changes in exchange rates would have already been discounted and reflected in the firm's current value. Operating exposure assesses the impact of changing exchange rates on a firm's operations and competitive position versus other firms in a certain period. While both transaction exposure and operating exposure deal with future cash flows, they differ in terms of what kind of cash flows are considered. Transaction exposure is about the fluctuation in the home currency value of foreign currency-denominated contracts for which the price has been fixed. Operating exposure is the fluctuation in future operating cash flows (whether denominated in the home or foreign currencies) in response to variations in actual exchange rates. While transaction exposure is short term, operating exposure affects any firm with foreign buyers, suppliers, or competitors through its impact on sales revenues and input costs. Therefore, operating exposure is a far more critical source of risk than transaction exposure for MNEs (Grant & Soenen, 2004, p. 53).

Measuring operating exposure requires forecasting and analyzing a firm's future individual transaction exposures and the future exposures of all the current and future competitors of the firm. The unexpected changes in exchange rates can affect a firm in both the short term and the long term. The short-term effect is mainly for the current and immediate contracts, while the long-term impact is more fundamental and may affect all cash flows of all units due to the changing price and cost and competitors' reactions. To illustrate how to measure operating exposure, we assume that firm ABC is a US-based international service company, "ABC US," with a French subsidiary, "ABC France," which sells locally and exports, but all sales are invoiced in euros. On the cost side, labor and other costs are local and in euros. The functional currency of ABC France is the euro, which this subsidiary uses to conduct its business and report its financial statements. The annual sales of ABC France are €10 million, and the costs are €7.5 million. Labor and materials (if any) are from Europe, and half of the services are exported to countries outside the eurozone.

Over the period from June 2021 to October 2022, the euro has depreciated in the market against the US dollar. Since the cash flows of ABC France are all in euros, there is little immediate change in its profitability. However, the profitability of ABC US is affected negatively even in the short term when the value of ABC France is converted to US dollars. Over the intermedium to long term, the effects of the euro's depreciation on ABC France and ABC US are more complex. With the unexpected fall in the euro, we can think of at least three scenarios for ABC France: (i) All variables remain constant. ABC France has no change in sales, costs, or operating cash flows since it is euro-functional. (ii) Volume increases, but other variables remain constant. This case is possible because the euro depreciation makes the French service more competitive with imports within Europe and cheaper outside of Europe. (iii) Sales price increases, but other variables remain constant. ABC France could raise its euro sales price to offset the euro's depreciation. Assuming there is no change in volume, the increase in euro price will increase the profit margin of ABC France. Indeed, there are other possibilities as well, and all these depend on the price elasticities and competitive position of ABC France. Therefore, we expect a variation in cash flows and profits and, thus, different values of ABC US under different scenarios analyzed.

This illustrative example shows that operating exposure is more subjective and forward-looking than transaction exposure because it is based on expected future cash flows and exchange rates. Therefore, it is also more critical to a firm's long-term survival and growth.

## Translation Exposure

It refers to the potential that an MNE's consolidated financial statements can be affected by changes in exchange rates. This exposure arises because assets, liabilities, equities, and earnings of a foreign subsidiary of an MNE are usually stated in the country's currency, and they must be restated in the reporting currency of the parent firm to prepare the consolidated financial statements. This translation or conversion can lead to unavoidable inconsistencies in calculating the consolidated earnings of the company if the exchange rate changes in the interim period. Continuing with the previous example, ABC France purchases a building worth €500,000 on September 1, 2021, when the exchange rate is US$1.18/€. The value of the building converted into dollars is US$590,000. ABC US decides to convert all of its foreign holdings into US dollars to present a consolidated balance sheet on March 31, 2022, when the exchange rate drops to US$1.11/€. Thus, the value of the building falls to US$555,000.

Translation exposure can portray a distorted representation of a company's international holdings if there is a significant change in the exchange rates between foreign and home currencies. There are two basic methods for accountants of MNEs to translate financial statements: the current rate method, in which all financial statement line items are translated at the "current" exchange rate with few exceptions (e.g., capital), and the temporal method, wherein specific assets and liabilities are translated at exchange rates consistent with the timing of their creation and line items such as inventory and net plant and equipment are restated regularly to reflect their market value. Regardless of the methods, the accounting principle of consistency must apply, which requires companies to use the same process over time to maintain uniformity in the books of account.

## Global Debt and Equity Markets



Over the past few decades, the world's financial markets have been increasingly connected due to at least three major forces: the growing number of MNEs, the universality of the US dollar, and the influential intermediary role of international financial institutions. Additionally, thanks to technological advances and financial innovation, which further accelerate the globalization of financial markets, MNEs with financing needs can access different sectors of global financial markets at a relatively lower cost.

## International Banking and Money Market

International banks differ from domestic banks in the types of services they provide. One important function of international banks is to facilitate the imports and exports of their clients by arranging trade financing and foreign exchange necessary to conduct cross-border transactions and investments. They borrow and lend in the international money market, underwrite international bonds, and participate in international loan syndicates to lend large sums to MNEs and sovereign governments. In conducting foreign exchange transactions, these banks usually provide services to help their clients hedge foreign exchange risk through various derivative products such as currency futures and options. Nowadays, many banks are structured as holding companies to function as both traditional commercial and investment banks.

International banking has grown tremendously in the past several decades, with regulatory arbitrage, financial liberalization, and financial innovation being the key drivers (McCauley et al., 2021). Regulations that raised the costs of domestic banks make it attractive for them to borrow and lend abroad. The transition of the broader international financial system from a tightly managed one with extensive exchange and capital controls to today's market-driven, integrated system is both a cause and a symptom of international banking's growth. In addition, the development of new financial products, including syndicated loans and derivatives, alters how banks manage risks in their global portfolios. ◘ Table 5.3 presents the world's 20 largest banks measured by total assets as of December 31, 2021. It indicates 6 of the world's 20 largest banks are from China, partly because the Chinese government had been pushing banks to lend more to infrastructure projects and small businesses while cutting key interest rates to release more liquidity for lending. For the rest of the largest banks, four each are from the United States and Japan, three are from France, two are from the United Kingdom, and one is from Spain.

Before we look at the international money and bond markets, it is crucial to clarify some basic terms used in this market. Internationally, despite having "euro"

**Table 5.3** The world's 20 largest banks, source: S&P Global (2022)

| Rank | Company name | Headquarters | Total assets (US$B) |
|---|---|---|---|
| 1 | Industrial & Commercial Bank of China Ltd. | China | 5536.53 |
| 2 | China Construction Bank Corp. | China | 4762.46 |
| 3 | Agricultural Bank of China Ltd. | China | 4575.95 |
| 4 | Bank of China Ltd. | China | 4206.53 |
| 5 | JPMorgan Chase & Co. | United States | 3743.57 |
| 6 | Mitsubishi UFJ Financial Group Inc. | Japan | 3176.84 |
| 7 | Bank of America Co. | United States | 3169.5 |
| 8 | HSBC Holdings PLC | United Kingdom | 2953.64 |
| 9 | BNP Paribus SA | France | 2905.83 |
| 10 | Credit Agricole Group | France | 2674.35 |
| 11 | Citigroup Inc. | United States | 2291.41 |
| 12 | Sumitomo Mitsui Financial Group Inc. | Japan | 2176.94 |
| 13 | Japan Post Bank Co. Ltd. | Japan | 1998.98 |
| 14 | Postal Savings Bank of China Co. Ltd. | China | 1981.53 |
| 15 | Mizuho Financial Group Inc. | Japan | 1957.87 |
| 16 | Wells Fargo & Co. | United States | 1948.07 |
| 17 | Barclays PLC | United Kingdom | 1874.4 |
| 18 | Bank of Communications Co. Ltd. | China | 1836.38 |
| 19 | Banco Santander SA | Spain | 1814.9 |
| 20 | Groupe BPCE | France | 1724.12 |

in the term, *eurocurrency* does not refer to euros deposited outside Europe. Instead, it is a general term for all currencies deposited outside their local country. The term has a historical background, as it originated in Europe. For instance, eurodollars are deposits of US dollars in banks outside the United States, while euroyen deposits are those denominated in Japanese yen outside Japan. Similarly, eurobonds are not bonds the European Central Bank issued, although news within Europe may report it this way.

**Eurobond**

In the international financial market, a eurobond is a global bond denominated in a currency not native to the country where it is issued.



We will follow the *international* terminology in the following sections.

The international money market is where foreign currency transactions are carried on among global banks, MNEs, and countries' central banks. It is one of the safest financial markets where currency transactions and investments made in this market are usually for a brief period (e.g., less than 1 year). The core of the international money market is the eurocurrency market, which emerged in Western Europe in the late 1950s and rapidly reached a global scale. Eurocurrency is a currency deposited at a foreign bank outside its home country. Unlike domestic deposits, eurocurrency deposits are less subject to domestic regulations related to reserve requirements or deposit insurance. Therefore, the operation costs of the eurocurrency market are lower, which explains the rapid growth of this market since its inception.

The majority of eurocurrency transactions are interbank transactions. Eurobanks with surplus funds and no retail customers to lend to will lend to other eurobanks that have borrowers but are short of funds. The rate charged by the eurobanks with excess funds is referred to as the interbank offered rate, the reference rate in the international money market. This rate is market specific, and the most important one is the London Interbank Offered Rate, or LIBOR, because London is the major eurocurrency financial center. LIBOR was a key benchmark for setting the interest rates charged on loans, mortgages, and corporate debt, but over the last decade, it has been burdened by scandals and crises. Effective from December 31, 2021, the Secured Overnight Financing Rate (SOFR) has replaced LIBOR for pricing new loans in the United States.

Besides the eurocurrency market, the international money market includes other segments involving the following financial products:

- Eurocredits, which are short- to medium-term loans lent by eurobanks to MNEs, sovereign governments, international institutions, and banks. The loans are denominated in currencies other than the home currency of the eurobank. If a borrower needs a large amount of funds, a syndicate is usually formed, and all banks in the syndicate band together and share the loan.
- Euronotes, which are short-term notes underwritten by a group of international banks. They usually have maturities from 1 to 6 months, are sold at a discount from face value, and pay back the total face value at maturity. Their interest costs are lower than the comparative eurocredits and thus become attractive to borrowers.
- Eurocommercial paper, which is an unsecured general obligation in the form of a promissory bearer note, issued on a discount or interest-bearing basis by large companies or banks and placed directly with the public through dealers. Its maturity typically ranges from 1 to 6 months. Most eurocommercial papers are denominated in the euro and the US dollar.

## The International Bond Market

This is a market for foreign currency bonds issued and traded across national boundaries. It contains various instruments created by international banks for MNEs, sovereign governments, and other institutions to raise long-term debt globally. Generally, all international bonds are divided into two categories: eurobonds and foreign bonds. The distinction lies in whether the borrower is a domestic or a foreign resident and whether the issue is in local or foreign currency.

A eurobond is underwritten by an international syndicate of banks and other securities firms using domestic currency but is sold or traded outside the borrower's domestic market. For example, a British company issues debt in the United States with the principal and interest payments denominated in pounds. Eurobonds can be a straight-fixed rate issue with a fixed coupon rate, set maturity date, and full principal repayment upon final maturity, a floating rate note with a variable coupon rate set at some fixed spread over the reference rate such as LIBOR, or an equity-rated issue, which is similar to a straight-fixed rate issue but can be convertible to stock at a specified price per share before maturity. On the other hand, a foreign bond issue is offered by a foreign borrower to investors in a national capital market and denominated in that nation's currency. As a comparison example, a British company issues debt in the United States with the principal and interest payments denominated in the US dollar as a foreign bond. Foreign bonds have nicknames: Yankee bonds for foreign bonds sold in the United States, Bulldogs for foreign bonds sold in the United Kingdom, and Samurai bonds for foreign bonds sold in Japan.

◘ Figure 5.2 presents the international debt securities outstanding for the largest 10 countries (defined by GDP in 2021) at the end of March 2022. Financial corporations in the United States issue the most significant amount of debt in the

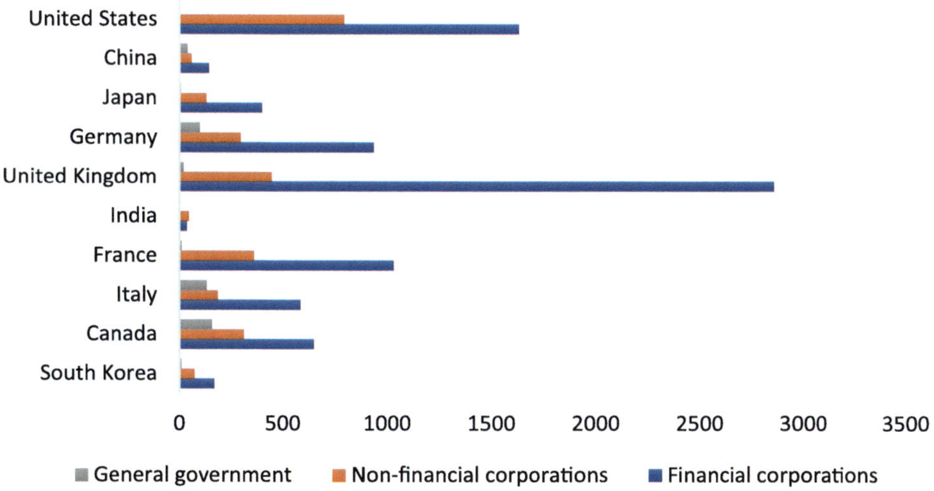


◘ Fig. 5.2 International debt securities outstanding in end March 2022, in billions of US dollars, source: (BIS, n.d.-b)

world bond markets, and non-financial corporations in the United States are active global borrowers. On the other hand, governments make minimal use of the international sector.

Compared to domestic and foreign bonds, eurobonds offer unique advantages to their issuers (Eiteman et al., 2016c, pp. 426–427). The first one is the absence of regulatory interference. Eurobonds fall outside the regulatory domain of any single nation. National governments usually impose fewer controls on eurobonds (sold within their markets but denominated in foreign currencies) than foreign bonds (sold within their markets and denominated in the local currency). Second, disclosure requirements in the eurobond market are much less stringent than those for domestic bonds. For instance, the SEC requires a large scope of disclosure rules for corporate bond issuance in the US market. As a result, many firms find that the registration costs and time needed for a eurobond offering are much less than those of a domestic issue. On the other hand, investors also find eurobonds attractive due to their tax anonymity and flexibility. Most eurobonds are issued in bearer form, meaning the owner's name and country of residence are not on the certificate. Because of this anonymity, interest paid on eurobonds is generally not subject to an income withholding tax. Another favorable attribute of eurobonds to local investors is that they provide exposure to foreign investments and thus offer diversification benefits. Eurodollar bonds, denominated in the US dollar and issued in a country other than the United States, are the largest component of the eurobond market. ◻ Figure 5.3 shows the quarterly gross issuance of eurodollar bonds from non-financial companies in the past decade. Overall, there has been an increasing trend over time, especially after the outbreak of the COVID-19 pandemic.

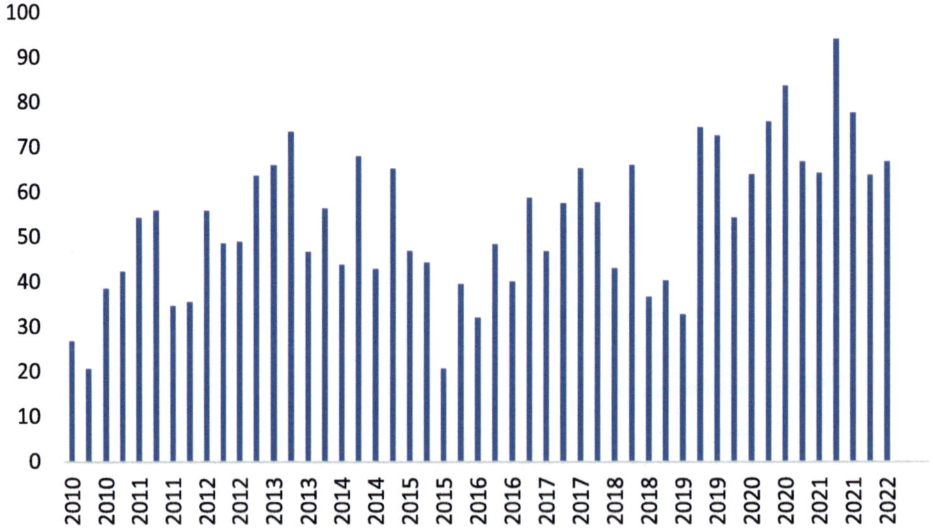


◻ **Fig. 5.3** Gross issuance of eurodollar bonds, in billions of US dollars, source: (BIS, n.d.-a)

How does an MNE choose between domestic and international debt financing? Well, this decision is based on several factors. Tawatnuntachai & Yaman (2008, p. 23) find that firms with a good reputation abroad and wanting to raise large amounts of funds tend to issue global bonds instead of domestic ones. Firms are also more likely to issue global bonds when the domestic economy weakens. In addition, firms with greater levels of international activity have better credit ratings (Reeb et al., 2001, p. 395), so their cost of debt financing in the global market is lower. A borrower can choose from several possibilities within the international debt market, including syndicated credits, notes, and bonds. The choice between bonds and syndicated credits is mainly influenced by the borrower's credit standing, the volume of funds required, and the degree of flexibility the borrower needs. Generally, borrowers with good credit ratings, well-known in the financial market, and requiring a limited quantity of funds choose to issue a bond, whereas borrowers with less familiar names or requiring substantial amounts use syndicated credits (Benzie, 1992, p. 24).

## The International Equity Market

This is a market or tool through which investors can invest in the equity of various global firms. It provides alternative ways for MNEs to raise long-term capital. This market consists of the primary and secondary sub-markets. Companies publicly sell new stocks for the first time, typically in the form of an initial public offering (IPO), in the primary market. Investors who buy shares of the issuing firm may not want to hold these shares indefinitely. The secondary market allows shares of issuing firms to be traded among investors. The two primary functions of the second market are to provide marketability and share valuation. Organized stock exchanges comprise the secondary stock market, which has grown tremendously and experienced changes in organizational forms in the past several decades. In developed economies, stock exchanges have been transformed from member-owned organizations or government institutions into privately owned for-profit corporations since the mid-1990s. Today, all major stock exchanges in these markets have their shares listed and traded on their exchanges. In emerging markets, however, stock exchanges were often established in the form of state-owned corporations, and their transformation into listed corporations has been more gradual. For instance, Shanghai Stock Exchange and Shenzhen Stock Exchange in China, the largest emerging market, operate as semi-public institutions and are membership institutions directly governed by the China Securities Regulatory Commission (CSRC).

As of 2021, world equity markets reached a record level of 160.95 trillion USD for value traded with a total of 51,632 listed companies, according to the World Federation of Exchanges (WFE). The number of IPOs was 679 in the Americas, 1278 in the Asia-Pacific (APAC) region, and 721 in the Europe, Middle East, and Africa (EMEA) region (721), with the capital raised through IPOs being 218.28, 191.79, and 88.06 billion US dollars in the three areas respectively. ◘ Table 5.4 exhibits the world's 10 largest stock exchanges at the end of 2021. Except for Euronext, which is a pan-European stock exchange, all other stock

5

**Table 5.4** The world's 10 largest stock exchanges, source: (WFE, 2022)

| | Exchange name | Country/Region | Value of share trading (USD millions) | Number of listed companies (domestic) | Number of listed companies (foreign) |
|---|---|---|---|---|---|
| 1 | NYSE | United States | 27,686,923.54 | 1925 | 600 |
| 2 | Nasdaq—US | United States | 24,557,073.95 | 2880 | 798 |
| 3 | Shanghai Stock Exchange | China | 8,154,689.12 | 2037 | – |
| 4 | Euronext | The Europe | 7,333,653.44 | 1740 | 255 |
| 5 | Japan Exchange Group | Japan | 6,544,303.49 | 3818 | 6 |
| 6 | Shenzhen Stock Exchange | China | 6,219,831.22 | 2578 | – |
| 7 | Hong Kong Exchanges and Clearing | China | 5,434,177.12 | 2388 | 184 |
| 8 | LSE Group London Stock Exchange | United Kingdom | 3,799,459.24 | 1646 | 352 |
| 9 | National Stock Exchange of India | India | 3,548,018.47 | 2053 | – |
| 10 | TMX Group | Canada | 3,264,137.36 | 3455 | 49 |

exchanges are within a country: two from the United States, three from China, and one each from Japan, the United Kingdom, India, and Canada. Most of these exchanges allow for listings of foreign companies, except the Shanghai Stock Exchange and Shenzhen Stock Exchange in China and the National Stock Exchange of India. Although Japan Exchange Group is open to foreigners, few foreign listings exist.

Generally, the secondary market has three main types of trading mechanisms. The first is a quote-driven system, where trades are all executed through dealers who act as market makers, post-prices they would be willing to buy and sell specific stocks on their account and keep an inventory of stocks. The dealers are the sole liquidity provider and generate profit from the bid-ask spread. Examples of a quote-driven market include Nasdaq and London Stock Exchange. The second type is an order-driven market, where all orders are displayed on an order book, and trades are only executed when the bid and ask prices are matched. In this market, traders buy and sell to each other directly; hence, dealers are not involved.

Nowadays, almost all exchanges use order-driven trading systems, and every automated trading system is an order-driven system. The third type is a brokered market, in which brokers help their clients find a counterparty willing to execute a trade. Due to their limited liquidity, this market is used mainly for large blocks of shares, which do not generate enough orders in order-driven or quote-driven markets. Regardless of the types of trading systems, a stock exchange is more attractive to investors if it is more liquid. *Liquidity* measures how easily an order is executed without affecting the market price. Amihud defines (il)liquidity as.

**Liquidity**

Liquidity is an elusive concept. It is not observed directly but rather has a number of aspects that cannot be captured in a single measure. Illiquidity reflects the impact of order flow on price – the discount that a seller concedes or the premium that a buyer pays when executing a market order – that results from adverse selection costs and inventory costs. (Amihud et al., 2015, p. 33)

Many proxies are being proposed to gauge stock market liquidity, one of which is trading volume. A deep market with a high trading volume can easily absorb orders, thus imposing limited trading costs. On the other hand, companies prefer more liquid stock exchanges since the cost of raising equity capital tends to be lower in these markets (Amihud et al., 2015, pp. 352–360). ◘ Table 5.4 shows the trading volume of the 10 largest stock exchanges in December 2021. All of them are very liquid, attracting both investors and issuers.

What are the possible approaches and instruments for a company to list shares or raise new equity capital in the global market? Eiteman et al. (2016c, pp. 409–419) outline five categories of equity alternatives available to this company, which consist of the following pathways:

- Initial public offering (IPO). It is the process of offering shares of a private company to the public in a new stock issuance for the first time. This process is lengthy and complicated, so it needs the assistance of investment banks (underwriters), which help prepare the regulatory filings and disclosures required. The company has to publish a prospectus before the IPO date to show its details (e.g., history, business model, financial results, risk, and business plan) to help potential investors assess the company.
- Seasonal offering. It refers to the offering of a large block of shares previously issued to the public (i.e., an offering after IPO). Capital raised through seasonal offerings can be used to fund operations or grow business. For example, the Goldman Sachs Group, a leading global financial services firm, announced that it had commenced a public offering of US$5 billion of its common stock for sale to the public on April 13, 2009. Since the company was already public with an IPO in 1999, issuing these additional shares constituted a seasoned equity offering.

- Depositary receipts (DRs). They are bank-issued negotiable certificates to represent shares of foreign companies. There are two basic types of DRs: American depositary receipts (ADRs), denominated in US dollars and traded in the US market, and global depositary receipts (GDRs), which refer to certificates sold outside the United States. ADRs are the primary way non-US companies are listed on a US stock exchange. Each ADR represents either a multiple or portion of the underlying foreign share, registered and traded in the same manner as any share of stock in the United States. Some popular ADRs include Alibaba Group (BABA), NIO (NIO), Taiwan Semiconductor Manufacturing Company (TSMC), and Nokia (NOK).
- Global registered shares (GRSs). They are shares that are traded and transferred across borders without the need for conversion; that is, they are identical shares that can be traded on different stock exchanges in other currencies. For example, the same share of a European firm purchased on the SIX Swiss Exchange can be sold on the New York Stock Exchange or vice versa. Both GDRs and GRSs are means for investors to invest in stocks of foreign companies without the need to trade on foreign exchanges. The difference is that a GRS enables the investor to have a direct claim on the foreign issuer, while investors of GDRs have claims on a domestic bank that mirrors the foreign stock.
- Euroequity issues. They refer to IPOs on multiple exchanges in multiple countries simultaneously, intending to raise more capital in its issuance by reaching as many different investors as possible. An excellent example of a euroequity issue is Investcorp, a holding company controlled by Bahraini investors. It sold 49% of its stake in Gucci Group, the Italian luxury goods maker, in an IPO on the Amsterdam Stock Exchange and New York Stock Exchange simultaneously in 1995.
- Cross-listings. They list a company's shares on exchanges other than its primary and original stock exchange. A cross-listing differs from a euroequity issue in that, in a cross-listing, shares of a company have been floated in the home market before they are listed in different countries. In contrast, a company does an IPO simultaneously on other exchanges in a euroequity issue. Several stock exchanges have a large proportion of foreign listings. For instance, foreign listings represent 24% and 34% of the New York Stock Exchange and the Singapore Exchange in 2021 (WFE, 2021).
- Directed public share issues. They are the issues targeting investors in a single country and underwritten, either in whole or part, by investment institutions from that country. These issues are typically used by firms in smaller capital markets with rapid growth to fund acquisitions or significant capital investments in a target foreign market. A directed public share issue is usually combined with a cross-listing on a stock exchange in the target market.
- Private placement. It refers to selling unregistered securities to a limited pool of qualified institutional investors (e.g., insurance companies and investment companies). A company may choose to raise equity capital through a private placement for various reasons. For instance, young firms choose private placements

because they may not meet specific public listing requirements; some firms may choose to remain private to avoid reporting burdens. As a result, the private placements market has increased in the past two decades. Fundraising through private placements reached a record of almost 1.2 trillion US dollars in 2021 (McKinsey., 2022, p. 6).

In addition to the access to a bigger pool of investors and capital, what are the other significant *benefits* of raising equity capital in the global market relative to the local market? Remember how the Sea Group raised its equity capital on the New York Stock Exchange in the United States rather than the Singapore Exchange domestically? For companies in emerging or less liquid markets, the first benefit of equity financing in the more developed market is improved liquidity and, thus, the reduced cost of capital. Amihud et al. (2015) examine the stock market liquidity in 43 markets globally and find that stocks listed in more developed markets (e.g., the United States and the United Kingdom) are much more liquid than those listed in stock exchanges of emerging and small markets (e.g., Indonesia, Malaysia) (p. 353). They also find that the price of liquidity is much higher in emerging markets than in developed markets, suggesting a higher cost of equity capital in emerging markets. The higher liquidity in developed markets results from various factors: specialized people, easy access to capital, good infrastructure, well-established regulatory and tax environments, and low levels of corruption. The second benefit is enhanced global visibility and reputation. Cross-border listings on the more famous stock exchanges, such as the New York Stock Exchange and the London Stock Exchange, enhance a company's public profile. In addition, many companies use it as an advertising strategy to attract foreign investors and to improve their image and brand value since these firms are more likely to be covered in the media. Related to this, these companies can attract more and better talent. Another benefit is to improve corporate governance. Raising equity capital publicly in more developed markets such as the United States and the United Kingdom typically requires companies to establish a clear and well-defined set of rules that govern their corporate structure.

On the other hand, raising equity abroad imposes additional costs on companies. The biggest ones are the commitment to providing complete and transparent disclosure of operating results and balance sheets and a continuous investor relations program. The mainstream view of the United States and United Kingdom regulatory institutions is that more transparent and comprehensive financial disclosures help reduce the cost of equity capital. Companies must adhere to these disclosure requirements to raise equity capital in these markets. However, complying with multiple regulatory bodies and reporting standards can also be costly.

## Debt Versus Equity Financing in the International Market

The two primary options to fuel a company's growth are leveraging business debt financing or fundraising for equity investors. But, as the question in the open case about the Sea Group asks, what are the advantages and disadvantages of debt and equity financing? The most significant advantage of using debt versus equity is control and ownership. With traditional types of debt financing, the company's owners do not abandon any controlling interests in their business. Additionally, debt financing is often less costly than equity financing because equity financing is a greater risk to the investor than debt financing is to the lender. Moreover, the payments on the debt are generally tax-deductible. The major disadvantage of debt financing is that interest must be paid to lenders, and payments must be made regardless of business revenue. This can be particularly risky for smaller or newer businesses without a secure cash flow. On the other hand, equity financing provides extra working capital with no repayment obligation, which is particularly important if the business does not initially generate a profit and gives the freedom to channel more money into the company's growing business. Equity can be preferable or more suitable than debt financing if the firm lacks creditworthiness. However, the price for equity financing and its potential advantages is that the firm's owners must share profit and control of the company with shareholders, which could lead to tension and even conflict if there are differences in vision, management style, and ways of running the business. Companies choose debt or equity financing, depending on which type of funding is most easily accessible, the state of their ▶ cash flow, and the importance of maintaining ownership control. In practice, most companies adopt a combination of debt and ▶ equity financing. The preference for equity versus debt financing differs across regions and countries. For example, European firms primarily rely on cash reserves and reinvested profits for their funding, while debt is their primary source of external finance. As a result, they rarely consider external equity. External finance represents less than 40% of firms' investment finance, with bank debt and leasing prevailing. Companies think they can invest and grow without diluting their ownership through external equity financing. Consequently, many European firms rely on internal finance and bank debt, showing a sluggish growth rate (European Investment Bank, 2018). This also makes them vulnerable when banks are less forthcoming with lending or during a banking crisis. To encourage firms to have more equity financing, the European Commission proposed, on May 11, 2022, that companies get tax incentives for raising money through share issues like they do when they borrow. This measure removes the tax bias favoring corporate debt and makes firms more stable (Reuters., 2022). Fan et al. (2012) studied firms' capital structure and debt maturity choices in 39 developed and developing countries and examined how the institutional environment influences firms' financing choices. They found that, for the period from 1991 to 2006, the highest five leverage ratios, measured as the proportion of total debt to the market value of the firm, are observed in South Korea, Indonesia, Brazil, Portugal, and Pakistan, while the lowest five are observed in Australia, South Africa, Canada, the United States, and Turkey (p. 33). Developing economies seem to dominate the higher range with more debt financing, while developed economies tend to be in the lower range with more equity financing.

## Trends and Challenges

After so many years of development and growth, the international monetary and financial environment now enters an era full of new trends and challenges. The management of MNEs needs to understand these changes to better manage the risks their firms face. The market's current status indicates a few trends, as outlined below.

**Technological innovations**: Technological advances have made the international financial market more efficient. Technological innovations such as electronic communications networks bypass human intermediaries, increasing competition, and reducing transaction costs. The advent of electronic trading has transformed many traditional stock exchanges requiring face-to-face communication at physical locations to ones where the communication of orders and executions is conducted entirely electronically. The New York Stock Exchange acquired the electronic trading platform Archipelago in 2006 as it moved increasingly toward electronic trading. The London Stock Exchange and the NASDAQ are entirely electronic. On the other hand, the application of digital technology to financial services—known as fintech—is reshaping the future of finance. The digitization of financial services and money creates opportunities to build more inclusive and efficient financial services and promote economic development. Fintech is rapidly transforming the financial sector landscape and blurring the boundaries of both financial firms and the financial sector. As financial products, payments, and business models evolve, so too are market players and the structure of the markets in which they compete. Giant telecom and information technology companies, retail chains, and small start-ups are joining traditional banks and non-financial institutions in providing services (The World Bank, 2022).

**Sustainability**: The banking and financial sectors have an increasingly vital role in supporting the economy's green transition. Addressing climate change is one of the most pressing priorities of our time. In battling against global warming, the banking sector is of particular importance due to its centrality in allocating resources to non-financial companies, its ability to impose costs on non-compliant companies, and its power to coordinate actions. Recently, a few initiatives have been taken by the banking and financial sectors to fight against climate change. For instance, the Net-Zero Banking Alliance (NZBA) was launched in April 2021. As of October 2022, the Alliance includes 118 members from 41 countries, representing about 39% of global banking assets, which are committed to aligning their lending and investment portfolios with net-zero emissions by 2050. Over time, firms with more sustainability issues, or brown firms, will find it more costly to raise capital. Kacperczyk and Peydró (2022) studied how firm-level carbon emissions affect bank lending in a sample of global firms with syndicated loans. They find that firms with higher (lower) direct greenhouse gas emission levels previously borrowing from NZBA member banks subsequently receive less (more) total bank credit. The economic mechanism is bank credit supply, and the results are consistent with bank preferences for green firms.

On the corporate side, recently, many firms have issued green corporate bonds specifically earmarked to raise money for climate and environmental projects. These bonds are typically linked to the issuing company's asset, backed by its balance sheet, and usually carry the same credit rating as the issuer's other debt obligations. For instance, the Mercedes-Benz Group uses sustainable financial instruments such as green bonds to finance significant future investments. Mercedes-Benz Group AG issued the first benchmark bond nominated in euros in September 2020, with a volume of €1 billion, a term of 10 years, and a coupon of 0.75%. In March 2021, the company issued a second green bond with the same volume and coupon rate as the first one but a longer term of 12 years. The Mercedes-Benz Group will use the net proceeds from the green bonds to develop and produce zero-emission vehicles with battery and fuel-cell electric drives (The Mercedes-Benz Group, n.d.). It has been revealed that US$2 trillion in green bonds demonstrating climate ambition aligned with the Paris Agreement has been issued by Q3 2022 (Climate Bonds, 2022).

5

**Transparency:** Regulatory authorities require more and more disclosures from participants in the financial markets. The global financial crisis in 2008 highlights the crucial importance for banks to disclose publicly more detailed information related to their financial position and exposures. In response to the global financial crisis, the Basel Committee on Banking Supervision (BCBS), the primary global standard setter for the prudential regulation of banks, developed the Basel III framework, which addresses shortcomings of the pre-crisis regulatory framework and provides a regulatory foundation for a resilient banking system that supports the real economy. Within this framework, banks must disclose much more detailed information on their credit risk, operational risk, leverage ratio, and risk-weighted assets (Bank for International Settlements, n.d.). Additionally and more recently, the European Commission adopted, on April 6, 2022, a technical standard to be used by financial market participants when disclosing sustainability-related information under the Sustainable Finance Disclosures Regulation (SFDR). Under these rules, financial market participants will provide detailed information about how they tackle and reduce any possible negative impacts that their investments may have on the environment and society in general, which helps assess financial products' sustainability performances (European Commission, n.d.-a). On the corporate side, disclosure of non-financial information has become compulsory for companies of specific sizes and jurisdictions. In Europe, for example, large companies must publish reports on the policies they implement concerning environmental protection, social responsibility and treatment of employees, and respect for human rights (European Commission, n.d.-b). In the United States, the SEC proposes rules that would mandate comprehensive climate change disclosures and integrate critical aspects of sustainability reporting with annual reports of public firms (SEC, 2022). While all these efforts aim to improve the financial markets' transparency, sustainability, and resilience, they may also increase the costs of disclosure and compliance of financial institutions and companies.

Meanwhile, the present international monetary and financial market faces many challenges. One of them is the riskier and more uncertain environment. The COVID-19 pandemic has been morphing from a health crisis into an economic crisis, leading to the most significant recession since World War II. It has rattled global financial markets. Countries have seen runs on risky assets (particularly equities and corporate bonds), unprecedented stock market crashes, widening credit and liquidity spreads, signs of strained global liquidity, and large capital flows (von Allmen et al., 2020, pp. 1–2). It has triggered unprecedented repercussions for the global economy, creating supply side disruptions, and depressed aggregate demand. To make things even worse, the outbreak of the Russia–Ukraine war increases geopolitical risks and weighs adversely on global economic conditions. With all these factors, the international monetary and financial market has become much more volatile than before. Companies face a market with a sharp increase in financing costs due to tightening financial conditions. Another challenge is that events such as the United States–China trade war starting in 2018 are threatening the decades-long integration and globalization process. The world's two largest economies seek to internalize more of their economic growth and bring other countries within their economic and political orbits, resulting in an increasingly polarized world. These new counter-globalization trends could be highly disruptive to the MNEs that have prospered during decades of relative international harmony, generating more barriers for them to raise capital in the global market.

## Review Questions

1. Briefly explain how international finance differs from purely domestic finance.
2. What is the international monetary system?
3. Outline the stages and characteristics of the international monetary system.
4. Why is it vital for European countries to have stable exchange rates? What are the significant actions taken to achieve this goal?
5. Outline the exchange rate arrangements classified by the IMF.
6. Who are the prominent participants in the foreign exchange markets?
7. Describe the three basic types of transactions in the foreign exchange market.
8. Distinguish the three approaches to forecast exchange rates in the fundamental analysis.
9. What is the international Fisher effect? Use an example to illustrate how theory can be used to forecast exchange rates.
10. What is the balance of payments (BOP) identity? How can it be used to understand future exchange rate movements?
11. BMW Group has been based in Munich since its founding in 1916. But by 2022, only 10.6% of the cars it sold were bought in Germany. China has become BMW's fastest-growing market, accounting for 33.1% of its global sales volume in 2022 (Carlier, 2023). Discuss the foreign exchange exposures faced by BMW.
12. How do international banks differ from domestic banks?
13. What is the core of the international money market? Briefly describe it.
14. Outline the major segments of the international money market.
15. What is a eurobond? How does it differ from a foreign bond? What are the unique advantages offered by Eurobonds to their issuers?
16. What major factors affect an MNE's choice between domestic and international debt financing?

17. What are the main functions of the primary and secondary sub-markets of the equity market?
18. Outline different pathways for a firm to list shares or raise equity capital in the global market.
19. What are the benefits for MNEs to raise equity capital in the global market relative to the local market?
20. Critically discuss the new trends in the international capital market.
21. What are the challenges multinational service firms face in raising global capital?



## Closing Case: A. P. Moller-Maersk Group and Its Foreign Exchange Exposure

The world's biggest container shipping company, A. P. Moller-Maersk Group, also known simply as Maersk, is an integrated container logistics company based in Copenhagen, Denmark, operating in 130 countries. The company is active in ocean and inland freight transportation and associated services, such as supply chain management and port operation. It is listed on the Copenhagen Stock Exchange, with a total market capitalization of US$36.00 billion as of January 2023.

Consolidated financial statements are financial statements of an entity with multiple divisions or subsidiaries, requiring the entity to integrate and combine all its financial accounting functions to show its financial conditions in standard statement reporting. For Maersk, the consolidated financial statements are presented in USD, the parent company's functional currency. In the translation to the presentation currency for subsidiaries, associates, or joint arrangements with functional currencies other than USD, the total comprehensive income is translated into USD at average exchange rates. In addition, the balance sheet is translated at the exchange rates at the balance sheet date. Exchange rate differences arising from such translations are recognized directly in other comprehensive income and a separate reserve of equity in the consolidated financial statements.

The functional currency of Maersk is typically USD, which means that the carrying amounts of property, plant, equipment, and intangible assets and, hence, depreciation and amortization are maintained in USD from the date of acquisition. For other activities, including container terminal activities and land-based container activities, the functional currency is generally the local currency of the country in which such activities are performed. Transactions in currencies other than the functional currency are translated at the exchange rate prevailing at the date of the transaction. Monetary items in foreign currencies not settled at the balance sheet date are translated at the exchange rate as at the balance sheet date. Foreign exchange gains and losses are included in the income statement as financial income or expenses.

**Questions**

1. What type of foreign exchange exposure is shown in the case of Maersk?
2. Why is the functional currency of Maersk the US dollar?

Sources: ((CompaniesMarketCap, 2023; Maersk, 2020; Reuters., 2021).

Maersk container ship, image by WikimediaImages from Pixabay

**Summary**

This chapter

- Illustrated the foreign exchange risk faced by multinational service firms.
- Introduced the foreign exchange market
  - Stages and characteristics of the international monetary system
  - Different exchange rate arrangements
  - Main currencies
  - Major participants
  - types of transactions
- Outlined different determinants of exchange rates and forecasting methods
  - Fundamental analysis: focus on economic theories linking exchange rates, price levels, and interest rates
  - Technical analysis: focus on historical prices or trends
- Explained three types of foreign exchange exposure
  - Transaction exposure
  - Operating exposure
  - Translation exposure

- Described the global capital market
  - Global debt market: eurocurrency market, eurocredits, euronotes, eurocommercial papers, eurobonds, foreign bonds
  - Global equity market: IPOs, seasonal offerings, DRs, GRSs, euroequity issues, cross-listings, directed public share issues, private placement
- Discussed trends in the global capital market and challenges faced by multinational service firms in raising capital globally

## References



Amihud, Y., Hameed, A., Kang, W., & Zhang, H. (2015). The illiquidity premium: International evidence. *Journal of Financial Economics, 117*, 350–368.

Bank for International Settlements. (n.d.). Retrieved from https://www.bis.org/bcbs/basel3.htm?m=2572

Benzie, R. (1992). *The development of the international bond market*. Retrieved from BIS https://www.bis.org/publ/econ32.pdf

BIS. (n.d.-a). *Debt securities issues and amounts outstanding*. Retrieved from Bank for International Settlements: https://stats.bis.org/statx/srs/table/c3?c=3P&p=20214

BIS. (n.d.-b). *Summary of debt securities outstanding*. Retrieved from Bank for International Settlements: https://stats.bis.org/statx/srs/table/c1

BIS. (n.d.-c). *Turnover of OTC foreign exchange instruments, by currency*. Retrieved from Bank for International Settlements: https://stats.bis.org/statx/srs/table/d11.3

BusinessWire. (2022, August 16). Sea Limited Reports Second Quarter 2022 Results. Retrieved from https://www.businesswire.com/news/home/20220815005740/en/Sea-Limited-Reports-Second-Quarter-2022-Results

Caramazza, F., & Aziz, J. (1998, April). *Fixed or Flexible? Getting the Exchange Rate Right in the 1990s*. Retrieved from IMF https://www.imf.org/external/pubs/ft/issues13/

Carlier, M. (2023, March 21). *BMW Group's key automobile markets 2022*. Retrieved from Statistica https://www.statista.com/statistics/267252/key-automobile-markets-of-bmw-group/

Chia, Y. M. (2017, May 8). *Tech company Garena raises US$550m, rebrands as Sea*. Retrieved from The Strait Times https://www.straitstimes.com/business/companies-markets/garena-raises-us550-million-rebrands-as-sea

Climate Bonds. (2022, November 9). Retrieved from Green Bond Market Hits USD2tn Milestone at end of Q3 2022 https://www.climatebonds.net/2022/11/green-bond-market-hits-usd2tn-milestone-end-q3-2022#:~:text=The%20total%20green%2C%20social%2C%20sustainability,45%25%20compared%20to%20Q3%202021.

CompaniesMarketCap. (2023). *Market capitalization of Maersk (DP4A.F)*. Retrieved from https://companiesmarketcap.com/maersk/marketcap/

Dornbusch, R. (1980). Exchange rate economics: Where do we stand? *Brookings Papers on Economic Activity, 1980*, 143–185.

Eiteman, D. K., Stonehill, A. I., & Moffett, M. H. (2016a). Foreign exchange rate determination. In D. K. Eiteman, A. I. Stonehill, & M. H. Moffett (Eds.), *Multinational business finance* (p. 262). Pearson.

Eiteman, D. K., Stonehill, A. I., & Moffett, M. H. (2016b). Transaction exposure. In D. K. Eiteman, A. I. Stonehill, & M. H. Moffett (Eds.), *Multinational business finance* (pp. 294–295). Pearson.

Eiteman, D. K., Stonehill, A. I., & Moffett, M. H. (2016c). Raising equity and debt globally. In D. K. Eiteman, A. I. Stonehill, & M. H. Moffett (Eds.), *Multinational business finance* (pp. 426–427). Pearson.

European Commission. (n.d.-a). Retrieved from https://finance.ec.europa.eu/sustainable-finance/disclosures/sustainability-related-disclosure-financial-services-sector_en#:~:text=The%20European%20Commission%20adopted%20on,Finance%20Disclosures%20Regulation%20(SFDR)

European Commission. (n.d.-b). Retrieved from https://finance.ec.europa.eu/capital-markets-union-and-financial-markets/company-reporting-and-auditing/company-reporting/corporate-sustainability-reporting_en

European Investment Bank. (2018, April 11). *Proof of Europe's crazy aversion to equity*. Retrieved from https://www.eib.org/en/stories/proof-of-europe-crazy-aversion-equity

Fan, J. P., Titman, S., & Twite, G. (2012). An international comparison of capital structure and debt maturiy choices. *Journal of Financial and Quantitative Analysis, 47*, 23–56.

Grant, R., & Soenen, L. (2004). Strategic management of operating exposure. *European Management Journal, 22*, 53–62.

Guild, J. (2022, March 15). *Why Singaporean tech firms grab and sea are seeing their stock prices tumble*. Retrieved from The Diplomat https://thediplomat.com/2022/03/why-singaporean-tech-firms-grab-and-sea-are-seeing-their-stock-prices-tumble/#:~:text=In%202017%2C%20Singapore's%20Sea%20Limited,rapidly%20expanding%20e%2Dcommerce%20sector

Hekman, C. R. (1985). A financial model of foreign exchange exposure. *Journal of International Business Studies, 16*, 83–99.

Hirschmann, R. (2022, December 12). *Number of monthly web visits on Shopee in Singapore from 1st quarter 2019 to 1st quarter 2022*. Retrieved from Statista https://www.statista.com/statistics/1012052/singapore-number-monthly-web-visits-shopee-quarter/#:~:text=Number%20of%20monthly%20web%20visits%20on%20Shopee%20Singapore%20Q1%202018%2DQ4%202021&text=In%20the%20fourth%20quarter%20of,the%20first%20quarter%20of

IMF. (n.d.-a). About the IMF. Retrieved from https://www.imf.org/en/About#:~:text=The%20IMF%20monitors%20the%20international,of%20its%20190%20member%20countries

IMF. (n.d.-b). The IMF in History. Retrieved from IMF https://www.imf.org/en/About/Timeline

IMF (n.d.-c). What is the IMF? Retrieved from IMF https://www.imf.org/en/About/Factsheets/IMF-at-a-Glance#:~:text=The%20IMF%20has%20three%20critical,policies%20that%20would%20harm%20prosperity

IMF. (2022, July 7). Annual report on exchange arrangements and exchange restrictions 2021. Retrieved from https://www.imf.org/en/Publications/Annual-Report-on-Exchange-Arrangements-and-Exchange-Restrictions/Issues/2022/07/19/Annual-Report-on-Exchange-Arrangements-and-Exchange-Restrictions-2021-465689

Kacperczyk, M. T., & Peydró, J.-L. (2022). Carbon emissions and the bank-lending channel. Working Paper.

Koetsier, J. (2021, December 27). *Top 10 most downloaded apps and games of 2021: tiktok, telegram big winners*. Retrieved from Forbes https://www.forbes.com/sites/johnkoetsier/2021/12/27/top-10-most-downloaded-apps-and-games-of-2021-tiktok-telegram-big-winners/?sh=635bb2a83a1f

Kumar, R. (2014). Stock markets, derivatives markets, and foreign exchange markets. In *Strategies of banks and other financial institutions: Theories and cases*. Academic Press.

Macro Trends. (n.d.). Sea—Stock price history. Retrieved from Macro Trends https://www.macrotrends.net/stocks/charts/SE/sea/stock-price-history

Maersk. (2020). *Accounting policies 2020*. Retrieved from https://investor.maersk.com/static-files/cb537fbf-22bd-4536-a34c-dfe35d0fc988

Malkiel, B. G. (2007). *A random walk down wall street: The time-tested strategy for successful investing*. W. W. Norton & Company.

McCauley, R. N., McGuire, P., & Wooldridge, P. (2021, September 20). *Seven decades of international banking*. Retrieved from BIS: https://www.bis.org/publ/qtrpdf/r_qt2109e.htm

McKinsey. (2022, March). *Private markets rally to new heights*. Retrieved from https://www.mckinsey.com/~/media/mckinsey/industries/private%20equity%20and%20principal%20investors/our%20insights/mckinseys%20private%20markets%20annual%20review/2022/mckinseys-private-markets-annual-review-private-markets-rally-to-new-heights-vf.pdf

Mulia, K. (2022, January 13). *As Shopee expands aggressively around the world, will it become the 'Amazon of emerging economies'?* Retrieved from KrASIA https://kr-asia.com/as-shopee-expands-aggressively-around-the-world-will-it-become-the-amazon-of-emerging-economies

Murdoch, S. (2021, September 10). *Singapore's Sea Ltd secures $6 billion in mega fund raising*. Retrieved from Reuters https://www.reuters.com/technology/sea-ltd-raises-about-6-billion-mega-fund-raising-2021-09-10/

Reeb, D. M., Mansi, S. A., & Allee, J. M. (2001). Firm internationalization and the cost of debt financing: evidence from non-provisional publicly traded debt. *Journal of Financial and Quantitative Analysis, 36*, 395–414.

Reuters. (2021, August 3). *Maersk lifts outlook as supply chain disruptions push up shipping rates.* Retrieved from https://www.reuters.com/business/shipping-giant-maersk-hikes-full-year-outlook-after-strong-second-quarter-2021-08-02/

Reuters. (2022, May 11). *EU proposes tax incentives for equity financing like those for debt.* Retrieved from https://www.reuters.com/business/finance/eu-proposes-tax-incentives-equity-financing-like-those-debt-2022-05-11/

Russell, J. (2017a, October 21). *Southeast Asia gaming and e-commerce firm Sea ends first day on NYSE up 8%.* Retrieved from TechCrunch https://techcrunch.com/2017/10/21/sea-closes-opening-day-on-nyse-up-8/?guccounter=1

Russell, J. (2017b, October 21). *Southeast Asia gaming and e-commerce firm Sea ends first day on NYSE up 8%.* Retrieved from TechCrunch https://techcrunch.com/2017/10/21/sea-closes-opening-day-on-nyse-up-8/

SeaMoney. (n.d.). Retrieved from https://www.seamoney.com/

SEC. (2017, September 22). Retrieved from https://www.sec.gov/Archives/edgar/data/1703399/000119312517291352/d363501df1.htm

SEC. (2022, March 21). Retrieved from https://www.sec.gov/news/press-release/2022-46

Statista. (2022, December 5). *SeaMoney quarterly active users Sea Limited Q4 2020-Q2 2022.* Retrieved from Statista https://www.statista.com/statistics/1349912/sea-limited-quarterly-active-users-of-seamoney/

Tawatnuntachai, O., & Yaman, D. (2008). Why do firms issue global bonds? *Managerial Finance, 34*, 23–40.

The Mercedes-Benz Group. (n.d.). *Daimler green finance investor report 2021.* Retrieved from https://group.mercedes-benz.com/dokumente/investoren/refinanzierung/daimler-ir-green-finance-investor-report-2021.pdf

The World Bank. (2022). *Fintech and the future of finance.* Retrieved from https://www.worldbank.org/en/publication/fintech-and-the-future-of-finance#:~:text=Fintech%20is%20transforming%20the%20financial,competition%2C%20while%20managing%20the%20risks

von Allmen, U. E., Jeasakul, P., Kang, H., & Khera, P. (2020). Macrofinancial considerations for assessing the impact of the COVID-19 pandemic. Retrieved from IMF https://www.imf.org/-/media/Files/Publications/covid19-special-notes/enspecial-series-on-covid19macrofinancial-considerations-for-assessing-the-impact-of-the-covid19-pan.ashx

WFE. (2021). *2021 Annual Statistics Guide.* Retrieved from https://www.world-exchanges.org/our-work/articles/2021-annual-statistics-guide

WFE. (2022). *Market Statistics—February 2022.* Retrieved from World Federation of Exchanges https://focus.world-exchanges.org/issue/february-2022/market-statistics

Yahoo Finance. (2022, August 16). *Sea limited reports second quarter 2022 results.* Retrieved from Yahoo Finance https://finance.yahoo.com/news/sea-limited-reports-second-quarter-103000649.html

## Further Reading

Eun, C. S., Resnick, B. G., & Chuluun, T. (2020). *International financial management.* McGraw Hill. This book provides a foundation for understanding and analyzing the international financial market. The book's first two parts introduce basic terms and concepts of international finance that are useful to comprehend the materials in this chapter.

Tirole, J. (2002). *Financial crises, liquidity, and the international monetary system.* Princeton University Press. The author, Jean Tirole, Winner of the 2014 Nobel Prize in Economics, examines the banking and currency crises in recent decades, the reforms being undertaken to prevent them, the role of the IMF in emerging markets and financial crises, and how global financial institutions might be restructured to this end. This book is helpful for someone keen to understand the economics behind the recent drive to improve the international financial architecture.

# Trade Protectionism and Economic Integration

## Contents




D. Klimkeit et al., *International Management in Service Firms*, Classroom Companion: Business,
https://doi.org/10.1007/978-3-031-50345-0_6

**Learning Outcomes**

After completing this chapter, you should be able to:

- Explain different reasons for state interventions in trade
- Outline the various instruments of state intervention in trade and discuss their impact on customers and companies
- Describe the role of GATT, the WTO, and GATS in global economic integration
- Discuss the effects of regional integration and distinguish stages of regional integration

## Introduction

6

While most economists agree that free trade is beneficial, most governments have put in place measures to restrict international trade and investment. This chapter reviews the various forms of protectionist measures and why governments put them in place. We will address the consequences of protectionism for customers and businesses. Then, we will outline global, regional, and bilateral economic integration that aims at liberalizing trade and investment. The role of international institutions like the World Trade Organization (WTO) will be discussed. We will give special attention to protectionism and liberalization in the trade of services and the Global Agreement on Trade in Services (GATS).

Work on telecommunications tower, image by Mike Goad from Pixabay

## Opening Case: Huawei in International 5G Mobile Networks

On first December 2018, Canadian police arrested Ms. Meng Wanzhou, Chief Financial Officer of Huawei, the Chinese telecommunications equipment manufacturer and daughter of Ren Zhengfei, founder of Huawei, in transit at Vancouver airport. She and Huawei were accused of evading American sanctions against Iran. Nine days later, two Canadian citizens, Michael Kovig and Michael Spavor, were detained in China. One thousand twenty days later, the "two Michaels," as they came to be referred to, and Ms. Meng were set free and simultaneously boarded home-bound planes in Canada and China. It became clear that the "two Michaels" were taken hostage by the Chinese authorities. Shortly before this prisoner exchange in the cold war style, a federal judge approved a plea deal between Ms. Meng and American prosecutors. Ms. Meng admitted to "material misrepresentations" about Huawei's business in Iran, and her prosecution was deferred.

This episode was just a facet of the conflict between Chinese firm Huawei and American authorities since Huawei was banned from selling its telecommunications equipment in the United States in 2012. So American mobile network operators renounced using it in their 5G network. When Donald Trump came into office as president of the United States, the conflict escalated further. Not content that only US network operators do not use Huawei equipment, he tried to convince his allies to ban Huawei from their mobile networks as well, particularly the 5G network. On 15th May 2019, authorities added Huawei to a list of companies that are seen to endanger US national security. Accordingly, Huawei's affiliates were banned from buying hardware or software from American firms without government approval. In doing so, the US administration used powers designed to stop the transfer of military technology.

There was a loophole, though, as suppliers could still sell items not produced in the United States. This loophole was to be closed in September 2019. Since then, the US administration has been seeking to stop companies worldwide from using software or hardware that originally comes from America to manufacture components based on Huawei's designs. This move has convinced allies like the United Kingdom to take a stricter stand on Huawei as well. Due to the effect on Huawei's supply chains, US regulation made using Huawei equipment riskier. So, on 14th July 2020, the British government also banned Huawei from its 5G network. Initially, Britain decided that Huawei components could be used in non-core parts of the 5G network if the required security procedures were applied. Australia had already banned Huawei in 2018. Japan passed respective laws. In June 2020, Canada and Singapore announced they would only use equipment from Nokia and Ericsson. In France, network operators not yet using Huawei were asked by the regulator not to introduce Huawei's equipment into their networks, and licenses for using Huawei were not renewed. Other countries like Germany, Italy, and New Zealand were more reluctant about a ban. Eventually, after a lengthy debate, the German government passed an IT security law in 2021 that did not mention Huawei. However, it stipulated a case-by-case assessment of critical components of 5G networks. Criteria have been defined, including whether a component's manufacturer is considered trustworthy. It is expected that due to the requirement for Chinese firms to collaborate with the state's intelligence service, Chinese manufacturers would not be regarded as trustworthy in this context.

Around 2019, Huawei overtook Nokia and Ericsson to become the world's largest telecommunications equipment provider. It played a significant role in changing the perception of China from being a location of cheap knockoffs to a home of technologically innovative firms. Huawei is owned by its employees and has a fierce self-belief. For China, it can play an important role in making the country more self-reliant. Concerns of governments that ban or contemplate banning Huawei go back to its role in providing backend equipment for mobile phone networks, especially, the fast 5G network. This network standard is seen as playing a pivotal role in the future for the advanced economic development of countries due to its enabling role for real-time applications such as the internet of things (IoT). Several governments worry that Huawei's equipment might contain a backdoor allowing the Chinese state to conduct espionage or even launch attacks against phone networks in case of conflict. Advocates of a ban on Huawei point to a Chinese law of 2017 that requires firms to cooperate with the country's intelligence services. The company argues that no evidence of such backdoors has been found and that allegations are politically motivated. Indeed, the issue is larger than the question of whether software codes contain backdoors or not. A technological cold war had developed between the United States and China. The discussion in Europe is instructive. Besides a fear of espionage, the risk of depending on an authoritarian regime for a vital part of a country's infrastructure is emphasized. This became acutely clear as Russia reduced or stopped the delivery of gas in 2022 in response to Western sanctions due to the invasion of Ukraine. The German interior minister pointed out that China might stop software updates for Huawei's equipment to pressure the government like Russia uses its gas to exert pressure. European companies Ericsson and Nokia will benefit from bans on Huawei, which aligns with the desire to promote European champions in modern high technology.

However, there are significant arguments put forward in Europe against banning Huawei. One is the weariness of worsening relationships with China and fears of Chinese countersanctions against European firms. Indeed, in late 2019, the Chinese ambassador to Germany threatened retaliation against German companies if they excluded Huawei from the 5G network in Germany. Connected to this, European governments did not want to be pressured by the American administration into taking a path they had not initiated themselves. Further reluctance against a ban came from the risk of falling further behind on modern technologies like IoT if the deployment of the 5G network gets delayed when Huawei is banned.

Telecommunications providers play an active role in countries debating their position on Huawei. For example, in Germany, Deutsche Telekom, which relies heavily on Huawei equipment, lobbied against any decision that might delay providing 5G to all its customers. By offering some basic 5G to 40 million customers in July 2020, drawing on Huawei and Ericsson equipment, it tried to present the situation as a done deal that can hardly be reversed. Mobile network operators in Europe play on the fear of falling behind on modern technology if a ban on Huawei causes delays in rolling out 5G. The situation varies from country to country because there is still no fully integrated single telecommunications market in the European Union. It is not straightforward for an operator from one EU country to provide services in another EU country. So, economies of scale are limited. There are more than 100 mobile phone operators in Europe. Operators rely strongly on Huawei in some markets and less in others. So, the cost of switching to alternative equipment providers would vary as well.

Sources: (Alvarez de Souza et al., 2022; Economist, 2019b, 2019c, 2020a, 2021a, 2021b).

**Questions**

1. Why has the Trump administration banned Huawei equipment for their 5G network and pressured other governments to do the same?
2. While strictly speaking, the ban on Huawei equipment relates to manufactured goods, how is it relevant for service providers?
3. How does a ban on Huawei equipment affect consumers, society, and various companies?

## Reasons for Protectionism

According to economic theory, countries are better off when each specializes in what it can do best and buys from other countries what they can do better. Following this is the idea of *free trade* that businesses and consumers should be free to buy from domestic or international sources and sell to customers at home and abroad without restrictions. Free trade is supposed to lead to more efficient utilization of resources when each country does what it can do most efficiently and leaves it up to others to do what they can do more efficiently. Most economists believe that free trade with minimum restrictions creates the most wealth and economic growth. Nevertheless, as seen in the opening case of Huawei, most governments put various forms of *protectionism* in place that restricts the free trade of goods and services.

**Protectionism**

*Protectionism* refers to governmental actions interfering in international trade to achieve economic, social, and political objectives (based on Daniels et al., 2021, p. 224)

| Economic Reasons | Non-Economic Reasons |
|---|---|
| • Reducing unemployment<br>• Protecting young industries<br>• Fighting dumping<br>• Strategic trade policy | • Human rights and the environment<br>• Foreign policy<br>• Protecting key industries<br>• Consumer protection<br><br>Service specific<br>• Protecting national culture<br>• Protecting data<br>• Preventing the spread of fake news |



**Fig. 6.1** Reasons for protectionism, own table based on content from Daniels et al. (2021), 224–223, Hill (2021), pp. 209–213, and own insights

Frequently, government intervention aims to protect domestic businesses from unwanted foreign competition. This frequently happens following lobbying by strong local interest groups. In the following section, we will review various, more sophisticated reasons why governments impose restrictions on international trade. First, we review economic arguments, then non-economic arguments. See Fig. 6.1 for an overview.

## Economic Arguments for Protectionism

**Reduce Unemployment:** Over the past decades, many manufacturing workers in developed countries like the United States lost their jobs as companies moved production to lower-cost countries, especially in Asia. While new jobs have sprung up in other areas, the mobility of workers is often limited, and some may lack the educational background that would enable them to learn the new skills needed for new jobs that open up. Especially small towns where most workers were employed by one firm are particularly hard hit if it closes down. Such unemployed workers are highly motivated to voice their discontent and have the time to do so. Politicians are tempted to respond by imposing import duties to protect local production from the low-cost international competition. Donald Trump's success in the 2016 presidential campaign in the United States could partly be attributed to this phenomenon. However, imports will become more expensive for consumers, as is the case for imported agricultural products in the European Union. Companies needing imported goods as product components will see their cost rise and may no longer be competitive. Also, the trade partner may retaliate by imposing import duties as well (Amiti et al., 2019; Economist, 2018d; Hart, 2012; Hill, 2021, p. 209; O'Leary et al., 2012).

The same argument also applies to the *service sector*. Some authors argue that resistance by service workers to new foreign market entrants will be less than in manufacturing. This is because, traditionally, most services require FDI to be where the customers are located. This would not reduce—we might add: perhaps even increase—net employment in the industry (Hoekman & Braga, 1997). However, drawing on modern information and communication technology, the cross-border trade of services (mode one) is increasingly possible. Many services have been offshored to outsourcing providers or shared service centers in countries like India or the Philippines, leading to significant job losses in developed countries where these tasks have been performed previously (Economist, 2019a). Therefore, other authors see the reduction of unemployment as a critical driver of protectionism in the service sector. For example, several attempts have been made in the United States to prevent the offshoring of service work by "Buy American" legislation (Borchert & Matoo, 2009).

**Protecting Young Industries:** Frequently, the argument is that nascent industries, especially in developing or emerging economies, need protection from strong, established global rivals until they have grown strong enough to brave competition. A case in point is the Brazilian automotive industry, which, so the argument goes, would not have been able to grow had there been full competition from the global automotive giants from the start (Humphrey, 2003). The reasoning is that initially, firms do not have the economies of scale they need to be competitive from a cost point of view. Only once they sell a large enough quantity can they survive the global competition without protection. Even the Global Agreement on Tariffs and Trade (GATT) officially acknowledges this as a legitimate reason for protective measures. The problem is that it is not easy to identify which nascent industries have the potential to be viable in the long run. The government may protect industries that will never be competitive, and the very protection provided reduces pressure to become competitive. In places like Taiwan and South Korea, new industries have thrived without government protection (Daniels et al., 2021, p. 226).

**Fighting Dumping:** You may have heard industry representatives claim that foreign competitors are dumping their products on the domestic market. We speak of dumping when products are sold abroad at a price that is either lower than the price charged in the home market or if sale prices do not cover the cost of products. Generally, dumping is seen as unfair competition. The rationale of companies engaging in dumping is that entering a new market with aggressively low-priced products can make many customers curious about their products and entice them to try them. Once established, the company raises prices and starts to make healthy profits. Typically, dumping requires either the firm engaging in dumping to obtain subsidies from its home government or cross-subsidize dumped products with revenues made elsewhere, such as in its home market. Typically, members of domestic industries who feel that foreign competing products are dumped appeal to the government with pleas to impose anti-dumping duties on the respective imported products. For example, US government has repeatedly raised anti-dumping charges against foreign steel makers, such as from China or Europe, to protect the US steel industry. In practice, it is not easy to prove that products are cheaper than what is charged to domestic wholesalers or that they are sold below production cost due to a lack of transparency and fluctuating exchange rates. Sometimes, critics accuse governments of arbitrarily using anti-dumping duties to avoid unwanted competition (Daniels et al., 2021, p. 229; Hill, 2021, p. 207).

**Strategic Trade Policy:** Some economists proposed *strategic trade policy* (Krugman, 1992). This policy applies especially to industries with strong economies of scale that only allow a few firms globally to be viable in this industry, as only a few firms can achieve the necessary scale. The argument goes that if a government believes that a promising local firm should and could be one of those few viable firms, it should subsidize the firm so it can achieve global scale and be a first mover or catch up with the first mover. Frequently, the aviation industry is given as an example. Boeing is said to have become a global champion due to subsidies from the US government in the 1950s and 1960s. At the same time, observers claim that Airbus has achieved parity with Boeing similarly due to support from European governments (Economist, 2005a).



## Non-Economic Arguments for Protectionism

Some arguments for protectionist measures are not primarily economic but political or social. Nevertheless, they often have economic implications.

**Human Rights and the Environment:** Many countries that have a democratic political system make it a point to support democracy and human rights in other countries as well. Trade sanctions are sometimes used to achieve this political aim, such as the sanctions against South Africa in the 1980s and 1990s due to the apartheid regime. By reducing revenues from international exports while reducing the sale of needed products to these countries, pressure is exerted on regimes to change their policies (Hill, 2021, p. 211). Internationally, a ban on trading ivory is in place to prevent the poaching of elephants for their tusks (Economist, 2019d).

**Foreign Policy:** Related to the previous argument, governments also use trade policy to further foreign policy objectives. Countries one wants to establish closer ties with may be given preferential trade treatment. In contrast, countries seen as not complying with international law or norms would be sanctioned by trade restrictions (Jordan, 1997). The probably longest-standing economic sanction is the embargo imposed in 1960 by the US administration against Cuba, aimed at weakening the communist regime in the hope that this would lead to a democratization of the country. Likewise, the US government has imposed a trade embargo against Iran, which is accused of seeking to build nuclear weapons. Following a 2015 agreement with Iran, sanctions were supposed to be relaxed but were reinforced by the Donald Trump administration (Economist, 2020c). More recently, many Western countries imposed a range of trade sanctions against Russia in 2022 due to its invasion of Ukraine to weaken the financing of the war and prevent Russia from invading other countries (Economist, 2022).

The following two arguments for government interventions in trade are *of particular relevance to service industries*. We will give examples from both service and non-service industries.

**Protect Key Industries:** Many countries protect specific national industries because, in times of crisis or conflict, they do not want to be dependent on other countries. This has been one reason for Germany to subsidize its coal mining industry until 2018, even though German coal mining was no longer competitive

Havana; Cuba has been the target of a US trade embargo since 1960, image by SweetMellowChill from Pixabay

due to its high cost. When Donald Trump put tariffs on imported steel, he invoked the importance of steel for national security (Economist, 2019e). Defense-related industries like aerospace or electronics are frequently protected (Hill, 2021, p. 209). In the Ukraine war crisis in 2022, Europe became acutely aware of its dependence on Russian oil and gas. This shows that the argument for reducing key industries' dependence on other countries cannot be dismissed entirely. However, sometimes the appeal to national security is questionable and only serves to protect domestic industries from international competition.

Government intervention to protect critical industries is *frequently applied to several service industries*. Governments often see utilities providing energy and water as essential industries they do not want to see dominated by foreign firms. The same applies to telecommunications, education, health care, media, and transportation, which are seen as essential for society and the country's independence. For example, even many poor developing countries make it a point to have their own national airline, which is also seen as a matter of prestige (Jones, 1996, pp. 169–172). The education of children and youngsters is frequently regarded as too sensitive to be in the hands of foreign-owned operators. The same applies to health care and media. In the opening case, besides data protection (see below), protecting key industries also explains the ban on Huawei in the United States and other countries.

**Consumer Protection:** Governments put in place regulations to guarantee the safety of consumers. This can, however, have the side effect of restricting or banning imports of products from other countries deemed unsafe or submitting them to lengthy safety controls (Hill, 2021, p. 210). In September 2020, when the first case of African Swine fever was detected in wild boar in the German state of Brandenburg, China imposed an import ban on pork from Germany, followed by Japan and Korea. Slaughter parts that used to go to Asia, such as paws, ears, and snouts, were difficult to market in Germany. So, the price of German pork had dropped, and pig farmers were making losses and raising fewer pigs. The closing down of several slaughterhouses was expected (Terpitz, 2022).

*In services* such as banking and insurance and especially in professional services such as legal advice, tax consulting, and medicine, governments regulate professional qualifications to ensure service quality to protect consumers. Professionals often need certification from a domestic professional body or university to practice. This is, however, frequently tied up with lobbying by domestic professional bodies and leading professional service firms who seek protection from unwanted competition (Quack & Schüßler, 2015).



## Service-Specific Arguments

The following arguments are specific to service industries, and all fall in the domain of non-economic arguments.

**Protection of National Culture:** Cultural industries such as music, literature, and media are service industries. Many governments have legislation intended to preserve the country's cultural heritage. The export of cultural artifacts is therefore restricted in many countries, especially developing countries that fear a sell-out of items of historical value. On the other hand, some countries restrict the import of cultural products suspected of driving out or marginalizing local cultural industries. This applies especially to audiovisual media, where some countries require a certain level of local content in media (Economist, 2003). In France, following a law passed in 1994, a minimum 40% quota of songs played on radio or television must be in French to push back English intrusion into French culture and support local cultural industries (France24, 2015). Several UNESCO conventions, such as the *Convention on the Protection and Promotion of the Diversity of Cultural Expressions* of 2007, support trade restrictions to preserve cultural heritage. However, they are discussed very controversially between proponents of trade liberalization and advocates of cultural diversity (Neuwirth, 2010).

**Protecting Data:** In today's world economy, data and information have become the most critical resource. And no one holds more data than social media firms like Meta and Tencent, e-commerce enablers like Amazon, and cloud hosting firms like Amazon Web Services and Google. As governments become aware of the importance of control over data, tech services like these are particularly vulnerable to politics and regulation. For example, Facebook and Twitter are not allowed to operate in China. India is very restrictive on US e-commerce firms like Amazon and requires that data from internet firms and financial services be only stored in India (Economist, 2019a). Partly, this is to protect consumers' data privacy, partly to avoid espionage by foreign secret services or businesses on sensitive data. This could relate to businesses' intellectual property and information relevant to a country's security. The ban on Huawei by the United States and other governments can also be seen in this context.

**Preventing the Spread of Fake News:** A different but related aspect regarding information is the widespread use of social media by authoritarian regimes to influence public opinion in other countries in their favor by spreading false information ("fake news") (Economist, 2019a). Russia has repeatedly been accused of spreading fake news in Western social media to destabilize democratic societies and interfere with elections. Instead of openly appearing as representatives of the country on whose behalf they post messages, agents ("trolls") appear under the apparent names of citizens of the country where the target audience resides. So, governments of democratic countries face the challenge of avoiding censorship of opinion while protecting their democracy from harmful covert foreign interference by authoritarian regimes (Economist, 2018a).

## Types of Trade Intervention and Their Impact on Businesses and Customers

Now that we have outlined the main arguments for why governments enact protectionist measures, we present the primary forms of state intervention in trade and investment and their effects in this section. ◘ Figure 6.2 provides an overview. Some interventions that are specific to services will be outlined.

| Instrument | Service Relevance |
|---|---|
| **Tariff** | Fees and immigration restrictions for the movement of persons<br>Services embodied in goods |
| **Quota** | Relate to the service provider |
| **Local content requirements** | Requirements for service providers |
| **Regulation & technical standards** | Certification of service providers<br>Restrictions on inputs for services |
| **Administrative procedures** | Certification requirements |
| **Subsidy** | Common in some industries |
| **Export tariffs & bans** | Political bans can apply |
| **Antidumping policies** | Less relevant |
| | **Flow of data via the internet** |
| | **Discriminatory access to networks** |

◘ **Fig. 6.2** Instruments of trade protectionism and their relevance to services, own table drawing, inter alia, on content from (Hoekman & Braga, 1997)

## Types of Trade Intervention

**Tariffs:** Tariffs are probably the most classic and well-known instrument of government trade intervention. A tariff is a tax on imported goods and services. In most cases, tariffs are calculated as a percentage of the imported good's value ("ad valorem"). In other cases, authorities levy a fixed amount of money per unit of imported goods, e.g., per barrel of oil ("specific tariff"). The immediate effect of a tariff is twofold: It generates revenues for the state and protects domestic firms from foreign competition by increasing the prices of imported goods. A further effect is on the consumers of imported goods as it makes the goods more expensive. So, government and domestic producers benefit while consumers are adversely affected. The same applies to businesses that buy imported goods made more expensive by a tariff. An effect that advocates of protective measures often forget is that domestic businesses that depend on imported goods become less competitive as the cost of their goods is driven up by the price increase of their imported inputs (Krugman et al., 2019, pp. 292–303). For example, US import duties on steel introduced by Donald Trump made products by American companies using steel as an important input more expensive and less competitive. As these industries account for a much higher share of US jobs than the steel industry, the net effect on US jobs is negative (Economist, 2018c).



*In services*, ad valorem tariffs levied at the border are difficult to apply. Due to the intangibility of services, customs officials can only observe service providers or consumers as they pass the border, but not a service crossing the border. The value of any service transaction is usually unknown to customs officials until it has been provided. *In services*, tariffs apply mainly to the cross-border movement of natural persons in terms of visa fees and entry or exit fees, analogous to specific tariffs for goods. In most countries, these are low and not a significant trade barrier. Immigration policies constitute a primary means of restricting market access for service providers. Tariffs are potentially more important for services embodied in goods, such as films, TV programs, or software sold on a CD or DVD. Indirectly, services can be affected by tariffs on goods that are necessary input for services, such as computers or telecommunications equipment (Hoekman & Braga, 1997).

Under the GATT agreement, tariffs were reduced significantly in the second half of the twentieth century. Instead, *non-tariff trade barriers* have increased in importance as governments have sought alternative ways of protectionism. These non-tariff barriers tend to be less easily detected by the WTO or others who monitor trade barriers.

**Quotas:** Import quotas restrict the physical volume or value of goods that companies can import into a country during a stipulated period, such as a year. Frequently, authorities issue licenses to firms that are allowed to import a stipulated quantity of a good into the country. For example, the United States has a quota for cheese imports, and licenses are given to certain trading companies that can import a specified number of pounds of cheese each year (Krugman et al., 2019, p. 308). Sometimes, importing countries negotiate quotas with exporting governments, which is somewhat misleadingly called a *voluntary export restraint*. Quotas can disadvantage smaller firms that do not have the resources to buy a license. Similar to tariffs, quotas can adversely affect firms that depend on imports as an input for their products (Krugman et al., 2019, p. 313). Due to an import quota of the EU agreed with the Chinese government for textiles from China, authorities held garments in ports, and retailers had empty shelves. Small retailers faced bankruptcy as they had already paid for the missing garments (Economist, 2005b).

*In services*, due to intangibility and simultaneity, quotas often relate to the service provider, not the services themselves. Regarding the movement of natural persons, they can consist of quotas for the immigration of personnel. An example of quantitative restrictions in services is the bilateral Air Service Agreements (ASA) and cargo-sharing arrangements administered by the UNCTAD Liner Code. ASA specifies which airlines can fly on a route, with which capacity, and which capacity airlines from third countries can offer. ASA are reciprocal and company-specific. Something similar applies to the Liner Code, giving shipping lines the right to acquire a specific part of shipping traffic (Hoekman & Braga, 1997).

**Local Content Requirements:** Local content requirements demand from manufacturers that a specific portion of the value added to a product sold in a market comes from local sources. This can mean local production or sourcing certain parts from local suppliers. In developing countries, governments frequently implement such policies to move up the value chain from the simple assembly of imported parts to becoming a producer of components. In developed countries, the motivation is often to maintain jobs in manufacturing industries that would otherwise move to lower-cost countries. The Buy American Act in the United States is an example, requiring government agencies to give preference to goods, of which at least 51% of the value-added is from the United States itself. Again, the impact is typically a price increase for consumers and businesses, as, without the requirement, production would usually happen in lower-cost locations (Krugman et al., 2019, pp. 315–317).

*In services*, local content requirements take on a different shape as they relate to the work of service staff rather than to the content of a tangible good. In some cases, they may be stricter. For example, several countries require that services such as legal advice, investment advice, insurance, or education must only be provided by residents or citizens of the respective country. Transportation of goods between two points within a country is sometimes only allowed to domestic providers (Hoekman & Braga, 1997). For example, in the European Union, a draft regulation was proposed: A truck driver from a home country (often in Eastern Europe) who delivers goods in a host country (often in Western Europe) is allowed to perform some additional local transportation within the host country before returning home. This was discussed very controversially (Schlautmann, 2018).

**Regulation and Technical Standards:** Many governments have precise requirements for products allowed to be sold within their borders. They can relate to safety standards for electrical equipment and motor vehicles, hygiene and content regulations for food, and requirements for labeling products. For example, in the European Union, there are strict regulations regarding genetically modified food that is considered undesired and therefore banned (Cavusgil et al., 2020, pp. 218–219). For consumers, such restrictions—besides ensuring safety—reduce the available goods and increase prices.

*In services,* this trade intervention is very relevant and mainly takes the shape of licensing or certification requirements for service firms, especially professional staff. Diplomas or certificates achieved abroad are frequently not recognized, both outlined above. In addition, environmental standards can apply to services such as emissions in the transport industry and restrictions on the number of visitors and zones allowed in tourism. This all adds up to restricting foreign service providers from offering their services (Hoekman & Braga, 1997). This is illustrated vividly by the opening case on possible bans on Huawei equipment, which affect telecommunications providers who use it in their 5G networks. Operators argue it would slow down the build-out of the network and make it more expensive.



**Administrative Procedures:** As tariffs have been reduced, governments' intent on protecting local businesses from international competition was becoming creative and devised bureaucratic administrative hurdles that are more difficult to pinpoint. Administrative procedures are bureaucratic regulations that make it difficult for foreign firms to enter the market. For example, customs procedures for imported goods may be lengthy and require much paperwork and inspections before goods can enter the market. This slows down the availability of goods for consumers. An example is a French regulation of 1982 that required all video recorders from Japan to be processed by a small customs office in Poitiers—far away from any port (Krugman et al., 2019, pp. 317–318).

*In services*, bureaucratic hurdles mainly relate to certification requirements for service providers addressed in the previous paragraph.

**Subsidies:** Subsidies are resources provided by governments to firms to facilitate exports or the production of goods at reduced prices to ensure the success of the firms in question in the face of international competition. Subsidies can take various forms, such as cash, low-interest loans, tax breaks, or government contracts at generous prices (Krugman et al., 2019, p. 305). The Chinese government is known for providing comprehensive subsidies to select companies, mainly state-owned enterprises, to facilitate their success in global markets (Economist, 2013a). WTO prohibits subsidies when they hinder free trade. However, what constitutes a subsidy in a particular case can be hard to define (Cavusgil et al., 2020, p. 220). For consumers, subsidies can make goods benefiting from subsidies cheaper than non-subsidized products.

*In services,* subsidies are also common in some industries, such as airlines. According to complaints by foreign airlines, airlines in the Gulf states, such as Emirates, Qatar Airways, and Etihad, owe their strong competitive position to subsidies worth billions of dollars (Economist, 2018b). Also, the construction, telecommunications, and rail transport sector receive subsidies in several countries. Especially subsidies for rail transport providers amount to 15–180% of the total value added (Hoekman & Braga, 1997).

**Export Tariffs and Bans:** Instead of on imports, sometimes tariffs are also placed on exports. In some cases, governments ban the export of some goods outright. This is to ensure enough supply of scarce goods in the country, aiming to boost national security and keep prices down by increasing supply to domestic customers (Hill, 2021, p. 206). This measure was used prominently at the beginning of the COVID 19 pandemic when governments restricted the export of scarce medical goods such as protective face masks (Fuest, 2020). An export ban can also be politically motivated and used as an instrument of foreign policy, for instance, in the sanctions against Russia due to the war in Ukraine addressed under the "foreign policy" argument above. In the importing country, the effect on consumers is higher prices in case of tariffs and the non-availability of goods in case of bans.

*In services*, the fact that tariffs are generally less relevant also applies to export tariffs specifically. Bans for political reasons can also apply to services, as seen in the sanctions against Russia, which can also affect some service firms.

**Antidumping Policies:** Also called *countervailing duties*, antidumping policies directly aim at penalizing foreign firms accused of dumping their products on the market. Therefore, antidumping duties are levied on imported goods like tariffs and aim to protect domestic firms from unfair competition. In 2016, about 6% of imports from China into the EU and about 9% of imports into the United States were subject to antidumping duties (Economist, 2017). This increases the cost of imported goods for consumers.

*In services,* antidumping duties tend to be less relevant.

## Service-Specific Interventions

The following two instruments are *specific to service industries.*

**Restrictions on Transborder Data Flows:** Service firms in industries like telecommunications, cloud services, and social media are impacted by government restrictions on the flow of data across borders. This can be based on protecting the data privacy of consumers and intellectual property of businesses or protecting minors from being exposed to pornography or other unwanted content on internet websites. Regulation can also amount to indirect barriers to trade and keep out foreign competitors (Hoekman & Braga, 1997). For example, India has banned 340 Chinese smartphone apps, including the popular TikTok and WeChat (Peer, 2022). Also, what was outlined above as an argument for trade interventions—protecting data—finds its counterpart in actual instruments of trade intervention addressed in this section. Due to the rising importance of digital data flows in the world economy, the term *digital protectionism* has been coined. Susan Aaronson argues that finding international rules to reduce digital protectionism will be difficult as it requires shared norms and definitions (Aaronson, 2019).

**Discriminatory Access to Distribution Networks:** To offer services, new service providers must access distribution networks or communication infrastructures, especially in the telecommunications industry. A dominant telecommunications carrier in a country may discriminate against service providers, for example, by rationing connection points to the infrastructure. In airfare, restrictions on ancillary services such as computer reservation systems or ground handling may reduce the competitiveness of a foreign airline entering a market. In the insurance industry, limitations on advertising can practically restrict market access (Hoekman & Braga, 1997).

## The Effect of Regulation on Businesses

The effect of trade interventions on consumers and business customers has been discussed above. Put shortly, most trade interventions hurt consumers and customers in the importing country, reducing the availability of goods and increasing prices, except for subsidies that lower the price of subsidized imported goods. We now want to discuss more systematically the effect on businesses.

**Effect on Foreign Companies:** For foreign companies, protectionist measures are all damaging. Measures like tariffs, country-specific technical standards, and administrative procedures increase the cost of their products entering as imports. Quantitative restrictions such as quotas reduce the salable quantity of products. Measures such as licensing requirements, technical standards, and administrative procedures delay market entry. The competitive advantage that businesses initially have is reduced by tariffs and subsidies for domestic competitors. Eventually, protectionist instruments may deter foreign firms from entering the market altogether.

6

**Effect on Domestic Companies:** The basic—and often desired—effect is that protectionist measures reduce foreign competition. Whether tariffs or non-tariff instruments, they typically constitute barriers that keep foreign firms away or make it cumbersome and expensive for them to enter the market. However, domestic businesses can also depend on inputs they import from abroad. Import restrictions reduce procurement options for domestic businesses either by banning their import or by raising their price so that it becomes prohibitive to buy them. As these inputs become more expensive, domestic businesses' cost increases, making their final product more expensive and, therefore, less competitive. Huawei is a case in point. So, protectionism typically benefits some domestic firms while it damages others. A sometimes-overlooked longer-term effect of protectionism is that even firms that may benefit from protection from foreign competition in the short term frequently become complacent. They invest less in innovation and feel under lower pressure to reduce costs. If protective measures are lifted one day, these firms may struggle to stand against the competition. This is, for example, the case in Brazil for industries like the automotive industry (Economist, 2012, 2016a).

## Economic Integration

The previous section has shown that protectionist measures frequently have many detrimental effects on both companies and consumers. After the World War II, the negative effect of protectionist policies became obvious. Governments understood that economic cooperation is required for their economic development. This led to creating institutions and agreements that aim at *economic integration*.

**Economic Integration**

*Economic integration* is a term used to describe political and economic agreements among nations and world regions in which preference is given to member countries (Daniels et al., 2021, p. 245)

**Fig. 6.3** Forms of economic integration, own diagram based on content from (Daniels et al., 2021, p. 245)

Economic integration can occur at three levels (see Fig. 6.3). Global integration means that most countries worldwide cooperate under the World Trade Organization (WTO) sponsorship. We speak of bilateral integration when two countries collaborate more closely, typically by reducing tariffs and other trade barriers. Regional integration refers to a group of countries collaborating more closely, forming an economic group or bloc, typically within one geographic region such as the European Union. Economic groups, whether bilateral or regional, play an important role in multinational enterprises. A company based in a country that is part of an economic group effectively has a larger market to address in which it can do business with fewer trade barriers (Daniels et al., 2021, p. 245). As Buckley et al. (2003) describe it, the "size of the country" is extended by an economic group, which is the key reason for pursuing economic integration. Even from a small state like Luxemburg, domestic companies can have a large home market as most trade barriers within the group—in this case, the European Union—have been removed. Companies not having their home base in an economic group can also benefit by conducting FDI in one group member country and then trading freely with other countries in that group. For example, many companies from China set up operations in Eastern Europe, frequently in Hungary, so that they can export from there to the rest of the European Union (Hanke, 2018).

We will now look at the three forms of economic integration more closely, primarily focusing on global and regional integration.

## Global Integration: GATT, the WTO, and GATS

### The GATT Agreement

During World War II, Western allies agreed that a new economic world order was needed to boost economic growth after the war. In 1941 Franklin Roosevelt and Winston Churchill drafted the Atlantic Charter to lower trade barriers and promote international economic cooperation. In 1947, 23 countries and territories signed the *Global Agreement on Tariffs and Trade (GATT)*. An intended formal organization to supervise the agreement never took effect at the time. International rules for trade in goods were set and enforced by the GATT agreement between 1949 and 1994 (Jackson, 2021, pp. 145–147). GATT aimed at abolishing quotas and reducing tariffs. The significant lowering of trade barriers contributed to an enormous increase in international trade in the second half of the twentieth century. A fundamental principle of GATT is "trade without discrimination." Member countries should open their borders the same way to each other. Related to this, the "Most favored nation" clause states that if a member country agrees with another member on reducing some tariffs, this should automatically apply to all other member countries unless the reduction is part of a comprehensive trade agreement. Over time, GATT also addressed some non-tariff barriers, such as industrial standards, government procurement, licensing, and subsidies. Members agreed that product standards for imported goods should be the same as for domestic ones. Most export subsidies were prohibited. Licensing procedures were streamlined. Over time, however, GATT encountered problems. Governments became more sophisticated at devising new trade barriers. Trade in services, which GATT did not address, became more important. GATT lacked the institutional setup to enforce countries' compliance with the agreement. This led to the creation of the *World Trade Organization (WTO)* in 1995 (Daniels et al., 2021, pp. 245–246).



## The World Trade Organization (WTO)

The WTO adopts and continues to apply the principles and agreements reached under the GATT but extends them. Now, services are also addressed, as well as the issue of intellectual property. WTO now has 164 member countries, representing 98% of world trade. Decisions are made by all members, typically by consensus. Parliaments of member countries then ratify the agreements. The functions of WTO are to administer the existing trade agreements, provide a forum for further trade negotiations, handle the settlement of trade-related disputes between members, monitor trade policies, and provide technical assistance and advice to developing countries (WTO, 2021b).

**Dispute Settlement:** The WTO has instituted a formal mechanism for settling trade disputes. This allows enforcing the rules of WTO. When governments believe that a member has breached their rights under the agreements of WTO, they can bring the case to WTO. Experts of WTO will analyze the case. After several steps, a panel of experts can pronounce a ruling. More than 600 cases have been brought to the WTO. The rulings of WTO have a binding character. If a member does not comply with the ruling, the other party has the right to apply countervailing measures, that is, sanctions (WTO, 2021b). Recently, WTO has pronounced on two separate cases, both supported by the EU for Airbus and supported by the US government for Boeing, as breaching WTO rules. Following this, the Biden administration and the European Commission have reached an agreement on the long-running dispute over unfair subsidies for these two airline manufacturers (Handelsblatt, 2021).

## The Global Agreement on Trade in Services (GATS)

The GATS agreement entered into force in 1995. All members of the WTO have signed it, thereby taking on the resulting obligations. GATS is the first multilateral agreement to treat trade in services. The agreement aims to contribute to the expansion of trade "under conditions of transparency and progressive liberalization and as a means of promoting the economic growth of all trading partners and the development of developing countries" (WTO, 2013, p. 2). The contribution of GATS to services trade is intended to be threefold:
(a) ensure increased transparency and predictability of relevant rules,
(b) provide a common framework for international transactions,
(c) promote progressive liberalization of services trade through negotiations.

**Application:** The GATS rules apply to any measure taken by member governments that affect the trade in services. It relates to a broad range of services from business, communication, financial, and tourism and travel-related services to recreational, cultural, sporting events, and many more. A notable exception is government services that are "supplied neither on a commercial basis nor in competition with one or more service suppliers" (WTO, 2013, p. 4). Examples include police, fire protection, monetary policy operation, and social security.

**Transparency:** As outlined in the first of the three contributions by GATS above, providing transparency is a key objective of GATS. Members of the agreement must promptly publish any measures they take that affect GATS's operation. They must provide annual information to the GATS council on all relevant legal and regulatory changes. Members also need to establish inquiry points where other members can obtain specific information on request (WTO, 2013).

**Most Favored Nation, Market Access, and National Treatment:** The *most favored nation* (MFN) treatment of GATT also applies to service firms under the GATS agreement. So, any favorable market access treatment granted by one member country to another automatically applies to all members. For a maximum period of 10 years, exemptions are possible. Comprehensive trade agreements are an exception. Otherwise, economic groups such as the European Union that provide preferential treatment to members could not exist. Members are free to decide in which service sectors and for which of the four modes of supply they are willing to grant which exact level of *market access* to foreign providers. The level of market access can relate to restrictions such as the number of service providers, the number of operations, or the number of natural persons supplying a service. The desired state is that none of these restrictions to market access are maintained, but each country can decide which of these restrictions it is willing to lift in which service sector. When a government commits to lifting such a restriction, this is called an "obligation" in WTO language. Each member enters a set of obligations, and they are made transparent. Besides the level of market access, *national treatment* is the term used for a second set of legal obligations that member countries enter. National treatment "implies the absence of all discriminatory measures that may modify the conditions of competition to the detriment of foreign services or service suppliers" (WTO, 2013, p. 6). In other words, foreign service providers should be treated like domestic providers. They should be granted equal opportunities to compete with domestic providers. As with market access, members can decide to what extent they grant complete national treatment in a sector or attach limitations to national treatment, in other words, which obligations they enter regarding national treatment (WTO, 2013).

**Unconditional General Obligations:** While many obligations under GATS are not mandatory for each sector of each member country, as outlined above, some of them are *unconditional general obligations*. These comprise (WTO, 2013, pp. 6–7):

- *MFN treatment*: MFN treatment generally applies to all sectors and all members; only limited exceptions for a limited period upon the accession of a member are allowed
- *Transparency*: Members must publish promptly all measures affecting the agreement and need to establish an inquiry point
- *Domestic regulation*: Members must have mechanisms where service suppliers may seek legal redress
- *Monopolies*: Members must ensure that monopolies do not act in a manner inconsistent with the MFN treatment
- *Business practices*: Members must consult, upon request, with other members on practices that restrain competition intending to eliminate such practices
- *Subsidies*: Members adversely affected by subsidies may request a consultation, and members need to give "sympathetic consideration" to such requests



**Limitations to National Treatment:** You may have noticed that national treatment is not one of the unconditional general obligations. The national treatment principle under GATS is more limited than under the GATT agreement. It only applies to specific sectors and modes of supply for which a member has voluntarily taken on an obligation. This is due to the nature of the services. National treatment of goods does not preclude tariffs. It does not mean complete free trade. As mentioned in the first part of this chapter, tariffs are challenging to implement for many services. So, universal national treatment would mean providing free access for foreign service providers, and virtually no WTO member is willing to grant this to all sectors and modes of trade (WTO, 2013).

**Trade Liberalization Under the GATS:** When the GATS agreement took effect in 1995, it did not include the ambitious liberalization of services trade. Instead, it took stock of the status quo and provided transparency and a framework for rule-based services trade. The further liberalization of services trade was written into the mandate for the future. As scheduled, in 2000, new talks were started; however, progress was limited and applied only to some sectors (WTO, 2013).

**Services Domestic Regulation:** As outlined above, regulations and technical standards are important barriers to trade in services. WTO has found that the cost of trading services is twice as high as that of goods. To a large extent, this is due to regulatory differences between countries and nontransparent and cumbersome regulations. Therefore, in 2017 a group of 59 WTO member countries formed an initiative on Services Domestic Regulation. The objective was to reduce the effects of licensing and qualification requirements and procedures, and technical standards for services. In September 2021, negotiations were concluded with an agreement on a uniform set of "regulatory disciplines." Participating members agreed to include respective obligations relating to services domestic regulation in their commitments to WTO under the GATS agreement. These obligations aim to make the regulatory environment more conducive to business and lower trade costs for services suppliers looking to access foreign markets (WTO, 2021a). As of June 2022, 70 countries accounting for 92.5% of world services trade have joined the initiative (WTO, 2022).

## Bilateral and Regional Integration

Progress in trade negotiations under WTO for further liberalization largely halted at the end of the first decade of the twenty-first century. It became increasingly difficult to find an agreement for further trade liberalization among the members of the WTO. Especially interests of developing and developed countries diverged significantly. Consequently, many bilateral and regional agreements have been concluded based on the assumption that reaching an agreement between two or a few countries is easier than reaching an agreement between all 164 WTO members. For regional integration, also geographic, cultural, political, and economic factors can play a facilitating role. Nevertheless, as the case of the CETA agreement between Canada and the European Union shows, bilateral agreements are not necessarily easy to reach.

A regional agreement creates an *economic bloc*. Some of the most well-known regional economic blocs are the European Union (EU), the US–Mexico–Canada Agreement (USMCA, formerly NAFTA), the Association of Southeast Asian Nations (ASEAN), and the Mercado Común del Sur (Mercosur) in South America.

## Effects of Regional Integration

Now, what effect does regional economic integration have on trade and businesses? First of all, it *creates trade*. As trade barriers come down, trade between countries that are members of the economic bloc increases because it becomes easier and cheaper to trade across borders. Consumers have a broader choice of goods and services at lower prices. Investments will shift to countries with comparative advantage in factors of production, such as inexpensive yet qualified labor (Balassa, 2011, pp. 25–29). In North America, many companies set up production in Mexico due to lower costs than in the United States. The same happened in the European Union, where many companies invested in Eastern Europe to benefit from lower costs as Eastern European countries joined the EU. Companies export from these countries to higher-cost countries such as the United States in USMCA or Germany in the EU.

At the same time, however, regional integration *diverts trade*. Even when a new economic bloc does not raise trade barriers for non-members, barriers become relatively higher for trade with non-members. As trade with members becomes much cheaper and easier, many businesses will shift their purchasing to suppliers from the new economic bloc. Suppliers from non-member countries will be left behind. Similarly, many consumers will shift their consumption to products and services from the now cheaper member countries. Trade gets diverted to some extent. This also has an impact on investments. As mentioned above, companies from outside an economic bloc will now have strong incentives to invest in one member state to reach a large common market within the economic bloc without trade barriers (Balassa, 2011, pp. 25–29). Investments by Chinese firms in the European Union are a case in point that combines investment in a trading bloc to address the large market and investing in lower-cost members, as frequently investments happen in Eastern European EU members.



For businesses within an economic bloc, integration means they can now address a larger home market (remember, "the country becomes bigger"). Through this, they can achieve *economies of scale*, that is, lower the cost per unit of output as the fixed cost of the operation spreads across a larger number of units. This, in turn, can lead to a further increase in trade (Balassa, 2011, pp. 120–143).

However, it also means *increased competition* for businesses within the economic bloc. As competing businesses in other member countries can now sell easily to customers in their home country, they face more competition than before (Balassa, 2011, pp. 101–119). As a consequence, for example, in the European Union, many banks sought to acquire other firms or merge with them to increase their size and be better positioned in competition (Economist, 2020b). For consumers, increased competition means lower prices for higher-quality goods and services (Balassa, 2011, p. 57).

The following insert shows a case of trade generation, economies of scale, and increased competition in a service industry.

**Luxury Hotels Have Washing Done in Poland**

When Danuta Jirgl gently strokes the large "A" on the breast pocket of the fluffy bathrobe, she often imagines which prominent hotel guest might be wearing "her" bathrobe in Hotel Adlon the following day. Perhaps Brad Pitt or Madonna? There is a distance of only 140 kilometers between her and the world of glamor, a 2-hour lorry ride, and a national border. There are worlds that separate the Polish washerwoman in Gryfino from the life of Berlin's luxury hotels, where she could barely afford a room for the night with her 450 euros a month. A little taste of the big, wide world arrives every day with a dozen delivery vans from Berlin laundry Fliegel to Gryfino. There, in a three-shift system, 50 Polish launderers per shift wait for the bedding, towels, and table linen from almost 40 Berlin hotels. Laundry driver Jacek Madej is one of the links to the other world. Every day, every week, he and his colleagues drive clean laundry from Gryfino to Berlin in the morning and usually deliver the dirty washing from the hotels to the laundry. Twenty-four hours after pick up, the laundry returns to the hotel ready for the wardrobe, in all weather, and top quality. Top quality is the credo of the laundry experts, and

Hotel laundry service; In a trading bloc, services such as laundry can move to low-cost locations, image by Tania Dimas from Pixabay

hotels confirm their excellent quality and enormous reliability. "We do not define ourselves by price, but exclusively by quality," assures manager Franz Josef-Wiesemann. Towels are even folded by hand in the desired appearance. "At this price, no one in Berlin can afford it," explains Wiesemann. At any rate, the Berlin hotels are impressed with the service and quality of the Fliegel laundry. And the clientele is growing steadily.

Note: This case is based on a newspaper article from 2006. Many things will likely have changed since then. Nevertheless, the case shows how creating an economic bloc such as the European Union can impact trade in a service industry.

Source: based on (Stengel, 2006)

## Stages of Regional Integration

When regional integration is discussed, terms like "free trade area," "customs union," or "common market" are frequently used. What is the difference between them? These terms can be seen as different levels or *stages of regional integration*, from the free trade area with the lowest level of integration to the economic union with the highest level (Balassa, 2011, p. 2, see ◘ Fig. 6.4).

**Free Trade Area:** The free trade area is the most common type of economic integration. Here, member countries have agreed to eliminate tariffs and other barriers to trade. Each member, however, continues to apply its own trade policy

| | Trade Barriers Removed | Common External Tariffs | Free Movement of Goods, People and Capital | Common Monetary and Fiscal Policy |
|---|---|---|---|---|
| Free-Trade Zone | + | | | |
| Customs Union | + | + | | |
| Common Market | + | + | + | |
| Economic Union | + | + | + | + |

**Fig. 6.4** Levels of regional integration, own diagram based on (Cavusgil et al., 2020, p. 230)



toward non-member countries (Cavusgil et al., 2020, p. 229). This can be seen by the fact that each member may apply different tariffs for goods and services imported from a particular third country. USMCA (the former NAFTA, comprising Canada, Mexico, and the US) is an example of a free trade area.

**Customs Union:** A customs union is based on the concept of the free trade area but goes one step further. External trade policy is harmonized to apply common tariffs and non-tariff trade barriers for imports from non-member countries. Agreeing on a joint external tariff can be challenging between countries that formerly had their own tariffs. MERCOSUR (a South American trade bloc) is an example of a customs union. Each third-party company faces the same tariffs in each MERCOSUR country (Cavusgil et al., 2020, p. 230).

**Common Market:** Building on the customs union, in a common market, the factors of production such as labor and capital, goods, and services can move freely within the economic group. This is the case in the European Union. Workers from EU member countries have the right to work in any other member country. Firms can transfer capital between their various operations within the EU (Cavusgil et al., 2020, p. 230). This led to concerns in Western European countries about an influx of cheap labor from countries like Poland, Bulgaria, and Romania when they joined the EU. So, a transition period has been agreed upon. In the meantime, economic development in countries like Poland created many reasonably paid jobs, reducing the incentive to move West for work (Wagner & Hassel, 2016).

**Economic Union:** Based on the common market, in an economic union, a common fiscal and monetary policy exists. A joint monetary policy requires having fixed exchange rates and the free convertibility of currencies. A single currency might be introduced, like the Euro in the EU. Countries aim for harmonization of their tax policies. This further facilitates the movement of products and production factors within the group (Cavusgil et al., 2020, p. 230). Among the members of the Eurozone, the exchange rate risk has been eliminated, and prices have become comparable. The EU is intended to be an economic union. However, it is a somewhat incomplete one as some members have not (yet) introduced the Euro, and a common fiscal policy is not yet realized.

## Review Questions

1. Define and explain the concept of "protectionism."
2. Outline the different arguments for protectionist measures.
3. Why do many governments engage in trade interventions despite the many benefits of free trade?
4. Explain the different types of trade intervention.
5. What are the effects of trade interventions on consumers and businesses?
6. Outline the GATT and GATS agreements and the role of the WTO.
7. How can the characteristics of services explain the differences between GATS and GATT?
8. Explain the various effects of regional integration.
9. Outline the stages of regional integration.
10. Explain what a regional economic bloc like the EU means for a company in a service industry of your choice.
11. What is your position on bilateral free trade agreements such as CETA?
12. Discuss whether to allow Huawei equipment in 5G mobile phone networks.

## Closing Case: The Struggle for the Ratification of CETA

"HEY, Canada, fuck you." As a result of a hack, this tweet from the Belgian foreign minister's account went viral on Twitter. Later, it was replaced with a friendly message: "Keep calm and love Canada." However, political decisions in Belgium are more in line with the original message. On 14th October 2016, the regional parliament of Wallonia voted to block a trade deal between the European Union and Canada, the Comprehensive Economic and Trade Agreement (CETA).

Europe has had a range of sectoral trade agreements with Canada since the 1970s. As the name suggests, CETA is meant to be a much more comprehensive treaty. Under negotiation since 2009, on 18th October 2013, an agreement in principle was reached on a deal between the European Commission and the Canadian government. Besides abandoning tariffs and extending import quotas, trade and investment in services are to be liberalized. Procurement by governments will be opened up for companies from the other continent. Takeover bids by foreign firms will be treated equally to bids from domestic firms. Especially important to services, certificates, for example, for engineers and architects, will be mutually recognized. Gaps in the protection of intellectual property will be closed. Proponents argue that consumers will be better off, increasing choice and reducing prices. The agreement would create jobs and help exporters. Small firms that struggle to go through a second round of safety tests would benefit from harmonized standards. Global norms would be set by Europe and North America rather than by other powers in the world. The European Commission believes CETA can boost bilateral trade by 23% or US$36 billion. According to one estimate, CETA could make Europe €11.8 billion richer per year. On fifth July 2016, the European Commission informed that the deal needs ratification by 36 parliaments, national and regional, in addition to the approval from the

European Council and the European Parliament.

Canada should be the least controversial of all nations with whom the EU plans to reach a trade agreement. In reality, there is much controversy, both among governments and the general public. Several countries have complaints against aspects of the deal: Bulgaria and Romania disagree that their citizens still need to apply for a visa to Canada, unlike other Europeans. In April 2016, the Dutch parliament passed a motion to prevent CETA from applying provisionally as intended, and the Walloon parliament voted against it. In Belgium, Walloon farmers who receive substantial subsidies fear cheap Canadian competition. The same applies to France.

Many Europeans fear CETA will reduce environmental standards, customer rights, and labor conditions. The biggest target for protesters is the Investor-State Dispute Settlement (ISDS) mechanism. It allows firms who invest abroad to sue governments that make decisions that damage their interests. For this, initially, as is usual for such agreements, a court of private arbitrators was planned. As a reaction to protests, private courts have been replaced by public courts, and their transparency has been improved, but protesters still do not agree. According to the European Centre for International Political Economy in Brussels, in no other country have protests been as strong as in Germany. On 27th September 2016, more than 100,000 protesters in a dozen cities across Germany voiced their concerns against CETA and TTIP, the planned free trade agreement between the EU and the US that was under negotiation at the time under the slogan "Stop CETA and TTIP!." Following approval by the European Parliament, since 27th September 2017, significant parts of CETA have been provisionally applied. Activists filed a case against the provisional application of parts of CETA before ratification by all governments at the German supreme court.

After a stalemate of 5 years, 2022 finally saw progress in CETA. In March 2022, the German supreme court dismissed the case against the provisional application of parts of CETA. This created pressure for the new German three-party governing coalition to act. The pressure was increased when Germany applied sanctions against Russia and lost Russia as a trading partner due to the war in Ukraine. There was an increasing awareness that the omission of trade with Russia needs to be compensated with increased trade with other countries on friendly terms with the EU. The German government decided to approve CETA but requires an interpretation statement to be added to the agreement. This would avoid renegotiating the actual treaty but appease the Green Party's and its electorate's concerns. The CETA treaty contains legal terms such as "indirect expropriation" or "unfair treatment," which are criticized as fuzzy and now to be stated more precisely. The German government wants investment protection declarations to be possible only in cases of direct expropriation and discrimination in clearly defined cases. The government sought approval from the European Commission and the Canadian government for these clarifications. However, besides Germany, governments of 11 other countries in the EU had not ratified CETA yet as of summer 2022. It is expected, though, that if Germany agrees, this will also lead to a jolt in other countries. As Chrystia

Skyline of Toronto, image by James Wheeler from Pixabay

Freeland, the Canadian trade minister, put it in Brussels in 2016:

> If the EU cannot do a deal with Canada, I think it is legitimate to say: Who the heck can it do a deal with? (Economist, 2016b)

Sources: (Delhaes et al., 2022; Economist, 2013b, 2016b, 2016c, 2016d, 2016e; Herwartz et al., 2022; Olk, 2022).

**Questions**

1. Given the many benefits of free trade, why is there so much controversy about the CETA agreement?
2. Why is it important for the EU in the situation around 2022 to finally ratify CETA?
3. Why have so many bilateral agreements like CETA been initiated over the past decade?

**Summary**

This chapter

- Outlines the concept of *protectionism*, defined as "governmental actions interfering in international trade to achieve economic, social, and political objectives."
- Explains *economic arguments* and *non-economic arguments* as well as *service-specific arguments* for state interventions in trade
- Outlines different *types of trade intervention*
- Explains the concept of *economic integration*, defined as "political and economic agreements among nations and world regions in which preference is given to member countries"

- Explains key institutions that play a role in *global integration*: the Global Agreement on Tariffs and Trade (GATT), the World Trade Organization (WTO), and the Global Agreement on Trade in Services (GATS)
- Discusses the effects of *regional integration* on trade and businesses
- Explains four *stages of regional integration*: free-trade area, customs union, common market, and economic union Stengel (2006)



## References


Aaronson, S. A. (2019). What are we talking about when we talk about digital protectionism? *World Trade Review, 18*(4), 541–577.

Alvares de Souza Soares, P., Koch, M., & Neuerer, D. (2022). IT-Sicherheit: Bundesregierung droht Huawei mit Rausschmiss. *Handelsblatt*, 2022, July 25(141), 8–9.

Amiti, M., Redding, S. J., & Weinstein, D. E. (2019). The impact of the 2018 tariffs on prices and welfare. *Journal of Economic Perspectives, 33*(4), 187–210.

Balassa, B. (2011). *The theory of economic integration (Routledge Revivals)*. Taylor & Francis Group.

Borchert, I., & Matoo, A. (2009). *The crisis-resilience of services trade.* The World Bank Development Research Group. Policy Research Working Paper. Retrieved from https://openknowledge.worldbank.org/handle/10986/4108

Buckley, P. J., Clegg, J., Forsans, N., & Reilly, K. T. (2003). Increasing the size of the 'country': Regional economic integration and foreign direct investment in a globalized world economy. In P. J. Buckley (Ed.), *The changing global context of international business*. Palgrave Macmillan.

Cavusgil, S. T., Knight, G., & Riesenberger, J. R. (2020). *International business: The new realities* (5th ed.). Pearson.

Daniels, J. D., Radebaugh, L. H., Sullivan, D. P., & Click, R. W. (2021). *International business: Environments & operations* (17th ed.) Pearson.

Delhaes, D., Olk, J., & Volkery, C. (2022, April 25). Schwachpunkt Handelspolitik. *Handelsblatt, 2022*(79), 11.

Economist. (2003, September 11). *Turning it off: Lighter regulation is this season's hit*. Economist.

Economist (2005a). Boeing and airbus: Air war. *Economist.*

Economist. (2005b, June 23, August 25). Knickers in a twist. *Economist.*

Economist. (2012, August 20). Untangling the custo Brazil. *Economist.*

Economist (2013a, April 27). China's economy: Perverse advantage. *Economist.*

Economist. (2013b, October 26). Canada doesn't get any sexier than this. *The Economist.*

Economist. (2016a, July 2). Of legumes and liberalisation. *The Economist.*

Economist. (2016b, July 16). Fear of the maple menace: The EU-Canada trade deal. *Economist*

Economist. (2016c, September 16). Why Germans are protesting against free trade. *The Economist.*

Economist. (2016d, September 17). Fortress mentality: Germans against trade. *Economist.*

Economist. (2016e, October 22). Wallonia is adamantly blocking the EU's trade deal with Canada. *Economist.*

Economist. (2017, December 7). China takes on the EU at the WTO. *Economist.*

Economist. (2018a, February 22). Russian disinformation distorts American and European democracy. The Economist.

Economist. (2018b, May 14). Airlines in America fail in their campaign against the Gulf carriers. *Economist.*

Economist. (2018c, August 9). Tariffs on steel and aluminium are creating some winners. The Economist.

Economist. (2018d, December 13). Trade war has given agricultural merchants a boost. The Economist.

Economist. (2019a, January 24). Globalization has faltered: It is now being reshaped. *Economist.*

Economist. (2019b, February 23). America and its allies disagree on Huawei. *Economist.*

Economist. (2019c, May 16). Donald Trump gets tough on Huawei. *Economist.*

Economist. (2019d, August 8). The ban on trading ivory is unfair but necessary. The Economist.
Economist. (2019e, December 5). The trump administration's trade policies clash with each other. The Economist.
Economist. (2020a, July 18). America's war on Huawei nears its endgame. The Economist.
Economist. (2020b, September 10). Why are European banks merging? The Economist.
Economist. (2020c, November 26). Donald Trump's sanctions in the Middle East have had little effect. The Economist.
Economist. (2021a, September 25). As Canada frees a Huawei boss, China lets two Canadians out of jail. *Economist*.
Economist. (2021b, October 23). Huawei should dissolve, disperse and seed China's high-tech future. The Economist.
Economist. (2022, March 12). Amid Russia's war, America Inc reckons with the promise and peril of foreign markets. The Economist.
France24. (2015). *French radio goes to war with language quotas in fight for musical freedom*. Retrieved from https://www.france24.com/en/20150928-france-radio-stations-rebel-over-french-song-quotas-stromae-boycott
Fuest, C. (2020, July 14, 2020). Corona verändert die Globalisierung, aber beendet sie nicht. *Handelsblatt*, (133), 48.
Handelsblatt. (2021, June 16, 2021). Handelskonflikt. *Fünf Jahre Waffenstillstand*, (113), 4.
Hanke, T. (2018, January 16). Protektion ohne Protektionismus. *Handelsblatt, 2018*(11), 12.
Hart, M. (2012). *Breaking free: A post-mercantilist trade and productivity agenda for Canada* (pp. 1–27). C.D. Howe Institute, Commentary No. 357.
Herwartz, C., Koch, M., & Olk, J. (2022, July 27). Deutschland ändert Handelsstrategie. *Handelsblatt, 2022*(121), 7.
Hill, C. W. L. (2021). *International business: Competing in the global marketplace* (13th ed.). McGraw-Hill Education.
Hoekman, B., & Braga, C. A. P. (1997). Protection and trade in services: A survey. *Open Economies Review, 8*(3), 285–308.
Humphrey, J. (2003). Globalization and supply chain networks: The auto industry in Brazil and India. *Global Networks, 3*(2), 121–141.
Jackson, S. D. (2021). *International trade in services: Effective practice and policy*. Routledge.
Jones, G. (1996). *The evolution of international business: An introduction*. Routledge.
Jordan, P. S. (1997). Country sanctions and the international business community. In American Society of International Law (Ed.), *Proceedings of the annual meeting* (pp. 333–342). Cambridge University Press.
Krugman, P. R. (1992). Does the new trade theory require a new trade policy? *The World Economy, 15*(4), 423–441.
Krugman, P. R., Obstfeld, M., & Melitz, M. J. (2019). *Internationale Wirtschaft: Theorie und Politik der Außenwirtschaft*. Pearson Deutschland.
Neuwirth, R. J. (2010). The culture and trade debate continues: The UNESCO convention in light of the WTO reports in China—Publications and audiovisual products: Between amnesia or Déjà-vu. *Journal of World Trade, 44*, 1333–1356.
O'Leary, C., Eberts, R., & Pittelko, B. (2012). Effects of NAFTA on US employment and policy responses. *OECD Trade Policy Working Papers 131*.
Olk, J. (2022, July 11). Brüssel und Berlin machen Tempo bei Handelsabkommen. *Handelsblatt*, 2022(131), p. 10.
Peer, M. (2022). Es geht auch ohne Chinas Techriesen. *Handelsblatt, 2022, August 11*(154), 23.
Quack, S., & Schüßler, E. (2015). Dynamics of regulation of professional service firms: National and transnational developments. In L. Empson, D. Muzio, J. Broschak, & B. Hinings (Eds.), *The Oxford handbook of professional service firms* (pp. 48–70). Oxford University Press.
Schlautmann, C. (2018, July 5). Straßengüterverkehr: Vorfahrt fürs Lohndumping. *Handelsblatt*, 2018(127), p. 17.
Stengel, M. (2006, April 8). Luxushotels lassen in Polen waschen. *Berliner Morgenpost*.
Terpitz, K. (2022, August 18). Tönnies, Vion & Co.: Wann schließt der erste große Schlachthof? *Handelsblatt, 2022*.

Wagner, B., & Hassel, A. (2016). Move to work, move to stay? Mapping atypical labour migration into Germany. In *Labour mobility in the enlarged single European market* (Vol. 32, pp. 125–158). Emerald Group Publishing Limited.

WTO. (2013). *The general agreement on trade in services: An introduction*. Retrieved from https://www.wto.org/english/tratop_e/serv_e/gsintr_e.pdf

WTO. (2021a). *Services domestic regulation: Rationale and content, potential economic benefits, and increasing prevalence in trade agreements*. Retrieved from https://www.wto.org/english/tratop_e/serv_e/sdr_factsheet_e_oct21.pdf

WTO. (2021b). *WTO in brief*. World Trade Organization. Retrieved from https://www.wto.org/english/thewto_e/whatis_e/inbrief_e/inbr_e.pdf

WTO. (2022). Georgia, Timor-Leste and United Arab Emirates join initiative on services domestic regulation. Georgia, Timor-Leste and United Arab Emirates join initiative on services domestic regulation.



## Further Reading

Balassa, B. (2011). The theory of economic integration (Routledge revivals). Taylor & Francis Group is a classic text on economic integration.

Hoekman, B., & Braga, C. A. P. (1997). Protection and trade in services: A survey. *Open Economies Review, 8*(3), 285–308 survey the literature on trade, protectionism, and liberalization in services.

Krugman, P. R., Obstfeld, M., & Melitz, M. J. (2022). *International trade: Theory and policy*, Pearson provide an introduction to international trade theory and practice.

WHO. (n.d.).The WTO provides comprehensive information on trade in services and progress in its liberalization on a dedicated gateway page: https://www.wto.org/english/tratop_e/serv_e/serv_e.htm.

# International Market Entry and Policy

# The Entry into Foreign Service Markets

## Contents




D. Klimkeit et al., *International Management in Service Firms*, Classroom Companion: Business,
https://doi.org/10.1007/978-3-031-50345-0_7

**Learning Outcomes**

After completing this chapter, you should be able to:

- Explain the motives for service firms'entry into foreign service markets.
- Outline the market selection process.
- Explain the criteria service firms usually use to select foreign markets.
- Identify and classify different entry modes.
- Evaluate the advantages and disadvantages of each entry mode.
- Explain the dynamics among the choice of different entry modes.
- Understand the rationales of different timing strategies for entry into foreign service markets.

## Introduction



This chapter starts Part II by examining how service firms enter foreign markets. It addresses service firms' motives for internationalization, the selection of markets to enter, modes of entry, and the timing of internationalization.

**Opening Case: Netflix's Global Expansion**

Open the Netflix app or website, and select Sign In to access your account. Now you can watch TV shows and movies in different genres, with varying subtitles of language, no matter you are in metropolitan cities like New York and Tokyo or a remote village in India, thanks to Netflix's wide global coverage.

Netflix's business model has transformed over the years. On August 29, 1997, Marc Randolph and Reed Hastings founded Netflix in Scotts Valley, California, offering a movie rental service. Users ordered movies on the Netflix website and received DVDs in the post. Upon finishing with them, users would post them back to Netflix in the envelopes provided. Netflix offered a per-rental model for each DVD but introduced a monthly subscription concept in September 1999. In 2000, Netflix introduced a personalized movie recommendation system, which used members' ratings to predict choices for all Netflix members. In 2006, Netflix accounts hit a record five million.

In January 2007, the company shifted its business model by launching a streaming media service, "Watch Now," allowing members to watch television shows and movies on their computers (PCs) via the internet. The service started with 1000 titles and only worked on PCs and internet Explorer. In January 2008, all its rental-disc subscribers were entitled to unlimited streaming at no additional cost. The same year, Netflix partnered with consumer electronics companies to allow streaming on the Xbox 360, Blu-ray disc players, and TV set-top boxes. The partnership was extended to Playstation and smart-TVs in 2009, and the Apple iPad, iPhone, and iPod Touch, the Nintendo Wii, and other internet-connected devices in 2010.

Today Netflix's online streaming services allow members to watch as much

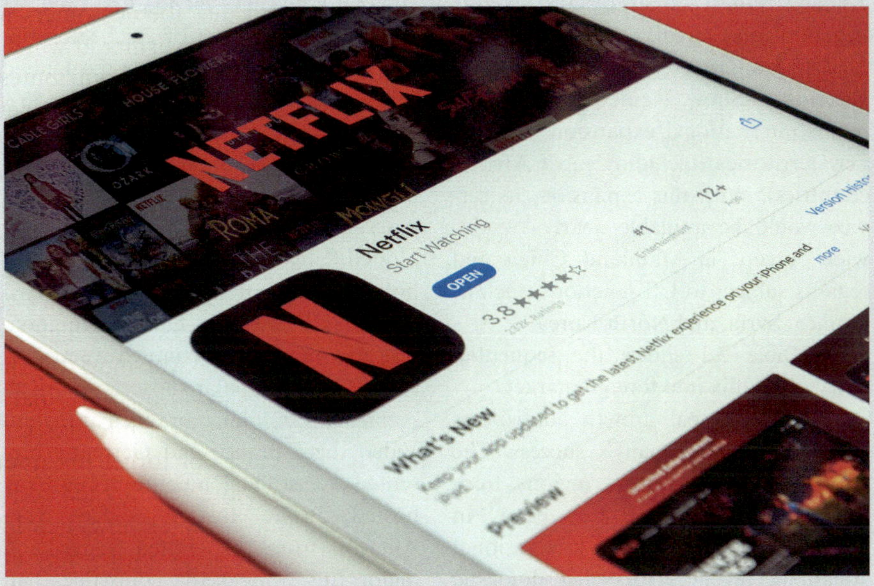


Netflix on a tablet, image by Souvik Banerjee from Pixabay

content as they want and access content anywhere and anytime on any internet-connected device. In addition to partnering with content providers to license streaming rights for a variety of TV shows and movies, the company also produces its in-house original content.

Netflix started international expansion by offering its streaming service to Canada on September 22, 2010. It took the company less than a year to reach one million subscribers, approximately 3% of Canada's population. "We're thrilled that Canadians have embraced Netflix so rapidly." Netflix CEO Reed Hastings said.

On July 5, 2011, Netflix announced its plans to launch its streaming service in Latin America. At the time, Netflix had 23 million subscribers in the United States and Canada. Entering the Latin American market would allow Netflix to potentially access approximately 600 million new subscribers. In September 2011, the firm began its expansion to 43 countries and territories in Latin America and the Caribbean, with content available in Spanish, English, and Portuguese, starting from Brazil. Following Brazil, Netflix continued its expansion in Latin America, including Argentina, Chile, Colombia, and Mexico, before further expanding into 38 countries in the following weeks.

In 2012, Netflix began its expansion into Europe, and by the end of that year, Netflix was streaming in the United Kingdom (UK), Ireland, Denmark, Finland, Norway, and Sweden. In 2013, Netflix launched in the Netherlands, and in 2014 Netflix continued its expansion further into other European countries.

In 2014, Netflix started to expand to Asia Pacific. In March 2015, Netflix launched its service in Australia and New

Zealand, and in the fall of 2015, Netflix began to enter Japan.

On January 6, 2016, at Consumer Electronics Show, Netflix announced a major international expansion into 130 new territories (including most African countries). With this expansion, its service would be available nearly "worldwide" except in Mainland China and regions subject to US sanctions, such as Crimea, Syria, and North Korea.

◘ Table 7.1 shows the sequential entry of Netflix into foreign markets.

Netflix's global growth contributes greatly to the company's success. The paid membership across regions from 2018 to 2021 is illustrated below in ◘ Fig. 7.1. In 2018, its international streaming revenues exceeded domestic streaming revenues for the first time. As of the second quarter of 2022, subscriptions from members outside the United States and Canada contributed to 56% of the company's revenue.

Netflix's performance varies in the international markets. In the European market, for example, when entering the United Kingdom in 2012, 74% of households in the United Kingdom had fixed broadband. But the United Kingdom was also an intensely competitive market since it had a popular subscription rival, Amazon's Lovefilm, rebranded as Instant Video then. France and Germany presented even stiffer competition. Germany hosted Prime Instant Video from Amazon from the United States, and major European media companies had

7

◘ **Table 7.1** Netflix international expansion from 2010, source: Author's own table. Data extracted from https://en.wikipedia.org/wiki/International_expansion_of_Netflix.

| Years | Markets | Entry modes |
|---|---|---|
| 2010 | Canada | Export |
| 2011 | 40 countries in Latin America and the Caribbean | Export |
| 2012 | Europe: United Kingdom, Ireland, Denmark, Finland, Norway, and Sweden | Export |
| 2013 | Netherlands | Export |
| 2014 | Continue expansion in Europe (e.g., France, Germany) and India | Export |
| 2015 | Cuba | Export |
| 2015 | Australia and New Zealand | Export |
| 2015 | Japan | |
| 2016 | Netflix announced a major international expansion into 130 new territories | |
| 2016 | Thailand | Strategic alliance |
| 2017 | China | Licensing content to a local company |

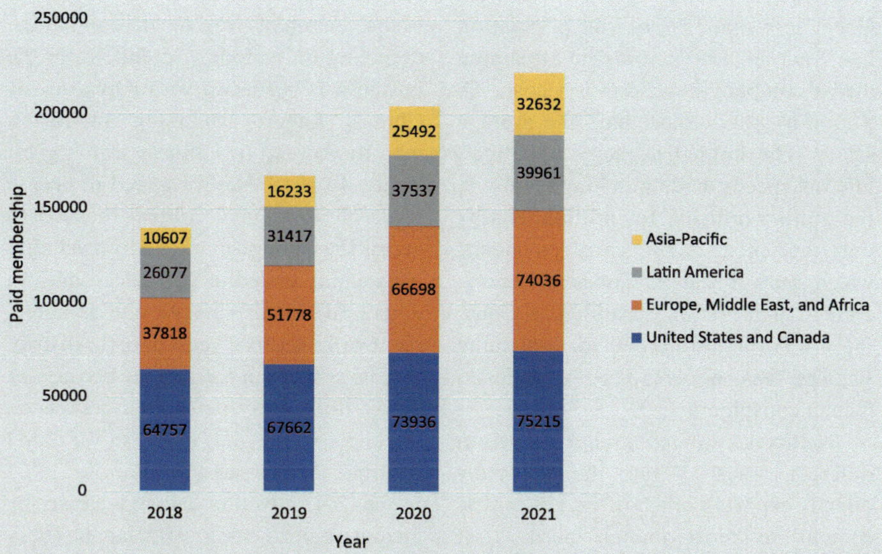


**Fig. 7.1** Netflix paid membership across regions (2018–2021), source: Author's own figure. Data extracted from Netflix financial statement

their own offerings, such as Watchever from media giant Vivendi, Maxdome from ProSieben, and Snap from twenty-first century Fox's Sky Deutschland. France had options in CanalPlay from Canal+ and Orangecast from Orange. In terms of price, Netflix priced its basic tier of service at €7.99 per month, the same as many of its competitors. Despite the intense competition, Netflix generally received a warm welcome throughout Europe. It heralded a milestone of one million United Kingdom members in less than 9 months after launching. At the end of 2018, Netflix accounted for 52% of all subscription online video services revenues in Europe, far more than Amazon Prime Video (21%), Sky (4%), HBO (3%), and Viaplay (3%).

The situation was quite different in Latin America. In Latin America, Netflix had no streaming competitors as it did in Canada or Europe. However, the growth in the region was slower than expected due to a few reasons. The digital infrastructure, that is, a lack of high-speed broadband internet penetration, hindered rapid growth. In Brazil, for example, only 20% of the population had an internet speed greater than 500 kB/s a second, while 800 kB/s a second were needed to stream Netflix's content. Furthermore, Netflix Chief Financial Officer David Wells said that being the first to offer streaming content in the region without a competitor, the company faced a big problem: Consumers in Latin America were more skeptical about the click-and-watch idea of watching movies and TV shows online. In addition, a banking system unused to recurrent monthly transactions exacerbated the problem.

In 2015, Netflix announced its expansion into Cuba; yet this expansion brought numerous complications too. In

Cuba, less than 5% of the population had internet access, and the streaming media company's subscription cost—$8 a month—was almost half the average salary. The limited capacity of Cuba's internet speeds made watching Netflix in the country difficult. In addition, Netflix only accepted credit card payments, which were illegal in Cuba. Therefore, even though Netflix expanded to Cuba, the infrastructure needed for streaming services was not readily available to Cuban consumers.

Netflix has entered foreign markets in different ways. While the company directly exported much of its US-centric content to most foreign markets, it adopted special arrangements to make its content available in some countries.

In China, Western media and tech companies have been trying to crack China's lucrative market for years. But, Beijing censors content heavily, and many services, including Google and Facebook, are blocked. Disney (DIS) and Apple (AAPL), although having received approval to launch their content (movies, e-books, games, and so on.) in China, the content services were abruptly shut down in China just 7 months after launching. As stated in a letter to Netflix shareholders, "The regulatory environment for foreign digital content services in China has become challenging." In January 2016, Reed Hastings, the CEO of Netflix, commented that government permission was needed, which took a long time; and the relationship was to be developed with the government and partners to facilitate the entry and operation in China. Considering the obstacles and risks, in 2017, Netflix announced that instead of launching its own service in the restrictive China market, it would license content to local companies, expecting only modest revenue from the business. It partnered with iQiyi, one of China's largest streaming platforms, majority-owned by Chinese search giant Baidu. In 2017, Netflix agreed to license some of its original content to iQiyi to access the Chinese market. However, that partnership ended in 2019, according to iQiyi CEO Gong Yu. "We had an agreement with Netflix 2 years ago, (to distribute) its content in China, but because of the verification system and users' tastes, the effect wasn't that great, so we didn't continue the partnership anymore."

In 2015, Netflix entered Japan by forming a partnership with Japanese talent agency Yoshimoto Kogyo to produce exclusive local shows for Netflix's coming foray into the Japanese market. The partnership involved funding by Netflix in exchange for exclusive streaming rights to the shows for a set period of time. Yoshimoto would retain the copyright, allowing it to sell the content elsewhere. The strategy involved offering a greater proportion of local TV shows and movies than in other countries. Whereas the streaming company's content usually consisted of about 20% of local-made programming, in Japan, this was pushed to 40%. The decision was based on current viewing trends in a country whose main channels generally see fewer foreign broadcasts than many other nations.

When entering the Thai market in 2017, Netflix partnered with the Thai mobile network Advanced Info Service (AIS). Such a partnership allowed AIS to offer its customers exclusive entertainment while promoting Netflix's international expansion. New AIS customers and existing customers switching from prepaid to postpaid plans with 4G Max speed unlimited, as well as platinum, gold and emerald customers, were offered unlimited access to Netflix content for the first 3 months, while current postpaid subscribers who would get the Netflix package before July 31, 2017, were able to get 1 month of unlimited access.

**Questions**

1. What drives Netflix's internationalization of its streaming service?
2. Observe the pattern of Netflix's international expansion. What is the rationale for Netflix's sequence of entry into the international markets?
3. Is Netflix a born global? How did it benefit from the speed of internationalization?
4. Do you think Netflix has chosen the best entry timing when entering Europe and Latin America?
5. Why did Netflix adopt different entry modes (export, licensing, and partnership) when entering different countries?

Source: (Brennan, 2018; Epstein, 2015; Etan, 2011; Frankel, 2012; Fritz, 2012; Hinchliffe, 2015; Julianne, 2011; Kharpal, 2019; Magdirila, 2017; McFadden, 2020; Mogg, 2015; Netflix, 2018 Financial Statement; Netflix 2022 Financial report; Netflix earns 50%+, 2019; PR Newswire, 2012; Riley, 2016; Schilling, 2015; Statistica, n.d.; The Nation, 2017; The Remarkable Netflix, 2022).

## Motives for Going Global

Various reactive or proactive reasons exist for firms to expand their operations internationally. Dunning (1993) introduced a model of internationalization motives including four categories: market seeking, resource seeking, efficiency seeking, and strategic resource seeking.

**Market Seeking:** Sometimes, a firm's home market is limited and cannot bring enough revenues. This could be due to a saturated, highly competitive, or small market (not enough customers). The firm thus could choose to expand to foreign markets if it observes a growing demand for its product/service, a trend change to favor its product/service, or the absence of or low competition, which would give the firm the first–mover advantage. Another market-seeking motive is to follow the main suppliers or clients abroad to retain business. The main clientele may establish themselves in foreign countries, and following them is essential for the focal firm.

**Natural Resource Seeking:** Manufacturing firms usually seek physical resources, such as minerals (oil, zinc, copper, and so on) and agricultural products (rubber, tobacco, sugar, and so on). Since most service industries rely on natural resources to a low extent, this motive is not very salient to service firms' expansion. An exception would be the tourism and hospitality industry, where the natural endowment of a country can be a major drawcard attracting tourists to a destination and, therefore, investments from companies wanting to benefit from this.

**Efficiency Seeking:** The purpose is to rationalize structures of established investments in order to benefit from the differences in factor endowments, cultures, institutional arrangements, and economic systems. The benefits often come from economies of scale and scope by concentrating activities in a limited number of places. As an example, value-adding activities that are capital, technological, or informational intensive are usually placed in developed countries, while value-adding activities that are labor or resource intensive are often placed in developing countries. Companies may also go overseas to lower the total amount of tax paid to governments. One such example is Goldman Sachs, an American multinational investment bank and financial services company headquartered in New York City, which holds $28.6 billion offshore and uses Bermuda as a tax haven to reduce the tax burden (CFI Team, n.d.). The following box gives more information about tax havens.



**Interesting Fact**
A tax haven, or offshore financial center, is any country or jurisdiction that offers minimal tax liability to foreign individuals and businesses. The most well-known tax havens include Bermuda, the Netherlands, Luxembourg, the Cayman Islands, and Singapore. Tax havens do not require businesses to operate out of their country or individuals to reside in their country to receive tax benefits.

**Strategic Resource Seeking:** Strategic resources are intangible resources dealing with the technology and core competence of the company (Dunning, 1993). Patents, knowledge, the skills of the employees, and strategic supplies necessary for developing comparative advantages are examples of strategic resources. An example is a Brazilian bank entering Frankfurt (Boehe, 2016). Banco Real is a Brazilian bank sold to ABN-AMRO in 1998. The former executives of Banco Real indicated a few strategic reasons for setting up a branch in Frankfurt, the most important financial hub in continental Europe. For instance, Banco Real could demonstrate how it worked to foreign partner banks, thus creating credibility. The resulting credibility facilitated obtaining credit lines that headquarters at home could use for pre-export financing. In this example, the bank from an emerging economy faced a lower reputation (Petrou, 2009), possibly due to the "liability of emergingness" (Madhok & Keyhani, 2012) and higher costs of capital (interest rates) than in developed economies. Being present in the world financial center could obtain various strategic resources, for example, building the reputation vis-à-vis their lenders, obtaining information on financing opportunities, and consequently improving their position to raise capital at lower interest rates abroad. In addition, having an international presence also augmented its reputation vis-à-vis its domestic clients; the bank thus could advertise the strength of its international network to its domestic clients. Another example is German enterprise software maker SAP SE, which established twenty research labs around the Americas, Middle East and Africa, Asia Pacific, and Europe (SAP website). In

2016, SAP further scaled up its R&D base in India by hiring the highest number of 1600 people in India. This allowed SAP to further enhance its second-largest R&D center outside of its headquarters in Germany to seek well-educated and experienced talents (Mishra, 2016).

Other than the reasons posited by Dunning, scholars have also proposed some other motives.

**Oligopolistic Reaction by Following the Leader:** Competitors in the same industry, particularly one that demonstrates an oligopolistic market structure, in the same country/region of origin tend to follow the first mover to make investments abroad with minimum delay (Flowers, 1976; Knickerbocker, 1973). For example, several Brazilian private banks followed Banco Real abroad only a few years later. Only 2 years after Banco Real's market entry, Itaú established its first foreign branches in Argentina in 1979. Its second major competitor, Bradesco, initiated its international expansion in the 1980s by opening branch offices in New York, Cayman, and London, most likely to gain comparable access to financial, reputational, and informational resources (Boehe, 2016).

**Risk Diversification:** Another reason to go global is to diversify the company's risk. By diversifying their operations in multiple countries/markets, companies become more immune to changing trends in consumption for each market. They are also less influenced by external factors affecting consumer behavior and purchase of their products/services, such as climate and diplomatic crises.

**Government-Driven:** Home governments could have policies and programs to encourage firms'overseas expansion. These could be government export promotion policies enabling entrepreneurs to internationalize using business education and training (Harris & Wheeler, 2005). One example is that the Singapore government provides grants for small and medium-sized firms to get consultancy to assess market readiness and list and sell their products and services on multiple overseas e-marketplaces. In recent years, Chinese law firms actively entered Belt & Road countries to follow their clients, promoted by the state through the One Belt One Road (OBOR) initiative (Li, 2019).

**Network:** Social and business networks are also potential catalysts (Coviello & McAuley, 1999) and enablers (Zain & Ng, 2006) for a firm's internationalization. Although globalization can be considered a great chance to increase business activities, various obstacles must be overcome before entering new markets abroad. Such obstacles include, for example, disadvantages in exploiting economies of scale and, thus, the inability to offer competitive prices (Welch & Luostarinen, 1988), problems in accessing monetary resources necessary to introduce business activities abroad, and lack of required market knowledge to start business activities abroad efficiently (Karlsen et al., 2003). Companies could utilize different kinds of formal and informal networks to overcome such obstacles to access various resources (Wu, Adbi & Mahmood, 2023). Networking has been described as a key motivation and enabler, particularly for international entrepreneurs who do not have a deep pocket (Dimitratos & Plakoyiannaki, 2003). Examples of network relations are personal connections, supplier-customer relations, contractual cooperation (e.g., strategic alliance), or other types of relations based on mutual gain and trust. For instance, a law firm could start its internationalization because it gets informal ad hoc referral relationships or has access to bilateral or closely-knitted law firm alliances or tightly coordinated formal networks.

Firms are often driven by various motivations to expand overseas. For example, Infosys Limited is an Indian multinational information technology company that provides business consulting, information technology, and outsourcing services. It established its first business process outsourcing center in Hangzhou, China, in 2008, aiming to not only cater to its multinational clients operating in the country but also take advantage of the quality workforce available at competitive costs compared to India (Infosys Newsroom, 2005, 2008). In the opening case, Netflix charted a deliberate course to global expansion from the start, mainly driven by market-seeking motives. In addition, since the content licenses they have secured are not based on the number of subscriptions, the incremental costs incurred for signing up a new subscriber are extraordinarily low. In other words, new subscribers do not increase content costs, the major cost category for the company. Expanding to more markets will allow efficiency and higher profitability.



## Specific Motives of Service Firms

Research has also shown that different motives may play a more important role for some types of service companies than for others. For example, Contractor et al. (2003) categorized services into capital-intensive and knowledge-based service sectors. The capital-intensive service sector (e.g., air transport, hotels/casinos, and restaurants/fast food chains) typically employs a "*seek-the-market*" strategy. In contrast, the knowledge-based service sector (especially in business services, e.g., professional service firms (PSFs) such as accounting, legal services, advertising, and market research) employs a "*follow-the-client*" strategy which implies it has clients already established in the host country. Since these services require the *simultaneity* of production and consumption and close and frequent interaction between the service provider and customer in the service process, service companies must be present in most or all of the countries where their client has a presence. This is evident in the case of the internationalization of Deutsche Treuhand-GmbH (DTG), the German part of the pedigree of audit firm KPMG. Internationalization steps were mostly the result of requests by clients who needed an auditor of their foreign subsidiaries' financial statements (Kewitz & Reihlen, 2006).

In addition, the importance of motives could vary at different stages of a firm's internationalization. In the service industry, following the client may be a motive in the early stage of internationalization. But its importance could decrease over time (Li & Guisinger, 1992). As the company gains more experience, it could expand its internationalization to seek market and to respond to a competing service firm's actions (Erramilli, 1990).

## Market Selection

### The Market Selection Process

For firms interested in conducting business internationally, the selection of the foreign location (where to sell the services), entry mode (how), and entry timing (when) is a complex and interconnected decision. Regarding location selection, a company could adopt a systematic or non-systematic approach (Andersen & Buvik, 2002). A systematic approach requires a structured and formalized decision-making process in which firms carry out a series of analyses before selecting some international markets. Most research on conducting a systematic international market selection suggests a similar process (Cavusgil, 1985; Root, 1994; Kumar et al., 1994; Sakarya et al., 2007; Johansson, 2009; Hollensen, 2017). In this book, we integrate the two models by Root (1994) and Johansson (2009) into one, illustrated in ◘ Fig. 7.2.

*In the first stage*, the goal is to use low-cost secondary data sources ("scanning") to narrow down the list of potential countries to find those warranting detailed investigation and analysis. Two main risks at this stage shall be minimized: ignoring prosperous markets and spending too much time analyzing unattractive markets (Root, 1994). To ensure a comprehensive assessment of the opportunities and risks in the macro-environment in the potential countries, a common tool, PESTLE, and its variations (PESTE, PEST, STEEPLE), are often used to survey the political, economic, social, technological, legal, and ecological conditions. The following box gives more details about PESTLE analysis.

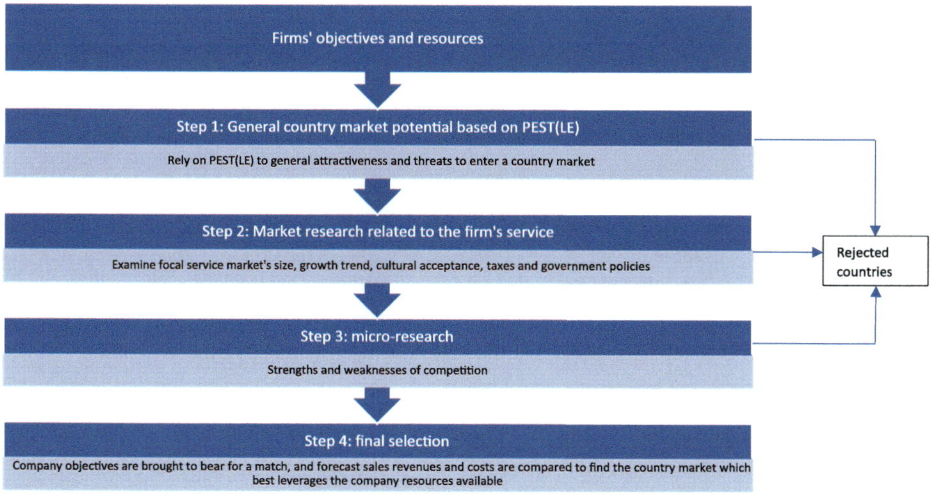


◘ **Fig. 7.2** Market selection process, source: Author's own figure

7

## PESTLE Analysis

PESTLE analysis is an important and widely used tool that helps show the big picture of a firm's external macro environment, particularly related to foreign markets. PESTLE is an acronym for the political, economic, sociocultural, technological, environmental, and legal contexts in which a firm operates. A PESTLE analysis helps managers better understand the opportunities and threats they face; consequently, the analysis aids in building a better vision of the future business landscape and how the firm might compete profitably. There are three steps in the PESTLE analysis. First, consider the relevance of each of the PESTLE factors to your context. Next, identify and categorize the information that applies to these factors. Finally, analyze the data and conclude. It is particularly important for managers to consider whether a factor constitutes an opportunity or a threat for the company to enter a country. For example, political stability would be viewed as an opportunity, while the labor force's low level of education would be a threat to a service firm contemplating a market entry. ◘ Table 7.2 illustrates the various PESTLE factors and how they affect a service firm's market selection and foreign operation.

**◘ Table 7.2 An overview of the PESTLE factors, source: Author's own table**

| PESTLE factors | Indicators | Example |
|---|---|---|
| Political factors | Those driven by home and host government actions and policies, e.g.,<br>• Corporate taxation<br>• Other fiscal policy initiatives<br>• Free trade disputes<br>• Antitrust and other anti-competition issues | The Chinese government has strict censorship for digital content services. Netflix thus had to license content to local companies, such as iQiyi, instead of launching its own service in China<br>The US government restricted any American company from conducting business in North Korea, Syria, and Crimea. So, even if Netflix wanted to operate there, they legally can't |
| Economic factors | Factors related to the broader economy, e.g.,<br>• Interest rates<br>• Employment rates<br>• Inflation<br>• Exchange rates<br>• Growth of the local and foreign national economies<br>• Availability of critical labor<br>• Local cost of labor | The fluctuating exchange rate affects its economy when buying others' content. However, Netflix can profit from its original content, like movies and TV shows<br>The loyal customers of Netflix complain about a steady hike in the subscription price. High-quality content can be the solution to satisfy the viewers to make them realize the content is money's worth |

(continued)

**Table 7.2** (continued)

| PESTLE factors | Indicators | Example |
|---|---|---|
| Social factors | Social factors influence the preferences of the consumer and their need<br>• Demographic considerations<br>• Social norms and customs<br>• Lifestyle and cultural trends<br>• Consumer beliefs<br>• Attitudes around working conditions | Japanese consumers prefer their locally produced media content. As a result, Netflix formed a partnership with Japanese talent agency Yoshimoto Kogyo to produce exclusive local shows for Netflix's offering in the Japanese market |
| Technological factors | Technological factors influence a firm's operation.<br>• Automation<br>• How research and development (R&D) may impact both costs and competitive advantage<br>• Technology infrastructure (like 5G, IoT, etc.)<br>• Cyber security | Brazil's market lacked high broadband internet penetration. Netflix will face more challenges in entering the market |
| Environmental factors | Changes to our physical environment that can present material risks and opportunities for organizations<br>• Carbon footprint<br>• Climate change impacts, including physical and transition risks<br>• Increased incidences of extreme weather events<br>• Stewardship of natural resources (like fresh water) | The media company operates almost online and leaves no direct environmental impact. However, its electricity consumption is quite heavy |
| Legal factors | Changes to the regulatory environment may affect the broader economy, certain industries, or even individual businesses within a specific sector<br>• Industry regulation<br>• Licenses and permits required to operate<br>• Employment and consumer protection laws<br>• Protection of intellectual properties | Some Netflix subscribers share their password and thus access to their Netflix accounts. Some use software to watch content only available outside their own country proxies and virtual private networks (VPNs). Such behaviors constitute copyright infringement. proxies and virtual private networks (VPNs). Instead of blocking users from other countries, the company must come up with a suitable strategy |

The second stage focuses on the market condition specifically about the firm's services, and aims to estimate the focal service market attractiveness in each of the countries shortlisted from stage 1. A few factors usually deserving considerations are the focal service market's size and growth, customer acceptance, tax, trade barriers, and government regulations. In addition to comparing target countries, further in-country segmentation can be done to achieve more precise target forecasts and to evaluate if there are significant differences in the focal service market conditions.

*In the third stage*, a firm will examine the competitive situation, especially entry barriers created by the competitors, such as competition intensity, competitors'market shares, positioning, and competitive strategies.

In the last stage, company objectives and strategies, resources, and capabilities are brought to bear for a match. The company will forecast sales revenues and costs to find the country market which best leverages the company's available resources and capabilities. A country market attractive for one company may not be attractive for another due to different product or service lines, market positioning (high quality vs. low cost), capabilities, resources, and strategies. For instance, a poor country in Africa will not be an attractive market for a retailer selling luxury brands to enter, while for a company selling inexpensive commodities, it may well be. If a company is very environmentally friendly, a market where customers appreciate and value this can be attractive. In contrast, a company that is much less environmentally friendly would rather have a handicap in that market.



When making such an international market selection, it is important to distinguish between countries and markets because real market differences may be unrelated to political or geographical boundaries. The Scandinavian countries, for example, are often treated as relatively homogeneous markets. Second, small- and medium-sized enterprises may not have the resources to develop operations on a national scale in larger countries such as the United States, China, and India (Young et al., 1989). They, hence, may have to consider their market selection in a limited number of states or cities within a country.

On the other hand, despite the range of studies proposing a systematic international market selection process, research has evidenced that many firms engaging in internalization for reactive reasons, for example, following existing or new clients, may not go through such a systematic market selection process. This is particularly true for small firms, who usually lack important resources like international managerial experience and know-how to obtain relevant information about potential foreign markets (Karagozoglu & Lindell, 1998). O'Farrell et al. (1996), drawing upon their survey of business service firms in Scotland and the South East of England, have asserted that international market selection is seldom formally planned. Instead, most exporting firms stated that "the choice was whether to do the job or not" (O'Farrell et al., 1996: 114). For them, the market selection issues were found to be irrelevant because their foreign-country market choice was primarily order-led or client-led (O'Farrell & Wood, 1998).

## Criteria for Location Selection and Data Sources

Firms adopting a systematic approach tend to examine several factors before selecting international markets. These factors can be divided into three categories: firm-specific factors, host country factors, and focal service market factors. ◘ Table 7.3 lists some factors that firms usually consider when selecting markets, together with the possible data source.

Before a company decides to go global, it should audit its resources and capabilities. The company should have clear competitive advantages regarding market knowledge, technology, portfolio of products/services, reliable partners, and other relevant parameters such as its competitive positioning.

Other than the firm's own resources and advantages, the firm needs to give consideration to a few factors about the host country. In fact, this is the part where PESTLE analysis is conducted. The first factor is the general economy size and

◘ **Table 7.3** Factors that firms usually consider when selecting markets, source: Author's own table

| | Factors | Information source |
|---|---|---|
| Firm | Firm's competitive advantage, such as<br>• Physical resources (natural, buildings, plant equipment)<br>• Financial resources (equity and borrowed capital)<br>• Human resources (individuals and teams, entrepreneurial and operation skills)<br>• Upstream knowledge (marketing, sales, distribution, after-sales service)<br>• Administrative knowledge (organizational structure, culture and systems)<br>• Reputational resources (brand names, reputation) | Firms' own assessment |
| Stage 1: Host country macro environment (PESTLE & CAGE) | Country attractiveness<br>• Economy<br>– Economy size and growth of the host country, e.g., country's GDP and GDP growth, population, etc.<br>– Inflation and cost situation<br>– Procurement/supply situation<br>– Currency volatility and inconvertibility risk<br>• Technology and infrastructure<br>• Environment or ecology factors<br>• Policies and free trade agreements favorable to foreign operations<br>• Social factors<br>– Demographic structure<br>– Social norms and customs<br>– Lifestyle and cultural trends | Public data sources such as government website |

(continued)

**Table 7.3** (continued)

| | Factors | Information source |
|---|---|---|
| | Country risk (Root, 1987)<br>• Political risk<br>– Instability of the policy system<br>– Risk due to government policies, such as expropriation risks, remittance control, price control, and local content requirements<br>• Legal risks<br>– Contract risk, litigation risk, compliance risk, dispute risk | Public data sources such as business environment risk intelligence index (BERI index)<br>Government website |
| | Differences between home and host country<br>• Geographic distance<br>• Economic distance<br>• Culture/psychic distance<br>• Administrative distance | Public data sources such as government website |
| Stage 2: Focal service market/industry attractiveness | Focal service's market/industry size and growth | Industry report<br>Primary data |
| | Customer receptiveness to the service | Industry report<br>Primary data |
| | Service-specific tax schemes, trade barriers and government regulations | Public data sources such as government website<br>Industry report |
| Stage 3: Focal service market competition and profitability | Intensity of competition<br>Competitors' positioning and market shares | Industry report<br>Primary data |

growth (Johansson, 2009), including the country's population, GDP, and GDP growth, which could give a basic picture of the readiness of infrastructure and the demand for the product/service.

The second factor to be considered is the host country's political, legal, ownership, operation, and transfer risks (Root, 1998), as shown in Table 7.3. When these risks are high, a multinational enterprise (MNE) may decide not to enter. If it does, it may limit the resource commitments and increase its capacity to exit from the market quickly if the environment deteriorates.

The third factor is market similarity, such as geographic proximity and psychic distance between home and host country. The geographic proximity of the home country and the host country will reduce the transaction costs of managing foreign subsidiaries and operations. At the same time, geographic proximity increases the probability of two countries sharing a similar culture and having a higher level of market similarity. The CAGE (Culture, administration, geography, economic) framework (Table 7.4) helps marketers evaluate market similarities and differences.

According to the classic Uppsala model of internationalization, companies select markets similar and physically close to their domestic market for initial entry as they are easier to learn and understand (Johanson & Vahlne, 1977; Nordstrom & Vahlne, 1994). For example, a US company might target Canada, the United Kingdom, and Australia before Japan, China, or South Korea. When a firm expands to markets similar to the home country, existing product and service specifications, pricing, and marketing strategies can be more readily transferred to the target markets. The firm can also more readily relocate its personnel to similar markets with a common language and culture. This is more important in services than manufacturing because of the need for frequent interaction between the supplier and client during service production (O'Farrell & Moffat, 1991). For more distant foreign markets, the firm will face higher uncertainty levels and more challenges in estimating and predicting costs, demand, competition, or environmental conditions. Such uncertainty is particularly threatening for service firms that usually prefer a high control and commitment

**Table 7.4** The CAGE framework, source: Recreated from Pankaj (2001)

| Cultural distance | Administrative distance | Geographic distance | Economic distance |
|---|---|---|---|
| **Attributes creating distance** | | | |
| Different languages | Absence of colonial ties | Physical remoteness | Differences in consumer incomes |
| Different ethnicities; lack of connective ethnic or social networks | Absence of shared monetary or political association | Lack of a common border | Differences in costs and quality of the following:<br>• Natural resources<br>• Financial resources<br>• Human resources<br>• Infrastructure<br>• Intermediate inputs<br>• Information or knowledge |
| Different religions | Political hostility | Lack of sea or river access | |
| Different social norms | Government policies | Different sizes of country | |
| | Institutional weakness where the necessary institutional arrangements supporting markets are absent, weak, or fail to fulfil their expected role. For example, legal regulations sometimes can be minimised or avoided due to ineffective law enforcement. | Weak transportation or communication links | |
| | | Differences in climates | |

(continued)

7

**Table 7.4** (continued)

| Cultural distance | Administrative distance | Geographic distance | Economic distance |
|---|---|---|---|
| **Industries or products affected by distance** | | | |
| Products have high-linguistic content (TV) | Government involvement is high in industries that are<br>• Producers of staple goods (electricity)<br>• Producers of other "entitlements" (drugs)<br>• Large employers (farming)<br>• Large suppliers to the government (mass transportation)<br>• National champions (aerospace)<br>• Vital to national security (telecommunications)<br>• Exploiters of natural resources (oil, mining), and<br>• Subject to high-sunk costs (infrastructure) | Products have a low value-of-weight or bulk ratio (cement) | Nature of demand varies with income level (cars) |
| Products affect the cultural or national identity of consumers (foods) | | Products are fragile or perishable (glass or fruit) | Economies of standardization or scale are important (mobile phones) |
| Product features vary in size (cars), standards (electrical appliances), or packaging | | Communications and connectivity are important (financial services) | Labor and other factor cost differences are salient (garments) |
| Products carry country-specific quality associations (wines) | | Local supervision and operational requirements are high (many services) | Distribution or business systems are different (insurance) |
| | | | Companies need to be responsive and agile (home appliances) |

mode to ensure supplier-client interaction. As a result, service firms tend to enter geographically, linguistically, and culturally similar markets, especially during the early stages of internationalization. As shown in the opening case, Netflix carefully selected its initial entry into adjacent markets in terms of geography, cultural, and economic distance. It first expanded into Canada, which was geographically close and shared many similarities with the United States. Netflix was thus able to develop its internationalization capabilities in places where the challenges of "foreignness" were less acute. From the experience and learning it gained in that process, Netflix developed the capabilities to expand into a more diverse set of markets in just a few years. In the second phase, Netflix became involved in a faster and more intense international expansion by entering markets in Latin America and Europe—Latin America was geographically close to the United States, and Europe shared relatively high similarities with the United States in terms of culture and economic development stage. In the third phase, Netflix used everything it had learned from the first two phases to expand to more distant markets: Asia Pacific. The following box provides more information about the Uppsala internationalization model.

**Uppsala Internationalization Model**

Next, an effort shall be made to assess the firm's service market attractiveness. Specific information about the focal service's market size and growth will be needed. Such data could be obtained from secondary sources, such as industry reports or government websites. Some companies also try to engage internal staff or external research agencies to collect primary data if more accurate data is preferred. In addition, customer receptiveness, that is, customers'attitudes toward the focal service and their perceptions of the country of origin and foreign business, are important factors when assessing the potential of markets (Sakarya et al., 2007). Such in-depth data shall be obtained from field research by the firm or some research agency. The industry-related government regulations, incentives, and trade barriers should also be researched, such as local content requirements, tax rates, subsidies available, and ownership restrictions. To obtain data about government regulations and incentives, a firm could refer to secondary sources like government websites or industry reports.

The Uppsala Internationalization Model was proposed by Swedish researchers to explain the internationalization process (Johanson & Wiedersheim-Paul, 1999; Johanson & Vahlne, 1977). Studying the internationalization of Swedish manufacturing firms, they developed a model of the firm's market choice and form of entry when going abroad. It presents a sequential approach, meaning that the firm internationalizes incrementally. The model assumes that a typical firm lacks foreign market knowledge, which is detrimental to internationalization. Therefore, the firm should first establish itself in its domestic market and then increase its commitment and resources in the target country in stages, progressing to the next stage once sufficient understanding and knowledge of the foreign market conditions have been attained.

Lastly, the market share and profitability shall be estimated based on an understanding of the market structure and the intensity of competition. When the intensity of competition is high, host country markets tend to be less profitable, and this reduces a service firm's probability of entry. Similarly, the greater the volatility of competition in a market, the less likely a business service firm is to commit itself to developing the market beyond responding to ad hoc project contracts. Hence, volatile markets are likely characterized by repeated entry and exit by business service companies unwilling to commit themselves to a direct investment entry mode. The data on competition could be obtained from some industry reports or tasked to internal staff or external research agencies to do more in-depth field research.

Looking back at the opening case, Netflix chose its markets based on their attractiveness, such as shared similarities, the presence of affluent consumers, and the availability of broadband internet. Yet Netflix also knowledge from the expansion experience and accordingly adjusted its international expansion and operation strategies. For instance, they discovered that international subscribers whose first language is not English prefer local-language programming. Netflix had to collaborate with local partners to develop more local content for foreign markets. Technology infrastructures differ across countries, requiring Netflix to deliver streaming services over a wide range of internet speeds. The development of other infrastructure, such as online payment, could hinder the market's growth. Foreign markets are dominated by incumbent streaming service providers, making it difficult for Netflix to earn market share.



## Modes of Entry

An entry mode is an institutional arrangement that a firm uses to sell its products and services in a foreign market in the first 3–5 years, which is generally the length of time it takes a firm to enter a foreign market (Root, 1994). The selection of an appropriate entry mode in a foreign market can have significant and far-reaching consequences on a firm's performance and survival (Davidson, 1982; Gatignon & Anderson, 1988; Root, 1994; Terpstra & Sarathy, 1994). For example, in 2011, Target, an American retail company, acquired 124 former Zellers department stores across Canada (O'Brien, 2015). The plan was to quickly convert these stores and enter the Canadian market in a brisk expansion, expecting to gain profit by 2013. However, within 2 years, Target closed down its Canadian business. An investment of over four billion dollars was a huge failure. A big reason for Target's failure in Canada is that it chose the acquisition of Zellers as the entry mode—many of the former Zellers stores it bought for conversion were situated in poor locations. Target also had to outlay a great deal of money to renovate the Zellers stores, which increased the financial pressures for early success. Customers were not always pleased with the store layouts and appearance, partly because of the limitations placed upon them by the former Zellers locations.

**Entry Mode**

An *entry mode* is an institutional arrangement that a firm uses to sell its products and services in a foreign market in the first 3–5 years, which is generally the length of time it takes a firm to enter a foreign market (Root, 1994).

## Entry Modes

There are a wide variety of entry modes that can generally be categorized into contractual entry modes and investment entry modes. A distinction is also made between equity-based and non-equity-based ► entry modes. Entry modes vary considerably regarding costs incurred by firms and benefits and disadvantages provided to firms.

### Contractual (Non-Equity-Based) Modes of Market Entry

**Export:** Exporting is the marketing and direct sale of domestically produced goods/services in another country. Export could be conducted directly or indirectly, as illustrated in ◘ Fig. 7.3.

Direct exporting involves an organization selling goods/services directly to customers in an international market, leveraging trade shows, representative offices, and e-commerce. Service companies could take use of digital technology for direct export. Some of such direct export of service includes medical personnel in the United States or Canada who read test results or compile medical reports about patients in another country via their hospital's telemedicine application or website. A translation company in China provides its services to clients in Europe via its own website. An education institution in the United Kingdom delivers its training course online to serve corporate clients in Indonesia. This aligns with the entry mode termed "electronic marketing," suggested by Grönroos (1999). Using Internet customer interest in the company's offerings, the company can export its services to foreign markets. However, it should be noted that even when a company internationalizes by using electronic marketing, it may not be able to manage its service operations wholly by itself. In foreign markets, it may have to rely on some local services, such as postal and delivery services, and the company's control over such partners may be very limited (Grönroos, 1999).

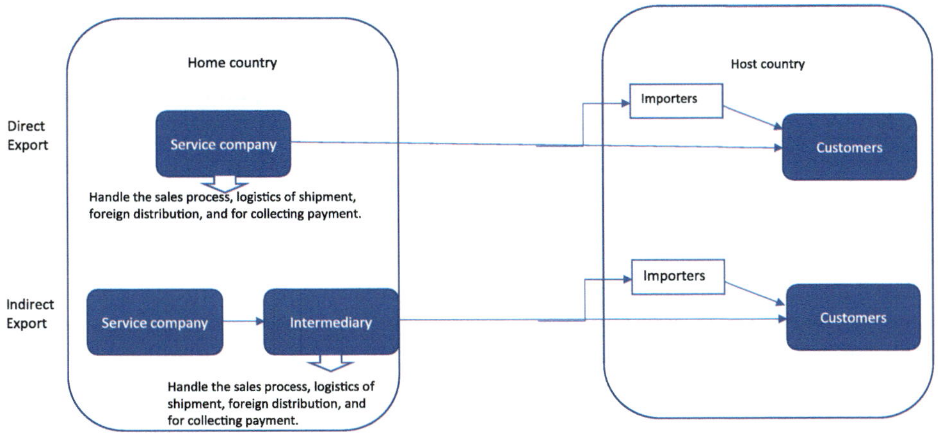


◘ **Fig. 7.3** An illustration of direct and indirect export, source: Author's own figure

**Direct Exporting**

*Direct exporting* involves an organization selling goods/services directly to customers in an international market, leveraging trade shows, representative offices, and e-commerce.

Indirect exporting involves an organization selling to an intermediary, such as export houses or foreign firms' buying offices in its own country. This intermediary then sells the goods to the international market and takes on the responsibility of organizing paperwork and permits, shipping, and arranging marketing. Export intermediaries offer indirect exporters several benefits in international markets: helping in identifying customers, financing and distribution infrastructure providers (Balabanis, 2000); overcoming knowledge gaps (e.g., country-specific knowledge); reducing uncertainties and risks associated with operating in foreign markets and monitoring the enforcement of contracts (Peng & York, 2001). Using large online marketplaces (aggregators) such as eBay, Amazon, Alibaba, and Expedia is another variation of indirect selling gaining popularity. Increasingly, these and other big aggregators offer distribution centers in other countries where a firm's products or services (e.g., airline service, package tours, or accommodation) can be closer to customers. In such cases, these big aggregators offer to handle all the paperwork, customs, and logistics—for a fee.



**Indirect Exporting**

*Indirect exporting* involves an organization selling to an intermediary, such as export houses or firms' foreign organizations based in the organization's country buying offices, in its own country. This intermediary then sells the goods to the international market and takes on the responsibility of organizing paperwork and permits, shipping, and arranging marketing.

Since exporting does not require the goods/services to be produced in the target country, no investment in foreign production facilities is required. Most of the costs take the form of marketing expenses. Exporting hence is typically the easiest way to enter an international market, and most firms begin their international expansion using this entry mode.

While relatively low risk, exporting entails some costs and disadvantages. Exporting firms face high transportation charges and possible tariffs. In addition, firms distribute and market their products in the new country through contractual agreements with local distributors and pay them for a variety of services. Due to the long distance, exporters have little control over the marketing and distribution of their products/services.

Lastly, by adopting a direct export, a service firm can maintain direct contact with the customers. The firm thus can obtain first-hand experience with the foreign market, making it possible to customize products and services to local tastes and preferences. The firm can also receive a higher profit margin since the firm does not need to pay for any markup to the intermediaries. However, direct export requires a firm to invest more time and resources, entailing higher financial risks. Due to the service firm's limited resources and experience in the host country, it takes time for the firm to have extensive market coverage. In contrast, an indirect export allows a service firm to enter a market quickly with minimum resource commitment, though the firm will have a lower profit margin and less opportunity to gain first-hand experience in dealing with foreign customers (Elango & Pangarkar, 2021).

**Licensing and Franchising:** A firm can also enter a foreign country via an international licensing agreement, in which the firm (the licensor) allows a local company (the licensee) to sell its products/services or to use its intellectual property (such as patents, trademarks, copyrights) in exchange for royalty fees. A famous example of licensing can be "Disney." It granted McDonald's the right to use the trademarks of Disney's characters for their Happy Meals while collecting a royalty fee from McDonald's.

**International Licensing Agreement**

An *international licensing agreement* is one in which the firm (the licensor) allows a local company (the licensee) to sell its products/services or to use its intellectual property (such as patents, trademarks, copyrights) in exchange for royalty fees.

Such an entry mode allows a company to quickly enter an international market with limited financial and legal risks. This is particularly useful for a firm with limited resources to set up operations abroad or when the firm perceives high uncertainty or barriers in the foreign market, for instance, due to an unstable political or economic environment, restriction on ownership, or greater distance between home and host country.

Licensing also has some drawbacks. For example, licensors have low central and tight control over the licensees. It is also possible that licensors lose the technical know-how to competitors if the technical know-how is to be shared with the licensee.

Another popular way to expand overseas is through franchising. Under an international franchise agreement, a firm (franchiser) grants a local company (the franchisee) in another country the right to use its brand name and to sell its products or services. The franchisee is responsible for all operations but agrees to operate according to a business model established by the franchiser. In turn, the franchiser usually provides advertising and marketing, training, site selection, new-product assistance, and other ongoing support. Franchising is widely used by service industries for their international expansion. Examples include consumer services like restaurant chains (e.g., McDonald's and Subway), hotel chains (e.g.,

Holiday Inn and Best Western), hair salons, and automotive repairs, as well as business support services such as accounting services, advertising services, and printing services.

**International Franchising Agreement**

*An international franchise agreement* is one in which a firm (franchiser) grants a local company (the franchisee) in another country the right to use its brand name and to sell its products or services.

The primary advantage of franchising is that the firm (franchisor) does not have to bear the development costs and risks associated with entering a new foreign market, just like in the entry mode of licensing. As a result, the firm could efficiently explore the market.



The disadvantage includes the difficulty of controlling franchisees. This is an especially salient issue in the service industry whereby the franchiser will require the franchisee to adhere to the same quality standards when delivering services. If the franchisee does not strictly obey the rules, it could have an adverse impact on the franchiser‘s reputation. Another disadvantage is the possible market cannibalization when a new territory is sold too close to an existing territory. One such example is Subway (Taylor, 2009). You may sometimes find one Subway on one corner of the street and then another Subway down the street. It is because Subway had opened up too many units without territory protection. This leads to sales cannibalization, where two nearby stores negatively impact each other's sales. Such cannibalization will reduce the Subway franchise's profitability, making the model less attractive.

License agreements are similar to franchise agreements in that they both relate to the shared use of business assets and intellectual property rights. License agreements differ from franchise agreements in that license agreements are more limited than franchise agreements and do not give the licensor control over how the licensee operates the underlying business. As a result, the franchise agreement is more complicated than the license agreement. It is generally seen that licensing is for products and goods. In contrast, the franchising model is used more in the service-providing industry.

**Turnkey Project:** A turnkey project is where the facility is built from the ground up and turned over to the client ready to go—turn the key, and the plant is operational. Turnkey projects are particularly useful to companies that provide services such as environmental consulting, architecture, construction, and engineering for government projects. This is a good way to enter foreign markets as the client is normally a government or financed by an international financial agency such as the World Bank, and hence the risk of not being paid is eliminated. An example of turnkey project is that is done by Alstom. In 2012, Alstom, a French multinational, had a 13-year contract with Dubai Roads and Transport Authority (RTA) to provide maintenance services for the Dubai tramway system. Alstom is responsible for the design, integration, and supply of this turnkey tramway project, which includes the supply of Citadis trams, track laying, signaling (using Alstoms Urbalis CBTC1), communications systems, integrated operation control center, platform screen doors, and ticketing system. Alstom will also be responsible for maintaining the transport system for 13 years (Alstoms Tramway System, 2014).

**Turnkey Project**

*A turnkey project* is where the facility is built from the ground up and turned over to the client ready to go—turn the key, and the plant is operational.

A company may want to enter a foreign market by taking on Turnkey projects for three reasons: (1) It is a way of earning great economic returns from the know-how required to assemble and run a technologically complex process. (2) The host country has strict restrictions on foreign investment. (3) The host country has relatively high political and economic risk, which does not warrant a longer-term investment. On the other hand, entering a market through a Turnkey project also means that the foreign company may not have a long-term interest in the country. In addition, since the know-how will be shared with the local clients, this could create a competitor.

**Management Contract:** A management contract is an arrangement by which one firm provides managerial know-how in some or all functional areas to another company for a specified period. This is in exchange for a lump sum payment or a continuing fee on a percentage of sales value or volume. Management contracts could be a useful entry mode where a firm has knowledge and expertise but cannot own the assets off-shore, and the other party lacks management expertise. It is used by both manufacturing and service operations when the foreign company can manage better than the owners.

**Management Contract**

A *management contract* is an arrangement by which one firm provides managerial know-how in some or all functional areas to another company for a specified period.

Sectors commonly use management contracts are utility services where some developing markets need assistance from developed markets to manage new infrastructure like water management. It is also widely used in the hotel industry. Empirical data highlights that during the late 1990s, the use of the management contract in North America, Europe, and Asia was around 41%, 37%, and 42% of hotels (Contractor & Kundu, 1998). In Australia and New Zealand, more than 50% of hotels use a management contract (Turner & Guilding, 2013). Marriott International, for example, had the highest number of hotels (1018) managed under a management contract, accounting for 26% of all hotels in their system at the end of 2013 (Turner et al., 2016).

Such a management contract entry mode has some advantages. As illustrated in the case mentioned above, the foreign company (Marriott International) was able to rapidly expand at a relatively low cost because it typically invested little to no equity in the hotels operated under a management agreement (Ivanova et al., 2016). Correspondingly, the foreign company carried no real-estate risk and little downside risk. They were also able to achieve economies of scale by spreading overhead costs, such as marketing expenses, across multiple hotels (Ivanova et al., 2016). In addition, with the specified management contract, Marriott International could maintain control over operations and brand standard compliance as it entered new and existing markets.



On the other hand, some problems could exist. A foreign company (Marriott International) and local partners (local hotel owners) could potentially conflict if they have different goals. For example, hotel chains are typically interested in achieving short-term cash flows that have an immediate impact on the management fees they collect. In contrast, hotel owners could prioritize long-term goals that sustain the value of their real estate (Guilding et al., 2001). The misaligned goals could result in lengthy and costly legal disputes or early termination of the management contract (Dev et al., 2010). In addition, sharing know-how with local partners will be associated with the risk of creating competitors.

**Service Networks***:* In professional service firms like law firms, audit firms, advertising, and market research firms, frequent international market entry happens not by setting up one's own subsidiary. Especially, but not confined to, the initial steps of internationalization, firms might instead create a reference network or *service network* with existing local firms in the major countries where their customers have operations. There is no equity investment and no strict formal contractual relationship as in management contracts or franchising. For example, when DTG, the German part of the pedigree of KPMG, internationalized, it referred audit clients who needed their foreign subsidiaries' financial statements audited to local audit firms in those countries. These local audit firms had established a trusting relationship with DTG and would refer their clients who needed an audit in Germany to DTG. Likewise, German market research firm GfK maintains a network of independent firms worldwide to combine local expertise and flexibility with global reach if a client needs international market research (Zimmer et al., 2009; Kewitz & Reihlen, 2006).

**Strategic Alliance:** A strategic alliance is a relationship between two or more organizations that—through combining their resources—can create significant and sustainable value for everyone involved. Firms could go into a strategic alliance for a variety of reasons, such as enhancing marketing efforts, building sales and market share, improving products, reducing production and distribution costs, and sharing technology and research capacity. The strategic alliance allows companies to share the risks and resources required to enter international markets, although returns also may have to be shared.

**Strategic Alliance**

A *strategic alliance* is a relationship between two or more organizations that—through combining their resources—can create significant and sustainable value for everyone involved.

Strategic alliances can be found in both manufacturing industries and service industries. In manufacturing industries, for example, in 2004, Cisco Systems Inc. and Fujitsu Limited formed a strategic alliance in the field of routers and switches. The companies have then worked together to customize the Cisco IOS XR operating system for high-end routers, enhancing product functionality and the support structure to meet the requirements of Japanese telecommunications carriers. In 2005, the strategic alliance introduced a Fujitsu and Cisco CRS-1 Carrier Routing System (Jose, 2005).

In service industries, for instance, in 2017, Samsung Pay cut a strategic partnership deal with PayPal and decided to link PayPal accounts to the Samsung Pay mobile payment platform. Via this strategy, Samsung Pay hoped to expand its customer base by partnering with PayPal, which was used by more than 200 million people, and PayPal expected to generate synergies by expanding offline payment areas (Samsung Newsroom US, 2017). Another example is that in 2019, Chinese telecom company Huawei's business arm, Huawei Cloud, and India's Infosys signed a memorandum on strategic cooperation to help clients transition quickly to the digital cloud. As part of the agreement, Infosys would join the Huawei Cloud Partner Network (HCPN), and the two companies would develop new cloud solutions. The new solutions will leverage Huawei Cloud and Infosys products and services to help customers securely adopt innovative cloud-based systems for their enterprise workloads (Huawei Cloud expands, 2019).

The disadvantages of strategic alliance, on the other hand, are lack of direct control and the possibility that the partner's goals differ from the firm's.

## Investment (Equity-Based) Entry Mode

Investment entry modes are about establishing or acquiring ownership in a company located in a foreign market. In other words, the activities within this category involve ownership of production units or other facilities in the overseas market, usually based on some equity or non-equity investment. This can be achieved by joint ventures (equity-based), acquisitions, or green-field investment.

**Joint Venture:** A joint venture, also called an equity joint venture (EJV), is an arrangement where foreign and local partners fund a separate entity (a partnership or a corporation) to manage their joint operation. The foreign firm has an equity position and a management voice in the foreign firm. This agreement gives the international firm better control over operations and access to local market knowledge. Another advantage is that through sharing the costs and benefits of the investment, the foreign company and local partner(s) can also share the risks. By investing in and joining a local firm, the international firm could gain market knowledge from the local partner firm and tap into the local partner's network of relationships with local supply chains and the government, which will smoothen the market entry and operation.

**Joint Venture**

A *joint venture*, also called an equity joint venture (EJV), is an arrangement where foreign and local partners fund a separate entity (a partnership or a corporation) to manage their joint operation. The foreign firm has an equity position and a management voice in the foreign firm.



The disadvantage is the conflicts between the partners, including: (1) Conflict over asymmetric investment and control power. It is often difficult to maintain a balanced relationship between the EJV partners. Once a firm's expansion strategy conflicts with the other party, the two may bargain about the relative share ownership for more control of the entity. Thus, the partner with stronger bargaining power will continue to lead an unsteady joint venture. (2) Mistrust over proprietary knowledge since it could be risky for the firm to share technology with the partner. (3) Performance ambiguity, that is, how to "split the pie" between partners. (4) Cultural clashes. Cultural differences in communication, leadership style, decision-making, and knowledge sharing could exist between foreign and local partners. In evaluating joint venture partners, if a proper compatibility and integration analysis is not performed, the cultural difference could lead to extensive conflicts in strategy, norms, and emotion among the international joint venture partners. Such conflicts have been shown as one of the most common causes of a JV failure. (5) If, how, and when to terminate the relationship.

As a result, when engaging in an EJV, the company needs to consider a range of issues, such as ownership, control, length of the agreement, pricing, technology transfer, choice of local partners (e.g., firm capabilities and resources, and alignment of objectives and culture), and government intentions carefully. For example, Starbucks adopted EJV in quite a few countries, such as Spain (18%), Israel (19.5%), and South Korea (50%). In 2001, Starbucks used an EJV to enter Spain, forming a partnership with the VIPS Group, a famous Spanish restaurant chain. Their first store opened the following year. Group VIPS created the joint venture with Starbucks because it regarded that becoming Starbucks' partner would contribute to its growth strategy (Starbucks to Enter Spain, 2001). In 2000, Group VIPS put an ambitious growth project into action to double its size in 3 years. Starbucks, in turn, chose Group VIPS because they needed a local partner to help the company to establish itself in the community. Álvaro Salfranca, Starbucks' Chief Executive in Spain, mentioned that VIPS group played a local role since they understood the country and operated the stores. At the same time, Starbucks set the heart, soul, and philosophy behind its Starbucks concept. Furthermore, both companies shared a vision and values to facilitate the smooth flow of their venture. Howard Schultz, Starbucks Coffee Company chairman, commented that VIPS Group was an ideal partner for Starbucks because the two had an aligned strategic and business vision (Santamaría & Ni, 2008).

However, it should be noted that not all joint ventures dictate profit sharing and management voice in proportion to capital contribution. The following box gives a special type of joint venture, that is, cooperative joint venture, where an agreement between the partners to collaborate does not necessarily involve equity investment.

**Cooperative Joint Venture (CJV)**

A special type of joint venture is a *cooperative joint venture (CJV)*, an agreement between the partners to collaborate that is not solely based on equity investment. A CJV does not have to be a legal entity, but it could be. The partners in a CJV are allowed to share profit on an agreed basis, not necessarily in proportion to capital contribution. This agreed basis of profit sharing also determines the entity's control and risks in the same proportion.

In China, although most joint ventures are equity joint ventures (EJVs), some investors establish CJVs. In a CJV, Chinese partners can hold and "lend" assets and licenses that are forbidden to foreign investors under Chinese law or undesired by the foreign partner until the venture terminates or foreign ownership rules are relaxed. Undesirable assets may include those with a high transfer tax or too complicated or costly for the foreign investor to obtain, such as land.

One example is E-Smart Technologies, Inc., a US company with wireless security technology for smart cards. E-Smart signed a CJV agreement with two Chinese companies in early 2004. Under the agreement, the CJV would operate nationwide value-added networks made up of E-Smart's operating platform and its multi-application, secure ID, and smart payment cards; market the system and technologies to the government and financial sectors; and maximize the technology's use in as many fields as possible. One of the Chinese CJV partners was majority owned and controlled by an entity of the Ministry of Information Industry (MII); the other was Chinese media and public relations personnel. E-Smart owned half of this joint venture (the maximum allowed by law for a value-added service venture), and the two PRC companies owned 30% and 20%, respectively. E-Smart contributed roughly $3 million in capital to the CJV over time after issuing all required permits and licenses, while Chinese partners do not contribute any equity. This $3 million would represent 100% of the CJV's registered capital. E-Smart owned exclusive licenses to provide and operate the system and technologies in China, and it would receive 20% of the CJV's gross operating income. The Chinese partners used their relationships with the authorities to obtain the needed licenses and approvals, participate in the market promotion and negotiations with customers, address network infrastructure issues, and help obtain financing. The board and operating management team would be determined by the parties in consultation with each other (USCBC, 2005).

**Sole Ownership (Wholly Owned Subsidiaries):** The entry mode of wholly-owned subsidiaries means the firm owns 100% of the overseas entity. There are two major ways to establish foreign wholly-owned subsidiaries. The first is a greenfield venture. That means the firm will enter the new international market by establishing a completely new operation and legal entity. Establishing greenfield wholly-owned subsidiaries offers a number of advantages. One of the advantages is that the firm, with its full ownership, could make its own strategic plan and tightly control the subsidiaries in its own way, which is much easier than changing the existing culture of an acquired unit or local partners in CJV, EJV, or franchise. In addition, compared with other entry modes, the firm does not need to bear the risk of losing its competitive advantages and know-how to its local partners, be they franchisees, CJV, or EJV partners. As a result, it is favored by those companies that operate in businesses where transferring competencies, skills, and expertise plays an important role. Furthermore, local presence and commitment allow the firm to move up the experience curve and understand the local economy. Last but not least, the firm could have 100% of its profits in wholly-owned subsidiaries.



**Wholly-owned Subsidiaries**

The entry mode of *wholly-owned subsidiaries* means the firm owns 100% of the overseas entity.

**Greenfield Venture**

The entry mode of *greenfield venture* means the firm will enter the new international market by establishing a new operation and legal entity.

The disadvantages of greenfield wholly-owned subsidiaries are clear too. Greenfield ventures are not only costly but also time-consuming to establish since the firm needs to take time to find the desired location, build new facilities, recruit and train local staff and ensure compliance with local regulations (Griffin & Pustay, 2012). Because of full ownership, the firm cannot get assistance from other parties. Bearing the full cost of the investment in the foreign country also means that the firm will bear the entire risk regarding future revenue and profit prospects. The risk lies in the uncertain foreign market, the unfamiliar political and economic environment, or the culture gap.

The second method is an *acquisition*, whereby the firm acquires another firm in the foreign market to enter directly. The other firm could be an established and well-built firm in that particular industry. Thus, the firm could gain the advantages of quick and established access to a new market by leveraging the acquirees'existing market knowledge, resource, and network. However, they are expensive. As Wharton professor Lawrence G. Hrebiniak explains, "Mergers fail because people pay too much of a premium. In addition, as in the example of "Target entering Canada" given earlier in this section, the acquirer has to reconfigure and rebuild the acquirees'resources and cultures to fit the acquirer's requirement, which causes extra cost. In addition, the variety and diversity of the foreign business practice or country culture could be a significant issue for the firm to deal with. According to Harvard Business Review, between 70% and 90% of mergers and acquisitions fail because, more often than not, key people leave, teams do not get along, or demotivation sets in the acquired company (Hell, 2022).

**Acquisition**

The entry mode of *acquisition* refers to the firm acquiring another firm in the foreign market to enter directly.

## Differentiating Supply Mode of Service and Entry Mode of Service Companies

We have to differentiate the entry modes from the supply mode of service. The two serve different purposes. The categorization of supply modes in Article I of GATS introduced in ► Chap. 3 addresses the trade flow coming from the service industry. With this purpose, the categorization looks into who produces the service from where and who consumes the service from where, which contributes to cross-border service flow. While the entry mode discussed in this chapter focuses on the strategy which a service company uses to enter an international market. A firm could adopt some entry mode to enter a foreign country to perform different functions, be it production, marketing, research and development, or other value-added activities. Connections between modes of service supply and entry modes can be established as outlined below.

Mode 1 cross-border supply of services involves service being produced in the home country and exported to the host country for consumption, similar to the export of goods, but mostly in an intangible form via information and communication technology. Correspondingly, direct export and indirect export would be the related entry modes, as illustrated in the section about export.

Mode 2 consumption of service abroad refers to when service is produced in the home country, and the consumption of the service also occurs in the home country but by customers from a host country. An example of the Mode 2 could be a consumer from host country A traveling to home country B, where the service firm is located and supplies service, perhaps for tourism, to attend an educational establishment, or to receive medical treatment. The actual provision of the touristic/educational/medical services would be accounted for as an export as the customers have their regular place of residence in another country. To facilitate this type of trade flow, a service company could use multiple entry modes to sell the service to customers in a foreign country. For example, a travel agency from Australia that sells the travel package could use direct export via its own website or indirect export via aggregators (e.g., Trip Advisor) to attract tourists from Japan to visit Australia. An education institution in the United Kingdom could use an indirect export by hiring an education agency in China; the agency will

**Table 7.5** Integrating entry modes and supply modes of service, source: Author's own table based on Daniels et al. (2021: 430), adding in the modes of service supply from WTO (2013) and making further amendments. Boxes in grey indicate collaborative arrangements

<table>
<tr><th rowspan="2">Production ownership</th><th colspan="4">Production location</th></tr>
<tr><th>Home country</th><th colspan="3">Foreign country</th></tr>
<tr><td rowspan="2">Equity arrangement</td><td rowspan="2">Export<br>• Cross-border supply<br>• Consumption abroad</td><td>Wholly-owned subsidiaries<br>• Greenfield<br>• Acquisition</td><td rowspan="2">Commercial presence</td><td rowspan="3">Presence of natural persons possible</td></tr>
<tr><td>(Equity) joint ventures</td></tr>
<tr><td rowspan="3">Non-equity arrangement</td><td rowspan="3"></td><td colspan="2">Management contracts<br>Turnkey contracts</td></tr>
<tr><td colspan="3">Presence of natural persons</td></tr>
<tr><td colspan="3">Licensing/franchising<br>Strategic alliances<br>Service networks</td></tr>
</table>



help the education institution recruit students and send students to the United Kingdom. The United Kingdom education institution can also form a strategic alliance or joint venture with another educational institution in China to develop an exchange program; through the exchange program, the students will be sent to a United Kingdom education institution to receive the service. Contrary to the sale of the service, the provision of the service itself would happen in the home country of the service firm, typically by the service firm itself, such as a university, a hotel, or a hospital.

Mode 3 Commercial presence in the consuming country refers to a service company that sets up its production base in a host country to produce the service for local customers. Here, both the service supply and consumption occur in the host country. It is usually facilitated with the entry modes of joint venture or wholly owned subsidiary, which makes local production possible.

Mode 4 Presence of natural persons abroad refers to when a foreign natural person provides a service within host country A as an independent supplier (e.g., a freelance consultant or a health worker). The natural persons have to be in the host country since the service supplied necessitates simultaneous production and consumption. Here, both the supply and consumption of the service occur in the host country. A service company could employ an export entry mode to supply service in this mode, whereby no production facilities are established in the host country. However, it could also happen in the context of other modes of entry. For example, one computer service company from India has entered a host country, Vietnam, using entry modes of turnkey, management contract, strategic alliance, joint venture or wholly owned subsidiaries. This Indian company could then send an individual expert to the host country Vietnam to support the project or subsidiary's operation for some days or weeks.

Daniels et al. (2021) have created a helpful diagram that combines the production location and equity participation in the operation. We use this as a starting point and enter the modes of service supply of WTO into the diagram, as shown in ◘ Table 7.5. In line with the modes of entry outlined above, we make some further amendments, leaving out modes we have not considered here (e.g. an entry mode in which the company has acquired a part of a stock-listed company in the target country, while the remaining shares are held by many small shareholders, equity alliances) and instead, add in (non-equity) strategic alliances and service networks.

## Ensuring Country-Specific and Cross-Country Competence

Based on the Ownership, Location- and Internalization (OLI) paradigm (Dunning, 1979), firms need certain internal strengths to overcome the additional costs of doing business abroad; those internal strengths are called Firm-Specific Advantages (FSA).

**Firm-Specific Advantage**

An *firm-specific advantage* (FSA) is the result of a firm‘s *unique resources* combined with the firm‘s typical *routines* in producing a service or a good and the firm's recombination skills.

In this definition, two components of FSAs deserve further attention.

*Unique resources.* Verbeke (2013) identified a few sources of unique standalone resources that could give the firm the advantages:

- Physical resources (natural resources, buildings, plant equipment).
- Financial resources (equity and loan capital).
- Human resources (individuals and teams, entrepreneurial and operational skills).
- Upstream knowledge (product and process-related technological knowledge).
- Downstream knowledge (marketing, sales, distribution and after sales service).
- Administrative knowledge (organizational structure, culture and systems).
- Reputational resources (brand names, reputation for honest business dealings)

*Routines.* The unique standalone resources are combined with some firm routines in unique ways valued by firms' stakeholders. Routines are stable patterns of decisions and actions coordinating the productive use of resources, thereby generating values, either domestically or internationally. Routines are more complex than stand-alone resources and hence difficult to be imitated by competitors.

FSAs give an advantage to a firm and separate it from its competitors. One example is Airbnb, which has unique standalone resources, such as brand recognition and limitless availability of places supported by the large number of hosts who list on Airbnb (currently totaling around seven million). The company also has its routines to help the company capture more demand and outperform other competitors. For instance, ► Airbnb.com allows hosts to identify suitable guests by showcasing the property with a lot of detail and in a standardized way familiar to guests. When a host decides to list a property, they need to take action concerning a range of areas: they need to provide certain information about the property (such as location and Wi-Fi password), ensure that the property has the safety features required under local laws and regulations (such as fire alarms, exit signs on doors and an emergency evacuation plan), and be able to signal to guests interested in booking their property whether or not it is available on specific dates. The Airbnb platform also forces hosts to take action when regulations or circumstances change in critical ways (Reinhold & Dolnicar, 2021).

Depending on the costliness of transferring FSAs internationally, FSAs can be distinguished into two types: non-location-bound FSAs and location-bound FSAs (Rugman & Verbeke, 1992).



*Non-location-bound FSAs* do not depend on their being used in one specific location. They can be transferred to other locations and used globally at low cost and without substantial adaptation. Cutting-edge technologies, marketing prowess, and strong brands are all examples of non-location-bound FSAs. These non-location-bound FSAs become a firm's cross-country competence.

Some FSA can only be used in one particular or a few locations, and they are *location-bound FSAs*. They cannot be easily transferred and used in other locations without significant adaptation. In that sense, the location-bound FSAs are a firm's country-specific competence. There are three drivers of the location-boundness of FSAs. First, the advantage is embedded in the home environment. It may be absent or lose value when going to other geographical contexts. For instance, some stand-alone resources, such as a good relationship with local government, a well-developed local distribution network, or local production-related factors (e.g., nature resources, labor, and raw materials), are used and linked to location advantages and hence are immobile and non-transferable. A firm can have deep knowledge of marketing and reputational resources in one location, but such knowledge or reputation may not have value in other countries. Some local best practices, that is, the highly effective and efficient routines in the home country, might not be the same abroad.

The second driver for the location-boundedness of FSAs is that the recombination capability is too complex to be transferred to foreign markets. For example, a firm's advantage may reside in its quality control practices, which need to function with the entire production system. In other words, such an advantage is organizationally embedded since it includes a range of activities involving cross-function coordination within the organization. Such advantages are costly to be transferred across national borders and thus location bound.

Third, the advantage is difficult to transfer due to its tacit nature. The extant research literature on knowledge transfer suggests that an FSA could be easily codifiable knowledge, that is, explicit knowledge, as documented information regarding a process, product, or service. While it is cheap and easy to transfer, it can also be easily imitated by other firms. This makes the transfer costs low, but the value that can be derived from it may also be low. Some FSAs are in the form of non-codifiable knowledge, that is, implicit or tacit knowledge (Kogut & Zander, 1993). Implicit or Tacit knowledge is knowledge garnered from personal experience and context. It is the information that is difficult to write down, articulate, present or teach in a tangible form (Nonaka & Takeuchi, 1995; Szulanski, 1996). For example, an IT specialist can troubleshoot a problem based on his experience. It would be very difficult for him to codify his knowledge into a document that could convey his know-how to a beginner. As a result, transferring it will require person-to-person communication and sending human resources abroad to build up experience over time by learning, which will be expensive and time-consuming. However, it is also difficult to imitate and thus a valuable FSA. In that sense, implicit or tacit knowledge is a major competitive advantage abroad.

Let us look into one case of a hotel expanding from Hong Kong to the United States, whereby the hotel's FSAs are location-bound. Hong Kong-based hotel groups such as the Peninsula have developed a high quality of services, partially because of Hong Kong's location characteristics as a regional business center and traveling destination. This quality of services is made possible by a high ratio of employees to rooms, among other factors. However, when Peninsula brought its hotels to the United States in the late 1980s, such practices were not feasible because labor in the United States was more expensive than in Hong Kong. Therefore, maintaining the same high ratio of employees to rooms, though viewed as a best practice in Hong Kong luxury hotels, was not efficient or cost-effective in the States. Consequently, the Hong Kong hotel groups had to rely more on other methods to assess and improve the quality of services in their US subsidiaries, such as focusing on more in-house training and recruiting more enthusiastic and younger staff.

## Selection of a Suitable Mode of Entry

In general, the entry mode varies regarding control levels, resource commitment, and risks. ◘ Table 7.6 summarizes the pros and cons of the above-mentioned entry modes. Generally speaking, equity modes with a higher ownership level can grant investors more control over their foreign business activities but also necessitate more resource commitment and hence incur higher risks compared to non-equity modes (e.g., Hill et al., 1990).

Choosing an entry mode means choosing the desired control level and resource commitment level, which will be associated with benefits and costs. Such a trade-off decision has been illustrated by a diagram in Frynas and Mellahi (2015), as shown in ◘ Fig. 7.4. In this diagram, the country risk is a decisive factor driving companies to choose a high resource commitment (for low country risk) or low resource commitment (for high country risk) mode to minimize risk while maximizing control as possible.

Four levels of factors could be considered when evaluating the risk of the market and deciding the control level required.

**Table 7.6** Pros and cons of the entry modes, source: Author's own table

| Entry modes | Advantages | Disadvantages |
|---|---|---|
| Exporting | Low commitment<br>Low risk | Low control<br>Lack of contact with foreign market<br>No learning experience |
| Licensing | Little or no investment<br>Low risk<br>Fast-entry<br>Means to bridge import barriers | Low control on licensees<br>Risk of creating a competitor |
| Franchising | Little or no investment<br>Fast-entry | Need for quality control<br>Risk of creating a competitor |
| Turnkey | High return based on sharing know-how<br>Suitable for entering foreign markets where the government is the client | No long-term interest<br>Risk of creating a competitor |
| Management contract | Low cost<br>Rapid expansion | Misaligned interests between foreign companies and local partners may cause conflict and early termination.<br>Risk of creating a competitor |
| Joint venture (strategic alliance, CJV and EJV) | Cost and risk sharing with local partners<br>Leverage on local partners' resources (such as local know-how, local distribution network, and relationship with the government) | Risk of conflicts with a partner<br>Lack of control<br>Risk of creating a competitor |
| Acquisition | Full control<br>Access to local assets (e.g., plants, distribution<br>Network, and brand assets)<br>Fast-entry | Costly<br>High risk<br>Difficulty in integrating different national/corporate cultures |
| Greenfield | Full control over the operation<br>Less risk of cultural conflicts | Costly<br>Time-consuming<br>High political and financial risks |

7

## Host Country Level Factors

There are some "hard uncertainties" which arise from the host country's environment, for example, political instability, economic instability (fluctuating exchange rate and inflation), poor diplomatic relations between the host country and the home country, regulatory restrictions, and law enforcement, and property protection. Usually, in environments characterized by high "hard" uncertainty, investors may have to choose a flexible entry strategy, reducing the resource commitment and the potential sunk costs. In this case, non-equity entry modes, such as export, licensing, and franchising, will be preferred. In addition, some countries have

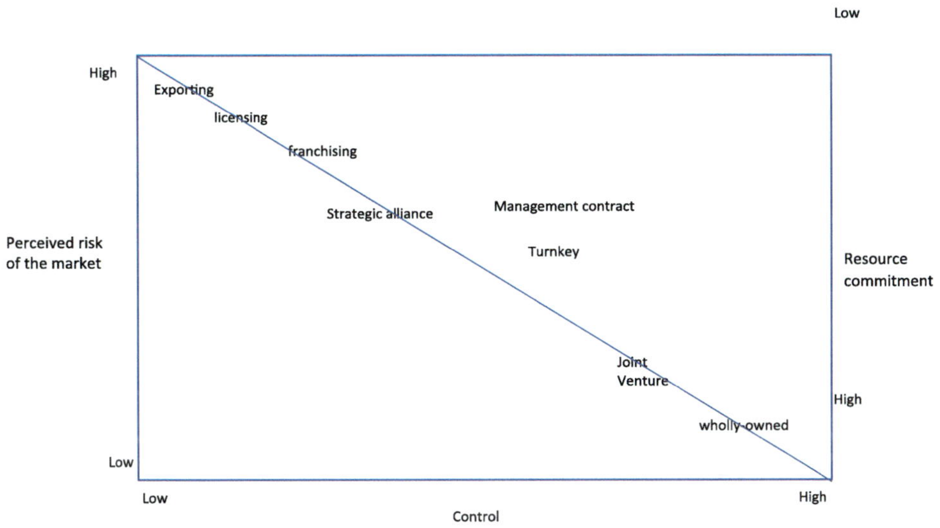


**Fig. 7.4** Entry mode selection based on the trade-off between resource commitment and control level. Author's own figure based on Frynas and Mellahi (2015)

ownership restrictions. For example, in Sep 2021, China tightened the restrictions on foreign ownership in the education industry: Ownership or control of private schools by foreign entities will no longer be allowed (China bars foreign curricula and ownership, 2021). The United States has laws addressing acquisitions. For example, one must be an American citizen to own a TV station in the United States, and a foreign firm is not allowed to own more than 25% of a US airline. In this case, the service firms may have to turn to other entry modes such as cooperative or equity joint venture or franchising as alternative ways to gain some control over the operation. In the opening case, in China, where government censorship for digital content was strict, Netflix used licensing to allow local firms to distribute their content. Although the return was lower, such an entry mode could help Netflix deal with the high market uncertainty in China.

## Industry Level Factors

Market attractiveness and product-market uncertainties need to be considered at the industry level. While foreign investors favor equity entry modes for greater profit sharing entering attractive local markets/industries, the product-market uncertainties may have more complicated implications for entry mode. Product-market uncertainty refers to unexpected changes in product demand, client preferences, and availability of substitute and complementary products (Brouthers et al., 2002). On the one hand, higher product-market uncertainties increase investors' propensity to share investment risks and reduce resource commitment in investments, similar to some country-level factors (e.g., the political and regulative environments). On the other hand, to quickly respond to and adapt to the change in the market, firms may also have the incentive to adopt high control entry mode.

### Firm Level Factors

The core capabilities of multi-domestic companies lie in exploiting non-location-bound FSAs or adapting location-bound FSAs, using host country-specific advantages. These companies have to deal with markets that require tailoring products and services to local circumstances. To do so, companies must be well aware of local circumstances and well-integrated into the local market. This will be easier to achieve by acquiring an existing company with a knowledgeable workforce and good connections in the local market or partnering with a local firm via joint venture or franchising than by setting up a new subsidiary from scratch.

## Specific Factors Related to the Service Industry: Type of Services

7

► Chapter 1 has introduced different types of services depending on the characteristics of services. The type of services has some important implications for the entry mode decision.

### Hard Service or Soft Service

As introduced in ► Chap. 1, services can be categorized as hard service and soft service. A hard service permits the separation of production and consumption. It could be produced in one country, embodied in some tangible form (such as a disk, blueprint, or document, and hence vehicle-based and object-based), and offered to another country via direct or indirect export mode. Examples include packaged software, engineering design, research service, life insurance, music, architectural design, education course, and some types of banking services.

With regard to soft services, the producer and receiver of a soft service should be in close physical proximity, enabling production and consumption to take place simultaneously. Examples of soft services include healthcare, advertising, hospitality, fast food, car rental, management consulting, and customized data processing. As a result, such a service cannot be exported where local production is absent. Instead, firms offering these services should choose the range of entry modes, such as licensing, or franchising, and investment entry modes, such as joint ventures, greenfield, or acquisition, to facilitate local production.

In the opening case, since the service provided by Netflix is a kind of hard service where production and consumption are decoupled, export is an appropriate way to enter most countries where adaption and localization are needed at a minimal level.

### Standardized Service or Customized Service

Another characteristic that influences the entry mode choice is the heterogeneity, namely, the degree of service standardization. Consumer services, such as fast food and car rental, followed by computer services, appear to be the most standardized. It is, therefore, not surprising that franchising is such a common method of entry for these services. Similarly, software firms that sell relatively standardized computer or software services can simply use export mode to enter a foreign market.

On the other hand, services such as advertising, banking, management consulting, and engineering are more customized and require one-on-one interaction with overseas customers. As a result, firms providing these services use entry modes characterized by a high degree of integration and control to facilitate local adaptation, such as joint venture and sole-ownership entry modes.

In the opening case, in Japan, where customers are not English speakers and localization is necessary, Netflix adopted a strategic alliance with a local firm to co-develop local programs. A strategic alliance was also formulated with the telecom company in Thailand to target those customers who had good access to the internet and hence were more likely to purchase Netflix's streaming services.

## Capital-Intensive Service or Knowledge-Intensive Service

Another dimension to examine services is the type of resources dominating the service operation, based on which we can identify capital-intensive and knowledge-intensive services.

As in ► Chap. 1, services could be classified based on the needed level of capital intensity (Contractor et al., 2003; Hertog, 2000; Windrum & Tomlinson, 1999). The level of capital intensity represents the volume of investment in fixed assets necessary to begin production and carry out operations in a given industry (Erramilli & Rao, 1993). Capital-intensive services whose presence abroad demands sizeable investments in installations and equipment, for example, telecommunications, hotels, and hospitals, will require higher resource commitment and control than those less capital-intensive services. At the same time, capital-intensive services will also face higher barriers to exiting the market where the cessation of the activity is advisable (Anand & Delios, 1997). As a result, those service companies tend to use shared-control modes, such as franchising, management contract, and joint venture, where the service companies can control the operation while committing fewer resources.

Knowledge-intensive services are those where knowledge has more importance than other inputs, and human capital dominates as opposed to physical or financial capital. Such services include professional service firms (PSFs), for example, accounting, management consultancy, engineering and architecture, marketing, and advertising service firms, among others. For these firms, direct foreign investment does not imply a large investment of resources in the host country, as it does not require sizeable investments in plants, machinery, buildings, and other physical assets; a firm's presence may be represented by a single office (Erramilli & D'Souza, 1995). Thus, these firms' exit costs are comparatively lower. On the other hand, the provision of knowledge-intensive services mainly requires investments in human resources, given that such services depend on the skills, talent, and knowledge necessary to satisfy the needs and expectations of the consumers (Erramilli & Rao, 1993). However, the provision of these services is also subject to a high level of variability, given that the final output fundamentally depends on the people involved in the process. This makes the quality control of these services critical, therefore requiring careful recruiting, training, and sharing of tacit knowledge (Palmer, 1995). Hence, such service companies prefer to adopt wholly owned subsidiaries to enter a foreign market.

### Services with Different Needs for the Physical Presence of the Customer

As mentioned in ► Chap. 1, Wirtz and Lovelock (2018) distinguish services by two criteria: (1) To what extent the actions performed by service providers are tangible, and (2) To what extent services are directed at people themselves or their possessions, which also impacts the need for the physical presence of the customer. They distinguish people-processing, possession-processing, mental stimulus-processing, and information-processing services. The four types of international services have different implications for the entry modes (Dolski & Hermanns, 2004).

- People processing services have to be provided in close customer contact and frequently require a wholly-owned subsidiary, JV, franchising, or management contract, which allows local presence in the host country, for example, a hotel.
- Mental processing services, for example, TV broadcasting, can be exported from any country. However, some local operations abroad are needed to facilitate the sale and delivery of the service to customers. For example, the TV station might employ local correspondents and someone who sells advertising space to local companies, due to which cross-border trade in combination with the presence of natural persons, joint ventures, strategic alliances, or a service network might be a suitable entry mode.
- Information-processing services, such as a bank, need to have at least a front office in the host country. Other parts of the service (back office) can be performed anywhere in the world, for example, in a shared service center, which could be facilitated by a wholly-owned subsidiary, joint venture, franchising or service network.
- Possession processing services enable all modes of market entry. For example, regarding repair services, the manufacturer can require that devices be sent to the firm's home country. It can have a cooperation partner in the host country who does the repair work, only provide remote service or set up a service operation of its own.



## Entry Timing: Overarching Timing and Country-Specific Strategies

Another international market entry decision is: When should the firm enter a foreign market? Two questions deserve a business' deliberate consideration: the timing of the internationalization process and the timing of entering a specific country.

### Timing of the Internationalization Process

The timing of the internationalization process can be understood in two important dimensions. The first one is the initial internationalization time which is the time between the initial establishment of a company and the initiation of foreign operations (Kabongo & Okpara, 2019).

## When to Start the Internationalization Process?

Two types of strategies can be generally identified for the initial internationalization timing strategy: the traditional internationalization process and the born global.

The traditional internationalization process literature argues that the international expansion process of firms should occur more slowly and sequentially, following the Uppsala model (Wiedersheim-Paul & Johanson, 1975; Johanson & Vahlne, 1977). As introduced before, this approach assumes that there is a lack of knowledge of the foreign market, which is detrimental to internationalization. Therefore, a firm should first establish itself in its domestic market before increasing its commitment and resources in a nearby country using low commitment entry mode (such as export). Many large multinational enterprises followed such an incremental model by not starting their internationalization until they had gained significant market share in their home market (Karra et al., 2008). For example, Nokia Corporation, a Finnish multinational telecommunications, information technology, and consumer electronics corporation established in 1865, only started its international expansion in the 1960s (Nokia Corporation, n.d.). Carrefour, a French multinational retail and wholesaling corporation, started its internationalization in Belgium in 1969 by forming a strategic alliance with GB Group, 10 years after its inception in 1958 (Carrefour, n.d.).

Recent international entrepreneurship studies suggest that many firms enter international markets much earlier in the firm's life cycle (Wu & Voss, 2015), which are typically termed as *Born Globals*. The literature suggests that to be considered a Born Global, a firm‘s internationalization debut ranges from within 2 years of inception (McKinsey & Co., 1993), to 6 years (Zahra et al., 2000), to 7 years (Jolly et al., 1992), to 8 years (McDougall et al., 1994). This diversity suggests that the definitional boundary for born globals is a matter of degree more than an absolute. From the decades of 1980s and 1990s, it has been witnessed with the appearance of such Born Globals. Many of these firms go global when they may not even have sales in their domestic market (Jolly et al. 1992; Knight & Cavusgil, 1996; McKinsey & Co., 1993; Oviatt & McDougall, 1994), thus contradicting the Uppsala model.

The early internationalization process is made possible for various reasons. For instance, liberalization of trade and technological advances in production, transportation, and communication (Madsen & Servais, 2017), particularly the Internet, provide firms with easy access to worldwide customers, distributors, network partners, and suppliers (McDougall & Oviatt, 2000). The increasingly global scope of cultural homogeneity and social change (Oviatt & McDougall, 1997) facilitates some industries' larger global customer base. The prior international experience and global networks of Born Globals' founders and decision makers play an important role in increasing the firms' speed of learning and internationalization (Oviatt & McDougall, 1997). The intense competition from imports in the firm's home market becomes the push factor for the Born Global.

Many Born Globals are knowledge-intensive service firms, though not all are. For instance, Skype, a Danish company providing free internet phone and messaging services founded in 2003, entered an agreement with the Polish web portal Onet.pl for an integrated offering in the Polish market in 2005 (Singh, n.d.;

Telecompaper, 2005). Other examples are Spotify, Logitech, and HTC, which all started their business by targeting international markets from the very beginning. Some conditions make this particularly suitable for these knowledge-intensive companies. For example, the market in the home country is not large enough to support the scale at which the firm needs to operate. Many of the firm's potential customers are foreign, multinational clients or clients having overseas operations where they will use the Born Global's products or services.

In the opening case, while Netflix was founded in 1997 as a DVD rental business, internationalization did not start until 13 years later (2010). Before its internationalization, it had attained sizable domestic sales. As a result, it followed a traditional internationalization process.

### How Fast to Internationalize?

The second dimension is the pace or speed of internationalization, which can be expressed as the number of countries or foreign markets the firm enters in a certain period (Meschi et al., 2017).



The traditional Uppsala model views internationalization as a gradual and risk-reducing process. Firms devote resources to international operations when they have sufficient experience to reduce uncertainties. However, since accumulating experience and knowledge takes time, internationalization under the traditional approach represents a slow process. This probably makes good sense considering the potential negative consequence of a failure on the firm's resource availability and reputation in an international business context (Musteen et al., 2010). Some firms have retreated into their domestic markets after an unsuccessful foreign entry. For instance, Starbucks opened in Australia in 2000 and grew to nearly ninety locations by 2008. However, Starbucks moved too quickly and grew faster than its popularity. In 2008, Starbucks closed more than 70% of its underperforming locations in Australia (sixty-one locations), leaving only twenty-three stores throughout the entire continent because it accumulated $105 million in losses in its first 7 years (Turner, 2018).

Nevertheless, recent studies argue that internationalization may occur faster (Hilmersson & Johanson, 2016). Many companies seek a faster internationalization strategy since they believe fast entry allows them to seize new opportunities and build first-mover advantages (Chetty et al., 2014). Speeding internationalization also allows the firm to search for new knowledge to complement and upgrade its current knowledge base, reduce the technological obsolescence risks and achieve cost efficiency by spreading their R&D fixed costs over a larger sales base (García-García et al., 2017). Especially in fast-moving industries such as mobile phones, it can be important to launch new products globally quickly before competitors can copy new features. The same applies to markets with global transparency so that competitors (and customers) immediately note what a firm is doing in some markets that it has entered. This can be because the product or service is very visible or the product has created a big echo in the media when being introduced in a country. When customer needs are similar across markets, such as for semiconductors, this can also be an argument for entering many markets quickly, as there is no need for local adaptation (Kutschker & Schmid, 2011: 992–995).

In the opening case, since 2010, Netflix has quickly expanded its business worldwide. A few factors could drive such a quick internationalization:

- Development of the internet, allowing Netflix to provide its service to worldwide customers.
- Global digital customers who share similar entertainment values and preferences.
- The content licenses Netflix has secured are not based on the number of subscriptions. The incremental costs incurred for signing up a new subscriber are extraordinarily low. Accessing as many customers as possible will allow Netflix to achieve the maximum value for the licensed content at a low unit cost.
- Knowledge obtained from one market could be leveraged into other markets.

## Timing Strategies for Entering a Specific Country

### First-Movers vs. Followers

Timing of entering a specific country refers to the order of entry into a new or existing space (e.g., market, industry, or geographic region) relative to competitors, technology development, product life cycle, or other contextual referents. Scholars exploring entry timing have largely drawn on the first-mover advantage perspective, although more research explores the advantages and disadvantages of a broad spectrum of temporal entry strategies ranging from first and early mover (or early follower) (e.g., Kerin et al., 1992; Lieberman & Montgomery, 1988, 1998) to late mover (e.g., Cho et al., 1998; Shamsie et al., 2004; Shankar et al., 1998).

Scholarly literature has suggested that a firm that first introduces a product or service to the market could enjoy a range of unique first-mover advantages that later entrants cannot overcome. For instance, first movers have more time to accumulate and master technical knowledge (Lanzolla & Suarez, 2006). They are able to preempt access to scarce assets, such as the best locations in a city to open its outlets, talented employees, or key suppliers (Boulding & Christen, 2008). First movers also have the advantage of defining consumer preference by influencing how different product attributes are valued and the ideal configuration of such attributes (Carpenter & Nakamoto, 1989). Additionally, first movers benefit from "branding" their products as the standard. This helps build an early base of customers who would find it inconvenient or costly to switch to the offerings of later entrants.

Bosch Healthcare is a good example of such a first-mover. The core of Bosch Healthcare was a startup called Health Hero Network before it was purchased by Bosch, the $63 billion leader in sensor technologies. Foreseeing that remote-patient monitoring could become a giant industry that improves patient care while offloading work from overstretched physicians and nurses, Bosch acquired Health Hero Network, received sixty-three patents, completed a raft of clinical studies, and made its technology recognizable to many hospitals and physicians. By doing this, Bosch Healthcare secured about half the remotely monitored patients worldwide and became the market leader in technologies to remotely monitor chronically ill patients in their homes. The remote-monitoring field is currently packed with start-ups, including big-name ventures such as General Electric and Intel. However, these firms lacked Bosch's many early-mover advantages and had to compete by offering expensive services at low prices (Wunker, 2012).

While there are some successful first movers like Bosch Healthcare, other first movers, such as eToys in Internet retailing, have failed. This is because first movers also face some disadvantages. For example, the first mover typically incurs high research and development costs, underdeveloped supply and distribution channels, immature technological infrastructures, and uncertainty of customer demands. The first movers' disadvantages could become advantages for the followers—the followers can exploit the experiences of the first mover and improve their offerings and business models; thus, they can capture market share more easily. One example is Six Degrees, the first social networking website that started in 1997 before Facebook but closed in 2001. When SixDegrees launched in 1997, only 21.6% of Americans were online. People then were using AOL dial-up connections. The addressable market was small, and the general public wasn't ready to share their lives online. The failure of Six Degrees illustrated the first mover disadvantage: high research and development cost for bringing in a new service, limited market base, and underdeveloped technological infrastructure. This is in good contrast to Facebook, which was launched to the public in 2006. At the time, 68.9% of Americans were using the Internet and were already familiar with other social networking predecessors—MySpace and Friendster. Facebook built on the awareness that its predecessors had created while improving their user experience to become the most valuable social network in the world (Press, 2018).



### Factors Influencing Optimal Timing of Entry

Then, what is the best timing strategy to enter a foreign market? The following checklist could help your decision.

- How mature is the industry? In a nascent industry, customer preferences are not well understood. The organizational form and functional requirements are not fully established (Dobrev & Gotsopoulos, 2010). As a result, early entrants are more likely to fail in nascent industries than in more mature industries.
- How much adaptation does the firm need to make for its service to meet the local demands? A product/service that necessitates less adaptation will accrue more rapid customer acceptance, favoring an early entry.
- Does the offer of the product/service necessitate some enabling technologies and infrastructures, and are they sufficiently developed? If the technological or other infrastructure is underdeveloped, the market will pick up slowly. A firm shall be cautious when considering an early entry.
- Do complementary goods influence the value of the product/service, and are they sufficiently available? Not all products or services require complementary goods, but for those that do (e.g., e-commerce and logistics service), the availability of complements will influence customer acceptance and the success rate of being an early entrant.

- Can the firm withstand early losses? The first mover bears the bulk of R&D expenses and may endure a significant period without revenues; the earlier a firm enters, the more capital resources it may need.
- Does the firm have the resources to accelerate market acceptance? Firms with significant capital resources can invest in aggressive marketing and supplier and distributor development, increasing the early adoption rate.
- Is the first mover advantage durable? Many companies believed that brand preference created by first constituting a valid source of first-mover advantage, only to find that, in many cases, consumers consider the alternatives available at the time of their first purchase, not which came first. As a result, to what extent the first mover advantage is durable or later entrants can enjoy the follower's advantage depends on the entry barriers. Such entry barriers could be a government permit or license to sell the products/services, customers having high switching costs due to loyalty, limited ability to learn or locked-in resources, or the firm having patent protection (Boulding & Christen, 2003), R&D and marketing capabilities, network effects (a phenomenon whereby increased numbers of people improve the value of a good or service), to secure clients (Franco et al., 2009).

  If there are significant entry barriers, the first mover can gain more benefits for a longer time. However, when there is an absence of or limited entry barriers, the first mover could suffer disadvantages. For example, the followers can quickly imitate the first mover's offering. Later entrants can utilize improved technology to deliver the service or produce the good with lower costs and higher quality than an earlier entrant committed to older technology, termed as vintage effects (Bohlmann et al., 2002). In addition, the first mover usually incurs higher costs due to the need to adjust design and production to suit the market preference. In contrast, later entrants do not need to, with better information about the market demand (Boulding & Christen, 2008).

In the opening case, when entering the United Kingdom, France, and Germany, Netflix seemed to have enjoyed a follower's advantage. The possible reasons are that those incumbents in the United Kingdom, France, and Germany had established acceptance for streaming services among consumers. Yet, they did not have a durable first-mover advantage. Instead, Netflix, with a better understanding of the consumers and its wide collection of content, could overtake them.

When entering Latin America and Cuba, Netflix seemed to have suffered from first-mover disadvantages, resulting from under-developed infrastructure and low awareness and acceptance of the streaming service among consumers.

However, Netflix entered Latin America and Cuba to plant the Netflix flag early. For example, concerning Cuba, one of the top priorities for the United States in normalizing its relations with Cuba was to improve Cuba's access to the internet. The United States allowed exporting communications equipment to Cuba and recently built a $31 million fiber-optic cable connecting Cuba to Florida (Epstein, 2015), hoping someday the entire island to be covered by the internet. Netflix, thus, could have a head start in a brand new market.

## Review Questions

1. Outline the motives for a service company to expand internationally.
2. Explain the criteria to be used to select a foreign market to enter.
3. Explain the pros and cons of the available entry modes.
4. Define and explain the location-bound FSAs and non-location-bound FSAs.
5. What factors should be considered when choosing an appropriate entry mode?
6. How do traditional multinationals and Born Global differ regarding the timing of the internationalization process?
7. Explain the rationale for a firm to choose a fast or slow expansion.
8. Doximity, a company headquartered in San Francisco, California, has created a digital network that connects physicians, clinicians, medical professionals, and patients, featuring video calls, voice calls, provider searches, news, and fax capabilities to streamline the healthcare process. The mobile app is used by over one million healthcare professionals across the United States, building stronger relationships between patients and their providers while unlocking efficiency across the healthcare spectrum. Is it better to enter a foreign market, like Vietnam, earlier or later than competitors? Justify your answer. (Source: Betz, 2023).



## Closing Case: Glorang's Expansion in South East Asia

Glorang is a Seoul-based Edtech startup founded by Taeil Hwang in 2017. Hwang started this company with an AI-powered platform helping students match with study abroad programs. Before the COVID-19 pandemic, Glorang pivoted its main business, the online class platform, and launched Gguge in 2020. Gguge offers after-school classes and extracurricular activities online for students between the ages of three and eighteen. The company has a team of thirty-five in Korea.

Launched by its parent company, Glorang Inc., in 2020, Gguge optimizes the learning effect of virtual classes based on its own IP licensing & algorithms. Gguge actively recruits the best teachers in each field for children's experiences. On the one hand, Gguge encourages students to explore topics based on their interests by offering more than 5000 online classes taught live via Zoom. On the other hand, Gguge actively recruits the best teachers in each field for children's experiences. The teachers help students engage with active learning methods, ranging from reading newspapers through solving puzzles to incorporating Minecraft and Pokémon games into the classes. Students can take a one-day course or subscription-based semester classes tailored to age-specific levels via Gguge.

What sets Gguge apart from its peers is its providing education services in local languages. In 2020, the company claimed Gguge had more than 100,000 users in South Korea.

In 2022, Glorang raised a $10 million Series A funding co-led by Korea Investment Partners and Murex Partners, along with Japan's PKSHA Capital. The new funding, which brings its total raised to $18 million, values Glorang at around $40 million.

The startup has aspirations to become the Outschool of Asia. Glorang CEO and founder Taeil Hwang said its business

A student doing online learning, image by Steven Weirather from Pixabay

model was similar to Outschool, the San Francisco-based after-school marketplace for children. Glorang would use Series A to expand its service to Japan and Malaysia by the fourth quarter of this year and Taiwan, Thailand, and Vietnam in the following years, Hwang said. It also planned to increase its headcount.

> The education market in the English-speaking and North American regions is undoubtedly large, but we [at Glorang] understand that each country's local Direct-to-consumer (D2C) education market in Asia can be just as substantial," Hwang said. "As a team that understands the local culture and strategies in Asia, we are confident that our platform will have a strong standing in Asia's ever-growing D2C education market… (Park, 2022).

The comment by Hwang makes particularly good sense after the coronavirus pandemic outbreak, which has forced students in many parts of the globe to become online learners; the education technology industry has experienced a surge in demand globally. The Asia Pacific is one of the fastest-growing regions in the adoption of EdTech, estimated to grow at a CAGR of 17.5%, increasing from $17.6 billion in 2019 to $64.5 billion in 2027.

The demand for EdTech in South East Asia seems especially promising for a range of reasons. Southeast Asia is home to a population of 700 million, of which 26% falls within the school-attending age group. Yet access to quality education is often limited and unevenly spread across the region, with literacy rates as low as 58% in Laos, 74% in Cambodia, and 76% in Myanmar, according to United Nations research. This gap is largely attributed to the region's sizeable rural population, often inadequate infrastructure, and a lack of trained educators and funding.

At a macro level, a material difference is the various stages governments are moving through in implementing changes to their education systems. Some countries have been advancing education with large-scale investments and upgrading education policies. In contrast, several countries struggle with access to funding, the challenges of public vs. private schooling systems, and inconsistencies in the curriculum and skill level of the students.



In South East Asia, private schools have materially advanced curricula vs. the public school systems. Private schools tend to have large balance sheets and resources, and students depend heavily on tutoring.

Asian parents have reasons for enrolling their kids early in independent schooling/tutoring. Competition is stiff, whether it's entering university for high school and college or in the workforce. They want to arm their children with the best education possible and feel that the formal schooling system is not enough. There's also peer pressure and the Kiasu attitude, that is, "the fear of losing out and being left behind" because all the other moms and dads send their primary and secondary kids to private tutors. Another reason for tuition is a lack of time on the part of parents. With most households having both parents working, it makes sense to give the children the tutoring they should be getting from mom and dad. Subjects, too, are not what they used to be. In addition, most countries in the region also have shrinking household sizes that can make higher-quality education more affordable since a family could have more resources for each child with fewer children.

In addition, due to several rounds of school lockdown during the Pandemic, a similar trend emerged throughout the region, with consumers demonstrating the increasing demand for K-12 online providers such as India's Toppr, Philippines' Edukasyon as well as higher education providers such as Vietnam's Topica and Singapore's Cialfo. This demand further increased demand for EdTech's top apps from six million installations in January to 20 million in August 2020.

In terms of the digital infrastructure in South East Asia, the internet economy continues to grow at a staggering pace there, as consumer trends over the last few years and disruption brought by the Covid-19 pandemic have massively accelerated internet penetration rates and a long-term shift to digital. Thanks to the huge digital push at the government level, internet penetration measured by percentage of population using the Internet has grown to a high level in most of the SEA countries (◘ Fig. 7.5). Countries like Brunei, Malaysia, Singapore, Thailand, Vietnam and Indonesia lead this digital intent.

Attributed to the above factors, South East Asia has seen rapid growth in the number of EdTech startup companies over the past 5 years, as shown in ◘ Fig. 7.6, with over 2000 firms operating at different stages of their lifecycle. Singapore stands at the first position with 503 EdTech firms in operation as of Aug 2022.

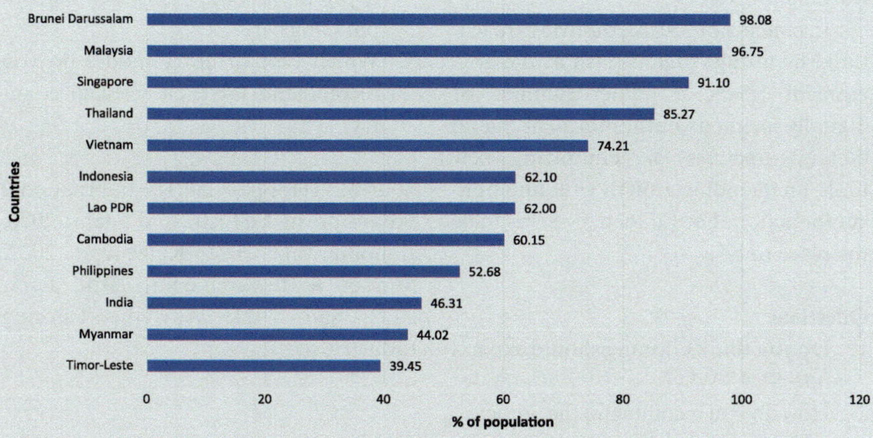


**Fig. 7.5** Individuals using the Internet (% of population) in 2021, source: author's own figure. Data extracted from World Bank (2023)

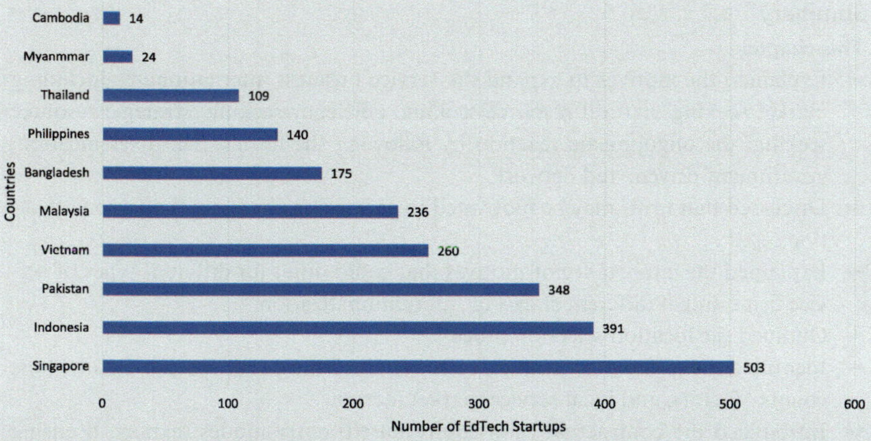


**Fig. 7.6** Number of EdTech startups by country as of Aug 2022, source: Author's own figure. Data extracted from Tracxn (n.d.) in Aug 2022

South East Asia also has some notable examples of companies that have followed the global trend of innovative technologies, such as AI, gamification, and adaptive learning, to enhance EdTech solutions. Ruangguru (Indonesia) is an example of a platform incorporating gamification in its online learning modules and successfully improving student engagement. Another notable example is Geniebook, Singapore's largest EdTech platform for English, Mathematics, and Science (EMS) syllabi, which uses AI to identify students' learning levels and rate of progress to personalize and adapt the learning process.

In conclusion, SEA countries are featured by a huge digital push at the government levels, a higher number of digitally inclined youth, prevalent digital literacy, openness to embracing new tools, an unending growth vibe, and hunger for action. For EdTech, it seems to be the place to be.

**Questions**

1. Do you think Glorang should expand into SEA? Why?
2. How do you recommend the sequence of its entry into those SEA countries if you think some countries are worth pursuing?
3. Which type of entry modes do you recommend for each selected country? Why?

Source: (Hoppe, 2021; International expansion in EdTech., n.d.; Jain, 2020; Jhunjhunwala, 2021; Kaizenvest, 2022; Market ► Research.com, 2020; Park, 2022; Shu, 2021; Why the Tutoring Industry, n.d.)



**Summary**

This chapter

- Explained the motives to expand the service business internationally, including market seeking, natural resource seeking, efficiency-seeking, strategic resource seeking, the oligopolistic reaction by following the leader, risk diversification, government-driven, and network.
- Discussed that firms may be motivated to go overseas by more than one motivation.
- Explained the importance of motives that could differ for different types of service firms and at different stages of internationalization.
- Outlined the location selection process.
- Identified the criteria for location selection, including firm-specific factors, host country factors, and focal service market factors.
- Introduced the contractual (non-equity based) entry modes (export, licensing and franchising, turnkey project, management contract, contract outsourcing, and strategic alliance) and investment (equity-based) entry modes (joint venture, equity joint venture, and sole ownership (greenfield and acquisition).
- Explained the country-specific and cross-country competence.
- Discussed that a suitable mode of entry is based on a trade-off between the desired control level and resource commitment level, which is decided by the country/market risks.
- Discussed the two issues for timing strategies: the timing of the internationalization process and the timing of entering a specific country.

## References

Alstoms tramway system starts operation on the worlds first 100% catenary-free line (2014, Novemeber 12). *Alstom*. Retrieved from https://www.alstom.com/press-releases-news/2014/11/alstoms-tramway-system-starts-operation-on-the-worlds-first-100-catenary-free-line

Anand, J., & Delios, A. (1997). Location specificity and the transferability of downstream assets to foreign subsidiaries. *Journal of International Business Studies, 28*, 579–603.

Andersen, O., & Buvik, A. (2002). Firms' internationalization and alternative approaches to the international customer/market selection. *International Business Review, 11*(3), 347–363.

Balabanis, G. I. (2000). Factors affecting export intermediaries' service offerings: The British example. *Journal of International Business Studies, 31*, 83–99.

Betz, S. (2023, April 10). *33 Telemedicine companies to know*. Builtin. Retrieved from https://builtin.com/healthcare-technology/telemedicine-companies

Boehe, D. M. (2016). Supervisory styles: A contingency framework. *Studies in Higher Education, 41*(3), 399–414.

Bohlmann, J. D., Golder, P. N., & Mitra, D. (2002). Deconstructing the pioneer's advantage: Examining vintage effects and consumer valuations of quality and variety. *Management Science, 48*(9), 1175–1195.

Boulding, W., & Christen, M. (2003). Sustainable pioneering advantage? Profit implications of market entry order. *Marketing Science, 22*(3), 371–392.

Boulding, W., & Christen, M. (2008). Disentangling pioneering cost advantages and disadvantages. *Marketing Science, 27*(4), 699–716.

Brennan, L. (2018, October 12). *How Netflix expanded to 190 countries in 7 years*. Harvard Business Review. Retrieved from https://hbr.org/2018/10/how-netflix-expanded-to-190-countries-in-7-years

Brouthers, K. D., Brouthers, L. E., & Werner, S. (2002). Industrial sector, perceived environmental uncertainty and entry mode strategy. *Journal of Business Research, 55*(6), 495–507.

Carpenter, G. S., & Nakamoto, K. (1989). Consumer preference formation and pioneering advantage. *Journal of Marketing Research, 26*(3), 285–298.

Carrefour. (n.d.) *France's leading retailer and pioneer in the world*. Ohlala!. Retrieved from https://www.ohlalafrenchfanfan.com/en/carrefour-the-french-pioneer-of-mass-retailing-in-the-world/

Cavusgil, S. T. (1985). Guidelines for export market research. *Business Horizons, 28*(6), 27–33.

CFI Team. (n.d.). *Tax Haven. Any country or jurisdiction that offers minimal tax liability*. Retrieved from https://corporatefinanceinstitute.com/resources/economics/what-is-tax-haven/

Chetty, S., Johanson, M., & Martín Martín, O. (2014). Speed of internationalization: Conceptualization, measurement and validation. *Journal of World Business, 49*(4), 633–650. https://doi.org/10.1016/j.jwb.2013.12.014

China bars foreign curricula and ownership in some private schools. (2021, May 17). *Nikkei Asia*. Retrieved from https://asia.nikkei.com/Politics/China-bars-foreign-curricula-and-ownership-in-some-private-schools

Cho, D. S., Kim, D. J., & Rhee, D. K. (1998). Latecomer strategies: Evidence from the semiconductor industry in Japan and Korea. *Organization Science, 9*(4), 489–505.

Contractor, F. J., & Kundu, S. K. (1998). Modal choice in a world of alliances: Analyzing organizational forms in the international hotel sector. *Journal of international business studies, 29*, 325–356.

Contractor, F. J., Kundu, S. K., & Hsu, C. C. (2003). A three-stage theory of international expansion: The link between multinationality and performance in the service sector. *Journal of International Business Studies, 34*, 5–18.

Coviello, N. E., & McAuley, A. (1999). Internationalisation and the smaller firm: A review of contemporary empirical research. *Management International Review*, 223–256.

Daniels, J. D., Radebaugh, L. H., Sullivan, D. P., & Click, R. W. (2021). *International business, global edition* (17th ed.). Pearson.

Davidson, W. H. (1982). *Global strategic management*. John Wiley & Sons.

Dev, C. S., Thomas, J. H., Buschman, J., & Anderson, E. (2010). Brand rights and hotel management agreements: Lessons from Ritz-Carlton Bali's lawsuit against the Ritz-Carlton hotel company. *Cornell Hospitality Quarterly, 51*(2), 215–230.

Dimitratos, P., & Plakoyiannaki, E. (2003). Theoretical foundations of an international entrepreneurial culture. *Journal of International Entrepreneurship, 1*, 187–215.

Dobrev, S. D., & Gotsopoulos, A. (2010). Legitimacy vacuum, structural imprinting, and the first mover disadvantage. *Academy of Management Journal, 53*(5), 1153–1174.

Dolski, J., & Hermanns, A. (2004). Internationalization strategies of service companies. *Management of International Services: Context—Concepts—Experiences*, pp. 85–110.

Dunning, J. H. (1979). Explaining changing patterns of international production: In defence of the eclectic theory. *Oxford Bulletin of Economics and Statistics, 41*(4), 269–295.

Dunning, J. H. (1993). Internationalizing Porter's diamond. MIR: *Management International Review*, 7–15.

Elango, B., & Pangarkar, N. (2021). Home country institutional impact on the choice of direct vs indirect exports: An emerging markets perspective. *International Marketing Review, 38*(2), 387–411.

Epstein A. (2015, February 9). *Why Netflix is entering Cuba even though the internet barely works there*. Quatz. Retrieved from https://qz.com/341368/why-netflix-is-entering-cuba-even-though-the-internet-barely-works-there



Erramilli, K. M. (1990). Entry mode choice in service industries. *International Marketing Review, 7*(5).

Erramilli, K. M., & D'Souza, D. E. (1995). Uncertainty and foreign direct investment: The role of moderators. *International Marketing Review, 12*(3), 47–60.

Erramilli, M. K., & Rao, C. P. (1993). Service firms' international entry-mode choice: A modified transaction-cost analysis approach. *Journal of Marketing, 57*(3), 19–38.

Etan, V. (2011, August 4). *Netflix Canada signs up one millionth subscriber*. The Hollywood Reporter. Retrieved from https://www.hollywoodreporter.com/tv/tv-news/netflix-canada-signs-up-one-219508/

Flowers, B. E. (1976). Oligopolistic reactions in European and Canadian direct investment in the United States. *Journal of International Business Studies, 7*(2), 43–55.

Franco, A. M., Sarkar, M. B., Agarwal, R., & Echambadi, R. (2009). Swift and smart: The moderating effects of technological capabilities on the market pioneering–firm survival relationship. *Management Science, 55*(11), 1842–1860.

Frankel, D. (2012, May 10). *Netflix continues Latin American content push with Fox deal*. Yahoo! Finance. Retrieved from https://finance.yahoo.com/news/netflix-continues-latin-american-content-183408977.html

Fritz, B. (2012, May 16). *Netflix faces problems in Latin America*. Los Angeles Times. Retrieved from https://www.latimes.com/entertainment/envelope/la-xpm-2012-may-16-la-et-ct-netflix-latin-america20120516-story.html

Frynas, J. G., & Mellahi, K. (2015). *Global strategic management*. Oxford University Press.

García-García, R., García-Canal, E., & Guillén, M. F. (2017). Rapid internationalization and long-term performance: The knowledge link. *Journal of World Business, 52*(1), 97–110. https://doi.org/10.1016/j.jwb.2016.09.005

Gatignon, H., & Anderson, E. (1988). The multinational corporation's degree of control over foreign subsidiaries: An empirical test of a transaction cost explanation. *Journal of Law, Economics and Organization, 4*(Fall), 305–336.

Griffin, R. W., & Pustay, M. W. (2012). *International business*. Pearson Education.

Grönroos, C. (1999). Relationship marketing: Challenges for the organization. *Journal of Business Research, 46*(3), 327–335.

Guilding, C., Kennedy, D. J., & McManus, L. (2001). Extending the boundaries of customer accounting: Applications in the hotel industry. *Journal of Hospitality & Tourism Research, 25*(2), 173–194.

Harris, S., & Wheeler, C. (2005). Entrepreneurs' relationships for internationalization: Functions, origins and strategies. *International Business Review, 14*(2), 187–207.

Hell, P. (2022). *Integrating individual differences to build team synergy during merger and acquisition* (Doctoral dissertation, The College of St. Scholastica).

Hertog, P. D. (2000). Knowledge-intensive business services as co-producers of innovation. *International Iournal of Innovation Management, 4*(04), 491–528.

Hill, C. W., Hwang, P., & Kim, W. C. (1990). An eclectic theory of the choice of international entry mode. *Strategic Management Journal, 11*(2), 117–128.

Hilmersson, M., & Johanson, M. (2016). Speed of SME internationalization and performance. *Management International Review, 56*, 67–94.

Hinchliffe, E. (2015, February 9). *Netflix launches in cuba*. USA Today. Retrieved from https://www.usatoday.com/story/money/2015/02/09/netflix-cuba/23134419/

Hollensen, S. (2017). *Global marketing* (7th ed.). Pearson Education Limited.

Hoppe, F. (2021, August 7). *COVID-19 helped accelerate Southeast Asia's digital future.* Now what? Fortune. Retrieved from https://fortune.com/2021/08/06/southeast-asia-covid-digital-consumers-growth/

Huawei cloud expands its partner network with Infosys. Huawei. (2019, April 23). Retrieved from https://www.huawei.com/en/news/2019/4/huawei-cloud-partner-network-infosys

Infosys newsroom. (2005, August 4). *Infosys signs agreement to set up software development centers in China*. Retrieved from https://www.infosys.com/newsroom/press-releases/2005/software-development-centers-china.html

Infosys newsroom. (2008, December 11). *Inaugurates its second center in China*. Infosys. Retrieved from https://www.infosys.com/newsroom/press-releases/2008/second-china-centre.html

International expansion in EdTech: Budgets, barriers and blueprints. (n.d.) *Brighteye ventures*. Retrieved from https://www.brighteyevc.com/post/international-expansion-in-edtech-budgets-barriers-and-blueprints

Ivanova, M., Ivanov, S., & Magnini, V. P. (Eds.). (2016). *The Routledge handbook of hotel chain management*. Routledge.

Jain, K. (2020, September 2). *Market research on the EdTech industry*. Plugandplay Apac. Retrieved from https://www.plugandplayapac.com/post/market-research-on-the-edtech-industry

Jhunjhunwala P. (2021, April 12). *Is Edtech Southeast Asia's largest untapped opportunity?* Business Times. Retrieved from https://www.businesstimes.com.sg/international/asean/edtech-southeast-asias-largest-untapped-opportunity

Johanson, J., & Vahlne, J.-E. (1977). The internationalization process of the firm—a model of knowledge development and increasing foreign market commitments. *Journal of International Business Studies, 8*(1), 23–32.

Johanson, J., & Wiedersheim-Paul, F. (1999). The Internationalization of the Firm. Four Swedish Cases. The internationalization of the firm, 27–42.

Johansson, J. K. (2009). *Global marketing: Foreign entry, local marketing and global management* (5th ed.). McGraw-Hill/Irwin.

Jolly, V. K., Alahuhta, M., & Jeannet, J.-P. (1992). Challenging the incumbents: How high technology start-ups compete globally. *Journal of Strategic Change, 1*, 71–82.

Jose S. (2005, May 24). *Fujitsu and Cisco deliver next-generation high-end routers based on strategic alliance*. Fujitsu. Retrieved from https://www.fujitsu.com/global/about/resources/news/press-releases/2005/0524-01.html

Julianne, P. (2011, July 5). *Netflix expands to 43 new countries*. CNNMoney. Retrieved from https://money.cnn.com/2011/07/05/technology/netflix_international/

Kabongo, J. D., & Okpara, J. O. (2019). Timing and speed of internationalization: Evidence from African banks. *Journal of Business Research, 102*, 12–20.

Kaizenvest. (2022). *EdTech landscape South and South East Asia*. Retrieved from https://irp.cdn--website.com/dfdb3685/files/uploaded/SEA%20EdTechAsia%202022%20copy.pdf

Karagozoglu, N., & Lindell, M. (1998). Internationalization of small and medium-sized technology-based firms: An exploratory study. *Journal of Small Business Management, 36*, 44–59.

Karlsen, T., Silseth, P. R., Benito, G. R., & Welch, L. S. (2003). Knowledge, internationalization of the firm, and inward–outward connections. *Industrial Marketing Management, 32*(5), 385–396.

Karra, N., Phillips, N., & Tracey, P. (2008). Building the born global firm: Developing entrepreneurial capabilities for international new venture success. *Long Range Planning, 41*(4), 440–458.

Kerin, R. A., Varadarajan, P. R., & Peterson, R. A. (1992). First-mover advantage: A synthesis, conceptual framework, and research propositions. *Journal of Marketing, 56*(4), 33–52.

Kewitz, T., & Reihlen, M. (2006). Strategischer Wandel im Internationalisierungsprozess am Beispiel der deutschen Treuhandgesellschaft: Vom Korrespondentennetzwerk zur 'Global Advisory Firm'. In M. Reihlen & A. Rohde (Eds.), *Internationalisierung professioneller Dienstleistungsunternehmen*. Kölner Wissenschaftsverlag.

Kharpal, A. (2019, May 10). *Netflix has a China strategy—But it doesn't involve launching there soon*. CNBC. Retrieved from https://www.cnbc.com/2019/05/10/netflix-has-a-china-strategy-it-doesnt-involve-launching-there-soon.html

Knickerbocker, F. T. (1973). Oligopolistic reaction and multinational enterprise. *The International Executive, 15*(2), 7–9.

Knight, G., Cavusgil, S., & T. (1996). The born global firm: A challenge to traditional internationalization theory. *Advances in International Marketing*, 8, 11–26.

Kogut, B., & Zander, U. (1993). Knowledge of the firm and the evolutionary theory of the multinational corporation. *Journal of International Business Studies, 24*, 625–645.

Kumar, S., Tamura, K., & Nei, M. (1994). MEGA: Molecular evolutionary genetics analysis software for microcomputers. *Bioinformatics, 10*(2), 189–191.

Kutschker, M., & Schmid, S. (2011). *Internationales Mangement*. Oldenbourg Verlag.

Lanzolla, G., & Suarez, F. (2006). Build it but they won't come: The role of information diffusion in early technology use. Working paper, Boston University.

Li, J. (2019). All roads lead to Rome: Internationalization strategies of Chinese law firms. *Journal of Professions and Organization, 6*(2), 156–178.

Li, J., & Guisinger, S. (1992). The globalization of service multinationals in the "triad" regions: Japan, Western Europe and North America. *Journal of International Business Studies, 23*, 675–696.

Lieberman, M. B., & Montgomery, D. B. (1988). First-mover advantages. *Strategic Management Journal, 9*(S1), 41–58.

Lieberman, M. B., & Montgomery, D. B. (1998). First-mover (dis) advantages: Retrospective and link with the resource-based view. *Strategic Management Journal, 19*(12), 1111–1125.

Lovelock, C. H., & Wirtz, J. (2018). Essentials of services marketing (3rd edition).

Madhok, A., & Keyhani, M. (2012). Acquisitions as entrepreneurship: Asymmetries, opportunities, and the internationalization of multinationals from emerging economies. *Global Strategy Journal, 2*(1), 26–40.

Madsen, T. K., & Servais, P. (2017). The internationalization of born globals: an evolutionary process?. In International business (pp. 421–443). Routledge.

Magdirila P. (2017, June 14). *AIS offers unlimited Netflix access in Thailand*. SP Global. Retrieved from https://www.spglobal.com/marketintelligence/en/news-insights/trending/EmQMvOyQAiUghDvYbAW9PQ2

McDougall, P. P., & Oviatt, B. M. (2000). International entrepreneurship: The intersection of two research paths. *Academy of Management Journal, 43*(5), 902–906.

McDougall, P. P., Shane, S., & Oviatt, B. M. (1994). Explaining the formation of international new ventures: The limits of theories from international business research. *Journal of Business Venturing, 9*(6), 469–487.

McFadden C. (2020, July 4). *The fascinating history of Netflix*. Interesting Engineering. Retrieved from https://interestingengineering.com/culture/the-fascinating-history-of-netflix

McKinsey and Co. (1993). *Emerging exporters: Australia's high value-added manufacturing exporters*. McKinsey and, Australian Manufacturing Council.

Meschi, P. X., Ricard, A., & Moore, E. T. (2017). Fast and furious or slow and cautious? The joint impact of age at internationalization, speed, and risk diversity on the survival of exporting firms. *Journal of International Management, 23*(3), 279–291.

Mishra B. R. (2016, June 9). I want India to be the most innovative place for SAP: Dilipkumar Khandelwal. Business Standard. Retrieved from https://www.business-standard.com/article/companies/q-a-with-dilipkumar-

Mogg, T. (2015, November 3) *Netflix launches in Japan, though it's doing things a little differently there*. Fox News. Retrieved from https://www.foxnews.com/tech/netflix-launches-in-japan-though-its-doing-things-a-little-differently-there

Musteen, M., Francis, J., & Datta, D. K. (2010). The influence of international networks on internationalization speed and performance: A study of Czech SMEs. *Journal of World Business, 45*(3), 197–205.

Netflix earns 50%+ of streaming revenues in Europe. 24i. (2019, March 7). Retrieved from https://www.24i.com/articles/netflix-earns-50-streaming-revenues-europe#:~:text=According%20to%20new%20research%20from,a%20distant%20second%20with%2021%25

Netflix 2018 Annual Statement. https://s22.q4cdn.com/959853165/files/doc_financials/annual_reports/2018/Form-10K_Q418_Filed.pdf

Netflix 2022 Annual Statement. https://s22.q4cdn.com/959853165/files/doc_financials/2022/ar/4e32b45c-a99e-4c7d-b988-4eef8377500c.pdf

Nokia Corporation. (n.d.) *Company profile, information, business description, history, background information on Nokia corporation*. Retrieved from https://www.referenceforbusiness.com/history2/35/Nokia-Corporation.html

Nonaka, I., & Takeuchi, H. (1995). *The knowledge creating* (p. 304).

Nordstrom, K., & Vahlne, J.-E. (1994). Is the globe shrinking? Psuchic distance and the establishemnt of Swedish sales subsidiaries during the last 100 years. In I. M. Landeck (Ed.), *International trade: Regional and global issue*. St. Martin's Press.

O'Brien, B. (2015, June 5). *4 lessons learned from famous market entry failures*. Traders Ready. Retrieved from https://www.tradeready.ca/2015/trade-takeaways/4-lessons-learned-famous-market-entry-failures/

O'Farrell, P. N., & Moffat, L. A. (1991). An interaction model of business service production and consumption. *British Journal of Management, 2*(4), 205–221.

O'Farrell, P. N., & Wood, P. A. (1998). Internationalisation by business service firms: Towards a new regionally based conceptual framework. *Environment and Planning A, 30*(1), 109–128.

O'Farrell, P. N., Zheng, J., & Wood, P. A. (1996). Internationalization of business services: An inter-regional analysis. *Regional Studies, 30*(2), 101–118.

Oviatt, B. M., & McDougall, P. P. (1994). Toward a theory of international new ventures. *Journal of International Business Studies, 25*(1), 45–64.

Oviatt, B. M., & McDougall, P. P. (1997). Challenges for internationalization process theory: The case of international new ventures. *Management International Review, 37*(2), 85–99.

Palmer, A. (1995). *Services marketing principles and practice*. Prentice-Hall.

Pankaj, G. (2001). Distance still matters: The hard reality of global expansion. *Harvard Business Review, 79*(8), 137–147.

Park K. (2022, April 29). *Glorang scores $10M series A to expand its edtech marketplace across Asia*. Tech Crunch. Retrieved from https://techcrunch.com/2022/04/28/glorang-scores-10m-series-a-to-expand-its-edtech-marketplace-across-asia/

Peng, M. W., & York, A. S. (2001). Behind intermediary performance in export trade: Transactions, agents and resources. *Journal of International Business Studies, 32*(2), 327–346.

Petrou, A. P. (2009). Foreign market entry strategies in retail banking: Choosing an entry mode in a landscape of constraints. *Long Range Planning, 42*(5–6), 614–632.

PR Newswire. (2012, October 18) *Netflix launches in Sweden, Denmark, Norway and Finland*. Cision PR Newswire. Retrieved from https://www.prnewswire.com/news-releases/netflix-launches-in-sweden-denmark-norway-and-finland-174749581.html

Press G. (2018, April 8) *Why Facebook triumphed over all other social networks*. Forbes. Retrieved from https://www.forbes.com/sites/gilpress/2018/04/08/why-facebook-triumphed-over-all-other-social-networks/?sh=502977d96e91

Reinhold, S., & Dolnicar, S. (2021). Sharing economy, collaborative consumption, peer-to-peer accommodation or trading of space? In S. Dolnicar (Ed.), *Airbnb before, during and after COVID-19*. University of Queensland. https://doi.org/10.6084/m9.figshare.14195945

Riley C. (2016, October 18). *Netflix admits its plan for China has failed*. CNN. Retrieved from https://money.cnn.com/2016/10/18/technology/netflix-china/index.html

Root, F. R. (1994). *Entry strategies for international markets*. Lexington Books.

Root, F. R. (1998). *Entry strategies for international markets.* John Wiley & Sons.

Rugman, A. M., & Verbeke, A. (1992). A note on the transnational solution and the transaction cost theory of multinational strategic management. *Journal of International Business Studies, 23*, 761–771.

Sakarya, S., Eckman, M., & Hyllegard, K. H. (2007). Market selection for international expansion: Assessing opportunities in emerging markets. *International Marketing Review, 24*(2), 208–238.

Samsung Newsroom US. (2017, July 17). *Samsung pay announces partnership to allow users to pay via Paypal.* Retrieved from https://news.samsung.com/us/samsung-pay-partnership-paypal/

Santamaría, B. & Ni S. (2008). *Entry modes of starbucks.* Retrieved from https://www.diva-portal.org/smash/get/diva2:121498/fulltext01.pdf

Schilling, M. (2015, June 9). *Netflix in Japan production pact with Yoshimoto Kogyo, say reports.* Yahoo. Retrieved from https://uk.movies.yahoo.com/netflix-japan-production-pact-yoshimoto-kogyo-reports-150019450.html?guccounter=1&guce_referrer=aHR0cHM6Ly93d3cuZ29vZ2xlLmNvbS8&guce_referrer_sig=AQAAANvTDXLLglegJmg3gzx5qfDkxqQ-iE9JWSSyhk82r7oIZHATn4_d3qGbbAIALFTvJRWazyRAiFCN6Z9XD_w0RP6xwsVhYA8tz3YGbp-kKSSocyntEZ3fuAD708PkW00d4sIJQZo78jHwylYN8QWEfsuix2xIZAVBjkVj36bSKU5Ww

Shamsie, J., Phelps, C., & Kuperman, J. (2004). Better late than never: A study of late entrants in household electrical equipment. *Strategic Management Journal, 25*(1), 69–84.

Shankar, V., Carpenter, G. S., & Krishnamurthi, L. (1998). Late mover advantage: How innovative late entrants outsell pioneers. *Journal of Marketing Research, 35*(1), 54–70.

Shu, C. (2021, October 19). *Singapore-based Geniebook's personalized learning platform raises $16.6M series A.* Tech Crunch. Retrieved from https://techcrunch.com/2021/10/18/singapore-based-geniebooks-personalized-learning-platform-raises-16-6m-series-a/

Singh R. (n.d.) *Skype.* Retrieved from https://www.ravisingh.com/social-medias/skype

Starbucks to Enter Spain with leading retail companies Grupo Vips and Europastry. Just Food. (2001, October 8). Retrieved from https://www.just-food.com/news/spain-starbucks-to-enter-spain-with-leading-retail-companies-grupo-vips-and-europastry/

Statistica. (n.d.) *Proportion of households with fixed broadband in the United Kingdom (UK) from 2012 to 2017.* Retrieved from https://www.statista.com/statistics/297704/uk-broadband-number-of-households-with-fixed-broadband/

Szulanski, G. (1996). Exploring internal stickiness: Impediments to the transfer of best practice within the firm. *Strategic Management Journal, 17*(S2), 27–43.

Taylor K. (2009, September 25). *Experts and insiders say Subway is haunted by a fundamental flaw that is forcing the chain to close hundreds of locations.* Business Insider. Retrieved from https://www.businessinsider.com/subway-franchise-model-forces-locations-to-close-2019-9

Telecompaper. (2005, June 28). *Onet.pl launches co-branded version of Skype for Windows.* Telecompaper. Retrieved from https://www.telecompaper.com/news/onetpl-launches-cobranded-version-of-skype-for-windows%2D%2D478217

Terpstra, V., & Sarathy, R. (1994). *International marketing.* Dryden Press.

The Remarkable Netflix. (2022, May 5). *Global expansion journey.* Centuro Global. Retrieved from https://www.centuroglobal.com/article/the-remarkable-netflix-global-expansion-journey-a-case-study

The Nation. (2017). *AIS partners with Netflix in Thailand.* March 01, 2017. https://www.nationthailand.com/in-focus/30307576

Tracxn. (n.d.) *Based on the update in Feb 2023.* Retrieved from https://tracxn.com/

Turner A. (2018, July 25). *Why there are almost no Starbucks in Australia?* CNBC. Retrieved from https://www.cnbc.com/2018/07/20/starbucks-australia-coffee-failure.html#:~:text=Starbucks%20didn't%20fit%20Australians,company%20to%20close%2061%20locations

Turner, M. J., & Guilding, C. (2013). Capital budgeting implications arising from locus of hotel owner/operator power. *International Journal of Hospitality Management, 35*, 261–273.

Turner, M. J., Hodari, D., & Blal, I. (2016). 13 entry modes: Management contract. The Routledge handbook of hotel chain management, 14, 1.

USCBC. (2005, January 2). *Cooperative joint ventures.* Retrieved from https://www.chinabusinessreview.com/cooperative-joint-ventures/

Verbeke, A. (2013). *International business strategy*. Cambridge University Press.
Welch, L. S., & Luostarinen, R. (1988). Internationalization: Evolution of a concept. *Journal of General Management, 14*(2), 34–55.
Why the Tutoring Industry in Asian Countries Is Surging. (n.d.) *Businesslogs*. Retrieved from https://businesslogs.com/why-the-tutoring-industry-in-asian-countries-is-surging/
Wiedersheim-Paul, F., & Johanson, J. (1975). The internationalization of the firm: Four Swedish case. *Journal of Management Studies, 22*(4), 305–322.
Windrum, P., & Tomlinson, M. (1999). Knowledge-intensive services and international competitiveness: A four country comparison. *Technology Analysis & Strategic Management, 11*(3), 391–408.
World Bank. (2023). *Individuals using the internet (% of population)—South Asia*. Retrieved from https://data.worldbank.org/indicator/IT.NET.USER.ZS?locations=8S
WTO (2013) to World Trade Organization. (n.d.). The reference is: World Trade Organization. (n.d.) Basic Purpose and Concepts: 1.3 Definition of Services Trade and Modes of Supply. https://www.wto.org/english/tratop_e/serv_e/cbt_course_e/c1s3p1_e.html
Wu, A., & Voss, H. (2015). When does absorptive capacity matter for international performance of firms? Evidence from China. *International Business Review, 24*, 344–351.
Wu, X., Adbi, A., & Mahmood, I. P. (2023). The social structure of insiders and outsiders: Toward a network community perspective on firm performance. Academy of Management Journal, (ja), amj-2022. https://doi.org/10.5465/amj.2022.0925
Wunker, S. (2012). Better growth decisions: Early mover, fast follower or late follower? *Strategy & Leadership, 40*(2), 43–48. Retrieved from https://www.newmarketsadvisors.com/uploads/7/0/3/6/70366435/better_growth_decisions.pdf
Young, S., Hamill, J., Wheeler, C. & Davies, J.R. (1989). International market entry and development: Strategies and management, Harvester Wheatsheaf, Hemel Hempstead, Hert.
Zahra, S. A., Ireland, R. D., & Hitt, M. A. (2000). International expansion by new venture firms: International diversity, mode of market entry, technological learning, and performance. *Academy of Management Journal, 43*(5), 925–950.
Zain, M., & Ng, S. I. (2006). The impacts of network relationships on SMEs' internationalization process. *Thunderbird International Business Review, 48*(2), 183–205.
Zimmer, M., Scherer, A., & von Wangenheim, F. (2009). Data—Information—Knowledge. Kundenintegration und Konfiguration in der Marktforschungsbranche. In D. Holtbrügge, H. H. Holzmüller, & F. Wangenheim (Eds.), *Management Internationaler Dienstleistungen mit 3K: Konfiguration—Koordination—Kundenintegration* (1st ed., pp. 233–253). Gabler.

## Further Reading

### More Readings About Internationalization Timing Strategy

Boulding, W., & Christen, M. (2008). Disentangling pioneering cost advantages and disadvantages. *Marketing Science, 27*(4), 699–716.
Chetty, S., & Campbell-Hunt, C. (2004). A strategic approach to internationalization: A traditional versus a "born-global" approach. *Journal of International marketing, 12*(1), 57–81.
Suarez, F., & Lanzolla, G. (2005). *The half-truth of first-mover advantage*. Harvard business review. Retrieved from https://hbr.org/2005/04/the-half-truth-of-first-mover-advantage

# The Multinational Service Firm and Its Strategies

## Contents




D. Klimkeit et al., *International Management in Service Firms*, Classroom Companion: Business,
https://doi.org/10.1007/978-3-031-50345-0_8

**Learning Outcomes**

After completing this chapter, you should be able to:
- Describe the characteristics of MNEs and Service MNEs.
- Explain how Service MNEs analyze their external and internal environment.
- Outline how Service MNEs configure their global value chain.
- Explain global environments given forces for integration and responsiveness and derive appropriate strategies for Service MNEs.
- Describe the different roles of subsidiaries and subsidiary managers.
- Define digital firms and explain the role of network effects for digital platforms.

## Introduction

This chapter introduces a key player in international services management: Multinational enterprises (MNEs), specifically multinational service firms. We will define MNEs and outline their characteristics. The consequences of the characteristics of services for the management of multinational service firms will be explained. We will introduce the global configuration of the value chain. Different strategies of MNEs can pursue and how they fit the MNEs' environment will be presented. Then we will focus on the various roles subsidiaries of MNEs can play and eventually address multinational service firms with digital business models.

Walmart store, Image by jimaro morales from Pixabay

## Opening Case: Walmart in Germany

In 2003, researchers at Bremen University, Germany, published a study entitled "Why did Wal-Mart fail in Germany?." Three years later, the executives of Walmart in Arkansas, United States, the world's biggest retailer, decided to close down its German operations, selling its 85 hypermarkets to a German competitor, Metro. Even Walmart's CEO, Lee Scott, admitted that Walmart's market entry in Germany was "somewhat embarrassing" (Economist, 2004). According to the study by Bremen University,

> Walmart "offers a textbook case of how not to enter a foreign market" (Knorr & Arndt, 2003, p. 5). What had gone wrong?

In December 1997, Walmart entered the German market by taking over the 21-store Wertkauf chain, followed by the acquisition 1 year later of Interspar's 74 hypermarkets, spending overall US$1.6 billion. However, Walmart only published results for Germany once, in 2003, where it lost 487 million euros. So experts estimate that Walmart never made profits during its 8.5 years in Germany. Market share remained small at just 1.1% in 2003, and Walmart never expanded its network of stores as planned but closed down some shops and laid off around 1000 staff.

The acquisition of Interspar was ill-informed as its outlets were not in good shape, in bad locations, and generated a low revenue. Strict zoning regulations in Germany made it difficult for Walmart to grow organically by setting up new hypermarkets in suitable locations. Talks with competitors Metro and Globus on acquiring some of their stores have failed. So, Walmart never reached the critical size necessary to put it in a bargaining position with suppliers to get price concessions from them.

During the first 4 years in Germany, Walmart had four CEOs. The first, Rob Tiarks, was an American from headquarters in Bentonville, Arkansas, who did not speak German and refused to learn the language. Instead, he required all mangers to speak English. He also proved unwilling to follow strategic advice by former Wertkauf executives, three of whom, therefore, left within 6 months. The second CEO, Allan Leighton, an Englishman, led Walmart Germany from his office in Leeds, UK. Six months later, Volker Barth, the first German CEO, replaced him. He failed to integrate Interspar, which had been very decentralized, into the more centralized Walmart organization.

Walmart was considered an unattractive employer, offering low pay and being very restrictive on business expenses. For example, mangers had to share double rooms on business trips, something unheard of in corporate Germany. In the United States, Walmart strictly refuses to accept trade unions. In Germany, however, they encountered an economy where unions traditionally play an important role. Walmart refused to acknowledge the centralized industry-wide wage bargaining process conducted by industry and union representatives. When the retailer wanted to lay off workers to reduce costs, it encountered legal hurdles in Germany, making the process complicated, costly, and lengthy. Walmart was also surprised to find that German regulation allowed them to open shops for only 80 h per week and enforced a strict opening ban on Sundays, not allowing the 24/7 model operated elsewhere. While Walmart is well known for low prices, it encountered well-established discounters, Aldi and Lidl, who were already offering rock-bottom prices in Germany. Due to its small scale and, therefore, limited bargaining power toward suppliers, Walmart was never able to undercut the established discounters on price. Its German headquarters and logistics centers had low utilization, driving up the cost. It was not even substantially cheaper than regular food retail chains like Edeka and Rewe.

Walmart believed that shoppers in Germany would like to be treated with the same courtesy as American customers. It stationed "greeters" at the entrance greeting arriving shoppers and employed staff at the cash desk to help shoppers pack purchases into plastic bags. On the shopfloor, in line with Walmart's "10-foot rule," shop assistants smiled at customers entering their 10-foot radius, looked them in the eyes, and asked if they needed help. German customers, however, did not appreciate this at all. Having been used to self-service shopping for decades, they felt uncomfortable being talked at by strangers and preferred to pack their purchases themselves. Several customers shocked, fled the shops, not buying anything. Repeatedly, customers complained that strangers had harassed them on the shopfloor. Furthermore, customers were wary that they have to pay the cost of this extra staff with higher prices for their purchases. Indeed, labor costs at Walmart were higher than the industry average in Germany.

Walmart also encountered further legal problems, having been fined for breaching several laws. Walmart tried to sell goods below cost, a practice strictly circumscribed in Germany. Walmart did not disclose financial information as required or participate in the refund system for plastic bottles that German law mandates for retail outlets.

To summarize, experts at the University of Bremen conclude:

> Wal-Mart's failure in the German market has been the inevitable result of its inability—caused by an astounding degree of ignorance of key principles of internationalization strategies and intercultural management—to select and implement an adequate entry and business strategy (Knorr & Arndt, 2003, p. 24)

**Questions**

1. Why has Walmart transferred policies from the United States to Germany?
2. Why have they failed with this approach?
3. What are the strategic requirements for global retail chains to be successful?
4. How can the characteristics of services introduced in ► Chap. 1 help analyze the problems of Walmart in Germany?

Sources: (Economist, 2004, 2006a, 2006b, 2013; Knorr & Arndt, 2003; Walmart, 2022).

## Multinational Enterprises (MNE) and Service MNEs

Whether you have a cup of coffee at Starbucks, eat at McDonald's, stay in a Hilton hotel, work out in a Gold's Gym, watch films on Netflix, stream music from Spotify, hail a ride from Uber, access your bank account at HSBC, date using Tinder, buy groceries at 7-Eleven, have your hair cut at Tony & Guy, shop at Amazon and receive your parcel via DHL, or make a phone call on your Vodafone SIM card—each time you are using the service of a multinational service firm. *Multinational Enterprises (MNEs)* are key players in international business, and multinational service firms (Service MNEs) make up an increasing portion of MNEs. So, let us investigate what MNEs and Service MNEs are and what characterizes them.

## Characteristics of MNEs



What distinguishes MNEs from other firms is that they have operations in more than one country. These operations outside the country where the firm is headquartered are called *affiliates* or *subsidiaries*. While such subsidiaries may frequently have considerable autonomy to go about their local business, eventually, they are controlled by global headquarters, either directly or indirectly via a regional headquarter, which in turn reports to global headquarters. Some MNEs may have more than one global headquarters. Still, the more typical case is having one headquarters, typically located in the country where the company was founded, the parent or home country. However, some MNEs move their headquarters to a country where they pay fewer taxes.

**Multinational Enterprise (MNE)**

A *Multinational Enterprise (MNE)* is a company that is headquartered in one country, but has operations in one or more other countries.[1] (Rugman & Collinson, 2012, p. 38)

As the definition shows, as soon as a firm sets up operations in one country outside of its parent country, it becomes an MNE. This implies that MNEs do not have to be big like the ones listed at the beginning of this chapter. A small and medium-sized firm that opens a subsidiary in a neighboring country is also an MNE. The operations that firms undertake outside of the home country, called *host countries*, can span anything from research and development, production, logistics, market-

1 In a more recent definition, Collinson & Rugman (2020: 18) emphasize the option of having multiple headquarters, but since this is rather rare, we prefer to stick to the more straightforward earlier definition.

ing, sales, and finance, to customer support. In services, subsidiaries could span the entire service value chain from designing a service, marketing, and selling it to providing the service and customer support or any part thereof. Certain internal service functions, such as accounting, are frequently moved into a shared service center in a lower-cost location such as India, the Philippines, Poland, or Costa Rica. In this case, the operation abroad is not oriented towards the local market but provides services for the MNE or other subsidiaries in its region.

MNEs must keep both types of countries mentioned above in mind, their home country and the host countries in which they have subsidiaries outside their home country (Rugman & Collinson, 2012, p. 40). Typically, an MNE is impacted much by the culture and institutions of its home country. Enter a subsidiary of a German MNE anywhere in the world, and you will find elements of German culture, the same for American MNEs and MNEs from other countries. Often, the MNE is listed on the stock exchange in its home country, has its headquarters there, and many important stakeholders, such as many of the firm's owners, workers in the home country operations, government, and the general public. These all have opinions of what the firm should and should not do. As a case in point, the opening case of chapter four has shown how a company like Ritter Sport from Germany that decided to remain active in Russia after the invasion of Ukraine by Russian armed forces was facing broad criticism on social media in its German home country (Economist, 2022). At the same time, MNEs must adapt to local conditions in each host country where they have operations. Local culture, language, regulation, institutions, competitors, and customer needs can differ from the home country, leading the subsidiary to fail if it does not adapt to local conditions. The opening case of Walmart's failure in Germany is a striking case in point. Further, in each host country, the firm faces a similar set of stakeholders as in the home country, including local staff, customers, suppliers, government, and the general public. For example, American food delivery firms like Doordash are struggling in Europe due to union-organized workers who demand relatively high salaries, strict labor laws, and customers who buy little and rarely give tips to delivery riders (Economist, 2021c).

MNEs share specific characteristics (see ◘ Fig. 8.1). Some characteristics have a global character. First, they have a *common global strategic vision* of what they want to do. Imagine the executive board of an MNE sitting in the boardroom, looking at a map of the world and discussing which product or service they want to provide in which part of the world and in which countries they want to place value-adding activities. Global leadership sees the whole world as its potential market and source of inputs. To implement the vision, the MNE draws on a *common pool of resources*. These can consist of financial resources that HQ provides to subsidiaries, but also know-how, patents, trademarks, branding, and experts who might be seconded into a subsidiary to help develop its market potential. Other characteristics have a more local character. The MNE needs to be *responsive to environmental forces* in the various countries where it operates. As outlined above, culture, language, technical standards, competition, suppliers, and customers will differ in each country and imply different requirements for the MNE. As the Walmart case has shown, this limits the transfer of successful practices from the

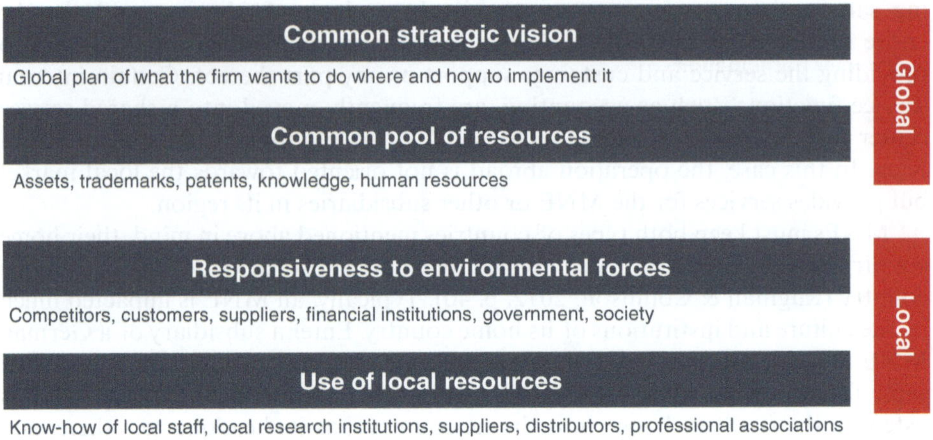


**Fig. 8.1** Characteristics of MNEs, own diagram based on content from (Rugman & Collinson, 2012, p. 40) and own thinking



home country to the host countries. To these three characteristics Rugman & Collinson (2012, pp. 40–41) addressed, we add a fourth one: the *use of local resources*. In addition to global resources, MNEs also use local resources. Besides other benefits, they help them respond to the local environment. MNEs draw on the know-how of local managers about the local market, culture, competition, and regulation—something Walmart Germany's first CEO Robert Tiarks refused to do. MNEs build networks with local suppliers, distributors, government authorities, professional associations, and research institutions to obtain local knowledge, get embedded in the local context, and succeed in the local market. This is particularly important for professional service firms that rely on local connections and learning from local know-how (Reihlen & Apel, 2007).

## The Impact of Characteristics of Services on Service MNEs

In ► Chap. 1, we outlined the distinctive characteristics of services: customer participation, simultaneity of production and consumption, intangibility, perishability, heterogeneity, and nontransferable ownership. Here, we will explain how these characteristics impact the international management of service firms (see ◘ Fig. 8.2). For details of the characteristics themselves, please refer back to ► Chap. 1. Other chapters apply service characteristics to their specific theme, especially ► Chap. 13 regarding global marketing.

**Customer Participation:** In services, the customer is typically present in the service process and plays an active role. This customer involvement can impact the quality of the service. For Service MNEs, it poses the challenge of avoiding a service failure due to the customer not playing its role properly as a coproducer of the service across all locations worldwide. Starbucks is asking every customer worldwide to provide their first name so it can be written on the cup. To some extent, this

| Distinctive Characteristics of Services | Implication for Service MNEs |
|---|---|
| **Customer Participation** | • Adapt to service quality perceptions<br>• Employ local staff<br>• Avoid customer-induced quality failures |
| **Simultaneity** | • Role of global branding<br>• Role of recommendations / credentials<br>• Local delivery point |
| **Intangibility** | • Role of recommendations / credentials<br>• Role of global branding<br>• Design of tangible elements<br>• Country of origin effect |
| **Perishability** | • Capacity management: geographic distance & regulatory conditions |
| **Heterogeneity** | • Global quality management<br>• Global training programs |
| **Non-Transferrable Ownership** | • Role of location & availability |

**Fig. 8.2** Distinctive characteristics of services and implications for Service MNEs, own diagram

requires educating the customer everywhere about the service provider's expectations of the customer to ensure an effective and efficient service delivery process. On the other hand, it requires some flexibility as customers' abilities and expectations of what their role should and should not include vary across cultures. In Germany, Walmart's customers expected more undisturbed self-service. Adapting to customer expectations and abilities is easier for local staff, so most MNEs employ local staff in customer contact positions (Ingwald et al., 2009; Meffert et al., 2015, p. 520). Managing customer participation will be addressed in more detail in ► Chap. 15.

**Simultaneity:** For most services, but not all, production and consumption of the service cannot be separated but happen simultaneously. So, most services cannot be produced and stored before customers use them. For Service MNEs, this means they need a local delivery point in each location worldwide where they offer their service. A global chain of gyms, a restaurant chain, a hotel chain, a law firm, and firms in many other service industries must establish a presence where they want to offer their services. Even e-commerce providers like Amazon need local logistics centers.

Further, simultaneity means that it is difficult for customers to ascertain the quality of the service before they decide to use it. This creates uncertainty for the customer. So, Service MNEs must provide reassurance of the quality of the service that customers can expect everywhere. Therefore, a strong global brand is essential to signal consistent global quality. Whether McKinsey consultants, Hilton hotels, Toni & Guy hairdressers, or Starbucks coffee, customers can expect the same quality worldwide. Likewise, globally available recommendations or credentials provide accounts from customers who have already experienced the service. Think of customer ratings of an apartment at Airbnb. Suppose a large number of customers have given good ratings. In that case, the average score provides a reasonable estimate of the quality that customers can expect, and Airbnb automatically translates the comments of previous guests into the local language of the customer based on the IP address (Maleri, 2004; Meffert et al., 2015, p. 521; Segal-Horn & Faulkner, 2010, p. 288).

**Intangibility:** Services are frequently described as a performance or the outcome of an interaction rather than a physical good (though a service can include a physical good as part of the package). Services cannot be touched. This also contributes to the uncertainty of customers who cannot inspect a service before consumption, hence the role of branding, recommendations, and credentials. At the same time, the tangible "hard" elements that sometimes form part of the service package attain particular importance as these can become quality indicators. Think of the furniture of a hotel or the seats of an airplane. Internationally, there may be different perceptions of what tangible elements signal high quality, which Service MNEs need to take into account. Before the firm provides a service, material surrogates such as a picture of an airplane can signal quality; however, their interpretation can vary internationally (Ingwald et al., 2009; Meffert et al., 2015, p. 521; Segal-Horn & Faulkner, 2010, p. 287).



**Perishability:** Most services are perishable. They cannot be stored unless embedded in a physical format, such as music or software on a CD. A hairdresser can only provide a haircut once the customer arrives and sits down. The income from a hotel bed or an empty airplane seat cannot be recovered. This requires good capacity management in Service MNEs. Due to geographic distance, predicting the required capacity for their international operations can be particularly challenging. Local regulatory changes, such as the introduction of a quota for local service providers, can occur anytime in one of the international locations of the MNE (Ingwald et al., 2009). At the same time, having several international locations where a service can be provided remotely can help with capacity management. Typically, a global business services organization that provides internal services for an MNE in several shared service centers worldwide can balance the workload between the different centers. When a center of one IT service firm in Singapore had an overload of work, a center in Prague could take over some of the workload (Klimkeit, 2019).

**Heterogeneity:** The quality of services varies because it is provided by people whose service quality cannot be standardized in the same way as the quality of the output of a machine. For Service MNEs, this calls for global quality management that attempts as much as possible to ensure consistent quality across the different operations worldwide. This includes a globally consistent training program for staff (Segal-Horn & Faulkner, 2010, pp. 287–288). Service MNEs that aim to provide premium quality service have these intensive quality management and training programs, such as the Ritz-Carlton hotels (Junger, 2004). We will also address global service quality management in more detail in ► Chap. 15.

**Nontransferrable Ownership:** A customer who pays for a service does not typically acquire ownership of a material good (though some tangible token might be part of the package). Instead, the customer receives the right to use labor and expertise, rented goods, a defined facility rental, access to shared facilities, or access to networks for a defined period. For Service MNEs, this implies that the availability of network access, such as in telecommunications, must be reliable in each location. The firm must choose the location of a service facility or rental good wisely. This is why rental cars are frequently available at airports or train stations (Bordoloi et al., 2019, p. 16; Wirtz & Lovelock, 2018, pp. 12–14). For example, the Legoland Malaysia Resort theme park is located in Johor Bahru, Malaysia, just across the border from the 5.5 million well-to-do potential guests in neighboring Singapore (Merlin Entertainment, 2022). The Interkauf shops that Walmart had taken over in Germany were not in convenient locations.

## Strategic Management in Service MNEs

Before Service MNEs enter foreign markets and engage in operational policies in areas like marketing, human resources management, financial management, service delivery and project management, and others, they must decide on their overarching goals and how to achieve them. They engage in *strategic management.*

**Strategic Management**

*Strategic management* is the process of strategic decision-making that sets the long-term direction for the organization. (Frynas & Mellahi, 2015, p. 7)

**Global Strategic Management:** When MNEs and Service MNEs determine their strategy, additional dimensions come into play when management engages in strategic management. MNEs need to decide in which countries they want to offer their products or services and in which locations they want to place which activities to ensure that customers in all the targeted markets worldwide receive the products or services they need. In other words, MNEs need to *configure their value chain.*

Once it has spread the various value-creating activities across different locations globally, the firm must coordinate them to ensure everyone is pulling in the same direction. In manufacturing, it wants to ensure procurement buys the supplies that production needs and production produces what sales need to deliver on its promise to customers. The same applies to the global delivery of services. The MNE needs to *coordinate its global value chain.*

An MNE must also decide to what extent it wants to globally standardize its offering versus adapt it to the culture, language, regulation, technical standards, laws, competitive situation, customer needs, and other variables in each country. A related decision is to what extent an MNE integrates and centralizes activities to save cost and achieves synergies versus allowing subsidiaries more autonomy to manage their activities locally. In other words, MNEs must decide on their *global integration and local responsiveness.* In the remainder of this chapter, we will address the configuration of the value chain, global integration, and local responsiveness. We will address the coordination of the value chain in ► Chap. 9 in the context of global organization. ◘ Figure 8.3 outlines the three key dimensions of *global strategic management*.[2]

**Global Strategic Management**

*Global strategic management* is the process of designing a coordinated strategy that sets the degree to which a firm globalizes its strategic behaviors in different countries through the standardization of offerings, and the configuration and coordination of activities in different countries. (simplified from Frynas & Mellahi, 2015, p. 15)

Strategic management consists of three phases: *strategic analysis*, *strategy formulation*, and *strategy implementation* (see ◘ Fig. 8.4).



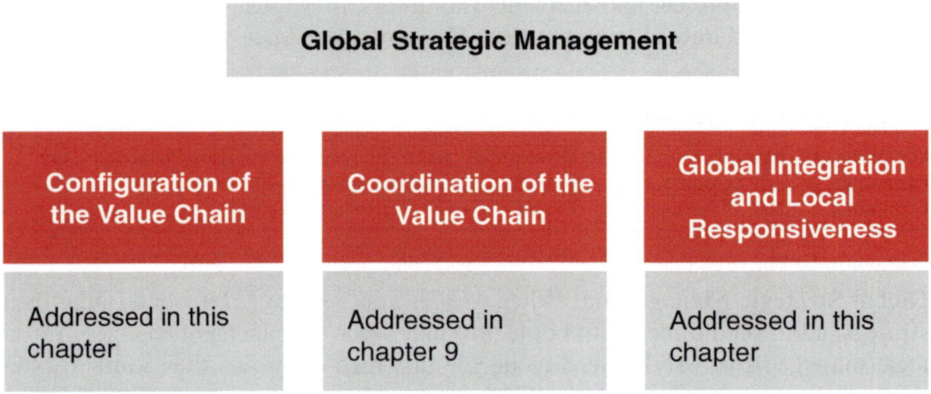


◘ **Fig. 8.3** Dimensions of global strategic management, own diagram, inspired by (Frynas & Mellahi, 2015, p. 14)

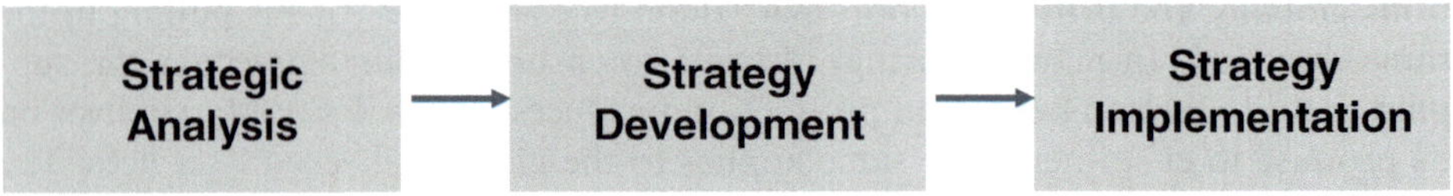


◘ **Fig. 8.4** Elements of strategic management, (Frynas & Mellahi, 2015, p. 6), (permission obtained)

2 The figure is inspired by Frynas and Mellahi (2015): 14 but different from them, we highlight the configuration and coordination of the value chain as two separate dimensions in their own right while considering their "integration dimension" as included in what we call "global integration and local responsiveness" (their "standardization dimension").

## Strategic Analysis

When MNEs conduct strategic analysis, they analyze their environment to identify opportunities and threats (external analysis) and their own strengths and weaknesses that derive from their resources and capabilities and the configuration of their value chain (internal analysis) (see ◘ Fig. 8.5).

## Analyzing the External Environment

**Macro External Environment:** Regarding strategic analysis, Service MNEs must first understand their external environment to identify opportunities they can exploit and possible threats to their business. This comprises, first of all, the global environment. Think of environmental forces with transnational impacts, such as the covid 19 pandemic, climate change, the dynamics of energy sources availability, international politics and conflict, demographic shifts, shifts in global power balances, and grassroots activist movements. Managers of MNEs analyze the more country-specific environment in countries that are particularly relevant to them. This includes their home country, host countries in which they are already active, and countries they contemplate entering. All the factors that we outlined in ► Chap. 4, such as the political, legal, and economic systems, are relevant here. Also, we consider the cultural context addressed in detail in ► Chap. 18 and the technological infrastructure and development. Taken together, all of these factors constitute the *macro environment* of an MNE. ► Chapter 7 has introduced the PEST analysis as an instrument to systematically analyze this macroenvironment, especially in view of countries a firm potentially wants to enter.

**Microexternal Environment:** Next, managers also zoom in on the specific industry in a country, both in countries they are already active in and in countries they are considering entering. Managers investigating the *microenvironment* want to understand the structure of their industry in a country: How many competitors are there? How powerful are the suppliers and customers towards firms in the market? How easy is it for firms to enter the market? Are there products that could replace products in the market, such as tablets that can replace laptops for many users? Michael Porter (2008) addresses these questions in his *Five Forces framework*. It

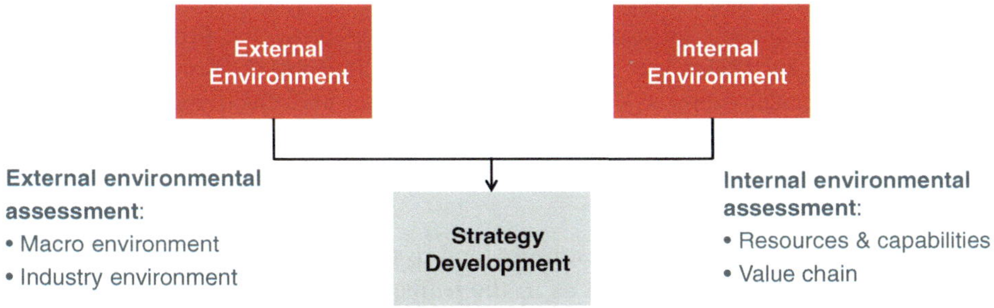


◘ **Fig. 8.5** Elements of strategic analysis, own diagram

investigates the threat of new competitors, the threat of substitute products, the bargaining power of buyers and suppliers, and the rivalry among existing competitors in the industry. These factors provide information about the intensity of competition in a market. When the threat of new entrants and substitutes and the bargaining power of customers and suppliers are high, competition in an industry is typically intense. Intensive competition typically exerts pressure on the prices firms can charge customers as they try to undercut each other's prices. This, in turn, reduces profit margins and therefore diminishes the profitability of companies. In countries where the company is already active, it can consider if it wants to leave that country if profitability has diminished over time. Alternatively, it can try to influence industry structure in its favor, for example, by introducing a customer loyalty program to make it more difficult for customers to switch. This is why airlines offer frequent flyer programs, awarding "miles" for each flight and providing benefits for collected miles. For countries where the company contemplates a market entry, the information gained about profitability in the industry in that country can be relevant information besides others for the market entry decision. ► Chapter 7 has addressed location choice for foreign market entry in more detail.



## Analyzing the Internal Environment

The macro and microenvironment analyses provide information on opportunities and threats in a Service MNE's environment. Before taking action, a Service MNE must first understand its resources and capabilities and how these are used in the value-creating activities the MNE conducts in its global value chain. Together, they help managers understand the firm's strengths and weaknesses. Therefore, managers conduct internal analyses to understand if they can take advantage of opportunities and fend off threats in the environment in different countries. They analyze the *internal environment* of the company.

**Resources:** MNEs have many *resources* both centrally and in various operations across the globe. Some are tangible, such as buildings, machinery, and equipment. Other resources are intangible. They include intellectual property, know-how, information, brands, skills, and the firm's processes.

**Resources**

[…] *resources* include all assets, […], organizational processes, firm attributes, information, knowledge, etc. controlled by a firm that enable the firm to conceive of and implement strategies that improve its efficiency and effectiveness. (Barney, 1991, p. 101, leaving out "capabilities" from the definition for a clearer delineation)

For most service firms, tangible resources tend to play a lesser role, though they can be very significant for some, such as in the transportation or telecommunications industries. Think of the grid and the rolling stock of train operators or the airplanes of airlines. Generally, though, due to the intangibility of most services, intangible resources such as the brand and know-how are particularly important. Taken together, resources are needed for the firm to implement its strategies. For example, an airline cannot implement its global expansion strategy without the required number of airplanes and know-how. Frynas & Mellahi (2015, p. 118) report how the BBC and Walt Disney have leveraged their archives of old films and recordings by re-releasing, for example, recordings of the Beatles or Disney films or selling licensed packages to other TV stations. These resources have shown to be very valuable. When MNEs analyze their resources, they also consider the geographic footprint of their resources. Especially physical resources such as plants are bound to specific locations. However, also intangible resources like know-how, while generally transferrable, are not necessarily present in all locations where the firm does or intends to do business. For example, a firm with all resources concentrated in Europe that plans to expand to Asia must build up or transfer the needed resources to operate successfully. Managers need to consider, though, that different countries may require different resources to be successful. For example, a food delivery service cannot draw on the network of restaurants in its home country but needs to develop a new network in each country it enters.

**Capabilities:** Resources are important, but firms need to be able to combine and integrate their resources to compete effectively. *Capabilities* provide a link between the firm's resources and the needs of the market to serve customers effectively. As Frynas and Mellahi outline, Google's programmers, marketing people, brands, and technical equipment, such as its servers, do not provide value to customers alone. The firm must be able to bring them together in a way that creates value. Capabilities can encompass a broad and frequently firm-specific range of things, such as effective customer service, the ability to identify new technological trends, effective human resource management, or the ability to anticipate the needs of customers. Internationally, additional capabilities are needed, such as effectively dealing with currency fluctuations and changes in international markets (Frynas & Mellahi, 2015, pp. 118–119).

### Capabilities

[…] *capabilities* are complex bundles of skills and accumulated knowledge, exercised through organizational processes, that enable firms to coordinate activities and make use of their assets. (Day, 1994, p. 38)

**The Global Value Chain:** In many industries today, companies face intense international competition, and service firms are no exception. Competition drives firms to provide better value for customers at lower prices. Consequently, many firms have decided to outsource some activities that are no longer considered core to outsourcing providers, frequently in low-cost countries like India or the Philippines. The philosophy is that companies should focus on things that need to be done by themselves and procure from outside what others can do cheaper and often better.

The question then becomes which activities to retain and which to outsource to other firms. A related question is where to locate which activities. Sometimes, instead of outsourcing, some activities are moved into a shared service center in a low-cost location that belongs to the firm. Through this, the firm can retain know-how in the firm and ensure the confidentiality of data while achieving lower cost and efficiency. For example, a software firm might have developers in Silicon Valley, have staff who test the software in a shared service center in India, and have offices for marketing, sales, and customer support in each country where they want to sell and implement their software. Some electronic or phone-based customer support might also be done in India or split across several centers across continents for time zone and language reasons. The firm might also use independent IT service firms to implement the software at customer sites worldwide. The *value chain* is a tool that helps to understand and analyze the current value-adding activities and by whom and where they are done, and then plan changes to them.



**Value Chain**

A firm's *value chain* represents "a collection of activities that are performed to design, produce, market, deliver, and support its [the firm's] products." (Porter, 1985, p. 36)

Michael Porter distinguishes two types of activities: primary and support activities. Primary activities are such activities that directly create or deliver a product or service for customers. In a classic manufacturing firm, they could include receiving inputs (inbound logistics), manufacturing the product (operations), marketing, selling, and distributing it to customers (outbound logistics), plus after-sales service. Support activities have an internal function and improve the effectiveness of the primary activities. They include typical internal functions like human resource management, IT, finance and accounting, controlling, and procurement (Porter, 1985, pp. 39–43).

**The Value Chain Applied to Services:** You might wonder to what extent the classic value chain of Michael Porter, with its focus on processing material inputs and outputs, applies to services. Indeed, while support activities tend to be similar across industries, primary activities are quite industry- and even firm-specific. Due to the simultaneity of production and consumption in most services, services cannot be first produced and then sold and distributed. Marketing and sales must come first, and only once a customer has agreed to buy a service it gets "produced," that is, provided or delivered to the customer. Segal-Horn and Faulkner (Segal-Horn & Faulkner, 2010, pp. 289–290) have pointed this out, drawing on the example of a hotel. First, the service gets designed (product design), then customers are made aware of it and enticed to buy it (marketing), then it is sold to a specific customer who agrees to buy it (distribution), then the service is provided (service provision), and eventually the quality of the service and customer satisfaction need to be monitored, and the service gets continuously enhanced (service monitoring & enhancement).

While Segal-Horn and Faulkner see it as very inappropriate to use a value chain starting with inbound logistics for services, we would qualify this statement. Using the classic value chain of Michael Porter as a starting point can point us toward the fact that inputs are also needed for providing services. For example, a hotel also requires inputs such as groceries for the kitchen that prepares the breakfast buffet provided to guests in the morning. However, the amount of groceries procured for breakfast depends on the number of guests staying at the hotel on a particular night. So, the placement of inbound logistics in the value chain would not be at the beginning, but after sales, after knowing how many customers have agreed to use the hotel service on a given day. This is again due to the simultaneity of production and consumption of most services. In many services, however, the input would be less tangible and frequently consist of information. Think of a management consultant, lawyer, tax advisor, advertising agency, bank, or insurance company. They all need information from their customers as input to provide their service effectively. This is connected to the role of the customer as a coproducer of services. Moreover, the output of firms in these service industries takes the shape of information as well, whether a tax return of a tax consultant, a management presentation of a consulting firm, or an insurance policy from an insurance firm. They are information processing services, and their output needs to be delivered to customers as well (outbound logistics), whether verbally, by mail, or electronically. So, asking the question "What is our input, and how does it get to us?" and "What is our output, and how does it get to the customer?" is also relevant for service firms. The answer will vary depending on whether the firm provides people processing, possession processing, mental stimulus processing, or information processing services. Consistent with our above argument, Haller and Wissing (2020, p. 101) do include inbound logistics in their proposal for a value chain for services. Based on the distinctive characteristics of services, one element we would add is customer integration. As the customer is involved in the service process, we include customer integration as an additional element in the service value chain.

◘ Figure 8.6 shows the resulting value chain for the services we propose. First, the service gets designed, including all the facilities and equipment needed. Then, the service firm engages in marketing and sales activities to promote its services to customers. Then inputs, whether material such as groceries or intangible like information, are procured. Next, the service is provided to customers. Outbound logistics are relevant for some services, such as film, music, or software, while for most others where simultaneity applies, it is less relevant, so we put it in grey in the figure. Finally, the service firm needs to monitor service quality and customer satisfaction. Customers are involved throughout inbound logistics, service provision, and service monitoring. Regarding the support activities such as infrastructure, technology management, and procurement, human resource management is of particular importance due to the importance of staff for service quality as perceived by the customer.

**Analyzing the Value Chain in Service MNEs:** Managers of Service MNEs take the value chain as described by Porter or service-specific versions as a starting point and adapt it to their industry and company. Once they have described the

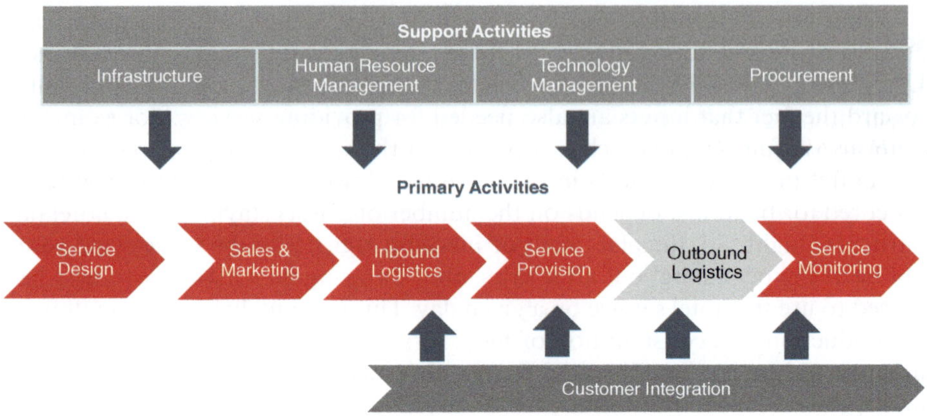


**Fig. 8.6** The value chain in services, own diagram inspired by (Porter, 1985, p. 37), (Segal-Horn & Faulkner, 2010, p. 290), (Haller & Wissing, 2020), and own thinking

8

firm's specific value chain, managers analyze it by asking various questions. First, managers can use the value chain to assess their strengths and weaknesses by comparing how well the firm performs each activity compared to its major competitors. Second, they analyze which activities create the most value for customers and which less. This can help decide which activities to retain in the firm and which to outsource. Third, it can guide an analysis of how much each activity contributes to the service's cost. In conjunction with the previous step, this can help identify activities that might be offshored to a lower-cost location. Fourth, by analyzing the company's value chain, managers can determine if the firm can compete at low prices because it can provide value activities cheaper than competitors (cost leadership). Alternatively, it may rather compete with high-quality, innovative services (differentiation) because its value activities are designed to provide higher quality and innovation than competitors. Managers also analyze their value chain's geographic scope or footprint to address the international dimension. In which locations do they perform which activities in the value chain? Are most of them concentrated in the home country or spread broadly into the various subsidiaries? Are certain activities done centrally, not in the home country, but in a shared service center in a low-cost country? Finally, managers must not forget the importance of linkages between the value activities. An isolated analysis of each activity might lead the firm to outsource certain activities without realizing how their linkage with other activities creates value for the customer. For example, only after subcontracting hardware manufacturing to Mitsubishi and then selling it to Mitsubishi did United States firm Apricot realize that its software business was critically dependent on hardware manufacturing (Frynas & Mellahi, 2015, pp. 132–133). The capability of Google to link all of its resources to create value is a positive example.

In the next section on strategy development, we will return to the value chain as we look at how managers can configure the value chain in different ways.

## Strategy Development

Once MNEs have understood the opportunities and threats in their external environment and their strengths and weaknesses internally, they develop strategies to compete successfully in global markets. Managers can develop strategies at various levels, such as the corporate and subsidiary levels. This section will mainly focus on corporate strategies developed for the MNE as a whole, while subsidiary-level strategies are addressed later in this chapter. In line with what we outlined above and in ◘ Fig. 8.3, we will focus here on the configuration of the value chain and the firm's strategy regarding global integration and local responsiveness.

## Configuring the Global Value Chain

As MNEs move from analyzing their existing value chain to making deliberate design choices by *configuring their value chain*, the critical choice they face is whether they want a *concentrated* or *dispersed* global value chain. In a concentrated global value chain, an activity like service design, service provision, or service monitoring is done in one location and provided for the whole world. In a dispersed global value chain, each activity is performed in each country where the MNE offers its services; each subsidiary would perform all activities in the value chain in their country (Porter, 1986). For example, an international chain of gyms might centrally design the service offering (which courses, which machines, common design features of the facilities, and general positioning as premium versus low cost). The operation of the gyms would happen locally, while service monitoring might be done partly centrally and partly locally. Its value chain would be relatively concentrated. Another chain of gyms might leave it up to each national subsidiary to design its service offering, adapting courses, machines, facilities, and positioning to local needs. The operation of the gyms and service monitoring would also happen locally. Its value chain would be very dispersed.

As the example shows, concentrated and dispersed value chains are ideal types or ends of a spectrum. In practice, the value chains of real MNEs will be somewhere along a continuum from fully concentrated to fully dispersed. A concentrated value chain carries several advantages for the MNE. The concentration of activities provides economies of scale as their fixed costs get distributed across a larger number of units, reducing the cost per unit. When a service is associated with a favorable country of origin effect, customers expect it to be conducted in the home country rather than offshoring it to a lower-cost location. Especially in knowledge-intensive services, concentration lowers the risk of unintended dispersion of know-how. Concentration also reduces the need for cross-country coordination (Holtbrügge, 2009, p. 10).

A distributed value chain also yields advantages for the MNE. It allows a better adaptation to local economic, political, legal, and other conditions worldwide, which is particularly important in industries where conditions vary widely between countries, such as healthcare services. Dispersing activities allows taking advantage of location economies such as low-cost labor compared to the more expensive home country of the MNE. Dispersing value activities increases flexibility and lowers risks because the MNE can offset adverse events in a country by shifting activities to other countries (Holtbrügge, 2009, pp. 10–11). The opening case on Russia and the War in Ukraine and the discussion of the effect of Covid 19 on international trade in previous chapters have demonstrated this vividly.

According to Michael Porter, when deciding how to allocate activities in the value chain, it is helpful to distinguish so-called "upstream" and "downstream" activities. *Downstream activities* are related to the customer and must be provided close to the customer in each country, such as sales and customer services. *Upstream activities* can be decoupled from the customer's location and conducted more centrally. Typically, this would be inbound logistics, operations (production), and support activities such as technology management or finance (Porter, 1986). For most services, more activities, especially operations ("service provision" in our model), would be considered downstream due to the simultaneity of production and consumption and the customer's involvement. The service provision of the gym chain in our example above needs to happen in each location where customers are. This is different for services embodied in goods, such as software that can be provided in low-cost locations, such as India, and then be sold to customers abroad, similar to goods (Kantsperger et al., 2004). Holtbrügge and Welge (2015, p. 146) provide a nice graphic display of concentrated and dispersed value chains in service firms and further distinguish two types of dispersed value chains (see ◘ Fig. 8.7). In a *parallel configuration*, each value activity is conducted in each national subsidiary of the firm, duplicating each activity. In an *integrated configuration*, some activities are duplicated in each subsidiary, while others are concentrated in only one country, whether the home country or a third country. Parallel configurations are required when it is necessary to adapt the service to local conditions. It is indispensable for people processing services and when the service cannot be provided

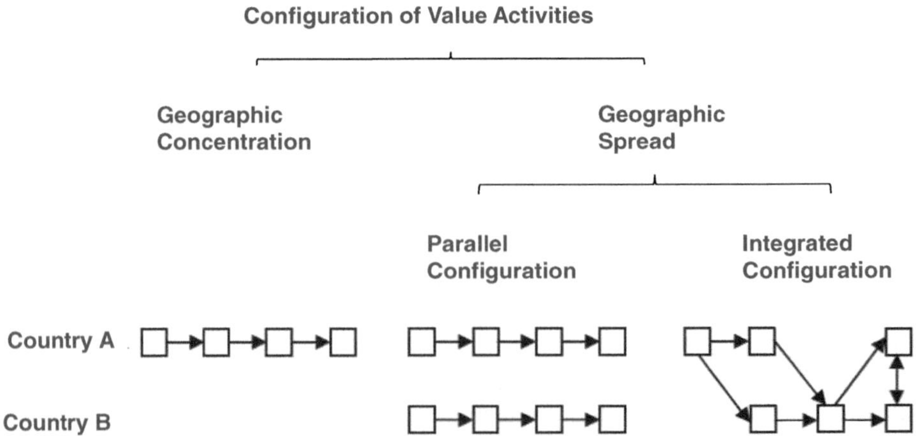


◘ **Fig. 8.7** Configuration of value activities in Service MNEs, adapted from (Holtbrügge & Welge, 2015, p. 146) (permission obtained)

via media (as in cross-border supply) or in an automated manner. It facilitates collaboration with customers. However, it requires that service provision can be multiplied unproblematically. This is not always the case when it is based on specific competencies that cannot be multiplied easily, such as the expertise of the highly skilled senior staff. In integrated configurations, for example, research and development in knowledge-intensive services can be concentrated in one country, while other service activities happen separately in the respective host country. This configuration is difficult to implement for people processing services with a very integrated character. This is different for possession processing services. In these, such as parcel delivery, only a multiplication of pick-up and drop-off systems is required (Kantsperger et al., 2004, pp. 127–128). A case in point is the laundry service in Berlin that picks up and drops off laundry at hotels in Berlin while the washing takes place in a village in lower-cost Poland just across the border outlined in ▸ Chap. 6. This requires, however, that transport cost does not offset the lower cost of the laundry location in Poland.

**Factors for Service Location Decision:** Once an MNE has decided on the general configuration of its value chain, the remaining question is how to choose the actual location of the various value-creating activities. Generally speaking, MNEs exploit location advantages or location economies when choosing locations. In other words: They choose the most productive location in the world or a region for a value-creating activity. In the academic and practice-oriented literature, various criteria for selecting locations for placing value-creating activities have been put forward. Reviewing them makes it clear that by the end of the day, they all boil down to three criteria: resource cost, business environment, and people skills & availability. Today, we need to add a fourth factor: digitalization. These four factors are also decidedly relevant to the location of service operations. They are, therefore, also the four factors used by advisory firm Kearney in its biannual Global Service Location Index (Kearney, 2019):

- *Resource cost* ("financial attractiveness" in the Kearney index) in service industries is primarily driven by the level of compensation of staff. However, it also includes infrastructure costs and tax and regulatory costs.
- *People skills & availability* include the size and qualification level of the labor force in a location, including the education level and language skills.
- *Business environment* addresses how easy it is to do business in a country, including the political and legal environment, the level of infrastructure such as telecommunications and transportation, and the protection of intellectual property.
- *Digitalization* ("digital resonance") has been added recently by Kearney to address the rising importance of digitalization. It includes things like the level of digital skills, digital activities of businesses, and the legal framework for digital business models, including cyber security.

Digitalization and the possibilities for automating tasks have enormously impacted location decisions. While in the past, firms have offshored many backend activities to lower-cost countries like India, automation makes it possible to conduct these activities at low cost in otherwise high cost developed countries. While the trend started in manufacturing, robotic process automation (RPA) can now automate many office tasks. So, several companies that initially offshored have now moved activities back home ("re-shoring") or to locations closer to home ("near-shoring"). RPA applications that run on a cloud-based system operate in "no location at all" (A.T. Kearney, 2014). However, they need qualified staff to set up and maintain the applications; for these teams, the four location criteria still apply, especially the digital skill requirements. For example, telecommunications giant Vodafone announced laying off 1700 service center staff in Romania, Egypt, and India as the firm implements automation solutions. In the Czech Republic, RPA replaces an estimated 4000 employees. However, this is partly offset by the 1200 staff who program and maintain the RPA robots (Kearney, 2019).

## Global Integration and Local Responsiveness



In today's global business environment, manufacturing and service multinationals face two seemingly opposing forces: *global integration* and *local responsiveness*. Global integration stands for the need for efficiency. This is due to the strong global competition that exists in many industries. Many MNEs face a range of strong competitors in many country markets. Intense competition means that firms try to undercut each other on prices, which exerts pressure to lower costs to remain competitive and profitable simultaneously, hence the drive toward global efficiency. Even where products cannot be globally standardized, MNEs look for ways of standardizing at least part of a product or use multilingual packages to reduce cost (Bartlett & Ghoshal, 1998, pp. 6–8). Airlines are a good example of the service sector. On most international routes, several airlines are competing fiercely for customers. So they attempt to standardize and rationalize as much as possible of their operations to keep their costs under control and offer competitive prices. Singapore Airlines is an example (Heracleous & Wirtz, 2010).

At the same time, most MNEs cannot neglect the need to adapt their products to local conditions, whether relating to local language, culture, economic conditions, legal and regulatory requirements, the competitive situation, or differing customer needs. They must be locally responsive. Despite global convergence, customer needs are far from homogenous (Bartlett & Ghoshal, 1998, pp. 9–11). Especially most services require responsiveness to local conditions. Besides some global pop bands, most performing arts, like concerts or theatre performances, are in the local language, addressing local tastes and cultural context. The same applies to most education services, which must comply with local government requirements.

The forces for global integration drive MNEs to standardize their product offering and processes, centralize value-creating activities and ensure strong global coordination. The forces for local responsiveness drive MNEs to locally adapt product offerings and operating processes and to decentralize activities to be closer to the various markets. Let us take a closer look at what drives these two forces.

## Forces Driving Global Integration

**Convergence of Consumer Preferences:** Global competition is—among other factors—driven by a convergence of consumer preferences. Almost worldwide, people use iPhones, drink Coca-Cola, eat at McDonald's restaurants, and have coffee at Starbucks, to name just a few classic examples. In several industries, this allows companies to offer broadly the same products or services in many markets worldwide and standardize them accordingly.

**Economies of Scale:** In manufacturing industries like electronics or automotive, large numbers of produced units are necessary to fully utilize the capital-intensive capacity of production plants. This drives companies to sell products in global markets while keeping the number of production sites small. Producing a large quantity in one place and selling it in multiple countries is frequently more efficient than having production sites in each country. By doing so, MNEs achieve *economies of scale* (Bartlett et al., 2008, pp. 88–89). Economies of scale are increasingly relevant in many service industries as they become more capital intensive. Many service industries today invest significantly in information technology and must run large-scale operations to leverage the investment made. Think of audit and management consulting, financial services, and software firms. Industries like hotel chains, telecommunications, IT, and airlines are capital intensive. For example, global advertising networks like WPP achieve economies of scale from bulk media time and advertising space purchases. Likewise, airlines, hotel chains, and car rental firms use their central computer reservation systems across the globe (Segal-Horn & Faulkner, 2010, pp. 290–293).

**Economies of Scope:** By using one asset for multiple processes, products, or business units, the cost of producing multiple outputs jointly is less than the cost of producing them separately. MNEs thus achieve *economies of scope*. Service firms like news agency Reuters use large-scale global electronic knowledge repositories to re-use codified knowledge gained across their operations. In tourism, customer data collected from flight bookings are used to cross-sell additional services such as insurance, accommodation, or car rental (Segal-Horn & Faulkner, 2010, pp. 290–293).

**Location Advantages:** To reduce cost, MNEs look to countries where production factors such as labor are available sufficiently and at a low cost. Manufacturing firms moved production to Southern Europe and Central America and then to the far east and Eastern Europe (Bartlett et al., 2008, pp. 88–89). Service firms moved parts of their service processes to shared service centers or outsourcing providers in countries like India or the Philippines. Thus, they achieve location economies or *location advantages*.

**Liberalization of Global Trade:** All three factors mentioned above require MNEs to integrate and coordinate their global value-creating activities to leverage economies of scope, scale, and location advantages. This was significantly facilitated by the liberalization of global trade since the end of the Second World War. Lower barriers to trade and investments made it economically and practically possible to realize the potential benefits from economies of scale, scope, and location (Bartlett et al., 2008, pp. 88–89).

**Global Competitive Strategies:** While the abovementioned factors are external, dynamics within several industries further drove firms to integrate globally. As competitors no longer manage their operations in various countries independently but as one integrated whole, they can leverage and transfer strengths in some markets to other markets. This exerts pressure on other firms in the industry to do likewise to remain competitive. For example, British Airways used its dominant position at Heathrow Airport to generate significant profits on its long-haul flights, especially across the Atlantic. This enabled it to subsidize its UK and European flights and thereby deter new entrants in Europe with low prices for a long time (Bartlett et al., 2008, pp. 89–90).

## Forces Driving Local Responsiveness



A range of factors drives companies to be responsive to local environments with economic, political, legal, cultural, competitive, and market differences, which we addressed in previous chapters. In the following, we will highlight some of them.

**Cultural Differences and Consumer Preferences:** Cultural differences impact consumption patterns. Take tea as an example. While in the UK, it is drunk with milk, in the United States, it is preferred as a summer drink over ice, while in countries like Saudi Arabia, it is drunk thick, hot, and heavily sweetened. So coffee house chains must adapt their offering accordingly (Bartlett et al., 2008, pp. 92–93). Cultural traditions also impact seasonal consumption patterns. In China, it is common to offer moon cakes as a seasonal gift during the mid-autumn festival. So international coffeehouse chains such as McDonald's McCafé and Starbucks offer branded moon cakes in China during the season (Han, 2017).

**Government Requirements:** To protect consumers, workers, local culture, and the environment, governments place many requirements on MNEs who wish to do business in their country, as outlined in previous chapters. In professional services, whether auditing, tax advice, law, or medical services, governments require diplomas or certificates from local educational institutions or professional bodies before a professional is allowed to practice.

**Resistance Against Globalization:** Increasingly, consumers reject globally standardized products. This is due to several reasons, including a preference for differentiated products, patriotism, or a desire to support local businesses. It creates opportunities for companies to offer localized products in response to local needs (Bartlett et al., 2008, p. 95). For example, in Germany, local cola drinks such as Fritz Cola, Afri Cola, Premium Cola, or Vita Cola have gained significant ground over the American brands Coca-Cola and Pepsi Cola. They have been launched by young startup firms and are considered authentic and based on clever marketing. In trendy bars, it is part of the good tone to have a local cola drink on the menu instead of the long-standing US drinks (Hegemann, 2015).

## Classification of Industries

Christopher Bartlett and Sumantra Ghoshal have found that the forces for global integration and local responsiveness vary in strength between industries.

In some industries, both forces are weak. These are shaped by an *international environment*. In these industries, there is no strong global competition by globally integrated multinational enterprises, so the pressure to lower costs and be globally integrated and coordinated is low. Also, customer needs do not vary much across countries, so the need to adapt products to country markets is not strong either. A service firm in this industry would design an innovative service in its home market and then diffuse the required know-how to its subsidiaries to deliver it locally in each host market. There would be little adaptation and little need to achieve global economies of scale or scope or leverage location economies (Bartlett et al., 2008, p. 98). Among service firms, railway operators might be considered as an example. Since they are geographically bound by the tracks and governments provide limited licenses to firms to operate trains on their rail network, there is no strong global competition. At the same time, how to operate a railway is more or less similar across countries.

In other industries, forces for local responsiveness are strong, while forces for global integration are weak. This is called a multinational or *multidomestic environment*.[3] In these industries, customer needs vary considerably across countries, and frequently, there are significantly different legal and regulatory requirements for businesses (Bartlett et al., 2008, p. 98). In services, law firms are an example. National law is very distinct in each country and requires deep local knowledge of lawyers. In addition, access to this market is strictly controlled by requirements to obtain diplomas from local universities and certificates from the national professional body to be allowed to practice. There is no need to be globally integrated for small- and medium-sized law firms not regularly involved in international affairs. A referent network with law firms operating in other jurisdictions will often suffice to refer clients to other firms in the network for legal advice in another country's legal matters. The largest law firms, however, do operate internationally and show a tendency to integrate more closely to provide integrated advice on cross-border transactions (Segal-Horn & Dean, 2009).

In a *global environment,* forces for global integration are strong, while there is little need to adapt to local conditions. Typically, products or services in such industries are relatively homogenous worldwide as they serve universal needs that require little local adaptation. When customers perceive products of different companies as being more or less the same, their price becomes the main differentiator. So, companies need to achieve economies of scale, scope, and location economies to lower their costs and offer low prices profitably. This drives the need for global integration. So value creation happens at a few centralized large-scale operations

3 We prefer the term *multidomestic* to avoid confusion with the term "multinational enterprise," as many MNEs are not in a multidomestic/multinational environment, but one of the other environments.

that serve an entire continent or even the world (Bartlett et al., 2008, p. 97). In services, this is a less common environment due to the need for customer involvement, which creates some heterogeneity in the service delivered. However, some standard software and IT services can be found here. Offering global cloud services to host data in a globally accessible server environment necessitates large-scale capital investments. A firm will not fully and efficiently use such huge infrastructure investments unless it offers the service globally. Customer requirements for cloud storage do not differ significantly, though legal requirements such as data privacy regulation may differ to some extent.

Companies operating in a *transnational environment* face the arguably most challenging pressures for local responsiveness and global integration simultaneously. Typically, in such industries, there is strong global competition by globally active MNEs, while consumer preferences and other requirements from the environment are not the same in each country. Frequently, this environment is the outcome of industries that once were global or multidomestic, but the need for local adaptation or global integration has increased. Especially the lowering of trade barriers increased competition, and technological advances facilitated a certain standardization of at least parts of products or services (Bartlett et al., 2008, pp. 98–99). Some examples from the service sector are financial services, telecommunications, management consulting, fast food chains, and e-commerce. For example, multinational telecommunications operators engage in stiff competition, requiring them to achieve economies of scale, scope, and location by using shared service centers in low-cost locations for back-office tasks. While the core service of providing a mobile or landline phone or internet connection does not vary much between operators, there are differences in legal requirements and customer needs between countries regarding how these services are packaged and sold (Melody, 1997). Regarding the opening case of Walmart in Germany, one can assume that the environment for a global retailer like Walmart is transnational. While fierce competition requires firms to buy large quantities from suppliers to achieve low purchasing costs and keep a close watch on other expenses, there is a broad range of local differences between country markets, as the case has shown.



## A Typology of Strategies

How are MNEs supposed to position themselves strategically, given their environment? Consistent with the four environments, according to Bartlett & Ghoshal (Bartlett et al., 2008), there are four possible strategies: *international, multidomestic, global,* and *transnational*. The basic rule here is: The strategy should be consistent with the environment. So, for example, a company in a multidomestic environment should pursue a multidomestic strategy. Otherwise, firms will run into difficulties. A firm in such an environment pursuing an international or a global strategy will not adapt sufficiently to the customer requirements in the various markets and will find it difficult to find customers. The opening case on Walmart in Germany has shown how Walmart has, in many ways, not been responsive enough to the requirements of the German market.

**International Strategy:** Companies pursuing an *international strategy* focus on developing key competencies in their parent country and transferring them to the various host countries. This typically relates to branding and the development of the products or services of the firm. Alphabet (Google) is an example. Their offerings are primarily developed centrally in their headquarters in Mountainview, California, and then made available worldwide with only minor modifications, such as the language of the user interface. This strategy is suitable when both forces for global integration and local adaptation are low. It works particularly when, as in the case of Alphabet, a firm has a competitive advantage that competitors in other markets lack. The advantage of this strategy is that resources and capabilities developed once at home can be used in multiple locations. However, the firm might miss local market opportunities as local operations focus on implementing the template from the parent country. Walmart's approach in 1997, when they entered the German market, appeared to fit mainly in this category, perhaps with elements of the global strategy due to the firm's emphasis on cost control. Their service offering and procedures were developed in the United States and applied without much adaptation in other countries like Germany. Had they been more open to the local context, they would likely have been more successful in the German market.

**Global Strategy:** Companies that follow a *global strategy* are focused on efficiency, driving down cost by centralizing activities in one or a few locations and by standardizing its offerings as well as processes and procedures. Through this, they achieve economies of scale and scope. Besides, they use location economies. So, a service firm might centralize its back-office operations that can be performed away from the customer in a shared service center in a low-cost location like India. Thus, they would combine location economies and economies of scope, as these centralized activities would serve multiple subsidiaries and business units. Generally, this strategy is suitable when strong forces exist for global integration while forces for local responsiveness are low (Bartlett et al., 2008, p. 204). Given the need for simultaneity and customer integration of most services, this strategy is less common for service firms. Examples of firms that come somewhat close might include international airlines such as KLM, British Airways, and Singapore Airlines, and express parcel delivery services such as Federal Express (van Dierdonck & van Looy, 2013).

**Multidomestic Strategy:** When a company pursues a *multidomestic* strategy, it emphasizes the adaptation to local conditions in each market it operates. Headquarters grants subsidiaries sufficient autonomy to respond to local market conditions and regulations. They might even develop local products or services for their local market. This strategy is suitable when there are strong forces for local responsiveness and low forces for global integration. Due to subsidiaries' autonomy, their managers will be motivated to drive business growth and pursue business opportunities. This is traditionally the case in professional service firms such as audit, law, and advisory firms, where local partners act like entrepreneurs of their own local businesses. By the same token, firms are highly innovative as they develop suitable offerings in each market. However, the strong emphasis on local adaptation comes at a high cost.

**Transnational Strategy:** Companies facing simultaneously high pressure for global integration and local adaptation frequently find that pursuing a transnational strategy serves them best. This strategy combines elements of the previously outlined strategies: leverage competencies on a global scale, achieve efficiency by economies of scale, scope, and location where possible, and adapt to local conditions where necessary. Unlike the international strategy, however, competencies are not only transferred from headquarters out into the subsidiaries but also shared between subsidiaries. This is based on the conviction that innovative practices and solutions can originate anywhere in the global firm. One professional service firm, for example, when it wanted to implement a new global IT system for managing staff training, identified a suitable system in the Turkish member firm. This was then rolled out globally to become the global training management system. This illustrates a difference to the multidomestic strategy: Innovations developed locally do not just remain local but might be shared across the firm, as other subsidiaries might also find them helpful. McDonald's can serve as an example. While it does activities like overall strategy, service design, marketing, supply chain, and others centrally to achieve efficiency, the menu, besides global standards, also includes some local food, such as offering vegetarian burgers in India and beer in Belgium (van Dierdonck & van Looy, 2013, p. 426). In Malaysia, McDonald's offers its own version of local favorite Nasi Lemak, called "Nasi McDo." Since most Malaysians are Muslim, McDonald's ensured this dish is "halal," certified by a stamp of the state authority supervising halal food, allowing Muslims to eat.



**The Strategies in Service Firms:** In addition to what was outlined above, to discuss further the appropriateness of the four strategies for service firms, it is helpful to look at the different types of services introduced in ► Chap. 1. People-processing services typically require a multidomestic or possibly transnational strategy as they require local interaction with and integration of the customer. If a Service MNE looks to implement a global strategy, this might be appropriate for some information processing, mental stimulus processing, and possession processing services. Especially information processing, drawing heavily on ICT today (think of cloud-based services as an example), allows more standardization and centralization than many other services. Possession processing, such as transportation and logistics, also allows at least partly more standardization and efficiency (remember the airline example) (Lovelock & Yip, 1996). The following insert illustrates the four strategies by outlining how they would look at consulting firm McKinsey.

**Evolution of Strategy at McKinsey & Company**

A company in London, UK, contacts McKinsey & Company to request a proposal for advice on a restructuring project. Had this happened in the 1960s when McKinsey pursued an international strategy, the request would have been forwarded to the McKinsey head office in New York. The project would then be staffed from New York and led by senior consultants from New York. The methodology would essentially have been developed in the United States, and McKinsey would apply it with little local adaptation. McKinsey would add some additional London-based consultants to provide some local input.

In the early 1970s, McKinsey had become a global company. In this case, a

Nasi McD, source: Dirk Klimkeit

manager from the London office would negotiate the project with the customer. McKinsey would use a globally standardized methodology that would not necessarily have been developed entirely in the United States. The project would be led by a senior consultant from the United States, supported by UK-based consultants trained in the global methodology in the United States.

Had McKinsey pursued a multidomestic strategy, the McKinsey brand name would have been used to attract and obtain the contract from the client. The project would then, however, be staffed and run by local London-based consultants. They would develop a customized British solution for the client.

By the 2000s, McKinsey had adopted a transnational strategy. The company would maintain centers of excellence for specific consulting topics worldwide. McKinsey would negotiate the project from London, but international experts would be involved. The firm would then staff the project with the most suitable consultants from around the world. The consultants would share a joint transnational corporate culture McKinsey developed through international training and previous projects. The solution for the client would be customized to the local situation but draw on the global firm-wide expertise of McKinsey.

Source: (Segal-Horn & Faulkner, 2010, p. 154).

**A Differentiated Approach:** Until now, we have addressed the four strategies at the level of the MNE as a whole. However, an MNE may have to adopt a differentiated approach for their different businesses, functions, and tasks. An MNE containing several different businesses might treat some of its businesses in a global manner and others in a transnational or multidomestic manner, as each business might be situated in a different environment. Within each business, functions might be treated differently. While research & development might be pretty global, marketing and sales might require a multidomestic approach. Differentiation might even go further and distinguish between different tasks within one function. Within marketing, the overall product policy might be treated in a global manner, advertising in a transnational way, as it requires local adaptation besides some standardization. At the same time, pricing and distribution might be more multidomestic (Bartlett & Ghoshal, 1998, p. 111). In a professional service firm, this might mean that the consulting business is treated in a global manner, while an audit can rely on a global methodology but needs adaptation to local accounting standards; hence a transnational approach might be favored. The tax consulting and legal advice business might be more multidomestic instead due to the very local nature of law and tax. Choosing the right approach for each function within the firm is critical to a Service MNE's success. This is illustrated by the following insert.

8

**Global Marketing Campaign in a Transnational Professional Service Firm**

One large professional service firm established a new Europe-wide central marketing team, which launched a marketing campaign in the context of the 2008 global financial crisis. Partners in the national subsidiaries were asked to talk to their clients about centrally defined topics using centrally designed brochures and PowerPoint slides. They had to report each week how many meetings they had had with clients addressing the campaign and what the outcome of them had been. Many partners, however, felt that the campaign did not match the issues of their local clients. They responded with a whole range of behaviors. Some ignored the campaign, some complained about it, and some pretended to participate while not really participating. In some cases where partners did address the campaign with clients despite knowing it was irrelevant to their client, the client's response was less than favorable. Marketing and sales tend to require a multidomestic or transnational approach, while this firm was attempting to conduct it in a global manner.

Source: (Klimkeit & Reihlen, 2016).

## The Role of Subsidiaries in Multinational Service Firms

Traditionally, international management scholars have mainly focused on MNEs' headquarters, as this is where many of the strategic decisions for the firm are made. However, increasingly, scholars have become aware that subsidiaries can play a range of essential roles for the MNE that go beyond executing what headquarters has designed and decided (J. Birkinshaw & Hood, 1998). Due to the need to integrate customers, customize to the needs of customers, and the simultaneity of production and consumption for most services, this is particularly relevant for Service MNEs. We will introduce three factors that determine the management of subsidiaries and then address them one by one. This is followed by an outline of the roles of subsidiary managers.

## Management of Subsidiaries

Mainly three factors determine how MNEs manage their subsidiaries: the strategic orientation of the MNE, the characteristics and roles of a subsidiary, and institutions in the home country (see ◘ Fig. 8.8).

**Strategic Orientation of the MNE:** One can observe that each MNE has a preferred way of managing its subsidiaries. This is connected to the four strategies of MNEs outlined above and to the preferred coordinating mechanism. The four strategies imply a different way of managing subsidiaries and, by implication, a different role for the subsidiary. Consider the international strategy. Headquarters holds core competencies, and subsidiaries sell and implement mostly standardized services according to the blueprint developed in the parent country. In MNEs pursuing a multidomestic strategy, subsidiaries take on a central role in the MNE. This is where many strategic decisions are made, and sometimes local services are designed specifically for the local market. When a global strategy is adopted, subsidiaries tend to be less powerful again and play a role designated to them by headquarters in view of the overall plan of the MNE, e.g., to leverage location economies. In transnational MNEs, subsidiaries play essential and diverse roles. While some may play a similar role to those in MNEs with a global strategy, others might become the global center of expertise for a particular service or theme. The

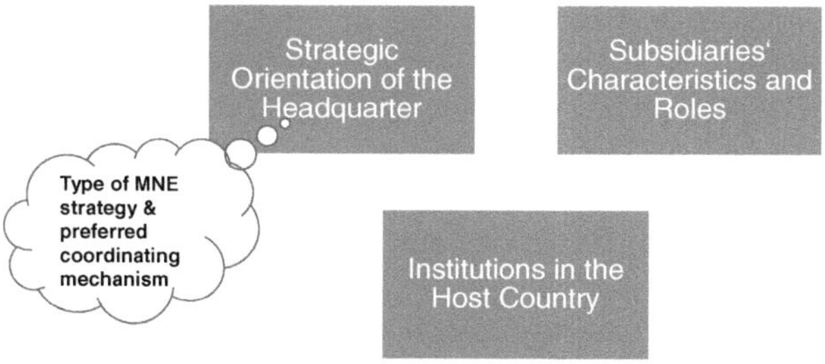


◘ Fig. 8.8 Determinants of the management of subsidiaries, own diagram

MNE would also pay more attention to the competencies of subsidiaries and expect them to share them and local innovations with other subsidiaries across the firm (Bartlett & Ghoshal, 1998, pp. 74–76).

Second, each MNE also has a preference for a global coordinating mechanism (centralization, formalization, and socialization). These also imply different approaches to managing subsidiaries. We will introduce them in ▶ Chap. 9 in the context of organizing the Service MNE.

**Characteristics of Subsidiaries:** While each MNE has a preference for how it manages its subsidiaries, you will notice that the headquarters of an MNE does not manage each subsidiary in the same way. There can be several reasons for this. Some reasons have to do with the characteristics of the country where the subsidiary is located. For example, the size of the market matters. Other things being equal, HQ management will pay more attention to and be tempted to involve themselves more in managing a subsidiary in a very large market such as China or the United States than regarding a subsidiary in much smaller markets. More is at stake regarding revenue potential and resources committed to that subsidiary. Other reasons for the different approaches of the MNE to different subsidiaries have to do with the characteristics of the subsidiaries themselves. For example, the maturity of the local management will play a role. Suppose local management is new in the role and does not have much management experience. In that case, HQ management will likely get involved more directly to help the subsidiary develop, whether in person or by sending expatriates to manage the subsidiary. For example, after the fall of communism in Central and Eastern Europe, most MNEs who set up subsidiaries in these countries initially sent expatriates to manage the subsidiaries. Over time, as local managers gained experience in managing an MNE subsidiary in a market economy, expatriates were replaced by local managers. A similar pattern can be observed in developing countries where experienced managers are scarce and are frequently developed internally over time (Bartlett & Ghoshal, 1986).



**Roles of Subsidiaries:** Based on the various factors that distinguish the subsidiaries of an MNE, HQ assigns each subsidiary a *role* that it plays in the MNE. To better grasp these roles, scholars have developed several different typologies of roles of subsidiaries (J. M. Birkinshaw & Morrison, 1995). Here, we will outline a frequently cited typology by Jarillo and Martínez (1990), which aligns well with the four strategies by Bartlett and Ghoshal (see ◘ Fig. 8.9). Jarillo and Martinez consider two factors that determine a subsidiary's role: the *degree of integration* and the *degree of localization*. Localization in this model is not to be confused with local responsiveness as in the integration-responsiveness model. Instead, it describes to what extent all or only a few value-creating activities in the value chain are located in-country. A high degree of localization would mean that a service firm designs services for the local market, markets and sells them, delivers them to local customers, and conducts service monitoring. Subsidiaries with a low degree of localization might only conduct one or few parts of the value chain in-country. This might mean simply providing a service designed elsewhere in the MNE. Even much of marketing, sales, and service monitoring would be done, for example, at a

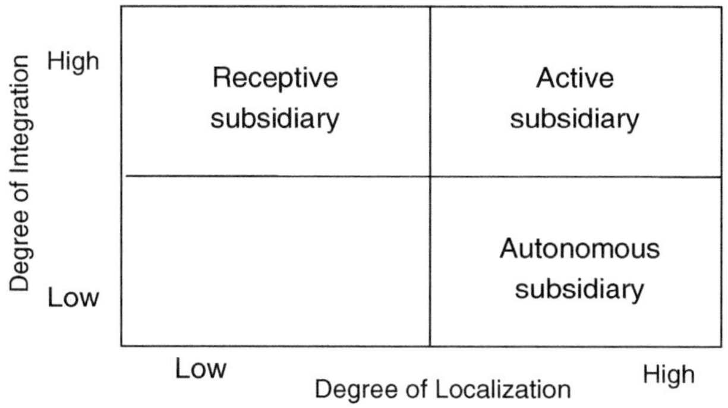


**Fig. 8.9** Subsidiaries' characteristics and roles, source: (Jarillo & Martínez, 1990, p. 503) (permission obtained)

regional headquarters. The degree of integration describes to what extent the activities a subsidiary conducts are integrated with the rest of the MNE. Combining the two dimensions yields several possible roles for the subsidiary:

- **Receptive Subsidiary**: A receptive subsidiary conducts only a few value activities locally but is well integrated with other parts of the firm. In manufacturing firms, it might be simply a sales outlet for products designed and produced elsewhere. Alternatively, it might be a pure production site for goods sold elsewhere, such as many textile firms produce in Bangladesh and then sell worldwide. In services, such as a fast-food chain, the subsidiary might operate restaurants. In contrast, the service concept, including layout and menu, supply chain, and marketing, might be managed by a regional headquarters.
- **Autonomous Subsidiary**: An autonomous subsidiary has most, if not all, value activities in the country and has a low degree of integration with other parts of the firm. If this is a service firm, in the extreme case, it designs, markets and sells, provides, and monitors local-for-local services. This could be a network of advertising firms such as WPP or Omicron that provide most of their services to domestic firms and only get together globally when a global client needs a worldwide campaign.
- **Active Subsidiary**: An active subsidiary contains most or all value activities locally; however, unlike the autonomous subsidiary, it is closely integrated with other parts of the firm. This firm might be a global or regional center of excellence for a product or service. As a service firm, it would design a service, coordinate marketing and sales, monitor service delivery, and continuously improve and develop it, all for its region or even the world market. The service delivery might happen locally in the various other subsidiaries or even be provided centrally in services that allow cross-border supply, such as digital platforms.

You might wonder why there is no subsidiary type in the fourth box. Consider this: A subsidiary that has only one or a few elements of the value chain must be well integrated with other parts of the MNE to have the missing parts of the value chain provided by them. So, the low-low combination is not a feasible option.

How do the types of subsidiaries relate to the four MNE strategies? The autonomous subsidiary is closely connected to the multidomestic strategy. By conducting all value activities locally, a subsidiary is well-positioned to be locally responsive. In MNEs with a global strategy, subsidiaries tend to be receptive, specializing in a focused role assigned by HQ to leverage economies of scale, scope, and location. For example, a subsidiary might be a sales outlet selling standardized products in its local market. The active subsidiary can be found in transnational MNEs that have awarded a global mandate to the subsidiary, e.g., as a global/regional center of excellence. Having said this, not all subsidiaries in a transnational MNE are active. In line with the differentiated approach of the transnational strategy, some subsidiaries might be just receptive. In fact, according to Jarillo and Martinez, most subsidiaries play a receptive role (Jarillo & Martínez, 1990). For Service MNEs, due to characteristics such as simultaneity, customer integration, and the implied need for customization for most services, many subsidiaries will do more than implement a globally designed standard service.



**Institutions in the Host Country:** Institutions in the host country are a third element impacting the management of subsidiaries by headquarters. Think of the values and norms in a country that constitute its culture, legislation, and regulation, the local education system, industry associations, industrial relations between organized workers and businesses, and other national differences introduced in ► Chap. 4. These differences constitute a barrier to a one-size-fits-all approach to managing an MNE. HQ may attempt to implement a new policy or procedure globally across the various subsidiaries. This will typically be informed by the institutions that prevail in the home country of the MNE. This might work reasonably well in countries similar to the home country, but in countries with significantly differing institutions, it may not work. Remember how Walmart's US-inspired approach towards dealing with managers, staff, and customers failed in Germany. Remember how the centrally designed marketing campaign in the professional service firm encountered many challenges due to differences in various European countries. Also, consider the following case: Many Western companies have implemented a system of performance management called "360° Feedback." In this system, not only do employees get feedback from their boss. Colleagues also provide feedback, and employees provide feedback to their superiors. One Chinese university also attempted to introduce this system, but the results were disappointing, and the attempt was considered a failure. As Liu argues, Confucianist thinking prevalent in China implies strict hierarchical relations. Leaders and subordinates have assigned positions in society. Respect for authority meant that few people dared to give negative feedback to leaders or students to professors or lecturers (Liu, 2012). Imagine you are the HR manager of the Chinese subsidiary of a US MNE, and global HR asks you to implement 360° feedback in the Chinese subsidiary, consistent with the US-designed approach. You are aware of the cultural institutions in China that would likely make successful implementation challenging. In this situation, you would feel squeezed between the request for *global conformity* by global HR and the challenges of *local fit* (see ◼ Fig. 8.10). In other words, you would need to find ways of dealing with these conflicting dual pressures (Kostova & Roth, 2002). In this situation, subsidiary managers need to become creative.

**Fig. 8.10** Dual pressures for global conformity and local fit, own diagram, including photo courtesy of Imagerymajestic/► FreeDigitalPhotos.net

Remember how the local partners in the professional service firm responded in various creative ways with the dual pressure of implementing and reporting on the marketing campaign while knowing that, in many cases, it would not be locally appropriate (Klimkeit & Reihlen, 2016).

## Roles of Subsidiary Managers

Bartlett et al. have developed a systematic approach to the various roles subsidiary managers need to play. While they propose these roles specifically for subsidiary managers in transnational MNEs, we believe they can be used well for understanding how to deal with the conflicting pressures in MNE subsidiaries more generally (Bartlett et al., 2008, pp. 654–656):

**Bicultural Interpreter:** Typically, managers in the headquarters of an MNE do not have a good understanding of the local context in each of their subsidiaries. So, it is up to subsidiary managers to communicate the relevant aspects of their domestic environment to global management in a way they can understand and stress its importance to effective management. At the same time, subsidiary managers need to interpret and communicate global strategy to staff in their subsidiary and make it meaningful in the local context. In the case of the professional service firm mentioned above, some local executives are said to have been good at explaining to local partners and managers why the campaign is important and why they should contribute to it (Klimkeit & Reihlen, 2016).

**National Defender:** Beyond explaining the local context to global managers, subsidiary managers also need to defend the interests of their subsidiaries. Global management in MNEs frequently tends to centralize and standardize policies and procedures. So subsidiary managers must consider the local context when they make global decisions. This is especially the case when a new policy being discussed at the global level threatens to cause problems for the subsidiary. Imagine an MNE plans to offshore IT support to India and operate a central English language IT helpdesk from there. Knowing that many staff in the subsidiary do not speak English well and would struggle to report IT issues in English, a subsidiary manager would protest against the planned new policy.

**Frontline Implementer of Corporate Strategy:** As a complement to the first two roles, subsidiary managers must also successfully implement the global strategy in their subsidiary. So, any action they take on global initiatives must achieve the outcome intended by global management but be effective in the local environment. For example, in the case of the professional service firm's marketing campaign, some local partners adapted the marketing material or addressed alternative locally relevant topics to achieve the campaign's aim while making it work in the local context. The most challenging part is that, in some cases, subsidiary managers have to convince local staff that a global initiative makes sense, even when they initially lobbied against it. After all local input has been heard and considered, once a global decision has been reached, subsidiary managers must implement it. Otherwise, they would not be loyal to the MNE that employs them. In the professional service firm, some local executives were reported to have been better than others in convincingly promoting the campaign locally despite their reservations against it (Klimkeit & Reihlen, 2016).

## Multinational Service Firms with Digital Business Models



We conclude this chapter by looking at a particular type of Service MNE that has recently become important in the global economy: Service MNEs with digital business models, or simply "digital firms," especially a sub-type: digital platforms.

## Digital Firms and Platforms

The development of the internet in recent decades enabled a new form of Service MNE that leverages the internet for doing business. Several terms are used in this context, such as digital firms, ICT firms, ibusiness firms, digital platforms, and others. In line with Monaghan et al. (2020), we use the term *digital firms*. Digital firms include internet platform businesses (e.g., LinkedIn), digital solution firms (e.g., PayPal), e-commerce (e.g., Amazon), and producers of digital content (e.g., Spotify, Netflix).

**Digital Firm**

[…] a *digital firm* relies on the internet for its production, operating, and delivery processes. (Monaghan et al., 2020, p. 12)

So, a firm with a physical offering, such as manufactured consumer goods like laptops, that only uses the internet to sell its products would not be considered a digital firm. *Digital platforms* are a sub-type of digital firms.

**Digital Platforms**

*Platforms* generate value by facilitating transactions between different groups of users. (Stallkamp & Schotter, 2021, p. 59)

Put differently, platforms "provide an internet-based platform, which allows users to interact with each other" (Brouthers et al., 2016, p. 514). The platform can relate to many things, such as lodging (e.g., Airbnb), ride-hailing (e.g., Uber, Grab), meal delivery (e.g., Just Eat, Grab food), social networks (e.g., Facebook, LinkedIn), gaming (e.g., Xbox), job portals (e.g., Monster, Stepstone), travel (e.g., TripAdvisor), video or picture sharing (e.g., YouTube, Instagram), or dating (e.g., Tinder). In some cases, one can distinguish producers and consumers as two different and complementary types of users, such as on video gaming platforms. In other cases, such as on social networks, it is more difficult to distinguish two separate user groups (Stallkamp & Schotter, 2021).

If you think of some of the example companies mentioned above, you will notice that most of them have been digital firms from the start. Therefore, these firms are called *born digital*. They have an online presence, a *space,* while physical *places* are less important. Compared to more traditional firms, this has several consequences for their internationalization and international management. When entering foreign markets, they require less investment in physical infrastructure, though this varies from business to business. So, e-commerce firms like Amazon need large logistics centers, and social network firms like Meta (Facebook) require large data centers. Once digital firms have established their online presence, they can instantly access global markets. They can directly engage with users across the globe and scale easily to many users across countries. Therefore, also economies of scale can be achieved quickly. When seeking employees, such firms can employ talent flexibly across the world, regardless of their location. For example, US-based furniture e-commerce firm Wayfair has offices in the UK, Germany, and Ireland but recruits remote workers across Europe. This reduces any longer-term commitment or reliance on specific locations (Monaghan et al., 2020). As Monaghan et al. summarize:

> » Instead of an evolutionary progression of internationalization, the internationalization process of born digitals is more likely to be very time-compressed, much broader in scope, and with much less of a physical footprint. (Monaghan et al., 2020, p. 19).

## The Role of Network Effects for Digital Platforms

In the remainder of this sub-chapter, we will focus on the internationalization of digital platforms. Since the value of a digital platform to its users depends on the number of other users, the key challenge when internationalizing for these firms is to build a large enough network in each country where they offer their service. This is due to the *network effect*—the more extensive a network is, the more valuable it becomes to its members. This creates a "chicken and egg problem" for the firms (Stallkamp & Schotter, 2021). Users do not want to be a member of a network with only a few users. Think of a food delivery service: Customers will not use a service with only a few local restaurants connected to the platform. Likewise, restaurants will not offer food via a platform with only a few customers. Likewise, think of people who prefer an alternative instant messaging service over the omnipresent WhatsApp. If none or a few members of their circle of friends use an alternative app, they are unlikely to use it as they will not have anyone with whom to exchange messages. Therefore, the network size becomes a critical competitive advantage for platform firms. Firms that achieve an early lead in a market can gain a lasting competitive advantage. So, platform firms tend to pursue aggressive growth strategies. The key question for these firms that want to internationalize then becomes: To what extent can the firm-specific competitive advantages (FSA) built in their home country be transferred to other countries?

To discuss the impact of the network effect deeper, it is helpful to distinguish between within-country and cross-country network effects. Where *within-country network effects* apply, FSA are only valuable within a country and cannot be transferred to other countries. They are location bound. Think of the above example of food delivery services. A food delivery platform like *Just Eat,* which has many users in one country, still has to set up an entirely new network of users in each country. So geographic distance can be a constraint on network effects. Besides distance, users frequently tend to prefer interacting with other users from their own country. Think of dating or social networking as an example. In this case, firms must solve the chicken and egg problem in each country and rapidly grow local networks. Where *cross-country network effects* apply, an existing user network provides a non-location-bound FSA, facilitating foreign market entry. Online travel or lodging booking is an example. Suppose a firm like Airbnb enters a new country market. In that case, customers in that country benefit significantly from the large existing pool of accommodation offered on the platform in other countries, as in many, if not most, cases, customers tend to book accommodation abroad via this platform. The size of the global user base matters for platforms such as online gaming platforms or smartphone operating systems. It is easier for platforms like these to enter a new market and less critical to rapidly build a local user base (Stallkamp & Schotter, 2021).



One can make a second distinction between direct and indirect network effects. *Direct network effects* exist when the benefit of the network to a user depends on the number of other (similar) users with whom they can interact. This is true for instant messengers like WhatsApp or social media like Facebook, as in the examples above. *Indirect network effects* occur when one type of user is attracted to a platform with a large base of another type of users who provide complementary products or services. This relates especially to service providers as one type of user and customers as another type of user. Think of drivers attracted to a ride-hailing platform like Uber, which has many users (customers) in a country. Likewise, software developers find it more attractive to develop software for operating systems with many users, such as Apple iOS and Android. This is why platforms like Microsoft's and Blackberry's smartphone OS with a small user base have found it challenging to attract software developers (Goldman, 2010) and developed many apps themselves. On job platforms, there is a mutual attraction between firms offering jobs and job seekers (Stallkamp & Schotter, 2021).

Stallkamp and Schotter have created a nice diagram combining direct vs. indirect network effects and location-bound vs. non-location-bound FSA (see ◘ Fig. 8.11). If a firm only has within-country direct or indirect network effects,

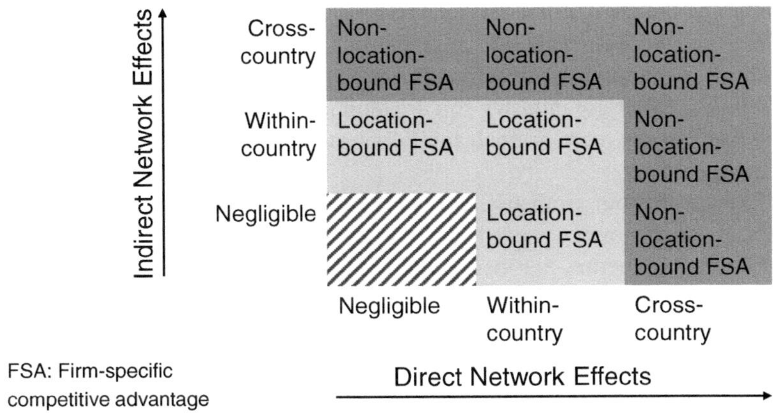


**Fig. 8.11** Geographic scope of network effects, source: (Stallkamp & Schotter, 2021, p. 65) (permission obtained)

this can create a location-bound FSA. In these industries, firms must develop other FSA like superior technology, branding, or management capabilities to internationalize successfully. Also, it must rapidly develop a large user base in each target market. If there is at least one type of cross-country network effect, direct or indirect, this can provide an important non-location-bound FSA. Looking at the online gaming platform example from the customer perspective, for example, Sony's Play Station's large global user network makes it attractive for players in a new country. Many games have been developed for it, even without an existing local user network (Stallkamp & Schotter, 2021).

Eventually, in platform industries, there is a tendency for a winner-takes-it-all effect, so platforms that manage to build the most extensive network tend to drive out competitors. For example, consider how platforms like YouTube, WhatsApp, or Airbnb have almost become monopolists everywhere. So, markets will likely consolidate globally in industries with cross-country network effects. In industries with within-country network effects, the winner-takes-it-all effect will likely happen at the country level. This is the case, for example, in food delivery, where we do not see one global champion but national or regional champions that drive out or take over local competitors (Stallkamp & Schotter, 2021).

### Review Questions

1. Define a multinational enterprise (MNE).
2. Outline the key characteristics of MNEs.
3. Explain how the characteristics of services impact Service MNEs.
4. Outline how MNEs analyze their external environment.
5. Explain how the value chain of service firms is different from manufacturing firms.
6. Do you think it makes sense to apply Porter's model of the value chain to service firms?
7. Describe the options for Service MNEs when they configure their value chain.

8. Outline the factors that Service MNEs consider when selecting locations.
9. Explain the factors that drive global integration and local responsiveness and the four environments resulting from their relative strength.
10. Consider a service industry you are familiar with: Explain whether it is characterized by an international, multidomestic, global, or transnational environment.
11. Explain the four strategies that MNEs can pursue and for which types of services which strategy is particularly suitable.
12. Outline the factors that determine how a subsidiary is managed by an MNEs headquarters.
13. Explain the tension that subsidiary managers often experience and the roles they can play to deal with it.
14. Explain the specific challenges that digital platforms face when entering foreign markets.
15. Outline direct and indirect, within-country and cross-country network effects.



## Closing Case: Grab in Southeast Asia

Commuters in most big cities of South-East Asia require much patience. Traffic jams keep people in taxis for hours or force them to sit at the back of motorbikes that dangerously weave through traffic. Uber, the American ride-hailing company, did not share this patience. In 2018, it announced that after 5 years and US$700 m of investment in Southeast Asia, it would sell its business there to Malaysian startup Grab, based in Singapore now.

Grab started smartphone app-based ride-hailing in Kuala Lumpur, Malaysia, in 2012. Today, the digital platform operates in more than 400 cities in eight countries across Southeast Asia. Since the firm has added many further services, such as food delivery, mobile payment, and financial services, Grab intends to be a "super app" for financial, commercial, and logistics services. In 2018, after 5 years in the region, US competitor Uber left Southeast Asia, selling its operations to Grab. Originating in the region, Grab has been better at adapting its services and marketing to local conditions. While Uber operates only cars, Grab also offers motorbike rides, and sometimes, as in Cambodia, three-wheel "tuk tuks" can be hailed via the app. In Jakarta, where a booked motorbike can be challenging to spot in the crowd of motorbikes, customers can also choose a rider and book it on the spot. The payment wallet in the Grab app allows topping up at convenience stores the same way as prepaid SIM cards and even with the riders. This has proven successful in a region where two-thirds of the population do not have a bank account. The feature "Grab Hitch" allows people commuting on motorbikes to announce their trip to others, offering a seat at the back of their motorbike. The offer "Grab Durian" even delivers the fruit beloved by many in the region farm-fresh to customers as well as various deserts made with Durian fruit like ice cream and mini tarts.

TukTuk, image by michael wave from Pixabay

**Questions**

1. Regarding the section on digital firms and platforms, what role do *places* versus *spaces* play for Grab?
2. Does Grab have direct or indirect network effects and location-bound or non-location-bound FSA?
3. Are there differences regarding the network effects between the different services Grab offers?
4. What are the implications for the internationalization of Grab?

Sources: (Economist, 2017, 2018, 2019, 2021a, 2021b; Grab, 2022).

**Summary**

This chapter

- Has defined an MNE as "a company that is headquartered in one country, but has operations in one or more other countries" and outlined characteristics of MNEs.
- Has outlined the effect of the characteristics of services on Service MNEs.
- Described internal and external strategic analyses and dwelled on analyzing the value chain of service MNEs.
- Discussed the configuration of the value chain as concentrated or dispersed and specific configurations of value chains of Service MNEs.
- Outlined factors for the service location decision: resource cost, people skills & availability, business environment, and digitalization.

- Described the forces for global integration and responsiveness and their varying effect on different service industries.
- Characterized the multidomestic, international, global, and transnational strategies of MNEs.
- Outlined three factors determining subsidiary management: the strategic orientation of the MNE, characteristics of MNEs, and institutions in the host country of a subsidiary.
- Described roles of subsidiary managers: bicultural interpreter, national defender, and frontline implementer of corporate strategy.
- Defined a digital firm as a firm that "relies on the internet for its production, operating and delivery processes" and explained that digital platforms "generate value by facilitating transactions between different groups of users."
- Distinguished various types of network effects for digital platforms.

## References



Barney, J. (1991). Firm resources and sustained competitive advantage. *Journal of Management, 17*(1), 99–120.
Bartlett, C. A., & Ghoshal, S. (1986). Tap your subsidiaries for global reach. *Harvard Business Review, 64*(6), 87–94.
Bartlett, C. A., & Ghoshal, S. (1998). *Managing across borders: The transnational solution*. Harvard Business School Press.
Bartlett, C. A., Ghoshal, S., & Beamish, P. W. (2008). *Transnational management: Text, cases, and readings in cross-border management*. McGraw-Hill Higher Education.
Birkinshaw, J., & Hood, N. (1998). Multinational subsidiary evolution: Capability and charter change in foreign-owned subsidiary companies. *Academy of Management Review, 23*(4), 773–795.
Birkinshaw, J. M., & Morrison, A. J. (1995). Configurations of strategy and structure in subsidiaries of multinational corporations. *Journal of International Business Studies, 26*(4), 729–753.
Bordoloi, S. K., Fitzsimmons, J. A., & Fitzsimmons, M. J. (2019). *Service management: Operations, strategy, information technology* (9th ed., international student edition). McGraw-Hill Education.
Brouthers, K. D., Geisser, K. D., & Rothlauf, F. (2016). Explaining the internationalization of ibusiness firms. *Journal of International Business Studies, 47*(5), 513–534.
Day, G. S. (1994). The capabilities of market-driven organizations. *Journal of Marketing, 58*(4), 37–52.
Economist. (2004, April 15). How big can it grow?, 2004.
Economist. (2006a, August 3). Heading for the exit: After struggling for years, Wal-Mart withdraws from Germany, 2006.
Economist. (2006b, November 4). Trouble at till: How retailers can avoid foreign adventures ending in disaster, 2006.
Economist. (2013, October 10). Crossing the divide: Why culture should be cool, 2013.
Economist. (2017, February 9). Grab battles Uber in South-East Asia, 2017.
Economist. (2018, March 28). Uber makes a tactical retreat from South-East Asia, 2018.
Economist. (2019, May 2). In South-East Asia, Grab and Gojek bring banking to the masses, 2019.
Economist. (2021a, May 15). Can South-East Asian tech's hot streak last?, 2021.
Economist. (2021b, December 4). Grab's $40bn Nasdaq listing is a key test for Asian tech, 2021.
Economist. (2021c, December 11). Why Germany is such tough terrain for food delivery, 2021.
Economist. (2022, April 16). The Russia remainers: Companies fear consumer boycotts, 2022.
Frynas, J. G., & Mellahi, K. (2015). *Global strategic management* (3rd ed.). Oxford University Press.
Goldman, D. (2010, August 5). *Blackberry's biggest problem: The app gap*. CNN Money, 2010. Retrieved from https://money.cnn.com/2010/08/05/technology/killer_apps/index.htm

Grab. (2022). *Grab Durian*. Retrieved from https://www.grab.com/sg/grabdurian/

Haller, S., & Wissing, C. (2020). *Dienstleistungsmanagement: Grundlagen—Konzepte—Instrumente* (8th ed.). Springer Fachmedien Wiesbaden GmbH.

Han, H. (2017). *Maccas, KFC and Starbucks cash in on mooncake demand in China*. Retrieved from https://www.sbs.com.au/language/chinese/en/article/maccas-kfc-and-starbucks-cash-in-on-mooncake-demand-in-china/hi2rby6zh

Hegemann, L. (2015, March 31). *Afri-Cola, Fritz-Kola, Premium Cola: Wie kleine Marken Coca-Cola und Pepsi ärgern*. Handelsblatt, 2015.

Heracleous, L., & Wirtz, J. (2010). Singapore Airlines' Balancing Act. *Harvard Business Review, 88*(7/8), 145–149.

Holtbrügge, D. (2009). Konfiguration in internationalen Dienstleistungsunternehmungen: Ein Rahmenkonzept. In D. Holtbrügge, H. H. Holzmüller, & F. Wangenheim (Eds.), *Management internationaler Dienstleistungen mit 3K: Konfiguration—Koordination—Kundenintegration* (pp. 3–27). Gabler.

Holtbrügge, D., & Welge, M. K. (2015). *Internationales management: Theorien, Funktionen, Fallstudien* (6th ed.). Schäffer-Poeschel.

Ingwald, J., Nott, A., & Holzmüller, H. H. (2009). Koordination im internationalen Dienstleistungsmanagement: Herausforderungen und Gestaltungsansätze. In D. Holtbrügge, H. H. Holzmüller, & F. Wangenheim (Eds.), *Management internationaler Dienstleistungen mit 3K: Konfiguration—Koordination—Kundenintegration* (pp. 29–56). Gabler.

Jarillo, J. C., & Martínez, J. I. (1990). Different roles for subsidiaries: The case of multinational corporations in Spain. *Strategic Management Journal, 11*(7), 501–512.

Junger, W. (2004). The Ritz-Carlton and total quality management. In M. A. Gardini & H. D. Dahlhoff (Eds.), *Management internationaler Dienstleistungen: Kontext—Konzepte—Erfahrungen* (1st ed., pp. 345–366). Gabler.

Kantsperger, R., Kunz, W. H., & Meyer, A. (2004). Wettbewerbsstrategien internationaler Dienstleistungsunternehmen. In M. A. Gardini & H. D. Dahlhoff (Eds.), *Management internationaler Dienstleistungen: Kontext—Konzepte—Erfahrungen* (1st ed., pp. 111–133). Gabler.

A.T. Kearney (2014). *The 2014 A.T. Kearney global services location index: a wealth of choices: From anywhere on earth to no location at all*. Retrieved from https://www.atkearney.com/documents/10192/5082922/A+Wealth+of+Choices.pdf/61c80111-41b2-4411-ad1e-db4a3d6d5f0d

Kearney. (2019). *Digital resonance: the new factor influencing location attractiveness: The 2019 Kearney Global Services Location Index*. Retrieved from https://www.kearney.com/digital/gsli/2019-full-report

Klimkeit, D. (2019). Global business services. *Intelligent Sourcing, 2019*, 26–37.

Klimkeit, D., & Reihlen, M. (2016). Local responses to global integration in transnational professional service firms. *Journal of Professions & Organization, 3*(1), 39–61.

Knorr, A., & Arndt, A. (2003). *Why did Walmart fail in Germany?* Globalisierung der Weltwirtschaft. Retrieved from https://dopus.uni-speyer.de/frontdoor/deliver/index/docId/3419/file/Wal-Mart.pdf

Kostova, T., & Roth, K. (2002). Adoption of an organizational practice by subsidiaries of multinational corporations: Institutional and relational effects. *Academy of Management Journal, 45*(1), 215–233.

Liu, X. (2012). Culture and quality assurance approach: A case study of 360-degree feedback in China. Proceedings of 2012 International Conference on Management Innovation and Public Policy, 1812–1815.

Lovelock, C. H., & Yip, G. S. (1996). Developing global strategies for service businesses. *California Management Review, 38*(2), 64.

Maleri, R. (2004). Zur Relevanz der Dienstleistungsbesonderheiten für das internationale Dienstleistungsmanagement. In M. A. Gardini & H. D. Dahlhoff (Eds.), *Management internationaler Dienstleistungen: Kontext—Konzepte—Erfahrungen* (1st ed., pp. 37–62). Gabler.

Meffert, H., Bruhn, M., & Hadwich, K. (2015). *Dienstleistungsmarketing: Grundlagen—Konzepte—Methoden* (8th ed.). Meffert Marketing Edition). Springer Gabler.

Melody, W. H. (Ed.). (1997). *Telecom reform: Principles, policies, and regulatory practices*. Den Private Ingeniørfond.

Merlin Entertainment. (2022). *How to get here*. Retrieved from https://www.legoland.com.my/plan-your-day/before-you-visit/directions/
Monaghan, S., Tippmann, E., & Coviello, N. (2020). Born digitals: Thoughts on their internationalization and a research agenda. *Journal of International Business Studies, 51*(1), 11–22.
Porter, M. E. (1985). *Competitive advantage: Creating and sustaining superior performance*. Free Press.
Porter, M. E. (1986). Changing patterns of international competition. *California Management Review, 28*(2), 9–40.
Porter, M. E. (2008). The five competitive forces that shape strategy. *Harvard Business Review, 86*(1), 79–93.
Reihlen, M., & Apel, B. A. (2007). Internationalization of professional service firms as learning—A constructivist approach. *International Journal of Service Industry Management, 18*(2), 140–151.
Rugman, A., & Collinson, S. (2012). International business. Pearson.
Segal-Horn, S., & Dean, A. (2009). Delivering 'effortless experience' across borders: Managing internal consistency in professional service firms. *Journal of World Business, 44*(1), 41–50.
Segal-Horn, S., & Faulkner, D. (2010). *Understanding global strategy*. Cengage Learning EMEA.
Stallkamp, M., & Schotter, A. P. J. (2021). Platforms without borders? The international strategies of digital platform firms. *Global Strategy Journal, 11*(1), 58–80.
van Dierdonck, R., & van Looy, B. (2013). Managing services across national boundaries. In P. Gemmel, B. van Looy, & R. van Dierdonck (Eds.), *Service management: An integrated approach* (3rd ed., pp. 411–429). Pearson.
Walmart. (2022). *Touchstones of Walmart Culture*. Retrieved from https://www.walmartmuseum.com/content/walmartmuseum/en_us/timeline/decades/1980/artifact/2648.html
Wirtz, J., & Lovelock, C. H. (2018). *Essentials of services marketing* (3rd ed.). Pearson.



## Further Reading

Frynas, J. G., & Mellahi, K. (2015). *Global strategic management* (3rd ed.). Oxford University Press provide an excellent overview of global strategic management generally.
Segal-Horn, S., & Faulkner, D. (2010). *Understanding global strategy*. Cengage Learning EMEA contains a chapter focusing on global strategic management in service firms.
Julian Birkinshaw has written extensively about the role of subsidiaries, Birkinshaw, J. M., & Morrison, A. J. (1995). Configurations of strategy and structure in subsidiaries of multinational corporations. *Journal of International Business Studies, 26*(4), 729–753 is a case in point.
Stallkamp, M., & Schotter, A. P. J. (2021). Platforms without borders? The international strategies of digital platform firms. *Global Strategy Journal, 11*(1), 58–80 is an exciting account of international strategies of digital platforms.

# International Organization and Change in Service Firms

## Contents




D. Klimkeit et al., *International Management in Service Firms*, Classroom Companion: Business,
https://doi.org/10.1007/978-3-031-50345-0_9

**Learning Outcomes**

After completing this chapter, you should be able to:

- Discuss organizational centralization and decentralization in Service MNEs.
- Outline and discuss various typical organizational forms of Service MNEs.
- Describe and select suitable forms of coordination for Service MNEs.
- Explain how organizational structures of Service MNEs are changing over time.
- Characterize how Service MNEs can manage change.

## Introduction

After multinational service firms have developed their strategy, they implement it. A core element of strategy implementation is to define and implement the proper organization that enables the firm to operate effectively in line with the strategy. Service MNEs decide how centralized versus decentralized they want to be. They decide which organizational form they want to adopt for their global operations. Once a Service MNE has established an organizational structure, it must coordinate and integrate activities in the global value chain across borders. Over time, firms also evolve their organization as they internationalize further and conditions change. Thus, the chapter will end with an outline of how MNEs can manage change.

Advertising in London, image by Paul Steuber from Pixabay

## Opening Case: WPP's Heterarchical Organization

In March 2018, Marc Pritchard, chief brand officer of Procter & Gamble, criticized WPP's model as a "Mad Men" operation, alluding to the successful TV series about a 1960s advertising firm on New York's Madison Avenue. Pritchard stated that WPP's model is "archaic" and overly complex at a time when campaigns and advertising need to be designed quickly across many different platforms.

WPP had started as a backstreet company called "Wire and Plastic Products," making wire baskets and trolleys. Sir Martin Sorrell built the most extensive global advertising group out of it, making US$20bn in annual sales. The company had grown by acquisitions: In 1987, Sorrell bought JW Thompson, then Ogilvy in 1989, and then Young & Rubicam. Today, it has more than 400 companies employing over 200,000 staff in over 100 countries. Only around one-third of WPP's revenue now comes from traditional advertising by famous creative firms that design and make TV and other media ads. A broad range of marketing activities, such as consumer research, digital marketing, public relations, and media planning and buying, generates the remainder. As Sorrell left WPP in 2018, he led the company for 32 years through various recessions and crises. The ad group has traditionally made much of its revenues from large, fixed client contracts, creating long-term relationships with multiple agencies.

As a consequence of a large number of acquisitions, WPP displays a broad geographic scope and portfolio of services. Sorrell decided to leave each agency with its own philosophy and identity as separate "brands" within the WPP network. The three major networks that form part of WPP's traditional advertising services, JW Thompson, Young & Rubicam, and Ogilvy & Mather, have different philosophies. This addresses the challenge of ad agencies that large clients regularly request that they do not serve direct competitors. Through this, the WPP group can serve a more extensive client base than would be possible in a more integrated, unified firm. Also, creative people prefer to work for smaller agencies. This is because they believe that in large agencies with large global clients, all they would do is adapt global campaigns to local conditions. This diversity allows WPP to be responsive to local market conditions in the various markets where the brands operate.

There is a conscious level of rivalry between the agency networks within WPP, which several times led them to pitch against each other in competition for a new client. Also, new business areas, such as new media, were addressed by extensions of the existing ad networks and new specialized agencies. Like this, WPP aims to get better at creatively searching for the best novel solution. Group management exercises little control. By employing the right people and allowing them autonomy, WPP finds that it is successful.

Despite this decentralized structure, WPP requires some practical coherence to ensure it can operate consistently across brands when needed. WPP uses several mechanisms to achieve this. ► Wpp.com was founded as a holding for all web-based activities of WPP across the different brands, aiming to reduce rivalry between the different agencies and catalyze collaboration regarding web-based services. Based on this, WPP sets up communities of practice where employees share knowledge across the brands. Projects play an important role. Many clients require more than individual ad campaigns but a whole range of services from WPP. While some clients prefer to work with the various component agencies of WPP separately, others want a one-stop shop with a customized team of specialists from different group agencies with tight central management. The heterarchical organization of WPP allows it to match these different client needs, be it more integrated when a multinational client needs a globally consistent ad campaign or more dispersed as required. In addition, WPP also deliberately conducts internal projects to strengthen links between the various agencies within the group. WPP sets up teams that cross the brands to share knowledge across the brands. These teams are recombined occasionally, making it possible to activate cross-brand networks when cross-brand collaboration is required.

Finally, WPP spends 20% of its revenues on continuously challenging established routines and experimenting with new ones. So, WPP runs many test beds for new approaches to resource management, client service, and cross-functional collaboration. In "SparkLabs," interactive workshops, a rethinking of existing work routines takes place.

More recently, this organizing model that served WPP well over several decades has been questioned. Given the large number of brands, employees, and locations, observers believe that WPP has become unwieldy, complex, and costly and needs to become nimbler, leaner, and better able to serve its clients. They believe WPP needs to become better at overcoming the long-standing rivalry between its member agencies. The departure of founder Sir Martin Sorrell is seen as an opportunity to reinvent the company to sustain its success under changing conditions.

**Questions**

1. Why has WPP decentralized most decision-making to the various agencies? What role does the type of work of WPP play? What is the advantage of this approach?
2. Why have they, at the same time, taken steps for global integration?
3. Why has WPP not adopted a formal matrix structure with two structural dimensions: geography and line of service?
4. Why does the organization of WPP seem to have reached a point where it needs adaptation?

Sources: (Economist, 2010, 2018a, 2018b, 2018c; Grabher, 2001).

9

## Organizational Structure

As outlined in ◘ Fig. 9.1, strategy implementation follows from strategy development, and setting the proper organization is a critical element of strategy implementation. The organizational structures, processes, and coordination mechanisms must be consistent with the chosen strategy. Think of how advertising firm WPP in the opening case, decided on a decentralized structure combined with various integration mechanisms across the brands. This allows the firm to win and retain talent

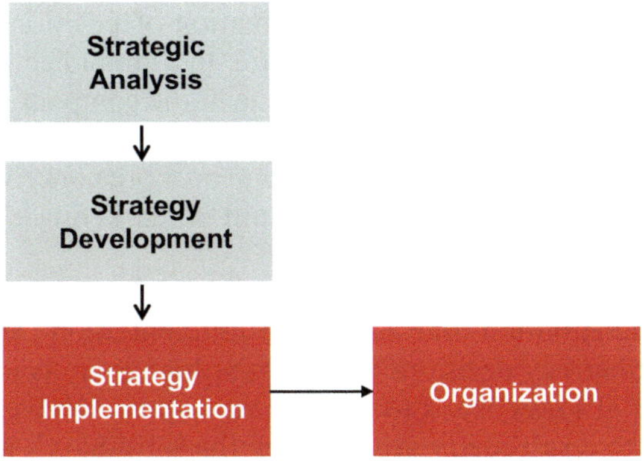


**Fig. 9.1** Organization in strategic management, adapted from (Frynas & Mellahi, 2015, p. 6) (permission obtained)

who demand autonomy, encourage them to identify with the local firm, and engage their creativity. At the same time, it enables globally integrated service when a client needs a consistent global advertising campaign.

When managers talk about *organization*, sometimes they refer to designing the organizational structures and processes of the company. This activity is called "organizing." Sometimes, when talking about organization, managers refer to the outcome of that activity: an organization.

**Organization**

An *organization* is "a consciously coordinated social unit, composed of two or more people, that functions on a relatively continuous basis to achieve a common goal or set of goals." (Robbins et al., 2017, p. 5)

An organization defines positions (jobs) and the relationship between them: Who is doing what and who is reporting to whom, how are positions grouped into departments, who can make which decisions, who is doing which part of a work process, and how does this relate to others who do other parts of this process? An organization is goal-oriented and designed to support the firm's strategy. Organization aims to direct staff behavior toward the firm's goals. Various types of service operations such as retail shops, hospitals, consulting firms, and public utilities are organizations.

A key element of organization is the *organizational structure* of a company.

**Organizational Structure**

An *organizational structure* defines how job tasks are formally divided, grouped and coordinated. (Robbins et al., 2017, p. 430)

Organizational structures consist of a combination of positions. A *position* is the smallest element of an organizational structure. In a simplified way, you can think of a position as a defined job done by someone in the company. In practice, sometimes several people working part-time can share a position. A company creates a position by permanently assigning tasks to one or more conceived persons (Vahs, 2019, p. 61). A receptionist, a senior consultant, a marketing expert, and a secretary are all positions in a consulting firm.

Regarding its organizational structure, a company must make two critical decisions: vertical differentiation and horizontal differentiation. Vertical differentiation refers to whether key decisions are taken at higher levels in the organization (centralization) or at lower levels (decentralization). In MNEs, it means whether decisions relating to a subsidiary are taken by the subsidiary's management or by global headquarters. Horizontal differentiation relates to how the company divides its tasks into positions and groups them into departments and business units. We will first address vertical and then horizontal differentiation.

## Vertical Differentiation



In Service MNEs, *vertical differentiation* is mainly about the level of autonomy that subsidiaries enjoy. Can subsidiary management make decisions regarding the local portfolio of services, locations of service operations in the country, staffing of the operation, and similar decisions, or does subsidiary management need to refer to headquarters for these decisions?

Centralization is based on the premise that the effective configuration and coordination of the value chain require headquarters to lead subsidiaries' activities. It has several advantages: It ensures that a subsidiary's activities support the overall aims of the MNE. The central direction of subsidiary activities can facilitate coordination and avoid duplicating activities, which is more likely if every subsidiary autonomously decides what to do (Daniels et al., 2021, p. 458). When decisions are centralized, it is also easier to drive strategic change throughout the MNE (Hill, 2021, p. 407).

Decentralization rests on the premise that the effective configuration of the value chain demands that local managers adapt to the local context. Decentralization has several advantages: Managers in direct contact with the local market, customers, competitors, and authorities make decisions. Subsidiary managers with much autonomy over local businesses tend to be motivated to drive business development. Subsidiary managers can be held accountable for the success of their subsidiaries as they have made the critical decisions that determine success (Daniels et al., 2021, p. 458). Decentralization also enables faster and more flexible responses to changes in local markets or regulations (Hill, 2021, p. 407). Remember how WPP has chosen a strategy that mainly relies on decentralization to achieve motivation of managers and staff in subsidiaries and be responsive to the local markets in which the agencies in the network operate.

This aligns well with the discussion in the previous chapter on subsidiary management. As you will remember, some MNEs leave their subsidiaries more autonomy than others. The centralization versus decentralization in organizational design allows the subsidiary more or less room for local decisions. The decision on centralization versus decentralization is not a pure either-or decision. You will remember that firms pursuing a transnational strategy conduct some activities, such as finance and management development, in a global, standardized manner. In contrast, other activities, like marketing and sales, are more locally responsive and adapted. The same applies here since centralization aligns with global integration and standardization while decentralization aligns with local responsiveness and adaptation. In some MNEs, more decisions are centralized, while in others, more decisions are decentralized.

This begs the question of how organizational centralization and decentralization align with the four strategies for MNEs outlined in the last chapter. If you think of the global strategy, it requires centralization as this is necessary for headquarters to drive standardization in services and processes, to determine optimal locations to achieve location economies, and to centralize activities to obtain economies of scale and scope (Yip, 2003). On the contrary, a multidomestic strategy requires decentralization. Only when subsidiary managers have the autonomy to make decisions can they be locally responsive, adapt to local culture, regulations, and market conditions, and quickly respond to changes. As you remember, MNEs that pursue an international strategy centralize critical competencies such as branding and product development at headquarters while leaving some local operational decisions to the subsidiaries. So, it mainly favors centralization, though not entirely (Hill, 2021, p. 408). For MNEs that follow a transnational strategy, the situation is more complicated. The strategy simultaneously requires global integration and local responsiveness, so the organizational solution is differentiated. Like global MNEs, transnational MNEs need to be centralized to achieve economies of location, scale, and scope and to standardize what can be standardized. Like multidomestic MNEs, they must be decentralized to facilitate adaptation to local conditions where necessary. So the transnational strategy requires a diligent combination of centralization and decentralization (Bartlett & Ghoshal, 1998, pp. 68–69).

## Vertical Differentiation in Service Firms

Given the need for customer participation and the simultaneity of production and consumption of most services, we would generally expect many service firms to adopt a structure that emphasizes decentralization more than centralization. However, a more differentiated perspective, drawing on key success factors of service firms, is needed. The more a service firm serves global clients that have standardized their operations across subsidiaries, the higher the pressure on the service firm to have centralized coordination and control to provide consistent service across borders. The greater the importance of scale to a service firm and the more capital-intensive it is, the more a service firm will likely have a higher degree of centralization to enable economies of scale. Think of capital-intensive telecommunications firms versus traditionally less capital-intensive and more people-intensive consulting firms (though their capital intensity has increased). If, however, the expertise of highly qualified and knowledgeable or creative service professionals, who tend to resent centralized control and standardized processes, is the key success factor of the firm, then that makes decentralization more suitable (Aharoni, 1996). This is precisely the case at WPP as a creative agency network.

Professional service firms are traditionally relatively decentralized; WPP as a PSF is a good example. Traditionally, local offices of PSFs enjoyed a high level of autonomy and had much discretion in customizing their services to local customer needs. Then, these firms implemented mechanisms to increase global coordination to facilitate serving global customers. Usually, these mechanisms tended to be more informal, such as drawing on global networks, a culture of reciprocity, a global mindset, and global client management systems (Greenwood et al., 2010). This is consistent with what we described for WPP. More recently, though, some of the most global PSFs have integrated further, emphasizing centralization more strongly to facilitate consistent global service for their global customers further. So, the PSF mentioned in previous chapters decided in 2012 to create a regional holding in Europe that took over ownership and control over European member firms. The firm now centralized critical decisions at the regional level (Klimkeit & Reihlen, 2016). Consequently, one can identify different types of PSFs in terms of centralization versus decentralization today. Boussebaa and Morgan (2015) distinguish between *federal* and *transnational* PSFs. The federal form has only weak central control and uses informal mechanisms to achieve global integration when needed, like at WPP. PSFs of the transnational type have greater centralization and central control. They challenge the autonomy of local offices to serve global clients better. They develop a "One Firm" global culture and strategy. International headquarters have increased responsibilities, defining shared standards, methodologies, training programs, and reward systems. Global client service partners, the global coordinators for activities relating to a client, have been given more authority to employ and coordinate staff from across the world in client projects. However, Boussebaa and Morgan also emphasize that there is much tension between these firms' global rhetoric and actual practices that often remain much more local. See the closing case of this chapter for an example.



## Horizontal Differentiation: Classic Organizational Structures for MNEs

*Horizontal differentiation* in Service MNEs is about how the MNE divides all the tasks that need to be done worldwide to design, deliver, monitor, and support its services for customers in various markets. This starts with defining positions and then departments that group a certain number of positions. Then the firm combines departments into business units. Here we will focus mainly on the level of business units as this is where the main differences between the various options in the international organization of Service MNEs lie.

**Functional Structure:** Early in the life of many firms that initially do not have a broad portfolio of products or services, they adopt a *functional structure*.

**Functional Structure**

A *functional structure* groups people in a firm together that perform similar tasks, drawing on similar expertise and resources.

This creates organizational units comparable to activities in the firm's value chain, such as service design, marketing, sales, service delivery, and service monitoring, but also supporting activities such as HR and Finance (see ◘ Fig. 9.2). Firms that develop a broader portfolio of services or internationalize frequently move away from the functional structure, but some retain it even when they become more international (Habib & Victor, 1991). In this case, each function has global responsibility for its part of the value chain, for example, marketing. As this example suggests, the functional structure is associated with centralized decision-making as one global head of marketing would eventually be responsible for all marketing worldwide. Accordingly, it is consistent with a global strategy emphasizing global integration over local responsiveness. Firms pursuing an international strategy sometimes also use such a structure, as it allows global functional heads to centralize and standardize activities. Expertise is grouped and facilitates the further development and sharing of functional knowledge. Roles are clear and precisely defined. However, cross-functional coordination can be burdensome for top management, and responding to changes in the firm's environment can be slow. People often narrow-mindedly focus on their function (Daniels et al., 2021, pp. 460–461). It can work well for firms with a relatively homogenous narrow range of products or services. Examples from the services industry include some firms in system catering, like fast food chains or some logistics service providers (Bruhn & Hadwich, 2016, p. 229).

**International Division:** For most MNEs, a functional structure is not the optimal choice since it is primarily inward-focused, looking at the company's various functional activities. Instead, MNEs may want to focus more outwards, on their overseas markets, service offerings, and customer groups. To serve this purpose, many MNEs create a divisional structure. The *international division*, the *worldwide area structure*, and the worldwide *product division structure* are classic types of divisional structures. Divisions that enjoy high autonomy and

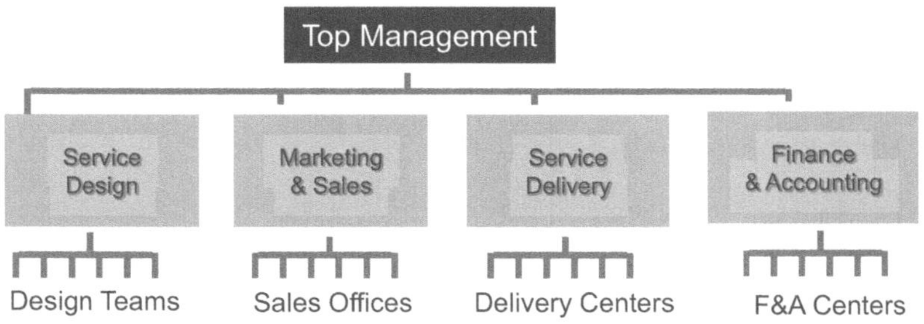


◘ **Fig. 9.2** Functional structure, own diagram

accountability are created, comprising all resources needed to serve their overseas geographic markets, customer groups, or product markets globally. Frequently, firms that start to internationalize initially create an *international division* (see ◘ Fig. 9.3).

**International Division**

In the *international division* structure, a dedicated international division conducts all international business of the firm while the other organizational units remain focused on the domestic market, frequently based on functions or product groups.

Walmart is an example of a firm that used this structure when it started internationalization in the 1990s (Hill, 2021, p. 410). Full-time specialists focusing on international business arise. They can make quick decisions regarding the firm's international business, gain experience, and share knowledge. However, there are also drawbacks. The division between domestic and international divisions can lead to poor coordination and tensions over priorities and resources between the two. This can make the global launch of a new service difficult. It could also inhibit concentrating certain activities for economies of location and scale. Therefore, as they expand further, many firms abandon this structure in favor of one of the following globally integrated structures (Daniels et al., 2021, pp. 461–462; Hill, 2021, p. 411).

9

**Worldwide Area Structure:** Some MNEs assume a *worldwide area structure* (see ◘ Fig. 9.4).

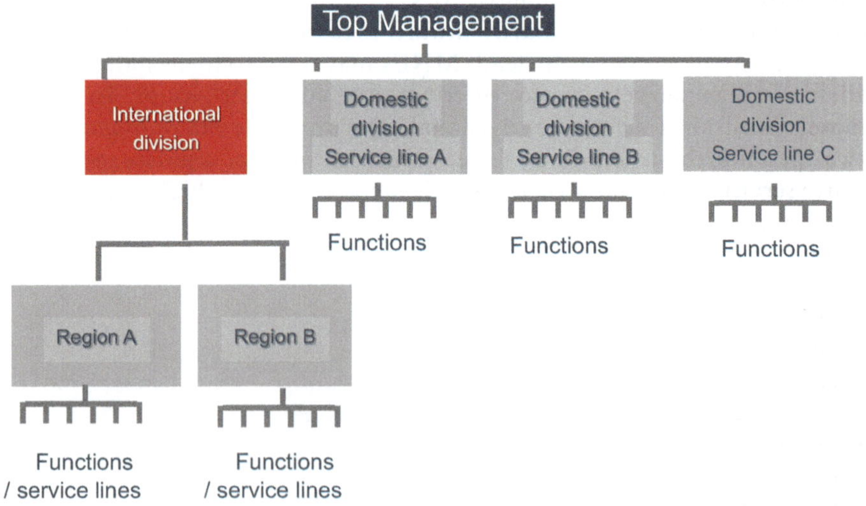


◘ **Fig. 9.3** International division, own diagram

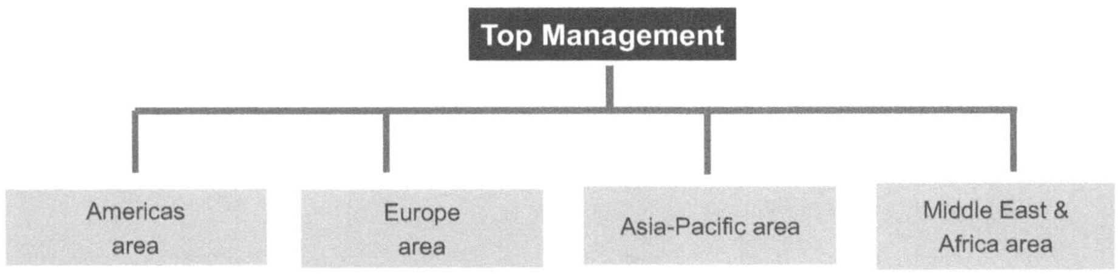


**Fig. 9.4** Worldwide area structure, own diagram

> **Worldwide Area Structure**
>
> A *worldwide area structure* divides the firm into geographic units with a high level of autonomy, typically the large geographic regions of the world such as North America, Latin America, Europe, the Middle East and Africa, and Asia-Pacific.

These divisions have the autonomy to design their own business within their region, complete with all value-adding activities required. This allows the firm to be responsive to local conditions in the various geographic markets. Each division can adapt its product offering and processes to local market needs (Hill, 2021, p. 411). UK-headquartered bank HSBC, which has operations in more than 60 countries, is a case in point. Their worldwide area structure allowed them to shift the focus to regions with high growth, such as Asia and the Near East (Daniels et al., 2021, p. 463). However, with this structure, each subsidiary may have little motivation or find it challenging to effectively transfer know-how to other divisions with a local focus. Using global locations for value-adding activities to achieve economies of scale and scope is also hampered by the local focus of each area division. So this structure is well suited for a multidomestic strategy but not for strategies that require more global integration, such as the global strategy (Hill, 2021, p. 412).

**Worldwide Product Division Structure:** Other MNEs prefer a *worldwide product division structure*.

> **Worldwide Product Division Structure**
>
> The *worldwide product division structure* divides the firm into highly autonomous units comprising groups of related products or lines of service.

While enjoying the same autonomy and completeness of value activities as the worldwide area structure, it is based on the idea that there should be worldwide coordination of all activities relating to a group of products or services (see Fig. 9.5). This facilitates the achievement of economies of scale, scope, and location as the heads of the divisions can consolidate each activity for each product group at the most efficient locations to the extent possible. In contrast to previously

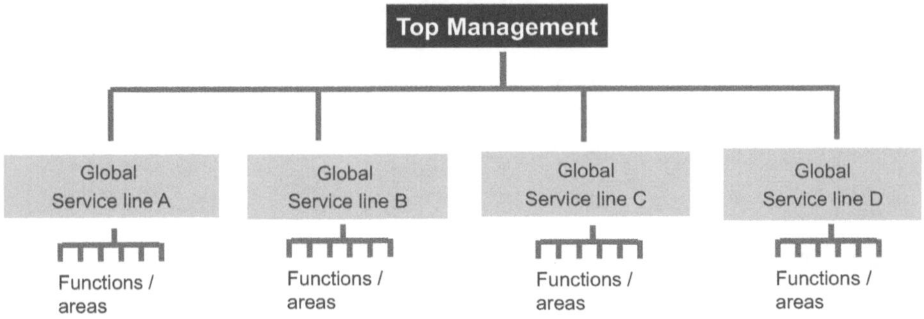


**Fig. 9.5** Worldwide product division structure, own diagram

9

mentioned forms, this structure facilitates the worldwide introduction of new services and the global transfer of competencies required to provide the respective services. It is particularly suitable for MNEs with a broad range of products or services and is, therefore, the most popular organizational form of MNEs (Hill, 2021, p. 412). At a professional service firm, this could mean that audit, tax consulting, and management consulting might be three divisions with global responsibilities, global competency development, and global knowledge sharing within the three divisions. A drawback is that operations within one country that belong to different product divisions might not be well coordinated. In a professional service firm, this could mean that a representative of one division, say tax consulting, has a sales meeting with a client where the client might say, "By the way, yesterday, a colleague of you from management consulting was here trying to sell me something as well," which can be embarrassing if the representative of the PSF does not know about the previous visit by the colleague to the same client. Therefore, global PSFs set up global account management that cuts across the lines of service to coordinate all activities relating to each major client. This will be elaborated further in ► Chap. 14. This structure is particularly consistent with the global strategy due to its ability to facilitate economies of scale, scope, and location.

**Global Matrix Structure:** Some MNEs try to combine what seems to be the best of both in their organizational structure—the local responsiveness enabled by the worldwide area structure and the global efficiency within the product divisions of the global product division structure. They set up a *global matrix structure*.

**Global Matrix Structure**

The *global matrix structure* has two dimensions that typically combine geographic area and product group dimensions. Responsibility for a given activity is shared between two leaders.

In the PSF example, the two leaders could, for example, be the leader of international tax consulting and the leader of the North American region. Together they

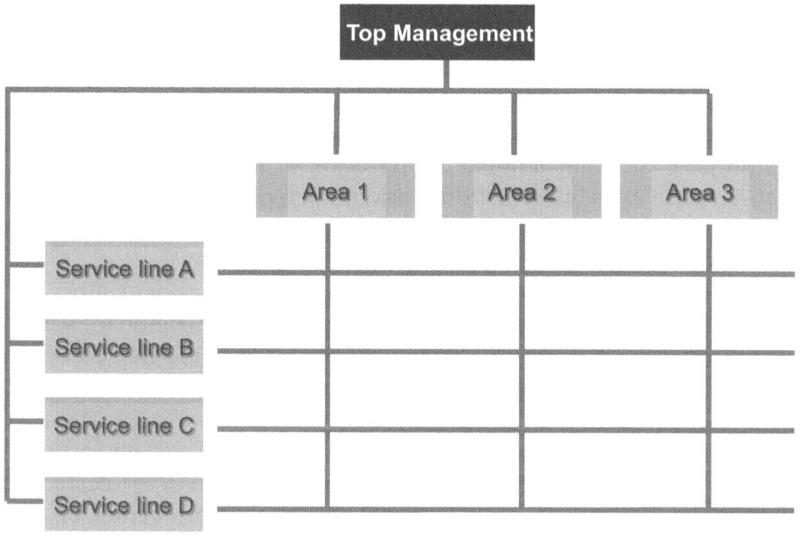


**Fig. 9.6** Global matrix structure, own diagram

should find a creative, innovative solution to providing international tax consulting services that would be adapted to the North American context while facilitating global consistency, competency building, and knowledge sharing within the international tax line of service (see Fig. 9.6). This requires much communication and coordination. Not surprisingly, MNEs that pursue a transnational strategy have traditionally chosen this structure. In practice, however, the matrix led to several challenges. The dual reporting lines led to much tension, conflict, confusion, and turf battles. Accountability was lost. In MNEs, these inherent challenges were amplified by the distance of time, language, and culture. So, many companies that initially instituted a global matrix have moved away from it, such as Dow Chemical and ABB, pioneers of global matrix structures. However, this does not mean that all matrix structures have failed. Today, large service firms like IBM, Microsoft, and Starbucks have learned how to make a matrix work successfully. Bartlett and Beamish are critical of instituting a matrix structure to implement the transnational strategy. They criticize that firms doing so only think in terms of an organizational structure, which is a static solution not fitting in a dynamic transnational environment. Instead, they recommend modifying the manager's thinking or mindset to become more transnational, keeping global integration, local responsiveness, and global knowledge sharing in mind. A suitable set of relationships, communication channels, administrative systems, and decision-making forums is seen as a solution rather than a formal matrix structure (Bartlett & Beamish, 2018, pp. 217–218). Remember, WPP did not create a formal matrix structure in the open case. Instead, it relies on its network of agencies, each focusing on its domestic market. It uses informal mechanisms to integrate globally when necessary for a client requiring cross-geographic or cross-line of service solutions.

## Horizontal Differentiation: Alternative Structures

**Transnational Network:** Given that frequently the matrix led to disappointing outcomes as an organizational form for MNEs pursuing a transnational strategy, what might be a good organizational form for transnational enterprises? Bartlett and Beamish propose the transnational organization or *transnational network*. It consists of three main elements: multidimensional perspectives, distributed and interdependent capabilities, and flexible integrative processes (Bartlett & Beamish, 2018, pp. 223–226):

- *Multidimensional perspectives:* The MNE has strong national subsidiary management to sense the needs of the local context, capable global business management to track what global competitors do and provide global coordination, and effective global management of the functions to build and transfer expertise in the functions.
- *Distributed and interdependent capabilities:* The MNE locates critical operations wherever they bring the greatest advantage. A unit in the best location for a given task can obtain a global mandate or be a global center of excellence, frequently outside the parent country. For example, the PSF mentioned previously looked for a new system to administer internal training globally. HR managers found the best existing system in the member firm in Turkey, turning this into the PSF's global system. A consequence of this specialization is an interdependence between the different subsidiaries, which are neither dependent on headquarters only as in international firms nor fully independent as in multidomestic ones. This interdependent, integrated network organization results in intensive flows of resources and information between the various units.
- *Flexible integrative processes:* As mentioned in the context of the transnational strategy in the previous chapter, Bartlett and Beamish recommend for transnational MNEs a differentiated approach for each function, business unit, and geographic unit, which in the context of organization implies differentiating what to centralize and what to decentralize. Some functions like research and development might be done in a centralized manner, while marketing and sales might benefit from a more decentralized approach. Subsidiaries in developing countries might need more involvement from headquarters than those in more developed countries. Coordinating the MNE will require a diligent combination of *centralization, formalization,* and *socialization*. We will outline these in a later section of this chapter.



**Heterarchies:** The world is changing fast—think of digitalization and artificial intelligence, Covid 19, global tensions and wars, and requirements from climate change. Therefore, MNEs look for ways of organizing that enable them to respond faster to changes and be more agile. MNEs experienced that sometimes, traditional organizational structures might hamper flexibility and agility. In addition, no matter how the company slices and dices its organization, whether by geography, product group, or function, structures tend to become rigid inhibitors of communication and collaboration across organizational units. As a result, MNEs seek new organizational forms that promise to be more flexible. Due to the focus of this book, we will not go into detail on this, but at least mention one of these forms that is particularly relevant for some service firms, called the *heterarchy*, or *heterarchical organization*. The organization of WPP in the opening case can serve as an example. On the one hand, a heterarchical organization is featured by a high tolerance for diversity, as reflected in the diverse brands that comprise the WPP network in the opening case. By deliberately encompassing rivalry of different philosophies, business models, and organizational forms, such a structure intends to create a broader set of options, like a "genetic pool" in an ecology, of how to best organize and deal with the requirements of the environment. On the other hand, diversity and rivalry are reined in by informal integrative mechanisms. A set of common rules and understandings exists as a joint basis for collaboration. Remember the internal projects WPP conducts to bring people from across the brands together to develop joint solutions and network, using various informal mechanisms rather than rigid structures. Finally, heterarchies are reflexive. That is, they expect their members to constantly question the appropriateness of their organizational behavior (Grabher, 2001).

## Organizational Structures in Multinational Service Firms

As you may have noticed, we provided some examples of service firms for the various structures outlined above. Indeed, research found that service firms generally select similar organizational structures as manufacturing firms under comparable framework conditions (Habib & Victor, 1991). For PSF specifically, authors found some form of matrix structures, while not necessarily formal-structural ones, as a result of the drive for more robust global integration while retaining the critical ability of PSF to remain responsive to local customers and context (Klimkeit, 2012). Greenwood et al. (2010) label transnational PSFs as "multiplex organizations." They find that while many MNEs have struggled to get on with a two-dimensional matrix, transnational PSFs have developed three axes and seem to be doing fine with them. Drawing on the example of the audit and advisory firm Ernst & Young (EY), the authors outline how their matrix contains the three dimensions of geographic region, lines of service, and industries. These are needed, as EY competes in different national jurisdictions, requires deep professional expertise related to various services, and serves clients in very different industries, requiring professionals also to understand their clients' industries. This complex structure creates tensions between the different dimensions of the matrix that the company needs to resolve by integrating mechanisms. There are mainly three mechanisms used: Professionals build extensive networks that cross the divisions and that they can draw on when needed for collaboration on overarching projects. They created account management systems coordinating all activities relating to the most important clients. They developed a culture of reciprocity that facilitates collaboration, such as providing staff to work on international projects. These informal mechanisms resemble those found at WPP; indeed, as WPP is also a PSF, this is no coincidence. More recently, Brock and Hydle labeled the popularity of the matrix organization in global PSFs as “almost universal” (Brock & Hydle, 2018, p. 122). In their study of two engineering consulting firms, one had a function/product/project matrix and the other a geography/function matrix. They confirmed the multiplex organization for PSFs of Greenwood and colleagues and added the balancing of global and local features as a further dimension of the organization of PSFs.

## Coordination of the Global Value Chain of Service MNEs

Once Service MNEs have set up an organizational structure for their global operations, they need to coordinate the activities that take place worldwide. If the firm has offshored parts of the service provision to a lower cost location, the interface between what gets done onshore, say in the UK, and offshore, say in India, requires coordination to ensure a seamless delivery of the entire service. Headquarters must ensure that the various subsidiaries and business units not only work in their self-interest but also in the interest of the MNE as a whole. Moreover, the MNE needs coordination to share competencies and knowledge across the firm, whether by training, secondments, or a knowledge management system. The following case of coordinating a global audit provides an example from a PSF.



### Coordinating a Global Audit

Audit firms have the role of auditing their clients’ financial statements as their traditional main task. That is, they verify whether the statements have been set up in line with generally agreed principles of accounting and represent an accurate and fair view of the financial performance and position of the client firm. When this is the case, this is then testified by the audit firm, providing its audit opinion. Global audit firms such as the “big four,” Deloitte, EY, KPMG, and PwC regularly audit the financial statements of all the national subsidiaries of the MNEs that are their clients to develop a consolidated audit opinion. Such a global audit is typically led and coordinated by a central audit team in the country, frequently the city or a nearby city, where the client is headquartered. They then involve local audit teams in all countries where the client has subsidiaries that must be audited, mirroring the client’s organization.

AuditFirm, one of the big four, had been contracted to audit the financial statements of a multinational client, Client. Client is headquartered in Canada, and the central audit team of AuditFirm, led by the global audit partner, is based in one of AuditFirm’s offices in Canada. Among others, the subsidiaries in Germany and the United States needed to be audited. AuditFirm facilitated a consistent audit conducted across the subsidiaries by a unified new global audit methodology that had just been rolled out across AuditFirm’s national member firms. In addition, the central audit team provided inter-office instruc-

Auditing; Global audit teams need cross-border coordination, image by Tumisu from Pixabay

tions to the teams in the United States and Germany. Inter-office instructions specify, for example, the scope of the audit, what exactly must be audited, possible critical elements in the client's financial statements, and timelines for reporting. The global audit partner had frequently worked with, socialized, and built a shared understanding with the partner of the US audit team. So, he knew him very well, trusted his abilities and procedures for the audit, and allowed him great latitude. This was, however, the first time for him to work with the German audit partner. So, he held close contact with regular touch-points by phone to ensure the audit was done well in line with requirements.

Source: (inspired by Barrett et al., 2005, but adapted for didactic purposes).

## MNE Strategy and Need for Coordination

The need for coordination varies between MNEs depending on the strategies they pursue. MNEs pursuing the multidomestic strategy need the lowest global coordination since subsidiaries focus on their local business, frequently developing products or services for their local market. For international MNEs, the need for coordination is somewhat higher since they must transfer their core competencies, such as branding and products or services, into the subsidiaries to implement them locally. The need for coordination is even higher in MNEs following a global strategy. To achieve global integration, HQ must devise and coordinate a globally dispersed value chain with the most efficient location for each activity. This dispersion requires a high need for coordination to ensure a smooth production or service provisioning flow. Likewise, the need for economies of scale and scope requires consolidation of activities and, therefore, a high level of coordination by HQ. The transnational MNE has the highest need for coordination. It combines the coordination needs of the global and international MNE while organizing the flow of knowledge and competencies not only from HQ outward but also between the various subsidiaries in the transnational network (Hill, 2021, p. 416).

## Coordinating Mechanisms

Scholars have developed typologies of various coordinating mechanisms companies use to coordinate their activities across business units. Naming sometimes varies, but *centralization*, *standardization/formalization*, and *socialization* are the most important. Here we follow the description and naming by Bartlett and Ghoshal as they have outlined them in the context of MNEs.

**Centralization:** *Centralization* requires subsidiary managers to go up the hierarchy to HQ and present the situation in which a decision must be made. The responsible manager at HQ then decides what to do.



**Centralization**

*Centralization* is based on the direct personal involvement of managers from headquarters in decisions relating to a subsidiary.

The advantage is that it is easy to establish. It only needs to be outlined who needs to be consulted for which type of decision. However, there are several drawbacks. Management at HQ can quickly get overburdened with many decisions they need to make relating to subsidiaries. The quality of decisions can suffer from this, but also from the fact that HQ is far away from the reality on the ground. At the same time, it can slow down decision-making when subsidiary managers are not allowed to make decisions themselves. It is detrimental to the motivation of subsidiary managers if they do not have the right to decide on matters they believe they understand best (Bartlett & Ghoshal, 1998, pp. 182–185).

**Formalization:** *Formalization* replaces case-based decisions as in centralization by general rules.

**Formalization**

*Formalization* implies that HQ management sets policies, procedures, and systems followed by subsidiary management.

It implies *standardization*, as each time a particular situation or case arises at a subsidiary, subsidiary managers can follow the standard procedure defined for this case. These standard procedures are then typically written down by HQ and communicated to subsidiaries, which is what the term "formalization" refers to in the strict sense. Formalization has the advantage that replacing case-for-case decisions by HQ makes operations much more efficient. However, establishing these procedures requires much effort and therefore cost. Many situations in subsidiaries deviate from the standard cases, and novel situations occur for which no rule has been defined. While formalization typically leaves some room for subsidiary managers' maneuvering and alleviates them from having to go to HQ for each decision, the system can become quite rigid if global management has defined many detailed rules that need to be followed strictly (Bartlett & Ghoshal, 1998, pp. 185–188).

**Socialization:** *Socialization* is based on subsidiary managers building close personal relationships with global management and managers of other subsidiaries over an extended period. Key subsidiary managers have been carefully recruited and socialized into the values and norms of global executives at HQ. As they have internalized the firm's culture, philosophy, and strategy, global leadership can trust them to make the right decisions themselves without being closely managed as in centralization or subject to strict procedures as in formalization. Networking extensively with managers of other subsidiaries allows subsidiary managers to arrive at decisions involving several subsidiaries by consensus between the respective subsidiary managers without involving HQ management.

**Socialization**

*Socialization* means that subsidiary managers are empowered to make decisions themselves, if needed, by liaising directly with peers in other subsidiaries, based on extensive networking and the internalization of the culture and philosophy of the firm.

This mechanism has several benefits: It is more flexible than formalization yet avoids the overload of HQ management with case-by-case decisions. Managers closest to the situation on the ground make decisions. It is more motivating to subsidiary managers than the other two mechanisms. However, it takes time and cost to build those networks and extensively train subsidiary managers to be trusted to make the right decisions. The consensus-based decision-making can, at times, be slow (Bartlett & Ghoshal, 1998, pp. 188–190).

The mechanisms are not an either-or for MNEs. Typically, each MNE employs all three in various situations at various times. However, you may remember what we said in ► Chap. 8 on managing subsidiaries: Each MNE has a preferred style of managing its subsidiaries. The same applies to the coordinating mechanisms. Some MNEs emphasize centralization more than the other mechanisms, some formalization, and some socialization. Having said this, MNEs take a differentiated approach. You will remember from ► Chap. 8 how transnational MNEs manage different types of activities in different ways, some in a more global and standardized way, some in a more multidomestic and localized way. The same applies to the coordinating mechanisms: The routine day-to-day operations of the firm, such as the flow of goods in a manufacturing firm, can be managed well at lower levels of the organization by using formalized procedures and systems. The flow of crucial resources, such as the allocation of financial resources, is a critical strategic choice of HQ management and is best coordinated via centralization. The flow of information and knowledge is best managed using socialization, drawing on personnel transfer between units and forums to exchange knowledge to foster learning across the MNE (Bartlett & Ghoshal, 1998, pp. 196–198).

## Coordinating Mechanisms in Service Firms

In a review of coordination mechanisms in MNEs, Martinez and Jarillo have grouped mechanisms into two broad groups: "structural and formal mechanisms" and "more informal and subtle mechanisms." The former contains centralization and formalization, while the latter comprises socialization (Martínez & Jarillo, 1989). Based on this distinction, Gardini investigated the use of coordination mechanisms in Service MNEs. According to Gardini, different types of services demand different coordination mechanisms depending on how standardized they are and how much interaction between the service provider and customer is needed (see ◘ Fig. 9.7).

Put simply: Formal mechanisms are most appropriate as the principal mechanism if there is a high degree of service standardization and low interaction with the customer. Think of system catering (e.g., fast food restaurants) or public transport, where the context is relatively unambiguous and formal mechanisms are needed to obtain efficiency. These services tend to have low-profit margins and

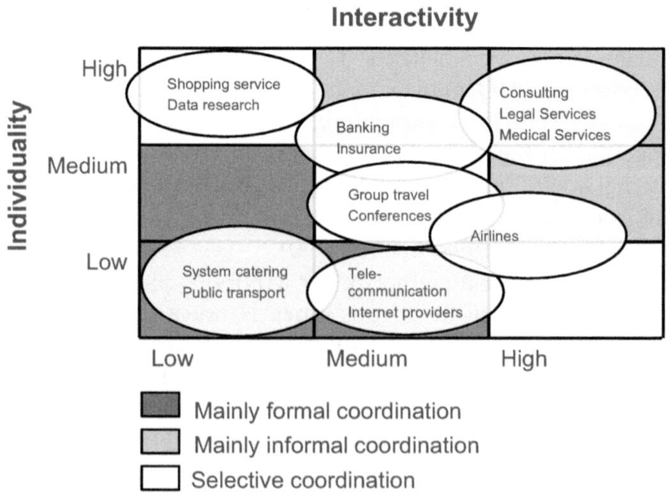


◘ **Fig. 9.7** Coordinating mechanisms in service firms, source: (Gardini, 2004, p. 20), translated from German language, permission obtained

must process large numbers of customers efficiently to be profitable. Suppose services require intensive interaction with customers and a high degree of customization of the service to the customer. In that case, more informal coordination mechanisms are appropriate as the primary form of coordination. Consulting, legal services, or advertising are examples. In these services, the task is more complex and ambiguous. This would make coordination by formal means difficult. In the international context, the attempt to apply formal means of coordination and control may be resented in some countries due to culture. Overall, Gardini finds that for many service firms that expand abroad, informal mechanisms are more appropriate to maintain high levels of quality when transferring a service concept abroad. This is because a joint organizational culture, a key element of socialization, on the one hand, can provide the needed frame of reference for staff to address the difficult quality assurance in service firms. On the other hand, it enables the flexibility and autonomy frequently needed to provide services. Companies like Ritz-Carlton, McKinsey, and Federal Express have created a distinctive identity based on a joint culture communicated internationally to guide staff. Empirical studies confirm the importance of a common set of values for coordinating subsidiaries of Service MNEs. This applies especially to PSFs with a homogeneous "One-firm Firm" culture like McKinsey, PwC, Goldman & Sachs, Baker & McKenzie, and Ogilvy & Mather (Gardini, 2004).

A more recent literature review on PSFs has shown that, traditionally, socialization has played a vital role in PSF: Firms use partner retreats, social events, and secondment abroad for socialization and networking. International mobility is used strategically for this purpose. PSFs provide incentives for international networking and collaboration. They use joint internal projects as a means of fostering international identification. However, as PSFs consistently increased their international integration to serve global customers across borders, formalization and centralization gained importance. They add layers of international hierarchy, and decision-making processes reduce local autonomy. Increasingly "abstract systems" like standard methodologies and templates as a coordinating mechanism are used. Moreover, PSFs saw the introduction of more formal bureaucratic structures and processes for budgeting, performance measurement, appraisal, and dismissal (Klimkeit, 2012).

## The Evolution of Organizational Structures

An organizational structure an MNE has adopted at one point in time may no longer be the optimal one at a later time. External conditions change, and the MNE needs to change as it increasingly internationalizes. Typically, international activities are initially conducted only on a case-by-case basis following international business opportunities. The main focus remains on the domestic market, and international business is not yet addressed by dedicated organizational structures. As overseas sales increase, at one point, the firm will want to put a department, such as the marketing department, in charge of international business. If the business in one country warrants it, the firm might set up subsidiaries abroad to address the local market. At some point, the firm might set up an international division to deal with all international business, with the advantages this brings as outlined above. As international business makes up an increasingly significant part of the firm's revenues, it is no longer appropriate to have the main part of the organization focusing on the domestic market and only one division addressing international business. The firm's strategy and outlook become increasingly global as it addresses opportunities worldwide and makes a significant portion of its business outside its home country. Then, typically, the international division is replaced by a globally integrated structure, whether a worldwide product division, worldwide area, or global matrix structure (Collinson & Rugman, 2020, pp. 285–289).

Stopford and Wells Jr (1972) developed a model addressing this organizational structure change as the firm internationalizes. While the model was developed in the early 1970s, later studies largely confirmed its basic tenets, with some additions (Egelhoff, 1988; Pla-Barber, 2002; Wolf & Egelhoff, 2002). By investigating the structures US MNEs have adopted as they internationalized, Stopford & Wells found some regularities. Structures correlated with two variables: "foreign sales as a percentage of total sales" and "foreign product diversity." If foreign sales make up a high percentage of an MNE's total sales, the MNE is highly internationalized and active in foreign countries. Foreign product diversity relates to many MNEs expanding their range of products or services to meet customers' needs in other countries. As firms start to internationalize, both variables are low, and most US MNEs adopted an international division structure. Subsequently, MNEs followed one of two paths: Some expanded internationally slowly while increasing their product range significantly at each step. These firms mostly adopted a global product division structure. Others expanded internationally more rapidly, entering many countries while extending their product range only slowly. Most of these instead adopted a worldwide area structure. Eventually, many MNEs ended up with both a broad product range and a high percentage that foreign sales made up of their total sales. These tended toward a matrix structure (Stopford & Wells Jr, 1972). While Stopford and Wells positioned this as a descriptive model, it has frequently been understood as prescriptive, advising what MNEs should do.



Nevertheless, there is a logic in the patterns observed by Stopford & Wells that has to do with the information processing capacity of MNEs. MNEs active in many country markets but with a narrow product range need to process mainly information about the many country markets. This can best be achieved by organizing geographically, with managers each focusing on one region or country. MNEs with a broad portfolio of products or services but relatively few country markets must process mainly information about their product or service portfolios. So having managers each focused on a group of similar products facilitates processing this information. Once both variables are high, some form of matrix allows processing of both types of information (Habib & Victor, 1991; Wolf & Egelhoff, 2002).

As mentioned above, more recent studies largely confirmed the findings of Stopford & Wells, though with some refinements and additions. For example, studies confirmed that the model applies to service firms the same way as to manufacturing firms (Habib & Victor, 1991).

## Managing Change in the Multinational Service Firm

There are many reasons for Service MNEs to engage in organizational change. Implementing a change in strategy, for example, from multidomestic to transnational, requires significant organizational changes for the MNE to increase global integration. Consider the case of the PSF that introduced a new European regional headquarters that took over control of the previously much more independent member firms in Europe. This was done to facilitate more consistent and integrated service provision to customers across borders. Many MNEs have internationalized through acquisitions of local firms in the host countries they wanted to enter, which led to a patchwork of diverse corporate cultures. To replicate success and create one culture, MNEs want to transfer principles and practices into foreign subsidiaries. Likewise, MNEs want to homogenize systems, methodologies, and processes across locations to provide efficient and consistent service for their international clients. For the same aim, some Service MNEs want to create a strong corporate culture across diverse national cultures (Denison et al., 2012; Lane & Maznevski, 2019; Lane et al., 2014).

## Resistance to Change

Although there are many reasons for the HQ of MNEs to drive organizational change, this does not mean that everyone throughout the global firm always welcomes such a directed change. Frequently, MNEs encounter various types of *resistance*, whether active or passive, against a change initiated by HQ.

**Resistance to Change**

*Resistance* can be understood as mental barriers that show in active or passive rejection of change. (Vahs, 2019, p. 334, translated from German language)

There is a whole range of reasons for resistance to change. Frequently, the change has not been communicated well to everyone in the MNE who needs to know about it: Why this change? What is the purpose of it? What does it entail? What does it mean for me? Accordingly, the awareness of the problem driving the change is not there. Frequently, top management may register changes in the global environment that necessitate organizational change. At the same time, this is unnoticed by managers and staff at lower levels, so the urgency of change is not broadly shared. Sometimes, people at the subsidiary level have low trust in top management at HQ, perhaps due to negative experiences with past change initiatives. Resistance could also arise due to a lack of participation by those affected. People do not necessarily mind change per se but are passive victims of change. For example, a subsidiary manager who could decide quite independently in the past might be placed under stronger control from HQ now. Here, change can be perceived as a personal degradation. Change often causes additional work on top of day-to-day operations. Incentives might be at odds with behaviors a change initiative requires (Vahs, 2019, pp. 339–340). Suppose the change initiative aims at strengthening knowledge sharing across the global firm. However, bonuses in a worldwide area structure are tied exclusively to profits generated in each country. In this case, there may not be strong incentives to share knowledge with other country operations.

While the above reasons for resistance can also apply similarly in domestic firms, additional reasons are specific to MNEs. In the international context, cultural differences challenge firm-wide change initiatives. They can create psychic distance and impact relationships, trust, and communication, which are essential bases for change. Likewise, language can constitute difficulties for change in MNEs as it can hamper communication. Time zones add a temporal distance and make synchronous communication difficult. Geographic distance means there will be less frequent face-to-face interaction. Differences between subsidiaries in terms of legacy or level of development can lead to different priorities and interests. Overall, change in MNEs is more complex than in domestic enterprises (Lane & Maznevski, 2019; Lane et al., 2014; Martin & Beaumont, 2001).



## Types of Change

Changes could occur in a planned manner, like homogenizing IT systems, or an unplanned way, such as responding to a new legal situation or attempting to save the company in an acute crisis. Different types of change carry implications for how to go about the change initiative (Lane & Maznevski, 2019). ◘ Figure 9.8 provides an overview.

**Anticipatory Change:** In anticipatory change, the need for change is identified at an early stage by top management. There is enough time to make changes to address shifts in the environment of the MNE. The challenge is, however, that many people in the firm will not see the need for change as the firm's performance is still good. So, management needs to employ intensive communication to create a sense of urgency. Anticipatory change proceeds at a slow pace.

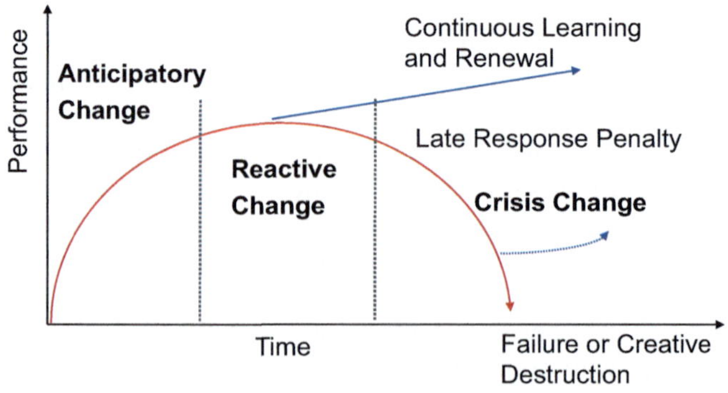


◘ **Fig. 9.8** Types of change, source: (Lane & Maznevski, 2019, p. 232) (permission obtained)

**Reactive Change:** When the firm's performance starts to suffer due to environmental shifts, the firm will go through a reactive change. More managers in the firm will see warning signals. However, the signals may not always be interpreted correctly by everyone. The increased awareness helps to speed up change initiatives to some extent.

**Crisis Change:** In times of crisis, the need for change is visible to everyone in the firm. Change is necessary for the firm to survive. This enables a change initiative to run at a fast speed. If the firm does not find the strength to change rapidly and deeply enough, it will fail.

## A Model for Change in Global Organizations

While there are many models for managing change, few specifically address how to manage change in MNEs. Lane and Maznevski (2019) developed a model for change in global organizations, drawing on many cases of change in MNEs. It is suitable for anticipatory and reactive change. Their model comprises three phases:

**Phase 1: Appraising the Readiness for Change:** Before starting the actual change initiative, one should assess the MNEs' readiness for change. How visible is the need for change to managers in the organization? What is the required management style for this initiative, and how appropriate is it in the various cultural contexts? What is the history of change initiatives in the subsidiary? If past initiatives went badly, this could cause resistance. How visible is the support and commitment of top management towards this initiative? Managers from the various subsidiaries and business units are selected as change agents who will drive the change in their area of work. How capable are they? What is the cultural perception of their power (position, expertise, personality) in the countries involved? Do they have the required cross-cultural skills? Are there differences between the subsidiaries, for example, in culture or relation to HQ, to be considered? Are the employees, as the target group for the change, willing and able to implement the intended change? If any of these questions have been answered "no," then action must be taken to enable the change before phase two starts.

**Phase 2: Initiating Change, Adopting New Behavior:** In phase two, the staff is enabled to perform the new behavior expected of them by the change initiative. Besides, the firm provides various forms of support to facilitate the change. For example, training is offered to staff to equip them with the necessary skills, knowledge, and competence. Resistance is overcome by communicating via various media types because of the cross-cultural context. For the same reason, local facilitators are used to communicate in a way appropriate to local culture. The firm invites affected staff to participate in the initiative at an early stage, and feedback mechanisms are established and used in a culturally appropriate manner. Success stories from subsidiaries where the change caught on well early are shared across the firm to demonstrate that the change can work.

**Phase 3: Reinforcing the Change:** To reinforce the change, in the third phase, the firm adjusts reward systems in line with the expected new behaviors and benchmarks actual behavior against goals. Combined with the communication of early wins, this demonstrates to staff that the new behavior benefits them. The firm adapts information and communication systems in line with the change goals to facilitate the new behavior. For example, a CRM system might facilitate customer information sharing across business units, or an ERP system might help change processes. These activities should help reinforce and consolidate the change.

## Practice Transfer in PSFs: When Will It Be Successful?

As outlined above, one key reason for change in MNEs is that HQ wants to transfer practices into the various subsidiaries. Managing change in MNEs is often tricky and frequently encounters resistance in various subsidiaries. The question is what factors facilitate a successful practice transfer and which factors hamper it. Klimkeit and Reihlen investigated this in a big PSF, an accounting firm. You will remember the example of the PSF from the previous chapter, where the firm created a new European marketing department in the new regional HQ. The centrally initiated marketing campaign led to various responses from local partners who found it unsuitable for their local context. Three main factors explained why some partners complied more with the new marketing practice while others resisted it: linking practices, local fit, and subsidiary resources (see ◘ Fig. 9.9).



Models of change management outlined above primarily focus on *linking practices* to facilitate the successful uptake of a change. As part of linking practices, *transfer leadership* relates to the role of leaders to translate the global/regional intention for change into a subsidiary's local context and make it locally understandable: Why do we need this change? What does it mean for the people in this subsidiary? Beyond transfer leadership, *compliance control* means: To what extent is there an effective control of whether people in the subsidiaries actually display the expected new behavior, or can they "go under the radar" if they resist the change? These two linking practices facilitate the change initiative's success in a subsidiary.

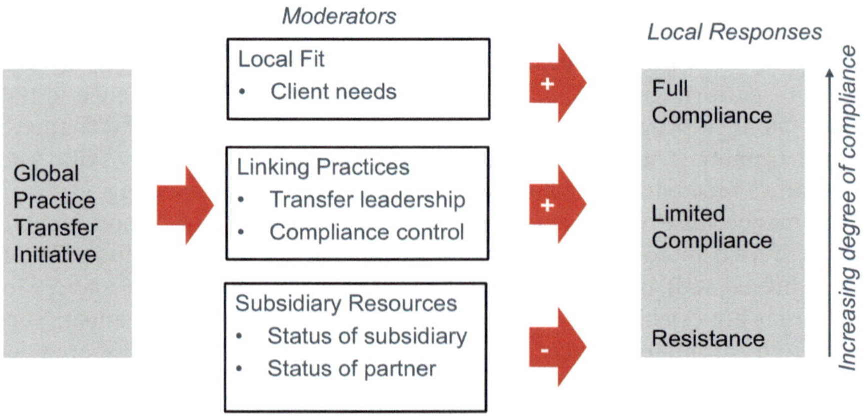


◘ **Fig. 9.9** Factors for successful practice transfer in PSF, adapted from (Klimkeit & Reihlen, 2016, 50) (permission obtained)

In addition, professionals in a PSF subsidiary will evaluate to what extent a new practice fits the local context (*local fit*). Given the importance of the relationship with customers in (professional) service firms, in the study by Klimkeit and Reihlen (2016), this related in particular to whether the marketing campaign was suitable for the needs of the firm's local clients. Local fit facilitates the successful uptake of a new practice in a subsidiary.

Finally, given a situation where practice does not fit the local context, the response by professionals in a subsidiary will also depend on their resources (*subsidiary resources*). If a subsidiary is big and influential in the MNE, and if the professional is in a senior position and has been there for long, then it is more likely that there will be resistance against the change initiative. So substantial subsidiary resources can negatively affect the successful implementation of change in a subsidiary of a PSF (Klimkeit & Reihlen, 2016).

## Exporting Cultural Change: Lessons from the Practice

Based on practical experience, Denison and colleagues make suggestions for successfully implementing change initiatives across subsidiaries of an MNE. The authors suggest a subsidiary-by-subsidiary approach because "All change is local, and then multilocal, long before it becomes global" (Denison et al., 2012, p. 93). In each subsidiary, convincing local management and staff needs to be conducted. A successful approach for managing change can work across borders if coupled with being open, curious, and respectful toward the local context. In one MNE, a practice of conducting structured meetings proved successful in the United States. This gained its credibility and subsequently worked well in other countries as well. Denison and colleagues highlighted the distinction between consistency and compliance: A global change initiative should have a consistent set of principles that help create momentum for the change. However, it should not be globally enforced by adhering to unified practices. For example, a US MNE, noticing that charity day teamwork was not well received in Europe, chose to use different team-building activities. As the authors state: "Change strategies designed to create momentum will beat change strategies designed to create uniformity every time" (Denison et al., 2012, p. 109). A lengthy discussion about one "correct" way to proceed in a change initiative is rarely motivating. A good idea can be to focus on those cultural elements that are shared and respect those not shared (Denison et al., 2012).

### ? Review Questions

1. Discuss the merits of centralization vs. decentralization for MNEs in general and for Service MNEs specifically.
2. Explain the various classic organizational forms of MNEs, their advantages and drawbacks, and their suitability for the various MNE strategies.
3. Why do some MNEs adopt alternative structures, and in which way are they different from the classic forms?
4. Why are Bartlett and Beamish critical of the matrix structure?

5. Identify the organizational form of a service firm of your choice and discuss its appropriateness.
6. Explain how the need for international coordination varies with the chosen MNE strategy.
7. Outline the three coordinating mechanisms and their advantages and drawbacks.
8. Discuss the appropriateness of coordination mechanisms for service MNEs and how this is evolving.
9. Identify a coordinating mechanism a company you are familiar with is using and discuss its suitability, possibly suggesting a better-suited one.
10. Explain how MNEs' organizational structures typically evolve over time.
11. Describe various reasons for resistance against directed change in MNEs.
12. Consider a need for change in a service MNE of your choice and describe steps to conduct this change successfully, drawing on the Lane and Maznevski model.



## Closing Case: Global Staffing in Four Professional Service Firms

The companies in this case study are four of the biggest professional service firms in the world. They provide services to the largest companies and governments. All four describe themselves as "global," offering consulting and outsourcing services. Initially, the firm used consultants from offices in the location where the client is based. As the firms internationalized, however, they aimed to staff projects globally according to expertise rather than geographic location. By the middle of the 1990s, the firms had created transnational resource management systems labeled *global scheduling systems* (GSS). These systems provided data on the consultants, such as their locations, qualifications and CVs, previous project experience, and when they were available to be staffed on projects. The GSSs were operated by staffing managers, who helped utilize resources and match consultants with new projects in the pipeline. The GSSs were seen as core to the firms' globalization, creating transnational pools of resources in an internal labor market across national boundaries. They were meant to serve clients with the best available talent for their projects.

However, the GSSs encountered several challenges and tensions. In practice, managers rarely utilized them. Instead, they staffed consulting projects primarily by drawing on local networks. This is because it was difficult to assess the quality of consultants based on their profiles in the system. As one consultant stated:

> The kind of people you are gonna get through that mechanism are gonna be pretty much the worst. So who do you pick? It's known brands; it's who you know. Because every firm has rotten apples and the last thing you want is rotten apples on your project. Because the client will sniff it out more quickly than you can ever imagine. (Boussebaa, 2009, p. 837).

Also, the GSSs were seen to be disregarding the importance of national-cultural factors. They did not consider how culturally close consultants were to the

Management Consultants, image by Joseph Murcira from Pixabay

manager needing them on a project. As one manager explained:

> People want the comfort of knowing that people are literally speaking the same language. When you are working in a team that is all from the UK, because we have all grown up in the same culture, we don't have any language barriers to overcome or any cultural barriers to overcome, which means you can make progress a lot quicker because nobody has to do the upfront explaining. And I think that is partly what drives some of the resourcing. (Boussebaa, 2009, p. 838).

Therefore, an unofficial process was used for staffing projects. Partners leading a project bypassed the GSSs to select consultants known to them. In addition, partners relied on their network to obtain recommendations for additional consultants with specific skills. Typically, partners relied on a global core team of consultants they continuously worked with on their projects and tried to have control over them in the long run. Conversely, consultants actively contacted partners for projects they wanted to work on and networked with them. By doing this, they became a member of a particular local group and were visible in the eyes of local senior staff and partners.

Sometimes, when needed specialists were unavailable locally, the GSSs were used, but the impression was that they failed to separate the good from the not-so-good consultants. So, instead, partners frequently contacted their counterparts abroad to request suitable staff. However, identifying qualified staff in other subunits did not always mean this led to the actual transfer of resources across borders. This is because each subunit was managed as a separate profit center. Professionals were recognized and rewarded for the work they did in the subunit. This provided an incentive against sharing resources across national borders. On the one hand, using resources from other units meant losing a part of profits to other offices. So, units preferred to use their own staff first regardless of whether they were the best qualified for the project or not. Subunits were also reluctant to export resources as it diminished profitability. When consultants worked on projects in other countries, they contributed to the profits of those other units, not the unit on which they were based. The subunit importing them would mainly just pay their salary cost, but not much more. Therefore, partners focused primarily on their local performance, not the firm's performance globally. This contradicts the concept of serving clients with the best talent worldwide rather than recruiting for projects based on nationality.

**Questions**

1. You are in charge of implementing a GSS across the firm. How would you deal with the situation? Analyze the problems and suggest a change management plan based on the model outlined in this chapter.

Sources: (Boussebaa, 2009).




## Summary

This chapter

- Defined organizational structure as "a fixed set of relationships formalized in rules."
- Discussed organizational centralization versus decentralization as options for vertical differentiation in MNEs and specifics of vertical differentiation in service firms.
- Outlined classic organizational structures in MNEs: the functional structure, the international division, the worldwide area structure, the worldwide product division, and the global matrix.
- Explained the transnational network structure and the heterarchy as alternative structures.
- Discussed organizational structures in service MNEs.
- Outlined the varying need for coordination, depending on the chosen MNE strategy.
- Explained classic coordinating mechanisms: centralization, formalization, and socialization.
- Discussed the appropriateness of coordinating mechanisms in service firms.
- Outlined how the organizational structure evolves as the firm internationalizes.
- Explained the need for change in MNEs and reasons for resistance against change.
- Described types of change: anticipatory, reactive, and crisis change.
- Outlined a model for change in MNEs.
- Discussed how *practice transfer* in professional service firms can be successful.
- Described some insights from the practice of exporting cultural change.

## References


Aharoni, Y. (1996). The Organization of Global Service MNEs. *International Studies of Management & Organization, 26*(2), 6–23.

Barrett, M., Cooper, D. J., & Jamal, K. (2005). Globalization and the coordinating of work in multinational audits. *Accounting, Organizations & Society, 30*(1), 1–24.

Bartlett, C. A., & Beamish, P. W. (2018). *Transnational management: Text and cases in cross-border management* (8th ed.). Cambridge University Press.

Bartlett, C. A., & Ghoshal, S. (1998). *Managing across borders: The transnational solution.* Harvard Business School Press.

Boussebaa, M. (2009). Struggling to organize across national borders: The case of global resource management in professional service firms. *Human Relations, 62*(6), 829–850.

Boussebaa, M., & Morgan, G. (2015). Internationalization of professional service firms. In L. Empson, D. Muzio, J. Broschak, & B. Hinings (Eds.), *The Oxford handbook of professional service firms* (pp. 71–91). Oxford University Press.

Brock, D. M., & Hydle, K. M. (2018). Transnationality: Sharpening the integration-responsiveness vision in global professional service firms. *European Management Journal, 36*, 117–124.

Bruhn, M., & Hadwich, K. (2016). *Internationales Dienstleistungsmarketing* (5th ed.). Kohlhammer.

Collinson, S., & Rugman, A. M. (2020). *International business* (8th ed.). Pearson Education.

Daniels, J. D., Radebaugh, L. H., Sullivan, D. P., & Click, R. W. (2021). *International business: Environments & operations* (17th ed.) Pearson.

Denison, D., Hooijberg, R., Lief, C., & Lane, N. (2012). *Leading culture change in global organizations: Aligning culture and strategy.* John Wiley & Sons.

Economist. (2010, November 6). King of the Mad Men, 2010.

Economist. (2018a, March 31). Technology has upended the world's advertising giants, 2018.

Economist. (2018b, April 21). Sir Martin Sorrell leaves WPP in a sorry state, 2018.

Economist. (2018c, June 16). Sir Martin Sorrell gets golden goodbye from WPP, 2018.

Egelhoff, W. G. (1988). Strategy and structure in multinational corporations: A revision of the Stopford and Wells model. *Strategic Management Journal, 9*(1), 1–14.

Frynas, J. G., & Mellahi, K. (2015). *Global strategic management* (3rd ed.). Oxford University Press.

Gardini, M. A. (2004). Internationalisierung von Dienstleistungen: Reflexionen zur Multikulturalität internationaler Dienstleistungskontexte. In M. A. Gardini & H. D. Dahlhoff (Eds.), *Management internationaler Dienstleistungen: Kontext—Konzepte—Erfahrungen* (1st ed., pp. 11–36). Gabler.

Grabher, G. (2001). Ecologies of creativity: The Village, the Group, and the Heterarchic Organisation of the British Advertising Industry. *Environment and Planning A, 33*(2), 351–374.

Greenwood, R., Morris, T., Fairclough, S., & Boussebaa, M. (2010). The organizational design of transnational professional service firms. *Organizational Dynamics, 39*(2), 173–183.

Habib, M. M., & Victor, B. (1991). Strategy, structure and performance of U.S. manufacturing and service MNCs: A comparative analysis. *Strategic Management Journal, 12*, 589–606.

Hill, C. W. L. (2021). *International business: Competing in the global marketplace* (13th ed.). McGraw-Hill Education.

Klimkeit, D. (2012). *Global integration and management of professional service firms: A review of the literature and suggestions for future research.* Retrieved from http://fox.leuphana.de/portal/en/publications/global-integration-and-management-of-professional-service-firms-a-review-of-the-literature-and-suggestions-for-future-research(d18d4b23-f567-49fb-9f36-42ed8d5461c9).html

Klimkeit, D., & Reihlen, M. (2016). Local responses to global integration in transnational professional service firms. *Journal of Professions & Organization, 3*(1), 39–61.

Lane, H. W., & Maznevski, M. L. (2019). *International management behavior: Global and sustainable leadership.* Cambridge University Press.

Lane, H. W., Spector, B., Osland, J. S., & Taylor, S. (2014). Global strategic change: A synthesis of approaches. In *Advances in global leadership.* Emerald Group Publishing Limited.

Martin, G., & Beaumont, P. (2001). Transforming multinational enterprises: Towards a process model of strategic human resource management change. *The International Journal of Human Resource Management, 12*(8), 1234–1250.

Martínez, J. I., & Jarillo, J. C. (1989). The evolution of research on coordination mechanisms in multinational corporations. *Journal of International Business Studies, 20*(3), 489–514.

Pla-Barber, J. (2002). From Stopford and Wells's model to Bartlett and Ghoshal's typology: New empirical evidence. *Management International Review (MIR), 42*(2), 141.

Robbins, S. P., Judge, T. A., & Campbell, T. T. (2017). *Organizational behaviour* (2nd ed.). Pearson Education Limited.

Stopford, J. M., & Wells, L. T., Jr. (1972). *Managing the multinational enterprise: Organization of the firm and ownership of the subsidiary*. Basic Books.

Vahs, D. (2019). *Organisation: Ein Lehr- und Managementbuch* (10th ed.). Schäffer-Poeschel.

Wolf, J., & Egelhoff, W. G. (2002). A reexamination and extension of international strategy–structure theory. *Strategic Management Journal, 23*(2), 181–189.

Yip, G. S. (2003). *Total global strategy II: Updated for the internet and service era*. Prentice Hall.

## Further Reading

Greenwood, R., Morris, T., Fairclough, S., & Boussebaa, M. (2010b). The organizational design of transnational professional service firms. *Organizational Dynamic, 39*(2), 173–183 provides a good account of the global organization of PSFs.

Henry W. Lane is one of the few authors writing about change management in a global context. Lane, H. W., Spector, B., Osland, J. S., & Taylor, S. (2014). Global strategic change: A synthesis of approaches. In Advances in global leadership. Emerald Group Publishing Limited provides an overview of approaches.

# Shared Services and Business Process Outsourcing

## Contents




D. Klimkeit et al., *International Management in Service Firms*, Classroom Companion: Business,
https://doi.org/10.1007/978-3-031-50345-0_10

**Learning Outcomes**

After completing this chapter, you should be able to:

- Distinguish between outsourcing and offshoring and outline the rationale for both.
- Outline the rationale for captive centers, criteria used for location choice, and options for the governance of shared service organizations.
- Explain key aspects of the management of shared service operations.
- Outline recent trends in shared services.
- Distinguish types of outsourcing.
- Describe how to manage outsourced services successfully.
- Outline specifics of outsourcing professional services and the trend of backsourcing.

## Introduction

Many firms have decided to outsource parts of support functions like IT, HR, procurement, or accounting to third-party providers, often in lower-cost "offshoring" countries. Besides reducing costs, other objectives are being sought, such as focusing on core activities, standardization, and continuous improvement. Other firms, especially MNEs, decided to achieve similar objectives by centralizing the provision of such support functions in one or a few locations, called shared service centers, to provide the service for all subsidiaries in a region or globally. We will outline the global landscape of service offshoring and its rationale and distinguish outsourcing from offshoring. Then, we will provide more details on both modes of service relocation.

Gateway of India, Mumbai, by Shridhar Amati from Pixabay

**Opening Case: British Airways' Shared Services in India**

The period following the terrorist attacks in the United States on September 11, 2001 was an enormously difficult period for many airlines, including British Airways (BA). Nevertheless, by 2005 BA had become the world's most profitable airline. How was this possible?

In 2002, CEO Rod Eddington launched the "Future Size and Shape" initiative. Creating a captive shared service center of BA in India played a major role in achieving a profit of GBP 135 m in 2003 after losing GBP 200 m in 2002. Initially, select parts of IT were outsourced to providers in India. Then, BA set up its own captive center, "Speedwing World Network Services" (WNS), in Mumbai, India. BA claimed it could hire more highly qualified employees there at only 20% of the cost compared to the United Kingdom. BA chose the captive mode to have greater control, ensure quality, and facilitate acceptance at BA internally. This was based on the assumption that the output of BA's own center would be more readily accepted than that from an external outsourcing provider. BA chose India as a location due to the excellent quality of staff available in the labor market. A Service Level Agreement (SLA) was reached for all processes transferred into the center. This provided transparency over processes and the handover procedure. Success was measured by the attained cost reduction and the level of acceptance by BA managers. After 12 months, WNS achieved a 40–60% cost reduction. By 2002, 1600 staff worked 24 h a day, 7 days a week. Beyond cost savings, the center continuously improved processes, increasing productivity. Additionally, BA took advantage of the 4-h time difference between the United Kingdom and India. Work in progress on resolving problems was handed over by staff in the United Kingdom to the team in India in the evening UK time. The following morning UK time, the problem had often been solved by staff in India.

The success of WNS attracted the attention of other airlines. So, BA started to offer services like revenue accounting and the management of frequent flyer programs to other airlines, thereby monetizing the services. By 2006, WNS counted 30 leading airlines and travel agencies among its customers of travel-related services.

**Questions**

1. What motivated BA to offshore services to India?
2. What benefits did BA expect from its captive center compared to outsourcing?
3. Why will BA have chosen to offshore accounting and the management of its frequent flyer program?

Sources: (Penter et al., 2009).

## The Landscape of Service Relocation

Observers generally see the large-scale outsourcing arrangement of Eastman Kodak with outsourcing providers in 1989 as the beginning of IT outsourcing (ITO) and business process outsourcing (BPO) . Following this, the market for

ITO and BPO. has grown enormously. This was in the context of the debate of the 1990s that firms should focus on their core competencies and outsource other activities to others who can provide them cheaper and often better. Companies outsourced more and more services and added more locations to the outsourcing landscape. It started with IT services, and then other business processes were outsourced. For example, in 1991, oil firm British Petroleum (BP) outsourced all European accounting services to Andersen Consulting, who consolidated them in Aberdeen, Scotland. Increasingly, firms also set up their own shared service centers, also called captive centers or global in-house centers (Willcocks et al., 2017).

**Locations:** India became a destination for outsourcing early, as firms outsourced IT and other services to firms like TCS, Infosys, and Wipro. By 2010, India dominated the offshoring market, having built capacity and economies of scale. Other countries followed to offer service offshoring. By 2016, 120 countries worldwide were available as service-offshoring locations, with India taking about two-thirds of the market, followed by the Philippines (Willcocks et al., 2017). ◘ Figure 10.1 shows some typical locations for service relocation. Several other locations in Asia, such as China, Malaysia, and Vietnam, have established themselves to cover the Asia-Pacific region. Countries in Eastern Europe, like Poland



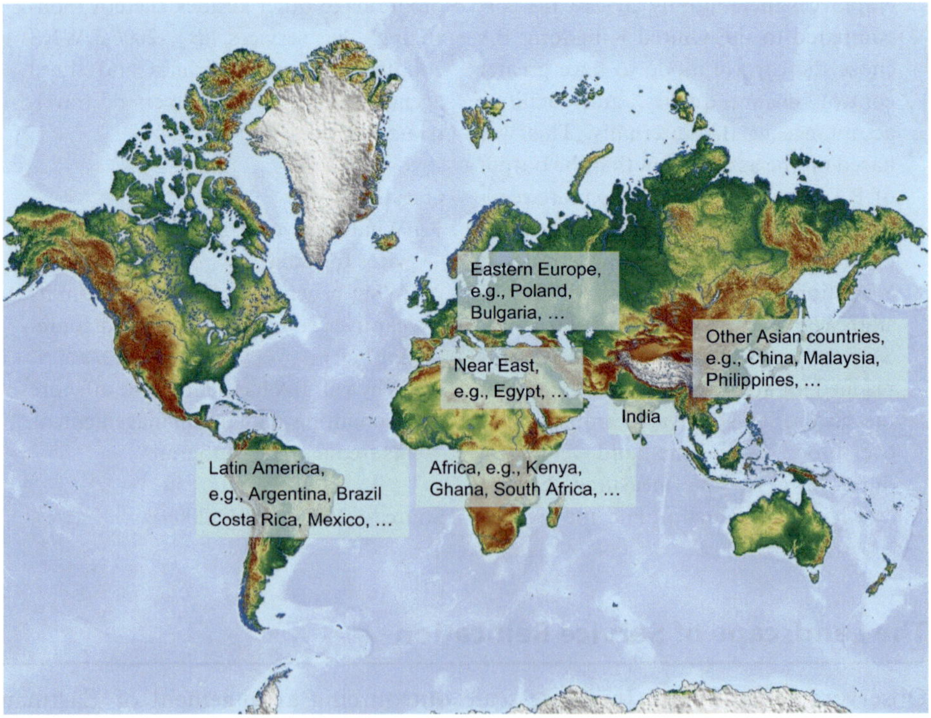


◘ **Fig. 10.1** Typical service offshoring locations, own diagram drawing on data from (Kearney, 2021), using world map by Mapswire from Pixabay

and Bulgaria, serve Europe the same as countries in the Near East, like Egypt and Africa. Locations in Latin America, like Mexico, Argentina, and Costa Rica, address the American continent (Kearney, 2021).

**Services Offshored:** The traditional focus of ITO and BPO. was on stable, discrete activities that were well understood and for which detailed contracts could be written with the providers, as this mitigated many of the risks involved (Willcocks et al., 2017). Information and communication technology development played a crucial role in enabling service offshoring. The higher the information intensity of a service is, that is, the higher the percentage of time dedicated to dealing with information, the better it is suited to be disaggregated. Companies can then relocate some of these disaggregated parts. Typically, supplementary services, rather than the core services of a firm, have been offshored because, for them, the separation of production and consumption is easier to achieve. In other words, providing them away from the customer is more feasible. Think of the accounting and frequent flyer program management services offshored by British Airways. Later, however, also more complex, knowledge-intensive services were offshored that are closer to the firm's core operations (Pisani & Ricart, 2016). Traditionally, mainly back office services, which are not provided in direct contact with the customers and can be divided into separate parts assigned to different people and managed by workflow systems, have been relocated (Sako, 2015).

The following are the most typical functions from which companies relocate generic, high-volume, and standardizable tasks by outsourcing or offshoring (Becker et al., 2009, pp. 39–41):

- Accounting and finance (e.g., billing and credit card processing).
- IT operations (e.g., network administration).
- Human resources (e.g., payroll and benefits administration).
- Procurement (e.g., processing orders and payment).

## The Offshoring/Outsourcing Matrix

Frequently, there is confusion about the terms offshoring and outsourcing. While they are related, they are distinct. Offshoring relates to moving services geographically, while *outsourcing* is shifting services across organizational boundaries to another company.

**Outsourcing**

*Outsourcing* refers to a company's purchase of products or services from another domestic or offshore company. (Bunyaratavej et al., 2011, p. 71)

*Offshoring*, on the contrary, can be defined as:

**Offshoring**

[…] *offshoring* connotes a domestic company sourcing products or services from a foreign-based company, either a subsidiary of the focal firm (captive or international in-sourcing) or an independent service provider (offshore outsourcing). (Bunyaratavej et al., 2011, pp. 71–72)

As the above definition suggests, offshoring and outsourcing are not an either-or decision but can be combined, which creates four options that can be displayed in a matrix (see ◻ Fig. 10.2). The bottom left quadrant shows a situation where a company conducts all activities itself in its home location. The top left quadrant shows a situation where the firm has outsourced some activities to a domestic outsourcing provider, say a French firm contracting services it previously conducted itself from an outsourcing provider in France. The bottom right quadrant shows a situation where a firm has moved some activities to a captive shared service center belonging to the firm itself in an offshore location, say the French firm sets up a shared service center for accounting in Poland. In the top right quadrant, outsourcing and offshoring are combined. A company moves services to an outsourcing provider abroad. For example, the French firm moves accounting processes to an outsourcing provider in Poland. When making statements that refer to outsourcing and offshoring, we will use the term "service relocation," as companies relocate services geographically or organizationally.



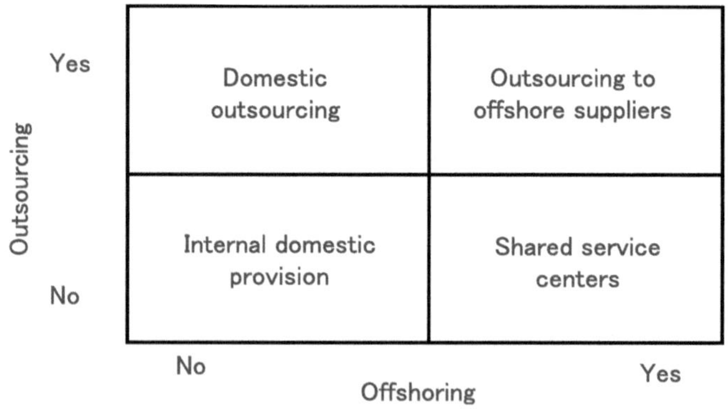


◻ **Fig. 10.2** The offshoring-outsourcing matrix, inspired by (Bunyaratavej et al., 2011, p. 72) and (Sako, 2015, p. 329)]

## The Rationale for Service Offshoring and Outsourcing

Why do companies outsource or offshore services? Since the start of service relocation, cost has been a key driving factor. For example, ITO leverages the economies of scale of a provider, the fact that the provider manages IT for a large number of customers, thereby better utilizing the infrastructure. Further, as service offshoring typically moves tasks to countries with lower salary levels, like India, this further drives cost savings. For firms engaging in captive offshoring to shared service centers, consolidating activities like accounting at one or a few locations generates further economies of scale. Remember how the intention to reduce cost has initially been a primary driver for British Airways' offshoring to India. However, in the meantime, companies have focused on other benefits of service relocation. The large number of qualified staff in labor markets like India, the Philippines, or Argentina drives firms to move their processes to be conducted there. For example, firms were often initially attracted to India by low labor cost but then remained and expanded due to the large pool of qualified staff (Bunyaratavej et al., 2011). This also was the case for British Airways.

Another driver, especially for outsourcing, is a strategy to focus on core activities while outsourcing activities not considered core to the business (Bunyaratavej et al., 2011). By relocating transactional, repetitive, routine activities, staff in the onshore operations can focus on more complex tasks adding more value.

Service relocation can also improve the quality of services. While in their original setting, these services had a low priority, for the outsourcing provider or shared service center, they become their core activity, therefore receiving increased attention. Service relocation providers are designed to continuously improve the processes transferred to them and have the skills to do so. Since the onshore users and offshore service providers typically strike service level agreements (SLAs), there is tighter control on the quality and cost of the service provision than in a traditional corporate function. Staffing becomes more flexible when processes for various customers (outsourcing) or business units/subsidiaries (captive centers) are combined. Companies can level peaks and troughs in services to one unit by shifting resources across different units (Lacity et al., 2008).

Sometimes, the creative staff in a shared service center can also get involved in developing new services or products. In several cases, shared service centers have been so successful that it was possible to commercialize the services and provide them to other firms, generating additional revenue. Remember how British Airways has provided services to other airlines. As will be outlined in more detail later, moving services into a shared service environment can drive far-reaching transformation in the company.

Finally, investing in a shared service center in a country can help generate goodwill among the government and customers in that country, facilitating market entry. For example, an aerospace company chose Malaysia for IT offshoring because it sells planes to that country, and having a center in that country fulfills the regulatory requirement of local manufacturing (Lacity et al., 2008).

## Offshore Shared Services

In this section, we will focus on shared services—a model where a semi-independent unit or units owned by a firm provide the services rather than an outsourcing provider. The units that provide the services in this model are called *shared service centers* (SSCs).

> **Shared Services**
>
> *Shared services* arrangements involve centralizing processes at a single location where the geographically dispersed units of an organization share the services centrally rather than have all the services provided locally. (McIvor, 2013, p. 9)

As the definition shows, shared services are based on moving specific processes, for example, accounts payable in accounting, from a range of business units or subsidiaries and centralizing their provision in a central unit, a shared service center. Since the company owns these SSCs, managers frequently refer to them as in-house or *captive centers*.



> **Captive Centers**
>
> A *captive center* is a global facility built, owned, staffed and operated by the firm itself at a subsidiary in a foreign location. (McIvor, 2013, p. 9)

## The Rationale for Captive Centers

We addressed the general rationale for service relocation above. The question is why companies set up captive centers instead of outsourcing the respective services to a third-party provider. There are several reasons. By keeping processes in-house, the firm has better control over them. It retains know-how about the respective processes. Once the company moves processes to a third party, it loses the know-how. Frequently, companies have concerns about the confidentiality of data that a third party would manage. Moving processes to an outsourcing provider puts the firm into a dependency on the provider, which an in-house solution can avoid. The company avoids the cost of setting up contracts with the provider. Contracts with outsourcing providers typically stipulate required service levels for specific services with a specified volume of staff for several years. Keeping processes in-house gives more flexibility to scale processes up or down (Becker et al., 2009, p. 21). Remember how British Airways chose a captive solution to have greater control, ensure quality, and facilitate acceptance at BA internally.

## Shared Services Location Strategy

Larger companies typically have not just one but several SSCs. In some cases, each function sets up its own centers so that there are HR, IT, and accounting centers, each conducting only processes from one function. In other firms, "multi-tower" centers house several functional teams in one location. Either way, in most cases, factors such as required language skills and time zone lead firms to set up several geographically dispersed centers. Larger firms typically have one or two centers in Latin America, Eastern Europe, and Asia (Klimkeit, 2019a). This allows them to support all business units of the firm in their time zone without having to work at night. At the same time, one can find staff speaking the major regional languages in the labor market.

Regarding the choice of specific locations for SSCs, we said much in ► Chap. 8 in the context of the global configuration of the value chain. As a reminder, we outlined the following four criteria for choosing locations from where to provide services:

- *Resource cost.*
- *People skills and availability.*
- *Business environment.*
- *Digitalization.*

These factors discussed in the literature are consistent with those for selecting service locations in Kearney's biannual Global Service Location Index, which

Wroclaw, Poland, has become a hub for shared service centers, image by ivabalk from Pixabay

the consulting firm primarily compiles for locations for shared service centers. Looking more closely at the Kearney ranking, based on industry surveys and insights from client projects, Kearney weighs the resources cost ("financial attractiveness") criterion at 35% of the total weight, as the cost is still a key driver in location decisions. The new digitalization category ("digital resonance") weighs 15%, and the other two 25% each. Countries like India, Sri Lanka, the Philippines, and Indonesia do particularly well on cost. Regarding the availability of skilled staff in the labor market, the United States fares best, followed by China and India. The business environment shows a different picture: Singapore, the Netherlands, and New Zealand are leading the table. Regarding digitalization, the United States, the United Kingdom, and Germany are in the top positions. As a reminder, "Digitalization" includes things like the level of digital skills, digital activities of businesses, and the legal framework for digital business models, including cybersecurity. The rising importance of digitalization, a criterion added in the 2019 report of Kearney, is affecting the overall ranking of global shared service locations. While India, China, and Malaysia have been the top three locations since Kearney started its report in 2004, providing the best overall combination across the four criteria, some countries have moved up significantly in the Kearney ranking. Especially the United States, due to the excellent level of digitalization, moved up in the ranking by 16 places to place six, and the United Kingdom moved up 11 places to place eight (Kearney, 2019, 2021). While a ranking like this is a helpful point of reference, by the end of the day, managers weigh the different criteria based on their company's priorities. See ◘ Fig. 10.3 for the top 20 countries in the 2021 Global Service Location Index.

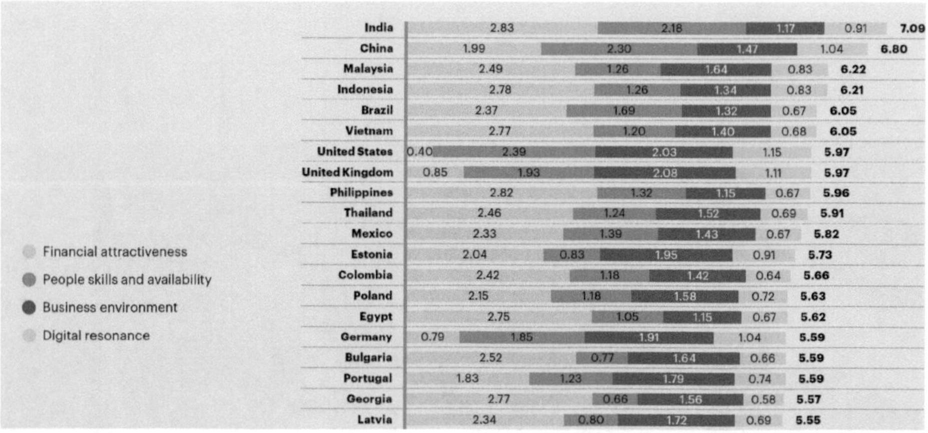


◘ **Fig. 10.3** Kearney Global Service Location Index 2021: top 20 locations, source: (Kearney, 2021, p. 10) (permission obtained)

## Governance of Shared Services Organizations

When a company has established the rationale for shared services and determined the location strategy, another critical question is how the shared services will be governed and organized. Which organizational unit will they belong to and report to? There are several models:

- *Shared group facility within a function*: In this model, SSCs report to the functions they serve. For example, a finance and accounting (F&A) SSC would report to the CFO (or a head of shared services within the F&A function). This has traditionally been very common and remains a frequent setup. The advantage is that a high quality of service provision can be ensured due to the functional focus (Lohrmann et al., 2015, p. 131). However, the company does not realize synergies between functions or provide cross-functional processes.
- *Shared group facility*: In this case, SSCs are part of a cross-functional setup, reporting to someone at the top management level with a cross-functional role for shared services. This has the advantage of gaining visibility and top-management support for shared services. Cross-functional synergies can be achieved (Lohrmann et al., 2015, p. 131). In practice, the head of shared services is often not a member of the top management but reports to a member of top management, such as the Chief Operations Officer (COO). This setup has become popular when creating Global Business Services (GBS) organizations (see below).
- *Shared group facility reporting to a functional leader*: In some cases, while the shared services organization of the firm comprises several functions, SSCs may still report to a functional head, often the CFO. This typically has historical reasons, as F&A was often the first function to set up SSCs, and other functions joined later. In this case, the CFO may be a primus inter pares, heading a team of functional shared services leaders who still retain control over their functions' shared services. The advantage is that cross-functional synergies are possible while retaining some control by the functions, which can benefit quality. However, deep cross-functional integration and synergies will typically not be on the CFO's agenda, who may continue to focus primarily on his or her own F&A function (Klimkeit & Christophers, 2022).
- *Regional facility*: In some companies, SSCs report to the regional management, which has set them up. For example, an MNE's Europe, Middle East, and Africa (EMEA) region may set up an SSC comprising one or several functional teams in Poland. An F&A SSC in Poland may serve and report to the EMEA F&A leadership (Klimkeit, 2018).

## Management of Shared Service Operations

Now, once a company has selected locations and determined the governance of shared services, how are they managed on a day-to-day basis? We will provide a part of the answer in ► Chap. 15, which addresses the management of ongoing global service delivery. Here we will focus on some aspects typical of shared services.

**IT Systems:** The global operations of SSCs are strongly reliant on specific IT systems. Two types of IT systems play a particular role: ERP systems and ticketing systems. *Enterprise Resource Planning (ERP)* systems capture all transactional data of a firm in one system. Whether related to procurement, logistics, accounting, sales, or human resources, all daily operations data are entered into the ERP system. Three features are particularly relevant for shared services: (1) The ERP system's workflow drives a consistent operation of processes to ensure the consistency and efficiency intended by shared services. (2) It also enables integration across the firm. When an MNE has a globally integrated ERP system, SSC staff, regardless of location, can access and enter data consistently across the world, enabling the remote support typical of SSCs. (3) An ERP system allows close monitoring and control of the work done in shared services, a hallmark of shared services, to ensure the intended efficiency gains. With the three features, various functions typically supported by SSCs, such as HR, procurement, or accounting, are integrated as modules into the system (Lindvall & Iveroth, 2011; PwC, 2016).

Besides ERP systems, *ticketing systems* play an essential role in shared services. They allow the routing and management of service requests from internal customers. Whether an employee of the firm reports an IT problem, an issue with the last payroll statement, or a question about an expense report, a ticket is opened in the ticketing system and then routed to staff in an SSC based on criteria like functional focus, location, and language of the employee. SSC staff updates the ticket status until its final resolution, and management has transparency to ensure tickets are resolved within the agreed service level and no service request falls by the wayside (EY, 2015a).



**Managing Performance:** As a basis for managing the performance of the SSCs setup by the firm, *service level agreements (SLAs)* are made. They define in detail the scope of services to be provided by the SSCs. They determine the tasks to be conducted by SSC staff, timelines such as maximum response time to service requests, the maximum time to complete a task, the number of transactions to be conducted within a timeframe, and escalation procedures. Besides, they also define the input required by employees in business units receiving service to enable the SSCs to perform their tasks. When the receiving units conduct a part of a process, the activity split, i.e., the division of labor between receiving unit and SSC within a process, is defined, including handover procedures. Key performance indicators (KPIs) are defined to better control the SLAs. They can include things like the reaction times mentioned above, acceptable error quotas, volumes of transactions processed, and efficiency indicators such as cost per process volume or transaction (Lohrmann et al., 2015, pp. 274–277).

**Continuous Improvement:** One of the reasons for moving processes into a shared services organization, in the long run, is to continuously improve the quality of processes while making them more efficient at the same time. Therefore, SSCs actively manage processes for *continuous improvement*. Some firms include the continuous improvement of processes in the SLAs. Others create dedicated teams for continuous improvement in the SSCs. Procter & Gamble is a case in point. Each SSC staff must attend continuous improvement training and dedicate a day per month to process improvement. This is then evaluated as part of the staff's annual performance appraisal. The company tracks ideas for improvement suggested by staff and—if suitable—ensures their implementation (EY, 2013).

## Global Business Services and Other Recent Trends and Issues

Since starting in the 1990s, shared service organizations have undergone several changes. One of the significant changes that the shared services in many firms went through is establishing a Global Business Services (GBS) organization. Traditionally, in many firms, the various functions like IT, accounting, and HR set up their own SSCs that were unconnected. The various SSC locations around the world were operating largely independently. GBS organizations bring all the SSCs of the firm across functions and locations together under one joint leadership. We will first address GBS and then some other recent trends and issues.

**Global Business Services:** Traditionally, even if some firms had several functional teams co-located in the same building of an SSC, in most cases, there was no further integration across the functions or locations in the world. As a result, companies missed opportunities for effective service delivery across continents and cross-functional end-to-end processes (see below). Experience was not shared between SSC locations. Duplication of efforts was frequent. Investments in technical innovation for individual SSCs did not pay off. Internal customers had to contact different SSC locations and teams via different channels, and their processes varied. One could not easily compare the performance of the SSCs, and a lack of standardization hindered the automation of processes. Therefore, in the 2010s, management consultants began recommending the Global Business Services (GBS) model for these companies. This requires all SSCs of the company to be brought under one organizational roof. Consultants expect several benefits, among others: economies of scale (e.g., use of a joint infrastructure), sharing of best practices, reduction of duplication, consistent channels of communication between internal customers and SSCs, higher efficiency by standardization of processes, better comparability of the performance of SSCs as well as more straightforward automation (EY, 2013, 2015b). A study conducted in 2018 has shown that companies implementing a GBS model indeed achieve such benefits, as well as further benefits. For example, staff in the SSCs benefits from global career development opportunities and the motivation from being part of a global team and working in a global environment (Klimkeit, 2019b). As a survey shows, by 2018, 41% of participating companies had implemented the GBS model at least partially, and 25% were planning to implement it (SSON, 2018).

The GBS model consists of the following elements: (1) SSCs are to bring together all functions for which the company has shared services. (2) All SSCs worldwide will be brought under one organizational roof with one joint GBS leader. (3) For each process conducted by GBS, there should be one global process owner who defines and oversees the continuous improvement of the process. (4) The SSCs of the company form a network for the coordinated delivery of its internal services. The company governs this via consistent key performance indicators (KPIs). (5) There should be intensive collaboration, knowledge-sharing, and standardization of processes in the global network (EY, 2013, 2015b).

The 2018 study mentioned above investigated global collaboration across the various SSC locations worldwide. A cross-location collaboration in delivering a service function, such as accounting, takes place in three ways: *24/5 Support*, *Global Specialization,* and *Business Continuity*.

First, in *24/5 Support*, a cross-location team, which one can, for example, reach via a joint mailbox, is organized for time-critical tasks so that tasks that come in after the business day of an SSC can be picked up by the SSC that is next in the sequence of time zones. So, GBS organizations achieve a 24-h availability. It turns time zone differences between SSC locations to its advantage.

Second, *Global Specialization* refers to specialized global centers which perform a function, e.g., payments, globally. This requires collaboration in service delivery. Here, processes like procure to pay (P2P, from procurement to payment to suppliers) are not conducted autonomously in one regional SSC; instead, interfaces with a global center arise. In this example, regional centers would conduct procurement and accounts payable. The payment would be processed in the specialized global center, requiring collaboration between this and the regional centers.

10

Third, in *Business Continuity*, cross-location collaboration in service delivery occurs when one SSC is ready to step in when another SSC cannot work due to an emergency to ensure the most critical processes continue. Collaboration in these three forms is made possible through the organizational combination of the SSCs in the GBS model (Klimkeit, 2019a).

Besides the advantages, however, companies implementing the GBS model may also encounter one or several challenges (Klimkeit, 2019b):

- *Global standardization*: While the global standardization of processes provides benefits, it can also become challenging. Requirements of the processes managed in SSCs often vary from country to country due to language, culture, legal, and other conditions. A transnational solution, as introduced in ► Chap. 8, was found to be helpful here: standardize as much as possible and adapt what needs to be adapted. For example, a GBS organization can standardize high-level process descriptions, while detailed work instructions vary between SSCs.
- *Functional silos*: While integrating various functions into one GBS organization should help to overcome functional silos, frequently, making this a reality is still challenging. What can help is to create cross-functional teams that operate an entire end-to-end process together. In one company, for example, integrated teams for the procure-to-pay process, which includes procurement specialists and staff working in accounts payable, were created.
- *Differences between SSCs*: The various SSCs included in a GBS organization often have different degrees of maturity, which can hamper collaboration. Some GBS organizations addressed this challenge successfully by secondments of managers from the more mature to the less mature centers and intensive exchange between locations.

- *Size and complexity of GBS*: By combining all existing SSCs across locations and functions into one organization, the GBS organization can become quite large and complex. As organization theory and practice show, large and complex organizations can become sluggish. To address this, GBS organizations often assign most supporting tasks to the SSCs in the same region as the service-receiving unit.

**End-to-End Processes:** Shared services have always been process-oriented. Several GBS organizations have recently organized service processes as cross-functional end-to-end processes (E2E). An example is the order-to-cash process, from a request from a customer coming in, finalizing the contract, delivering the service, sending an invoice to tracing the payment, and recording it in the accounting books. It can involve functions like sales, legal, accounting, and finance. Collaboration is typically driven by workflow systems. Cross-functional teams are sometimes created under one joint manager and deliver the entire E2E process to one business unit or country subsidiary. Such an internal organizational design streamlines and facilitates an efficient flow of the E2E process significantly. This is especially the case when these teams physically sit together in the office, facilitating quick informal coordination by team members. To ensure global consistency, GBS organizations introduce the role of a Global Process Owner (GPO). The GPO ensures processes are conducted as consistently as possible and continuously improved. Sometimes, the GPO is located within the GBS organization, sometimes outside. If the GPO is located outside, he or she needs to be in close contact with SSC staff conducting the processes daily so that the processes can realistically be implemented in practice (Klimkeit, 2018, 2020).

**Robotic Process Automation (RPA):** With the development of digital technologies, automating routine computer-based processes conducted by office workers is made possible through a technology called Robotic Process Automation (RPA). While the technology originated outside of shared services, it has a particularly high relevance for shared services. This is especially true because many of the processes that SSCs have traditionally taken on are routine, repetitive, transactional, and conducted in large volumes and hence can be automated most easily. Therefore, RPA potentially constitutes a threat to SSCs. In practice, however, SSCs found various ways of avoiding job losses due to RPA. They shifted more processes or parts of processes from the business units to the SSCs. They transfer staff freed up by automation to other processes requiring staff. Generally, SSCs are using the opportunity presented by RPA to "move up the value chain" into more complex, knowledge-intensive tasks. This can include controlling, legal work, or parts of functions like finance & accounting or HR closer to the firm's core business than parts traditionally conducted in SSCs. While this trend started before RPA, it has received a significant boost by automating more repetitive and transactional tasks. The effect is that the GBS organization can potentially improve its standing in the company, moving away from the image of a "cheap back office operation" (Klimkeit & Reihlen, 2022).

**Moving to a More Transformational Role:** In addition to taking on more complex tasks, some most advanced GBS organizations are increasingly becoming driving agents of corporate transformation, including digital transformation. Some characteristics of GBS organizations predispose them toward this role. They are often the most cross-functional and global parts of the company. They have a young workforce that is dynamic and eager to drive change. They already deal with many of the company's data, processes, and systems. Shared services work rests on digital technology. The processes traditionally conducted in SSCs lend themselves to automation so that SSCs can become a testing ground for automation. In the case of Alcon Corp., for example, the GBS organization piloted agile ways of working and subsequently rolled them out to the entire IT organization of the company (Klimkeit & Christophers, 2022). In a pharmaceutical firm, the setting up of the GBS organization drove the integration of the various business units' previously separated finance and accounting departments into one central accounting department, also outside of GBS (Klimkeit, 2019b).

## Offshore Services Outsourcing

### Different Types of Service Outsourcing

*Information Technology Outsourcing (ITO)* and *Business Process Outsourcing (BPO)* are the more frequently used types of outsourcing.



**Information Technology Outsourcing (ITO)**

*Information technology outsourcing (ITO)* means "to rely on external service providers for hardware, software, telecommunications, cloud computing resources, and automation tools." (Willcocks et al., 2017, p. 1)

ITO is focused on outsourcing IT infrastructure and related services. *Business Process Outsourcing* (*BPO*) . refers to a broader set of outsourced functions that relate to the functions' effectiveness and efficiency rather than the technologies supporting them.

**Business Process Outsourcing (BPO)**

*Business process outsourcing (BPO)* is referred to as "the vendor taking responsibility for executing a business process such as customer contact, and delivering it to the client as a service." (McIvor, 2013, p. 6)

BPO can include functions, especially regarding back-office support, such as accounting, HR, human resources, or procurement. BPO can be selective or total. *Selective outsourcing* relates to moving a limited number of process activities to a provider. *Total outsourcing* refers to outsourcing an entire process to an external

Manila; The Philippines have become a major hub for BPO and ITO, image by Kris from Pixabay

vendor (McIvor, 2013). This can, for example, relate to travel management or recruiting.

## Management of Service Outsourcing

Much of what we said about managing the delivery of services in globally distributed shared services organizations also applies to outsourcing. Here we will focus on specifics deriving from the fact that outsourcing is a contractual relationship between two independent firms, the customer and the service provider. Leslie Willcocks and Mary Lacity, who have researched outsourcing over decades, have compiled recommendations on establishing an outsourcing agreement and ongoing outsourcing management, vetting statements from providers with their research findings.

**Establishing the Outsourcing Arrangement:** Willcocks and Lacity found that many of the best practices for establishing an outsourcing agreement that providers claim would indeed benefit the client as well (Lacity & Willcocks, 2012). We outline a selection:

- *Client's objectives*: Clients have various reasons for outsourcing business processes. When the client's procurement department drives outsourcing, cost-saving is the primary aim. However, if the client expects innovation, this requires the engagement of its top management and investment in building a strong collaborative partnership. Then, benefits like access to global markets and innovation go beyond cost-saving. Sometimes, clients expect all at the same time.

- *Client readiness:* The client must be ready for outsourcing. This includes understanding the current internal cost, headcount, processes, and realistic expectations of what outsourcing can achieve. Frequently, clients do not have a good measurement of their in-house processes and provide unrealistic information about their current processes to the provider, which skews the baseline from which a company can measure success. Lacity and Willcocks found it essential to have an internal evaluation before moving processes to a provider.
- *Pricing*: There are different options for pricing the outsourcing service—a lump sum, pricing per unit, and pricing based on actual cost. Clients often prefer a lump sum but underestimate future growth in demand. This is a suitable option if the outsourced service can be defined in detail and conditions are predictable. Often, companies underestimate the hidden cost of outsourcing. The ongoing cost for managing the outsourcing on the client side is typically 4–12% of the contract value. Lacity and Willcocks found this hidden cost to be the main risk in outsourcing.

**Managing Outsourced Services:** Willcocks identified good practices for the ongoing management of outsourced services (Willcocks & Lacity, 2012), some of which we will outline here:

- *Client capabilities and management*: When companies outsource processes, the client needs to retain certain skills and capabilities to manage the relationship with the outsourcing provider. However, they relate more to managing inputs provided to the outsourcing provider and checking the outputs of the provider rather than managing the provider's resources. While some clients retain too few capable staff to manage the outsourcing, others retain too many and interfere too much in managing the processes and resources at the outsourcing provider. The client needs to retain some people who can conduct troubleshooting and that can evaluate the provider's proposals and activities.
- *Provider capabilities and management*: Efficiency has more to do with providers' management capabilities than with pure economies of scale: standardization, rationalization, IT-enablement of processes such as self-service portals, and close monitoring and controlling make outsourcing efficient. However, providers do not always have the capabilities to serve a particular client. Beyond the domain expertise, the providers need to be managed well to meet SLAs, be able to acquire, retain, deploy and motivate talent, use suitable technology, improve processes, and maintain security and confidentiality of client data.
- *Relational governance*: Besides contracts, *relational governance* is vital to make outsourcing a success. It is notable that sometimes customers blame providers for things that go wrong but fall under their own responsibility. Client and provider need to develop shared norms, communication, trust, cooperation, and share information to make the relationship a success. Governance by contracts and relational governance are not mutually exclusive but complement each other. Outsourcing works best with a combination of the two.

## Outsourcing of Professional Services

It is interesting to take a closer look at professional service firms (PSFs) in this context as they outsource services to others, and providers of outsourced services are PSFs themselves. Think of major outsourcing providers like Wipro, Tata Consulting Services, Accenture, or Genpact. They are PSFs. In many PSFs, the standardization of tasks and their offshoring is increasing. This implies that PSFs disaggregate initially integrated professional tasks into components, some of which can be routinized and standardized and subsequently outsourced, offshored, or automated. The deregulation of some professional services, such as legal services, facilitates the disaggregation of professional tasks. Deregulation and disaggregation allow some tasks to be conducted by semi-professionals or non-professionals. The more a PSF has split a task into components, the easier it can be conducted by non-professionals. For example, in financial services, contracts relating to derivatives can be drafted and reviewed by a contract specialist. However, to what extent outsourcing or offshoring takes place depends on the governance of a PSF (Sako, 2015).

It is noteworthy that PSFs move not only support activities but core activities of services delivered to clients offshore (Caratti et al., 2016). Offshoring among PSFs has been pioneered by accounting firms, consulting firms, and investment banks, especially in offshore captive centers like India. In these locations, accounting firms conduct activities like client tax returns and audit work that do not require judgment. Investment banks conduct tasks like financial modeling and analytics offshore. Consulting firms do market research and PowerPoint documentation in offshore locations. Law firms move legal support work such as litigation document review and legal research offshore. Most PSFs are traditionally professional partnerships with a high autonomy of individual partners. This makes it more difficult for these PSFs to obtain consent from all partners for an outsourcing or offshoring decision. Often, the individual practice areas or partners can decide what to outsource. Outsourcing of professional services led to the rise of new entrants into the industry: Knowledge Process Outsourcing (KPO) providers. They provide business research, R&D, engineering services, financial research, patent filing, and legal research. Sometimes, they have spun off from captive centers. For example, Genpact had been part of General Electric initially. In other cases, entrepreneurs who had worked for PSFs before and identified a business opportunity setup KPO providers. KPOs enable PSFs to outsource tasks that involve a large volume. However, the challenge for PSFs is that by outsourcing the more uncomplicated and repetitive tasks to KPO providers, they lose the training opportunities traditionally provided to junior professionals as part of their development (Sako, 2015).

## Trends in Outsourcing: Backsourcing

Regarding trends in outsourcing, we want to highlight especially one: backsourcing. Backsourcing refers to moving the processes once outsourced back into the company. This does not have to mean bringing them back to the home country of the MNE. For example, the firm might bring processes from an outsourcing provider in China into a captive center owned by the firm in Southeast Asia. According to a recent publication by Mederos (2021, pp. 20–26), there are currently mainly four reasons for backsourcing:

- *Perceived hidden cost*: Frequently, there are costs due to outsourced services taking much longer to complete than expected. One participant in Mederos' research stated that a process that had taken 2 days now took 6 days after outsourcing. Sometimes, rework due to language barriers was required, increasing cost.
- *Diminished quality*: A decrease in the quality of processes provided by outsourcing suppliers is observed frequently by managers. Mederos attributes this partly to a continuous demand for decreasing prices, which also diminished quality, requiring rework by clients.
- *Corporate politics*: Some executives used outsourcing to achieve other internal objectives. Once leadership changes, this can lead to changes in outsourcing arrangements. New leaders want to make their mark on the organization, and a decision to backsource processes can be one way of achieving this.
- *The effect of COVID-19 and RPA*: COVID-19 led to the disruption of widely spread global supply chains. This drove several governments like Japan and the United States to provide funding for their companies to backsource activities previously outsourced to firms in offshore locations. While initially related to medical supplies, it triggered a general debate about the global spread of value chains and their associated risks. Companies can regain control of their processes through robotic process automation (RPA) while saving money. Having a process conducted by a software robot is still cheaper than having it performed by humans in a low-cost location. Both COVID-19 and RPA are together encouraging a drive towards backsourcing.



## Review Questions

1. Outline the key locations of service relocation and typical services involved.
2. Define outsourcing and offshoring, explain the difference, and how these can be combined.
3. Explain the rationale for service relocation and specifically for captive centers.
4. Explain the key criteria used for determining suitable locations for service offshoring.
5. Outline the various options for services offshoring.
6. Outline what needs to be considered when managing shared service operations.
7. Describe some recent trends in services offshoring.
8. How is the concept of GBS different from traditional shared services?
9. Given its benefits and challenges, how do you see the concept of GBS?
10. Define and explain the concepts of ITO and BPO..
11. Explain what needs to be considered when establishing and managing outsourcing arrangements.
12. How is the outsourcing of professional services special?
13. Why have several companies decided to backsource services that were previously outsourced?

## Closing Case: KAS Bank's Bot Program

KAS Bank, founded in 1806, was an independent Dutch bank providing fund administration and custodian services to institutional investors and financial institutions. In 2014, KAS Bank initiated a program to reduce operating costs. So, it outsourced various IT functions to an outsourcing provider, including transferring IT assets and employees. Outsourcing was considered a success. Beyond significant cost reductions, it provided flexibility in pricing by applying a pay-per-use mechanism.

Encouraged by this, the management looked for ways of achieving further cost reduction. In 2016, the RPA program was introduced, first investigating the automation of some standard processes. The bank considered processes that were transactional, routine-based, repetitive, and low in complexity. Further, it investigated the impact of automation for every potential process considered for automation, such as the potential for cost reduction and needed support. Two business processes were automated first within 6 weeks. Overall, KAS Bank automated 20 finance processes using five robots (bots), including treasury management and client data management. Bots took over processes conducted manually by using Excel spreadsheets before. While cost reduction was the main driver in the beginning, later, improving the quality of processes by avoiding rework came into focus.

Various challenges occurred, however, regarding KAS Bank's bot pro-

Computer work, image by StartupStock Photos from Pixabay

gram. First, employees had little understanding of what bots are and how they work, and many were skeptical about whether they could perform tasks previously performed by humans. Further, while the bank planned that bots would conduct an entire end-to-end process, operations personnel who conducted these tasks previously only knew a part of the process that was their focus. This made it difficult for the programmers of the bots to program the entire process. Additionally, employees previously knew whom to contact in case of questions regarding the process, such as handovers. Now that bots had taken over many process tasks, uncertainty and resistance grew. When bots became operational, they regularly required inputs from operations personnel, and outputs from the bots needed to be checked by personnel and forwarded to clients. However, in practice, the input provided to the bots was not always accurate and complete. Thus, the bot could not process data and labeled the incomplete task as an exception. This applied to about 20% of transactions, requiring human personnel's attention to correct the input so the bot could process the data correctly. So, operations personnel still needed to engage in work they previously did, but differently. Now, exception reports needed to be studied and errors corrected instead of data entered. Some personnel analyzed the causes of errors and helped designers redesign the process to prevent future errors. This provided career development opportunities to become a process improvement manager. Others were discouraged by being restricted to handling exceptions now and quit their job.

**Questions**

1. What do we learn from the case about using RPA in an outsourcing/offshoring environment?
2. How could the challenges have been avoided or mitigated?
3. Do you see a rationale for backsourcing at KAS Bank?

Sources: (Oshri & Plugge, 2020).



**Summary**

This chapter

- Distinguished between outsourcing, defined as "a company's purchase of products or services from another domestic or offshore company" and offshoring, defined as "a domestic company sourcing products or services from a foreign-based company, either a subsidiary of the focal firm (captive or international in-sourcing) or an independent service provider (offshore outsourcing)."
- Outlined the rationale for services outsourcing and offshoring and specifically for captive centers.
- Explained criteria used for location choice: resource cost, people skills and availability, the business environment, and the level of digitalization.
- Outlined options for the governance of shared service organizations.
- Explained critical aspects of the management of shared service operations: IT systems, performance management, and continuous improvement.

- Outlined Global Business services and other recent trends in shared services: end-to-end processes, robotic process automation, and the move to a more transformational role.
- Distinguished types of outsourcing: ITO, defined as "to rely on external service providers for hardware, software, telecommunications, cloud computing resources, and automation tools" and BPO., defined as "the vendor taking responsibility for executing a business process such as customer contact, and delivering it to the client as a service."
- Described how to manage outsourced services successfully.
- Outlined specifics of outsourcing professional services.
- Explained the trend of backsourcing previously outsourced services.

## References


Becker, W., Kunz, C., & Mayer, B. (2009). *Shared service center: Konzeption und Implementierung in internationalen Konzernen*. Kohlhammer.

Bunyaratavej, K., Doh, J., Hahn, E. D., Lewin, A. Y., & Massini, S. (2011). Conceptual issues in services offshoring research: A multidisciplinary review. *Group & Organization Management, 36*(1), 70–102.

Caratti, S., Perrin, B., & Scully, G. (2016). An accounting firm perspective of offshoring. In J. Kotlarsky, I. Oshri, & L. P. Willcocks (Eds.), *Shared services and outsourcing: A contemporary outlook: 10th global sourcing workshop 2016, Val d'Isère, France, February 16-19, 2016, Revised Selected Papers* (pp. 137–165). Springer International Publishing.

EY. (2013). *Delivering tomorrow's companies today: How global business services can transform your business*. Retrieved from https://webforms.ey.com/gl/en/services/advisory/delivering-tomorrows-companies-today%2D%2D-the-cfo-perspective%2D%2D-at-a-glance

EY. (2015a). *Digitizing global business services: The future of Global Business Services*.

EY. (2015b). *Global business services: Enabling global market operations Survey Results 2015*. Retrieved from https://webforms.ey.com/Publication/vwLUAssets/ey-global-business-services-enabling-global-market-operations/$FILE/ey-global-business-services-enabling-global-market-operations.pdf

Kearney. (2019). *Digital resonance: the new factor influencing location attractiveness: The 2019 Kearney Global Services Location Index*. Retrieved from https://www.kearney.com/digital/gsli/2019-full-report

Kearney. (2021). *The 2021 Kearney Global Services Location Index: Toward a global network of digital hubs*. Retrieved from https://www.kearney.com/digital/article/-/insights/the-2021-kearney-global-services-location-index

Klimkeit, D. (2018). How Companies are Implementing the Global Business Services (GBS) Target Operating Model: Good Practices Identified in an Exploratory Study in Asia and Europe. In EY (Ed.), *How can Global Business Services drive value across continents? Findings from research in Global Business Services operations* (pp. 4–15).

Klimkeit, D. (2019a). Global business services. *Intelligent Sourcing, 2019*, 26–37.

Klimkeit, D. (2019b). Shared Services weltweit integriert: Ergebnisse einer Studie zur Implementierung des Global Business Services-Modells in der Praxis. *Der Betriebswirt, 60*(2), 24–28.

Klimkeit, D. (2020). Das neue Aufbrechen funktionaler Silos: Cross-funktionale Integration und Kollaboration in Global Business Services-Organisationen. *IM+io Best & Next Practices Aus Digitalisierung | Management | Wissenschaft, 2020*(3), 92–95.

Klimkeit, D., & Christophers, L. (2022). Global Business Services als Transformationstreiber: Eine Fallstudie der heutigen Möglichkeiten von Shared Services. *Der Betriebswirt, 63*(1), 13–26.

Klimkeit, D., & Reihlen, M. (2022). No longer second-class citizens: Redefining organizational identity as a response to digitalization in accounting shared services. *Journal of Professions and Organization, 9*(1), 115–138.

Lacity, M. C., & Willcocks, L. P. (2012). What providers say about establishing the outsourcing arrangement. In M. C. Lacity & L. P. Willcocks (Eds.), *Advanced outsourcing practice: rethinking ITO, BPO and cloud services* (pp. 25–46). Palgrave Macmillan UK.

Lacity, M. C., Willcocks, L. P., & Rottman, J. W. (2008). Global outsourcing of back office services: Lessons, trends, and enduring challenges. *Strategic Outsourcing: An International Journal, 1*(1), 13–34.

Lindvall, J., & Iveroth, E. (2011). Creating a global network of shared service centres for accounting. *Journal of Accounting & Organizational Change, 7*(3), 278–305.

Lohrmann, M., Rau, T., & Riedel, A. (2015). *Shared services und business process outsourcing: Umsetzung, Herausforderungen und aktuelle trends*. Wiley-VCH.

McIvor, R. (2013). *What do we know about services outsourcing?* Retrieved from https://www.icas.com/__data/assets/pdf_file/0009/7839/117-What-Do-We-Know-About-Services-Outsourcing-McIvor-Lit-Review-ICAS.pdf

Mederos, L. A. (2021). *The future of outsourcing: Strategic outsourcing controls and the Backsourcing evolution*. Palgrave Macmillan.

Oshri, I., & Plugge, A. (2020). What do you see in your bot? Lessons from KAS Bank. In I. Oshri, J. Kotlarsky, & L. P. Willcocks (Eds.), *Digital technologies for global sourcing of services* (pp. 145–161). Springer International Publishing.

Penter, K., Pervan, G., & Wreford, J. (2009). Offshore BPO at large captive operations in India. *Information Technology & People, 22*(3), 201–222.

Pisani, N., & Ricart, J. E. (2016). Offshoring of services: A review of the literature and organizing framework. *Management International Review, 56*(3), 385–424.

PwC. (2016). *Shared services: Multiplying success*. Retrieved from http://www.pwc.com/ph/en/consulting/consulting-publications/shared-services-multiplying-success.html

Sako, M. (2015). Outsourcing and offshoring of professional services. In L. Empson, D. Muzio, J. P. Broschak, & B. Hinings (Eds.), *The Oxford handbook of professional service firms* (pp. 327–347). Oxford University Press.

SSON. (2018). *State of the Shared services and outsourcing industry report—2018*. Retrieved from https://www.ssonetwork.com/business-process-management/whitepapers/just-published-global-state-of-the-sso-industry

Willcocks, L. P., & Lacity, M. C. (2012). What providers say about managing outsourced services. In M. C. Lacity & L. P. Willcocks (Eds.), *Advanced outsourcing practice: Rethinking ITO, BPO and cloud services* (pp. 47–68). Palgrave Macmillan UK.

Willcocks, L. P., Lacity, M. C., & Sauer, C. (2017). Introduction. In L. P. Willcocks, M. C. Lacity, & C. Sauer (Eds.), *Outsourcing and offshoring business services* (pp. 1–22). Springer International Publishing.




## Further Reading

Consulting firm Kearney biannually provides an overview of the best locations for shared services and outsourcing locations, also addressing general trends in the industry. Retrieved from www.kearney.com/digital/gsli

The website of the Shared Services and Outsourcing Network (SSON) contains a wealth of reports on outsourcing and shared services, including the annual *State of the Shared Services and Outsourcing Industry Report*. Retrieved from www.ssonetwork.com

# International Corporate Governance

## Contents




D. Klimkeit et al., *International Management in Service Firms*, Classroom Companion: Business,
https://doi.org/10.1007/978-3-031-50345-0_11

**Learning Outcomes**

After completing this chapter, you should be able to:

- Outline the importance and aims of corporate governance (CG)
- Distinguish different types of agency problems
- Explain various mechanisms of corporate governance
- Outline the key dimensions by which CG systems in the world differ
- Explain specifics of corporate governance in service firms, especially PSFs

## Introduction

This chapter investigates various aspects of appropriate and ethical behavior of service firms and their management and staff in the international context. We will first outline the various types of agency problems and why good corporate governance is essential to mitigate these problems. We introduce a range of mechanisms for mitigating agency problems. Key dimensions by which CG systems differ across the world are explained. The chapter concludes with an outline of different types of CG in professional service firms.

Money on a world map. Image by svlkimkin from Pixabay

## Opening Case: Four Corporate Scandals

At the start of the 2000s and continuing during the 2008 financial crisis, several corporate scandals shook the confidence of investors and the public in businesses and their published financial statements. In the following, we will report four of them briefly.

**Barings Bank:** This case is about the failure of one of the United Kingdom's oldest banks due to the actions of just one employee. Nick Leeson, a trader in Barings' Singapore office, generated about 10% of the firm's profits in 1993. He had developed a fine sense of the stock markets in Asia, and the top management of Barings held him in high regard. Later, however, Leeson created significant losses. Consequently, he requested additional funds from head office, which top management provided him without questions. Nick Leeson took very high stakes in the Japanese Yen. Following an earthquake in Japan, which caused a stark drop in the value of the Yen, he lost GBP850 million, which led to the collapse of Barings Bank. For several months he had been able to cover up the losses he had previously made.

**Enron:** Enron had activities in the energy market and developed into an energy trader, including gas and electricity. The published financial statements for the year 2000 showed solid profits and an excellent financial position of the firm. However, this was partly due to the use of Special Purpose Entities that Enron set up to conceal the debt and losses of the firm from the consolidated financial statements. Some of these entities were used to transfer funds to some of Enron's directors. In 2001, Enron had to declare a loss of US$1b and a write-off of US$1.2b and filed for bankruptcy. This became the biggest bankruptcy in US history until then. The audit firm Arthur Andersen, who was supposed to identify and point out irregularities in the financial statements, helped cover up the irregularities by shredding documents that proved them. Arthur Andersen had a conflict of interest as the firm earned more from lucrative consulting services to Enron than from the audit and was worried about losing the consulting contract had they pointed out the irregularities. Enron's CEO was sentenced to a 24-year jail sentence.

**Parmalat:** Parmalat was a prominent Italian firm specializing in long-life milk. The founding family still owned the majority of the shares. The firm had expanded through a series of acquisitions of other companies. Due to this, the firm had taken on a sizeable debt burden. In 2003, Parmalat could not serve its debt even though it was supposed to have significant cash reserves. An investigation found that the cash reserves did not exist, so the firm had to file for bankruptcy. The firm's debt amounted to an equivalent of GBP10b, so some media labeled the firm as "Europe's Enron." The founder, Calisto Tanzi, had conducted transactions with other firms he owned that each time transferred funds away from Parmalat and then provided false accounting information about the firm.

**Royal Bank of Scotland:** Like several other banks, before the 2008 financial crisis, the Royal Bank of Scotland (RBS) dealt with mortgage-backed securities that were considered very risky. In 2008, due to the subprime mortgage crisis, they significantly dropped in value. The staff of RBS received short-term performance bonuses that encouraged excessive risk-taking. If the risky transaction was successful, bankers received high bonuses; if it failed, there was no penalty to staff. RBS had grown through many acquisitions of other banks under CEO Goodwin. Observers commented that often the prices paid were too high. Despite the bad performance, executives of RBS received excessive remuneration packages. Eventually, the British government had to take over RBS to save it, which led to public outrage at the generous pension the CEO received. A report eventually found fundamental deficiencies in the governance of RBS that led to bad decisions.

**Questions**

1. Why have such scandals and collapses occurred?
2. What might be done to prevent them from happening again?

Sources: (Mallin, 2019, 2–3; 266–268)

## Aims, Goals, and Theories of Corporate Governance

11

Barings Bank, Enron, Royal Bank of Scotland, Satyam, Steinhoff, Carillion, Wirecard, Swiss Air: Many, if not most, of the corporate scandals and collapses of the past two decades happened at service MNEs, which is probably no coincidence. At the same time, service firms such as banks, audit firms, media, and rating agencies play an important role in ensuring good *corporate governance* at a company to prevent such scandals and collapses from happening. So corporate governance is essential for international service firms from two perspectives. Corporate governance deals precisely with the two questions above: why have scandals and collapses such as the ones in the opening cases occurred, and what could be done to prevent them from happening again?

Now, what is corporate governance (CG) ? The Organization for Economic Co-operation and Development (OECD) provides a rather broad definition: "a set of relationships between a company's board, its shareholders and other stakeholders" (Mallin, 2019, p. 9). Sir Adrian Cadbury, very influential in corporate governance not just in the United Kingdom, described CG as "The system by which companies are directed and controlled" (Cadbury, 1992, p. 15) and stated as the aim of CG: "to align as nearly as possible the interests of individuals, corporations, and society" (Mallin, 2019, p. 9). We believe that the following definition summarizes the key points well:

**Corporate Governance**

A *corporate governance* system is the combination of mechanisms which ensure that the management (the agent) runs the firm for the benefit of one or several stakeholders (principals). (Goergen & Renneboog, 2008, p. 100)

These definitions show that CG is about setting the firm's direction and controlling its implementation. The definition by Goergen and Renneboog emphasizes well the purpose of CG. At the same time, it highlights the mechanisms used to achieve this purpose in practice. These make CG tangible, and we will treat them in detail in this chapter. Each country's CG system has a specific combination of mechanisms, and in some countries, the focus of CG is on one stakeholder, while in others, several stakeholders are addressed. We will explain this below.

## Why Corporate Governance is Important

So why is CG important? It helps to make sure that an adequate system of controls is in place in a company. It helps avoid situations where one single person has too much power. It fosters transparency and accountability. It defines relationships between the firm's management, shareholders, other stakeholders, and the board of directors. By the end of the day, corporate governance helps ensure that the company is managed in the best interest of its shareholders and other stakeholders (Mallin, 2019, p. 10). We want to highlight this last sentence as what we see as the key *aim of corporate governance*:

» The aim of corporate governance is "to ensure that the company is managed in the best interest of the shareholders and the other stakeholders" (Mallin, 2019, p. 10).

Companies that ignore the benefits of good CG can eventually collapse, as those in the opening cases. Good CG instead can help prevent collapses and restore investor confidence because there are mechanisms in place that ensure that their investment is safeguarded and the firm is managed in their best interest.

Until now, CG may still appear somewhat abstract to you. So, we want to give you a short preview of essential mechanisms of CG. Some mechanisms have an informal character: Many companies have strong social norms that tell managers and staff what is right and wrong. Some firms explicitly write these expectations of appropriate behavior into corporate codes of conduct. Also, by and large, managers are interested in maintaining a good reputation, which tends to be a deterrent from misbehavior damaging the firm for personal benefit. Many other mechanisms are more formal. Governments put legal requirements or regulations in place to enforce good CG by law. Companies institute a board of directors or supervisory board that controls the management on behalf of the shareholders. Firms use incentive schemes to align the interests of managers more with those of shareholders. The firm's owners can also play a role in monitoring the management, especially the large shareholders, so-called blockholders. Various other stakeholders can also be involved, such as banks interested in monitoring the management of firms that have received a sizeable loan from them. Auditors check whether the financial statements provide a true and fair view of the financial performance and position of the firm (Thomsen & Conyon, 2012, p. 46). These mechanisms should ensure that the firm is managed in the best interest of shareholders and other stakeholders and that scandals and collapses are avoided.

## Theories of Corporate Governance

Traditionally, the main problem of corporate governance is due to the separation of ownership and control in publicly listed companies (see ◘ Fig. 11.1). As long as a firm is managed by its owners, such as an entrepreneur or a family, those who make managerial decisions and those who take the financial risk from them are identical. So, managers will be careful about managing the firm and the decisions they make, for example, significant investments, as they will bear both the return and risk of their decisions. At one point, to raise additional capital, some owners decide to take their company to the stock market and issue shares that anyone can buy. While they typically retain a significant portion of the shares, others will now hold another part. Moreover, these other shareholders will not be involved in the company's management. They must trust the management to manage the firm in their best interest. The original owner may frequently withdraw from day-to-day management and entrust management to a manager hired from outside. In this case, the original owner must also trust the manager hired to manage in their best interest. This situation is addressed by the *principal–agent theory* or *agency theory* (Jensen & Meckling, 1976). The owners are called the *principals*, the managers the *agents*.

> **Principal and Agent**
>
> The *principal* is anyone who hires someone else to do a particular job, while the *agent* is the person hired.



Principal–agent relationships exist in many contexts: boss and employee in a company, patient and doctor, house owner and real estate agent tasked to sell the house, citizens and government in a democratic state. The problem is that different parties can have different interests. The boss may want the employee to work hard, while the employee may prefer to take it easy (Thomsen & Conyon, 2012, pp. 5–17). In the same way, the manager may want a large office with expensive furniture, an expensive company car, perhaps with a chauffeur, or even a company jet or helicopter, expensive dinners with business partners, and other things that make life comfortable for the manager, while the owners of the firm pick up the bills for these amenities. The question is to what extent they benefit the business or just the manager personally.

◘ **Fig. 11.1** Agency problem type I: the owner-manager problem, own diagram

The principle–agent problem is primarily fostered by what is called *information asymmetry*. The manager who runs the firm's day-to-day operations knows much more about the firm's situation and the management activities undertaken than the shareholders, who only have the information made publicly available by the firm. Likewise, a manager who applies for a management position knows his or her actual capabilities much better than those hiring. So, there are two types of information asymmetry: *adverse selection* and *moral hazard* (Rutherford et al., 2007).

*Adverse selection* refers to a situation when the agent has hidden knowledge. This applies especially in a hiring situation: The company board may scan the CV and references from former employers and conduct a job interview with a candidate for an executive position. However, only the candidate will know how intelligent, experienced, knowledgeable, and hard-working he or she is (Rutherford et al., 2007). Investors contemplating buying shares of a company are in a similar situation: They make their investment decisions based on the limited public information available. Based on this, the company may seem to be in good condition, while only the firm's management may know that, in reality, it is in deep trouble, which does not show up yet in the published accounts.[1] This was the case at Enron, where until shortly before the scandal became public, on the outside, Enron appeared as a healthy, successful company, and investors kept buying its stock.

**Adverse Selection**

*Adverse selection* happens when there is information in a hiring or investment situation known to an agent that the principal does not know so that the decision by the principal can later turn out as misguided.

The *moral hazard* problem arises because the principal cannot observe the actual behavior of the agent. For example, a manager may spend much of the day playing golf or having expensive meals at the company's expense rather than working hard for the firm. Shareholders can only observe the published information about the firm and track some indicators of the firm's performance. This lack of transparency can encourage the manager to take advantage of the situation and manage in a way that benefits only himself or herself but not the company. There is a further aspect of moral hazard. Consider the following interesting finding: Insurance firms found that in the houses of people who have fire insurance, a fire occurs more frequently than in households without fire insurance. Why? People who know that the insurance will pay for the damage in case of a fire become somewhat more careless and will not check twice that, for example, they have extinguished candles before they leave the house. The same occurs in companies: Since managers are not dealing with their own money but the shareholders' money, they might tend to be less diligent about its use. This might lead to risky investments as managers do not lose

1 The full theoretical explanation of the adverse selection problem is more complex, but we won't go into the details in our context here.

their own money if the investment project fails. So, when managers do not carry any risk, they lose the incentive to avoid it (Thomsen & Conyon, 2012, p. 21). This was the case at Enron, Barings Bank, and RBS. In all these companies, managers took high risks as they did not have to carry the risk of failure, at least until the companies collapsed and they lost their jobs.

**Moral Hazard**

A *moral hazard* happens when the principal cannot observe the agent's actions, and the agent deals carelessly with resources provided by the principal as the principal bears the risk.

The question is what the principals can do about moral hazard. Basically, two options directly address the root causes of moral hazard: *incentives* and *monitoring*. Since the lack of transparency is one root cause, the shareholders as principals can monitor the manager more closely by, for example, putting in place a board of directors that monitors the manager more closely than the shareholders can do. Alternatively, they can ask the manager to publish annual or quarterly financial statements and contract an auditor to testify that they are correct. Especially at Barings Bank, the top management had too much trust in Nick Leeson and therefore monitored him too little, putting the bank at risk. Incentives address the fact that managers are not affected financially by their actions. By providing bonuses for good performance or offering stocks or stock options, the interests of managers become more aligned with those of the owners. Bad performance will lead to a lower or no bonus and a fall in the firm's stock price and, therefore, the value of the stock or option the manager holds. These mechanisms, however, generate costs and can have drawbacks, as we will see later (Padgett, 2012, 2–3, 24, 96).



**The Owner-Manager Problem:** We want to focus now more on the agency problems that can occur between owners and managers of a business. There are two main types of problems: *perquisites* and *empire building*. Perquisites or perks, sometimes called fringe benefits, comprise what a manager consumes on the job. Perks may include expensive offices, accommodation, corporate cars and jets, and many other things. The manager obtains the benefit of the perk while the shareholders pick up the bill for them.

**Perquisites (Perks)**

Perquisites or perks [...] consist of on-the-job consumption by the firm's managers. While the benefits from the perks accrue to the managers, their costs are borne by the shareholders (Goergen, 2018, p. 8).

Especially when executives responsible for corporate failure receive perks, this can create public outrage (Goergen, 2018, pp. 8–9). Take the excessive remuneration packages for executives in the opening case of RBS as an example. In another case,

Thomas Middelhoff, former CEO of German retailer Arcandor, spent 80,000€ of company funds for private jets to commute from his home in Bielefeld to the Arcandor office in Essen to avoid the traffic jams on the motorway. Eventually, Arcandor went bankrupt, and Middelhoff was sentenced to jail (Jakobs, 2019). David Yermack found that publicly listed firms where the CEO can make private use of the corporate jet underperform their benchmark by 4%. He also found a significant correlation between CEOs' private use of corporate jets and membership in long-distance golf clubs (Yermack, 2006).

While perks may generate public outrage, *empire-building* typically creates more extensive financial damage to the firm. Empire building is also sometimes called the free cash flow problem.

**Empire Building**

*Empire building* consists of the management pursuing growth rather than shareholder value maximization (Goergen, 2018, p. 9).

While there is a certain connection between growth and shareholder value, growth itself does not necessarily create value if it is not profitable. If a firm acquires another firm that is making losses and does not manage to make it profitable, it destroys shareholder value. To generate value for shareholders, managers should only invest in projects where the expected cash flow is greater than the initial investment in the project (a positive net present value, NPV). Any cash flow that remains after the company has invested in all projects with an expected positive NPV is called free cash flow. This money belongs to the shareholders, and the firm should disburse it to them as dividends. However, some executives continue to invest in projects even though their NPV is negative. The question is, why would managers do so? Because they benefit personally from growing the firm. Being CEO of a larger firm means more responsibility, more staff, a larger budget, higher status and prestige, and—as research has found—higher salary, as there is a correlation between executive compensation and firm size (Jensen, 1986). RBS is a good example of empire building, where the bank had grown through acquisitions of other banks at often too generous prices.

**The Expropriation of Minority Shareholders:** Traditionally, the assumption in corporate governance has been that the original owners of a firm listed on the stock exchange would only retain a tiny portion of the firm's shares, which would also apply to all other shareholders. So, the management would face a large group of small anonymous shareholders. This would then foster the owner–manager problem as the main problem of CG, as outlined above. In practice, however, this only describes the US and the UK situation, the so-called "Anglo-American system of corporate governance." In most other countries, most stock-listed firms have large shareholders who can exert significant control over the firm. These large shareholders, or blockholders, can be the original owning families, other companies, the government, and others. This creates two classes of shareholders: the blockholders and the minority shareholders. The blockholders can have significant control and influence on the firm's decisions, while the minority shareholders lack both. What follows from this is that the primary agency problem in these firms is the majority–minority shareholder problem or *expropriation of minority shareholders*. This can take several forms. We will focus here on what is called *tunneling* and *transfer pricing*. Goergen (2018, p. 12) provides an excellent example to illustrate tunneling. Imagine a large shareholder who owns 51% of firm A while owning firm B entirely. The large shareholder could now use his control of firm A to ask the firm to transfer funds to firm B. On every Dollar transferred, he would make a gross gain of $1, while the net gain would be $0.49 ($1–$0.51). This net gain would occur at the expense of the small shareholders who lose this money. So the large shareholder would effectively steal from the small shareholders, hence the term "expropriation" (see also Johnson et al., 2000). Somewhat less blatant is the use of *transfer prices* between related companies so that company B provides services to company A while overcharging them compared to what would be a typical price in the market. Each transaction diverts money from company A to company B, resulting in the same effect. The minority shareholders are expropriated while the large owner makes a gain. Both tunneling and the described use of transfer prices are also called *related-party transactions* since there is a relationship between the two companies involved as they are majority-owned by the same person (Goergen, 2018, pp. 12–13).

**Related-Party Transactions**

*Related party transactions* occur when a transacting party has the ability to substantially influence or exercise control of another transacting party because of a financial, common ownership, or familial relationship with that party (Levine et al., 1997, p. 46).



Parmalat is an example of a firm where the large owner Calisto Tanzi conducted related-party transactions between Parmalat and another firm he owned, thereby draining away funds from Parmalat.

Related-party transactions are very relevant to service firms since they frequently involve services, like in the example of secretarial services above. In a study on related-party transactions in 112 publicly traded companies, most companies were in service industries. Many of the transactions involved services such as management services, legal services, marketing, real estate, accounting, and investment banking (Gordon et al., 2004).

**The Extended Agency Problem:** Distinguishing between large and small shareholders is already one important extension of the traditional agency theory. Thomsen and Conyon (2012, pp. 6–8) suggest one further extension by broadening the perspective to various other company stakeholders beyond owners and managers (see ◘ Fig. 11.2). Larger firms have a board that monitors and controls the management. The firm's employees are important stakeholders; in some countries, they can be represented on the board. Government has expectations of companies

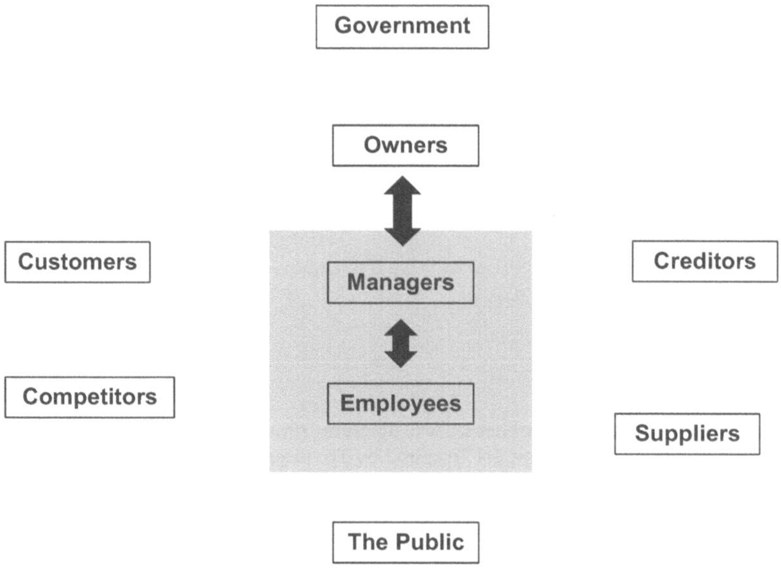


**Fig. 11.2** The extended agency problem, own diagram inspired by Thomsen and Conyon (2012, p. 7)

and might be (partial) owners of firms. Banks monitor the management of their major customers to ensure they serve their loans. Customers and suppliers also have their expectations as stakeholders. The media can expose corporate scandals. Auditors check the firm's financial statements, and analysts provide their opinion about the firm to (potential) investors. While the main focus primarily remains on the owners, managers increasingly pay attention to the other stakeholders. To what extent they do that varies between countries, as we will see later.

So, in sum, three types of agency problems can be distinguished (see Fig. 11.3). Type I is the classic owner–manager problem. Type II is the agency problem between majority and minority shareholders. As mentioned before, in most countries, many listed companies have large shareholders besides many smaller ones, so there is always the risk that the large owners use their influence in a way that may be detrimental to the small owners. Type III agency problem is the one between shareholders and other stakeholders. Due to the diverse interests and expectations of the various stakeholders, there is almost always potential for tensions and conflict. Shareholders might expect high dividends, reducing the company's cash reserves, thereby ringing alarm bells with creditors like banks. Shareholders may want the firm to close down an operation that is making losses, which would run counter to the interests of employees who would lose their jobs, local suppliers, local government, and society (Thomsen & Conyon, 2012, p. 20). The conflicting interests of the various stakeholders of a firm (type III agency problem) will be addressed further in ▶ Chap. 12, which deals with business ethics and corporate social responsibility (CSR).

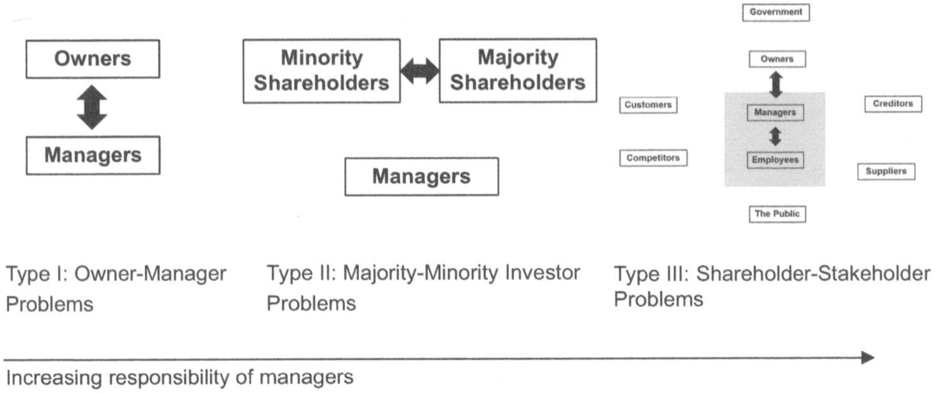


**Fig. 11.3** Types of agency problems, own diagram, drawing on content from Thomsen and Conyon (2012, p. 20); diagram "Type III" inspired by Thomsen and Conyon (2012, p. 7)

## Mechanisms of Corporate Governance

Given the agency problems outlined above, the question is how to solve them. In other words: How do the shareholders of a company ensure that the managers (and blockholders) manage the firm in the owners' best interest? This is where the mechanisms of corporate governance, which aim to mitigate agency problems, come into play. Given the focus of this book, we will only outline them briefly.



**Informal Governance: Social Norms:** Many companies have sound social norms prescribing appropriate behavior that are widespread and anchored throughout the firm. If managers would have to assume that as soon as staff are not closely monitored, they will deviate from what they are supposed to do, it would be difficult to run the company. Companies like Enron are frequently seen as examples of firms that lacked such social norms. To the extent that managers act morally, this goes a long way toward mitigating the agency problems. However, it is not a perfect solution, as many cases of immoral behavior show. In an international context, social norms vary, posing a challenge for MNEs (Rezaee, 2009).

**Informal Governance: Trust and Reputation:** Companies depend much on their good reputation in the eyes of customers, the government, and the public. Appearing in the media with a big scandal is not beneficial for the business. So, companies have a self-interest in behaving appropriately to avoid scandals that damage the company's reputation and endanger the firm. Companies that consistently demonstrate that they put investors' money to good use, avoiding inappropriate behavior, can attract investment. The same applies to managers. Managers do not want their names to be connected to a scandal as it damages their position in the managerial labor market. In countries with inadequate CG legislation, the pressure from the media can play an important role in improving CG if this is supported by societal norms and values (Dyck & Zingales, 2002). However, as many corporate scandals show, this informal mechanism is not a perfect solution. So, more formal mechanisms are needed to complement the informal ones.

**Regulation:** Government legislation and regulation protect investors. Law ensures that managers who misappropriate shareholder funds will be prosecuted. Corporate law stipulates required practices for good corporate governance. Depending on the country, this might include mandating the publication of annual financial statements, which need to be testified by an auditor, an annual meeting of shareholders, the election of a board of directors that controls the management, and many other requirements. There are also legal provisions to protect minority shareholders and other stakeholders like employees and creditors (Aguilera et al., 2013). Beyond government legislation, stock market operators also set requirements for companies that want to list their shares to protect investors. The many requirements of the New York Stock Exchange by the Securities and Exchange Commission (SEC) are an example (Mallin, 2019, p. 62).

**Ownership: Large Owners:** Imagine you own shares in several companies. You own shares worth 100 € in company A, yielding an annual payout of 2.50 € and an annual value increase of 5%. Will you read the annual and quarterly reports and press releases? You get an invitation to the Annual General Meeting (AGM) in Hannover, Germany—will you attend it? If yes: Will you submit agenda topics? Will you ask questions to the management? Probably not. Why? The time and money required would exceed your benefit as a small shareholder. Look at the shareholder structure of the French company L'Oréal in ◘ Fig. 11.4. At first sight, it becomes evident that the Bettencourt family (34.7% of the shares) and Nestlé (20.1%) each hold a sizeable number of shares (L'Oréal Finance, 2023). Together they hold a controlling majority of the company. Will they take the time to read the various reports published by the company, attend the AGM, and submit agenda topics? Certainly yes. Why? They have invested a sizeable amount of money in the firm and will want to ensure it is put to good use to generate profits for them. Besides their motivation to monitor the management, large shareholders will have

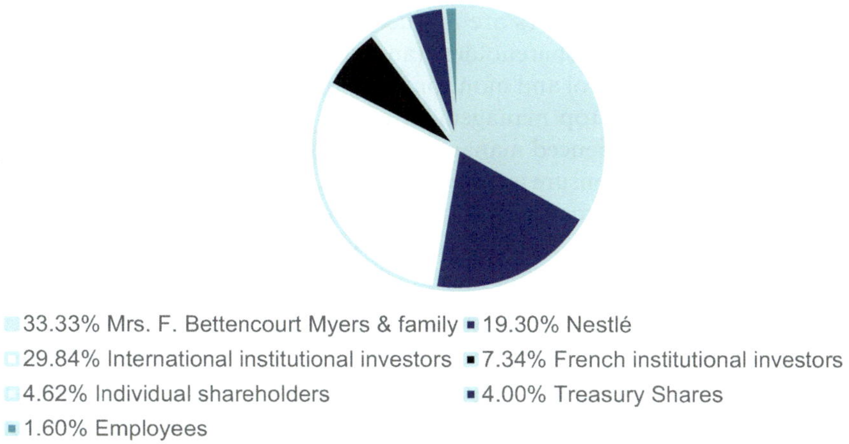


◘ **Fig. 11.4** Shareholder structure of L'Oreal as of 31 December 2022, share ownership in %, own diagram based on data from (L'Oréal Finance, 2023)

a better ability and more resources for monitoring than small ones. So, they can monitor management also on behalf of the small shareholders who can free-ride on their efforts. However, large shareholders bring their own set of challenges. They can create the agency type II problem. They may use their influence in a way that is not in the best interest of the small shareholders, such as putting family members in management positions that may not be the best available managers for the job (Padgett, 2012, pp. 27–29). At Parmalat, the large owner Calisto Tanzi abused his position to siphon off money to his other firms.

**Shareholder Activism:** While shareholders who are not major blockholders tend to be less actively monitoring the management, they can still do so. The Annual General Meeting (AGM) is the primary forum for that. They can make proposals, vote on proposals, contribute to the debate, make public statements in the media, organize social pressure, and walk away from a company they no longer want to support by selling their shares. Active shareholders can keep management on its toes (Poulsen et al., 2010). Social or environmental activist groups sometimes buy shares of companies and get organized to exert pressure on management. For example, there is the Association of Ethical Shareholders in Germany which are active at the AGMs of all companies listed in the German prime stock index DAX (Association of Ethical Shareholders, 2022).

**The Threat of Takeover:** The threat of being taken over by another company can exert pressure on management to perform well. If the performance of top management is bad, the share price will drop, so the company becomes inexpensive to buy. A so-called raider, such as a private equity fund, may buy the firm. The first thing they will do is to replace management with new management that they expect to perform better. If the share price then increases, the raider can sell the company at a higher price and make a profit. In reality, takeovers do not always create value. Nevertheless, there is empirical evidence that a realistic threat of being taken over does exert pressure on management to perform well in the interest of shareholders (Masulis et al., 2007).

**Boards:** Boards of Directors are a crucial element of corporate governance. The board is elected by the shareholders (and in some countries, employees elect a part of the board) to control and monitor the management on their behalf. Boards appoint and dismiss the top management of the firm. Besides, board members, who are frequently experienced managers, advise management, draw on their network to benefit the firm, ensure a suitable strategy, and decide on key matters such as auditing the financial statements and compensation of executives (Adams et al., 2010). In a later section of this chapter, we will outline the differences between boards in different countries' CG systems.

**Incentive Systems:** You will remember that besides monitoring management, providing incentives is another option to address the agency problem type I. Therefore, many stock-listed firms offer performance-based incentives to managers as part of remuneration to align the interests of managers more closely with those of the shareholders. This could be bonuses, stock grants, or stock options. However, incentives can become part of the problem if not correctly designed. They can lead to short-term thinking and excessive risk-taking (Mallin, 2019, pp. 243–249). This can be seen in the opening cases of RBS, Enron, and Barings Bank.

**Stakeholder Pressure: Creditors, Auditors, and Analysts:** Finally, several outside stakeholders play a role as mechanisms for corporate governance. *Creditors*, especially banks that provide a significant loan to a company, have an interest in monitoring the management of a company. Their capital provided to the firm and the agreed interest payments are at stake. However, this plays a prominent role only when a firm has significant debt (Diamond, 1984). *Auditors* check the financial statements of stock-listed firms to testify that they have been set up correctly in line with generally agreed principles of accounting and present a true and fair view of the firm's financial position and performance. Thereby, they can help ensure that the financial information provided to shareholders is reliable, which reduces the information asymmetry between management and shareholders. However, as the role of Arthur Andersen in the Enron scandal has shown, for various reasons, auditors may not always spot irregularities (Asthana et al., 2010). *Analysts* employed by stockbrokers, investment banks, or rating agencies issue analyses of listed companies, resulting in recommendations to buy, hold or sell the company's shares. This provides handy information for investors without their own analysis capabilities. However, also analysts may have conflicts of interest. They are often criticized for issuing too positive or optimistic reports (Lin & McNichols, 1998).

## International Corporate Governance Systems

In the international context, countries vary in which of the outlined mechanisms are used to what extent and in which shape. Therefore, it has become common to talk about different CG systems.

**Corporate Governance System**

We define a country's *corporate governance system* as a set of governance mechanisms in use in a given country or context (Thomsen & Conyon, 2012, p. 68).

To simplify the analysis of the complex CG systems worldwide, typologies or taxonomies have been created that highlight the major differences. We will discuss here four major dimensions (see ◘ Fig. 11.5):

| | |
|---|---|
| Market-based system | Bank-based system |
| Dispersed ownership | Concentrated ownership |
| Stakeholder-based system | Shareholder-based system |
| Unitary (one-tier) board | Dual (two-tier) board |

◘ **Fig. 11.5** A taxonomy of corporate governance systems, based on content from Thomsen and Conyon (2012, pp. 69, 75–76)

We must add, though, that these dimensions and the classification of countries along them constitute a simplification of reality. In reality, CG systems are more complex. For example, while it is more common for US firms to list on the stock market for financing than for German firms that are more likely to take up bank loans, not all US firms are listed, and not in all German firms banks play a significant role. Things are also changing over time. For example, while traditionally, in Germany, banks held significant shares in the biggest German stock-listed companies, these blockholdings by banks have been reduced (Thomsen & Conyon, 2012, pp. 68–69).

## Shareholder vs. Stakeholder System

You will remember how agency problems type I and II outlined above focused on protecting shareholders. In contrast, agency type III extended the perspective to address the interests of other stakeholders, such as employees and creditors. In some countries, the CG system mainly focuses on protecting shareholders, and the focus is on mitigating the agency type I (and type II) problem. This system is called the shareholder system. The United States is a country typically associated with the shareholder focus. In other countries, managers are expected to consider the interests of other stakeholders besides the shareholders, especially employees, to a greater extent. Accordingly, this system is labeled as a stakeholder system, and the CG system is also supposed to address the type III agency problem more explicitly. Continental Europe and the Scandinavian countries are classic examples. This is also connected to political systems. Countries mainly governed by socialist or social democratic parties tend toward a stakeholder system, while those ruled mainly by conservative governments favor a shareholder system (Goergen, 2018, p. 70). Consider how Jeff Skilling, the former CEO of the US company Enron, stated in the congress committee where he was questioned following the scandal: "Everything I did was in the interest of the shareholders of the company" (Gibney, 2005). Compare this to how the responsibility of the management board of listed companies in German corporate governance is described: "The Management Board is responsible for independently managing the enterprise in the interest of the enterprise, thus taking into account the interests of the shareholders, *its employees, and other stakeholders*, with the objective of sustainable creation of value" (Regierungskommission Deutscher Corporate Governance Kodex, 2015, p. 6, emphasis added).

## Market-Based vs. Bank-Based Systems

One can divide CG systems into market-based and bank-based systems. Market-based systems have a well-developed capital market, and many companies issue shares in the stock market to obtain financing. This is supported by strong protection of shareholder rights (La Porta et al., 1997). In bank-based systems, capital markets are less well-developed, and companies are more likely to turn to banks to obtain loans for financing. The latter applies to Germany, France, and Japan (Mayer, 1988). Historic regulation, especially of financial services, has played a role here. In the United States, banks are not allowed to hold more than 5% equity stakes in non-financial companies, while other financial institutions are only allowed to hold a limited stake. In Japan and Germany, on the contrary, less restrictions allowed the development of a more substantial role of banks in corporate governance (Roe, 1996, pp. 98–99, 169–186). Private households in market-based systems are more likely to invest directly in the stocks of companies. In contrast, this is less prevalent in bank-based systems, and households tend to put their money in a bank, which then provides it to corporations (Allen & Gale, 2001, pp. 49–50). In countries like Germany, banks can play the role of custodians for shareholders and vote on their behalf at the AGM. Banks may also sit on the board of companies, which is not the case in market-based systems (Mallin, 2019, p. 279). So, in bank-based systems, banks can play an essential role in CG.

Deutsche Bank. In Germany, banks like Deutsche Bank can play a significant role in corporate governance, image by Sabine Lange from Pixabay

## Concentrated vs. Dispersed Ownership

Take a look at ◘ Fig. 11.6. It shows the average control stake, that is, the voting rights, of the largest shareholder of stock-listed companies across the United States and a range of European countries. What do you notice?

While in the United States and United Kingdom, the average stake of the largest shareholder is relatively small—between 9% and 14%—it is much more significant in most other countries. Indeed, in the United States and United Kingdom, only 2% of stock-listed firms are controlled by a majority shareholder. In other countries, two-thirds of listed companies have shareholders who hold most of the shares and exercise control. In the United States and United Kingdom, in most listed firms, the largest shareholder does not even have a 25% blocking minority. In Continental Western Europe, one shareholder or a group of shareholders (remember the case of L'Oréal above) frequently has a controlling majority (Goergen, 2018, pp. 26–31). In other words, while in the United States and United Kingdom, it is common for ownership of stock-listed companies to be *dispersed*, in most other countries, it is rather *concentrated*. There are several consequences of this. In countries with dispersed ownership, there is no direct personal communication with investors. Communication occurs via the company's published information and shareholders' buy or sell decisions. If shareholders are not happy, they will sell their shares, and the share price will drop, which sends a signal to management. When ownership is concentrated, there will be an ongoing personal dialogue with the major shareholders. For the same reason, the responsibility of management in companies with dispersed ownership is diffused (to the public or "the (anonymous) shareholders"). In contrast, in firms with concentrated ownership, it is much more direct and personal (Becht & Mayer, 2001). Remember the L'Oréal



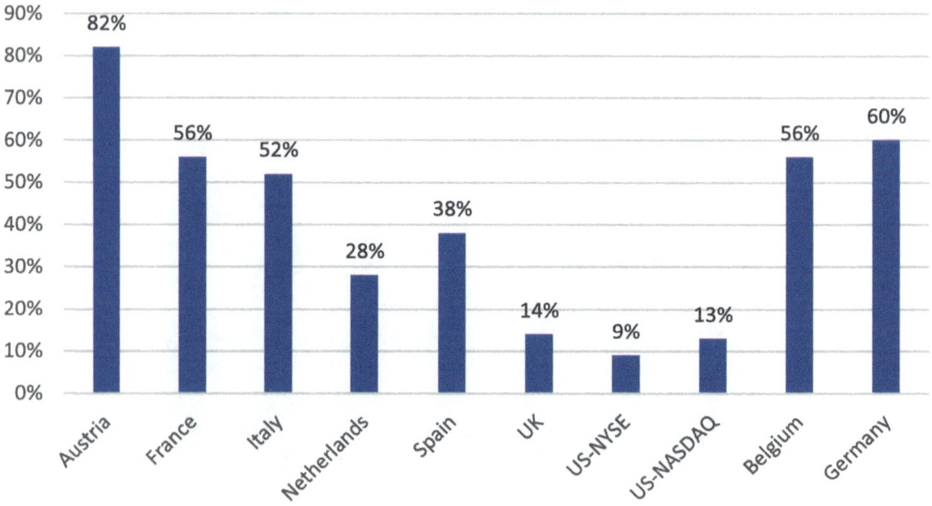


◘ **Fig. 11.6** Average control stake of largest shareholder (rounded), All data from 1996, except Belgium (1994) and United Kingdom (1993), based on data from (Goergen, 2018, p. 30)

example. Mrs. Bettencourt and the person at Nestlé in charge of the L'Oréal shareholding of Nestlé will undoubtedly have the phone number of L'Oréal's CEO. When they call, the CEO will certainly pick up the phone and talk to them as they are the firm's controlling shareholders. Consequently, in countries with dispersed ownership, the classic type I agency problem between owner and manager is of major concern as many small owners find it difficult to control and monitor the management closely, as outlined above. In countries with concentrated ownership—most countries in the world—the type II agency problem is more acute as the majority shareholders might abuse their power in a way that benefits them but damages the interest of the smaller shareholders, as outlined above (Goergen, 2018, p. 12).

## One-Tier vs. Two-Tier Board

We mentioned boards as an essential mechanism of corporate governance. In practice, there are two types of board systems: *unitary (one-tier)* and *dual (two-tier)* systems (see ◘ Fig. 11.7). The dual system has two boards: a management board and a supervisory board. The management board is in charge of the firm's day-to-day management, while the supervisory board exclusively focuses on monitoring and controlling the management board. The supervisory board gets elected by the shareholders and appoints management board members. In some countries, like Germany and Austria, employees can also elect some of the supervisory board members. Members of the supervisory board are exclusively outsiders, that is, non-executives of the firm. In the unitary system, there is just one board composed of

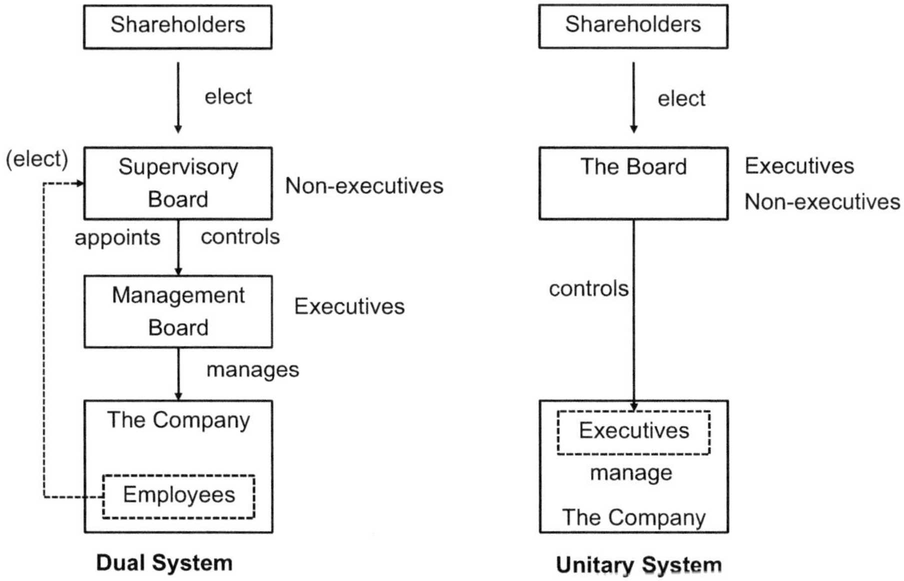


◘ **Fig. 11.7** Board systems, inspired by Thomsen and Conyon (2012, p. 75)

executives, such as the CEO and CFO, and independent non-executives. The members of the board get elected by shareholders. The unitary board is common, for example, in the United States, United Kingdom, Japan, Italy, and most companies in France. The case of France is interesting because companies can choose, and most do choose, the unitary system. The dual board is common, for example, in Germany, Scandinavia, and China. There is a discussion on the advantages and drawbacks of both systems. Proponents of the two-tier system argue that the directors of the supervisory board can be more independent from the firm's executives and, therefore, better monitor and control the management board. Proponents of the one-tier board argue that it has better information about what is going on in the firm due to the membership of the executive directors. In contrast, the supervisory board in a two-tier system has very little information to enable it to monitor effectively (Goergen, 2018, p. 115). We would add that in the dual system, responsibilities are more clearly separated: One board manages, and the other controls. However, shareholders cannot directly elect the board's executives. They can only do so indirectly via the supervisory board. The unitary system provides shareholders with more direct influence on the appointment of key executives. However, the question is whether shareholders have enough information to make an informed decision.

**Chairman—CEO Duality:** In countries with a unitary board, there is a further issue to consider: Should the CEO also be the board's chairperson? While this is commonly the case in the United States, in the United Kingdom, it is prohibited. The pros and cons of separating the roles have been discussed intensively. Arguments in favor of separation are: Duality can create a conflict of interest as the chairperson needs to monitor and control his or her own work. Can he or she really represent the interests of the shareholders? It dilutes the system of checks and balances. One person may have too much power, reducing the board's effectiveness. Separation guarantees better independence of the board (Rechner & Dalton, 1991). Arguments against separation are: The CEO has the greatest reputational and financial risk and, therefore, the greatest incentive to monitor. The CEO has a much greater insight into the strategy and operations of the firm than an independent chairman who must rely on the CEO to provide that information. Having two different leadership positions could lead to confusion about who of the two speaks on behalf of the company (Brickley et al., 1997).



## Corporate Governance in Service Firms

We started the review of CG mechanisms with informal mechanisms, particularly corporate values. Thomsen finds that corporate values are influenced significantly by interactions with important stakeholders of the firm (besides by their ownership structure and the board). In service firms, where human capital and the retention of employees plays a crucial role, the corporate culture will tend to emphasize employee satisfaction and, therefore, employees as stakeholders (Thomsen, 2004).

Regarding the agency problems, we mentioned how relevant related party transactions (type II problem) are to service firms because many of these transactions involve providing services to the company in focus. A trend among professional service firms also makes the traditional owner–manager problem (type I problem) more relevant for some of them. Traditionally, most PSFs, especially accounting and law firms, and many consulting firms and others, have been partnerships. That is, the partners, who are also the owners of the firms, have managed them (Empson, 2012). Therefore, there was no separation of ownership and control; accordingly, the owner–manager problem did not occur. Increasingly, however, many larger PSFs changed governance to a corporate structure such as limited liability partnership (LLP), private corporations, and corporations listed on the stock exchange. For example, partnerships now constitute a minority among large advertising, consulting, and architecture firms. Some accounting and law firms have also been listed on the stock exchange in countries like the United States, United Kingdom, and Australia. Thus, the agency type I problem now also becomes relevant for them. However, there are some specifics to PSFs that create specific agency issues. As you know by now, monitoring and control are essential in CG. However, the complex and non-routine characteristics of professional services make it challenging to apply formal controls, especially by external owners who may have a limited understanding of the services provided. In partnerships, there can also be internal agency problems when, as the firm grows, management is delegated to a sub-group of partners that may have different objectives and time horizons than the broader group of partners (owners). Listing on the stock market creates the potential for having large owners (blockholders). Therefore, the agency type II problem can also arise (Pickering, 2015).

In the remainder of this chapter, we will outline various forms of governance found in professional service firms.

## Types of Governance in PSFs

In PSFs, Harlacher and Reihlen (2014) found four types of legal forms: the public corporation, the private corporation, the Limited Liability Partnership (LLP), and the general partnership. In private corporations and general partnerships, ownership lies with the professionals (partners) working there. While in private corporations, partners' liability for actions of other partners is usually limited, in general partnerships, it is unlimited. In public corporations, ownership lies with the external shareholders of the firm, so a separation of ownership and management occurs. Over the past 20–30 years, the LLP has been introduced, with elements of partnership and corporation, with limited liability for partners. Harlacher and Reihlen (2014) distinguish four types of governance in PSFs:

**Founder-Dominated Governance:** In these PSFs, ownership resides with only the founder or founders of the firm. For example, until the 1990s, consulting firm Bain & Company was owned by only Bill Bain and seven senior professionals. Control is concentrated on a few professionals. In most cases, this form is found in smaller firms. Most firms move to another type as they grow.

**Collegial Governance:** In these PSFs, control remains internally, with the firm's partners sharing control over decision-making. So, partners can participate widely in decisions. Some of these PSFs are still general partnerships, while others have moved on to an LLP. For example, the New York-based law firm Wachtell, Lipton, Rosen, and Katz is still a general partnership. There is no partnership agreement, only a "handshake between friends" (Harlacher & Reihlen, 2014, p. 144). This can be found among non-diversified PSFs with customized services that are still relatively small. This type can work well when professionals share common values and beliefs. It is also most likely to be found in an environment with a low risk of litigation against the PSF.

**Managerial Governance:** In PSFs with this type of governance, partners' autonomy and self-governance are replaced by more managerial control, hierarchical decision-making, and formalization. These firms often have limited liability and are frequently externally owned. While the large audit firms have been largely excluded from external ownership, they lobbied for the LLP and frequently adopted this legal form where possible. Capgemini is a good example, offering a broad range of IT consulting, management consulting, and outsourcing services. They have centralized decision-making where central group management sets rules and procedures for the decentral operating units with some autonomy. Some of the Big Four audit firms have created regionally integrated partnerships. While such firms legally remain partnerships, partners have lost voting right as critical decisions are now made by a body of elected executives at the regional level (Klimkeit & Reihlen, 2016). The managerial governance can be explained by the large size and high level of specialization in a broad range of services, for which collegial governance is no longer appropriate. The increased need for capital investments favors external ownership. This governance form also occurs when the risk of litigation is high. This is one factor driving large audit firms toward managerial governance as the risk of litigation has increased.



**Entrepreneurial Governance:** The entrepreneurial type of PSF governance has commonalities with the managerial type, such as hierarchical decision-making and decentralized control rights. However, it is more decentralized. The global advertising network WPP we introduced in ► Chap. 9 is an example of entrepreneurial governance with external ownership. Another example, US law firm Greenberg Traurig LLP, is internally owned. At the law firm, power is centralized in the CEO position. Committees, common in the collegial form, are seen as too slow. At the same time, individual partners have much autonomy in providing their services and can easily set up new practice areas. This is to maximize the capturing of market opportunities, and indeed, the firm has quickly expanded internationally. Management is not very formalized; however, finances are controlled strictly. This type can be found in large PSFs due to the focus on fast growth and the diversification of services offered. This type of governance is suitable for low to medium levels of litigation; otherwise, PSFs would require more formalization.

### ❓ Review Questions

1. Define and explain the term "corporate governance."
2. Why should we care about corporate governance?
3. Why is CG less of an issue in family-owned and -managed firms?
4. How can adverse selection and moral hazard be distinguished?

5. Why can empire-building often cause greater damage than perks?
6. Why are the described related-party transactions categorized as an "expropriation of minority shareholders"?
7. Define the three types of agency problems.
8. Why is the agency type III problem labeled as the "extended agency problem"?
9. Should managers also pay attention to other stakeholders besides the shareholders?
10. Outline the various types of CG mechanisms.
11. Why is a combination of various mechanisms necessary to mitigate agency problems?
12. Outline the four described dimensions by which CG systems differ.
13. How would you characterize the CG system of your country along the four dimensions?
14. How can the four types of governance systems in PSFs be distinguished?
15. How is the relevance of the type I and type II agency problem different for PSFs, and how has this partly changed?

## Closing Case: Wirecard

When Matthew Earl, a London-based short seller, called the BaFin whistleblower hotline to report suspicious business practices at Wirecard, the person who answered the phone said he did not understand English well enough. When Earl called again, the respondent simply hung up. When the Wirecard scandal became public in 2020, Felix Hufeld, head of the German financial services watchdog BaFin, stated that the case was a "complete disaster" and a "shame for Germany" (Holtermann & Schnell, 2020, p. 53). The German minister of the economy added that he would have expected such a situation

Mobile payment. Image by Photo Mix from Pixabay

anywhere but not in Germany. Wirecard became the biggest scandal in the history of the German prime stock market segment DAX30.

These statements highlight a crucial point: Everyone with influence—auditors, board, regulators—seems to have failed in their role. On June 18, 2020, Wirecard's auditor EY said it could not find €1.9b that was supposed to be held in accounts in the Philippines. Wirecard then withdrew its financial statements for the last fiscal year, and CEO Markus Braun resigned. On June 22, Wirecard admitted that the €1.9b "probably does not exist." Later that day, Braun was arrested, accused of fraudulent accounting techniques to inflate reported revenues. On June 25, insolvency proceedings started.

Wirecard was founded in 1998 to enable secure online payment by credit card. In 2002, Markus Braun became the CEO. In the 2010s, Wirecard showed rapid growth. Investors loved Wirecard for the grand visions of its CEO. He liked to paint the big picture and talked about data, artificial intelligence, and the Internet of Things. In 2018, Wirecard replaced Commerzbank in the DAX30 Prime Standard of the German stock market, and its share price rose to 195 euros. There was much hype about the company, and many in Germany expected it to become the new SAP, a new star of the digital economy. Most did not want to hear or believe that the Wirecard story might not be true. The prominent Japanese investor SoftBank invested $1b in 2019, appeasing the doubts of other investors. In 2019, more than five years after the first reports of accounting irregularities, only 2 out of 26 analysts recommended selling Wirecard's shares. Until Braun resigned, half a dozen banks still issued buy recommendations.

Wirecard obtained about half of its alleged revenues from so-called Third Party Acquirers (TPA) in countries where it did not have a presence, especially in Asia and the Near East. An article in the Financial Times in October 2019 claimed the TPA business was more than doubtful. About half of the TPA profits allegedly came from a partner firm in Dubai. However, a journalist found that the alleged customers of this firm had never heard of it or could not be found. In 2019 investor Softbank pressed for a special audit by another audit firm, and KPMG was commissioned with this. KPMG used forensic methods that assumed fraud and found several irregularities. This raised questions about EY, who had audited Wirecard's financial statements for 11 years and testified it. Why didn't EY verify with the trustee in the Philippines that the alleged balance of €1.9b existed? EY defended itself by claiming that there were clear indications that this was an elaborate and sophisticated fraud involving a wide variety of parties around the world from different institutions, with the aim of deceiving.

Analysts, asset managers, regulators, and auditors seem to have ignored the red flags. Bernd Ziesemer of the Cologne School of Journalists claimed that the board members of Wirecard lacked competence for a multinational tech firm. The role of BaFin, the German regulator, was especially questionable. In 2016, short sellers released a

11

report accusing Wirecard of corruption, fraud, and weak money laundering controls. In 2019, the Financial Times published an investigation into dubious accounting practices. In response, BaFin filed a criminal complaint about two FT journalists and several short sellers. It banned short selling of Wirecard stocks, something unprecedented in Germany's stock market. What made things worse were allegations of insider trading of Wirecard shares by BaFin employees. On January 29, 2021, finance minister Olaf Scholz fired Hufeld and his deputy at BaFin. The supervision of Wirecard had been split between BaFin and other agencies, some not at the federal but state level. Scholz announced he would look worldwide for a new leader of Bafin. Mark Branson, the previous boss of the Swiss financial watchdog, was convinced to take on the tough job of reforming BaFin. In line with the finance minister's preference, he is an outsider with international experience who knows the banking industry. Now BaFin is supposed to have complete oversight of complex companies. A task force will conduct a forensic audit of firms suspected of fraud. Whistleblowers are now to be taken seriously. Hopefully, the person operating the whistleblower hotline will also receive English language training.

As the German finance newspaper Handelsblatt concludes in an analysis of the Wirecard case:

> "Wirecard is an instructive piece about the abysses of the business world, about technology faith, investor greed, sloppiness, and about a hunger for greatness that leads to ruin"
> (Holtermann & Schnell, 2020, p. 53).

**Questions**

1. Which agency problem can you identify at Wirecard?
2. Which mechanisms of corporate governance have failed at Wirecard?
3. Can you identify parallels between Wirecard and Enron?
4. Despite the awareness raised by scandals like Enron and the improvements in CG systems made worldwide following the scandals at the beginning of the twenty-first century, how can such a scandal still occur?

Sources: (Economist, 2020a, 2020b, 2021a, 2021b, 2022; Holtermann & Schnell, 2020)

**Summary**

This chapter

- Has defined corporate governance as "the combination of mechanisms which ensure that the management (the agent) runs the firm for the benefit of one or several stakeholders (principals)"
- Has defined the primary aim of CG as "to ensure that the company is managed in the best interest of the shareholders and the other stakeholders"
- Has outlined the classic agency problem, where "the principal is anyone who hires someone else to do a certain job while the agent is the person hired"

- Explained adverse selection and moral hazard as two forms of information asymmetry, which foster the classic agency problem between owners and managers of stock-listed firms
- Defined perks as "on-the-job consumption by the firm's managers" where "the benefits from the perks accrue to the managers, their costs are borne by the shareholders"
- Defined empire building as "the management pursuing growth rather than shareholder value maximization"
- Besides the classic agency problem (type I), the expropriation of minority shareholders by majority shareholders was outlined as the agency type II problem, consisting primarily of tunneling or the use of transfer prices in related-party transactions
- The extended agency problem (type III) was explained as the clash of interests between shareholders and other stakeholders
- Various forms of mechanisms of CG were outlined that aim at mitigating the agency problem
- A CG system was defined as "a set of governance mechanisms in use in a given country or context"
- CG systems around the world were distinguished by the dimensions
- Market vs. bank-based systems
- Dispersed vs. concentrated ownership
- Stakeholder vs. shareholder-based systems
- One-tier (unitary) vs. two-tier (dual) board systems
- Specifics of corporate governance in (professional) service firms were addressed, distinguishing various types of governance in PSFs



## References


Adams, R. B., Hermalin, B. E., & Weisbach, M. S. (2010). The role of boards of directors in corporate governance: A conceptual framework and survey. *Journal of Economic Literature, 48*(1), 58–107.

Aguilera, R. V., Goyer, M., & Kabbach-Castro, L. R. (2013). Regulation and comparative corporate governance. In M. Wright, D. S. Siegel, K. Keasey, & I. Filatotchev (Eds.), *The Oxford handbook of corporate governance* (pp. 23–45). Oxford University Press.

Allen, F., & Gale, D. (2001). *Comparing financial systems*. MIT Press.

Association of Ethical Shareholders. (2022). *About us*. Retrieved from https://www.kritischeaktionaere.de/en/about-us/

Asthana, S. C., Balsam, S., & Krishnan, J. (2010). Corporate governance, audit firm reputation, auditor switches, and client stock price reactions: The Andersen experience. *International Journal of Auditing, 14*(3), 274–293.

Becht, M., & Mayer, C. (2001). Introduction. In F. Barca & M. Becht (Eds.), *The control of corporate Europe* (pp. 1–45). Oxford University Press.

Brickley, J. A., Coles, J. L., & Jarrell, G. (1997). Leadership structure: Separating the CEO and chairman of the board. *Journal of Corporate Finance, 3*(3), 189–220.

Cadbury, A. (1992). *Report of the committee on the financial aspects of corporate governance*. Gee.

Diamond, D. W. (1984). Financial intermediation and delegated monitoring. *The Review of Economic Studies, 51*(3), 393–414.

Dyck, A., & Zingales, L. (2002). The corporate governance role of the media. In The World Bank Group (Ed.), *The right to tell: The role of mass media in economic development* (pp. 107–140).
Economist (2020a, June 27). *How Wirecard fooled most of the people all of the time*. Economist, 2020.
Economist (2020b, June 27). *Wirecard's scandal shows the benefits of short-sellers*. Economist, 2020.
Economist (2021a, February 4). *Germany's finance minister promises to overhaul financial regulation*. Economist, 2021.
Economist (2021b, May 27). *Battered Bafin's new boss Branson*. Economist, 2021.
Economist (2022, June 18). *How one journalist exposed the Wirecard scandal*. Economist, 2022.
Empson, L. (2012). Beyond dichotomies: A multi-stage model of governance in professional service firms. In M. Reihlen & A. Werr (Eds.), *Handbook of research on entrepreneurship in professional services* (pp. 274–294). Edward Elgar Publishing.
Gibney, A. (Director). (2005). Enron. *The smartest guys in the room*.
Goergen, M. (2018). *Corporate governance: A global perspective* (1st ed.). Cengage Learning EMEA.
Goergen, M., & Renneboog, L. (2008). Corporate governance and shareholder value. In D. Lowe & R. Leiringer (Eds.), *Commercial management of projects: Defining the discipline* (pp. 100–131). John Wiley & Sons.
Gordon, E. A., Henry, E., & Palia, D. (2004). Related party transactions and corporate governance. *Corporate Governance, 9*, 1–27.
Harlacher, D., & Reihlen, M. (2014). Governance of professional service firms: A configurational approach. *Business Research, 7*(1), 125–160.
Holtermann, F., & Schnell, C. (2020, June 26). Der Fall Wirecard. *Handelsblatt, 2020*(121), 52–60.
Jakobs, H.-J. (2019, August 23). Vom Himmel zur Hölle und zurück. *Handelsblatt, 2019*(162).
Jensen, M. C. (1986). The agency cost of overvalued equity and the current state of corporate finance. *American Economic Review, 76*(2), 323–329.
Jensen, M. C., & Meckling, W. H. (1976). Theory of the firm: Managerial behavior, agency costs and ownership structure. *Journal of Financial Economics, 3*(4), 305–360.
Johnson, S., La Porta, R., Lopez-de-Silanes, F., & Shleifer, A. (2000). Tunneling. *American Economic Review, 90*(2), 22–27.
Klimkeit, D., & Reihlen, M. (2016). Local responses to global integration in transnational professional service firms. *Journal of Professions & Organization, 3*(1), 39–61.
La Porta, R., Lopez-de-Silanes, F., Shleifer, A., & Vishny, R. W. (1997). Legal determinants of external finance. *The Journal of Finance, 52*(3), 1131–1150.
Levine, M. H., Fitzsimons, A. P., & Siegel, J. G. (1997). Auditing related party transactions. *CPA Journal, 67*(3), 46–50.
Lin, H., & McNichols, M. F. (1998). Underwriting relationships, analysts' earnings forecasts and investment recommendations. *Journal of Accounting and Economics, 25*(1), 101–127.
L'Oréal Finance. (2023) *Share ownership*. Retrieved from https://www.loreal-finance.com/eng/share-ownership
Mallin, C. A. (2019). *Corporate governance* (6th ed.). Oxford University Press.
Masulis, R. W., Wang, C., & Xie, F. (2007). Corporate governance and acquirer returns. *The Journal of Finance, 62*(4), 1851–1889.
Mayer, C. (1988). New issues in corporate finance. *European Economic Review, 32*(5), 1167–1183.
Padgett, C. (2012). *Corporate governance: Theory and practice*. Palgrave Macmillan.
Pickering, M. E. (2015). An exploratory study of organizational governance in publicly-quoted professional service firms. *Organization Studies, 36*(6), 779–807.
Poulsen, T., Strand, T., & Thomsen, S. (2010). Voting power and shareholder activism: A study of Swedish shareholder meetings. *Corporate Governance: An International Review, 18*(4), 329–343.
Rechner, P. L., & Dalton, D. R. (1991). CEO duality and organizational performance: A longitudinal analysis. *Strategic Management Journal, 12*(2), 155–160.
Regierungskommission Deutscher Corporate Governance Kodex. (2015). *German Corporate Governance Code*. Retrieved from https://dcgk.de/files/dcgk/usercontent/en/download/code/2015-05-05_Corporate_Governance_Code_EN.pdf
Rezaee, Z. (2009). *Corporate governance and ethics*. John Wiley & Sons, Inc.
Roe, M. J. (1996). *Strong managers, weak owners: The political roots of American Corporate Finance*. Princeton University Press.

Rutherford, M. A., Buchholtz, A. K., & Brown, J. A. (2007). Examining the relationships between monitoring and incentives in corporate governance. *Journal of Management Studies, 44*(3), 414–430.

Thomsen, S. (2004). Corporate values and corporate governance. *Corporate Governance: The International Journal of Business in Society, 4*(4), 29–46.

Thomsen, S., & Conyon, M. (2012). *Corporate governance: Mechanisms and systems*. McGraw-Hill Higher Education.

Yermack, D. (2006). Flights of fancy: Corporate jets, CEO perquisites, and inferior shareholder returns. *Journal of Financial Economics, 80*(1), 211–242.

## Further Reading

ECGI. (n.d.). *The European Corporate Governance Institute has an extensive collection of CG codes from around the world on its website*. Retrieved from https://ecgi.global/content/codes.

Mallin, C. A. (2019). *Corporate Governance* (6th ed.). Oxford University Press contains descriptions of CG systems in many countries worldwide.

# International Ethics and Corporate Social Responsibility

## Contents




D. Klimkeit et al., *International Management in Service Firms*, Classroom Companion: Business,
https://doi.org/10.1007/978-3-031-50345-0_12

**Learning Outcomes**

After completing this chapter, you should be able to:

- define and identify stakeholders that a multinational service firm has to deal with
- identify different stakeholders' interests and goals and the implication on a multinational service firm's strategy and operation
- explain the ethical dilemmas a multinational service firm faces in its international operation
- outline the moral approaches a multinational service firm can employ to deal with the ethical dilemmas
- identify forms of inappropriate conduct of multinationals abroad
- define corporate social responsibility
- explain the three models that a multinational service company could rely on when designing and implementing corporate social responsibility
- understand the causes and consequences of corporate social responsibility greenwashing

## Introduction

This chapter first outlines ethical questions that face service firms in their global operations and the moral approaches multinational service firms could adopt to deal with the ethical dilemmas. It then identifies some typical inappropriate conduct of multinationals abroad. The chapter further highlights that considering the intangible characteristics of services and the corresponding difficulty for customers to assess services, service multinationals engage in corporate social responsibilities to gain legitimacy in the foreign market. The chapter thus illustrates a few frameworks that guide companies to act responsibly towards their people, local communities, the environment, and other stakeholders.

Road in India image by ► Pexels from ► Pixabay

## Opening Case: Uber in India

It turned out to be a bad week for Uber—Uber was banned in Delhi, India, on Monday, 8 Dec 2014, after one of its drivers was charged with raping a female passenger over the weekend. The police were checking whether the company should have vetted its drivers better.

In fact, Uber, a San Francisco-based ride-sharing company, has faced criticism and protests from various stakeholders since it first entered the Indian market in 2013.

As India's economy has grown over the last 40 years, hundreds of millions of people have moved to urban areas from villages. India now has three cities, Mumbai, Delhi, and Kolkata, with more than 15 million residents, and it has dozens more with more than a million. Yet India's urban infrastructure has not kept up. By the turn of the last century, transportation scholars began warning of an urban transportation crisis that had driven air and noise pollution, traffic, and road fatalities to some of the highest levels in the world. It is especially difficult for India's poor to get around. A tiny slice of the wealthiest Indians can afford private cars and drivers to ferry them. Others are left with fewer choices: bicycles, scooters, bicycle rickshaws, motorized rickshaws, and buses so crowded that passengers hang out the door. Most Indian cities lack adequate public transportation, and walking can be perilous because of the foul air and the dearth of sidewalks. In Bangalore, three pedestrians are killed on the roads every 2 days.

This presented an opportunity for Uber, which thought technology would enable it to provide rides cheaper than other forms of transportation and more accessible to a wider swath of Indians.

The entry of Uber was good news for consumers and local communities. Before the hailing service existed, getting a cab in most Indian cities was expensive and difficult. People even had to call a taxi one day in advance. Compared to other options available to most Indian riders, Uber, together with another local ride-hailing service provider, Ola, represented an improvement in transportation access and a steep price drop for consumers. In Bangalore, a 22-mile Uber ride that lasted nearly an hour cost only 548 rupees, or about $8.50. That was on UberX, the company's middle-tier service; with UberGo, which uses smaller cars, it might have been a dollar or two cheaper. A taxi taking the same route might have cost more than $10. With these prices and convenience, Uber is becoming an everyday option for India's rising middle class. Citizens of a certain professional class, such as tech workers and frequent travelers, said Uber and Ola had become part of the fabric of Indian urban life. Before Uber, "folks were rather locked up at home," said Christian Freese, the general manager for Uber's Bangalore office, where the company has placed its only dedicated engineering center outside San Francisco. "Now you can see people go out, especially on the weekend. You just press a button and the car is there." As a matter of fact, as many as 96% of riders said they use Uber because it is convenient, according to Public First's report. Uber saves riders over 16.8 crore hours a year (Abrar, 2022).

At the same time, the entry of Uber initially became a good option for Indian drivers. Since the entry of Uber into the

Indian market in 2013, many poor, semi-literate Indians have left their jobs to join up, taking out a loan for a car and expecting to increase their earning potential significantly. "They gave us the impression that the sky was the limit in terms of money. They said what we earned all depended on us. I was told by an Uber agent that some drivers were earning up to 90,000 rupees [£1015] a month," said Kumar, one of such poor Indians. He became a "driver-partner," in Uber parlance, in early 2016. By working about 10 h a day, he was able to manage his monthly installment on the car loan, the cost of fuel and maintenance, and enjoy savings of around 50,000 rupees—an astronomical sum for any Indian driver. "For the first time in my life, I could put some money away," he said.

However, at the end of 2016, Uber further reduced the rate per km to provide better value to customers and deal with competition from the local ride-hailing players. "We used to get an incentive of 2000 rupees every day once we had completed a dozen rides. This was cut back to just once a week for doing 40–50 rides. And they hiked their commission from 20% to 25%," said New Delhi Uber driver Naresh Kumar. These rates—along with the other measures—were a disaster for drivers. They could not reduce the size of their monthly car repayments. Those who wanted to sell the car and get out could not do so because the resale value would not be enough to repay the loan. While the ride rates had fallen, petrol and diesel prices had increased. Many drivers angrily accused Uber of making false promises, even "guarantees" about income. In 2018, hundreds of drivers for ride-hailing giant Uber and its local rival Ola went on a strike in the two biggest Indian cities, Delhi and Mumbai, demanding higher fares to meet rising fuel costs that were eating away at their incomes.

Additionally, the company faced push-back from local taxi drivers and unions, who argued that Uber was operating illegally and threatening their livelihoods. Taxi and auto-rickshaw drivers across major Indian cities from Delhi to Mumbai and Bengaluru to Kochi took turns to protest against what they said was a threat to their livelihoods from cab aggregators Uber and Ola. Black and yellow cabs were hit because, in general, Uber and Ola rides were far cheaper than theirs, though the app-based cab services could charge higher fares through a practice known as surge pricing.

On the other hand, Uber faced pressure from the Indian government and regulators to comply with local laws and regulations regarding a range of issues, such as transportation services, including licensing, insurance requirements, and pricing practices. For the past several years, the Modi government has been trying to set rules for cab aggregators, particularly since the rape of a passenger by an Uber driver in December 2014. Soon after that incident, India's home ministry advised all states to ban taxi aggregators. In 2017, a new law was under consideration seeking to bring taxi aggregators under the Motor Vehicles Act. Following this, various state governments must follow the guidelines fixed by the transport ministry while issuing licenses to such companies. States would be free to add additional rules since transport is a state subject.

Uber also had to deal with local government regulations regarding its pricing structure. Uber's revenue depends on the pricing model they use to calculate consumer fares and driver earnings. Uber fears that its pricing model, including dynamic pricing, would likely continue to be challenged, banned, limited in emergencies, and capped in certain jurisdictions.

> "In 2016, following the filing of a petition in the Delhi High Court relating to surge pricing, we agreed to not calculate consumer fares in excess of the maximum government-mandated fares in New Delhi, India," Uber added.

The company said that additional regulation of its pricing model could increase its operating costs and adversely affect its business.

> "As a result, we may be forced to change our pricing model in certain jurisdictions, which could harm our revenue or result in a sub-optimal tax structure," Uber added.

Ever since the rape of a passenger by an Uber driver in December 2014, Uber continued to face challenges in India from other stakeholders, including accusations of lax background checks for drivers and incidents of sexual assault by drivers. Uber said on its website that every ride-sharing driver is investigated using a criminal background check. The company said it reviews each driver's motor vehicle record. But in the reported case in India, the company was accused of not performing a check of the driver's criminal record. These issues resulted in further pressure from human rights groups and other international stakeholders.

In addition, Uber faced regulatory pressure from its home country regarding bribery and corruption. Uber said in May 2017 and August 2017 it received requests from the Department of Justice concerning allegations of "small payments to police in Indonesia and other potential improper payments in other countries in which we operate or have operated, including in Malaysia, China, and India." This investigation remained ongoing. Uber said it was cooperating in the investigation.

> Additional compliance requirements may compel us to revise or expand our compliance program, including the procedures we use to verify the identity of platform users and monitor international and domestic transactions, Uber said.

To address these challenges, Uber engaged in stakeholder communication and collaboration with local communities, regulators, taxi drivers, and its home country government. The company invested in local infrastructure, such as mapping and navigation systems, and established a local call center to provide customer support in different languages. Uber also worked with the Indian government to address regulatory concerns and obtain necessary licenses and permits. Yet the complex nature of its service business model and the international environment makes it even more challenging to balance the expectations of different stakeholders.

**Questions**

1. Which groups of stakeholders can you identify for Uber in India?
2. How do their interests and appeals differ?

Source: (Abrar, 2022; Bhattacharya & Balachandran, 2017; Dhillon, 2018; Jaeger, 2019; Khatri, 2019; Manjoo, 2017; Shah, 2018; Skariachan, 2016; Voice of America, 2014)

## Stakeholders of Multinational Service Firms

### A Stakeholder Perspective

The global environment in which multinational service firms operate is fraught with significant environmental, economic, technological, political, social, ethical, and human subjects issues (Lawrence & Weber, 2011). A stakeholder perspective is useful for understanding service firms' complex environments. The stakeholder perspective, detailed by Freeman (1984), highlights the interdependence of a company and its stakeholders.

> **Stakeholders**
>
> *Stakeholders* are any group of individuals who could be affected by the actions that companies perform to achieve their objectives.

Because, as the definition states, stakeholders are affected by the actions of the company, they have certain interests and expectations toward the company. Under this paradigm, companies will try to satisfy their stakeholders, both internally (employees, management, and shareholders) and externally (customers, suppliers, authorities, local communities, media, and so on.).

### Primary Stakeholders and Their Conflicting Interests



Then who are the primary stakeholders? Although the answer to the question depends on the business model and industry in which the company operates, there are a few commonly agreed important primary stakeholders, and they have different interests towards the company, for example:

- **Shareholders** are interested in dividends and obtaining capital gains by investing in the company. They want the company to continue growing and generating more profits, positively affecting dividends distributed and capital gains.
- **Employees and management** are interested in high salaries, benefits, a healthy work environment, promising career paths, and adequate training and development programs. In turn, employees affect the company with their commitment and performance. Management makes decisions that have a significant impact on a company's success.
- **Customers** are interested in a company's products, services, and privacy protection. An increasing number of customers are also interested in business ethics and appreciate socially and environmentally responsible companies that are not just pursuing profit.
- **Suppliers** have an interest in the purchase of inputs by the company. They want companies to pay on time, keep ordering from them, and buy in bulk. They do

not like companies switching to other suppliers since this will reduce their revenue.
- The **government** is interested in companies paying taxes on time and complying with regulations. The government also requires companies to run environmentally responsible businesses, refrain from anti-competitive behavior, and adopt fair employment practices. Another interest is the jobs and income businesses create in the economy.
- **Creditors** want the company to pay principal and interest on time. Therefore, they pay attention to the company's liquidity and solvency.
- **Local communities** are concerned about the jobs created by the company. They want the company to recruit local workers. They also desire the company to carry out environmentally responsible business practices, not generate negative externalities, and support local community programs.

Each stakeholder seeks to protect their own interests and achieve their own goals. These interests and goals are often conflicting, thus making it challenging for companies to fulfill all their wishes. ◘ Table 12.1 lists some of the conflicting interests among stakeholders.

While the stakeholder situation of companies operating only in their domestic market is already complex, the complexity of stakeholder groups increases for

◘ **Table 12.1** Conflicting interests among stakeholders, source: Author's own table

| | |
|---|---|
| Higher wages vs higher dividends | Shareholders generally want the company's profits to increase because it affects the dividends and capital gains. So, they are reluctant to see businesses pay high wages to employees |
| Higher short-term earnings vs business expansion | The expansion increases the business size and scale of the company's operations. It creates new jobs, which the local community and government appreciate<br>However, to expand, companies must spend more to buy capital goods such as machinery and equipment or build new factories. It all results in less short-term profit and, therefore, lower dividends. Shareholders with a short-term investment horizon may not like it |
| Efficiency vs loss of a job | Companies must be more frugal and take efficiency measures in difficult times like a recession. Thus, they can still operate healthily. One option is to layoff staff during difficult time. Shareholders and management may prefer this option but not staff |
| Quality and cheap products vs Less profit | Customers want higher quality but cheaper products. But, it means higher costs and lower profits for the company, an option that shareholders and management do not want |
| Foreign business relocation vs domestic employment | When the company decides to relocate production facilities overseas to increase efficiency, it benefits the owner because its profits improve. But the same harms the existing staff, who may lose their jobs. The home country's government and local communities also dislike it because it reduces job opportunities in the domestic economy |

MNEs with every country they enter. Basically, they face a similar set of stakeholders in each country. In addition, some concerns, such as fighting climate change, are voiced by stakeholders globally. The business relocation example in the table above gives an impression of the often divergent interests of stakeholders from various countries. In the opening case, Uber faced conflicting pressures from multiple stakeholders in India. On the one hand, customers and local communities in India were eager for the convenience and accessibility of ride-sharing services. They also expected Uber to provide affordable and safe transportation options in a country where public transportation is often unreliable, and taxis are expensive. This pushed Uber to reduce the price. On the other hand, the local drivers were unhappy about the lower fares, which made it difficult for them to meet their ends. Local competitors were angry since the low fares threatened their market share. Local government also challenged the dynamic pricing model with the maximum government-mandated fares.

Facing various conflicting goals pursued by stakeholders and given limited resources and bounded rationality, businesses have to prioritize their stakeholders based on managerial discretion, legitimacy concerns, assessment of environmental specificities, and power relations (Jamali & Mirshak, 2007; Yang & Rivers, 2009). The following box shows the stakeholder analysis model presented by Hawkins (2007).



**Stakeholder Analysis Model**

Hawkins (2007) presented a stakeholder analysis model that MNEs can use to trade off the competing interests of their stakeholders. Her model indicated four steps:

*Step one*: Identify a company's current internal, external, and potential future stakeholders.

*Step two*: Identify each stakeholder group's specific interests, issues, and concerns.

*Step three*: Evaluate the degree to which each stakeholder group has the power to influence the company's actions.

*Step four*: Determine the company's responsibilities for responding to the various stakeholder groups and their interests, issues, and concerns.

Hawkins' (2007) model aids in determining the stakeholders and interests, issues, and concerns they have. However, the model does not provide a means to make judicious trade-offs among the identified competing interests.

## Ethical Dilemmas and Moral Approaches

In domestic business environments, national laws and traditions establish a shared ethical framework on what businesses can and cannot do. A French company operating in France knows that it must comply with well-established labor, environmental, and governance rules backed by reliable enforcement mechanisms.

However, when a service firm expands overseas, it usually engages suppliers to source the merchandise necessary to provide the service or recruit service staff who could have close contact with the customers in the host country. In this case, diversified legal and cultural environments in multiple locations and the firm's arbitration strategy and coordination mechanisms pose more complex ethical dilemmas. For example, the company may face substandard regulatory frameworks and weak enforcement mechanisms in a host country, which present the opportunity of obtaining benefits through arbitration practices that would be unacceptable at home. Just like pharmaceutical companies sometimes decide to test new therapeutic methods in societies with weak health regulations (Ast, 2018). In a similar vein, international café or restaurant chains, when sourcing their products from suppliers, may find their suppliers engaging in unethical practices due to the weak local laws in protecting workers. For example, in the café sector, the majority of global output comes from just the top five producers: Brazil, Vietnam, Colombia, Indonesia, and Ethiopia (Deshmukh, 2021). Yet slavery in the coffee industry is an ongoing issue in the international community. Data collected from Vietnam's National Child Labor Survey of 2012 showed that an estimated 34,000 children under the age of 17 were being exploited on coffee plantations. Of these 34,000 children, 9% were 5–11 years old, 28% were 12–14 years old, and 63% were 15–17 years old (Irwin, 2021).

Many dilemmas arise about the moral legitimacy of capturing such benefits, including but not limited to the following.

## Labor Standards

In the 1960s and 1970s, companies in developed economies began to relocate production facilities in emerging countries to cut labor costs. Offshoring raised moral dilemmas in a few aspects.

The first is the *issue of sweatshops*. Sweatshops are crowded workplaces with poor, socially unacceptable, or illegal working conditions. On the one hand, sweatshops violate the duties of justice because the company offers lower pay and working conditions to employees in the host country for the same kind of work. On the other hand, sweatshops may be necessary for economic development in emerging countries, and some would argue they ought to be encouraged.

*Child labor* is an especially critical issue in such debates. Managers from a Western multinational would not consider hiring children in their home country since it is illegal and against the moral sense of the community. In some emerging economies, however, child labor is common and essential for the child's subsistence.

Other dilemmas involve differences in *worker safety standards*. The SS. United States was one of the most luxurious cruise ships of the 1950s. In the 1990s, the company decided to refurbish it, which required removing asbestos from the vessel. Asbestos is a natural mineral and carcinogen that causes mesothelioma. Conducting the task under the US strict worker safety norms cost $100 million (Ast, 2018). The company decided to outsource the job to Turkey, which cost only $2 million. When the Turkish authorities did not allow it for fear that workers would get cancer, the ship was towed to the Russian port of Sevastopol, where asbestos was removed for even less, thanks to even lower standards in worker safety.

## Environmental Standards

Multinational firms expanding overseas raise several dilemmas about using natural resources in societies with poor environmental regulations. Some emerging economies seek to attract foreign direct investment by lowering environmental standards. This phenomenon is known as the "race to the bottom." Multinationals thus relocate their polluting activities to countries with weaker environmental regulations to avoid the compliance costs of their home countries (Berry et al., 2021). This phenomenon has created countries as "pollution havens." Although service firms typically require fewer natural resources and conduct fewer production activities, such a dilemma could indirectly involve service companies, particularly when their clients are in the relevant industries. For example, in 2023, a group of indigenous Australians filed human rights complaints against 12 international banks, including Australia's ANZ and NAB, ING of the Netherlands, DNB of Norway, and Singapore's DBS, over a US$1 billion (S$1.3 billion) loan to a company building a controversial gas project that they say threatens their traditional lands and sea, as well as the future of their culture. Environmental groups have also criticized the project, saying it will fuel climate change by releasing huge amounts of planet-warming greenhouse gases (Fogarty, 2023).



## Human Rights

Companies sometimes face dilemmas linked to operations in countries with governments accused of violating human rights, and they adopt different approaches to deal with the dilemmas. For instance, Google accepted the Chinese government's request to censor keywords like Tiananmen Square and Dalai Lama in its search engine. CEO Eric Schmidt stated,

> » I think it is arrogant to enter a country where we are starting our operations and tell the country how to govern itself (Flemish & Trevino, 2010).

In the opposite case, in 2020, the New York Times, The Wall Street Journal, Axios, and others published reports that connected Uyghurs in forced detention to the supply chains of many of the world's best-known fashion retailers, such as Adidas, Lacoste, H&M and Ralph Lauren. Many of those brands reassessed their relationships with Xinjiang-based cotton suppliers and issued statements expressing concerns about human rights in their supply chain. For example, H&M posted "deep concerns" about reports of forced labor in Xinjiang, and confirmed that the retailer had stopped buying cotton from growers in the region. Shortly after, numerous fashion brands, including Nike and H&M, were trending in Chinese social media, with netizens calling for widespread boycotts (Friedman & Paton, 2021; Paton & Ramzy, 2020).

## Cultural Diversity

When doing business internationally, companies should generally respect the customs and culture of the communities where they operate. Traditional values can be lost to the homogenizing trends introduced by globally integrated production processes and product promotion. Some change is inevitable since local practices may not deserve protection if they violate important minimum global norms. However, when should a norm be respected because of cultural diversity considerations or ignored because it violates a global minimum?

One dilemma arising from cultural diversity is the norms of gender equality. Western corporations typically promote gender equality at home. Such gender equality could be challenged when the firm expands to societies intolerant of women due to religious practices. In Saudi Arabia, for example, women are forbidden by law to practice many professions. While companies usually justify discriminatory practices out of respect for local traditions, these arguments can be problematic: "*As in Saudi Arabia today, South Africa maintained a system where a broad segment of society was discriminated against in all walks of life and under the authority of men without any fear of being considered responsible for their actions. The only difference was that the victims in South Africa were black; In Saudi Arabia, are women*" (King, 2001).

In some cases, soft discrimination exists. While Mexico does not have formal restrictions against women in the labor market, a widespread macho culture often operates as a glass ceiling (Mayer & Cava, 2005). Companies face an unwritten rule that women should not be in charge of a male team. Using the gender equality standard of the home country (not considering gender as relevant for defining team leadership) could be costly for the company, as employees may not perceive a female boss as a legitimate authority. However, respecting local traditions and denying promotion to a talented executive solely because of gender considerations would violate the principle of equal opportunity.

Sometimes, cultural diversity dilemmas manifest themselves in international marketing decisions. Developed countries usually have strict regulations against dangerous substances such as tobacco. As changes in customer preferences and health laws generated a decline in cigarette consumption in developed economies, tobacco companies are shifting their attention and marketing efforts to emerging markets with different regulatory standards. For example, US tobacco executives have to decide how to market tobacco in the Central African Republic, one of the 22 countries that do not have a minimum age for purchasing tobacco products (Benowitz, 2022). Should the company use the home standard (abstain from marketing tobacco to people under 18) or adopt the host standard and cultural norm about the age at which people should be responsible for choosing to smoke?

## Corruption

Corruption is a concept that agglomerates practice ranging from multi-million dollar payments to high government officials to a few dollars bribe to a low-level bureaucrat. It is estimated that businesses and individuals pay more than $1 trillion in bribes yearly, squandering public resources and depriving millions of food, education, and other government services to which they are entitled (UN Press, 2018). Transparency International, an association founded in 1993 by former employees of the World Bank, publishes on its website the perception of corruption around the world (corruption perception index), which nicely shows how widespread the problem is (see ▶ https://www.transparency.org/cpi for the index).

Bribery in foreign operations was not always considered morally wrong. Some even saw it as a normal operating expense in emerging economies. For example, while severely punishing bribery at home, German corporate law considered foreign bribes tax-deductible as expenses before it was outlawed in 1998 (AP News, 1998).

Nowadays, it is beyond doubt that bribing foreign officials to win a contract is immoral, just like in the opening case, Uber had to cope with the home country's bribery and corruption allegations. However, less clarity exists in other situations. For example, is it acceptable to bribe a low-level bureaucrat to speed up a procedure he is supposed to do anyway? Small payments are tolerated in some countries and even rationalized by the need to supplement the meager salaries earned by public officials (Spicer, 2009). In April 2012, Walmart was reported to have paid more than $24 million to Mexican officials to speed up permits to open new branches. In this case, payments were made to expedite a process that officials should have executed anyway. Is $24 million a "small payment" for a company the size of Walmart? (The Wharton School, 2012). The following box gives more information about how businesses perceive anti-corruption acts.



**Business' Views About Anti-Corruption Acts**

The conflicting views are shared by business practitioners. A survey conducted by KPMG in the United Kingdom found that while 80% of respondents agreed that the UK Anti-Corruption Act was an admirable attempt to address the problem of corruption, 58% believed that the Act was impractical and ignored the reality that bribery is an accepted way of doing business in many countries.

Other similar studies have revealed widespread international criticism of the US Anti-Corruption law as hypocritical in light of the American business practice of offering gifts to potential customers or clients (e.g., trips to conferences, golf outings, tick-

> ets to entertainment and sporting events, use of luxury facilities such as spas, condos, and country clubs).
>
> Source: (Guillermo & Elizabeth, 2016)

To what extent the relationship between a company and its stakeholders is appropriate also varies across cultures. In China, "guanxi" is the informal network of favor exchange between companies and public officials. It is common practice for business people to spend time with counterparts in building guanxi outside the office, such as at the golf course or dinner banquet. Since it is not a specific payment for a particular service, guanxi does not fit into the conventional definition of bribery. But *guanxi* opens doors and creates opportunities for business relationships and dealings. Advocates of guanxi argue that the definition of bribery is based on a Western concept of impartiality that is not necessarily shared by all cultures. Critics contend that in itself, *guanxi* is not corrupt; yet strong *guanxi* connections and obligations can serve as an incentive for corruption. In fact, guanxi is similar to Western mafia practices of "today you scratch my back, and tomorrow I will scratch yours." It is unclear whether these exchanges of favors constitute a form of corruption or a legitimate way of doing business in the Chinese market.

## Moral Approaches

Dealing with these ethical issues is often perplexing. How, exactly, should we think through an ethical issue? What questions should we ask? What factors should we consider? The first step in analyzing ethical issues is obvious but not always easy: Get the facts. Some ethical issues create controversies simply because we do not check the facts. But having the facts is not enough. Facts by themselves only tell us what is; they do not tell us what ought to be. In addition to getting the facts, resolving an ethical issue also requires an appeal to values. Philosophers have developed five different approaches to values to deal with ethical issues.

**The Utilitarian Approach:** Utilitarianism was conceived in the nineteenth century by Jeremy Bentham and John Stuart Mill to help legislators determine which laws were morally best. Both Bentham and Mill suggested that ethical actions provide the greatest balance of good over evil (Ast, 2018). To analyze an ethical issue using the utilitarian approach, the firm manager first identifies the various courses of action available. Second, the manager asks who will be affected by each action and what benefits or harms will be derived from each. Third, the manager chooses the action that will produce the greatest benefits and the least harm. Ethical action is the one that provides the greatest good for the greatest number. Consider the example of a pharmaceutical firm testing a drug to cure a deadly disease in a developing country where regulation is weak. Having the tests done in a country with lower standards could greatly accelerate the release of the drug, potentially saving the lives of millions. The cost would probably be a handful of preventable deaths in an emerging country. Some could argue, from a utilitarian point of view, that the benefits of conducting the tests far outweigh their cost. Hence, it would be morally permissible.

**Kantian Deontology or the Rights Approach:** The second important approach to ethics has its roots in the philosophy of the eighteenth-century thinker Immanuel Kant and others like him, who focused on the individual's right to choose for herself or himself. According to these philosophers, what makes human beings different from mere things is that people have dignity based on their ability to choose freely what they will do with their lives, and they have a fundamental moral right to have these choices respected. People are not objects to be manipulated; it is a violation of human dignity to use people in ways they do not freely choose (Velasquez et al., 2015).

Kantian deontology suggests that organizational structures should treat all people with equal dignity and respect. It advises managers to identify the rights of the different groups affected by a decision and to choose a course of action that does not violate any. Because of its non-consequentialist nature, Kantian ethics avoids the problem of the aggregation of benefits and damages that affect utilitarian models (Ast, 2018).

**The Common-Good Approach:** This approach to ethics assumes a society comprising individuals whose own good is inextricably linked to the good of the community. Community members are bound by the pursuit of common values and goals. In this approach, we focus on ensuring that the social policies, social systems, institutions, and environments on which we depend are beneficial to all. Examples of goods common to all include affordable health care, effective public safety, peace among nations, a just legal system, and an unpolluted environment (Velasquez et al., 2015).



**The Fairness or Justice Approach:** The fairness or justice approach to ethics has its roots in the teachings of the ancient Greek philosopher Aristotle, who said that "equals should be treated equally and unequals unequally." Favoritism gives benefits to some people without a justifiable reason for singling them out; discrimination imposes burdens on people who are no different from those on whom burdens are not imposed. Both favoritism and discrimination are unjust and wrong. The basic moral question in this approach is: How fair is an action? Does it treat everyone in the same way, or does it show favoritism and discrimination? (Velasquez et al., 2015)

In the example where pharmaceutical companies test new drugs in societies with weak health regulations, based on Kantian deontology, the common-good approach, and the fairness or justice approach, this option would be illegitimate because it does not respect the dignity of the individuals who will be subjected to the tests, is not safe or fair to the subjects of tests.

**Virtue Ethics:** The virtue approach to ethics assumes that there are certain ideals toward which we should strive, which provide for the full development of our humanity. These ideals are discovered through thoughtful reflection on what kind of people we have the potential to become.

Virtues are attitudes or character traits that enable us to be and act in ways that develop our highest potential. They enable us to pursue the ideals we have adopted.

Honesty, courage, compassion, generosity, fidelity, integrity, fairness, self-control, and prudence are all examples of virtues (Velasquez et al., 2015).

In dealing with an ethical problem using the virtue approach, we might ask, what virtue is at stake? What kind of person should I be? What will promote the development of character within myself and my community? In the pharma company's example, the subsidiary manager in a developing country may decide based on his or her own ethical beliefs. If the manager believes that "being fair and honest is important," he or she will choose not to conduct the test for the drug in developing countries.

Utilitarian, Kantian, common-good, and fairness and justice approaches, despite their difficulties, are capable of offering criteria of good corporate behavior on which to build globally applicable rules. Virtue ethics, on the contrary, is unable to provide answers to dilemmas at the level of the corporation in relation to business in society.

Other than the above-mentioned value-based moral approaches, Enderle developed a taxonomy of four typical moral approaches that guide policy when domestic and foreign standards differ (Enderle, 2015).

*The Foreign Type* adapts the practices of the subsidiaries to the laws and customs of the host country under the notion of "when in Rome, do as the Romans." This is just like Google having accepted the Chinese government's request to censor keywords like Tiananmen Square and Dalai Lama in its search engine.

*The Imperial Type* applies home standards virtually unchanged across the world. H&M in dealing with the human rights in their supply chain in China, adopted this approach.

*The Interconnected Type* implies an "ethics of reciprocity": a well-known code that states that one should treat others as they themselves would like to be treated, which derives from the ethics of Immanuel Kant, outlined above. The relevant ethical standards arise from both sides, the home, and the host country, and are driven by mutual advantage, underlying the discussion about negotiating justice in international trade and investment. One example is the apparel sector in Bangladesh. Bangladesh has been perceived as having weak legal protections for workers, low enforcement of regulations, and low minimum wages for many years. A series of high-fatality industrial accidents in 2012–2013 led the government and multinational firms to take steps to improve workers' safety and labor rights. In 2013, a group of 29 US-based multinational retailers (including Gap and Wal-Mart) formed the Alliance for Bangladesh Worker Safety. Member companies required all factories in their supplier base to participate in workplace safety measures, such as building safety audits and worker training and empowerment programs. Overall, the Alliance covered between 600 and 700 garment factories and 1.21 million workers in the country. The Alliance formed a key part of the Government's 2013 action plan to improve safety conditions, with MNE groups sharing the responsibility of overseeing safety in the factories they covered (Boudreau, 2020).

*The Global Type* companies do not believe belonging to a country is relevant for international business practice. It is exemplified by dealing with ethical issues such as global warming, which are so important that national borders become almost irrelevant. Citizens turn out to be cosmopolitan; multinational firms change into global entities; and nation-states fade away. In principle, this type can comprehend the whole Earth, although until now, it is not fully realized. This approach implies a "universal ethics": The relevant ethical standards apply to all actors on the planet Earth regardless of their different local traditions and cultures.

## Inappropriate Conduct of Multinationals Abroad

When dealing with dilemmas, some international firms are involved in inappropriate conduct or misbehaviors, such as corruption, the overexploitation of natural resources, or the abuse of workers, particularly those adopting a *Foreign Type* approach, as illustrated in the previous section.

## Environmental Misbehaviors

Environmental misbehavior in multinationals is on the "pollution haven" hypothesis, where multinationals relocate their production activities to developing economies due to their lower environmental protection standard. In the late 1990s, the Finnish company Botnia planned the construction of a pulp mill in the city of Fray Bentos (Uruguay), on the shores of the Uruguay River near the border with Argentina. Environmental advocacy groups heavily resisted the project, accusing Botnia of making extra profits by following lower environmental standards than in the home country. Another frequent international environmental misbehavior is related to toxic waste. For instance, until 2017, China accepted 70% of the world's electronic waste—discarded computers, cell phones, printers, televisions, microwaves, smoke alarms, and other electronic equipment and parts, due to the lower disposal cost there (Cho, 2018). It is estimated that heavy metals pollute about 10.18% of arable land in China, and 13.86% of grain production is thus contaminated (Zhang et al., 2015). After China stopped accepting this e-waste out of concern for its environment, European and North American companies began shipping more of it to Southeast Asia, such as Vietnam and Thailand.



## Governance Misbehaviors

There are also multinational firms involved in corruption. According to a report issued by the Mexican Employers Association in 2011, companies operating in Mexico spend more than 10% of their revenue on corrupt acts. The country is a huge market for Walmart—one in every five Walmart stores is in Mexico. In September 2005, the Walmart scandal was brought to light and resulted in the company's stock value dropping by as much as $4.5 billion. Evidence unearthed by internal and external investigations revealed the widespread use of bribes, alleged to total over $24 million. The bribes were paid to facilitate the construction of Walmart stores throughout Mexico (Guillermo & Elizabeth, 2016).

Beyond corruption, another vital area of multinational governance misbehavior is tax evasion. Multinationals arbitrage differences in tax regimes thank to their operations across jurisdictions. They reduce their tax burden and enjoy tax incentives through international legal structures or transfer pricing, and public perception has considered this unethical even if it is legal (Godar et al., 2005; Matute et al., 2021; Mehafdi, 2000).

Some other governance misconducts include financial irregularities, which include intentional misstatements or omissions of information to financial transactions that are detrimental to the interests of the Institution. These may consist of violations of relevant Federal, State, or institutional laws, rules, and procedures. These acts include but are not limited to embezzlement, fraud, and forgery or falsification of reports, documents, or computer files to misappropriate assets. The opening cases of Enron and Parmalat in ▶ Chap. 11 are some examples of such financial irregularities.

## Social Misbehaviors

Multinational firms also show social misbehaviors: child labor, discrimination, and human rights violations. For example, in September 2005, the International Labor Rights Fund filed a lawsuit on behalf of Walmart supplier sweatshop workers in China, Indonesia, Bangladesh, Nicaragua, and Swaziland. The workers were denied minimum wages and legally mandated health care and forced to work overtime without compensation. Other worker rights violations in Walmart's foreign factories producing goods for Walmart included locked bathrooms, wages so low they did not allow workers to survive on them, pregnancy tests, and workers being fired and blacklisted if they tried to defend their rights (International Labor Forum, 2005). In terms of discrimination, unlike in developed countries, women working for multinationals in developing ones are paid more poorly compared to domestic firms. In an article published by the World Economic Forum in 2020, a larger gender wage gap was found in multinationals compared to domestic firms in developing countries (−$2.53 vs. −$1.20) (World Economic Forum, 2020).

Although we get to know those potential misbehaviors, in many occasions, it is not easy to identify the inappropriate conduct of multinationals abroad. The following box illustrates some reasons.

**What Makes It Challenging to Identify Inappropriate Conduct of Multinationals Abroad?**

In the international context, it is challenging to identify multinationals' misbehaviors because the appropriate standards of behavior are less clear for three reasons.

First, there is a large diversity of what countries consider legal. The enforcement of laws also varies, with some nations having a more effective and unbiased application of laws and regulations than others. In addition, what is legal might not always be considered ethical, and what is illegal might not always be illegitimate, just as in the case where multinationals pay less to sweatshop workers. In multinationals, there is a broader diversity of judges because their activities affect multiple stakeholders across countries. The same action might be considered appropriate by one group of stakeholders but as misbehavior by another (e.g., closing a foreign facility to improve profits is acceptable by shareholders, but misconduct from the perspective of the local community).

Second, multinationals' globally dispersed operations offer them unique opportunities to arbitrage activities across borders. Multinationals can select international locations to reduce compliance with norms, for instance, locating polluting operations in countries with lower standards or relocating to jurisdictions with low tax rates. This arbitrage can be used to reduce operational costs or risks legally and to hide illegitimate or even illegal corporate behavior.

Third, the diversity of locations makes it challenging to identify the intentionality and associated responsibility of multinationals' misbehavior. Sometimes, multinational managers actively engage in inappropriate acts abroad. Headquarter managers may invest in particular locations because they know they can get away with activities shunned in the home country, like not following environmental or labor standards. Headquarter managers may not know that employees in subsidiaries outside the home country fail to follow norms. Subsidiary employees may make decisions they know are improper (e.g., non-compliance with safety or environmental standards abroad) but good for their career and the firm, even if the multinational formally disallows such behavior. On the other hand, misbehavior may be an unintentional outcome of activities. Sometimes employees may become accomplices to the wrongdoing they do not initiate (e.g., bankers unknowingly helping clients launder money). Multinationals may also unknowingly misbehave indirectly when partner firms hide contestable local practices (e.g., subcontractors using child or slave labor in the inputs sold to the firm). In such cases, multinationals may suspect the misconduct of their partners but choose to ignore it.

All these cases raise interesting questions about the responsibility of the multinational for the misbehavior and accountability of its employees and partners across locations.

Despite the challenges in identifying those inappropriate conducts, in 2022, the European Commission adopted a proposal for a Directive on corporate sustainability due diligence. The proposal aims to foster sustainable and responsible corporate behavior throughout global value chains, assuming that companies play a key role in building a sustainable economy and society. The companies will be required to identify and, where necessary, prevent, end, or mitigate adverse impacts of their activities on human rights, such as child labor and exploitation of workers, and on the environment, for example, pollution and biodiversity loss. For businesses, these new rules will bring legal certainty and a level playing field. For consumers and investors, they will provide more transparency.

See ▶ https://ec.europa.eu/commission/presscorner/detail/en/ip_22_1145 for more details.

## Corporate Social Responsibility (CSR)

### What Is CSR?

The inappropriate conduct by multinationals has harmed multiple stakeholders. For instance, home country's workforce suffers due to the multinational's outsourcing arrangement. In the host country, the environment could be harmed by polluting production activities, threatening local communities; employees in the subsidiaries could be discriminated against or abused. The affected parties ignored long enough may take action against the firm, such as a product boycott or turn to the government for redress. Multinationals thus risk losing societal legitimacy. In addition, the intangible characteristics of services lead to potential information asymmetries, making people seek clues that help them diminish the uncertainty inherent in service consumption. Analogously, service firms also look for mechanisms so that consumers trust the firms and their service quality (Casado-Díaz et al., 2014).

In response to such a legitimacy risk, service firms increasingly incorporate the concerns of stakeholder groups within their strategic outlook by engaging in corporate social responsibility (CSR) initiatives. CSR can be defined as follows:

**Corporate Social Responsibility**

The *corporate social responsibility (CSR)* of business encompasses the economic, legal, ethical, and discretionary expectations that society has of organizations at a given point in time (Carroll, 1979)

This can be manifested in the opening case, where Uber engaged in various socially responsible activities to engage with local communities, regulators, and taxi drivers.

### Models of CSR

Academics have suggested different models to initiate and implement CSRs. In this chapter, we introduce three of them. These models share some overlappings and generally cover four corporate social responsibilities, including legal, ethical, philanthropy, and strategic responsibility, as illustrated in ◘ Table 12.2.

Archie Carroll was one of the first academics to distinguish between different kinds of CSR engagement, using the "pyramid of corporate social responsibility" (Carroll, 1991). Fundamentally, a firm is responsible for producing an acceptable return on its owners' investment. An important component of pursuing economic gain within a law-based society is a legal responsibility—a duty to act within the legal framework drawn up by the government and judiciary. In the opening case, Uber actively worked with the Indian government to address regulatory concerns

**Table 12.2** CSR frameworks, source: Author's own table

| | **Carroll (1979)** | **Rangan et al. (2015)** | **Porter and Kramer (2002, 2006), Kramer and Porter (2011)** |
|---|---|---|---|
| | Firms could engage in CSR by addressing different responsibilities | Firms could engage in CSR in three ways | Firms could create shared value via CSR by |
| Legal responsibility | Act within the legal framework drawn up by the government and judiciary | | |
| Ethical responsibility | Not harm its stakeholders and its operating environment | | |
| Philanthropy | Proactive behaviors benefiting society | Theater 1: Do good to society, but not designed to produce profits or directly improve business performance | |
| Strategic responsibility | Proactive, strategic behaviors benefiting the firm and society | Theater 2: Deliver social or environmental benefits in ways that improve firms' effectiveness and efficiency<br>Theater 3: Improved business performance is integrated with achieving social or environmental results | Strategy 1: Reconceiving products and markets<br>Strategy 2: Redefining productivity in the value chain<br>Strategy 3: Enabling local cluster development |

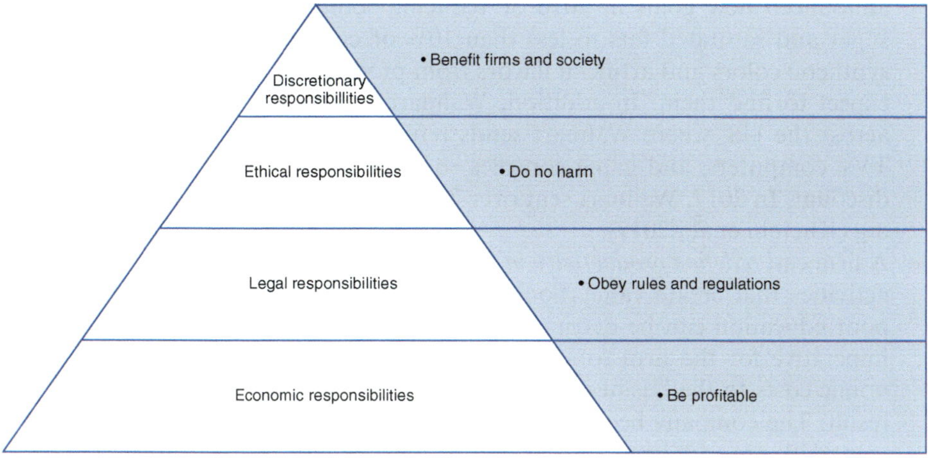


**Fig. 12.1** Corporate social responsibilities pyramid by Carroll (1991), source: Author's own figure based on Carroll (1991)

and obtain necessary licenses and permits, which shows it was fulfilling legal responsibility. Taken one step further, a firm has an ethical responsibility to do no harm to its stakeholders and within its operating environment. Finally, firms have a discretionary responsibility, which represents more proactive, strategic behaviors that can benefit the firm or society, or both. Uber also invested in local infrastructure, such as mapping and navigation systems, and established a local call center to provide customer support in different languages, which was a manifestation of engaging in discretionary responsibility. As a firm progresses up Carroll's pyramid, its responsibilities move from being fundamental to becoming more discretionary or voluntary. A socially responsible firm encompasses all four responsibilities within its culture, values, and day-to-day operations. Figure 12.1 shows the pyramid.

In a series of Harvard Business Review articles, Porter and Kramer (2002, 2006) and Kramer and Porter (2011) posed the concept of "creating shared value" via CSR. They have posited a context-focused strategic CSR approach, requiring firms to use their unique resources and expertise to address social and environmental needs in the corporate context to achieve a convergence between social and economic goals. They have suggested three ways of creating shared value via CSR.

- A firm can *reconceive products and markets* by meeting social ► needs while better serving existing markets, accessing new ones, or lowering costs through innovation. One example is CARD Pioneer Microinsurance Inc. Insurance in the Philippines. It initially sold insurance services exclusively afforded by the rich. Then the company fitted the insurance service to the poor who needed it the most. Because of CARD Pioneer, the poor can now collect claims fast without resorting to moneylenders with high interest rates. CARD Pioneer has been rewarded by the market, as the poor have been the fastest-growing market of the Philippine insurance industry (Tagpuan, n.d.). Another example is Walmart, which reconceived products by following a lot of initiatives to create value for society. From 2011 to 2015, Walmart drove an initiative with suppliers. It announced new goals in 2016 of reducing sodium by 20%, bringing added sugar and saturated fats to less than 10% of calories, and removing certified synthetic colors and artificial flavors from products in which customers do not expect to find them. In addition, Walmart utilizes four refurbishing centers across the US, where Walmart sends returned and damaged phones, tablets, TVs, computers, and game consoles so they can be repaired and resold at a discount. In 2017, Walmart sent over 7.5 million electronic items for refurbishing (Kherchi et al., 2019).

- A firm can *redefine productivity in the value chain*. The value chain is the firm's activities that create value. Social problems such as pollution, drought, and poor education can be detrimental to the firm's value chain. This creates an imperative for the firm to actively address these problems, which incur economic costs to the business. Solving these problems creates a twofold positive result: The company becomes more productive, and the societal and environmental ills are addressed. One example from Walmart is that in 2009, it reduced its packaging and rerouted its trucks. These actions not only reduced the emission of greenhouse gases but also helped Walmart cut its cost on a large scale (Liu, 2014). In the opening case, Uber's effort in investing in local infrastructure, such as mapping and navigation systems, and establishing a local call center to provide customer support in different languages, would be a good example of redefining productivity in the value chain.
- A firm can *enable local cluster development*. Companies do not operate in isolation from their surroundings. To compete and thrive, they need reliable local suppliers, a functioning infrastructure of roads and telecommunications, access to talent, and an effective and predictable legal system. Correspondingly, a firm can implement CSR by developing partnership collaborations across sectors to tackle local issues. In 2017, Walmart China and China Women's Development Foundation announced a joint program to help women in various industries achieve economic independence by leveraging many of Walmart's business resources (Kherchi et al., 2019). In addition, Walmart and the Walmart Foundation have provided funding for training, coaching, and tech tools to more than 50,000 prospective and current retail workers to enhance the economic mobility of workers (Walmart Inc., 2018, p. 39). These efforts for strengthening local clusters ensure firms develop an ecosystem for sustainable growth (Kherchi et al., 2019).



Rangan et al., (2015) pointed out that most companies have long practiced a multifaceted version of CSR that runs from pure philanthropy to environmental sustainability to the active pursuit of shared value. They classified CSR into three theaters:

- **Theater one: focusing on philanthropy.** Programs in this theater are not designed to produce profits or directly improve business performance. Examples include donations of money or equipment to civic organizations, engagement with community initiatives, and support for employee volunteering.
- **Theater two: improving operational effectiveness.** Programs in this theater function within existing business models to deliver social or environmental benefits

in ways that support a company's operations across the value chain, often improving efficiency and effectiveness. Thus, they may, though do not always, increase revenue, decrease costs, or both. Examples include sustainability initiatives that reduce resource use, waste, or emissions, which may, in turn, reduce costs; and investments in employee working conditions, health care, or education, which may enhance productivity, retention, and company reputation. In the opening case, Uber's effort in investing in local infrastructure can probably fall into Theater Two CSR.

- **Theater three: transforming the business model.** Programs in this theater create new forms of business specifically to improve business performance while achieving social or environmental results.

The following box shows some examples of CSR initiatives falling into the three theaters.

**Cases: CSR Initiatives Falling Into the Three Theaters**

Let us look at how the large midwestern bank **PNC** unified a multitude of theater one philanthropic and community service projects, spread across numerous business units, behind a single cause. From 2010 to 2015, PNC, funded the Grow Up Great initiative with $100 million to offer schoolreadiness resources, such as resources, materials, or programs aimed at preparing children for success in formal schooling, to disadvantaged communities. Before the program's advent, each **PNC** market had a CSR budget that regional managers allocated as they thought best, resulting in a well-intentioned but incoherent array of initiatives. Roughly 30% of aggregate funds went to the arts, 25% to sports, 20% to civic activities, 5% to education, and 3% to health. Then CEO Jim Rohr unified **PNC** behind Grow Up Great because of his long-standing commitment to early childhood education, the eagerness of many employees to engage with a local cause, and the program's alignment with the bank's community-development-oriented identity. By pruning its disparate CSR programs, gradually easing out those without an early education focus, and encouraging regional managers to redirect their discretionary budgets to early education, **PNC** has built a well-funded initiative that correlates better with its employees' motivations and is likely to yield significant benefits to the communities the bank serves and relies on.

The family-owned Mexican baking company **Grupo Bimbo** demonstrates alignment in theater two. Bimbo is the largest bakery in Mexico, with a workforce of nearly 100,000 and a similar number of small retailers in its network. Its comprehensive CSR programs focus on social welfare: It provides free educational services to help employees complete high school and offers supplementary medical care and financial assistance for dependents' care to close the gaps in government health coverage. It also has a strong microfinance program to help its mom-and-pop retailers manage working-capital shortages and pay for small capital additions. As theater two initiatives, these are all explicitly intended to increase efficiency and effectiveness, and indeed they have improved employee performance and retention and strengthened Bimbo's distribution chain.

**Hindustan Unilever's** Project Shakti ("empowerment") in India provides a good example of the theater three initiative. Instead of using its customary wholesaler-to-retailer distribution model to reach remote villages, the company recruited village women, provided them with access to microfinance loans, and trained them in selling soaps, detergents, and other products door-to-door. Over 65,000 women entrepreneurs participated, nearly doubling their household incomes, on average, while increasing rural access to hygiene products and thus contributing to public health. These social gains have been met by business gains for the company: As of 2012, Project Shakti had achieved more than $100 million in sales. Its success has led **Hindustan Unilever** to roll out similar programs in other parts of the world. As Project Shakti demonstrates, theater three programs need not be comprehensive. Most are narrow initiatives undertaken with a focused market segment or product line in mind but with significant potential to alter the company's social or environmental impact and financial performance. Theater three initiatives almost always call for a new business model rather than incremental extensions.

Source: (Rangan et al., 2015)

## Critical Discussion of CSR

12

These CSR models provide a general framework helping firms embrace their international operational and strategic planning process to respond to their stakeholders and society for long-term viability. However, some companies engage in CSR initiatives with the aim of only achieving or increasing their level of legitimacy. When companies offer misleading communication and try to influence their stakeholders' perceptions, they incur the phenomenon known in the literature as "greenwashing".

**Corporate Social Responsibility (CSR) Greenwashing**

*Corporate social responsibility (CSR) greenwashing* refers to the practice of companies making false or exaggerated claims about their environmental or social efforts in order to improve their public image or brand reputation.

The term "greenwashing" was coined by New York environmentalist Jay Westerveld in a 1986 essay about the hotel industry's practice of placing notices in bedrooms promoting the reuse of towels to "save the environment." He posed that these institutions often made little or no effort toward reducing energy waste. Encouraging towel reuse saved them laundry costs. He concluded that often the real objective was to increase profit. He labeled this and other profitable but ineffective "environmentally-conscientious" acts as greenwashing (Watson, 2016).

Today greenwashing can take many forms in practice, such as using misleading language or images to make a product seem more eco-friendly than it really is, exaggerating the impact of a company's sustainability or socially responsible efforts, or making false claims about the company's commitment to reducing its carbon footprint. One example is Uber, which has faced criticism for greenwashing its ride-sharing services. Uber has claimed that its services help reduce traffic congestion and emissions by encouraging carpooling and reducing the number of cars on the road. However, some critics argue that the company's overall business model is not environmentally friendly, as it encourages people to take more rides and relies on large fleets of gas-guzzling vehicles. Additionally, the company's claims of reducing emissions may be overstated, as studies have shown that ride-sharing services like Uber may actually increase traffic congestion in some areas. Furthermore, Uber has pledged to electrify its entire fleet by 2030, but critics argue that this commitment lacks specificity and may not be achievable given the company's current business practices. Additionally, the company has been criticized for its treatment of drivers, who are not classified as employees and do not receive benefits like health insurance or paid time off. These criticisms suggest that Uber's claims of being environmentally responsible may be exaggerated or misleading, and the company may be using greenwashing to promote its services (Transport & Environment, 2020).

Such greenwashing is not rare. In January 2021, the European Commission, working with national consumer authorities, scanned consumer websites for breaches of EU consumer protection laws, the results of which was published in a report. The study, for the first time, focused on greenwashing and looked at green claims from a variety of consumer products. It concluded that in 42% of the websites examined, claims were likely false and deceptive and might well constitute actionable claims for unfair commercial practices (Park, 2022).

Greenwashing can lead consumers to make purchasing decisions based on false or incomplete information, which can have negative consequences for both the environment and the company's reputation. In recent years, such greenwashing has been getting attention from regulatory bodies, activists, and consumers. There have been a number of lawsuits in the United States in the past year against Coca-Cola, Blue Triton Brands (which manufactures Poland Spring, Deer Park, and other water brands), and others, for making broad sustainability claims despite the fact the vast majority of their bottles end up in landfills and are not recycled. These lawsuits have been filed by various environmental advocacy groups like the Sierra Club (Park, 2022).

Corresponding to this, the Green Guides issued by the Federal Trade Commission in the United States and the European Union's directive on Unfair Commercial Practices provide explicit direction regarding what qualifies as misleading information. Under both regimes, using vague terms such as "sustainable," "green," "eco," and the like, are not acceptable if false or misleading. Additionally, claims need to be supported by clear factual evidence and qualified so as not to overstate their benefits. Moreover, the environmental benefit claim must pertain directly to the product as manufactured or used (Park, 2022).

Beyond the threat of enforcement actions or litigation, which is costly, loss of business looms is an even more significant long-term cost. Driven by growing concerns about climate change and ecological degradation, as well as increased awareness about the impact of consumer behavior on the environment, consumers have become increasingly conscious of greenwashing. They are becoming more skeptical of vague or general claims of environmental responsibility and are more likely to look for concrete evidence of a company's environmental practices (Nguyen et al., 2019), such as their supply chain practice, the third-party certifications or labels that verify a company's sustainability claims, like the Forest Stewardship Council (FSC) label for sustainable forestry or the Energy Star label for energy-efficient appliances.

Customers are balking when greenwashing is blatant. A quick review of YouTube, for example, reveals content created by millennials or Gen Z consumers warning of the worst greenwashers and poking fun at many well-known brands. This sort of notoriety is bad for brands, potentially undoing decades of goodwill and turning off the next generation of consumers who are willing to spend more money for brands that deliver on their environmental commitments (Park, 2022).

Overall, companies that engage in CSR greenwashing are more likely to face reputational damage and loss of consumer trust, which can have a significant impact on their bottom line. They are, therefore, pressured to be more authentic and transparent about their responsible business practices and to back up their responsible claims with concrete evidence.

## Review Questions

12

1. How do a firm‘s stakeholders' interests differ, and how do such different interests affect the firm’s international strategy?
2. What are some typical ethical dilemmas a multinational firm has to face during its international expansion and operation? Which moral approach do you prefer to adopt and why?
3. What are the different ways of engaging in corporate social responsibility, and how do they benefit a multinational firm?

### Closing Case: The Green Starbucks Cup: Green or Greenwashing?

If you go to Starbucks' website, you will be able to find a dedicated page illustrating their various CSR commitments (► https://www.starbucks.com/responsibility/reporting-hub/), covering a wide range of business aspects and employee relationships such as supporting local communities, educating and empowering workers, gender equality and minorities, energy and water consumption, waste reduction, and so on. But in general, Starbucks' social responsibility strategy is based on three pillars: community, ethical sourcing, and the environment. Here is what the company does to have a positive impact in each of those areas:

Starbucks coffee, image by ► Pexels from ► Pixabay

For the first pillar, to have a positive impact on the communities it works with and in, Starbucks develops community stores that partner with local non-profits. The non-profits these stores work with offer services aimed at meeting the needs of the communities they are located in. Starbucks, in turn, donates $0.05–$0.15 per transaction to the non-profit partner. In addition, Starbucks has pledged to hire at least 10,000 veterans and military by 2018 and focuses on diversity and inclusion in the workplace. The company also provides training opportunities for youth in their communities and has even developed the Starbucks Foundation, whose goal is to strengthen those communities further. These are just a few of their many community-centric initiatives.

The second pillar, Ethical Sourcing, dictates the way that Starbucks purchases its products. The company is committed to ensuring that its coffee, tea, cocoa, and manufactured goods are responsibly and ethically produced and purchased. They say their "success is linked to the success of the farmers and suppliers who grow and produce [their] products," and so they only purchase those products from farms and manufacturers that adhere to a certain standard of ethical treatment.

Regarding the third pillar, Starbucks refers to the planet as their "most important business partner," and takes a comprehensive approach to reducing its environmental impact. To do this, they build LEED (Leadership in Energy and Environmental Design, a green building certification program used worldwide) certified stores. With these stores, Starbucks are committed to recycling and conserving water and energy, and pursue strategies that address climate change on a global level. Generally, Starbucks tries to be as environmentally friendly as possible in every aspect of its operations.

However, there has been criticism about the company's CSR claims.

Regarding the second pillar, Starbucks has sourced 99% of its coffee ethically since 2015. However, in 2018, slave labor was revealed on a Starbucks-certified coffee farm in Brazil. Brazilian labor inspectors discovered the incident. The farm held the CAFE Practices certification—owned by Starbucks in partnership with SCS Global Services. Workers reported dead bats and mice in their food, no sanitation systems, and work days that stretched from 6 AM to 11 PM. Workers' take-home pay was significantly reduced due to deductions required to cash their checks. In 2020, The Guardian detailed how five coffee farms in the Starbucks supply chain had been found to employ children under the age of 13 to work incredibly hard 40-h weeks picking coffee beans.

For the third pillar, coffeehouses rely heavily on the use of fossil fuels and natural resources. Since most Starbucks stores are in places where coffee is not grown, it has to be shipped thousands of miles to get there. With more than 4500 Starbucks stores in 47 countries, it takes a lot of money, time, and energy to build, heat, cool, and power these stores. Starbucks has recently received harsh criticism for its inefficient water usage. Continuous water flowed from dippers, which are used to wash dishes. This resulted in an estimated daily loss of 6.2 million gallons of water. So, the company is looking at alternatives to the dipping wells system, some of which have already been used in 2022.

In 2018, Starbucks announced that it would build 10,000 "Greener Stores" by 2025, with a focus on reducing energy and water usage, using sustainable building materials, and reducing waste. Yet critics pointed out that the initiative did not go far enough to address the significant environmental impact of Starbucks' global operations. For example, the initiative did not address the company's use of single-use plastic cups, which are a major source of waste and pollution. Furthermore, the initiative was criticized for lacking specific targets and for not being independently verified.

In addition, vegan charity PETA has accused Starbucks of "greenwashing," since it refuses to drop the surcharge for its non-dairy alternatives despite acknowledging that cow's milk is the company's biggest source of carbon dioxide emissions. The award-winning actor Alan Cumming wrote a letter to Starbucks Canada Senior Vice President Lori Digulla. It stated:

"More than a year ago, Starbucks acknowledged that cow's milk is the company's biggest source of carbon dioxide emissions. Yet it continues to penalize customers for making green and humane choices by charging them extra for vegan milk…" "If Starbucks really wants to help the planet, it must do more than just talk about its goals. It's time to take action" (Dodhiya, 2021).

**Questions**

1. How can you categorize Starbucks' CSR commitment using the frameworks proposed by Carroll's Pyramid, Porter and Kramer (2002, 2006), Kramer and Porter (2011), and Rangan, Chase and Karim (2015)?
2. Do you agree with the critics that Starbucks' CSRs are greenwashing? What will be the likely impact on Starbucks?
3. What caused the so-called greenwashing or unethical practices related to Starbucks?

Source: (Dodhiya, 2021; Ethically Engineered, 2022; Lewis, 2021; Starbucks Website, n.d.; Starbucksathome, n.d.; Vandeveld, 2015)

**Summary**

This chapter

- Has defined stakeholders as "any group of individuals who could be affected by the actions that companies perform to achieve their objectives."
- Had identified shareholders, employees and management, customers, suppliers, government, and local community as a company's primary stakeholders and shown that they have different interests and goals and hence have different expectations for the company.
- Has explained the ethical dilemmas a multinational service firm faces due to different regulations, standards, and cultural norms in the global arena.
- Has outlined the moral approaches a multinational service firm can employ to deal with ethical dilemmas.
- Has identified the inappropriate conduct of multinationals, including environmental, governance, and social misbehaviors.
- Has defined that corporate social responsibility of business encompasses the economic, legal, ethical, and discretionary expectations that society has of organizations at a given point in time.
- Has explained three models of corporate social responsibility.

## References

Abrar, P. (2022, August 25). *Uber India created Rs 44,600 cr in value for economy in 2021: Report*. Retrieved from https://www.business-standard.com/article/companies/uber-india-created-rs-44-600-cr-in-value-for-economy-in-2021-report-122082400981_1.html

AP News. (1998, November 10). *Germans: No tax break for bribes*. Retrieved from https://apnews.com/article/b2c5f4c1e26c055d9176af27e8177b47

Ast, F. (2018). The moral Dilemmas of global business. In *Globalization*. IntechOpen.

Benowitz, S. (2022, July 23). *22 Countries do not have a minimum age for purchasing tobacco products*. Retrieved from https://thepavlovictoday.com/22-countries-do-not-have-a-minimum-age-for-purchasing-tobacco-products/

Berry, H., Kaul, A., & Lee, N. (2021). Follow the smoke: The pollution haven effect on global sourcing. *Strategic Management Journal, 42*(13), 2420–2450.

Bhattacharya, A., & Balachandran, M. (2017, July 27). *The Indian government wants to take on Uber and Ola*. Retrieved from https://www.weforum.org/agenda/2017/07/the-indian-government-wants-to-take-on-uber-and-ola/

Boudreau, L. (2020). Multinational enforcement of labor law: Experimental evidence from Bangladesh's apparel sector. In *Private enterprise for development in low-income countries working paper*.

Carroll, A. B. (1979). A three-dimensional conceptual model of corporate performance. *Academy of Management Review, 4*(4), 497–505.

Carroll, A. B. (1991). The pyramid of corporate social responsibility: Toward the moral management of organizational stakeholders. *Business Horizons, 34*(4), 39–48.

Casado-Díaz, A. B., Nicolau-Gonzálbez, J. L., Ruiz-Moreno, F., & Sellers-Rubio, R. (2014). The differentiated effects of CSR actions in the service industry. *Journal of Services Marketing, 28*(7), 558–565.

Cho R. (2018, August 27). *What can we do about the growing E-waste problem*? Retrieved from https://news.climate.columbia.edu/2018/08/27/growing-e-waste-problem/

Deshmukh, A. (2021, October 1). *The world's top coffee producing countries*. Retrieved from https://www.visualcapitalist.com/worlds-top-coffee-producing-countries/

Dhillon, A. (2018, December 4). *'My life is spent in this car': Uber drives its Indian workers to despair*. The Guardian. Retrieved from https://www.theguardian.com/global-development/2018/dec/04/my-life-is-spent-in-this-car-uber-drives-indian-workers-to-despair

Dodhiya, M. (2021, April 19). *Starbucks' Earth month initiative slammed as 'greenwash'*. Retrieved from https://www.totallyveganbuzz.com/news/starbucks-earth-month-initiatives-slammed-as-greenwash/

Enderle, G. (2015). Exploring and conceptualizing international business ethics. *Journal of Business Ethics, 127*, 723–735.

Ethically Engineered (2022, November 19). *Is Starbucks greenwashing? A breakdown*! Retrieved from https://www.ethicallyengineered.com/is-starbucks-greenwashing/

Flemish, R., & Trevino, L. K. (2010). Google goes to China. In *Managing business ethics*. John Wiley and Sons.

Fogarty, D. (2023, April 4). *DBS among international banks to get human rights complaints over loan to gas company*. Retrieved from https://www.straitstimes.com/business/dbs-gets-human-rights-complaint-from-indigenous-australians-over-loan-to-gas-company

Freeman, R. E. (1984). Strategic management: A stakeholder approach. Boston: Pitman Goodpaster, K. 1991. Business ethics and stakeholder analysis. *Business Ethics Quarterly*, 1, 53–73.

Friedman, V., & Paton, E. (2021, March 29). What is going on with China, cotton and all of these clothing branding. *The New York Times*. Retrieved from https://www.nytimes.com/2021/03/29/style/china-cotton-uyghur-hm-nike.html

Godar, S. H., O'Connor, P. J., & Taylor, V. A. (2005). Evaluating the ethics of inversion. *Journal of Business Ethics, 61*, 1–6.

Guillermo, J. C., & Elizabeth, P. (2016). *Good corporation, bad corporation: Corporate social responsibility in the global economy*. Open SUNY Textbooks. Retrieved from https://milnepublishing.geneseo.edu/good-corporation-bad-corporation/chapter/10-corruption-in-international-business/

Hawkins, L. (2007). *Stakeholder analysis. (A presentation delivered at the 2007 Colorado conference on volunteerism & service learning)*. Retrieved from http://www.hawkinstrategies.com/Files/CFO/Paper.pdf.

International Labor Forum. (2005). *2005 List: The 14 worst corporate evildoers*. Retrieved from https://laborrights.org/in-the-news/2005-list-14-worst-corporate-evildoers

Irwin, S. (2021, April 26). *Is your coffee brewing slavery?* Retrieved from https://thefreedomhub.org/blog/is-your-coffee-brewing-slavery/

Jaeger, J (2019, April 16). *Uber discloses its bribery and corruption risk*. Retrieved from https://www.complianceweek.com/anti-corruption/uber-discloses-its-bribery-and-corruption-risk/26906.article


12

Jamali, D., & Mirshak, R. (2007). Corporate social responsibility: Theory and practice in a developing country context. *Journal of Business Ethics, 72*, 243–262.
Khatri, B. (2019, April 15). *Here's why uber is having a rough ride in India*. Retrieved from https://inc42.com/buzz/heres-why-uber-is-having-a-rough-ride-in-india/
Kherchi, I., Fellague, M., & AhlemHaddou, S. (2019). Creating shared value in marketing "wal-mart retailing company model". *Sustainable Development, 1*(02), 90–103. Retrieved from https://www.asjp.cerist.dz/en/downArticle/672/1/2/123662
King, C. I. (2001). *Saudi Arabia's apartheid*. The Washington Post. Retrieved from https://www.washingtonpost.com/archive/opinions/2001/12/22/saudi-arabias-apartheid/6dc54ab8-37bc-4a87-86f4-c0b489fc8b8e/
Kramer, M. R., & Porter, M. (2011). *Creating shared value* (Vol. 17). FSG.
Lawrence, A. T., & Weber, J. (2011). *Business and society: Stakeholders, ethics, public policy* (13th ed.). McGraw-Hill/Irwin.
Lewis, J. (2021, August 3). *The dark truth behind Starbucks' coffee plantations*. Retrieved from https://www.mashed.com/476972/the-dark-truth-behind-starbucks-coffee-plantations/
Liu Y. (2014). *Walmart—Creating shared value*. Retrieved from https://blogs.ubc.ca/yunmoliu/2014/11/09/walmart-creating-shared-value/
Manjoo, F. (2017 April 14). Uber wants to rule the world. *The New York Times*. Retrieved from https://www.nytimes.com/2017/04/14/technology/uber-india.html
Matute, J., Sánchez-Torelló, J. L., & Palau-Saumell, R. (2021). The influence of organizations' tax avoidance practices on consumers' behavior: The role of moral reasoning strategies, political ideology, and brand identification. *Journal of Business Ethics, 174*, 369–386.
Mayer, D., & Cava, A. (2005). Social contract theory and gender discrimination: Some reflections on the Donaldson/Dunfee model. *Business Ethics Quarterly, 5*(2), 257–271.
Mehafdi, M. (2000). The ethics of international transfer pricing. *Journal of Business ethics, 28*, 365–381.
Nguyen, T. T. H., Yang, Z., Nguyen, N., Johnson, L. W., & Cao, T. K. (2019). Greenwash and green purchase intention: The mediating role of green skepticism. *Sustainability, 11*(9), 2653.
Park, K. (2022, December). *Green trademarks and the risk of greenwashing*. WIPO. Retrieved from https://www.wipo.int/wipo_magazine/en/2022/04/article_0006.html
Paton, E., & Ramzy, A.. (2020, July 23). Coalition brings pressure to end forced Uighur labor. *The New York Times*. Retrieved from https://www.nytimes.com/2020/07/23/fashion/uighur-forced-labor-cotton-fashion.html
Porter, M. E., & Kramer, M. R. (2002). The competitive advantage of corporate philanthropy. *Harvard Business Review*, 80(12), 56–68.
Porter, M. E., & Kramer, M. R. (2006). The link between competitive advantage and corporate social responsibility. *Harvard Business Review*, 84(12), 78–92.
Rangan, K., Chase, L., & Karim, S. (2015). The truth about CSR. *Harvard Business Review, 93*(1/2), 40–49.
Shah, A. (2018, October 22). *Uber, Ola drivers strike in India, demanding higher fares*. Reuters. Retrieved from https://www.reuters.com/article/us-uber-ola-strike-idUSKCN1MW1WZ
Skariachan, D. (2016, July 28). *Uber, Ola face increased resistance from traditional transport*. Retrieved from https://www.livemint.com/Companies/49KCcygZrWIxIXn53RkzMP/Uber-Ola-face-increased-resistance-from-traditional-transpo.html
Spicer, A. (2009). The normalization of corrupt business practices: Implications for integrative social contracts theory (ISCT). *Journal of Business Ethics, 88*(S4), 833–840.
Starbucks Website. (n.d.). *Committed to transparency—People, planet, coffee*. Retrieved from https://www.starbucks.com/responsibility/reporting-hub/
Starbucksathome Website. (n.d.). *CAFE practices*. Retrieved from https://www.starbucksathome.com/gb/story/cafe-practices
Tagpuan (n.d.). *Three ways to create shared value*. Retrieved from https://tagpuanph.wixsite.com/creatingsharedvalue/three-ways-to-create-shared-value
The Wharton School. (2012, May 9). *Everyone's problem: Looking beyond the Wal-Mart Bribery case*. Retrieved from http://knowledge.wharton.upenn.edu/article/everyones-problem-looking-beyond-the-wal-mart-bribery-case/

Transport & Environment. (2020, March 19). *Uber pollutes more than the cars it replaces—US scientists*. Retrieved from https://www.transportenvironment.org/discover/uber-pollutes-more-cars-it-replaces-us-scientists/

UN Press, (2018). *Global cost of corruption at least 5 per cent of world gross domestic product*. Secretary-General Tells Security Council. https://press.un.org/en/2018/sc13493.doc.htm

Vandeveld, K. (2015, September 24). *Corporate social responsibility: How Starbucks is making an impact*. Retrieved from https://www.whywhisper.co/the-blog/2015/9/24/corporate-social-responsibility-how-starbucks-is-making-an-impact

Velasquez, M., Andre, C., Thomas Shanks S. J., & Meyer, M. J. (2015, August 1). *Thinking ethically*. Retrieved from https://www.scu.edu/ethics/ethics-resources/ethical-decision-making/thinking-ethically/

Voice of America. (2014, December 14). *Concerns raised for Uber, ride-sharing services*. https://www.51voa.com/VOA_Special_English/concerns-raised-for-uber-ride-sharing-services-60191.html

Walmart Inc. (2018). 2018 GLOBAL RESPONSIBILITY REPORT. https://corporate.walmart.com/content/dam/corporate/documents/purpose/environmental-social-andgovernance-report-archive/wal-071-2018-grr-full-book1.pdf

Watson, B. (2016). The troubling evolution of corporate greenwashing. *Sat, 20*, 15.

World Economic Forum. (2020). *How multinationals influence the gender wage gap on a global scale?* Retrieved from https://www.weforum.org/agenda/2020/03/women-multinationals-gender-wage-gap-developing-countries/

Yang, X., & Rivers, C. (2009). Antecedents of CSR practices in MNC subsidiaries: A stakeholder and institutional perspective. *Journal of Business Ethics, 86*(2), 155–169.

Zhang, X., Zhong, T., Liu, L., & Ouyang, X. (2015). Impact of soil heavy metal pollution on food safety in China. *PLoS ONE, 10*, e0135182. https://doi.org/10.1371/journal.pone.0135182

## Further Reading

Cuervo-Cazurra, A., Dieleman, M., Hirsch, P., Rodrigues, S. B., & Zyglidopoulos, S. (2021). Multinationals' misbehavior. *Journal of World Business*, 56(5) For more information about multinationals' misbehaviour, refer to.

Cuervo-Cazurra, A., Dieleman, M., Hirsch, P., Rodrigues, S. B., & Zyglidopoulos, S. (2021). Multinationals' misbehavior. *Journal of World Business, 56*(5), 101244.

Werther, W. B., Jr., & Chandler, D. (2010). *Strategic corporate social responsibility: Stakeholders in a global environment*. Sage (For more information about the stakeholder perspective of CSR, refer to).

# The Ongoing Management of Multinational Service Firms

# Global Service Marketing

## Contents




D. Klimkeit et al., *International Management in Service Firms*, Classroom Companion: Business,
https://doi.org/10.1007/978-3-031-50345-0_13

**Learning Outcomes**

After completing this chapter, you should be able to:

- explain the product strategy when marketing services in the global market
- assess the pricing strategy for services in the global market
- identify the key issues when distributing services in the global market
- analyze how communication strategies should be developed in the global market
- evaluate the special issues in developing the marketing mix for digital services

## Introduction

Companies expand internationally to reach more customers, gain higher profit opportunities, balance sales across countries if one country experiences problems, and compete with other brands expanding internationally and with global firms in their home markets. What is the best way to reach those international customers?

This chapter addresses to what extent and how service firms adapt their marketing mix to the country markets they have entered. The marketing mix includes the four Ps—product, price, promotion, and place. We will look into the implications that the unique features of services have on the international marketing mix, as opposed to that of manufactured goods.

### Opening Case: Airbnb's Struggle in China

When first entering the Chinese market in 2015, Airbnb struggled.

China's fast-growing middle class has been driving a boom in domestic tourism, with younger millennials increasingly looking for alternative options to the traditional tour group vacations of their parent's generation. According to China Tourism Research Institute, there were 120 million outbound Chinese tourists in 2015, an increase of 12% from the previous year. Meanwhile, Daxue Consulting predicted there would be 200 million Chinese overseas travelers by 2020. If Airbnb accessed this market successfully, its brand reputation across China could soar and allow them to scale rapidly.

At the same time, foreign businesses often face stiff competition from their Chinese counterparts upon entry into the Chinese market. Airbnb was no exception. Players leading this market included ► Tujia.com, Mayi.com, Xiaozhu.com, and Zhubaijia.

- Founded in December 2011, Tujia acquired bulk and standard new housing sources working with real estate developers and room owners. Tujia mainly targeted the tourism destination cities market and provided accommodation services for travelers in China by using a model similar to that originally constructed by Airbnb. They used their local knowledge to build services that directly address trends in Chinese consumer behavior. Recognizing that Chinese consumers disliked industry intermediaries, they managed 10,000 of their listed properties themselves rather than solely con-

Airbnb app on a smartphone, apartment, image by Peggy from Pixabay

necting travelers with local homeowners. Accordingly, their services became very popular as they operated over 400,000 rooms in 250 destinations across China in 2016.

- ► Mayi.com, founded in November 2011, offered beyond 300,000 short-term accommodations, including tickets to tourist attractions and car rentals. It focused on family customers, with 80% of its bookings coming from family travelers. Mayi was acquired by Tujia in 2016.
- Launched in August 2012, ► Xiaozhu.com platform provided about 140,000 rooms. It advocated personalized accommodation space to encourage the landlord to share their own life experiences, allowing users to enjoy deep and unique experiences. It mainly targeted first and second-tier cities and had listings in over 400 locations globally, and raised US$65 million in November 2016.
- Founded in March 2012, Zhubaijia focused on the outbound tourism market with over 250,000 rooms across 70 countries. It targeted domestic outbound tourists who would rent houses abroad for a short period, which was different from Xiaozhu and Tujia. Over 60% of its revenues came from short-term overseas accommodations in 2016.

Airbnb, therefore, faced the challenges of replicating its global popularity in China. Airbnb made a series of efforts to cater to the local demand.

- Airbnb started by changing its name to Aibiying, which roughly translates as "welcome one another with love."
- Next, it expanded its local staff and secured funding from major Chinese investors, including China Investment Corporation, the state sovereign-wealth fund.

- On the marketing side, the company's Chinese team ensured it stayed attuned to local cultural trends and tastes. For example, Airbnb expanded its "Experiences" platform across China and agreed on a partnership with the Chengdu Research Base of Giant Panda Breeding. Airbnb also probed unusual avenues for brand building by engaging in a collaborative exhibition of modern artists at Beijing's UCCA Centre for Contemporary Art. The ambition was developed through a campaign that featured Chinese artisans sharing their knowledge as part of the "Airbnb Experience" program, a move that smartly connected the company's brand with Chinese cultural heritage. A documentary followed with the second season of "Adventure Life" co-produced by Tencent Video, an affiliate of the China tech giant. "Adventure Life" captured the journeys of Chinese celebrities to destinations around the world and explored the relationships they built along the way. Travelers under 35 years old accounted for 60% of Airbnb's China users, and the show's focus on "slow travel" reflected the viewpoint of these tourists who longed for more than mere list checking. Viewers could fantasize about cycling through Canada with a 72-year-old man, creating a crop circle in England, or studying the art of a Japanese tea ceremony. Each episode featured a major domestic star such as actress Zhou Xun, social media celebrity Angelababy, or model Liu Wen. The stars stayed in Airbnb-listed properties and interacted with their hosts and locals. The show emphasized Airbnb's key advantage over its domestic Chinese competitors: a global presence of the "Airbnb Experiences" program.
- Airbnb also ensured its interface was increasingly localized and adapted. For example, Apirbnb used a localized version of google maps, which was blocked in China, so that its customers could navigate effectively. It also integrated its app with Chinese social networks, such as Weibo and WeChat. Airbnb's collaboration with Tencent extended beyond the series and leveraged the company's dominant presence in entertainment and social media circles. Airbnb and Tencent's QQ Music partnered for promotional purposes, and Airbnb launched an "adventure guide" on WeChat with "adventure coupons" worth RMB 1000 ($142) and chances to win accommodation. Offline activities included "adventure concerts" at various Beijing venues and a "coffee adventure" campaign with local roastery Seesaw Coffee.

Despite the loalization efforts, the reality turned out to be less optimistic, and Airbnb failed to go mainstream in China. To older generations, staying at someone's home or couch surfing remained alien concepts, while to younger people, hostel chains were cheaper and easier to access. Local rivals, backed by tech giants such as Alibaba, Meituan, and Ctrip, fought for customers by offering generous subsidies and charging lower fees and less per night on average than in other regions—this is a strategy Chinese tech companies often use when trying to establish control of a newly emerged sector. Airbnb stayed out of that price war, and, as a result, rentals in China accounted for just 1% of its global revenue. Airbnb was also slow to incorporate the dominant mobile payment methods, Alipay and WeChat Pay.

In light of the pcoronavirus disease 2019 (COVID-19) crisis starting in late 2019, Airbnb launched its +"Rest Assured Stays" program to promote listings with exceptional cleanliness and high sanitation standards. The company had been aggressively offering coupons to guests and hosts to re-engage its users and rebuild consumer confidence in the travel industry. For example, Airbnb offered a host a US$ 100 coupon to boost the number of hosts.

Since the COVID-19 pandemic, strict zero-Covid policies have compounded Airbnb's problems by sharply curbing domestic and cross-border travel, with foreign tourists barred from entering the country. Authorities also made it difficult for citizens to obtain or renew passports and limited outbound travel. Citizens re-entering the country were required to quarantine in special hotels for up to 4 weeks.

Airbnb's presence in China has also been a source of controversy. Airbnb said it had been upfront with users regarding what data was shared with Chinese authorities but noted in its annual report that complying with Beijing's policies could materially adversely affect its brand reputation. Vivian Wu, a former Airbnb host in Beijing, said she stopped having guests after local authorities scrutinized the platform. "They wanted guests to report to the police," she said. "Police also called to tell me it was illegal."

In 2022, Airbnb Inc. shut its operations in China, choosing to focus instead on outbound Chinese tourism as the country continued its aggressive approach to containing Covid-19.

**Questions**

1. What drives the standardization versus localization strategy of Airbnb?
2. What did Airbnb do to tackle the barriers to promoting its service in China?
3. What could be the reasons Airbnb does not engage in a price war with its Chinese competitors?

Source: (Canaves, 2019; CIW Team, 2017; Cortese, 2020; Daxue Consulting, 2016; Griffith, 2022; Lee & McMorrow, 2022; Tobin, 2022; Xiang et al., 2021; Zhou, 2022)

13

## Product Policy

When expanding into a new market or region, your customer's requirement for the service should be your priority if success is to be achieved. Should you offer the standardized service in foreign markets as in your domestic market or customize the service to foreign contexts? How do the characteristics of service influence the standardization versus customization decision? This section gives a detailed discussion of these two issues.

## Standardization Versus Customization of Services

A recurrent theme in global marketing is whether companies should aim for standardized or country-tailored market offerings. Consider the following two contrasting examples. McDonald's represents a classic example of service standardization. Consistency can be found in its widely recognized golden arches, employee uniforms and restaurant design, the similar menu (with minor modifications to cater to location-specific peculiarities, such as lamb burgers in India), and the standardized food preparation process (Ritzer, 2011). In contrast, Amazon Prime Wardrobe has recently launched a personal shopping service exclusively for Prime members. Customers complete a survey about their styles and fit preferences, and a team of stylists provides personalized recommendations from more than half a million items across brands (Lindecrantz et al., 2020). The two brands represent a fundamental difference in their international marketing strategies: McDonald's emphasizes service standardization, while Amazon emphasizes service customization.

### Service Standardization

Service standardization refers to a non-varying sequential process, similar to the mass production of goods, in which each step is laid out in order, and all outcomes are uniform (Shostack, 1987). The objective of standardized services is to reach as many customers as possible while satisfying a rather limited number of customer needs (Simonson, 2005).

**Service Standardization**

*Service standardization* refers to a non-varying sequential process similar to the mass production of goods. Each step is laid out in order, and all outcomes are uniform.

A few factors favor the standardization strategy:

1. **Common customer needs:** For many product/service categories, customer needs are similar across countries. For example, for courier services, customers look for the same kind of functional benefits, i.e., speed and reliability, around the world. For other services such as streaming (Netflix), consumers overlap in terms of the emotional benefits being pursued (e.g., enjoyment); hence, global content offered is made possible.
2. **Global customers:** In business-to-business marketing, the shift toward globalization means that many business clients are multinational corporations (MNCs). These MNCs have operations around the world and hence are essentially global customers. Buying and sourcing decisions are commonly centralized or globally coordinated, or at least regionalized. As a result, such customers typically demand services or products that are harmonized worldwide.

3. **Global uniformity and image and predictability:** The standardization in service industries such as restaurants, hotels, retailing, and tourism (Ritzer, 2011) helps a service company establish global uniformity and image (Albaum et al., 2016: 434–441), which gives customers the *predictability*. Such predictability implies that regardless of location, customers can expect to receive a consistent standard of service. This is particularly valuable for service given its experience-based nature—customers cannot evaluate the quality sufficiently unless they consume it. Just like when you travel abroad, you may be worried that the food in the local restaurant could be too unusual and unpredictable. You may feel more confident and safer going into McDonald's for a predictable Burger and Fry set.
4. **Technology advancement:** The development of technology has facilitated the delivery of standardized and consistent service performance (Ding & Keh, 2016). For example, the growth in self-service technologies (Meuter et al., 2000) such as ATMs, pay-at-the-pump at many filling stations where customers can pay for their fuel by inserting a credit, debit card, or fuel card into a slot on the pump, automated hotel checkout, vending machines, and Internet transactions has made standardized service delivery more possible.
5. **Easier planning and control:** (Albaum et al., 2016: 434–441) Standardization removes the discrepancy between teams and employees. IT process standardization, for example, brings a standard way of reviewing and testing software code. By bringing in a rigorous testing process that the entire team follows, software errors can be brought down, and high-quality software can be delivered. A standardized service process also makes it possible to convey the standardized business model to the franchisees and monitor their performance.
6. **Economies of scale** (Albaum et al., 2016: 434–441): With a standardization strategy, a service company treats all its markets as a single market. This allows the business to concentrate standardized value activities in a few locations to produce service components on a large scale, which results in lower costs. This will be given more discussion in ► Sect. 4.2.
7. **Transfer of learning:** By standardizing processes and tasks, it becomes easier to document, transfer, and retain knowledge. Such documented knowledge first helps give training to new staff or rotated staff. In addition, often, when an employee with unique work knowledge quits the organization, the working knowledge is lost. It takes time and money to regain the working knowledge lost this way. Standard protocols ensure that a single employee is not responsible for a critical business process. Proper documentation and a standard off-boarding process enable smooth and proper knowledge transfer so that the knowledge stays in the organization even when the employee leaves the organization.
8. **Reduce costs:** Standardization can reduce costs in a few ways. First, it eliminates repetitive tasks, bringing down the costs associated with these steps. These repetitive steps can be effectively automated to reduce the strain on employees, just like using ATMs to replace manual services. The time saved thus can be channelized into productive activities that improve process output quality. Second, standardization can help reduce stock costs. This can involve using

standardized parts, equipment, or materials that can be purchased in bulk at a lower cost. By reducing the number of unique items in inventory, companies can minimize the amount of working capital tied up in inventory and reduce the costs associated with storage, handling, and obsolescence. Standardization can also streamline production and supply chain processes, leading to further cost savings.

## Service Customization

In contrast to standardization, customization refers to some level of adaptation or tailoring of the process to meet the individual consumer's needs (Shostack, 1987). In service, customized services may result from employees' proactive contributions, such as offering helpful information and suggestions (Keh et al., 2013). One example is a service staff in a restaurant who gives customized recommendations when guests are placing their orders. Or the customization of services could be facilitated by a predetermined "envelope of variety" (Hart, 1995), namely a range within which a service can be meaningfully customized. For instance, when you go into a car service workshop, you can choose your customized service package from a variety of services offered by the workshop.

**Service Customization**

*Service customization* refers to some level of adaptation or tailoring of the process to meet the individual consumer's needs.

Forces that push forward the service customization include:

- *Consumer preferences*. Consumer tastes and preferences can vary substantially across countries or regions in many categories. Customized services thus cater to consumers' individual aesthetic and functional preferences. In addition, perceived uniqueness induced by customization may also enhance the consumer's experience, as in the example of Amazon Prime Wardrobe (Franke & Schreier, 2008; Tian et al., 2001).
- *Cultural differences*. Each culture is made up of visible and invisible elements. Visible elements could be language, the kind of food or cooking method that has been followed for ages, or even the kind of clothing that has been used traditionally. The invisible elements of a culture are the beliefs, values, morals, and intellectual perceptions held by a specific community or society. These cultural elements vary across counties. A company needs to factor in these visible and invisible cultural elements when designing and offering its services. For instance, Disneyland Shanghai tried incorporating Chinese cultural elements into its service. One big nod to Chinese culture is the Garden of the Twelve Friends, located in the huge area in front of the castle. Each animal in the Chinese zodiac is associated with a Disney character, just like the Year of the Pig is matched to Hamm from Toy Story (see ► https://www.designingdisney.com/parks/shanghai-disney-resort/shanghai-disneyland-garden-twelve-friends/ for more

details). Incorporating such Chinese cultural elements shows an appreciation of the Chinese belief system and becomes a popular Chinese pastime. The spot has become a great place for selfies—every visitor can take photos with the animal representing their birth year (Cochran, n.d.).

- *Environmental conditions*. Local circumstances (e.g., climate and infrastructure) are another factor that can encourage companies to adapt their products or services. For example, when entering the Philippine market, Netflix provided adaptive streaming because the Internet speed in the country was perceived as not good enough for video streaming for most Internet users. Adaptive streaming means that the quality or the bitrate that comes into your device is measured in milliseconds by the conditions around you so that the pictures are constantly adjusted according to conditions, and you do not see buffering (Estopace, 2016). Uber offers Uber Boat by Thames Clippers. Uber Boat departs from key London piers every 20 min. The fleet of 18 high-speed catamarans links London's attractions, offering an alternative way to see the city sights, and has become the fastest and most frequent fleet on the river Thames (Tripadvisor website, n.d.).
- *Economic development level*. A country's economic development level greatly impacts customers' purchasing power and lifestyle. Again, Uber is well-known for its hailing services, allowing users to book a car in most developed countries. However, in developing countries, Uber offers a bigger range of services, catering to the economic development level, which has important implications for infrastructure maturity and buying power. For example, in Thailand, Uber offers motorbikes (UberMOTO), other than providing its standardized service, Uber taxis. This is because over 1500 new cars in Bangkok hit the streets daily, and the average daily commute takes 2 h. That congestion has made moto-taxis a common form of transport in Bangkok (Balea, 2016). While in In India and Pakistan, Uber customers can request a ride in a rickshaw—an open-air, bike-drawn vehicle common in Asian countries. The feature works like the company's ride-hailing service in the United States, though fares are significantly cheaper. Rides start at a minimum fare of just 74 US cents (Salinas, 2018).
- *Government policy*. The government could prescribe various product and technical standards, censorship, and social policies to influence the service's configuration and encourage or discourage some service activities. For example, in Sep 2021, China implemented new regulations tightening party oversight of private schools and restricting foreign players in the education sector. The new rules halt teaching foreign curricula in schools from kindergarten to grade nine (K-9). This means that international schools operating in China must adapt their standardized international curriculum and teach the same lessons as state-run public schools. In addition, the government may impose various restrictions on international players to protect the local business. For instance, the government could restrict foreign airlines' landing rights or ability to pick up passengers at an intermediate stop ("third freedom" rights), which provides a way to protect home-based airlines on international routes (Thomas et al., 1998). Moreover, technical standards have also developed historically, such as different electric power plugs and voltage or TV signals between the United

States and Europe. For example, in the United States, the NTSC (National Television System Committee) standard is used, while in Europe, the PAL (Phase Alternating Line) standard is used. The two standards differ in resolution, refresh rate, and color encoding. The formats are not compatible (NTSC vs. PAL, n.d.). The differences in TV signals can affect the availability of certain channels and programming in different regions. Some channels may be available in one region but not the other or may have different programming due to differences in licensing agreements or local regulations. This makes it necessary to adapt the service to the local requirement.

Though offering various benefits, service customization/localization is said to be associated with lower efficiency, lower productivity, and higher costs (Hart, 1995). The benefits of customization may be outweighed by the monetary and psychological costs that a consumer encounters, including the increased price of customized services, the delay in receipt of the custom-made service, and the need for consumers to invest time in specifying their preferences before the service can be purchased and consumed (Bardakci & Whitelock, 2004; Huffman & Kahn, 1998).

In summary, both benefits and drawbacks accrue to service standardization and customization. Most service companies make a coordinated effort of standardization and localization. McDonald's, even with its well-known standardized service model, has introduced a variation in its marketing mix. Localization of the menu can be found in a range of countries: Teri Tama Burger as a spring menu item in Japan and custom-made club sandwiches in Greece. (Mourdoukoutas, 2015). In France, to adapt to the French culture of sitting down to a meal, French McDonald's are spacious, with tastefully decorated restaurants that encourage people to take their time while eating. The cozy McCafe's, with its plush chairs and sofas, has become an extension to many restaurants (Beardsley, 2012). To achieve the best outcome, the managers need to locate the standardization and localization of the marketing mix along a continuum or seek ways to combine standardization and adaptation instead of treating it as an either-or choice.

## Modularization of Services

### What Is Service Modularization?

One way to gain the benefits of standardization and localization is through service modularity. Service modularity divides services into distinct standardized components; these standardized components can then be combined to form novel services to meet customer needs (De Blok et al., 2010; Pekkarinen & Ulkuniemi, 2008). For airline flight services, examples of service modules could be catering services, tax-free sales, flight security services, and entertainment. For a logistics service, modular structures are recognizable such as warehousing, transportation, order picking, packaging, delivery, express carriers, value-added logistics centers, or any combination of these service modules, which allow the customers to choose the best suite suiting their needs.

**Service Modularity**

*Service modularity* divides services into distinct standardized components; these standardized components can then be combined to form novel services to meet customer needs.

Like product modularity, service modularity allows keeping some elements standardized while adapting others, as in McDonald's example, thus yielding a range of benefits. First, service modularization enhances efficiency by concentrating the standardized service components into a few places to achieve specialization and economies of scale (Miozzo & Grimshaw, 2005; Pekkarinen & Ulkuniemi, 2008; Voss & Hsuan, 2009). Second, service modularization creates flexibility by mixing and matching common service components for different offerings for innovation and adaptation (Pekkarinen & Ulkuniemi, 2008; Sundbo, 2002; Voss & Hsuan, 2009). Third, as the solutions in industrial markets are becoming increasingly complex (Hobday, 1998), breaking down services into standardized modules for further integration can mitigate the adverse effects of complexity (Rahikka et al., 2011). Service modularity is therefore a potential solution to balance the opposing goals of customization and standardization in service provision (Meyer & DeTore, 1999; Sundbo, 1994).

## Design of Service Modularization

The principle of modularity is well-established in product development and software engineering. However, in recent years, this principle has been extended to different service industries, such as financial services, hospitals, logistics, IT, or health care. To design the service modules, a company needs to specify three aspects:

- **Module specification:** A service is decoupled and put into defined functional elements, i.e., standardized modules. A traveling service can be broken down into different modules: visiting the cultural highlights of Florence, museums tour, tour exploring food and dishes, and transport.
- **Minimizing relative independence:** Components comprising a module should be mutually interdependent, but the interdependence with other modules should be minimized (Campagnolo & Camuffo, 2010; Peters et al., 2018). Using the travel example, changing the public transport, e.g., from bus to tram, within the transportation component does not affect the design of a museum tour.
- **Interface specification:** The interface keeps the two or more service modules by providing common rules that govern the interdependencies between the two. In the traveling example, a travel company should arrange how the different modules are connected, e.g., making sure that the transportation, museum tour, and cultural highlights components are linked seamlessly. The interface specification is essential for connecting modules into various service configurations to address customers' diverse needs and wishes. In modular products, interfaces are typically standardized and manage the connections and interdependencies across multiple physical components that comprise the final product. However,

in modular services, interfaces are generally seen as supporting the flow and movement of clients and information from one object involved in the service component to the next (Pekkarinen & Ulkuniemi, 2008; Voss & Hsuan, 2009). The interfaces hence could be standardized or customized depending on different levels of human involvement.

- In a service with more human involvement, customers play an important role in working with an interface. In the travel service example, such an interface is usually an agent, either a human travel agent or a travel website which allows a customer to choose different components of their travel package. The customer will co-create and co-produce the ultimate service offering by specifying his or her special requests with the agent as a means of customization. For example, a customer must first convey his or her interest to a travel agency to co-create a tour package including a museum tour, a food and dish exploring tour, and a travel component. Then the customer has to agree on and stick to the timeline and arrive at the right venue (interface) suggested by the travel agency to ensure the multiple service modules are connected smoothly.

With the service modularization design, the service offering is a bundle of modules that can take different forms depending on the customer in question and still function independently. The application of service modularity can be found in B2C markets. For example, DHL offers a wide range of optional services (service modules)—from non-standard deliveries and billing options to climate-neutral shipping. Its configuration page allows customers to configure their shipment arrangement by choosing modules that suit their unique purposes. You can refer to the link ► https://help.sellercloud.com/omnichannel-ecommerce/shipping-with-dhl-ecommerce/ for their customization page.

Another example is Netflix, which has a few important modules. The first is a personal recommendation system, which suggests and pushes shows and movies based on customers' watching history. The second module is the streaming part, which provides the visual product, including shows, TV series, movies, documentaries, and talk shows. Another add-on module is the subtitle service. It comes in four or five different languages and needs to be run simultaneously with the picture and the audio. The recommendation system "interfaces" with a customer's watching history to identify the genre of a customer's tastes and interests. Then the recommendation system puts forward the visual product of the identified genes from the streaming part. The streaming service is connected to the subtitle service. All these small modules are combined to create the "magical" Netflix service experience (Yu, 2018).

In business services, an example is SAP. SAP SE is a German multinational software company based in Walldorf, Baden-Württemberg. It offers enterprise resource planning (ERP), in which a range of standardized modules in different domains and lines of business, such as material management (MM), warehouse management (WM), production plan (PP), sales and distribution (SD), finance and costing (FICO), and human capital management (HCM), are available for customers to choose. SAP also has a cross-module configuration (the interface), using which the SAP consultant helps integrate different modules based on the customers' specified demand. Should the customers have more special requirements for the service, SAP programmers can develop a tailored solution based on the standardized modules in the ABAP environment. Such service modularization helps with customer success by providing the flexibility to choose modules relevant to their business and industry. In addition, the service provider (SAP), by applying the principle of modularity, can achieve reductions in time and cost of delivering customized services.

## Hard and Soft Services

The multidimensional nature of services impacts the feasibility and the extent of standardization versus customization of service. As introduced in ▶ Chap. 1, services can include hard and soft elements. Hard elements have a physical appearance or can be coded into documents, software, and other forms, permitting the decoupling of producers and consumers. In contrast, soft elements are intangible. The producer and receiver of a soft service should be in close physical proximity, enabling production and consumption to take place simultaneously.

For some services, the majority part is hard service, for which standardization can be achieved at a high level. In the example of Netflix, the platform and most content are highly standardized. Customization is achieved by algorism, and limited adaptation is offered in terms of language (subtitles) and content to cater to different countries.

In contrast, for a service like hospitality, though standardization can be achieved for its hard service component (such as hotel buildings, decoration, furniture, facilities, and room reservation system), for its soft elements, for example, guest services, event planning, catering, and house-keeping, some *customized standardization* will be more suitable. Take event planning, for example. A hotel can provide relatively standardized packages for clients to choose from. Still, customization of types of food, wine, and decoration style should be possible when interacting with customers for their specific requirements. For guest service, the hotel staff could be required to follow some standard procedure, for example, greeting customers, offering drinks upon guests' arrival, and helping guests with check-in and check-out. He/she should also give customized advice if a guest puts forward some special query about the best sightseeing sites in town. On the one hand, such a "customized standardization" helps employees avoid mistakes and deviations in providing "customized" service. On the other hand, it will increase customer satisfaction.



## The Front Office and Back Office

Standardization versus customization can be facilitated by separating the front and back offices. According to the customer contact approach put forward by Chase (1981) and Chase and Tansik (1983), not all services are equal in terms of what they can achieve in the way of efficiency because of varied levels of customer contact when delivering the service.

Customer contact refers to the customer's physical presence in the service delivery system. Although different terms are in use, such as "on/off stage," "front/back-stage," "frontline/backline," "front/back office" seems to be most common. The front–back office model of service organizations is probably the most common way of conceptualizing the impact of customer contact on a service delivery system.

The front office of service includes the activities that require customer contact and, as such, is directly experienced by customers. These activities comprise client-facing duties commonly found in marketing, sales, public relations, and customer service. These high-contact activities are more difficult to control due to all kinds of disturbances caused by the customer, requiring interpersonal skills and being close to the customer. Take insurance services as an example. The front-office services include those driving customer experience, engagement, and behavior, such as marketing and sales distribution, product personalization, underwriting, policy administration, and claim management (first response to clients' demand for claims). Due to the need to have close contact with customers and to respond to customers' different requests, front-office service components will have a higher level of customization.

The back office contains low-contact processes and activities that cannot be seen or experienced by customers and hence can be carried out remotely by customers (Shostack, 1982, 1984; Grove & Fisk, 1992; Johnston & Clark, 2001). Examples of back-office processes are activities related to human resources management, operations, IT, accounting, and compliance. They often require technical skills and can be located close to resources. In the insurance service example, the back office services focus on streamlining in-house operations, such as data and forms processing, commission management, claims management (studying inclusions and exclusions and claimant eligibility), policy processing, and IT data processing. These low-contact parts are usually the "technical core" or a service process that can be sealed off from the environment, thus being more standardized for higher efficiency (Thompson, 1967).

► Chapter 15 treats the distinction between the front and back office in more detail in the context of the service blueprint.

## Price Policy

As in the domestic market, the price at which a product or service is sold directly determines a company's revenues. A firm's market research should include an evaluation of all variables that may affect the price range for its product or service. If the company's price is too high, the product or service will not sell. If the price is too low, export activities may not be sufficiently profitable or may create a net loss. The basic pricing challenges companies face in domestic marketing (e.g., skimming versus penetration pricing) also apply to global marketing. However, the complication of pricing in the global market accelerates due to its complex nature, for example, inflation, cross-border variations in willingness to pay, and competition.

To understand the structure of a price, we first need to examine those basic factors that influence the setting of an export price. These factors include cost, company goals, customer demand and value, competition, distribution channels, and government policies.

## Factors Influencing Pricing

**Cost:** The costs of service set the floor of a company's pricing strategy: The company wants to set at least a price that will cover all costs needed to produce and sell its products/services.

The first cost is production cost. Production cost differentials between countries can lead to wide price gaps. Management must consider all relevant costs of producing, marketing, and distributing services. The cost of producing a service generally includes fixed costs, variable costs, and semi-variable costs (Wirtz & Lovelock, 2016). Take a hotel as an example. Fixed costs may include rent/mortgage of the property, property taxes, and other related expenses (e.g., insurance), fixed monthly bills (e.g., cable and Internet), human resources (e.g., staff salaries and other payroll-related expenses), and franchise fees if applicable. Variable costs include hourly labor, utility costs, marketing and distribution costs, linen, toiletries, cleaning products, food and Beverage inventory, credit card commissions, other payment processing fees, and technology costs (e.g., hotel management software fees, guest room technology). Semi-variable costs fall in between fixed and variable costs. They represent expenses that rise or fall in a stepwise fashion as the volume of businesses increases or decreases. Examples are hiring a part-time employee to work in the hotel or the extra shuttle buses to meet increased demand during the peak seasons.

In addition, a company also needs to consider the factor of discounts. Channel partners often ask for discounts or other incentives to buy from a service firm. For example, when hiring a travel agency to sell the hotel service, the travel agency usually asks for a discount. Discounting can have a significant impact on the hotel's margins and profit.



There are additional costs that the importer typically bears. These include tariffs, customs fees, currency fluctuation, transaction costs (including shipping), and taxes. These costs can add substantially to the final price paid by the importer.

The above cost will vary depending on where the service is produced and how the service is distributed. For example, prices for services tend to show larger differences across countries than for goods due to the higher share of labor input into services and the high dispersion of wages across countries (Europa, 2022).

**Company goals:** When developing a pricing strategy for its global markets, the firm needs to decide what company goals it wants to accomplish with its strategy. These goals might include maximizing current profits, penetrating the market, projecting a premium image, and so forth. Company goals could vary across different markets and over time. For example, initially, when a company enters a foreign market, it is not rare that the company sets a lower price to penetrate the market.

Once the firm establishes its position in the market, it may shift the objective to profit-gaining or image-building, aligning with the price in other markets.

**Customer demand:** Customers' willingness to pay for service sets a ceiling to the price. Consumer demand is a function of purchasing power, tastes, habits, and substitutes. These demand conditions will vary from country to country. Customers in countries with low per-capita income may have lower purchasing power and are more price sensitive than those in developed markets. Denmark has the most expensive haircuts in the world, with an average price of $75.20 across genders, while in Nigeria, a trim costs $13.43 for a Nigerian woman but just $1.83 for a man (Alex, 2021). This disparity, though partially explained by the wage of service staff, is attributed to the purchasing power to a great extent.

Even with similar per-capita income, customers in different countries tend to show big differences in their values, for example, in terms of their priority towards price versus quality. When Walmart tried to operate its "everyday low price" in Japan, it did not receive a positive response as in its home country United States, because Japanese customers were highly sophisticated and more conscious about freshness and quality than low price (Inagaki & Lewis, 2020).

Cultural symbolism can also influence pricing decisions. In China, the number "eight" has traditional associations with prosperity due to similarities in the pronunciation of the number "eight" (ba) in Chinese to "to be rich" (fa) and "to be lucky" (fu). Hence, the use of the number "eight" in price promotions (such as paying 88% or $888) in the gift shop can bring higher positive emotional responses among Chinese tourists, increasing their purchasing intention (Wang et al., 2021).

**Competition:** Differences in the competitive situation across countries could also lead to cross-border price differentials. A service company may face a different number of competitors, and the nature of competition could also vary across countries. For example, when supermarket chain Carrefour entered Egypt in 2002, over 80% of the distribution market was handled by small-scale grocery stores located in most neighborhoods and focused on convenience (Oxford Business Group, n.d.). In such a market, Carrefour would have more space to set its price—they could set a high price to create a premium image or a low price based on bulky purchases, either of which could help it stand out from competitors. This was very different from when Carrefour was in South Korea, where it faced fierce competition from local and international chains, such as Shinsegae, Lotte, and Tesco. Being the price taker might be the only option (The New York Time, 2006). To be the price leaders or price takers depends on the competition landscape in different country markets.

**Distribution channels:** Another driver behind global pricing is the distribution channel. Countries such as France and the United Kingdom are characterized by large retailers (e.g., Carrefour and Tesco) who can order in bulk and bargain for huge discounts with manufacturers. When entering Japan, Walmart found it difficult to get discounts from local suppliers because Japan's food retail scene was extremely fragmented. Historically, even the biggest domestic participants could not establish an upper hand (Inagaki & Lewis, 2020). This made it difficult for Walmart to maintain its low price as a competitive advantage.

**Government policies:** Government policies can have a direct or indirect impact on pricing policies. Policy factors such as sales tax rates (e.g., value-added taxes), tariffs, and price control directly influence prices. In 2022, India increased GST for various categories of goods and services. For instance, hotels with rent below Rs 1000 per day, which were exempted from GST before, would now be taxed a GST of 12% (Motiani, 2022). Such a tax increase will have important implications for a service company's cost structure and profit margin. Government policies could also have an indirect impact on pricing by influencing operational costs. For example, when a high government deficit increases the interest rate, inflation, and exchange rate fluctuation, a service company will incur a higher cost. The government's social policy (e.g., health) could influence labor costs. The environmental regulations and technical standards could increase/decrease costs.

## Pricing Strategies and Their Application in Service Industries

Considering those factors, a service company could use one or a combination of the following approaches to get the pricing in the global market.

**Cost-based pricing:** Cost-based pricing is a way to build a profit margin directly into the price of the product or service: You calculate the cost to deliver a service and then add a profit margin (plus), for example, 10%. It is a straightforward way to price the service. It will be more appropriate in a country market where a service company faces less competition and has favorable consumer response since it doesn't consider the customer or competitors. Otherwise, a company may leave money on the table by focusing on cost.

However, using the cost-based pricing strategy in services is usually more complex than it is in manufacturing. It is generally harder to determine the financial costs of creating a process or intangible real-time performance for a customer than to identify the labor, materials, machine time, storage, and shipping costs related to producing and distributing a physical good. In addition, many service companies have a higher ratio of fixed costs to variable costs than usually found in manufacturing companies, attributed to the labor and infrastructure needed to deliver the services. For example, service businesses may have high fixed costs, such as expensive physical facilities (hospitals or colleges), a fleet of vehicles (airlines or cruise companies), or a network (railroad, telecommunication services).



For service companies with high fixed costs and complex product lines with shared infrastructure, such as in college, hospital, or retail banking, a more complex activity-based costing (ABC) approach could be worthwhile (Wirtz & Lovelock, 2016). ABC links resources needed to perform an activity. A set of activities comprising the processes are identified, and the related costs are estimated. It increases understanding of overheads and cost drivers and makes costly and non-value-adding activities more visible, allowing managers to reduce or eliminate them.

■ **Table 13.1** The activity-based costing approach of a hospital

| Activity | Activity rate (estimated) | Patient usage | Patient costs |
|---|---|---|---|
| Admissions | $80 per admission | 1 admission | $80 × 1 = $80 |
| Operating room use | $1000 per hour | 3 h | $1000 × 3 = 3000 |
| Dispensing medications | $35 per administration | 3 times per day/5 days | $35 × 3 × 5 = 525 |
| Radiology testing | $350 per image | 2 images | $350 × 2 = 700 |
| Diagnostic lab | $180 test | 5 tests | $180 × 5 = 900 |
| Medical assistance | $30 per visit | 5 visits per day/5 days | $30 × 5 × 5 = 750 |
| Cleaning and laundry | $100 per day | 5 days | $100 × 5 = 500 |
| Discharge | $150 per discharge | 1 discharge | $150 × 1 = 150 |
| | | | Total = $6605 |

Source: Author's own table. A total of $6605 of overhead costs is associated with this patient's hospital stay

A hospital, for example, might identify the activities, such as admissions, operating room use, dispensing medications, radiology testing, diagnostic lab, medical assistance, cleaning, and laundry and discharge, whose general costs must be shared among patients. Each activity rate is estimated based on the activity's budgeted overhead cost divided by the number of occurrences expected during the year, as shown in ■ Table 13.1. For each patient stay, the number of times each activity occurs is multiplied by the overhead rate for that activity. The sum of all the activity costs is the amount of overhead applied to servicing the patient.

**Value-based pricing:** Value-based pricing takes into account two key questions related to customers: 1. Can they pay? 2. Will they pay? The determinant factor in this pricing strategy is how much the customers are willing to pay rather than how much a product or service costs to produce or deliver. The willingness to pay depends on the net value customer perceive from receiving a service (Lovelock & Wirtz, 2016).

Net value = perceived value – perceived cost.

On the one hand, value is subjective, and not all customers have the skills or knowledge to judge the quality and value they receive, particularly for the credence services, for which customers cannot access the quality of service even after consumption. The invisibility of back-stage facilities and labor makes it hard for customers to see what they get for their money. For example, when a homeowner calls an electrician to repair a defective circuit, the electrician arrives carrying a small bag of tools. He goes into the closet, locates the problem, replaces a faulty circuit breaker, and everything works in about 15 min. Then the electrician showed the bill to the homeowner. The homeowner was shocked by the bill of $200 and could not see the value. This is because customers often fail to recognize the fixed costs that business owners need to recoup. In the electrician's case, fixed costs include the office, telephone, insurance, vehicles, tools, and office support staff. The variable costs of a home visit could also be higher than it appears—15 min of service in the house may be associated with 20 min of driving and 5 min of loading/unloading time to move the needed tools and supplies from the van. The firm also needs to add in a margin to make a profit (Wirtz & Lovelock, 2016).

To manage the perception of value, effective communication, and even personal explanations are needed to help customers understand the value they receive. The electrician could quickly explain it in a simple service of fixing wires. In more complicated service offerings such as strategy consulting, marketers must find ways to communicate the time, professional research expertise, and attention given to the details that go into, for example, completing a best practice in a consulting project.

On the other hand, a customer's overall costs are more than the price of the product/service itself. For example, when considering booking a hotel room, customers will calculate monetary and non-monetary costs. *The monetary cost* includes not only the price of the room service but also the related costs such as transportation costs from the hotel to transportation junctions and various tourist sites, the parking cost, the cost of buying food, beverages, and others from the nearby stores. *The non-monetary costs* are other costs a customer may associate with the purchase, such as search cost (e.g., the effort invested in identifying, comparing, and selecting among services), the time cost (e.g., time spent commuting from the hotel to the destinations), the convenience cost (e.g., service hours do not coincide with the customers' available time), and the psychological cost (e.g., a customer may feel anxious due to language barriers or unclear check-in process, or a status-conscious customer may feel uncomfortable of lodging in a low-priced hotel).



A service firm can create a competitive advantage by minimizing the customers' monetary and non-monetary costs. Some possible approaches include:

- Provide sales promotions, such as discounts, rebates, and member rates, to reduce monetary costs.
- Reduce the search costs by providing information in multiple channels, helping customers access, compare, and evaluate the services.
- Reduce the time and convenience costs by shortening traveling, waiting, and delivery time. For example, an e-commerce site could collaborate with logistic partners to ensure quick delivery and develop a tracking system to allow customers to plan their time conveniently.
- Reduce the psychological cost by enhancing staff's communication competence and aligning the firm's positioning with target customers' identity.

**Competitive pricing:** Competitive pricing focuses neither on costs nor on customers. Instead, competitive pricing is about the existing product or service market. In competitive pricing, a service company is to research the pricing strategies of many competitors to establish a pricing range. The range should have a high and a low end, and the service price should fall somewhere between those bookends to be competitive.

However, competitive pricing could be less relevant for service industries due to a few reasons:

- Personal relationship matters for services that are featured by high personalization and customization, such as hair styling, family medical care, or some B2B businesses.
- Switching costs need to be considered. While switching costs may not be high for every type of service, it could be for some. This is particularly the case in which customers have to be involved in a relatively long-term contract with the service provider, and penalties apply if the contract terminates early. Typically B2B services are some examples. Just like those firms purchasing a heavy machine and the related services from Caterpillar. It will be too costly for them to switch to another service provider since such switching will be associated with not only the cost of the machine but also the relevant supporting hardware and software, as well as the costs of training workers and engineers. Similarly, a customer may be less likely to change to a new insurance company after he/she signs a contract with an existing insurance company, since there will be cancellation fees within a certain period of time.
- Some services are time and location-specific. For example, a customer may only hope to be a member of a Gym nearby his/her home.

**Skimming versus penetration pricing:** Skimming pricing sets the highest possible price out of a product's distinctiveness in the introduction stage to attract customers most interested in the product or service to maximize short-term profits. The high price is set until the small market at that price is exhausted. The price may then be lowered to tap a second successive market or income level (Albaum et al., 2016). The rationale of this strategy is to skim surplus from customers early in the product life cycle and exploit a monopolistic position or the low price sensitivity of early adopters (e.g., Dean, 1976; Marn et al., 2003).

This technique is used when a new product faces no to little competition in the market and has a great extent of consumer acceptability. Skimming pricing is adopted by the company due to the following reasons (Dean, 1976):

- In the early stages, the demand for the product is inelastic till the product occupies a good position in the market.
- In the initial phase, the demand for the product is not known, and the high price helps in covering the cost of production.
- In the beginning, there is a huge requirement of capital for producing the product, resulting in high production costs. Further, a huge amount is invested in promotional activities, which also adds to its cost. When the product is charged high, it will easily cover the production and promotion expenses.

A variation in the skimming strategy is *sliding down the demand curve*. The strategy involves starting with a price that the market will bear and moving from this point toward cost pricing at a measured pace. The pace must be slow enough to pick up profits but fast enough to discourage competitors from entering the market. This is primarily used by companies introducing product innovations. Companies following this strategy seek to recover development costs as they become established in the market (Albaum et al., 2016).

A penetration strategy involves charging a low price at the product launch to rapidly reach a wide fraction of the market and initiate word-of-mouth (WOM), which helps create a mass market (Albaum et al., 2016; Dean, 1976; Nagle et al., 2011, p. 127). Penetration pricing is designed to enlarge market share and exploit economies of scale or experience (Tellis, 1986). When the demand picks up, the firm can increase the product's price. Penetration pricing results in lower profits in the short run; however, the firm hopes to obtain higher profits based on a bigger market base in the long run. The reasons behind adopting penetration pricing are as follows (Albaum et al., 2016; Dean, 1976):

- If the price is adjusted to target a mass market, the resulting increase in volume can drive down costs to a level where the price generates a profit. In industries characterized by rapidly declining costs, penetration pricing can expedite this process.
- The demand is highly elastic, or foreign purchasers buy primarily on a price basis.
- Other well-established brands already provide new products offered by the firm. The low price will lure customers familiar with other brands to switch to the new product.
- It can help in increasing sales of the product in a short period.
- It restricts new entrants from entering the market.



We could see more service companies use penetrating pricing instead of skimming pricing when launching new services. This is reasonable given the experience and credence nature of the services. It is hard for customers to evaluate a new service before and even after receiving it. So the service company has to reduce the costs for the customers. One example is the Streaming service Netflix (Keenan, 2022). The late 1990s was the heyday of rental services. Netflix entered the market with a new promise: Waiting 1 or 2 days for a DVD to arrive will allow customers access to a better movie library without fees. A customer could rent four movies at a time for $15.95 per month without a return date. That's a big difference from Blockbuster, its main competitor at the time. For a single, three-day rental, the rental service charged $4.99. The price point for a Netflix rental was around $1 per DVD. It's history from there. By providing value to consumers, Netflix disrupted the rental market so much that Blockbuster went bankrupt.

**Yield management:** Yield management is a pricing strategy based on understanding, anticipating, and influencing consumer behavior to maximize revenue or profits from a fixed, time-limited resource (Netessine & Shumsky, 2002). For example, a hotel forecasts a higher demand in the peak season and will charge $200 for a room to those willing to pay such a high price, while the same room is charged $100 during non-peak season. As a pricing strategy, yield management uses data to ensure the right room is sold to the right customer, at the right time, for the highest possible price. Yield management is commonly utilized by businesses in hospitality, air travel, and other tourism-related sectors, featured by perishable and fixed inventory. There are three conditions to make yield management possible: 1. There is a fixed amount of resources available for sale. For example, on an aircraft, there are 200 seats. 2. The resources sold are perishable. If some seats cannot be sold for a trip from Singapore to Munich before the aircraft takes off, the airline company cannot re-*sell* those unsold *seats* for the same trip after the aircraft takes off. So the inventory (seats) is perishable. 3. Different customers are willing to pay a different price for the same service. Customers with urgent needs are willing to pay a high price for a seat, while those traveling for leisure only want to pay a low price for the same seat.

## Relation to Domestic Prices in Service Industries

When developing a global pricing strategy, one of the most critical issues is whether to maintain the same price between the domestic market and different foreign markets. Some believe that a higher-than-domestic price should be charged in foreign markets to cover the additional exporting costs, others believe a lower-than-domestic price should be offered to penetrate the foreign market, or a unified/similar price as the domestic price should be adopted worldwide to avoid being accused as dumping (Albaum et al., 2016).

In practice, companies may employ all three approaches in different markets. If you have experience eating at McDonald's around the world, you will probably find the price of a McDonald's meal is not always the same. A Big Mac will cost you US$ 5.15 in United States and US$ 5.25 in Canada, but the same will cost you US$ 6.71 in Switzerland and US$ 2.34 in South Africa. McDonald's prices certainly vary, so much so that The Economist magazine uses a "McDonald's Big Mac Price Index" to compare the cost of living in major business cities worldwide. How does McDonald's coordinate its service prices across the markets?

Price coordination is a great challenge nowadays due to the price and cost transparency made possible by the Internet. The Internet provides abundant free, easily obtained information, allowing customers to see through the costs and compare the prices offered by different companies or the same companies in different markets by simply clicking. This makes it necessary for companies to carefully gauge whether to charge a unified price or justify the price differentiation across markets.

To make such a decision, a service company's manager has to consider whether offering different prices in different markets could be justifiable and feasible.

First, to what extent the local resources are involved in the production is crucial in justifying the price differentiation. In coordinating the prices for products, firms selling physical products may have to maintain similar price levels with no or few cross-border variations since many companies conduct centralized production, and price differences can only be justified by the exporting cost and taxes in local markets. However, many services are labor-intensive in that the offering of the service necessitates a heavy local workforce involvement for accomplishment. Such examples include people-processing services, such as hotel and lodging services, transportation services, education services, medical services, and beauty shops, and possession-processing services, such as automobile repair services. In these industries, labor cost is a significant proportion of service costing. Considering the variation in labor cost and per capita income in different countries, it is easier to justify the price differences. In fact, uniform pricing will be the least possible for people-processing services.

Second, for the services that contain standardized product components or do not involve local resources as much, offering a unified price or differentiated prices will depend on the elasticity of demand. High price elasticity suggests low prices; price inelasticity favors high prices. For example, Spotify offers a standardized service—music streaming worldwide, though with some localization and mass customization. An individual plan is priced at US$ 1.037 per month in India but 15.40 per month in Denmark (Vahid, 2023). The different pricing is offered because Spotify targets the mass market. This means Spotify needs to ensure its service is affordable for as many customers as possible. Therefore, it has to consider the average national wage, purchasing power, and elasticity of demand, which ranges in the destination countries. In contrast, a translation company, Cambridge Proofreading, offers translation services to worldwide customers. Though the service is quite customized, its translation service is sourced in a centralized way—the center allocates the manuscripts to a few translators. No workforce in the customers' countries is necessarily involved. Considering that the customers tend to be business or academic institutions for whom the translation service is a necessity, the company charges a unified price for its service.

Third, a necessary condition to allow different prices across markets is that the relevant markets must be separated effectively. The markets of physical products may not be effectively separable. For example, a handbag is priced at $200 in a retailer's shop in Italy but at $800 in China. An illegitimate company may be able to purchase a handbag in Italy and resell it in China at $700 if the tariffs, transportation costs, or other related exporting costs are less than the price differential. Thus, a gray market is created. Such a gray market will eat up the profit of the legitimate retailers in China and that of the handbag's manufacturer. Therefore, manufacturers should be cautious when pricing their products differently in different markets. However, most services are unlikely to have such a gray market. Many services are perishable and must be produced and consumed simultaneously. The purchase of the service is also more about the right to use a service/facility instead of the ownership. Even if a customer purchases the right to live in a hotel room at a lower price, he/she cannot sell the right to another customer. As a result, it will be less likely to have a gray market for services. This makes charging different prices for a service in different countries more feasible.



## Distribution Policy

Distribution of service is about getting the service to the customer. A few questions should be carefully considered when choosing a distribution strategy. Should a company seek to perform the whole service process itself? If not, who and at what stages of the process should be involved to deliver the benefits to customers? In addition, a service company has to bear in mind three characteristics of service as introduced in ▶ Chap. 1 and their implication on distribution strategy (Wirtz & Lovelock, 2016):

- Service cannot be owned. Therefore, it is irrelevant to talk about transferring service ownership through distribution channels.
- Pure soft services are intangible and perishable. Therefore, stocks cannot exist.
- The inseparability of most services should logically require the firm itself or an intermediary to serve as the local delivery point and co-produce service with customers in a foreign market.

Similar to distributing a physical product, a service company usually makes three decisions when configuring distribution channels.

**Length of distribution channel:** Channel length refers to the number of intermediaries between the producer (or manufacturer) and the consumer. If the producer sells directly to the consumer, the channel is very short. If the producer sells through an import agent, a wholesaler, and a retailer, a long channel exists. A service company could arrange its distribution channels in three ways: purely direct sales without engaging intermediaries, purely indirect sales by engaging intermediaries such as franchises, agents, brokers, and electronic channels, and a combination of both. ◘ Figure 13.1 shows the possible distribution channel configuration a service company could have. It should be noted that when a company like McDonald's uses a national master franchisee in a country, there are even two levels of intermediaries between the service firm and the customer, making the channel very long.

**The intensity of the distribution channel:** Another channel strategy is the intensity of the distribution channel (Jobber, 2001). According to Kotler (2000) and Fein and Anderson (1997), companies have to decide on the number of intermediaries to use at each channel level. Three approaches are available:

- An intensive distribution strategy where producers use as many outlets as possible. For example, Vodafone Group Plc, a British multinational telecommuni-

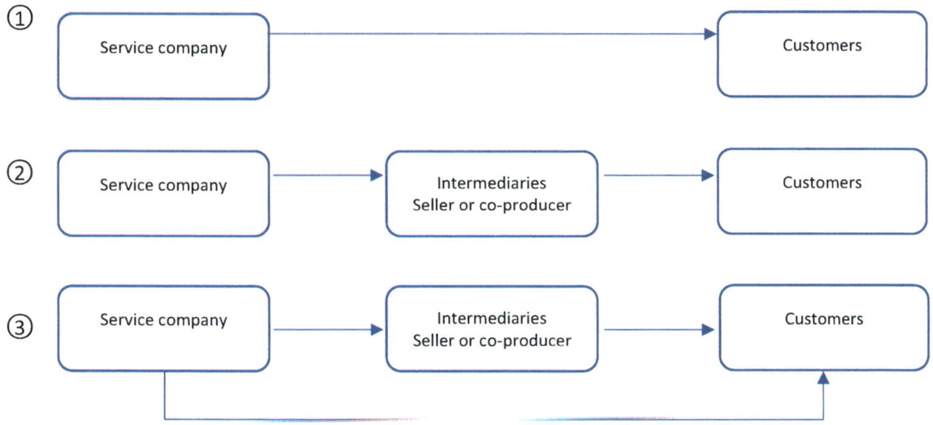


◘ **Fig. 13.1** Distribution channel configurations, source: Author's own diagram

cations company, has 700 large stores, 3300 mini-stores in bigger towns and cities, and 5800 rural mini-stores as of 2015 (Sahu, 2015). This is because the firm targets the mass market, and the buyers scatter across a wide region—a long and intensive distribution channel helps provide convenient access for the geographically huge market.

- A selective distribution strategy where fewer but selective intermediaries are used. An example is an e-commerce giant that allows a qualified group of vendors to sell on its platform.
- An exclusive distribution strategy where the producer gives a limited number of retailers the right to sell its products/services in their specific territories. One example is that in mainland China, McKinsey only has four offices in Beijing, Chengdu, Shanghai, and Shenzhen (McKinsey website, n.d.). This is because the number of customers is expected to be less or concentrated in a limited number of areas. The service provider can effectively sell directly to the customers by appointing salespeople and using exclusive distribution channels.

**Roles of intermediaries:** In addition, for a service company, it is important to distinguish between intermediaries as co-producers and their role as mere sales agents. While the former is an active part of the production process, the latter does not actually deliver a service itself but only sells the service. For example, a website selling a hotel room is not significantly involved as a co-producer of hotel services. However, it can be difficult to distinguish between these two situations. In addition to merely selling the theater ticket, a travel agency may provide valuable service for customers in arranging specific seats. To a great extent, the roles played by the intermediaries decide how many resources a service company has to commit to selecting, evaluating, and training the intermediaries.

An international service provider shall consider six aspects when configuring the distribution channels in different countries.



**Retail concentration:** In a concentrated retail system, a few retailers supply most of the market. In a fragmented retail system, there are many retailers, none of which have a major market share (Hill, 2009). You may notice that the European countries—with some large outlets, chains, and malls—also tend to have more small companies, retail outlets, and even mom-and-pop shops that provide products and services to both businesses and consumers. Some Asian markets, like Japan, South Korea, Taiwan, and Australia, also have a mix of large retail operations and smaller stores. In emerging markets such as India and Egypt, mom-and-pop shops dominate the country. For example, in India, most grocery retail happens at kiranas—small and mid-sized mom-and-pop outlets, which account for 75–78% of the consumer goods market. Store owners typically have a strong and regular customer base in their neighborhood, with home delivery and taking orders on the phone a common phenomenon (Reuters, 2021).

Retail concentration is probably the most important determinant of channel length. Suppose a country has a fragmented retail system, like the retail system for food products in Japan, where many small and independent retailers operate in different regions. This can make it difficult for food service providers to establish direct relationships with suppliers, and wholesalers will play a key role in bridging this gap by aggregating products from multiple suppliers and distributing them to retailers and food service providers. Hence, fragmented retail systems tend to promote the growth of wholesalers to serve retailers, which lengthens channels (Hill, 2009). When the retail sector is very concentrated, it makes sense for the firm to deal directly with retailers, cutting out wholesalers. A relatively small sales force is required to deal with a concentrated retail sector, and the orders generated from each sales call can be large. Such circumstances tend to prevail in the United States, where large food companies may sell directly to supermarkets rather than going through wholesale distributors (Hill, 2009).

**Channel exclusivity:** Choices made by competitors can also influence distribution strategies. Sometimes desired middlemen may not be available to distribute goods/services because competitors may have exclusive contracts with local retailers or wholesalers. An exclusive distribution channel will make it difficult for outsiders to access (Hill, 2009). For example, in Japan, exclusive distribution channels are common in many industries, including electronics, automotive, and consumer goods. It is typical that the Japanese manufacturer has a network of hundreds of primary wholesalers who are solely its own. The manufacturer takes good care of its distribution network, and it is considered to be an extension of the company itself. Distributors are dedicated to one manufacturer in each product category and will only sell the brand they are contractually committed to selling. To offer any other brands would be a violation of Giri (loyalty) to the manufacturer. In return, the manufacturers guarantee the distributors an attractive markup (Hill, 2009). As a result, large manufacturers, who enjoy higher prestige, greater political power, and social legitimacy than smaller firms, dominate the distribution system in Japan (Martin et al., 1998). In this case, the service company has to make its own arrangements by opening branches or sales depots to distribute the service directly to the customers.

**Channel quality:** Channel quality refers to the expertise, competencies, and skills of established intermediaries in a nation and their ability to sell, support, and co-produce the products and services of international businesses. The quality of distribution members is usually good in most developed countries but is variable at best in emerging markets and less developed countries. Firms will need to evaluate potential distribution partners carefully, establish clear performance metrics to ensure that the distribution channel is effective and profitable, and devote considerable resources, such as regular communication, training, and incentive, to improve the performance of distribution members. For example, Walmart's expansion into the Indian market has been hindered because there was no organized supply chain. There was no forecasting or understanding of demand. There was also no refrigerated cold chain for fresh produce in India, leading to much waste. The transparency of consumption was absent in that the farmer and the small manufacturer ended up selling to the middlemen who may or may not be so transparent about pricing. To address the issues, Walmart worked with the government in areas like training and development for supply chain employees. Walmart also worked with the government to set up large warehousing and distribution facilities (Knowledge at Wharton Staff, 2008).

**Business culture:** In countries like the United States, Germany, the United Kingdom, and Canada, where the business culture is well-defined and policy-based, most transactions have a high level of transparency. On the other hand, in relationship-centric countries like France and Italy in Europe, Japan, China, South Korea, and India in Asia, or certain parts of Africa, personal "connections" are usually more important than the Western economic principle of profit maximization in conducting business (Millward, 2013). Therefore, working with local distributors has been very important in building initial connections with the local business community and government regulators.

**Government policies:** Government policies also influence the configuration and management of distribution. Segments like education, real estate, insurance, or finance tend to be driven by in-country laws and regulations. Because of those different laws and regulations, the channel structure in those segments varies greatly from country to country. For example, concerning the distribution of insurance services, ancillary insurance intermediaries are intermediaries who engage in insurance distribution activity, not as their principal professional activity. Such intermediaries distribute insurance products that cover the goods/services in their main business. For example, travel agencies and car rental companies are the most common types of ancillary intermediaries. They could distribute insurance to provide coverage to tourists and cars. In certain jurisdictions, there are no limitations on the type of profession that can provide insurance intermediation as an ancillary activity (e.g., Austria, Belgium, Estonia, France, Korea, Luxembourg, Portugal, South Africa, Switzerland, and the United Kingdom). In other countries (e.g., Argentina, Chile, Colombia, and Japan), no professionals outside the insurance industry can perform insurance intermediation services as ancillary activity (OECD, 2019).

The government could also have regulations on contracting between a service company and an agent/distributor. For example, in Saudi Arabia, terminating an agent/distributor agreement can be difficult even though Saudi policy permits the registration of a new agreement objecting to an existing distributor (International Trade Administration, n.d.).



**Internet infrastructure:** The Internet is helping to shorten channel length. Consumers can now buy directly from manufacturers through their websites, reducing the number of intermediaries in the supply chain. This has also led to the emergence of large online retailers like Amazon, which have disrupted traditional retail models. In addition, large stores like Wal-Mart and Tesco have also shortened channel length by buying directly from manufacturers and bypassing intermediaries.

## Impact of the Characteristics of Services

The characteristics of the service also influence the decision of distribution channel configuration. Services are not homogeneous, and this should be reflected in the role played by intermediaries. While some services can be handled by a large number of intermediaries, others cannot easily be provided by intermediaries at all. The characteristics of services and customers' expectations need to be considered before an intermediary strategy is developed.

As mentioned in ► Chap. 1, service is a process and can be categorized as people-processing, possession-processing, mental-stimulus processing, and information-processing (Wirtz & Lovelock, 2016). The characteristics of different types of service will have two implications on channel configuration: 1. To engage intermediaries or not; 2. If engaging intermediaries, what roles should they play.

**People-processing service:** People-processing services, such as airline service, hotel service, hair salons, coach tours, and hospitals, are directed at the customer. Thus, the customer must physically enter the service system. For this type of service, active cooperation of the customer is needed in the service delivery process. For example, for a manicure service, you would have to cooperate with the manicurist by specifying what you want, sitting still, and presenting each finger for treatment when requested. As a result, this type of service experiences highly variable outcomes, making it difficult to control the service quality with intermediaries' involvement.

Direct sales with a selective or exclusive presence in the foreign market will be more favorable for two reasons: 1. It is easier to control the quality; 2. The service provider is in regular direct contact with consumers of its service, making an immediate response to customer comments and requests possible. This can facilitate improving services, developing new ones, or building good relationships and trust with customers. Intermediaries, if engaged, do not participate in the co-production but more as a sales branch to provide some supplementary services. For example, a restaurant has multiple outlets to approach customers directly. At the same time, the restaurant could also employ some intermediaries, such as a travel agent or a third-party food recommendation app, to reach more customers, fulfilling the functions of information, consultation, and order-taking.

Sometimes, the service firm providing people-processing services may engage intermediaries as co-producer. For example, a fast food chain or a hairdressing company, when expanding overseas, often adopts the franchise model by engaging local franchisees (intermediaries). The franchisees will be more active in providing customized service to the local customers. To ensure consistent quality, the franchisors always need to provide regular training to the service staff, offer operational support, and put in a monitoring system.

**Procession-processing service:** Possession-processing service is directed at some possession, such as a malfunctioning heater, a broken smartphone screen, a parcel that needs to be sent to another city, or a sick pet dog, not the customer. Customers tend to be less involved in these services compared to people-processing services. The involvement may be limited to dropping off or collecting the item. In such instances, production and consumption are separable, giving more flexibility to the service firm in designing and delivering such services for cost-efficiency, for example, by setting up self-service stations. However, in some instances, the customer may prefer to be present during service delivery, perhaps to comfort the pet dog while it receives an injection at the veterinary clinic. For this type of service, due to the higher participation from customers, relying on intermediaries with a local presence will be more appropriate. Intermediaries could take on more critical roles in providing core and supplementary services.

**Mental-stimulus processing service:** Mental-stimulus processing services only involve mental work. Examples are education, news, psychotherapy, professional advice, and certain religious activities. For instance, the Boston Symphony Orchestra's concerts are intangible. It can be attended, viewed, or heard live. It can also be digitized and made available via downloads, YouTube, and the like because the core content of services in this category is information-based (in text, speech, music, visual images, or video). In the education sector, students can access a lecture online and view key parts repeatedly if needed, which might be more effective than sitting in a classroom for a face-to-face class. Overall, the customer is not required to be present at all, and not even an object of the customer is required. They can choose to access the information remotely when they need it. Services in this category can be "inventoried" for consumption at a later date or consumed repeatedly. As a result, a direct channel with minimal local presence will be possible. Like Spotify and Netflix, they allow customers to place orders to access their streaming service directly. Intermediaries, even being involved, do not need to participate in the co-production but serve as a sales branch. This is also reflected by the strategy adopted by Spotify and Netflix, collaborating with local telecommunication service providers to sell their services. Here the local telecommunication service providers are the intermediaries playing the role of a sales arm, providing some supplementary services such as order-taking, information, consultation, billing, and payment.

**Information-processing service:** Information-processing services are the services that provide information. The information can be processed by information and communications technology (ICT) and/or by professionals who use their brains to process information. Some services highly dependent on the effective collection and processing of information are financial and professional services such as accounting, law, marketing research, management consulting, and medical diagnosis. Information, though it is the most intangible form of service output, can be transformed into more permanent and tangible forms like letters, reports, books, or files. The provider of such services presents information to the customer either face-to-face, in hard copy, or through electronic channels. Customers do not need to be present during the production of the service. Services in this category can be "inventoried" for consumption at a later date or repeatedly. However, unlike most mental stimulus processing services, many types of information processing services are professional and highly complex, and specialized. They also require more customization effort, which means customers will be required to actively contribute to service production through face-to-face negotiation, virtual discussion, or documentation (like specifying demand in a consultation service). Therefore, direct channel with the necessary local presence will be more appropriate. Intermediaries' involvement will be minimized because they may lack professional training and knowledge and hence cannot co-produce or even sell the service. The back-office parts of these services can often be conducted in a central location away from the customer, such as payment processing at a bank.

## Global Dispersion of Service Modules

Dispersion of service modules follows the disaggregation process as firms reallocate discrete service modules in their value chain to be performed by internal and external parties (e.g., domestic or overseas subsidiaries, franchisees, and outsourcing contractors) across geographical boundaries (location choice). The trend in global strategy is to concentrate each service module as much as possible for various benefits, as introduced in ► Chap. 8, although not necessarily all activities in the same country. Firms increasingly reconstruct themselves as a flexible, modular collection of services shored from various locations (Lewin et al., 2009b).

Following the customer contact approach, the dichotomy of front and back-office services increases the possibility of service globalization by relocating back-office services. Many back-office service modules have the potential to be concentrated to make use of the location advantages to build more efficient and effective value chains. You may still remember the discussion in ► Chap. 8 "Factors for service location decisions." Correspondingly, service could configure their value chain globally to reap location advantages (Kedia & Mukherjee, 2009).

First, firms may disperse their service modules to foreign locations for the advantage of resource cost mentioned in ► Chap. 8, which is termed as labor arbitrage (Kogut, 1985). For example, some US banks and insurance companies now send checks and claims to be processed in East Asia or Ireland. McKinsey & Company, the management consulting firm, now sends some of its work for clients from high-cost countries to its offices in low-cost countries like India.

Second, service firms could also locate their service modules in locations with needed people skills, which could be termed as knowledge arbitrage. For example, IBM has 19 research labs on six continents, such as Almaden United States, Cambridge United Kingdom, Haifa Isreal, Dublin Ireland, Tokyo Japan, and Zurich, Switzerland. These labs are collaboration hubs where more than 3000 researchers cross-pollinate ideas that lead to major breakthroughs (IBM website, n.d.).

Third, a positive business environment, in the forms of government support, infrastructure, and digital resonance, in some foreign locations also incentivizes firms to offshore their service modules to such locations. Indian, Chinese, and Malaysian governments have actively promoted their global service-provider industry by creating investment-friendly policies, improving national infrastructures, and offering high-quality and affordable labor force to attract global sourcing activities from foreign firms (Kearney, 2014; Lewin et al., 2009a, b).

Other than those mentioned in ► Chap. 8, some MNC firms disperse their service modules to reap the benefit of time arbitrage (Carmel, 2006). To provide its global customer support service, Hewlett-Packard maintains a global chain of activity in more than 30 Response Centers worldwide. These 30 centers are integrated into a global network headed by four major centers: Bracknell (United Kingdom), Atlanta (Georgia), Mountain View (California) in the United States, and Melbourne (Australia). Each center is staffed during extended daytime hours, 7 days a week, by between 12 and 200 engineers. Problems that cannot be resolved in a smaller center may be transferred to one of the major centers. Because of time-zone differentials, at least one of the major centers is always in full operation at any time (Lovelock & Yip, 2016).

However, many service businesses also have front-office service modules. A service company should consider locating these service modules close to clients' locations. Take DBS Bank from Singapore as an example. DBS, aiming to grow its fin-tech and digital banking service, has DBS Tech India and Taiwan as its global technology hubs. Here the back-office service modules have been concentrated on leveraging the high-quality ICT talents in these two locations. At the same time, DBS also has its front offices in 18 markets globally (DBS Newsroom, n.d.).

Modern technology can often be used to convert "front-office" to "back-office" activities, thereby loosening ties to client-linked and resource-oriented locations. For example, during the Covid pandemic, insurance companies have developed a system to automate some front-office functions. Claims management is now conducted via the Internet, without involving human agents to collect the documents and forward them to the back office. Distribution and sales chains are moving to a completely digital and affinity-based ecosystem. Chatbots and virtual agents can, therefore, play a critical role in increasing cross-sell and up-sell opportunities (Simon, 2020).

## Communication Strategy

International communication is a fundamental activity in a multinational company's marketing mix. Once a service is developed to meet customer needs and is properly priced and distributed, the intended customers must be informed of the product's availability and value. International communication consists of those techniques and activities which the marketer uses to inform and persuade the customers to buy. When choosing the proper communication techniques and activities, service marketers need to consider the barriers they will face in foreign countries and the implications that the special characteristics of services have on the communication tools.



## Barriers to Promotion in Foreign Countries

When promoting services in foreign markets, marketers should bear a few barriers in mind.

**Language barriers:** Language is one of the most daunting barriers that international advertisers need to surmount. Marketing translation failure can decimate even the best marketing campaign. For example, HSBC Holdings, a UK-based financial institution, serves millions of people around the world. Due to its global reach, HSBC has to speak the language of its patrons. In 2009, as part of its multilingual marketing strategy, HSBC Bank expanded its "Assume Nothing" slogan to several other languages. This was a great idea because HSBC prided itself on security and transparency with its customers. However, what wasn't wise was their failure to proofread the translated message to ensure it retained the original meaning. Unfortunately, instead of reading "Assume Nothing," many translated slogans ended up reading "Do Nothing." To rectify the translation mistake, HSBC had to spend $10 million on a re-branding campaign. After spending such a large sum of money, they came up with a new slogan, "The World's Local Bank," which they managed to translate effectively and is still used in many markets today (Sitsanis, 2019). Braniff Airlines also hit a big snag when trying to promote their upgraded leather seats using the slogan "Fly in Leather" slogan—it turned out that in Spanish, the slogan read "Fly Naked," which was certainly not the message they were trying to relay.

Besides the mistranslation in advertisements, language can be perceived as a major barrier to internationalizing professional services, as communication is an important element of the service interchange. In fact, language barriers are the root causes of many problems or obstacles in health care, aviation, maritime, business, and education. For example, in the healthcare sector, patients described experiences where language barriers contributed to inferior patient assessment, misdiagnosis, delayed treatment, incomplete understanding of the patient condition, risks of medication errors and complications, and prescribed treatment (De Moissac & Bowen, 2019).

**Cultural barriers:** Cultural insensitivity could lead to a severe adverse impact on a service company's campaign. For example, in 2005, the fast-food giant McDonald's spent thousands on a new TV ad targeting Chinese consumers. The ad showed a Chinese man kneeling before a McDonald's vendor, begging him to accept his expired discount coupon. The ad caused an uproar over the fact that begging is considered a shameful act in Chinese culture and was pulled due to a lack of cultural sensitivity on McDonald's behalf (China Daily, 2005). Another example is the Philippine Long Distance Telephone Company (PLDT), a Philippine telecommunications, Internet, and digital service company. Although PLDT's "Hello Billy" series of commercials became hugely popular in the early 2000s, one sore point that stood out was the stereotypical portrayal of homosexuals in some of its episodes. In the commercial, the gay character Joey was made out to be a schemer who spread false rumors about his best guy friend's fiancée to break up the impending marriage of his guy friend whom he was in love with. In the end, protests by gay rights groups forced PLDT to scrap the commercial in question (Filipiknow, 2022).

**Government regulation:** Advertising is one of the more controversial elements of international marketing, and it is subject to different levels of government control in different countries. Most nations have some laws regulating advertising, and advertising groups have self-regulatory codes. Advertising regulation takes several forms. One pertains to the message and its truthfulness. In Germany, for example, it is difficult to use comparative advertising and the words better or best. Australian Consumer Law contains the rule of disclosing commercial relationships between review platforms and businesses (Australian Competition and Consumer Commission, 2013). Another form of restriction relates to control over advertising certain products/services. In Singapore, the health care service must ensure that any advertisement provides information that is not exaggerated, false, or misleading; the advertisement must not contain any photograph, picture, video, or film showing the appearance or a feature of any individual before and after, or only after, receiving any treatment (Singapore Statutes Online, n.d.).

In addition to the regulations related to communication, trade barriers to service markets tend to be much more cumbersome than for their physical goods counterparts. Many parts of the world have service trade barriers under many different guises. Most cumbersome are the non-tariff trade barriers. For example, there could be measures restricting producers of exported goods to provide post-sales service in the importing country. After-sales servicing on exported TV sets must be provided by a local service company of the importing country (UNCTAD, 2012).

**Country of origin:** Consumers tend to hold either positive or negative perceptions of a country's image based on stereotypic beliefs, and these perceptions are transferred to products/services that originate in these nations affecting a buyer's perceptions and behavior (Andehn et al., 2016; Gurhan-Canli & Maheswaran, 2000). This is the country of origin effect. For example, Germany is seen as robust, Japan as cutting-edge, and England as solid and reliable (Baker & Ballington, 2002). "It's French; it must be stylish" (Kotler & Keller, 2009, p. 659). Billionaires prefer Swiss banks since the country has a long, kindred history of banking secrecy and client confidentiality, reaching back to the early 1700s.

**Country of Origin**

*Country of origin (COO)* can be defined as the total of all descriptive and inferential informational beliefs that one has about a particular country and has consistently been treated as a construct that includes several facets explained by the political, economic, technological or social domains of a country (Olsen & Olsson, 2002).



Sometimes, the reference of COO is explicitly communicated by a brand (e.g., British Airways), visualized by the Swiss cross, for instance, (e.g., Victorinox), or communicated in the phrase "Made in…" (Berentzen et al., 2008). The COO can also be communicated by a brand's claim. For example, Audi uses the German language: "Vorsprung durch Technik" ("advance by engineering") as its slogan in its international promotional materials (Peters, 2011) to emphasize Audi's German heritage, which is well known for superior engineering performance.

The research on COO is mostly done on tangible goods. By transferring country-related images to products or services, COO effects seem especially useful when other quality cues are missing and/or the brand is not well known. Correspondingly, COO can be more relevant for services due to their peculiar characteristics, like intangibility, heterogeneity, and perishability. Consumers tend to rely much more on extrinsic cues in their quality assessments of services (Lovelock & Wirtz, 2016). In the case of a service company entering a foreign market, perceived risk can be even higher because less reliable information is available, and consumers have limited feedback from the personal experience of others (Coulter

& Coulter, 2003). Therefore, consumers rely heavily on alternative quality indicators such as COO to diminish perceived risk.

At the same time, adopting a COO in a service context could be more complicated. International service providers, such as McDonald's and Walt Disney, often face the strategic dilemma of positioning their service offerings in other cultures partly because of the "American" appeal of their market offerings or COO effects (Cateora & Graham, 2007). While positioning a market offering based on its US consumer cultural values and lifestyle seems to be a logical and viable strategy for US firms, it may potentially conflict with prevailing consumption norms in host countries with different cultural values and lifestyles, which may ultimately induce anti-American sentiments in this era of anti-globalism. For example, when McDonald's first entered the French market, it struggled due to widespread anti-American sentiment. An activist who smashed a newly built McDonald's restaurant was celebrated as a hero (Hill, 2015). The following box provides more research findings about COO.

**More About COO**

Research and practice reveal a few important findings about COO in the service context:

1. COO effects are not stable but change over time (Millward, 2013). For instance, consumers are slowly learning about South Korea as one of the most important beauty trendsetters in Asia and the world. When those home-grown plastic surgery services, skincare, and cosmetic brands such as Korean beauty firm AmorePacific expand overseas, they will owe much of their positive brand equity to this COO effect.
2. COO influences consumers' behavior in multiple ways. Schooler and Sunoo (1969) were the first to postulate that COO was composed of a cognitive dimension, which emphasizes the perceived characteristics of a country, and an affective one, which reflects attitudes and feelings towards a country and its people. For example, in the service context, Ofir and Lehman (1986) asked skiers to compare the ski Resorts in Switzerland, Austria, and France. Results turned out that skiers considered the Swiss more friendly, honest, challenging, and romantic, while the French more modern, entertaining, and expensive. Lascu and Giese (1995) reported that US consumers expected German retailers to have better product offerings, services, and advertising, while Mexican retailers would have lower prices and larger discounts.
3. COO also impacts consumers' willingness to purchase and pay for a service. Research has shown that consumers preferred services from their own country, an economically developed country or a culturally similar country. For instance, Pinkaeo and Speece (2002) found that for life insurance, a high-contact service, consumers prefer the providers of their own country, probably because they perceive the local providers better understand

their needs. Hence, the expected service quality is higher than that of foreign insurance companies.

4. Consumer characteristics influence the salience of the COO impacts. Novices, i.e., those who are not experts on a product, tend to use COO to evaluate service outcomes (Maheswaran, 1994). In contrast, the COO loses its impact on a purchase decision when consumers are more familiar with the service. Consumers‘ ethnocentrism predicts their preference towards domestic products over foreign products. Ethnocentrism represents deeply-held beliefs that homemade products should be purchased over foreign-made products (Yagci, 2001).
5. COO effect varies across product/service categories. While South Korea has achieved top 10 status as a country from which to buy manufactured goods because of Korean brands like Samsung, Hyundai, LG, and Kia, it may have a weak overall country brand in terms of tourism—ranked 49th overall by Futurebrand (Martin Roll, 2021). Michaelis et al. (2008) reported that a positive COO effect leads to a higher level of initial trust only in the case of a risky service but not in low-risk services.
6. COO in the service context could be broken down into multiple components:
   - *Country of brand (COB)* is the country where consumers perceive the brand originated (Pinkaeo & Speece, 2002).
   - *Country of design/know-how (COK)* is the country in which the service procedure is designed (Guilhoto, 2018; Pinkaeo & Speece, 2002).
   - *Country of staff (COS)* refers to the nationality of service providers or the person who delivers the service, such as sales representatives of insurance (Guilhoto, 2018; Pinkaeo & Speece, 2002; Veale & Challen, 2010).
   - *Country of training (COT)* is the country where the person delivering the service is trained (Veale & Challen, 2010).
   - *Country of physical evidence (COP)* refers to the country of the provision of evidence, such as facilities, equipment, stationery, decoration, and, more recently, websites, that can help consumers to get more information about the service and to form their quality evaluations (Guilhoto, 2018).

A service company could have an aligned COO by touching on some or all the dimensions. For example, an American international school establishes its brand (COB) and core curriculum and procedure (COK) in the United States. When it establishes a campus and sells its education service in China, it adopts the US style in designing the facilities (COP) and tries to recruit foreign teaching staff (COS) instead of local educators to align the nationality of the service providers with its COO, the United States. However, due to globalization, services from many countries compete in local markets. A particular service can have more than one COO, i.e., branded in one country, designed in a second coun-

13

try, but delivered by personnel of another country and adapted the service outlet to the local aesthetics.

In consideration of the impact of a COO, a service firm could implement strategies to cope with COO stereotypes. Before exploring strategic options to deal with COO, firms should conduct market research to investigate the extent and impact of COO stereotypes for their services. Such studies would reveal whether and which element of the COO matters to consumers and to what extent the COO hurts or helps the service evaluation. Depending on the results, service firms could then develop strategies to cope with the COO.

For those with a favorable match between service and COO, it is worthwhile to reflect COO in multiple ways:

- Use a brand name that reflects the COO. For example, the Korean style has always been one of the trendsetters in the fashion scene in Asia and expands to Korean hairstyles. As a result, some hair salon from Korea names their company with the word "Korean hair salon" or brand names in the Korean language, such as "Apgujeong Hair Studio," to reflect its COO.
- Provide physical evidence that reflects the COO. In a Korean hair salon outlet, we can see the image of Korean celebrities, Korean languages, and other Korean-related symbols.
- Promote the brand's COO. As in the Korean hair salon's case, the company tends to highlight it is a Korean brand.
- Ensure and convey that the staff are trained in the COO. A Korean hair salon can convey that all its hairdressers receive training in Korea.

For those with an unfavorable match between service and COO, the recommended strategy is to weaken the connection between the company and the COO. For example, the company could emphasize benefits other than COO, use non-country branding or form a joint venture with a favorable match partner, or hire local staff to show its local relevance. For example, Tencent, the China-based Internet giant, hired the Argentine soccer player Lionel Messi as the brand spokesperson in its global ad campaign to launch WeChat, an online messaging service (Millward, 2013).

**Level of "noise" (promotion activities of other firms) in a country:** "Noise" has a negative connotation in marketing, meaning there is so much promotional clutter, like advertising, that consumers tire of it and have a difficult time remembering specific messages. If there is much noise in the sense of advertising by other companies, it is difficult for a new entrant into a market to catch the attention of consumers or customers. Internationally, the level of noise varies. In highly developed countries like Japan and the United States, there is much advertising across all imaginable channels vying for customers' attention. Think of all the flashing electronic billboards on Tokyo's Shibuya crossing that visibly demonstrate this high noise level. Compare this to Mali in West Africa. In Mali, 90% of the population was illiterate, limiting the reach of printed advertising. The few newspapers

Flashing electronic billboards on Tokyo's Shibuya crossing demonstrate a high noise level for marketing, image by StockSnap from Pixabay

consisted of only a few pages, and there was only one TV channel, broadcasting from 6 pm to 9 pm. The higher the noise level in a country, the more the multinational firm needs to find ways of cutting through the noise to capture the attention of customers or consumers.



## Impact of the Characteristics of Services on Communication Strategy

Service's special characteristics discussed in ► Chap. 1 pose challenges and opportunities for communication and promotion in the international market.

**Intangibility and experience nature of service:** The intangibility, experience nature, and credence quality of services introduced in ► Chap. 1 pose challenges for customers to evaluate the service before or even after the service encounter, hence could easily trigger cognitive dissonance. That is, customers may feel discomfort when perceiving a gap between their expectations and the actual service experience. This is particularly true in international marketing, given that the geographic and psychological distance may further aggravate such dissonance. For example, some cultures may expect personalized service, while others prioritize efficiency. A culture that may prioritize personalized service is Japan. In Japanese culture, there is a strong emphasis on hospitality and the concept of "omotenashi," which refers to the spirit of selfless hospitality. This means that Japanese customers may expect service providers to go above and beyond to make their experience personalized and comfortable. For example, in a restaurant, the server may take note of the customer's preferences and tailor the menu or presentation of the food accordingly. On the other hand, the United States is an example of a culture that may prioritize efficiency. In American culture, there is often a focus on getting things done quickly and efficiently. This means that American customers may prioritize prompt service and not expect as much personalization. For example, in a fast-food restaurant, the customer may prioritize quick service and accuracy over personalized attention from the staff. If a Japanese customer is not informed about the difference, he or she may feel unhappy about the experience in a US restaurant.

Service also requires more explanation and demonstration than manufactured goods, especially in countries where the service is not yet well known. An example is ride-hailing services such as Uber and Lyft. When these services were first introduced, customers were unfamiliar with them in many countries. The companies thus faced several challenges related to cultural differences and regulatory challenges. For example, in some countries, sharing a ride with a stranger may not align with local cultural norms or be considered unsafe. Additionally, there may have been regulatory challenges related to obtaining necessary licenses or permits or complying with local laws and regulations. To address these challenges, Uber and Lyft had to invest in significant marketing and education campaigns to build awareness and understanding among potential users. They also had to work closely with local authorities to understand and comply with the regulatory environment.

To counter the insecurity of customers, it is important to use branding and credentials. These will be discussed in more detail in the later section.

**Perishability:** Perishability is the lack of storage ability for a service. It is impossible to stockpile some services and keep them for later use (Zeithaml et al., 1985). This has implications for the marketing communication tool of sales promotion and other communication strategies. When an organization faces seasonal demand, a communication strategy, such as sales promotion, becomes necessary to help even out peaks and troughs and encourage customers to use the service when they normally would not. In this situation, an organization may also need to communicate additional benefits of their service to customers to encourage purchase. For example, a hotel resort that traditionally targets the family holiday market but wants to target business customers during the off-peak season. If the market perception is that the resort is family-oriented only, it would have to alter its positioning in its communication to attract the business market. It could do this by outlining the business benefits, such as Internet facilities, executive lounges, and secretarial services.

**Heterogeneity:** The heterogeneity of service poses some challenges. Service businesses operate through diverse elements and interactions. A bank may offer customer service through a helpline or website and cash withdrawals through ATMs and counters. Customers may have different experiences when interacting with the bank in different ways. Furthermore, in most industries, the service delivery process involves the interaction between service providers and customers. Service customers (or prosumers) have to participate proactively in a successful service delivery process. For example, without clients specifying the request clearly, a management consultant cannot deliver a satisfactory solution. As the behaviors of both service providers and customers are subjective and unpredictable, it is hard to maintain the standard delivery outcome. The heterogeneity is even more pronounced in international marketing due to the variation in infrastructure, customers expectations, and local staff's working culture across countries. This will make it challenging to manage customer expectations and convey consistent messages all the time, possibly leading to dissatisfaction and backlash. For example, when a Western consultant provides management consultancy service to a Chinese business client, he or she may find the clients tend to give the information more indirectly and prefer a solution that emphasizes harmony more than efficiency. In this case, the Western consultant must be equipped with sufficient cultural sensitivity and skills to manage expectations and recommend adapted solutions.

Service companies should try to align integrated communication to ensure the consistency of messages and trust. This is particularly true of professional services and service shops. For example, a consumer is likely to be more satisfied by a medical clinic if they are attended to by the same doctor, while less confident if they have a different doctor each time. Likewise, some consumers may be more comfortable eating at a McDonald's restaurant on an oversea trip than in choosing an independent restaurant because they know the menu will be familiar, and the service staff will use familiar scripts in dealing with them ("Would you like fries with that?"). The overall quality of service will be similar to other McDonald's restaurants they have visited.

**Simultaneous production and consumption of service:** Simultaneous production and consumption result in consumers being involved in a series of encounters with service producers. This provides opportunities for the front-office employees to influence customers' perceptions and promote the service. During each encounter, a service company has a chance to communicate with its customers. Without any effort on the company's part, customers will pick up messages, whether good or bad. With more planning, the company can ensure that every encounter is turned into an opportunity to convey positive messages that encourage repeat purchases from customers and encourage them to pass on the message to others. This poses more challenges in managing an international service provider team, which we will discuss more in the next section.

Given the characteristics of intangibility, experience-based nature and credence quality, perishability, heterogeneity, and simulations production and consumption, a few components can be enhanced to strengthen the marketing effort: front-line employees, the physical environment of the service encounter, branding, and credentials.

## The Role of Employees in Service Marketing

People are the main focus when it comes to service marketing. The service credibility and success rely on a service company's ability to develop a healthy relationship with the customers. In addition, because many services require customers to be present or even participate in the service production together with the service staff, the front-line operational personnel have the opportunities to build and manage the customer relationship, influence target customers' perceptions of a service company and play the role as "part-time marketers." Therefore a service manager must pay close attention when defining customer communication protocols, choosing the right employees, and providing training to equip front-office staff with the necessary skills, as an important part of international marketing efforts. The following aspects should be particularly taken good care of:

**Product/service knowledge:** Say a front-office staff is giving a product demo, and the customer has a question about a certain feature. If the staff can provide a quick and comprehensive response about the service, the customer will likely be satisfied with the service and close the deal. This is especially important for complex services, such as professional business services like management consultancy, medical services, or financial advisory services, for which customers may have limited knowledge about the service and need more help understanding it. So it is important to give timely training to the front-office staff and ensure they have a consummate understanding of service. Staff should master the knowledge about the price, possible ways of customization, how to use the service, how and where to get technical support, and plans to roll out new products/services. In an international service company, it also helps that the employees are equipped with the knowledge regarding the differences in the service offerings provided by different country subsidiaries, particularly when customers can choose the service from different subsidiaries of the service company. Then the employees will be armed and confident to discuss it in detail, combat objections in real-time, confidently answer questions, and provide a solution to the customer.

**Communication skills and cultural sensitivity:** Excellent front-office staff should have communication skills like active listening, speaking, and writing clearly, effectively, efficiently, and politely. In a multinational service company, the front-office staff are also expected to be able to communicate in a culturally sensitive way. Cultural sensitivity is a set of skills that enables staff to learn about and understand people different from themselves. In a multinational service company, the front-line workers are considered interactants and should have intercultural communicative skills. As a result, the service company should have a policy and procedure to recruit and retain front desk staff who reflect the cultural and linguistic diversity of the communities served. Job descriptions and recruiting advertisements shall include skill sets and areas of knowledge related to cultural and linguistic competence. For the existing staff, policies, and training should be provided to guide employees about the protocol for dealing with cultural diversity. For example, in a hotel, it will be useful to have policies and procedures to serve individuals with special communication needs or those who speak little or no local language.

**Marketing skills:** It is important to equip service personnel with the marketing concepts and skills of "meeting the needs of the customer through the creation of value" as they are part of the "production" process of delivering the service to the consumer and "part-time marketers" when interacting with customers. For example, staff can influence future purchases by encouraging customers to book a repeat service or giving them brochures/vouchers to pass on to friends. In addition, an ability to spot cross-selling opportunities calls for empathy on the part of front-line staff. A bank clerk who sees a customer repeatedly using a service that does not adequately fulfill his or her needs could be trained to cross-sell another service that better meets the customer's needs. Training should make the employees aware of the services available and give them skills in effectively approaching customers and referring them to appropriate personnel.

**General manners:** The general manner of staff's interaction with customers is important in formulating a positive customer experience and encouraging customers to return and to tell their friends about their good experience. So, training should emphasize those behaviors that positively affect customers' evaluation of their encounters.

## The Role of Service Outlets: Provide Tangible Cues, Symbols, and Physical Evidence

Physical evidence is particularly important in establishing a consistent and credible image for cross-border sales of services due to intangible and heterogeneous characteristics of service offerings (Hyder & Fregidou-Malama, 2009).

From the outside, service outlets can be seen as billboards conveying messages about the services which take place within them. They are powerful tools for appealing to both customers and non-customers. The general appearance of an outlet can promote the image of a service organization. A brightly colored and clean exterior can convey that the organization is fast, efficient, and well-run. An interior with a cool color like blue can facilitate an image of fidelity and assurance. Consistent use of logo, design of office, dressing code, and documentation template in all the outlets around the world helps convey a consistent image of professionalism.



Service outlets can also provide valuable opportunities to show service production processes to potential customers, which is more difficult to achieve through conventional media. For example, a fast-printing shop can display sophisticated printing equipment. A restaurant can set up an open kitchen to showcase the cooking process to customers. An airline company can show the tidy appearance of employees as a clue of their professional service. This helps promote an organization's processes as much as its outcomes.

Service outlets could also be used as a way to showcase the COO. For example, a Spanish restaurant could decorate its outlets by using bright and bold colors like red, orange, and yellow, showing framed prints or posters of famous Spanish artists or landmarks, and playing traditional Spanish music. All these will help create an authentic and welcoming atmosphere for Spanish COO for diners.

## The Role of Branding and Credentials for International Services

Since services are intangible and cannot be tested before consumption (experience good or credence good), a strong brand recognized internationally is particularly important to imply the quality as a peripheral cue to reduce the perceived risks resulting from intangibility (Brady et al., 2005). Use Singapore Airlines as an example. The palette of the Singapore Airlines badge uses bright colors, but in their calm and deep shades, softening the bold lines of the emblem and adding distinction to the lettering—the combination of yellow and blue stands for the sun and the sky. At the same time, yellow is also a color of energy and movement, while blue is the commonly known symbol of protection, reliability, and trustworthiness (1000logos, 2022). Besides the logo, the Singapore Airlines brand is personified as the "Singapore Girl." The Singapore Girl is the name of the airline's female flight attendants. They wear the country's distinctive "sarong kebaya" as a uniform, created by French haute couture designer Pierre Balmain in 1968. The SIA logo and "Singapore Girl" are easily recognizable and convey an image of care, trustworthiness, warmth, and efficiency in delivering a unique in-flight experience. When customers see the brand, it authenticates the communication as genuine, safe, and from a known and trusted airline service (Danao, 2018) (see also the Singapore Airlines case in ► Chap. 15).

A brand also eases a customer's effort when repurchasing a product/service. Consider the purchase of car insurance. The brand purchased on the previous occasion now has some meaning for the purchaser. It could be a brand that conveys images of safety, security, and confidence that claims will be paid out, or it could have negative images associated with the brand owing to some unsatisfactory service received. The next time insurance is required, a purchaser will either automatically repurchase the brand without searching for alternatives or look for another service provider. Either way, the choice has been simplified compared to the last purchase.

If a service organization is not well known under its own brand, it can be useful to use other third-party endorsements or credentials to indicate the quality of the service. Such credentials could be the logos of industry association members, awards or accreditation received from certification bodies, credentials of past projects of a consulting firm, or ratings by previous guests on a third-party website. For example, many hotels show the ratings given by consumers through the hotel booking website Agoda. Such ratings are shown on the Agoda website and at the hotel's counter, their social media, websites, email signature, and business events. Management consultants put together lists of successful past projects as credentials to demonstrate their ability to prospective new customers. The branding and credentials are particularly important for those people-processing services, given the higher level of heterogeneity due to the interaction between a service provider and customers, and in an international context, where economic, geographic and cultural distances make it more challenging for customers to have a clear expectation of a foreign service provider.

## Techniques of Promotion in the Service Context

The promotional element in the four Ps of marketing is the core of marketing communication, which targets customers. It includes the tools of advertising, personal selling, sales promotions, Internet/electronic communication, publicity, sponsorship, and word of mouth. These communication tools need to reflect the different characteristics of services and the importance of the service experience. This means some of the accepted notions of marketing communication for tangible products may not easily translate when communicating a service. For example, marketing a service differs from promoting a tangible product because consumers often need to be educated about a service. Additionally, these tools need to reduce the dissonance between expectations and performance and thus create shared meaning.

### Advertising

Advertising is the communication tool that most customers are familiar with. An advertisement usually aims to create awareness and develop a value proposition among customers. It could also be used to inform, persuade and remind customers about a brand and its other marketing mix. You may find advertisements on a range of mediums such as broadcast media (television, radio), print (newspapers and magazines), outdoor (billboards, vehicles), cinema, directional media (directories, catalogs), and electronic (Internet, SMS, kiosks).

Advertising for services is different from that for goods. Due to their intangible nature, services are perceived as riskier by customers. This implies that an advertisement should try to make the service more tangible ("tangibalize") and reassure customers that this service is less risky than the alternatives.

In addition, advertising is a cultural phenomenon to a large extent. As discussed in the section "Barriers to promotion in foreign countries," the host country's culture, regulation system, and other factors may influence the creation of an ad campaign and its effectiveness. For example, with regard to the way of tangibalizing the service, there is debate about whether to use rational or emotional appeals. Albers-Miller and Stafford (1999) find that in Taiwan, which features a collectivistic culture, more emotional appeals are used for services. They gave the reason as emotional appeals related to belongingness and affiliation can help alleviate the abstractness of the service offering. For example, including a tangible emotional cue, such as a happy family sharing KFC chicken, in the advertisement helps customers develop a positive view of the food service. This is in direct contrast to much US research that advocates the use of informational and rational ads for services (e.g., Grove et al., 1995; Stafford & Day, 1995)—the research explains that in culture featured by individualism, advertisements with information and rationalization conveying a competitive edge (productive, modern) are more effective. Such cultural differences imply the importance of deciding on a standardized or localized advertising approach, which is argued to depend on the goals of the advertising campaign and the target audience.

Standardizing advertising involves creating a single advertisement that is used across multiple markets or regions. This approach can be effective for products or services with a universal appeal or that are marketed toward a global audience. Standardized advertising allows for consistency in messaging and branding and can be more cost-effective since a single advertisement can be used across multiple markets.

Localizing advertising, on the other hand, involves creating separate advertisements tailored to the cultural and linguistic nuances of each market or region. This approach is more effective for products or services that have a strong cultural or regional appeal. Localized advertising allows for more targeted messaging and can better resonate with local audiences.

In many cases, a hybrid approach that combines standardized and localized advertising may be most effective. This could involve creating a core advertisement that is used across multiple markets but also includes localized elements such as language, imagery, or cultural references to better resonate with local audiences. One such example is a multinational fast-food chain that uses a standardized advertising campaign but adapts certain elements to better resonate with local audiences. The fast-food chain may create a core advertising campaign that features a single tagline or slogan, a consistent brand message, and a recognizable visual identity. This core campaign could be used across multiple markets to ensure consistency and cost-effectiveness. At the same time, the core campaign will be translated into different languages to better communicate with local audiences. In different markets, the fast-food chain may partner with local influencers or celebrities to promote the brand.

## Personal Selling

Personal selling is a two-way communication process in which a salesperson engages with a potential customer to sell a good or service. It is usually appropriate for more complex services requiring demonstration, customization, or explanation. This is a dominant form of communication in business-to-business markets, owing to the high complexity and transaction values associated with purchases (Morris et al., 2001).

In a service environment, the sales process can provide indicators of quality and pre-evaluation information. This is especially important for the services high in credence qualities, i.e., the service that cannot be observed by the consumer immediately after purchase, making it difficult to assess its utility. An example is financial advice. A customer has limited ways to evaluate financial products but relies on the salesperson (Sharma & Patterson, 1999). For a customer in a sales appointment with a financial adviser, if the adviser appears trustworthy or has been with the customer in the past, the customer tends to perceive a higher quality and credibility of the service. In addition, the communication skills of the salesperson are important in this case, where no physical product is available to evaluate. Suppose a salesperson can communicate effectively by understanding customers' needs, providing clear explanations of financial concepts, and giving balanced advice to the customer. In that case, he/she is more likely to be able to increase the conversion rate.

In international marketing, personal selling is particularly important because it allows companies to navigate cultural differences and adapt their sales message to local customs and preferences. For example, in some cultures, building a personal relationship with a potential customer may be more important than making a quick sale. In other cultures, customers may expect a more direct and to-the-point sales approach. To be successful in international personal selling, an international service company needs to give proper training to their sales employees, as explained in the Section "The role of employees in service marketing."

### Sales Promotions

The area of sales promotion covers tactics such as contests, sweepstakes, coupons, pricing discounts, point-of-purchase materials, and rebates. Service is featured by intangibility and experience nature, so customers perceive high risks and costs of trying out a new service. Sales promotion effectively reduces the monetary and non-monetary costs to incentivize customers to try the service. For example, a tuition center, by providing a free trial session or a discount for the first few sessions, can reduce the opportunity cost of customers and encourage them to enroll on trial to experience the service while incurring close-to-zero marginal costs. Similarly, beauty salons can also provide coupons to induce brand switching or trial by reducing customers' perceived costs and risks. In addition, sales promotion can reinforce a consumer's cognitive and emotional commitment to their existing service provider before settling down into an automated pattern of habitual buying. Discounts and rebates have also been used to retain customers or cross-sell services to customers. For example, some educational institution provides a rebate once a customer finishes one course; the rebate could be used for the customer to pay for another course. Furthermore, sales promotions can be very useful to smoothen the demand for services featured by perishability and experience peaks and troughs, as illustrated before in yield management.

However, it should be noted that sales promotion is not a tool to generate long-term results such as brand loyalty or long-term sales (Ehrenberg et al., 1994). A few shortcomings of using promotions should be notable. Promotions focusing on price discounts (such as 10% off) rather than value-adding (two-for-one deals) run the risk of diluting brand equity. What is worse, they may reduce profits if the customer is going to buy the service anyway. In addition, if a service company already has a regular discount program, withdrawing the program may upset existing customers who are used to the deals and expect them. For example, Redmart, a Singapore online grocery e-commerce site, used to waive delivery fees for orders over $80. When it informed the customers that the waiver was no longer offered, some customers felt dissatisfied and immediately switched to other e-commerce sites, such as Amazon (Redmart, 2022).



For most multinationals, the sales promotion policy is a local affair owing to a few factors. The first factor is economic development. Low incomes and poor literacy in developing countries make some promotional techniques unattractive but render other tools more appealing. One study of promotional practices in China, Singapore, Malaysia, and New Zealand finds that as the industrialization of a market increases, along with the increasing sophistication of consumers and multinationalization of the industry, the use of passive value-added techniques (such as sampling, demonstrations, and free gifts) decreases (McNeill, 2012). Second, for most product/service categories, there is a great deal of variation in market maturity. In countries where the product is still in an early stage of the product life cycle, trial-inducing tools such as samples, coupons, and cross-promotions are appropriate. In more established markets, one of the prime goals of promotions will be to encourage repeat purchases. In this case, a bonus pack could be used by including a free service or consultation with the purchase of a larger service package. In-pack coupons could be used to offer discounts on future services or to incentivize customers to book additional appointments. Third, cultural perceptions of promotions differ widely across countries. According to one study, Taiwanese consumers have less-favorable attitudes toward sweepstakes than consumers in Thailand or Malaysia. Nor are Taiwanese concerned about losing face when using coupons. Malaysians, on the other hand, favor sweepstakes over coupons. Shoppers in Europe redeem far fewer coupons than their counterparts in the United States (Kotabe & Helsen, 2022). Fourth, companies need to decide how to allocate their promotional dollars between consumer promotions—which are directly aimed at the end-user ("pull")—and trade promotions ("push")—which target the middlemen. Because of differences in the local trade structure, the balance of power between manufacturers and trade is tilted in certain countries. Assume a software company that wants to promote its cloud-based data storage service in a country where a few large retailers dominate the market. These retailers may demand significant discounts or other concessions from the software company to carry out its service, which could impact its profitability. Lastly, government regulations regarding sale promotion practices vary across countries. Certain practices may be heavily restricted or simply forbidden. Amazon was not allowed to offer free shipping to its customers in France. In response, Amazon introduced shipping fees for a symbolic one euro cent (Griswold, 2014). In Germany, coupon values cannot be more than 1% of the product's value. Vouchers, stamps, and coupons are banned in Norway (Kotabe & Helsen, 2022).

### Public Relations

For global marketers, building up good relationships with various stakeholders for mutual benefits (e.g., employees, press, distributors, customers, and government authorities) is an important part of their communication strategy. This helps the company obtain favorable publicity, build a good "corporate image," and handle unfavorable rumors, stories, and events.

Public relations can be conducted to enhance the brand image by calling attention to a firm's involvement with the community, such as cause marketing, staff volunteering, and raising funds for charities and other not-for-profit organizations. These are part of the company's corporate social responsibility, which will be detailed in ► Chap. 12. Public relations can also be used to tangibalize the service through experiential marketing in various ways, for example, interactive webinars and conferences, event marketing, contests, in-person surveys, open-house day, and in-store experiences. One example is HSBC, which hosts Investment Outlook events to give customers opportunities to meet their most senior investment teams worldwide. By allowing its Global Investment Committee to share the latest views and an incisive perspective on major asset classes and investment themes, HSBC can provide tangible cues of its service and establish its authority in the financial service industry (HSBC website, n.d.).

These public relations will help convey the company's value to the customers (learn) and build up their positive attitude towards a service company (feel), which in the end convert to customers' trust and positive behavior outcome (do).

## Sponsorship

Sponsorship is a common method for generating publicity and getting the external community involved in the organization. Its objectives are usually concerned with brand awareness, corporate image, and positioning. For example, HSBC sponsors various sports events such as Golf, Rugby, and Tennis. HSBC sponsors Rugby events and programs all over the world, such as the Hong Kong Sevens and the Sevens World Series, comprised of tournaments in Dubai, South Africa, New Zealand, the United States, Australia, Hong Kong, Japan, England, and Scotland, knowing that its mass customers are interested in Rugby games (HSBC website). This sponsorship provides good opportunities to remind customers about HSBC as "The world's local bank" during the games.

A service company will need to decide whether to sponsor a major global event or a local one. Being a sponsor of major global events such as the Olympics or the World Cup Soccer allows the company to raise its profile, build its brand image and stand out from competitors worldwide, particularly in the key markets. Second, the "feel-good" association with big events provides employees with a recruitment and motivational tool. Finally, when the sponsorship involves the provision of in-kind services (e.g., information technology), it gives a global stage for the sponsoring firm to showcase its skills. However, sponsoring a major global event could also have some pitfalls. The event organizers could sell too many sponsorships, leading to too much "noise." The payback of the sponsorship can prove elusive. Measuring the effectiveness of a particular sponsorship activity is extremely hard. In addition, the sponsoring company may be subject to ambush marketing done by competitors. Ambush marketing is a promotional strategy in which a company attempts to associate itself with a particular event, such as a sports competition or cultural festival, without paying for official sponsorship or advertising rights. One example of ambush marketing was done by UAE airline during the 2022 FIFA. Qatar Airways was FIFA's official airline partner and had exclusive rights to utilize the governing bodies' official trademarks relating to the FIFA World Cup among airlines. However, featuring retired Dutch international footballing superstar Clarence Seedorf and UFC legend Khabib Nurmagomedov, UAE airline, in their advertisement, promoted that the UAE airline was running six flights a day from Abu Dhabi to Doha during the World Cup. Notably, there was no mention of the World Cup in the campaign, with the tournament instead referred to as "the biggest football tournament of 2022." With accommodation at a premium during the tournament, many supporters chose to stay in the UAE before traveling to the games (Kitchen & Harper, 2023).



In contrast, sponsoring a local event can be an effective promotional strategy for service companies, particularly those looking to build brand awareness and connect with their target audience in a specific geographic area. By sponsoring a local event, service companies can position themselves as community-minded organizations and build goodwill among potential customers.

## Word of Mouth

Word of mouth is informal communication between consumers about products and services (Westbrook, 1987). Advice from friends or family who can share their first-hand experience of the service will probably determine which company a service is purchased from, as friends and family are deemed objective and credible.

While word of mouth is outside the firm's control and technically not part of the marketing communication mix, it can be influenced by marketing activities. One way to encourage positive word of mouth is to offer referral programs to encourage loyal customers to recommend the service to friends. Many different service companies have used this. For example, Uber, the ride-share app, builds referrals into its product—assigning each customer a personalized referral code once their account is activated. Every time a new account is created using a customer's referral code, both parties get their next Uber trip free. Word of mouth is so important to Uber that Uber claimed more than 95% of its riders had learned about Uber from other riders, including groups outside of the digital realm, such as older demographics.

A key issue for managing word-of-mouth communication is that customers must be encouraged to speak positively about a service encounter as close to the event as possible. This is because the evaluation of the event is more extreme when it is closer to the encounter (Christiansen & Tax, 2000). This could be done by offering a bonus coupon to give to a friend, with the coupon having an expiry date not long after the encounter date.

The level of search quality determines the importance of word of mouth. Different services have varying search qualities, so word of mouth can be more important for certain services than others. For example, word of mouth is more important for promoting professional services, such as doctors, lawyers, accountants, and consultants, owing to their high credence qualities and difficulty in evaluation and comparison. You will notice, for instance, that these organizations rely less on traditional promotion, such as advertising, and more on developing networks and referrals.

Another merit of word of mouth is that it appears to be a common feature across cultures (Christiansen & Tax, 2000). Therefore, in creating shared meaning between organizations and consumers, word of mouth can be useful in international marketing and multicultural societies such as Australia, New Zealand, Singapore, and the United States.

## Opinion Leaders: Influencers and Celebrities

One important type of word of mouth is that of influencers and celebrities, as they serve as opinion leaders. Unlike normal customers, these influencers and celebrities have many followers. They are perceived to have more in-depth and professional knowledge about the service and can provide information and advice to others. They are also perceived as more credible due to their publicity and reputation. As a result, influencer and celebrity endorsement is important in building and maintaining a positive and consistent corporate image. Famous and popular individuals could act as the company's image ambassadors, which helps gain more traction with the audience they command.

In the context of international marketing, service companies can partner with popular influencers in different regions to tap into their existing audiences and gain access to new potential customers. These influencers can create content that showcases the service and share it with their followers, potentially generating significant exposure for the service company. Some examples include food bloggers giving evaluations of restaurants and travel bloggers providing reviews of hotels and destinations. When Uber launched its service in Delhi, Bangalore, and Mumbai, they brought out a Rider Zero campaign where they roped in key influencers from every city to try out Uber's service for the first time "secretly." For example, from Delhi, it was Zaheer Khan, Ranvijay, Neha Dhupia, and NDTV Host Rajiv Makhni. From Mumbai, it was Anil Kapoor, Arbaaz Khan, and Rahul Bose. From Bangalore, it was Raghu Dixit and Vasundhara Das. The idea was to reach out to millions of followers of these celebrities on Twitter to create a significant buzz around the Uber cab service (Malpani, 2015).

It is worth noting that influencers and celebrities do not need to be paid for their endorsements if the value can be achieved for both parties. In addition, due to the flourishing of social media, some influencers are hired by a company to endorse the service; but for those who are not, it won't be easy to control the types of messages spreading out. In addition, it is important to recognize that the effectiveness of opinion leaders can vary depending on the culture and region in which they operate. In some cases, relying on a local opinion leader with a deep connection with the local community will be the best option. This is particularly the case if a company is selling to a geographically constrained audience, like Uber promoting its service in India, opting for local-level influencers to make use of relevant local tagging might make all the difference for the campaign. In other scenarios, for example, ► Starwars.com, the service of which is not tied to a fixed location, does not need to worry about local campaigns since the purpose is to generate awareness among worldwide customers.



## Internet and Electronic Interfaces

To use the Internet for communication, organizations can use their own website, social media, and emails to communicate branding, products, new information, and company background. They can also use other electronic media, such as third-party websites and Internet forums, to advertise or communicate with customers to reach customers worldwide.

In fact, many traditional communication or promotion tools can now be moved online to access customers worldwide. For example, advertisements can be shown online as interactive display ads or pay-per-click search advertising. Personal selling can be conducted in a virtual demonstration or real-time chat. Sales promotions can be provided online as e-coupons or online loyalty schemes. Public relations can be implemented as online webinars, newsletters, and campaigns that could drive viral marketing. Service providers can also sponsor an online event instead of an offline one. Word-of-mouth can be facilitated by encouraging customers to recommend the service on social media. Online opinion leaders such as influencers and celebrities can help endorse the service.

Other than those, the Internet also provides some special promotional tools. Many organizations now reduce misperceptions of service by providing tangible evidence. Some financial institutions, for example, provide evidence of tangible outcomes using online widgets and toolkits. CIMB, a Malaysian universal bank headquartered in Kuala Lumpur, embeds various calculator tools, such as auto financing installment calculator, property installment calculator, and credit card payment calculator, in its website (► https://www.cimb.com.my/en/personal/day-to-day-banking/tools.html). The benefit of such online tools is that consumers can discuss a new loan with their family and make decisions jointly with the tools at home. The 24-hour convenience of the Internet offers key benefits for household decision-making. Many universities provide virtual campus tours to allow students from worldwide to have a feeling of campus life before signing up for the education program.

The Internet can also be used to reduce the perceived risk of a service supplier. Many users spend much time searching for information using chat rooms, bulletin boards, and third-party sources before purchasing. Travel, for example, can be a highly risky purchase—you select a hotel to stay at, but it is too late to discover a problem on arrival in peak tourist season. By using sites such as YouTube to watch travel Vlogs or Tripadvisors to read travel reviews, a customer can see the "tangiblized" travel service, lower the perceived purchase risks and hence make an informed decision.

Another important feature of the Internet is the "opt-in" feature. That is, customers must agree (opt-in) to be involved in an organization's marketing activities, usually as a result of relevance or an incentive (e.g., E-mail opt-in, "Like" of a brand on Facebook) (Seth Godin, 1999). This is different from interruption marketing, e.g., a TV commercial that is shown to a customer without his/her consent and disrupts the customer's activities. As a result, Internet communication tools, banner advertising, and pop-up features are not as effective as initially thought because consumers do not opt-in to receiving advertisements, i.e., they can choose not to click the banner advertising or close a pop-up ad (Van Doren et al., 2000). The reported click-through rate of banner advertisements is close to 0.06% (Hesterberg, n.d.). Viral marketing, if designed and implemented well, can create curiosity and desire and generate demand for a product or service. However, plenty of viral marketing efforts do not resonate with the target audience and just go unnoticeable. In some cases, nuances in socioeconomic messages, for example, due to cultural insensitivity, can change the results of viral marketing in unpredictable ways.

When leveraging the Internet and electronic interfaces for international marketing, marketers have to take care of a few things. First, service companies should ensure their website is localized to meet their target audience's language and cultural preferences. This includes translating content into the local language, adapting graphics and images to appeal to local tastes, and designing the website to be user-friendly for local consumers. Second, service companies need to identify local consumers' media usage habits. This is because the dominant social media platforms and third-party sites are not always the same in different countries. For example, in 2023, the most popular social media platforms in Europe and North America are Facebook, Instagram, Pinterest, YouTube, and LinkedIn (Statcounter, n.d.); in China, the Most Popular Social Media Platforms are WeChat, Sina Weibo, Douyin (Tiktok), Little Red Book and Kuaishou as of Sep 2022 (Guide to Most Popular Chinese Social Media Sites, 2022). Regarding the digital device used to access the Internet, 57.56% of the traffic comes from mobile in the United States, while in India, 79.50% of the traffic comes from mobile in 2023 (Similar Web, 2023). These factors should be considered when designing and implementing international marketing campaigns on digital platforms.

### Summary of Promotional Techniques

Each of the communication tools outlined can be used separately or together to develop an integrated communication strategy to manage perceptions and create shared meaning for a service. In doing so, the limitations and benefits should be considered, and the consistency of the messages from multiple channels should be ensured to succeed in the integrated communication strategy.

## The Marketing Mix of Digital Service

Since the COVID-19 pandemic, technology has been increasingly used for many services and forced digital transformation of our work and lives. The year 2020 and 2021 has seen more services offered online/electronically, termed digital service, than ever. The usage and relevance of digital services are now more significant. While digital services still share some of the characteristics of services, such as intangibility, many do not necessarily share other characteristics, such as simultaneous production and consumption, perishability, and heterogeneity, since they can be processed without consumers being present, stored as electronic data and standardized to a great extent. The special characteristics of digital services have some implications for the marketing mix in the global market.



## Digital Service Product: Balance Between Standardization and Customization

Think about our daily life. You may find on the train you take out your mobile phone and click on Netflix to enjoy the show. When reaching home, you click on Uber Eat and order some food. After finishing your meal, you sit down, turn on your computer, and watch some online courses from Udemy. All of these, i.e., Netflix show, Uber Eat, and Udemy, are digital services. Digital services are becoming increasingly popular as more and more people have access to the Internet and mobile devices.

**Digital Services**

*Digital Services* are services that are supplied digitally. This includes both *classical services*, i.e., services that have always been considered to fall within the scope of the General Agreement on Trade in Services (GATS), like legal services or consulting services, that can now easily be provided over the Internet, and *new generation services* like Internet telephony, blogs, social networks, and search engines. The unifying trait of these services is their digital supply and reliance on the Internet, and data flow to be provided (Willemyns, 2021).

Willemyns (2021) categorizes digital services into digital infrastructure services and digitally enabled services in consideration of GATS.

**Digital infrastructure services** are the services necessary for/incidental to enable the access and use of the Internet. They are generally either telecommunications and/or computer services.

- **Carrier services:** Network management services, and hosting and IT infrastructure provisioning services include a range of services enabling access to the Internet. In other words, they are the Internet backbone and access services.
- **Cloud computing:** Though it is not a service in itself that can be supplied and consumed, it is a means of providing the service. Three general ways to supply services through the cloud include:
  - software as a service (SaaS): the cloud provider hosts and manages the software application, and the consumer uses the providers' application on various client devices;
  - cloud platform as a service (PaaS): the consumer-producers can create and/or acquire applications developed with the programming languages and tools supported by the provider;
  - cloud infrastructure as a service (IaaS): The consumer can rely on the provider for the processing, storage, networks, and other fundamental computing resources located in the cloud.

**Digitally enabled services** are those supplied over the Internet, constituting the bulk of digital services. This includes, amongst many others, online lending services, online legal services, video-on-demand services, search engines, e-payment services, and Internet telephony. ◘ Table 13.2 gives examples of digitally enabled services based on the category McColl-Kennedy (2003) suggested.

As shown in ◘ Table 13.2, most digital services tend to be easily modularized for standardization, given their information nature (information-processing or mental stimulus processing service). Two levels of customization can be achieved. The localization is achieved as needed in the form of language and content to cater to different country contexts. Mass customization blends flexibility and personalization in the service offering at the individual customer level.

**Table 13.2** Type of digital services

| Digital services | Nature |
|---|---|
| Digital infrastructure services | |
| Carrier services, network management services and hosting and IT infrastructure provisioning services | |
| Cloud computing service | |
| Digitally enabled service | |
| Search engine<br>• Google | Information processing service |
| Aggregators:<br>• Price comparison sites: Google shopping, ► shop.com, Shopsavvy<br>• Metamediaries/Super-affiliates: Taobao, Amazon | Information processing service |
| Broker-based services<br>• online exchange and trading: Forex CFD Online Trading<br>• online auctions: ebay, ► Auction.com, Copart | Information processing service |
| Agent-based service:<br>• online travel and tourism services: Tripadvisor, Airbnb<br>• online employment placement agencies: INDEED, Monster<br>• online real estate service: Zillow, Trulia<br>• online transportation: Uber, Grab | Information processing service |
| e-finance services<br>• e-banking<br>• online insurance<br>• e-payment services | Procession processing service |
| Online consulting<br>• online legal services<br>• e-health | People processing service |
| Social network<br>• LinkedIn, Facebook, YouTube | Mental stimulus processing service |
| Internet telephony (Voice over Internet Protocol: VoIP)<br>• Skype, Zoom | Mental stimulus processing service |
| Video-on-demand services<br>• Netflix, Disney+, Spotify | Mental stimulus processing service |
| Online training and education<br>• Udemy, Coursera | Mental stimulus processing service Or people processing service |

Source: Author's own table based on Willemyns (2021) and McColl-Kennedy (2003)

13

For example, the content offered by Netflix is standardized in most countries. Localization is achieved at the national level in two ways. First, to cater to customers worldwide, Netflix developed the technology and processes to translate their apps and interfaces, subtitles, and voice dubbing of content. Second, to cater to the customers' preferences in terms of content, Netflix also created localized content. For example, Sacred Games, Netflix's hit series in India, was set in Mumbai. The show was saturated with Indian cultural references, and most of the dialogue was in Hindi. Currently, the show sits at a rating of 8.8/10 on the IMDB website, with 96% positive Google reviews (Smartling, n.d.).

Mass customization is carried out at the individual customer level. Netflix has about 150 million subscribers around the world. They all turn to Netflix for the same service. Yet when they boot up their apps, no two subscribers will see the same home screen. Netflix does not laboriously create new home screens for each of its customers. Instead, it divides its subscriber base into segments ("taste communities") and serves each segment with a customized version of its product. Each viewer is treated with a set of tiles reflecting their viewing histories, coupled with individualized recommendations for future viewing. Even the poster art changes to reflect viewers' unique aesthetics. Everyone gets an experience of their own (National Research Corporation, 2019). Such mass customization is made possible through digital technologies, such as artificial intelligence, big data, and machine learning. Netflix uses machine learning algorithms to predict viewer patterns and understand when there will be general increases and decreases in viewers for a certain movie or show (Geeksforgeeks, 2021).

## Price: Special Pricing Tactics

While setting the price of digital services, a service firm must consider general factors such as cost, demand, and government regulation. In addition, there are some special pricing tactics for digital services owing to their digital nature. The use of tactics could vary across different types of digital services.

### Pricing Based on Subscription Business Model

Subscription business models are based on selling a product or service to receive monthly or yearly recurring subscription revenue. It is a powerful business model because it creates an environment where the default customer behavior is retention, as opposed to one where churn is the default (CB Insights, 2020).

The price of a subscription can be set in a few different ways.

1. *The flat-rate pricing model* charges a single, fixed rate for a particular service (McKnight & Boroumand, 2000). This fee does not fluctuate regardless of the time or effort required to complete. Let us say you're a freelance graphic designer and charge a flat rate of $400 for a logo design, regardless of whether it takes 1 h or 20 to complete. Another example is that the New York Times offers unlimited access to the digital version of its newspaper for $17 every 4 weeks. The flat rate pricing is ideal for quick and repeatable services.

2. *The tiered pricing model* allows companies to offer multiple packages with different features and product combinations available at different price points. The number of packages can vary, but most subscription companies offer two or three pricing tiers. For example, Chargebee is a subscription billing software that powers end-to-end billing for SaaS businesses. The features are bundled in different tiers at different price points: US$ 249/month, US$ 549/month, and a customized package. A tiered pricing program results in better customer satisfaction than a "one price fits all" policy (Gerstein & Friedman, 2015).
3. *Per unit/user model* is adopted by the majority of subscription companies. Pricing scales evenly along with the number of users—the more users, the more a company will charge. For example, a SaaS application provider might want to charge a business subscriber for each user of its application (for example, $5.99 per user per month) rather than simply setting a flat fee (for example, $50/month for unlimited application usage
4. *The Freemium model* is a business model in which a company offers basic or limited features to users at no cost and then charges a premium for supplemental or advanced features (Holm & Günzel-Jensen, 2017). The freemium business model dates back to the 1980s, though the term was coined in 2006. There are different ways of applying the freemium model. For example, a company could implement the traditional fermium model, in which a fully-functional product is free forever but has significant feature limitations or rate limits. Dropbox Basic account and Apple's free iCloud subscription are perfect examples. This freemium model tends to have difficulty converting customers from a free version to a paid version, termed a "penny gap." Some companies adopt Freeware 2.0, which is a free-forever, fully-functional product. It is usually the company's main product or a standalone product line in a larger company (Rock Content Writer, 2021). Companies usually monetize the product through add-ons for power users or special features. YouTube is an example.



Overall, the subscription business model is an effective pricing strategy for international marketing because it allows service companies to offer their services to customers across the globe while also ensuring predictable and recurring revenue. By adopting these strategies, service companies can optimize pricing plans, attract and retain customers, and drive business growth in international markets.

### Dynamic Pricing

Dynamic pricing, also called real-time pricing, demand pricing, or surge pricing, is a pricing strategy in which businesses set flexible prices for products or services based on the current market demands (Neussner et al., 2022). It is a yield management pricing strategy enabled by digital technology such as big data and machine learning. Businesses can change prices based on algorithms that consider competitor pricing, supply and demand, and other external factors in the market. It is suitable for many service sectors because of the perishability nature of the services, and hence widely used in pricing services such as hospitality, airline, and transportation. For example, such dynamic pricing is adopted by new digital services such as Uber and Grab, two companies that offer ride-hailing services (Xiong et al., 2021).

In this industry, snowy, rainy, or stormy days and the rush hour dictate the prices (a great example of surge pricing) to get extra benefits from these environmental or time-based conditions.

### Auction-Based Pricing

The Internet has facilitated the participation of many users worldwide, making forward auctions and reverse auctions more tenable—these have become more widely used than before.

Forward auctions take the form of a single seller offering an item for sale, with buyers competing to secure the item by bidding the price upward. Forward auctions are widely used when the goal is for the seller to receive the most money possible for the item being offered at auction. Thus, a forward auction can be utilized to sell goods and services of all types, whether conducted online, offline, or a hybrid. One example is eBay. A service seller can list his/her service, for example, a customized design for an eBay store home page, to eBay (▶ https://www.ebay.com.sg/itm/183785993513?hash=item2aca7fb529:g:-r0AAOSwjalcwtlG). Interested customers will offer their prices to bid for the service.

A reverse auction is the other major form of auction. In a reverse auction, a single buyer informs potential sellers of their intent to buy a specified good or service. Sellers place bids for the amount they are willing to be paid for the good or service, and at the end of the auction, the seller with the lowest amount wins. Reverse auctions are most typically used for procurement by private companies, public sector agencies, and nonprofit organizations. One such reverse auction website is ▶ https://www.ebridgeglobal.com/ .

### Digital Service Companies' Pricing Strategy in an International Context

Like any service company, digital service companies' pricing strategies can differ in different countries due to local market conditions, economic factors, cultural preferences, available payment methods, and local government regulations.

**Local market conditions:** Subscription pricing can vary depending on the level of competition in a given market. In some markets, there may be multiple competitors offering similar services at lower prices, which can impact the pricing strategies of subscription-based companies.

**Economic factors:** Economic factors such as the local cost of living and disposable income can also impact subscription pricing. For example, in countries with higher disposable income, customers may be more willing to pay higher subscription fees. Such an example can be found in Netflix, which charges different prices in different markets. In the United States, Netflix offers three subscription plans: standard with ads, basic, standard, and premium, with prices ranging from $6.99 to $19.99 per month (Netflix Help Center, n.d.). In India, Netflix offers four subscription plans: mobile, basic, standard, and premium, with prices ranging from INR 199 (US$2.43) to INR 799 (US$ 9.76) per month (Netflix Launches Mobile Plan for India, 2019).

**Cultural preferences:** Different cultures may have different preferences when it comes to pricing models. In some developed countries with well-established subscription-based services, such as the United States and Canada, consumers may be more accustomed to paying a monthly fee for access to a service such as Netflix, Spotify, or Amazon Prime. This is because these services have been popular in these markets for many years and have become a part of the cultural fabric. On the other hand, in some emerging markets where subscription-based services are relatively new, consumers may be more hesitant to commit to a monthly subscription fee and prefer to pay-per-use or use a hybrid pricing model instead. Similarly, auctions may be more or less effective in different cultures, depending on factors such as consumer behavior and preferences, levels of trust in online transactions, and attitudes toward bargaining and negotiation. An example can be seen in the case of eBay's expansion into China. eBay launched its online auction platform in China in 2003 but struggled to gain traction in the market. One of the factors was that eBay focused on auctions, while both sellers and customers wanted fixed-price sales (Why eBay Failed in China, 2018). Online auction sales in the United States had increased from $8.4 billion in 2001 to $28.2 billion in 2004, representing a 33% annual growth rate. But the online auction market size in China was rather small compared to that in the United States. According to IResearch, a Shanghai-based Internet market research firm, online auction sales in China had increased from $51 million in 2001 to $434 million in 2004, representing a 104% annual growth rate (Hou, 2007). To address these challenges, eBay eventually shifted its strategy in China to allow both auction and fixed-price formats (Baidu & eBay, 2006).

**Local payment methods:** Subscription pricing and dynamic pricing can also be impacted by the availability of local payment methods and currencies. For example, in countries where credit cards are not widely used, companies may need to offer alternative payment methods, such as mobile payments or bank transfers. When Netflix first launched in India in 2016, it offered only credit card payment options to subscribe to its service. This limited the company's potential subscriber base, as credit card penetration in India was relatively low, with only around 30 million credit cards in circulation in a country of over a billion people. To address this issue, Netflix partnered with local payment providers in India to offer more payment options to subscribers, such as debit cards, net banking, and mobile wallets. This helped the company increase its subscriber base in India significantly, making it easier and more convenient for users to pay for the service (Bhagat, 2016). The same was observed in Uber's pricing model in India, where cash was king because credit cards and other digital payment systems weren't widely used (Manjoo, 2017). Uber broke from its tradition of only accepting payment via card but began a pilot in 2016 that allowed users in Hyderabad, a city in India with a population of nearly eight million, to pay for their rides using cash (Russell, 2016).



**Local regulations:** Different countries may have different regulations and legal frameworks around auctions and bidding, which can impact the viability and effectiveness of subscription- or auction-based pricing strategies. An example of how regulations and legal frameworks around auctions and bidding can impact auction-based pricing strategies can be seen in the case of Uber's launch in India and South Korea. In 2020, New Delhi announced a new guideline. The guideline put a cap on the so-called surge pricing, the fare Uber and Ola charge during hours when their services see peak demand. Uber and any other app-operated, ride-hailing firm can charge a maximum of 1.5 times the base fare (Singh, 2020). When Uber launched its ride-sharing platform in South Korea in 2013, it initially used its standard auction-based pricing model, where prices fluctuated in response to supply and demand. However, South Korean authorities challenged the legality of Uber's pricing model, arguing that it violated local transportation laws, which require taxi fares to be set and approved by the government. Uber faced significant legal challenges and public backlash, ultimately leading to the company being banned in South Korea in 2014 (Kim & Cho, 2021). To address these challenges, Uber eventually adapted its pricing model in South Korea to comply with local regulations. It introduced fixed-rate pricing and partnered with local taxi companies to provide a more familiar and accepted service.

## Place: Disintermediation and Reintermediation

When you hope to get access to Netflix or Spotify, you probably simply go to their website or get their App from the app store, click the payment button, and then access their services. Similarly, a firm that needs market research or data service could click on the service company's website to place the order. Given its digital nature and wide reach of Internet access, a digital service company may not need the support of intermediaries to distribute the service to customers. The removal of the intermediaries is typically termed "disintermediation," whereby traditional intermediaries are eliminated (Alba et al., 1997; Quinn, 1992).

However, should you not know about Netflix, Spotify, or any market research company's website, you will likely use some search engine or some aggregator to search and compare those service providers through which to click into their online outlets. Here, the intermediary seems important to ensure the digital service can reach the customer and hence has to be re-introduced into the distribution channel. This is called re-intermediation, i.e., the creation of new intermediaries between customers and suppliers providing services such as supplier search and product evaluation (Agrawal et al., 2006).

Such re-intermediary is made possible with online agents, brokers, and aggregators accessible worldwide at a much lower cost. For example, an online market research company could be present on an online aggregator. This is particularly the case when a digital service first enters a foreign market—it is important for the service company to make its digital service available on a local aggregator site, which customers are familiar with, or even in a physical channel. For example, when launching its service in Indonesia in 2016, the Sweden-based company Spotify partnered with the biggest local wireless network provider Indosat Ooredoo to enable millions of Indonesians nationwide who didn't use credit cards to sign up for a three-month trial of Spotify Premium (Maulia, 2016).

## Promotion

### Opportunities for Cross-Selling and Up-Selling

When purchasing a digital service, customers have to interact with the digital platform, which provides opportunities for cross-selling and up-selling based on mass customization.

For example, when you book a room using the Airbnb service, the standard checkout time is 11 am, while your flight is 8 pm. Here you may find that you have the option of choosing late checkout by paying a bit more. This exemplifies up-selling, which involves encouraging the buyer to purchase the upgraded version of a product or service. In the case of Airbnb, it involves offering late checkout when you place an order of booking a room. You may have found that not a few hosts are doing similar up-selling via Airbnb: extra services of housekeeping, food delivery, honeymoon gifts, or even a personal driver are all options.

Another example is from Grab. Grab is the leading super app platform in Southeast Asia. Starting from a ride-hailing service, it now provides everyday services that matter to consumers. It offers a wide range of on-demand services in the region, including mobility, food, package and grocery delivery services, mobile payments, and financial services across 428 cities in eight countries. With the super app model, Grab will be able to predict with a great deal of accuracy what customers may be looking for, be it price or product. It rolled out the subscription program GrabUnlimited: $8.99/month based on a 3-month subscription. With this plan, users can receive a variety of discount vouchers that can be used for purchasing transportation, food, and other goods and services. This program helps increase customer loyalty and usage frequency and promotes cross-selling across services (Grab website, n.d.). See ► Chap. 8 for a detailed case study of Grab.



### More Ways to Tangibilize the Service

Compared to non-digital services, digital service has more ways to be tangibilized. Just as mentioned in the pricing tactics of digital service, service companies can provide a fully functional free version for a limited time or a free version with limited functions to allow customers to experience the service. Business service firms can now turn their successful projects into case studies and show them on their website, social media, or YouTube as credentials. They can also offer free online webinars and consultation sessions to give clients more first-hand experience. This is justifiable cost-wise, given that many digital services have a very low marginal cost

**Review Questions**

1. What is the rationale for achieving standardization and customization of service products?
2. What are the possible ways to balance standardization and customization of service products?
3. What factors should be considered when pricing service products for the global market?

4. How do the country differences and service characteristics influence a service company's distribution channel configuration?
5. What factors should be noted when making an integrated communication plan when promoting services internationally?
6. Elaborate on the special issues in developing a marketing mix for digital services.
7. Choose a service company that you are familiar with, and discuss how the company has done or should do for its marketing strategies when expanding overseas.

## Closing Case: Starbucks in Vietnam

Starbucks has more than 30,000 outlets around the globe. Yet it only has a mere 46 locations in Vietnam in 2020 after having opened its first store in Vietnam in Ho Chi Minh City in February 2013.

Vietnam has a population of 97.34 million. Vietnamese consume roughly two million bags of coffee annually, and the Southeast Asian nation is the world's second-largest coffee exporter. The middle class is growing in Vietnam, and the market for specialty coffee and tea shops in Vietnam is worth more than $1 billion, according to Euromonitor International. However, Starbucks has less than 3% of Vietnam's billion-dollar coffee and tea market.

When looking into Starbuck's marketing mix, a few factors can be identified.

Traditional Vietnamese iced coffee, also known as cà phê sữa đá, is one of the most popular beverages in the country. What makes this Vietnamese coffee

Starbucks, image by Pexels from Pixabay

so different is its stronger robusta beans that have a higher caffeine content than Starbucks' mild Arabica beans. Starbucks' Arabica beans contain up to 1.5% caffeine. But if a Vietnamese customer wants a stronger dose, the robusta beans in the cà phê sữa đá can give them the energy boost they need with a whopping 2.7% caffeine content. Starbucks did not seem to care about its weaker caffeine content and did not deviate far from its American-style coffee.

Second, the French colonialists introduced coffee into Vietnam in the nineteenth century, and today, coffee production plays a very important role in the country's economy. In 2016, the Southeast Asian country produced 1,650,000 metric tons of coffee. As a result, local cafe owners do not need to go through the hassle of importing coffee—they've got a huge pile of strong, eye-opening robusta beans right outside their door.

Third, there are quite some coffee varieties in Vietnam that might surprise a Westerner. For example, Cà phê trứng is a Vietnamese beverage made of egg yolks, sugar, condensed milk, and robusta coffee. Some are made with yogurt and fruit. Starbucks, on the other hand, restricted its Vietnamese menu mostly to the usual flat whites and lattes. There's a huge demand in the market for traditional Vietnamese coffee that Starbucks failed to fill.

Fourth, Starbucks had to face thousands of local coffee shops in Vietnam. The local vendors controlled almost 80% of the restaurant business. In addition, Starbucks prices ranged from 55,000 dongs ($2.59) for a black coffee—about half the average daily wage—to 85,000 dongs ($4) for an Asian Dolce Latte. These prices were slightly higher or similar to offerings from Highland Coffee and Trung Nguyen, two domestic chains. Yet the thousands of street-side cafes in Hanoi offer shoe-shine, free Wi-Fi, and traditional drip-filtered iced coffee for just 10,000–15,000 dong (47–71 US cents).

One noteworthy point is that Vietnamese customers do not visit Starbucks just for coffee. As you can probably imagine, the average price of coffee in a Vietnamese Starbucks outlet is higher than the local cafes. This doesn't stop customers from visiting Starbucks. However, the frequency of their visits is certainly affected. Vietnamese customers, especially people with good jobs who can afford expensive coffee, visit Starbucks to break the usual routine and experience something different every once in a while. Special occasions like a date can also drive people to visit this American coffee chain. It's like when someone in a first-world country goes to a five-star hotel occasionally to pamper themselves. But it's a "once in a blue moon" type of thing—not something that can be done frequently.

The Covid-19 pandemic has forced several food and beverage chains to close outlets amid plunging revenue. Starbucks not only closed a few outlets but also opened new ones. Patricia Marques, General Manager of Starbucks Vietnam, said that the company found it challenging to expand the number of outlets in Vietnam due to difficulties negotiating rent prices. At the same time, in central districts, Starbucks has observed that customers tended to order more takeaways, so it was considering opening small takeaway outlets where customers can pick up their drinks right away.

As of 2023, the Seattle-based coffee chain has operated 87 outlets across seven Vietnamese provinces. Marques said the company would continue targeting outlet growth in the country after reaching its milestone. Marques said Starbucks' long-term goal in Vietnam was to become consumers' "everyday café."

**Questions**

1. What explains the failure of Starbucks in Vietnam?

   The following ▫ Table 13.3 shows the prices of a Starbucks tall (small) hot latte in US$, adjusted to reflect the relative cost of other goods in 2017. Why did Starbucks charge different price levels in different countries?
2. Do you think Starbucks can become a Vietnamese consumer's "everyday café"? How should Starbucks shape its marketing mix to achieve this goal?

Sources: (Haigh, 2019; Linda, 2022; Nguyen, 2022; Petty, 2014; Ross, 2017; Saigoneer, 2017; Saini, 2020)

▫ **Table 13.3** Prices of a starbucks tall (small) hot latte in US$ in 2017

| Country | Comparative cost, Starbucks Tall Latte |
|---|---|
| Vietnam | 8.18 |
| China | 7.18 |
| Malaysia | 7.23 |
| India | 7.99 |
| Singapore | 4.71 |
| Germany | 3.83 |
| Australia | 2.86 |
| United States | 2.75 |

Source: Author's own table. Data extracted from Ross (2017)

**Summary**

This chapter

- discussed the product strategy when marketing services in the global market, including
  - the need to balance standardization versus customization for service products
  - using service modularization to balance standardization versus customization
  - considering how the types of services, including hard and soft services, and front-office and back-office, influence the strategy of standardization versus customization
- evaluated the pricing strategy for services in the global market, including
  - the factors influencing international pricing of services
  - pricing strategies
  - the relation of the prices between foreign markets and domestic market
- identified the key issues when distributing services in the global market, including
  - how differences between countries and markets affect the distribution strategy
  - how the characteristics of services influence the distribution strategy
  - how to arrange the global dispersion of service modules
- analyzed how communication strategies should be developed in the global market, including
  - considering barriers to promotion in foreign countries
  - factoring in the impact of service characteristics when formulating communication strategies
  - application of promotion techniques for service companies
- evaluated the special issues in developing the marketing mix for digital services:
  - digital service products provide more opportunities for standardization, while localization and customization can be achieved at national and individual levels
  - special tactics applicable to digital services include subscription-based, dynamic, and auction-based pricing
  - digital services require some level of re-intermediation
  - digital services provide more opportunities for cross-selling and upselling, as well as more ways of tangibalization.



## References

1000logos. (2022, July 15). *Singapore Airlines Logo*. 1000logos. Retrieved from https://1000logos.net/singapore-airlines-logo/

Agrawal, A., Cockburn, I., & McHale, J. (2006). Gone but not forgotten: Knowledge flows, labor mobility, and enduring social relationships. *Journal of Economic Geography, 6*(5), 571–591.

Alba, J., Lynch, J., Weitz, B., Janiszewski, C., Lutz, R., Sawyer, A., & Wood, S. (1997). Interactive home shopping: Consumer, retailer, and manufacturer incentives to participate in electronic marketplaces. *Journal of Marketing, 61*(3), 38–53.

Albaum, G., Duerr, E., & Josiassen, A. (2016). International marketing and export management (8. Bs.).

Albers-Miller, N. D., & Royne Stafford, M. (1999). An international analysis of emotional and rational appeals in services vs goods advertising. *Journal of Consumer Marketing, 16*(1), 42–57.

Andehn, M., Nordin, F., & Nilsson, M. E. (2016). Facets of country image and brand equity: Revisiting the role of product categories in country-of-origin effect research. *Journal of Consumer Behaviour, 15*(3), 225–238. https://doi.org/10.1002/cb.1550

Australian Competition & Consumer Commission. (2013). Online reviews—A guide for business and review platforms. Retrieved from https://www.accc.gov.au/system/files/Online%20reviews%E2%80%94a%20guide%20for%20business%20and%20review%20platforms.pdf

Alex, (2021). Study reveals how much it costs to get a haircut around the world. September 10, 2021. Vividmaps. https://vividmaps.com/costs-ofhaircuts-around-the-world/

Baidu and eBay EachNet Expand Strategic Cooperation in China. (2006, November 8). Retrieved from https://ir.baidu.com/static-files/608f70f1-df84-4baf-b177-96ef3c2b3f37

Baker, M. J., & Ballington, L. (2002). Country of origin as a source of competitive advantage. *Journal of Strategic Marketing, 10*(2), 157–168.

Balea, J. (2016). *Uber launches motorbike service to go after Grab and Go-Jek*. Tech in Asia. Retrieved from https://www.techinasia.com/uber-launches-motorbike-service-ubermoto

Bardakci, A., & Whitelock, J. (2004). How "ready" are customers for mass customisation? An exploratory investigation. *European Journal of Marketing, 38*(11/12), 1396–1416.

Beardsley, E. (2012). *Why McDonald's in France doesn't feel like fast food*. NPR. Retrieved from https://www.npr.org/sections/thesalt/2012/01/24/145698222/why-mcdonalds-in-france-doesnt-feel-like-fast-food

Berentzen, J. B., Backhaus, C., Michaelis, M., Blut, M., & Ahlert, D. (2008). Does "made in…" also apply to services? An empirical assessment of the country-of-origin effect in service settings. *Journal of Relationship Marketing, 7*(4), 391–405.

Bhagat, H.R. (2016). Netflix enters India, to bring quality global content: Chris Jaffe & Chitavan Patel. *The Economic Times*. Retrieved from https://economictimes.indiatimes.com/opinion/interviews/netflix-enters-india-to-bring-quality-global-content-chris-jaffe-chitavan-patel/articleshow/50479609.cms?from=mdr

Brady, M. K., Bourdeau, B. L., & Heskel, J. (2005). The importance of brand cues in intangible service industries: An application to investment services. *Journal of Services Marketing, 19*(6), 401–410. https://doi.org/10.1108/08876040510620175

Campagnolo, D., & Camuffo, A. (2010). The concept of modularity in management studies: A literature review. *International journal of Management Reviews, 12*(3), 259–283.

Canaves, S. (2019, December 6). *Local Celebrities and global projections, how Airbnb is courting Chinese travelers*. Jingculture & Crypto. Retrieved from https://jingculturecommerce.com/local-celebrities-and-global-projections-how-airbnb-is-courting-chinese-travelers/

Cateora, P. R., & Graham, J. L. (2007). *International Marketing* (13th ed.). McGraw-Hill.

Carmel, E. (2006). *Building your information systems from the other side of the world: How Infosys manages time zone differences*. MIS Quarterly Executive, 5(1), 43–53.

CB Insights. (2020, February 26). *7 Surprising industries turning to subscription business models*. CB Insights. Retrieved from https://www.cbinsights.com/research/report/subscription-business-model-industries/

Chase, R. B. (1981). The customer contact approach to services: Theoretical bases and practical extensions. *Operations Research, 29*(4), 698–706.

Chase, R. B., & Tansik, D. A. (1983). The customer contact model for organization design. *Management Science, 29*(9), 1037–1050.

China Daily. (2005, June 23). McDonald's ad banned due to insulting plot. *China Daily*. Retrieved from http://www.chinadaily.com.cn/english/doc/2005-06/23/content_453733.htm

Christiansen, T., & Tax, S. S. (2000). Measuring word of mouth: The questions of who and when? *Journal of Marketing Communications, 6*(3), 185–199.

CIW Team. (2017, March 4). *An overview of China's "Airbnb": Xiaozhu, Tujia, Zhubaijia. March 4, 2017*. China Internet Watch. Retrieved from https://www.chinainternetwatch.com/14626/chinas-airbnbs/

Cochran, J. (n.d.). *Look at how different Shanghai Disneyland is from other Disney Parks*. Retrieved from https://www.frommers.com/slideshows/848246-look-at-how-different-shanghai-disneyland-is-from-other-disney-parks

Coulter, K. S., & Coulter, R. A. (2003). *The effects of industry knowledge on the development of trust in service relationships*. International Journal of research in Marketing, 20(1), 31–43.

Cortese, A. J. (2020, July 9). *Airbnb's battle against local unicorns resumes as China's home-sharing market recovers*. KrAsia. Retrieved from https://kr-asia.com/airbnbs-battle-against-local-unicorns-resumes-as-chinas-home-sharing-market-recovers

Danao, M. (2018, February 14). *How Singapore Airlines became the best airline brand in Asia*. Referral Candy. Retrieved from https://www.referralcandy.com/blog/singapore-airlines-marketing-strategy

Daxue Consulting. (2016, July 26). *Airbnb officially enters China: Lessons in market strategies for Chinese consumers*. Retrieved from https://daxueconsulting.com/airbnb-officially-enters-china/

DBS Newsroom. (n.d.). *DBS to acquire Citi's consumer banking business in Taiwan*. Retrieved from https://www.dbs.com/newsroom/DBS_to_acquire_Citis_consumer_banking_business_in_Taiwan_sg

De Blok, C., Luijkx, K., Meijboom, B., & Schols, J. (2010). Modular care and service packages for independently living elderly. *International Journal of Operations & Production Management, 30*(1), 75–97.

De Moissac, D., & Bowen, S. (2019). Impact of language barriers on quality of care and patient safety for official language minority Francophones in Canada. *Journal of Patient Experience, 6*(1), 24–32.

Dean, J. (1976). Pricing policies for new products. *Harvard Business Review, 54*(6), 141–153.

Ding, Y., & Keh, H. T. (2016). A re-examination of service standardization versus customization from the consumer's perspective. *Journal of Services Marketing., 30*(1), 16–28. https://doi.org/10.1108/JSM-02-2015-0088

Ehrenberg, A. S., Hammond, K., & Goodhart, G. J. (1994). The after-effects of price-related consumer promotions. *Journal of Advertising Research, 34*(4), 11–22.

Estopace E. (2016, June 6). *Netflix's answer to slow Internet: Adaptive streaming*. Philstar Global. Retrieved from https://www.philstar.com/business/technology/2016/06/06/1590535/netflixs-answer-slow-internet-adaptive-streaming

Europa. (2022, December 15). *Comparative price levels of consumer goods and services*. Retrieved from https://ec.europa.eu/eurostat/statistics-explained/index.php?title=Comparative_price_levels_of_consumer_goods_and_services#Overall_price_levels

Fein, A. J., & Anderson, E. (1997). Patterns of credible commitments: Territory and brand selectivity in industrial distribution channels. *Journal of Marketing, 61*(2), 19–34.

Filipiknow. (2022). *11 Controversial and banned Filipino advertisements*. Retrieved from https://filipiknow.net/controversial-advertisements-in-the-philippines/

Franke, N., & Schreier, M. (2008). Product uniqueness as a driver of customer utility in mass customization. *Marketing Letters, 19*, 93–107.

Geeksforgeeks. (2021, November 10). *How does Netflix use machine Learning? Geeks for Geeks*. Retrieved from https://www.geeksforgeeks.org/how-does-netflix-use-machine-learning/

Gerstein, M., & Friedman, H. H. (2015). Smart pricing strategies for the internet age: A prime. *Journal of Accounting and Finance, 15*(2), 25–36.

Godin, S. (1999). *Permission marketing: Turning strangers into friends and friends into customers*. Simon and Schuster.

Grab Website. (n.d.). Retrieved from https://www.grab.com/sg/grabunlimited/

Griffith, E. (2022, May 23). Airbnb shuts down its local business in China. *New York Times*. Retrieved from https://www.nytimes.com/2022/05/23/business/airbnb-china.html

Griswold, A. (2014, July 11). *France banned free shipping. So Amazon made it cost one cent*. Retrieved from https://slate.com/business/2014/07/france-banned-free-shipping-so-amazon-made-it-cost-one-cent.html

Grove, S. J., & Fisk, R. P. (1992). The service experience as theater. *Advances in Consumer Research, 19*, 455–461.

Grove, S., Pickett, G. M., & LaBand, D. N. (1995). An empirical examination of factual information content of services advertisements. *The Service Industries Journal, 15*(2), 216–233.

Guide to Most Popular Chinese Social Media Sites & Platforms for Marketing (Update 2022) (2022, September 12). Gentlemen Marketing Agency (GMA). Retrieved from https://marketingtochina.com/top-10-social-media-in-china-for-marketing/

Guilhoto, L. D. F. (2018). The effects of country-of-origin on the service sector: A multidimensional approach. *RAM. Revista de Administração Mackenzie, 19*, eRAMR180006.

Gurhan-Canli, Z., & Maheswaran, D. (2000). Cultural variations in country-of-origin effects. *Journal of Marketing Research, 37*(3), 309–318. https://doi.org/10.1509/jmkr.37.3.309.18778
Haigh M. (2019, December 23). *Why Starbucks and other international chains are way less popular than local coffee shops in Vietnam*? Dec 23, 2019CNBC. Retrieved from https://www.cnbc.com/2019/12/19/starbucks-coffee-bean-tea-leaf-are-losing-to-local-vietnam-chains.html
Hart, C. W. (1995). Mass customization: Conceptual underpinnings, opportunities and limits. *International Journal of Service Industry Management, 6*(2), 36–45.
Hill, C. W. (2009). *International business* (7th ed.). Aufl.
Hill, C W. (2015). *International business: competing in the global marketplace. 10e [edition]*. McGraw Hill Education, New York, NY.
Hobday, M. (1998). Product complexity, innovation and industrial organisation. *Research Policy, 26*(6), 689–710.
Holm, A. B., & Günzel-Jensen, F. (2017). Succeeding with freemium: Strategies for implementation. *Journal of Business Strategy, 38*(2), 16–24. https://doi.org/10.1108/JBS-09-2016-0096
Hou, J. (2007). Price determinants in online auctions: A comparative study of eBay China and US. Journal of Electronic Commerce Research, 8(3).
HSBC Website. (n.d.). Retrieved from https://www.privatebanking.hsbc.com/investment-services/investment-outlook-programme/
Huffman, C., & Kahn, B. E. (1998). Variety for sale: Mass customization or mass confusion? *Journal of Retailing, 74*(4), 491–513.
Hyder, A. S., & Fregidou-Malama, M. (2009). Services marketing in a cross-cultural environment: The case of Egypt. *Journal of Services Marketing, 23*(4), 261–271.
IBM Website. (n.d.). Retrieved from https://research.ibm.com/labs/
Inagaki, K., & Lewis, L. (2020, November 17). Why Walmart's might couldn't crack Japan. *Financial Times*. Retrieved from https://www.ft.com/content/db42cb7e-5f87-4e46-b923-e9ef5a9d4600
International Trade Administration. (n.d.). *Distribution and sales channels*. Retrieved from https://www.trade.gov/country-commercial-guides/saudi-arabia-distribution-and-sales-channels
Jobber, D. (2001). *Principles and practice of marketing* (3rd ed.). McGraw-Hill.
Johnston, R., & Clark, G. (2001). *Service operations management*. Pearson Education Limited.
Kearney, A. T. (2014). *Global services location index—A. T. Kearney*. Global Services Location Index 2014.
Kedia, B. L., & Mukherjee, D. (2009). Understanding offshoring: A research framework based on disintegration, location and externalization advantages. *Journal of World Business, 44*(3), 250–261.
Keenan, M. (2022, September 9). *Penetration pricing: Win market share and profitability*. Shopify. Retrieved from https://www.shopify.com/retail/penetration-pricing
Keh, H. T., Ren, R., Hill, S. R., & Li, X. (2013). The beautiful, the cheerful, and the helpful: The effects of service employee attributes on customer satisfaction. *Psychology & Marketing, 30*(3), 211–226.
Kitchen, D., & Harper, L. (2023, January 12). *Ambush marketing and the 2022 and 2023 FIFA World Cups*. Retrieved from https://imbusiness.passle.net/post/102i4zn/ambush-marketing-and-the-2022-and-2023-fifa-world-cups
Kim, J., & Cho, H. (2021). Case 6. The Korean experience of sharing economy and its policy implications.
Knowledge at Wharton Staff. (2008, July 10). *Wal-Mart India's Raj Jain: 'The biggest challenge is there is no organized supply chain'*. Retrieved from https://knowledge.wharton.upenn.edu/article/wal-mart-indias-raj-jain-the-biggest-challenge-is-there-is-no-organized-supply-chain/
Kogut, B. (1985). Designing global strategies: Comparative and competitive value-added chains. *Sloan Management Review (pre-1986), 26*(4), 15.
Kotabe, M. M., & Helsen, K. (2022). *Global marketing management*. John Wiley & Sons.
Kotler, P. (2000). *Marketing management* (10th ed.). Prentice Hall.
Kotler, P., & Keller, K. (2009). *Marketing Management*. Global edition. Pearson Education Inc..
Lascu, D. N., & Giese, I. (1995). Exporting country bias in a retailing environment: Implications or retailer country of origin. *Journal of Global Marketing, 9*(1/2), 41–58.
Lee, D., & McMorrow, R. (2022, May 4). Airbnb gives up on China as zero-Covid policy crushes tourism. *Financial Times*. Retrieved from https://www.ft.com/content/f491744b-10a9-4f0a-b4b5-d9d8851aff24

Lewin, A. Y., Massini, S., & Peeters, C. (2009b). Why are companies offshoring innovation? The emerging global race for talent. *Journal of international business studies, 40*, 901–925.

Lewin, A. Y., Perm-Ajchariyawong, N., Sappenfield, D., & Aird, C. (2009a). *Is the global outsourcing industry in for a no-holds-barred competition?* ORN Service Provider Survey Report.

Linda. (2022, December 6). *The low cost of coffee in Vietnam makes it a popular destination for coffee lovers*. The Commons Cafe. Retrieved from https://www.thecommonscafe.com/the-low-cost-of-coffee-in-vietnam-makes-it-a-popular-destination-for-coffee-lovers/

Lindecrantz, E., Gi, M. T. P., & Zerbi, S. (2020, April 28). *Personalizing the customer experience: Driving differentiation in retail*. McKinsey. Retrieved from https://www.mckinsey.com/industries/retail/our-insights/personalizing-the-customer-experience-driving-differentiation-in-retail

Lovelock, C. H., & Yip, G. S. (2016). Developing global strategies for service businesses. *California Management Review, 38*(2), 64–86.

Maheswaran, D. (1994). Country of origin as a stereotype: Effects of consumer expertise and attribute strength on product evaluations. *Journal of Consumer Research, 21*(2), 354–365.

Malpani, P. (2015, June 16). *Uber's uber cool & unconventional marketing strategy in India*. Retrieved from https://www.linkedin.com/pulse/ubers-uber-cool-unconventional-marketing-strategy-india-malpani

Manjoo, F. (2017, April 14). *Uber wants to rule the world*. First It Must Conquer India. Retrieved from https://www.nytimes.com/2017/04/14/technology/uber-india.html

Marn, M. V., Roegner, E. V., & Zawada, C. C. (2003). Pricing new products. *McKinsey Quarterly, 3*, 40–49.

Martin Roll. (2021, November). *How nations and brands overcome country of origin challenges*. Retrieved from https://martinroll.com/resources/articles/marketing/how-nations-and-brands-overcome-country-of-origin-challenges/

Martin, D., Howard, C., & Herbig, P. (1998). The Japanese distribution system. *European Business Review, 98*, 109–121.

Maulia E. (2016, March 31). *Spotify partners Indosat with 'affordable' Indonesian service*. Nikkei Asia. Retrieved from https://asia.nikkei.com/Business/Spotify-partners-Indosat-with-affordable-Indonesian-service

McColl-Kennedy, J. R. (2003). *Services marketing*. John Wiley & Sons Inc.

McKinsey Website. (n.d.). Retrieved from https://www.mckinsey.com/cn/contact-us

McKnight, L. W., & Boroumand, J. (2000). Pricing Internet services: Approaches and challenges. *Computer, 33*(02), 128–129.

McNeill, L. S. (2012). Sales promotion in the supermarket industry: A four country case comparison. *The International Review of Retail, Distribution and Consumer Research, 22*(3), 243–260.

Meuter, M. L., Ostrom, A. L., Roundtree, R. I., & Bitner, M. J. (2000). Self-service technologies: Understanding customer satisfaction with technology-based service encounters. *Journal of Marketing, 64*(3), 50–64.

Meyer, M. H., & DeTore, A. (1999). Product development for services. *Academy of Management Perspectives, 13*(3), 64–76.

Michaelis, M., Woisetschlager, D. M., Backhaus, C., & Ahlert, D. (2008). The effects of country of origin and corporate reputation on initial trust: An experimental evaluation of the perception of Polish consumers. *International Marketing Review, 25*(4), 404–422.

Millward S. (2013). Boosted by Messi's endorsement, WeChat scores 100 million users outside of China. 15 Aug 2013. https://www.techinasia.com/tencent-wechat-100-million-overseas-users

Miozzo, M., & Grimshaw, D. (2005). Modularity and innovation in knowledge-intensive business services: IT outsourcing in Germany and the UK. *Research Policy, 34*(9), 1419–1439.

Morris, M. H., Pitt, L. F., & Honeycutt, E. D. (2001). *Business-to-business marketing: A strategic approach*. Sage.

Motiani, P. (2022, August 19). Holidays to become costlier from July 18 as all hotel rooms to be taxed under GST. *Economic Times*. Retrieved from https://economictimes.indiatimes.com/wealth/tax/holidays-to-become-costlier-from-july-18-as-all-hotel-rooms-to-be-taxed-under-gst/articleshow/92841840.cms

Mourdoukoutas, P. (2015). *Three trends haunting McDonald's: Localization, customization, and cheap labor*. Forbes. Retrieved from https://www.forbes.com/sites/panosmourdoukoutas/2015/06/18/

three-trends-haunting-mcdonalds-localization-customization-and-cheap-labor/?sh=18ba4b5f6d81
Nagle, T. T., Hogan, J. E., & Zale, J. (2011). *The strategy and tactics of pricing: A guide to growing more profitably* (5th ed.). Prentice Hall.
National Research Corporation. (2019). What healthcare can learn from Netflix: An executive Q&A with Steve Jackson, President of NRC Health and Jeffrey Rakover, Senior Research Associate at Institute for Healthcare Improvement. Retrieved from https://www.marketscreener.com/quote/stock/NATIONAL-RESEARCH-CORPORA-13255969/news/What-healthcare-can-learn-from-Netflix-An-executive-Q-A-with-Steve-Jackson-President-of-NRC-Health-29356817/
Netessine, S., & Shumsky, R. (2002). Introduction to the theory and practice of yield management. *INFORMS Transactions on Education, 3*(1), 34–44.
Netflix Help Center. (n.d.). *Plans and pricing*. Retrieved from https://help.netflix.com/en/node/24926
Netflix Launches Mobile Plan for India at INR 199/month. (2019 July 24). Retrieved from https://about.netflix.com/en/news/netflix-launches-mobile-plan-for-india
Neussner, W., Ebner, D., & Lackner, M. (2022). Value creation by dynamic pricing through digitization and industry-wide perspective. *International Journal of Economics and Finance, 14*(1), 115–115.
Nguyen D. (2022, June 25). *Starbucks closes third Vietnam outlet*. June 25 2022. VN Express. Retrieved from https://e.vnexpress.net/news/companies/starbucks-closes-third-vietnam-outlet-4480332.html
NTSC vs. PAL. (n.d.). *Diffen*. Retrieved from https://www.diffen.com/difference/NTSC_vs_PAL
OECD (Organisation for Economic Co-operation and Development). (2019). *Insurance intermediation: Regulatory/supervisory framework and market conduct*. Retrieved from https://one.oecd.org/document/DAF/AS/WD(2019)4/en/pdf
Ofir, C., & Lehman, D. R. (1986). Measuring images of foreign products. *Columbia Journal of World Business*, 105–109.
Olsen, S. O., & Olsson, U. H. (2002). Multientity scaling and the consistency of country-of-origin attitudes. *Journal of International Business Studies*, 149–167.
Oxford Business Group. (n.d.). *Egyptian retail continues to expand and adapt to changing trends*. Retrieved from https://oxfordbusinessgroup.com/reports/egypt/2019-report/economy/spending-power-despite-threats-to-consumer-spending-the-sector-continues-to-expand-and-adapt-to-changing-retail-trends
Pekkarinen, S., & Ulkuniemi, P. (2008). Modularity in developing business services by platform approach. *The International Journal of Logistics Management., 19*(1), 84–103. https://doi.org/10.1108/09574090810872613
Peters, N. (2011). *The country-of-origin affect on perception of services: Entry mode decisions as a determinant of usability*. GRIN Verlag.
Peters, V. J. T., Meijboom, B. R., & De Vries, E. (2018). Interfaces in service modularity: A scoping review. *International Journal of Production Research, 56*(20), 6591–6606.
Petty M. (2014, July 23). *Starbucks seeks to expand in cafe-clogged Vietnam*. July 23, 2014 Reuters. Retrieved from https://www.reuters.com/article/us-vietnam-starbucks-idUSKBN0FS13B20140723
Pinkaeo, K., & Speece, M. (2002). Country of origin effects on expectation of service quality for life insurance among Thai consumers. In Ramizwick & T. Ping (Eds.), *AP—Asia Pacific advances in consumer research* (Vol. 5, pp. 295–301). Association for Consumer Research.
Quinn, J. B. (1992). *The intelligent enterprise*. Free Press.
Rahikka, E., Ulkuniemi, P., & Pekkarinen, S. (2011). Developing the value perception of the business customer through service modularity. *Journal of Business & Industrial Marketing, 26*(5), 357–367.
Redmart. (2022, June). *Anyone notice redmart free shipping is no longer free*? Retrieved from https://www.reddit.com/r/singapore/comments/vcn4jw/anyone_notice_redmart_free_shipping_is_no_longer/
Reuters. (2021, March 22). India's $883 billion retail landscape dominated by kirana stores. Business Today. Retrieved from https://www.businesstoday.in/latest/economy-politics/story/india-883-billion-retaillandscape-dominated-by-kirana-stores-291474-2021-03-22.
Ritzer, G. (2011). *The McDonaldization of society 6* (Vol. 6). Pine Forge Press.
Rock Content Writer (2021, August 11). *Find out the Best Examples of Freemium models*. Rockcontent. Retrieved from https://rockcontent.com/blog/examples-of-freemium-models/

Ross K. (2017, April 18). *Countries where buying Starbucks is the most and least extravagant.* Valuependuin. https://www.valuepenguin.com/countries-where-buying-starbucks-most-and-least-extravagant

Russell J. (2016 February 9). *Uber begins to see the payout from accepting cash payments.* Retrieved from https://techcrunch.com/2016/02/08/uber-begins-to-see-the-payout-from-accepting-cash-payments/

Sahu, R P. (2015, October 19). *Vodafone plays the retail tune.* Business Standard. Retrieved from https://www.business-standard.com/article/management/vodafone-plays-the-retail-tune-115101901208_1.html

Saigoneer. (2017, May 3). *Vietnam Has the Third-Most Expensive Starbucks drinks in the world: Survey.* Saigoneer. 03 May 2017. Retrieved from https://saigoneer.com/saigon-food-culture/9957-vietnam-has-third-most-expensive-starbucks-drinks-in-the-world-survey

Saini, L. (2020, January 10). *Why Starbucks is failing in Vietnam*? Better Marketing. January 10, 2020. Retrieved from https://bettermarketing.pub/why-starbucks-is-failing-in-vietnam-e77a87c3eccb

Salinas S. (2018, June 9). *Uber and Lyft are racing to own every mode of transportation—They're getting close.* CNBC. Retrieved from https://www.cnbc.com/2018/06/09/uber-and-lyft-are-racing-to-own-every-mode-of-transportation.html

Schooler, R. D., & Sunoo, D. H. (1969). Consumer perceptions of international products: Regional vs. national labeling. *Social Science Quarterly*, 886–890.

Sharma, N., & Patterson, P. G. (1999). The impact of communication effectiveness and service quality on relationship commitment in consumer, professional services. *Journal of Services Marketing, 13*(2), 151–170. https://doi.org/10.1108/08876049910266059

Shostack, G. L. (1982). How to design a service. *European Journal of Marketing, 16*, 49–63.

Shostack, G. L. (1984). Designing services that deliver. *Harvard Business Review, 62*, 133–139.

Shostack, G. L. (1987). Service positioning through structural change. *Journal of Marketing, 51*(1), 34–43.

Similar Web. (2023). https://www.similarweb.com/platforms/

Simon, N. (2020, January 3). *5 insurance front-office processes you can improve with AI.* Mantra Labs. Retrieved from https://www.mantralabsglobal.com/blog/5-insurance-front-office-processes-you-can-improve-with-ai/

Simonson, I. (2005). Determinants of customers' responses to customized offers: Conceptual framework and research propositions. *Journal of Marketing, 69*(1), 32–45.

Singapore Statutes Online. (n.d.). *Healthcare services (advertisement) regulations 2021.* Version of 23 Feb 2023. Retrieved from https://sso.agc.gov.sg/SL/HSA2020-S1033-2021?DocDate=20211230&ProvIds=pr5-&ViewType=Advance&Any=3+Factories+Persons+In+Charge+Regulations&WiAl=1

Singh M. (2020 November 28). *India sets rules for commissions, surge pricing for Uber and Ola.* Retrieved from https://techcrunch.com/2020/11/27/india-sets-rules-for-commissions-surge-pricing-for-uber-and-ola/?guccounter=1&guce_referrer=aHR0cHM6Ly93d3cuZ29vZ2xlLmNvbS8&guce_referrer_sig=AQAAAD4iwHX5O57Av-T9wGf84PYo5lr5uEzdGvH6a6S7JN_PLqw58Qw1wRFZJ2eM9921dK5X2ptx8MEon1UoGXWOFtcyiBqRNPblHWRjZGgyYTx_OfjsUIRmsEsKdbacuv8a8OH6NlUF6NOdJ8hI2dE8eOAkQLvP1niRQS3g7uUDiUKb

Sitsanis N. (2019, October 30). 7 Translation marketing blunders that cost millions. *Speakt.* Retrieved from https://speakt.com/7-translation-marketing-blunders-that-cost-millions/

Smartling. (n.d.). *5 Great examples of localization done right.* Retrieved from https://www.smartling.com/resources/101/examples-of-localization/

Stafford, M. R., & Day, E. (1995). Retail services advertising: The effects of appeal, medium, and service. *Journal of Advertising, 24*(1), 57–71.

Statcounter. (n.d.). *Social media stats North America April 2022–April 2023.* Retrieved from https://gs.statcounter.com/social-media-stats/all/north-america

Sundbo, J. (1994). Modulization of service production and a thesis of convergence between service and manufacturing organizations. *Scandinavian Journal of Management, 10*(3), 245–266.

Sundbo, J. (2002). The service economy: Standardisation or customisation? *Service Industries Journal, 22*(4), 93–116.

Tellis, G. J. (1986). Beyond the many faces of price: An integration of pricing strategies. *Journal of Marketing, 50*(4), 146–160.

The New York Time. (2006). *Carrefour quits Korea*. 28 Apr 2006. Retrieved from https://www.nytimes.com/2006/04/28/business/worldbusiness/carrefour-quits-korea.html

Thomas, H., O'Neal, D. E., & Alvarado, R. (Eds.). (1998). *Strategic discovery: Competing in New Arenas* (Vol. 7). John Wiley & Sons.

Thompson, J. D. (1967). *Organizations in action: Social science bases of administrative theory*. Transaction Publishers.

Tian, K.T., Bearden, W.O., and Hunter, G.L. (2001) *Consumers' need for uniqueness: scale development and validation*. Journal of Consumer Research, 28, 50–66.

Tobin, M. (2022, May 24). *Airbnb is shutting China business to focus on outbound Asia Travel*. 24 May 2022. Bloomberg. Retrieved from https://www.bloomberg.com/news/articles/2022-05-23/airbnb-to-shut-china-business-focus-on-outbound-asia-travel#xj4y7vzkg

Tripadvisor Website. (n.d.). *Uber boat by Thames Clippers*. Retrieved from https://www.tripadvisor.com.sg/Attraction_Review-g186338-d1188478-Reviews-Uber_Boat_by_Thames_Clippers-London_England.html

UNCTAD. (2012). *Classification of non-tariff measures*. February 2012 version. Retrieved from http://wits.worldbank.org/wits/docs/multi-agency_classification_of_ntms.pdf

Vahid (2023). *Spotify premium price by country 2023|cheapest country*. February 19, 2023. Retrieved from https://howtospotify.com/spotify-premium-price/

Van Doren, D. C., Fechner, D. L., & Green-Adelsberger, K. (2000). Promotional strategies on the world wide web. *Journal of Marketing Communications, 6*(1), 21–35.

Veale, R., & Challen, R. (2010). Is it what you know or where you are from? Revealing the influence of a country of birth and country of training on consumer expectations of service quality. In *Proceedings of the International Service Research Conference (AMA SERVSIG), June, Porto, Portugal*.

Voss, C. A., & Hsuan, J. (2009). Service architecture and modularity. *Decision Sciences, 40*(3), 541–569.

Wang, D., Martin, B. A., & Yao, J. (2021). Do discount presentations influence gift purchase intentions and attitudes of Chinese outbound tourists? *Journal of Travel Research, 60*(5), 1104–1122.

Westbrook, R. A. (1987). *Product/consumption-based affective responses and postpurchase processes*. Journal of marketing research, 24(3), 258–270.

Why eBay Failed in China. (2018 July 13). Retrieved from https://marketingtochina.com/ebay-failed-china/

Willemyns, I. (2021). *Digital services in international trade law*. Cambridge University Press.

Wirtz, J., & Lovelock, C. (2016). Service marketing communications. *World Scientific Book Chapters*, 210–264.

Xiang, Y., Liu, L., & Dolnicar, S. (2021). Airbnb in China—Before, during and after COVID-19. In S. Dolnicar (Ed.), *Airbnb before, during and after COVID-19*. University of Queensland. https://doi.org/10.6084/m9.figshare.14195930. Retrieved from https://uq.pressbooks.pub/airbnb-978-1-74272-321-1/chapter/airbnb-in-china-before-during-and-after-covid-19/

Xiong, F., Xu, S., & Zheng, D. (2021). An investigation of the uber driver reward system in china–An application of a dynamic pricing model. *Technology Analysis & Strategic Management, 33*(1), 44–57.

Yagci, M. I. (2001). Evaluating the effects of country-of-origin and consumer ethnocentrism: A case of a transplant product. *Journal of International Consumer Marketing, 13*(3), 63–85.

Yu X. (2018 September 18). *Case study of Netflix modules*. Retrieved from https://blogs.commons.georgetown.edu/cctp-820-fall2018/2018/09/18/week-3-case-study-of-netflix-modules/

Zeithaml, V. A., Parasuraman, A., & Berry, L. L. (1985). Problems and strategies in services marketing. *Journal of Marketing, 49*(2), 33–46.

Zhou, V. (2022). *For some Chinese hosts, Airbnb's exit marks a return to a smaller world*. Restofworld. Retrieved from https://restofworld.org/2022/china-airbnb-exit-impact/

## Further Reading

Javalgi, R. G. R., Cutler, B. D., & Winans, W. A. (2001). At your service! Does country of origin research apply to services? *Journal of Services Marketing, 15*(7), 565–582 For more about the country of origin in service context, refer to Javalgi.

# Global Account Management

## Contents




D. Klimkeit et al., *International Management in Service Firms*, Classroom Companion: Business,
https://doi.org/10.1007/978-3-031-50345-0_14

**Learning Outcomes**

After completing this chapter, you should be able to:

- Explain why global account management is essential for service MNEs
- Outline key criteria used to select global accounts
- Describe which elements of the account the account manager analyzes
- Outline the roles of the global account manager
- Describe typical members, responsibilities, and organizational options of account teams
- Outline knowledge management on accounts and the role of information systems
- Explain how account teams manage customer relationships
- Outline account planning, including the major challenges

## Introduction

Many firms with international business want to coordinate all activities they do for their major global customers, whether sales or service delivery. This is particularly important for Service MNEs who rely on maintaining close customer relationships. Many business customers of Service MNEs expect consistent and coordinated service worldwide. We, therefore, start this chapter by outlining the importance of global account management (GAM) for Service MNEs. Then we address selection criteria for global accounts, understanding the account, the global account manager and team, knowledge management and information systems, relationship management, and global account planning.

Marriott resort in Phuket, Thailand, image by Michelle Raponi from Pixabay

## Opening Case: Global Account Management at Marriott International

In 2002, Accenture, a major customer of Marriott International hotel group (Marriott), became a publicly listed company. This led to strong cost reduction pressures, especially for travel-related expenses. Marriott needed to adjust to keep this significant customer. In a short time, the Accenture account team of Marriott offered a new "corporate apartment program" to provide homes for relocating Accenture employees. As an outcome, Marriott significantly increased its business with Accenture.

Marriott International is one of the major hospitality groups in the world, comprising 30 brands, including well-known names such as Ritz Carlton, St Regis, W Hotels, JW Marriott, Marriott, Sheraton, Le Meridien, Westin, and Aloft. Besides hotels, executive apartments and conference centers are on offer. Together, they comprise 8000+ properties in 139 countries and territories. For 2021, Marriott posted earnings of $2.3 billion (EBITDA).

With its global account management (GAM) program, Marriott became a pioneer in the hospitality industry. Marriott's globally dispersed customers have a wide range of travel needs, and with its broad portfolio, Marriott can provide what they need. So, it is attractive for customers to become a global account of Marriott. In 1996, Marriott launched its program "Lodging 2000." This was driven by several reasons: Increasingly, customers demanded coordination of their suppliers, a single point of contact, standardization, and consistency in service quality. Given its broad portfolio of diverse brands, Marriott was previously struggling to meet these demands. Marriott also noticed how competitors increased their competitive advantage. As a response, Marriott reorganized its sales to address the demand of its major global customers and created the Global Sales Organization (GSO) as a strategic account organization within marketing and sales. This brought sales, marketing, and customer service together. Marriott provided the GSO with a central global leadership, an integrated approach, and centralized customer relationships across all the business segments, and support services for each account. Sales, done independently by each brand previously, became coordinated to avoid unnecessary duplication and present a single face to the customer. Marriott realigned the salesforce around major customers instead of around hotels or brands. Coordinated clusters of "sales engines," organized around key strategic accounts, were created. "Alliance Accounts" and "Multinational Accounts," the most complex and high-value accounts, got the most attention. The assigned global account manager for these accounts develops the strategy for the account and initiatives with customers and involves all the required internal resources to serve the account customer best. Specialists from various functions get assigned to these accounts. Following an analysis of the customer's organization, Marriott customizes teams to an account's needs. Salespeople are matched at the same level as key buyers at the customer in the various business units and locations. The account teams have the discretion to adapt to the customer's needs. Local sales representatives can, at the same time, access global statistics and attend to local cultural differences.

To become a global account, a customer needs a minimum revenue level for Marriott to afford the GAM overhead. Marriott expects a minimum of 25$ million in hotel bookings annually for an account to be a global account. Marriott's account managers handle between three and six accounts. They are the principal point of contact for a customer but can involve others to provide service or solve customer problems. Account managers are expected to be creative and to develop the relationship further. They receive 30% of their compensation in the form of a bonus. Of this, one-third depends on their contribution to relationship-building (evaluated by the customer, peers, and their boss), while two third of the bonus depends on hitting sales targets. Account managers research online news databases and other sources to understand the customer better and identify opportunities for reengineering the customer's travel processes. By managing the entire mix of hotels for a customer, Marriott can provide cost savings for the customer while increasing revenue for itself. For example, Marriott was able to help IBM reduce cancellation costs by creating an internal bulletin board for IBMers to book canceled conference spaces and thereby avoid cancellation fees.

However, the introduction of the GAM program was not without problems. Since each hotel was franchised and managed independently, hotel managers perceived GAM as a loss of control. Marriott, therefore, created an internal campaign to sell the GAM idea. Continuous communication of the GAM vision, mission, and plan took place. The urgency was communicated, training offered, and success celebrated. The results demonstrate the success of GAM. Accounts that make up the GSO portfolio generated over US$4 billion in 2001, accounting for 20% of Marriott's worldwide revenues. In 2002, the Strategic Account Management Association (SAMA) awarded Marriott International the prestigious SAMA Performance Award, recognizing Marriott's success in its sales force restructuring.

**Questions**

1. Why has Marriott decided to launch a global account program?
2. Which criteria does Marriott use for selecting its global accounts?
3. How important are Marriott's services to customers like Accenture or IBM regarding their total cost, and how easy is it for customers to replace Marriott as a supplier? What follows from this?
4. What drawback can there be from locating account management within the sales department?
5. Which challenges did Marriott encounter, and how did it address them?

Sources: (Hennessey & Jeannet, 2004, 8, 13, 145–146; Marriott International, 2021, 2023; McNeill, 2005; Sengupta et al., 1997; Shi et al., 2005, 2010)

## The Importance of Global Account Management for Service MNEs

### Global Account Management

» I am sorry, but we are dropping your company as a supplier to us because you are unable to serve us on a globally integrated basis.

» I am pleased to tell you that we have designated your company as a worldwide supplier because you have demonstrated your ability to serve us on a globally integrated basis. (Yip & Bink, 2007, p. 3).

Firms serving MNEs as clients today frequently hear statements like the first or the second of the above quotations from their clients. This indicates how today, multinational customers and multinational suppliers collaborate. Previously, in many MNEs, the national subsidiaries were free to decide about suppliers. This often implied that different national subsidiaries of one MNC customer might be buying from the national subsidiaries of an MNC supplier. However, the relationships would be between national subsidiaries and not at the level of the overall MNE (Yip & Bink, 2007, p. 3). The need to manage customers globally is related to the globalization of countries, industries, and companies. As MNEs expand their activities across borders, they expect their suppliers to follow them to all countries where they are active. Multinational customers increasingly seek to deal with their suppliers on a globally coordinated basis. They demand one global contract, consistent global pricing, standardized products or services, and a global account relationship. To achieve this, many MNEs have significantly reduced the number of suppliers (Capon & Senn, 2010). This demand of MNEs for global coordination further implies a global customer–supplier relationship. Such relationships typically involve coordination by global units on the side of the customer and supplier. Advertising agencies are a good example. Many advertising agencies have seen that their largest customers engage in *supplier rationalization*. Instead of working with up to a hundred different agencies worldwide, many advertising clients want to work as much as possible with only a few agencies worldwide. There are two reasons for this: to achieve greater consistency in their advertising messages globally and to achieve greater global coordination of their purchasing (Yip & Bink, 2007, pp. 4–7).



Wilson and Speare (2002, pp. 6–9) summarize the drivers of global account management (GAM) in four points:

- *Economic factors*: Globalization has encouraged companies to venture abroad, increased global competition, and enabled the growth of global brands
- *Market factors*: Many industries consolidated internationally, innovation continues to accelerate, and procurement moved from a transactional to a more strategic approach

- *Technology*: The introduction of customer relationship management (CRM) systems greatly facilitated managing accounts across borders
- *Customers*: Customers increasingly expect suppliers to enter a global relationship and supply them consistently across the world

Remember how Marriott's customers demanded global coordination of their hospitality suppliers, a single point of contact, standardization, and consistency in service quality. The global account manager at Marriott can act as a single point of contact for the customer, involving all necessary specialists across its brands when needed.

For these reasons, for a long time, companies have been using *account management* or *key account management* to handle their most important customers in a dedicated manner.

**Account Management**

*Account management* means "focusing [...] efforts on major customers (actual and potential) and developing the appropriate strategies, line organizations, systems and processes, and human resources to serve them." (Capon et al., 2006, p. 5)

This implies that there will be one manager, typically supported by a team, to take the overall responsibility for all business the supplier does for a customer. *Global Account Management* (GAM) extends this idea globally, for the most important customers, at least in the most important markets (Yip & Madsen, 1996).

**Global Account Management**

*Global Account Management* is "an organizational form and process in multinational companies by which the worldwide activities serving a given multinational customer are coordinated centrally by one person or team within the supplying company" (Montgomery & Yip, 1999, p. 10).

It will become apparent, though, that global account management is more than just account management for global customers. As Kumar et al. (2019) summarized in a literature review, global account management is unique compared to domestic account management, displaying different strategies and team behavior. Global account management faces the challenges of cross-country coordination and communication, which require special skills (Ellis & Iwasaki, 2018).

A study among 106 global accounts in 16 MNEs in the United States and Europe found that by enhancing the internal coordination of information and activities, GAM improves the capability of the supplier to obtain information on the account and process it. At the same time, it puts the supplier in a better bargaining position toward the account (Birkinshaw et al., 2001).

## Global Account Management in Service MNEs

Services typically require, sometimes more, sometimes less, close interaction with the customer. This is especially true when services are complex and highly customized to the client, as in many business services, particularly professional ones. Large business service firms, however, tend to fragment into various business units that provide different services. In such a setting, having global account management can help to maintain a consistent and continuous relationship with the client beyond individual customer contacts and projects. This helps to create a trusting atmosphere between the service provider and customers (Nätti & Palo, 2012). This is also important as services are typically intangible and, therefore, difficult for the client to assess before purchasing and experiencing them. This is particularly true for complex, professional services where service providers must build credibility and trust to convince customers to purchase.

Furthermore, particularly in professional services, the most critical resource is knowledge, much of which professionals obtain through customer interaction. To provide service to cater to the customer's needs, customer-related knowledge needs to be obtained, shared internally, and utilized. A global account management program provides a context for transferring knowledge gained from customer interaction within the service firm. Global account teams are typically set up so that they cross the various units that provide service to the client. This enables a synergistic service offering (Nätti & Palo, 2012). Without the necessary customer-specific knowledge, a PSF cannot build the right service offering for clients (Nätti et al., 2006). PSFs recognized already a long time ago the benefit of coordinated global sales and service delivery for large companies in multiple countries worldwide. Large audit firms, for example, offer standardized auditing of an MNE's financial statements across its subsidiaries worldwide. Like this, the customer needs to manage only the relationship to one audit firm, not separate ones in each country where it has subsidiaries. Therefore, PSFs were the first group of firms that recognized the need to serve global customers in a dedicated manner through a global account management program. The same applies to other service industries like consulting or advertising. Beyond professional services, MNEs in other service industries are also engaging in global account management, as the examples of DHL, Maersk, Citibank, ING, and Marriott show (Hennessey & Jeannet, 2004, pp. 1–4).



## Selection Criteria for Global Accounts

Since an accounting program requires significant resources, companies are selective about which customers to include. This is especially the case for global accounts, which require a particularly high cost to meet customer's demands globally (Ellis & Iwasaki, 2018). This highlights companies' criteria for selecting the right companies as global accounts (Yip & Bink, 2007, pp. 94–100):

**Geography:** For an account to be a global account, the customer needs to have some geographic spread. This can mean that it operates and sells in at least two or three continents and has a growing percentage of its business outside its home market. However, suppose a customer is present in many countries but does not have business relationships with the supplier in these countries. In that case, it is not likely to qualify as a global account. Therefore, companies often consider the number of countries where they and the customer already have a business relationship. When there is a very good fit between the supplier's and customer's key markets, this will help develop the relationship worldwide and the added value that the companies can provide to each other.

**Organization:** Only if the customer coordinates its activities worldwide would suppliers see it as an attractive partner in a global relationship. A customer may have a comprehensive footprint of activities but no global coordination. In this case, there is no reason for the supplier to work with it in a globally coordinated way. Global value is limited if the two companies cannot collaborate in compatible global organizations. Customers with global coordination and a centralized purchasing department will probably expect a coordinated and integrated response from their suppliers. As an experienced global account manager explains:

» If you get a global agreement with a non-global customer, all you've got is a hunting license! (Yip & Bink, 2007, p. 96).

In other words: Such an agreement allows the supplier to attempt to convince each and every subsidiary's purchasing team to buy from it. However, the agreement does not oblige all subsidiaries to purchase from the supplier.

**Potential Revenue:** Managers typically aim to achieve profitable growth, which also plays a role in account selection. Potential revenue with a customer is frequently seen as more important than current revenue, as the expectation is that the relationship will, in time, lead to more revenue. This extra revenue can come from combined purchasing. When a customer makes a global deal, it often aims to combine as much volume as possible in one purchase to get a better deal. A global relationship would lead to growing trust between the two companies and more insight into the needs and wants of the customer. This puts the supplier in a position to target the customer with products and services that will bring more revenue. When a global supplier obtains similar revenue from two global customers, the customer with a small but growing market share in its industry may be more interesting than the customer with a large market share but with only minimal growth potential. The supplier can grow with its client. Remember how Marriott expects a minimum of 25$ million in annual hotel bookings for an account to be a global account to justify the cost of global account management for a customer.

**Strategic Importance:** How strategically important a customer is to a supplier also matters. The strategic importance of a customer is first reflected by the amount of business the supplier has with this customer compared with its total revenue. A supplier does not want to lose a customer that generates a significant part of its revenue. It can also matter which line of service or product group a customer buys. Not all lines of service are equally important to the supplier. If a customer already buys services that the supplier wants to focus on in the future, that is beneficial. If the customer is a well-known brand and by serving it, the supplier affiliates itself with that brand, that can also factor into selection criteria.

**Fit** Generally, suppliers look for a good fit between them and their customers. This can be a strategic fit because the customer's strategy fits the suppliers. For example, there might be opportunities to market products together. When the two companies have a similar culture, it is easier to work together without tension. For a global supplier, a customer with a global mindset will usually fit better.

Regarding the criterion of "fit," a study among 106 accounts of 16 MNEs confirmed that similar strategies and structures of the supplier and customer are associated with better performance. In particular, the sales growth of the supplier was driven by a similar strategic importance attributed to the relationship by both sides and if both configured their activities similarly and had similar executive support. The latter also drives the degree to which the two parties establish a true partnership (Toulan et al., 2006).

The following box shows examples of selection criteria some leading service firms used.

**Account Selection Criteria of Leading Service Firms**

**Marriott International** focuses on *high-value customers*. Global accounts must spend at least US$25 million on travel and accommodation. They need centralized purchasing and activities in countries worldwide that coincide with Marriott's global footprint. They must show the willingness to enter a partnership and exhibit a cultural fit with Marriott.

**PricewaterhouseCoopers (PwC)** identifies the potential value of an account with two factors: the inherent value of the account and PwC's capability to exploit this potential of a global relationship.

**IBM** considers companies to be a global account that value having a global relationship with IBM and who appreciate being served by a global sales team. Customers need to have a considerable global or at least regional presence, a high growth potential, and a need for leading technology solutions.

Source: (Wilson et al., 2002, pp. 30–31)



By the end of the day, each company will define and prioritize its own selection criteria. The selection process is, however, not restricted to the start of the GAM program. Successful GAM programs regularly test customers against the criteria to see if they are still suitable for the GAM program. According to Yip and Bink (2007, p. 102), companies should not be afraid to shift customers to another form of account management when they no longer fit the criteria to be global accounts. However, firms must handle this with diplomacy. For example, when Hewlett-Packard found over 250 global accounts to be too many, it decided to reduce the number significantly. Instead of directly informing the dropped accounts, HP gradually reduced the services provided to avoid offending them.

## Understanding the Account

After selecting accounts, global account managers want to develop a thorough understanding of the account to support it best. Such understanding includes the customer's industry, business, strategy, the existing business of the supplier with the client, and the relationship potential (Hennessey & Jeannet, 2004, pp. 46–134).

**Understanding the Customer's Industry:** Global account managers want to understand the industry that their customer is part of: What is the value chain in that industry, who are the participants, what requirements are there for companies in that industry, what are the critical success factors (Hennessey & Jeannet, 2004, pp. 46–66)? This is particularly important for professional service firms such as audit or consulting firms. For example, the auditor must understand the industry and the client's business to assess its financial statements. Likewise, a consultant must have an insight into an industry to provide adequate advice suitable for companies in that industry. Therefore, consultants in larger consulting firms frequently specialize in one industry (Greenwood et al., 2010).

**Understanding the Customer's Business:** The analysis of the customer's industry already tells an account manager much about the customer's business. Regarding the further analysis of the customer's business, Hennessy and Jeannet focus on understanding what they call the "global logic" of the customer—to what extent are demands from the business and industry requiring the customer to be global? Do customers of the customer have similar needs across the world? Are the customer's product features the same across countries? Does the customer meet the same competitors in most countries where it does business? Are there pressures to achieve economies of scale? You will remember from ► Chap. 8 that these are the questions to assess the strength of the forces for global integration, which is no coincidence. An account manager wants to understand the forces for global integration on the customer since these would typically drive the customer to benefit from global account management by its suppliers and a global relationship with its suppliers. Suppose the supplier is well globally integrated and coordinated, and the customer faces strong pressures for global integration. In that case, the supplier can help the customer achieve the global integration demanded by its environment (Hennessey & Jeannet, 2004, pp. 79–96).

**Understanding the Customer's Strategy:** To be a valuable supplier to a company, account managers want to understand the customer's strategy. Through this, they can help the customer achieve its strategy and thereby develop its own business with the customer. Frequently, the customer may be a business unit of a corporation, not the entire corporation, so the strategy at the business unit level would be analyzed: What is the portfolio of products or services, the position in the value chain, the geographic footprint, the market segments covered and the competitive strategy? How does the customer deal with demands for global integration from its environment? Remember how, at Marriott, account managers conduct research in online news databases and other sources to understand the customer better and identify opportunities for reengineering the customer's travel processes (Hennessey & Jeannet, 2004, pp. 111–125).

**Understand the Existing Business and Relationship Potential With the Customer:** Finally, the account manager wants to get a good understanding of the current business the supplier already does with the customer and opportunities for further business. One way of doing this is to map product line by product line or service line by service line, the *sales penetration* or "market share" the supplier has with the customer compared to competitors. As a starting point, the account team can review sales statistics. However, obtaining information on competitors' sales to the customer can be more difficult (Hennessey & Jeannet, 2004, p. 125).

To assess the *potential for the relationship* with the customer, it can be helpful to understand how the customer perceives the importance of the supplier. Kraljic (1983) proposes classifying the situation by how risky the supply of a product or service is for the customer and how much the supplier's product or service impacts the customer's profit. When the products or services of the supplier have a substantial impact on the customer's profitability, the customer will be more intent on maintaining a good relationship with the supplier than when buying, say, pens for office use. The risk of supply also encourages a customer to build a good relationship with the supplier. In the matrix proposed by Kraljic (1983, p. 112), four different groups of purchased items exist, in line with four ways the customer perceives the supplier. While the original matrix contains much information that can distract understanding, we have simplified it for our purposes here to focus only on the four types of items purchased. We also relabeled the axes in line with the explanations given by Kralj (see ◘ Fig. 14.1):

- *Noncritical items* (low impact on the customer's profits; low supply risk): The customer is mainly interested in the price and may want to integrate supplier contracts to achieve economies of scale globally. However, the customer would not take a very aggressive approach due to the low risk and impact.



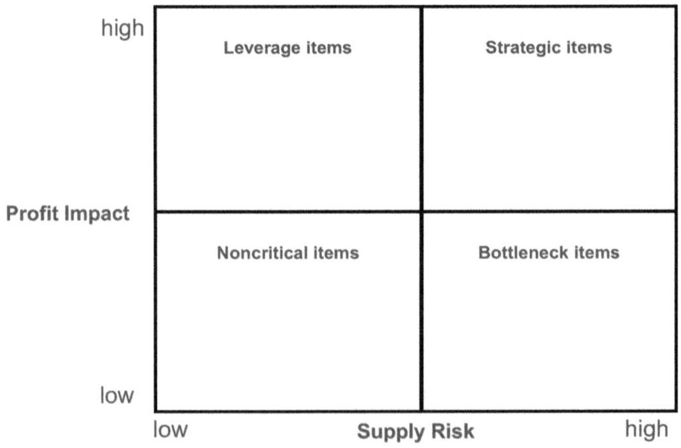


◘ **Fig. 14.1** The purchasing matrix, adapted from Kraljic (1983, p. 111)

- *Leverage items* (high impact on the customer's profits, low supply risk): Here, what the supplier provides makes up a large percentage of a customer's total cost and is therefore important, but many suppliers can supply it, so it is relatively easy for the customer to switch to other suppliers. The customer will typically attempt to squeeze the price because a slight reduction in the purchasing price already has a significant effect. Still, it would not be wise to exploit the situation too much not to endanger supplier relationships or provoke adverse responses from suppliers.
- *Bottleneck items* (low impact on the customer's profits, but high supply risk): Often, for bottleneck products, there is only one supplier, for example, only one that has the required licensing. The customer will want to find alternative suppliers to create competition between suppliers. It will be interesting in a good relationship.
- *Strategic items* (high impact on the customer's profits and supply risk): The item typically makes up a large percentage of the cost of the customer's product. Moreover, the customer may depend on just one or a few suppliers: Often, these are tailor-made products made specifically for a customer. There is a strong interest in cooperation by the customer.

The implications for the supplier are as follows (Yip & Bink, 2007, pp. 105–108): For *strategic items*, the supplier would share the customer's strong interest in cooperation. The supplier would aim to build a good strategic relationship in this situation. A supplier and a customer can engage in projects that improve quality, reduce costs, improve processes, and even develop new products together. For *noncritical items*, when the customer aims to consolidate purchases, this can be a threat for the supplier but an advantage for globally integrated suppliers, who can attempt to get a large share of that service with the customer. Once the supplier has a critical share, the customer becomes more dependent on the supplier and will be more willing to work on the relationship and projects that benefit both. For *bottleneck items*, smart account managers of a supplier would not take too much advantage of the situation because it would decrease trust and drive the customer to find other suppliers. Instead, one would extend the business relationship by providing further services that generate value for the customer in more areas. The customer will be interested in a good relationship as well. For *leverage items*, the supplier would try to develop a competitive advantage, for example, by becoming a global supplier to the customer. Understanding the customer is especially important in this case. The supplier would want to identify any added value it can provide to become a more strategic supplier for the customer.

One might argue that Marriott's services to customers like Accenture or IBM are leverage items as they contribute significantly to their costs, but many competing hospitality providers exist. What Marriott does for its accounts is consistent with the above recommendations for leverage items.

## The Global Account Manager

Now it is time to take a closer look at the key person who leads the management of an account—the global account manager. Which roles does the account manager play? Wilson and Speare (2002, pp. 127–156) and Yip and Bink (2017) suggest the following:

- *Boundary-spanning coordinator*: The account manager brings together the different business units and subsidiaries to provide one joint offer for the customer. The manager bridges different interests within the firm for the benefit of the account. This requires a good network within the firm.
- *Entrepreneurial strategist*: The account manager ensures that the supplier gets as much as possible from the global relationship with the customer. The manager constantly looks for opportunities to develop the relationship further. A strategic development plan for the account is often used to plan for this actively.
- *Long-term vision*: The account manager develops objectives regarding the account's development and specific actions to achieve these. The manager keeps everyone involved with the account informed.
- *Team leader/manager*: The global account manager plays a team leader role for members of the global account team. Often the manager must rely on informal authority because he or she has no formal authority over the members. The manager selects members in contact with the account, typically representing a business unit or subsidiary/region. Based on informal authority, the manager needs to create a team spirit and encourage cooperation.
- *Information broker*: The global account manager collects all information available in the company on the account. Frequently, this role is delegated to a dedicated account knowledge manager. The manager also spreads the collected information by maintaining a platform on the intranet, via global account reports, newsletters, and conference calls with the global account team members.
- *Relationship facilitator/builder*: The global account manager has an overview of the network at the supplier and with the customer. Beyond this, the manager actively establishes connections that benefit the account.
- *Negotiator*: The global account manager negotiates an umbrella contract with the customer. If the contract is global, purchases are negotiated at a global level. However, different price levels across countries can be a challenge.
- *Ambassador*: The global account manager is the first point of contact for the customer. Sometimes, the manager may even be based at the customer's office like an ambassador of a country. The account manager is typically in the country where the customer's headquarters are.
- *Politician*: The global account manager influences decision-makers at both the customer and internally at the supplier. The manager analyses the customer's internal politics to determine who is important for decision-making.

As the roles above suggest, the position of global account manager requires more skills than that of a domestic account manager. Political and entrepreneurial skills are needed to span geographic and functional boundaries worldwide (Wilson & Millman, 2003). So the global account manager may require specific training (Ellis & Iwasaki, 2018). The following box illustrates the requirement of a global account manager at a global advertising agency.

### The Global Account Manager at J. Walter Thompson

The global advertising agency J. Walter Thompson (JWT) has 200 offices in 90 countries. In its requirements for global account managers, JWT clearly points out that the people working on a global account must be entrepreneurial. For its global positions, JWT typically considers managers who have succeeded in a local office and are looking for a new global challenge in their careers. The position of the global account manager is considered as senior as that of a country office leader.

New York; Manhattan, NY, is a traditional hub for advertising groups like JWT, image by Pexels from Pixabay)

Source: (Yip & Bink, 2007, p. 114).

## The Global Account Team

### Members of the Global Account Team

Without a team, the global account manager will not be able to achieve much. Besides the manager, the global account team (GAT) typically comprises an executive sponsor who champions the account at the executive level and maintains contact with customer executives, local account managers from countries where the supplier is in contact with the customer, and supporting staff (Hennessey & Jeannet, 2004, p. 182). One of the supporting staff can be the role of the account knowledge manager, who takes care of collecting and sharing information. This will be addressed in more detail later. Having executives involved can help connect to counterparts in the customer company (Shi & Gao, 2016) and encourage the customer to involve equivalent levels of executives in the relationship with the supplier. Like this, both sides are better positioned to coordinate activities globally within their firm (Ellis & Iwasaki, 2018). Further, the team may contain functional experts who hold relationships with counterparts at the customer. For example, the insurance firm Zurich states to its customers:

> To help you handle your risks, we have instituted the Account Team: an internationally experienced expert in risk management leads a group of insurance, financial and technical specialists. This team is dedicated to your industry and will ensure continuity of service for your company (Yip & Bink, 2007, p. 133).

The design of the GAT impacts its performance. The following design factors were found to be essential for GAT performance (Atanasova & Senn, 2014):

- The team structure provides adequate geographic and functional coverage for the account
- Team members have a wide variety of backgrounds and expertise.
- Team members have adequate skills, such as creativity, understanding of the customer, relationship building, networking, strategic thinking, and interdisciplinary collaboration.
- The team and its members have clear goals relating to the firm's global accounts, and roles and responsibilities of team members are clearly defined.
- The team is sufficiently empowered to make decisions about customer business and organizational routines to improve results for customers.
- The team leader has a strong relationship with top management and influence in the firm.



▪ Figure 14.2 summarizes the typical members of an account team

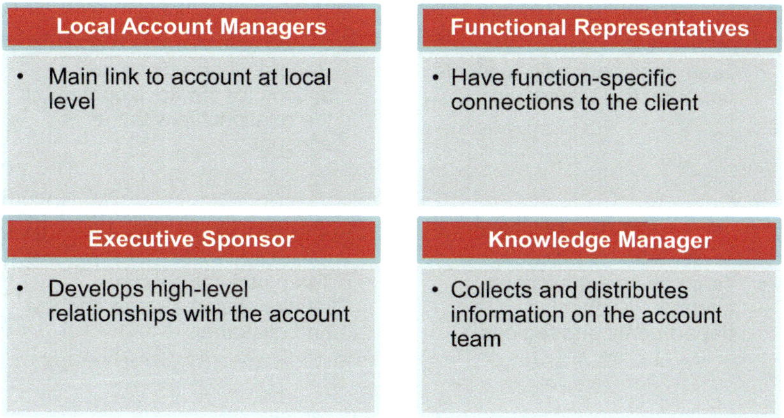


**Fig. 14.2** Members of the account team, based on content from Hennessey and Jeannet (2004, pp. 182–183) and Yip and Bink (2007, pp. 130–135)

## Responsibilities of the Global Account Team

Now, what are the responsibilities of the global account team (Yip & Bink, 2007, pp. 128–130)?

- *Global account planning*: Team members must provide input for the account plan from the functions or regions/countries they represent on the team to integrate local and functional contacts and activities. The global account plan records all objectives and actions relating to developing the relationship with the account. This will be addressed in more detail later.
- *Information and communication*: Team members provide information about their activities with the account to the account manager, who creates an information base to store and share it. At the same time, the team will be the communication channel for the various business units and regions. Like the account manager, the team members act as ambassadors for the account in the company.
- *Strengthening the relationship network*: Yip and Bink recommend that the account team not have a bowtie relationship with the customer, where the account manager is the only contact with the customer. Instead, it should have a diamond structure with many relationships between supplier and customer. If many members of the account team have contacts with the customer in their function or region, they can provide better insight into opportunities that exist at the client.
- *Locating opportunities*: Account team members act as the eyes and ears of the account manager and can therefore play a vital role in identifying opportunities. They have better insight into specific parts of the customer's organization,

**Fig. 14.3** Responsibilities of the account team, based on content from Yip and Bink (2007, pp. 128–130)

such as a local subsidiary. They can look actively for business opportunities, drawing on all the information they can obtain. Based on the information from team members, the account manager can decide which opportunities to pursue. Account management provides transparency about all opportunities and their status.

See Fig. 14.3 for a summary of account team responsibilities.

The following example of Global Account Teams at IBM illustrates responsibilities in account teams in a professional service firm.



**Account Team Responsibilities at IBM**

IBM is a leading provider of IT services, including software and consulting. The firm gives responsibilities on the Global Account Team to very senior people. They are fully dedicated to the account team. Members of the account team receive targets to achieve over three years. This recognizes the long-term importance of global customer relationships. The team contains specialists dealing with gathering and sharing information about the account globally and has responsibility for locating global opportunities with the account. For about 100 global accounts, IBM has established a separate business unit. This unit contains global account teams taking care of these biggest accounts of IBM that justify having a separate organization. Smaller accounts are managed on a local basis. Like this, there is no friction between global and local interests. All global account data must be entered into an IT system. Only such customer projects get support from the company where all the relevant information relating to that account and opportunity has been entered into the system.

Source: (Yip & Bink, 2007, 82; 128–129; 191)

## Organizational Structure

There are different structures to organize global account teams (GAT). All global account teams within one company generally have a similar setup. Most companies use one of the following three main structures (Yip & Bink, 2007, pp. 135–137):

- *Formal direct GAT*: In this structure, team members are fully dedicated to a global account and report to the global account manager. There are often local part-time members in addition to the full-time core team members. This intensive organizational structure is justifiable only when the business with global accounts is big enough. This is especially relevant in service industries, where putting much effort into maintaining close customer relationships is essential.
- *Formal indirect GAT*: In this structure, team members have other main roles besides their role on the account team. On the GAT, they officially represent a business unit or region of the supplier. They report to their line manager. This is a good structure for any firm that cannot afford fully dedicated account teams but wants many people paying attention to accounts. The team in this structure is small enough to feel responsible for the supplier's success at the account. Team members act as champions for the account in their own business units or regions.
- *Informal GAT*: In this structure, everyone involved with the account is a member of the GAT. The account manager has little or no authority over account team members. It can be seen as just a virtual team. The manager may not even know everyone involved with the account. In some cases, account teams attempt to meet at least once a year. The advantage of such a structure is that it can be set up and changed quickly. There are several disadvantages, however. Such GATs tend to be large. Transparency is low. It is challenging to keep track of all that happens concerning the account. The account manager has only limited influence. The turnover of members is high.

◘ Figure 14.4 summarizes the three structural options for account teams.

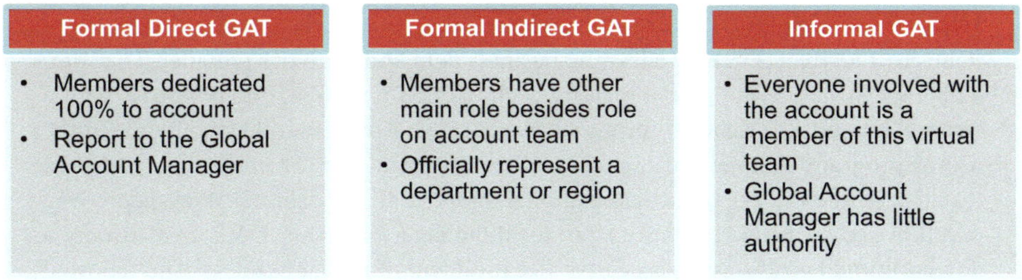


◘ **Fig. 14.4** Organizational structures of global account teams (GATs), based on content from Yip and Bink (2007, pp. 135–136)

## Place in the Company's Overall Organization

Connected to the organization of the GATs is the question of how the company integrates the account teams into the company's overall organizational structure. Historically, GATs often grew out of existing sales or marketing departments. Remember how this was the case at Marriott. However, a GAT must cross the functional silos, so it is beneficial if it is not located within one function. One can structure the GAM program to transcend the silos and recruit team members across functions. Suppose the organizational structure of a supplier is not well suited to support a customer globally. In that case, the company can set up the GAM program in a separate unit outside the existing silos. This provides account teams with some autonomy. The teams can serve customers globally without struggling with the existing organizational silos (Hennessey & Jeannet, 2004, pp. 184–186). For formal direct GATs, Yip and Bink recommend positioning them within a separate business unit dedicated to global accounts, facilitating intensive account management. Remember the case of IBM above. IBM set up a separate business unit for its global accounts to support large customers (Yip & Bink, 2007, p. 136). In other cases, the GAM program is more integrated with existing structures. Members with GAM roles also have local responsibilities other than their global role in the GAM program.

Besides, Hennessey and Jeannet (2004, 104–105) also distinguish between centralized and decentralized GAM programs. In the case of a centralized GAM, the corporate headquarters of the supplier manage the GAM program with people who are quite separate from the supplier's local operations. This allows all global accounts to be well coordinated and shows senior executives' support for the program. Local managers, who may see this as a threat to their interests, may, however, resent this. In decentralized GAM programs, managers in the country where the customer is headquartered manage a global account. This avoids local resistance to the GAM program but makes global coordination more challenging. This structure is frequently found among suppliers where the country units of the firm are powerful. The following example illustrates a decentralized and integrated structure at Dun & Bradstreet.



**GAM Structure at Dun & Bradstreet**

Dun & Bradstreet (D&B) is a leading business data and analytics provider. The company was structured in global regions, each with its president, and countries with a general manager. Instead of setting up a separate business unit, D&B integrated the GAM program with the existing regional/country structure. Through this, the GAM could leverage the existing organizational support at the regional level. Moreover, D&B hoped to avoid resistance from local managers like this. D&B created only a few additional positions: an executive vice president of global business, who reported directly to the CEO, three new regional global customer managers (RGCMs), and 40 local global customer managers (GCMs). D&B recruited RGCMs from senior sales managers in each region committed to the new global concept. Each GCM served several global accounts. They might be based at regional headquarters or in a country and often have dual reporting lines (global and local).

Source: (Hennessey & Jeannet, 2004, pp. 105–106)

## Knowledge Management and Information Systems

Especially in (professional) service firms, it is essential for global account teams to obtain detailed knowledge about the customer, its business, and industry and apply knowledge to serve the customer best worldwide. To achieve this, successful GATs systematically share the knowledge they obtain about the customer within the global team and beyond. Successful GATs build effective knowledge management and use supporting information systems to facilitate it.

Successful GATs in knowledge-intensive business service firms move from a *transactional relationship* with the customer to a *collaborative relationship*. A transactional relationship is focused on selling and delivering services to the customer. The collaborative relationship means "learning about customer needs and wants, and knowing how best to create, satisfy, and sustain the relationship" (Nätti & Palo, 2012, p. 1841). A collaborative relationship requires everyone in contact with the customer to share insights and knowledge within the GAT and across the various functions at the supplier. The GAT then uses broader knowledge resources to identify opportunities and customize its services to the customer. Managing customer knowledge is a vital aim of a global account management program (Nätti & Palo, 2012). At least the global account manager needs to have a good overview of the account and the supplier's activities with the account. It can lead to embarrassing situations if the account manager does not have as good an overview as the procurement officer of the customer.

## Account Knowledge Management in Professional Service Firms

In professional service firms, connections between service lines tend to be loose, and each service line maintains its relationships with customers. A GAT can provide an opportunity to share customer knowledge across the various service lines. Think of an audit firm comprising audit, tax, management, and legal advice. Beyond the specific technical knowledge, knowledge relating to customer needs, organization, responsibilities, characteristics, and new developments is relevant for auditors, tax consultants, management consultants, and lawyers (Nätti et al., 2006).

It is necessary to share explicit and tacit knowledge on accounts in PSFs. *Explicit knowledge* can be written down in documents and shared via electronic platforms. In contrast, *tacit knowledge* is based on experience, in this case, relating to customer interaction, and can only be shared orally by intensive engagement between people. In developing customer relationships, tacit knowledge is the most valuable. Explicit knowledge shared via electronic repositories can quickly go out of date and require updating (Nätti et al., 2006).

## Information Systems

Managing knowledge in a global account requires appropriate information systems. While an IT system alone does not guarantee good knowledge management (KM), having good KM in global account management is difficult without it. Fundamental IT systems of the company need to allow tracking sales and delivery of services to customers at the global, not just local, level. Global account managers want to have an overview of customer orders and what services the firm provides to their account in which country across the world (Capon186-189), and how profitable their customer relationship is (Cheverton, 2008, p. 200). Having transparency of the major global customers allows for determining global accounts in the first place. This is not trivial; not every company tracks such information in one global system. Moreover, companies may have different names in different countries (Hennessey & Jeannet, 2004, pp. 201–202). This requires something called *metadata management*. In metadata management, a central person or team enters central terms like customer names, which can be picked from a dropdown list rather than allowing everyone to type in a company name. Otherwise, several unrelated entries for the same customer may be made, each with a different spelling of the customer's name.

The most relevant systems for global account management are the ERP system and the CRM system. We will briefly outline them now.

**The ERP system:** As you may remember from ▶ Chap. 10, an enterprise resource planning (ERP) system tracks a company's procurement, manufacturing or service delivery, logistics, shipping, accounting, sales, and human resources. For many firms, the ERP system is the primary information source for much of what the company does. It is, therefore, also well suited to provide vital information for a global account program. However, often multinational enterprises do not have one global ERP system but a set of different unconnected local ones. Even when all subsidiaries use one system, such as from global market leader SAP, they might have different versions of SAP. This can make it challenging to have an integrated view of all the company does with one customer globally. Companies must deal with this when a global account management program starts by providing data integration (Yip & Bink, 2007, p. 147).



**The CRM system:** A customer relationship management (CRM) system is even more directly relevant to global account management. A CRM system collects information specifically relating to the relationship with customers. This enables the supplier to demonstrate to the customer that it is globally coordinated. One person or team, the global account manager and the GAT, can have complete visibility of all business and opportunities with a customer. By providing comprehensive information on the account, a well-managed CRM system can facilitate an understanding of the customer that makes the global account manager a good business partner for the customer. It should also allow strategic data analysis and include customer feedback and strategic information on the customer's strategy and industry (Hennessey & Jeannet, 2004, pp. 205–206). While SAP is the global market leader for ERP systems, for CRM, it is Salesforce. In a CRM system like

Salesforce, there is one record for each customer, and all opportunities relating to that customer are entered and tracked throughout their lifecycle. If the CRM is well maintained, the global account manager can see the stage of each opportunity with the customer, from prospecting, via submitting a proposal to the customer and negotiations to closing, either won or lost. Through this, the potential new business opportunities with the customer can be identified, prioritized, and well-supported. Even before a company becomes a customer, a so-called "lead" can be entered for a potential new customer who has shown interest in a service offering of the supplier. Once the interest manifests, the account team can convert the lead into a customer with an attached opportunity. It then also enters critical contacts at the customer to keep track of the most important contact points at the customer (Salesforce, Inc., 2023).

While CRM systems are important for successful global account management, in practice, results are mixed. Many companies invest many financial resources in CRM systems without achieving the expected improvement in their customer relationships (Hennessey & Jeannet, 2004, p. 206). There are several reasons for this. Often, companies focus on technology alone, disregarding other elements like employees' attitudes and motivation, incentives, and the organization of customer relationship management (Cheverton, 2008, p. 202). Often, a CRM system is overloaded with transactional data but provides no strategic information. It is frequently focused internally and does not include customer feedback (Hennessey & Jeannet, 2004, p. 206). The quality of data in the system is often not good and regularly updated as changes at the customer occur (Capon et al., 2006, p. 189). Maintaining the system is often not integrated into daily sales routines. To make CRM systems successful, Yip and Bink recommend incorporating its use into daily work routines. Companies should set up rules on which information to enter and where in the system (Yip & Bink, 2007, pp. 148–149). We would add that rules such as the one outlined for IBM previously in this chapter can be helpful, where teams can start a new project only when the appropriate information on the opportunity has been entered into the CRM system previously.

So, we must look beyond IT systems to make managing knowledge on global account teams successful. Employees play a crucial role in KM. They are the ones who carry the critical tacit knowledge about customers in their minds. To share this tacit knowledge, opportunities for real-life sharing of experience are vital. This can be an annual physical meeting of the GAT, but also monthly video conferences are helpful for such exchanges. IT systems aimed at knowledge sharing often face a downward spiral: When they are poorly maintained, employees have little motivation to look for information; when few go there to search, it is less motivating to post and update information in the system. This problem is less pronounced in ERP systems, as companies generate much of their content as part of the normal daily operations of the firm. For other systems like CRM systems, creating a culture where the use of the system is a natural part of operations is helpful (Yip & Bink, 2007, pp. 149–150). It can be beneficial to link a system that facilitates knowledge sharing to other systems. Imagine a professional service firm that has created a system with short descriptions of successfully completed client projects ("credentials"). The credentials in the system are regularly used to portray the firm's competence in proposals to prospective clients. This system can be linked to the CRM system so that each time an opportunity in the CRM system is flagged as "closed/won," a draft credential is automatically created in the credential database with all relevant information from the CRM system pre-populated in the credential database. This would trigger an email with a link to the draft credential to the opportunity owner, who would just need to add a few more pieces of information and publish the credential with the click of a button.

## The Global Account Knowledge Manager

To address the issues of account KM, it can be beneficial to have a dedicated person in charge of KM for the account: the global account information manager or knowledge manager. By taking care of the KM system, the knowledge manager can prevent the system from getting clogged with unstructured and irrelevant information while helping ensure that relevant information gets posted. At professional service firms such as IBM, a dedicated team gathers relevant information on the account. An account knowledge manager would regularly create reports with updates on the account for the GAT. Sometimes, only the knowledge manager can upload information into the system (Yip & Bink, 2007, p. 151). The role could also extend beyond a single account. Imagine a PSF where the account knowledge managers of the various accounts within one industry, such as the telecommunications industry, are in contact with each other, coordinated by an industry knowledge manager, and share insights on trends and issues in that industry. Each account knowledge manager would then share these insights with his or her GAT.

## Relationship Management



Customer relationship management typically occurs in business-to-business (B2B), where customers are other businesses. In services, we call them business services. While in consumer services, customers tend to be a large and relatively anonymous group from the service provider's perspective, in B2B, suppliers treat each customer more or less individually. Some call this a "market segment of one" (Wilson et al., 2002, p. 65). In B2B, relationships tend to be longer-term, especially in business services. So cooperation and maintaining the relationship become essential, and both sides can benefit from such longer-term relationships between suppliers and business customers (Wilson et al., 2002, pp. 64–78).

## Customizing and Mirroring the Customer

How the account teams are organized within one company could result from the company's preference. In one firm, for example, the most important global accounts will have direct formal global account teams; in another, they might be informal.

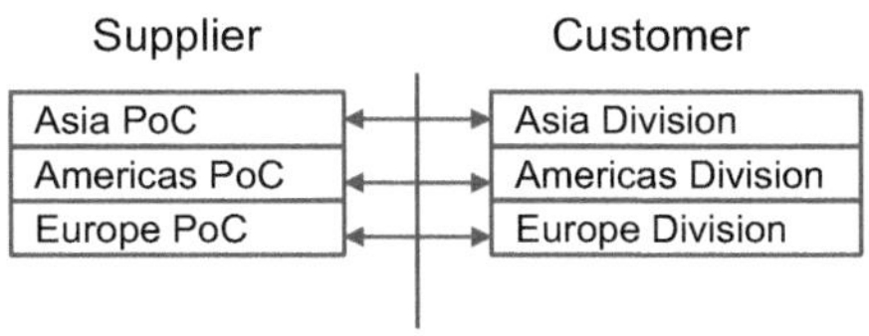


**Fig. 14.5** Mirroring the customer organization, based on content from Yip and Bink (2007, pp. 174–175)

At the same time, to some extent, the organization of the account may need to be *customized* to adapt to the customer. This is especially pronounced in advertising agencies where an account team can be entirely customized to a customer to work in a way that best suits the customer (Yip & Bink, 2007, pp. 174–175). Consider the French advertising giant Publicis. When winning the contract to provide advertising for the Nivea brand of consumer products firm Baiersdorf in 2021, Publicis announced it would set up a particular agency unit called "One Touch" to do advertising exclusively for the Nivea account (Bialek, 2019). In the realm of information and communication tools, suppliers sometimes set up internet-based client portals customized to an account that contains all information relevant to the customer, such as about existing contracts and responsible account managers. While the general structure of such client portals might be similar, the supplier will customize the specific content and layout to each customer (Yip & Bink, 2007, pp. 174–175).

A special kind of customization is called *mirroring*. In this case, the account closely mirrors the customer's organizational structure to enable well-aligned working relationships with the customer. This requires having first a good understanding of the organization of the customer. The supplier should staff these contacts at the same level as the customer. This can make managing the relationship easier (Yip & Bink, 2007, pp. 174–175). If the customer, for example, has three procurement teams in Germany, Japan, and the United States, then the supplier would have three points of contact (PoC) in these countries to maintain close relationships (see Fig. 14.5).

## Educating the Customer

Once a supplier has set up an account team customized to the customer, it will want to inform the customer about it. The customer will want to know the right contacts at the supplier. The supplier will want to inform the customer about what it can do for it because global account management eventually aims to generate more customer business. The supplier can achieve this best if it helps the customer achieve its goals. As Yip and Bink phrase it, the message toward the customer should be "How can we help you to achieve your objectives?" (Yip & Bink, 2007, p. 175).

## Account Coordination Mechanisms

Global account management requires coordination in terms of centralizing and integrating its activities worldwide to some extent to serve the major customers globally. Two forms of global account coordination can be distinguished (Shi & Gao, 2016):

- *Global account operational coordination* (GOC): This form of coordination means that a supplier coordinates its marketing mix and value chain activities across borders. This relates mainly to the supplier's activities. Coordination occurs at an operational level to implement strategies across local units and functions of the supplier.
- *Global account relational coordination* (GRC): This form of coordination relates to a supplier's purposeful activities to organize joint activities with the customer at various levels, such as senior executives, global account managers, and local account managers. These are more strategic-level initiatives taking place between supplier and customer. It frequently implies the communication of critical information between executives at both firms and strategic decision-making enforced across hierarchical levels, down to the front-line employees.

Shi and Gao found in their study that successful global account management requires internal cross-country coordination at the supplier and relational coordination between the supplier and customer. Both forms of coordination are complementary, and both lead to two aspects of successful GAM: (a) enhancing market outcomes for the supplier in terms of sales growth, market share, and profitability, and (b) increasing the likelihood that the relationship with the customer will last for a long time (Gao & Shi, 2011). Less formal coordination mechanisms are needed when a cultural fit exists between supplier and customer. When customers' needs and competitors' actions change frequently, the supplier needs to increase both forms of coordination to obtain more knowledge about the customer and design solutions to fit the customer's needs (Shi & Gao, 2016).



## Challenges in Managing Account Relationships

A global account manager is likely to encounter the following challenges when managing the ongoing relationship with the customer, especially in view of ensuring effective and efficient service delivery to the global customer (Harvey et al., 2003):

- *Multiplicity of units and authorities*: The multiple units of a global customer require constant prioritization, and internally, the multiple levels of authority need to be dealt with.
- *Maintaining flexibility*: The supplier must flexibly adapt to changing conditions and emerging opportunities.
- *Securing internal support*: To successfully serve the customer, the account manager must secure internal coordination and support within the supplier organization.

- *Multidimensional tasks*: The account manager must consider the technical, legal, economic, and political dimensions of a global account.
- *Multiskill demands*: Effective delivery for a global account requires multiple skills of the global account manager and team, as follows from their multiple roles and responsibilities.

## Assessing the Relationship

When managing the relationship with the customer, a global account manager will want to assess the relationship. Arnold et al. (2001) suggest a helpful tool for this purpose that focuses on the balance of power between customer and supplier. This follows from how globally integrated both sides are. We mentioned above that the supplier needs to be globally coordinated and integrated to serve a global customer. The same applies to the customer. Managing a global relationship will be difficult if the customer is not globally integrated. If both sides do not have international coordination, the customer and supplier will only have a *country-by-country relationship*. There is no potential for global account management. Only if both sides are well integrated across borders is there a high potential for a relationship at the global level—a *global fit*. When the customer has its subsidiaries well integrated, but the supplier does not, the balance of power favors the better-integrated customer. The customer can play the supplier's local units off against each other, who may try to undercut each other on prices—a *prize squeeze*. When the supplier is better integrated, in theory, the balance of power shifts to the supplier. However, the situation is not beneficial to the supplier. The supplier's global agreement with the customer in such a setting becomes a *hollow agreement*. This is because the global headquarters of the customer will not be able to enforce such an agreement with their local units. The local units may still buy a particular category of services from another provider (Arnold et al., 2001). ◘ Figure 14.6 provides an overview of the four situations.

Finally, the global account manager will also want to assess how profitable the relationship with a customer is. A global account program is expensive and only warranted if it leads to a more profitable relationship with the customer. This

| | Price squeeze | Global fit | Country-by-country relationship | Hollow agreement |
|---|---|---|---|---|
| Customer's international coordination | High | High | Low | Low |
| Supplier's international coordination | Low | High | Low | High |
| Relationship potential | Low | High | none | Low |

◘ **Fig. 14.6** Fit between supplier and customer, based on content from Arnold et al. (2001)

requires having an integrated accounting system across the company, which is not always the case. It may be challenging to have global visibility of all dealings with the customer as it may appear under different names in different countries (Yip & Bink, 2007, pp. 171–173). As outlined above, the supplier needs good metadata management to address this issue. This includes creating a *company tree* in the IT system that shows all customers' local units under their global parent company.

## Global Account Planning

GATs want to identify new avenues to serve the client systematically. Creating an account plan allows for this. Typically, account managers from all countries where the client operates are involved and align their national account plans with the global plan. Inviting the customer to an account planning session can be beneficial to achieve a better alignment with the customer's plans. Shipping company Maersk, for example, invites customers every year to set goals and develop action plans together (Hennessey & Jeannet, 2004, pp. 6–7).

An account plan typically contains global goals for the account and activities that aim at achieving the goals. Since account management is an ongoing activity, an account plan is not just set up once and for all. Typically, account managers review and update it every year. Most firms have a yearly meeting where the global account manager and executives discuss how last year's account plan goals have been achieved and set the goals for the following year. Further, they discuss the resources needed to achieve the plan's objectives. Having the firm's executives involved is important for the global account manager to get approval for the required resources (Capon et al., 2006, pp. 153–178). The following box shows typical elements of an account plan.

**Elements of an Account Plan**

- Situation analysis
  - Understanding the customer's industry (processes and dynamics)
  - Understanding the customer (requirements and needs, challenges, performance, strengths and weaknesses, and strategies)
  - Understanding the supplier's competition (presence on the account, wallet share, strengths and weaknesses, relationships)
  - Understanding the supplier (strengths and weaknesses, services, resources)
  - Understanding the relationship (existing relationships of team members)
- Opportunities and threats for business with the account
- Framework for account action
  - Vision and mission for the account
  - Strategy for the account
  - Resources committed to strategy execution
  - Action plan
  - Budgets and forecasts

Source: (Capon et al., 2006, pp. 155–158)

**Planning With the Customer:** Global account managers often find including the customer in account planning beneficial. This can work fine if the relationship is strong and enough trust has been built. The supplier and customer can plan what they want to do together and identify projects to conduct jointly. In this context, it is beneficial if both sides inform each other of plans that can impact the other side so that the other side can adapt accordingly. Especially if the customer informs the supplier of planned activities where it may need help from the supplier, the supplier can plan its resources accordingly. Beyond this, customers and suppliers can use account planning to set up projects to facilitate future collaboration, such as joint IT systems (Yip & Bink, 2007, p. 178). At global integrated logistics provider Fritz, account teams meet quarterly with customer representatives to evaluate performance, discuss problems, and find solutions. A list of action items is agreed upon for follow-up each time (Hennessey & Jeannet, 2004, pp. 152–153).

## Challenges in Global Account Management

In practice, companies engaging in global account management encounter various challenges (Yip & Bink, 2007, pp. 179–182):

- *Local versus global attitudes*: Frequently, there are frictions between global and local interests at the supplier. Local account managers may resent a loss of responsibility when the company launches a global account management program. While in the past, they have had complete autonomy in their customer relationships, now they must report their activities to the global level. They may not be allowed to pursue local opportunities that are at odds with global priorities. This can also lead to motivational issues among local account managers (Ellis & Iwasaki, 2018). This can be addressed by including local account managers on the global team and communicating closely with them. When local managers undertake activities that benefit the global program, their compensation should reward them for this. Remember how at Marriott, hotel managers perceived GAM as a loss of control since each hotel was franchised and managed independently. Marriott, therefore, created an internal campaign to sell the GAM vision, mission, and plan and convey its urgency.
- *Lack of global capabilities—supplier*: As we already mentioned when we discussed the balance of power between supplier and customer, some suppliers are not as globally integrated as they think. In other words, they do not have global capabilities. They may have operations across many locations worldwide, but the global account manager may not have authority over local account teams. So, a subsidiary may resist charging a price set by the global account manager if they traditionally charge a higher price to the customer.
- *Lack of global capabilities—customer*: Similarly, when the customer is not well integrated across borders, this can cause challenges for the account relationship. You will remember the problem of the *hollow agreement*. Besides what was mentioned above, if the customer only wants to transfer existing business with the supplier into one global contract, the value for the supplier is limited. It may only lead to a lower sales price than before the integration.

- *Downward pricing spiral*: Some customers may use the account relationship to negotiate lower prices for the services provided at every meeting with the supplier. As you will remember, that risk is especially high when the supplier is not well coordinated so that the customer can play local units of the supplier off against each other. To prevent this, the supplier needs good coordination between its subsidiaries to avoid such a situation. Instead, in a trusting account relationship, the customer and supplier will attempt to find ways of lowering the cost of collaboration for both sides.

## Review Questions

1. Define global account management and why companies engage in it.
2. Why is global account management particularly relevant for service firms?
3. Outline typical selection criteria for global accounts. Why is potential revenue sometimes seen as more important than current revenue?
4. Explain how global account managers analyze their accounts. Why is it important to also understand the industry of the customer?
5. Explain how the potential for the relationship can be analyzed.
6. Outline the roles of the global account manager.
7. Explain the roles of the global account team.
8. Describe the options for organizing the account team and their benefits and drawbacks. What are the implications for their placement in the overall company's organizational structure?
9. Why should a global account program conduct knowledge management, and which role can ERP and CRM systems play?
10. Why are CRM systems often not successful?
11. Explain why and how account teams should mirror the customer.
12. How can the relationship with the account be assessed?
13. What is your opinion on whether and if yes, under what conditions it is advisable to involve the customer in account planning?
14. Explain the challenges that can occur in global account management.



## Closing Case: Young & Rubicam and the Star Alliance

Star Alliance was set up by five airlines in 1997, becoming the first alliance in the aviation industry. The alliance initially included Lufthansa, United, Air Canada, SAS, and Thai Airways, several of which already had bilateral cooperation agreements. As part of the alliance, the airlines, with different geographical focuses, coordinated flight schedules, advertising, frequent-flyer programs, access to business lounges, and purchasing of things like cabin interiors. To customers, the alliance facilitated miles collection on their frequent flyer cards, better connections, and lounge access. For member airlines, the primary benefit is access to further customers to fill their seats. The Star Alliance contacted the advertising group Young and Rubicam (Y&R) to launch the new Star Alliance brand globally. Y&R, as an international advertising group, had many

Star Alliance airplane, image by Cor Gaasbeek from Pixabay

global accounts. The agency Wunderman, part of the Y&R group, was made responsible for all non-media advertising activities of Star Alliance.

Since Star Alliance was initially a purely virtual organization without a central marketing department, it set up a marketing and communications committee (MCC) to provide a counterpart for Y&R. Each airline member sent one representative into the MCC with one vote per airline. Decisions needed to be unanimous. Overall, in the 1990s, the Star Alliance had 24 committees to decide on connectivity, purchasing, and customer relationships. Chairman roles were shared around to ensure all members felt represented. All member airlines were enthusiastic about the potential benefits that the Alliance could bring, so they could make progress within the MCC.

To meet Star Alliance's needs, Y&R mobilized its global force. Y&R's headquarters in New York centrally controlled the account. By working with Y&R, Star Alliance could access the expertise in Y&R's 539 offices in 80 countries. However, not all went smoothly for Y&R initially. The advertising group had not previously worked with a client that was a virtual global organization like the Star Alliance. The traditional model, where an agency took the lead and coordinated customer relationships, proved ineffective for this account. With the absence of a headquarters, the agencies of Y&R had to win the trust of each of the Star Alliance member airlines. Creating a global brand from scratch, working across different languages, cultures, and time zones, required creativity, flexibility, and persistence from the Y&R network.

Each member airline had its vision for Star Alliance, which was not always easy to reconcile. Y&R responded by getting the airlines of Star Alliance onto a consistent platform globally. This meant agreeing on a common target audience: international business travellers. Y&R also put together a team that represented all the different cultures in the Alliance. This way, any cultural-specific issues could be carefully considered before cobbling together the marketing campaigns for Star Alliance.

Y&R needed to evolve to work better with Star Alliance. Over time, new processes were introduced within Y&R that improved client service but also addressed concerns of Star Alliance about Y&R's centralized organization and Western bias. For example, Y&R's team composition became more diverse regarding national background. New initiatives were developed, but because of the September 11, 2001, terrorist attacks, the marketing budget for the Star Alliance was reduced from $59m to $5m, which meant that these initiatives could not be pursued.

Later, Y&R increasingly assumed the role of an international coordinator and planner. Soliciting input from local partner agencies increased participation. Y&R set objectives and strategies and then passed them on to their local member agencies to provide comments on how an idea would work locally and how they could implement it. The local Y&R agencies often collaborated with a local client airline to agree on the best way to execute a strategy or idea.

The most striking feature of the customer for Y&R was the diversity of cultures within Star Alliance. The Y&R agencies organized regular conference calls among the MCC representatives where marketing initiatives were to be approved. After the calls, Wunderman executives frequently noticed the lack of active participation by Alliance members from certain national cultures. Later, delays with campaign signoffs occurred because the members who had not participated in the discussions had issues to clarify. Like this, Y&R had to constantly balance getting consensus on campaigns while not destroying the creative momentum of the group.

Y&R managers perceived cultural diversity as the most significant challenge. However, Star Alliance members used culture as an excuse to delay a campaign when issues resulted from personal interpretations by individual members. Nevertheless, through the relentless effort of Y&R and its member agencies, they overcame these challenges, and Star Alliance successfully launched worldwide in May 1997.

The challenge for Y&R to coordinate projects grew as the Star Alliance grew. The MCC increasingly became bureaucratic and unwieldy as it grew from five airlines with five representatives to 15 airlines with 30 representatives. At one point, over 50 people with diverse perspectives attended the meetings. Y&R also realized that it involved an excessive number of people in the project to serve the client. Due to the virtual nature of Star Alliance, Y&R managed many functions that typically the client would manage. The agency became the de-facto marketing department and project manager for Star Alliance. At one point, Y&R set up the MCC's regular meetings and agreed on timing with all the airline representatives. Y&R set up a process management system that listed critical deliverables and their timing and completion status by the various airlines. It was also not in the best interest of the Star Alliance to be so dependent on the advertising agency.

To be an effective global supplier to the Star Alliance, Y&R had to put various measures in place. First, the Y&R agencies mirrored the structures of their client. To serve the Star Alliance, Y&R established a global account management structure. Second, a strong support team was created for the account managers because the Star Alliance account was very demanding regarding resourcing. Staffs who worked on the Star Alliance account were dedicated to it almost full-time. This created challenges in meeting their other responsibilities on other projects, as it was customary to work on more than one project at a time. Third, Y&R launched a regular client satisfaction survey to ensure ongoing communication with Star Alliance. This put Y&R in a position to determine client satisfaction levels, assess individual Y&R offices involved, and determine the value Y&R was creating. Results were presented both internally and to the client.

The relationship between Star Alliance's MCC and Y&R changed gradually as Star Alliance became more real. In 2002, Star Alliance registered as a limited liability company in Germany with 65 permanent employees at its global headquarters in Frankfurt. Star Alliance set up a full-time marketing department, which took over the strategic planning that the agencies conducted previously. Wunderman took over managing the Star Alliance account from Y&R headquarters in New York. In this new context, Wunderman's role turned back to the more traditional role of an agency.

From the perspective of R&Y and Wunderman, Star Alliance was a success story:

» "It started from nothing, and within five years, it has managed to build a brand and be the leading airline alliance in the world. It has won the battle over other alliances" (Yip & Bink, 2007, p. 186).

As of 2023, Star Alliance comprises 26 airlines, operating over 50 global hubs and serving 1200 airports. In 2021, the Alliance set up a subsidiary management company in Singapore in addition to the Frankfurt office.

**Questions**

1. To what extent is Y&R customizing its approach and mirroring its customer, the Star Alliance?
2. Is Y&R educating the customer?
3. What is your assessment of the balance of power between Y&R and the customer?
4. How is Y&R dealing with this situation?
5. Which barriers to global account planning can you observe? How is Y&R dealing with them?
6. Following the successful launch of the Star Alliance brand, what could a joint account planning of Y&R with the customer Star Alliance comprise?

Sources: (Economist, 1998, 2011a, 2011b, 2013; Star Alliance, 2023; Yip & Bink, 2007, pp. 182–186)

**Summary**

This chapter

- Defined global account management as "An organizational form and process in multinational companies by which the worldwide activities serving one or more multinational customers are coordinated centrally by one person or team within the supplier company."
- Outlined why global account management is essential for service MNEs.
- Described key criteria used to select global accounts: geography, organization, potential revenue, strategic importance, and fit.
- Described elements of the account analysis: a customer's industry, business, strategy, and the relationship potential.
- Explained roles of the global account manager.
- Described typical members of global account teams and their responsibilities: account planning, information and communication, strengthening the network, and locating opportunities.
- Described options for organizing global account teams (GAT): formal direct GAT, formal indirect GAT, and informal GAT.
- Characterized knowledge management on accounts and the role of information systems, especially ERP and CRM systems, and the role of the global account knowledge manager.
- Explained how account teams manage customer relationships, especially by customizing their account team to the customer and mirroring its organization.
- Distinguished operational and relational coordination of global accounts and how a GAT can assess the relationship with the customer.
- Outlined account planning.
- Described major challenges of global account management: local vs. global attitudes, lack of global capabilities of supplier and customer, and a downward pricing spiral.


## References




Arnold, D., Birkinshaw, J., & Toulan, O. (2001). Can selling be globalized? The pitfalls of global account management. *California Management Review, 44*(1), 8–20.

Atanasova, Y., & Senn, C. (2014). Global customer team design: Dimensions, determinants and performance outcomes. In D. Woodburn & K. Wilson (Eds.), *Handbook of strategic account management: A comprehensive resource* (pp. 379–403). John Wiley & Sons, Ltd..

Bialek, C. (2019, November 21). Werbeagenturen: Neustart für Publicis in Deutschland. *Handelsblatt, 2019*(225), 22.

Birkinshaw, J., Toulan, O., & Arnold, D. (2001). Global account management in multinational corporations: Theory and evidence. *Journal of International Business Studies, 32*(2), 231.

Capon, N., & Senn, C. (2010). Global customer management programs: How to make them really work. *California Management Review, 52*(2), 32–55.

Capon, N., Potter, D., & Schindler, F. (2006). *Managing global accounts: Nine critical factors for a world-class program*. Thomson.

Cheverton, P. (2008). *Global account management: A complete action kit of tools and techniques for managing key global customers*. Kogan Page.

Economist (1998, September 26). *Mergers in mind, 1998*.

Economist (2011a November 11). *Open the skies, 2011*.
Economist (2011b, November 12). *The airmiles-high clubs, 2011*.
Economist (2013, July 17). *SkyTeam and the world of tomorrow, 2013*.
Ellis, N., & Iwasaki, A. (2018). Making sense of global key account management (GAM): A case study from Japan. *Journal of Business & Industrial Marketing, 33*(7), 1052–1064.
Gao, T., & Shi, L. H. (2011). How do multinational suppliers formulate mechanisms of global account coordination? An integrative framework and empirical study. *Journal of International Marketing, 19*(4), 61–87.
Greenwood, R., Morris, T., Fairclough, S., & Boussebaa, M. (2010). The organizational design of transnational professional service firms. *Organizational Dynamics, 39*(2), 173–183.
Harvey, M. G., Novicevic, M. M., Hench, T., & Myers, M. (2003). Global account management: A supply-side managerial view. *Industrial Marketing Management, 32*(7), 563–571.
Hennessey, H. D., & Jeannet, J.-P. (2004). *Global account management: Creating value* (11th ed.). John Wiley & Sons Ltd..
Kraljic, P. (1983). Purchasing must become supply management. *Harvard Business Review*, September-October 1983, 109–117.
Kumar, P., Sharma, A., & Salo, J. (2019). A bibliometric analysis of extended key account management literature. *Industrial Marketing Management, 82*, 276–292.
Marriott International. (2021). *2001 Annual report*. Retrieved from https://marriott.gcs-web.com/static-files/33ba0a19-8a68-4f3f-9f73-fef2c458c22e
Marriott International. (2023). *We are Marriott International*. Retrieved from https://www.marriott.com/marriott/aboutmarriott.mi
McNeill, R. (2005). Go-to-market frontier: Global account management (GAM). *Journal of Global Business and Technology, 1*(1), 12–31.
Montgomery, D. B., & Yip, G. S. (1999). Statistical evidence on global account management programs. *Thexis: Fachzeitschrift Für Marketing, 16*(4), 10–13.
Nätti, S., & Palo, T. (2012). Key account management in business-to-business expert organisations: An exploratory study on the implementation process. *Service Industries Journal, 32*(11), 1837–1852.
Nätti, S., Halinen, A., & Hanttu, N. (2006). Customer knowledge transfer and key account management in professional service organizations. *International Journal of Service Industry Management, 17*(4), 304–319.
Salesforce, Inc. (2023). *Trailhead*. Retrieved from https://trailhead.salesforce.com/
Sengupta, S., Krapfel, R. E., & Pusateri, M. A. (1997). The strategic sales force. *Marketing Management, 6*(2), 28–34.
Shi, L. H., & Gao, T. (2016). Performance effects of global account coordination mechanisms: An integrative study of boundary conditions. *Journal of International Marketing, 24*(2), 1–21.
Shi, L. H., Zou, S., White, J. C., McNally, R. C., & Cavusgil, S. T. (2005). Executive insights: Global account management capability: Insights from leading suppliers. *Journal of International Marketing, 13*(2), 93–113.
Shi, L. H., White, J. C., Zou, S., & Cavusgil, S. T. (2010). Global account management strategies: Drivers and outcomes. *Journal of International Business Studies, 41*, 620–638.
Star Alliance. (2023). *About Star Alliance*. Retrieved from https://www.staralliance.com/en/about
Toulan, O., Birkinshaw, J., & Arnold, D. (2006). The role of interorganizational fit in global account management. *International Studies of Management & Organization, 36*(4), 61–81.
Wilson, K., & Millman, T. (2003). The global account manager as political entrepreneur. *Industrial Marketing Management, 32*(2), 151–158.
Wilson, K., Speare, N., & Reese, S. (2002). *Successful global account management: Key strategies and tools for managing global customers*. Kogan Page.
Yip, G. S., & Bink, A. J. M. (2007). *Managing global customers: An integrated approach*. Oxford Univ. Press.
Yip, G. S., & Bink, A. (2017). Global account managers: The linchpins of GAM programmes. *Journal of Brand Strategy, 6*(2), 146–159.
Yip, G. S., & Madsen, T. L. (1996). Global account management: The new frontier in relationship marketing. *International Marketing Review, 13*(3), 24–42.

## Further Reading

Yip, G. S., & Bink, A. J. M. (2007). Managing global customers: An integrated approach. Oxford Univ. Press provides an excellent overview of global account management, including examples of companies, many of which in the services sector.

# Global Service Delivery and Project Management

## Contents



The original version of the chapter has been revised. A correction to this chapter can be found at https://doi.org/10.1007/978-3-031-50345-0_19


D. Klimkeit et al., *International Management in Service Firms*, Classroom Companion: Business, https://doi.org/10.1007/978-3-031-50345-0_15

**Learning Outcomes**

After completing this chapter, you should be able to:

- Explain the service blueprint and its role in designing cross-border service delivery
- Outline the specific challenges of managing cross-border projects and ways of dealing with them
- Describe what to consider on ongoing international service delivery
- Outline how to measure and manage quality in international service delivery
- Explain how to manage the participation of customers in international service delivery

## Introduction

After previous chapters dealing with the strategy, organization, governance, and market entry of service multinational enterprises (MNEs) set the stage, this chapter will address the heart of international services management: How are services delivered for customers across borders? It starts with introducing the concept of the service blueprint as a tool for designing the delivery of services and discussing options for its international design. Since many services, especially business services, are delivered in the form of projects, the bulk of this chapter will address the specifics of international project management. As some services are instead provided on a more ongoing basis rather than in projects, we will address the international provision of ongoing services as well. We will complement this by addressing the issue of how to ensure consistent service quality internationally and how to manage the participation of customers in the service process in international service delivery.

Flower delivery, image by Capsule Cosplay from Pixabay

## Opening Case: Say It with Flowers—Worldwide: Fleurop-Interflora

In 1908, Max Hübner, a florist in Berlin, Germany, and 98 colleagues set up Fleurop, an association for transmitting flowers as gifts. In 1910, in the United States, Florists' Transworld Delivery (FTD) Association was founded for the same purpose. In 1927, Hübner set up the European network Fleurop-Interflora across many European countries. After the end of the second world war, Fleurop delegates met with Interflora British Group and FTD representatives to join forces to deliver flowers worldwide under the name of Interflora Inc. (Interflora). In the 1950s, business boomed, and in the 1960s, the slogan "say it with flowers" was created. In the 1980s, Interflora established a global electronic order transmission system to simplify the transmission of flower orders. Since the 2000s, the Internet has become the driving force behind Interflora's fast development. At Interflora, flowers are not sent physically to the destination; instead, Interflora exchanges orders for flower delivery within a network of florists. Only at a florist at the receiver's location are flowers put together and delivered. Interflora exclusively draws on its network of florists. The company organizes the financial transaction between the florists involved. Today, more than 40,000 florists in over 150 countries are involved, processing more than 25 million orders a year, making it the largest floral delivery company in the world.

The process of international flower delivery at a company like Interflora runs as follows. There are two customers: the person placing the order and the receiver of the flowers. Both are in contact with the company. The person placing the order would traditionally go to the nearest florist who is part of the network and place the order. Today, he or she could also use the Internet for this purpose. If a customer contacts a local florist, she will receive the order and enter it into the information technology (IT) system. The system, including a database of orders and florists, will have been set up in the background already. An invoice is created for the customer placing the order, and the customer pays the required money. The IT system transmits the order to a florist in the receiver's location, drawing on the database. The florist in the destination puts together the bouquet, drawing on flowers she will have procured independently of the order previously, and organizes the delivery, drawing on a database of delivery service providers created previously. The delivery service provider fetches the bouquet from the florist, drawing on a delivery van that it will have procured before and maintains on an ongoing basis, independent from a specific delivery order. The delivery service provider schedules the delivery, drawing on drivers it will have hired before, independent of the specific flower order. The driver transports the bouquet to the receiver and presents it to the receiving customer. The driver informs Interflora about the successful delivery to the receiving customer.

**Questions**

1. In which parts of Interflora's service process do the customers participate?
2. Which parts of Interflora's service process are visible to the customers?
3. Which aspects of Interflora's activities are independent of a particular order?
4. How are the various tasks of flower delivery divided between different countries?

Sources: (Fleurop-Interflora, n.d.; Fließ, 2004).

## The Service Blueprint of Cross-Country Service Processes

You will remember how we introduced the service value chain in ► Chap. 8 to analyze the various service activities that create customer value. When designing efficient cross-country service processes in detail, an instrument is needed that provides more detail than the value chain. The *service blueprint* is such an instrument. It was developed by Shostack (1982, 1984) and further developed by Kingman-Brundage (1991) and others such as Fließ and Kleinaltenkamp (2004). Each author added further elements to the blueprint. We will outline a simplified version of the blueprint outlined by Fließ (2004) and its application in an international context as addressed by the same author.

**Service Blueprint**

[A *service blueprint*] specifies in detail how a service process is constructed. Service blueprints map customer, employee, and service-system interactions. They show the full customer journey from service initiation to the final delivery of the desired benefit, which can include many steps and service employees from different departments (Zeithaml & Bitner, 2003, p. 238).

Blueprints visualize how customers and service providers interact, how different departments of the service provider play a role, and how some activities are visible to the customer (onstage) while other activities happen behind the scenes (backstage) (Zeithaml & Bitner, 2003, p. 238). A blueprint provides a two-dimensional picture of a service process: The horizontal axis shows the temporal sequence of activities from inception to completion. The vertical axis outlines various interaction areas divided by "lines" (Fließ & Kleinaltenkamp, 2004). Fließ distinguishes five lines, creating six areas: line of interaction, line of visibility, line of internal interaction, line of order penetration, and line of implementation (Fließ, 2004, p. 188). While we consider most of them very helpful, for this textbook, we leave out the line of internal interaction and line of implementation. This is mainly to reduce complexity as we believe that the added benefit of those two lines does not warrant the increase in complexity they generate in our context. This is mainly because, in the next step, we will add further lines to address the international context. The remaining three lines distinguish substantially different areas of interaction relevant to international service delivery. See ◘ Fig. 15.1 for our version of the service blueprint.

The *line of interaction* separates activities conducted by the customer from the service provider's activities. They define contact points between customers and service providers. In the opening case of Interflora, the first customer places the order and pays, while the second customer receives the bouquet. The service provider, for example, receives the order and delivers the flowers to the receiving customer. The *line of visibility* separates those activities of the service provider that are visible to the customer from those that are not. The visible activities above the line are called

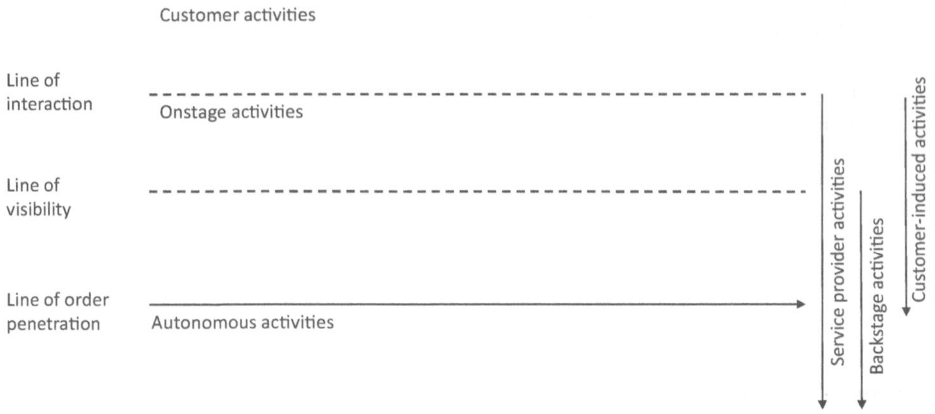


**Fig. 15.1** The service blueprint, adapted from (Fließ, 2004, p. 188) (simplified, permission obtained)

the front office or onstage, and the invisible ones below are back-office or backstage activities. For example, the delivery of the flowers is visible, while the binding of the bouquet and the transportation to the house of the receiving customer are invisible. The *line of order penetration* separates those service provider activities induced by an order from the customer from those activities of the service provider that are independent of a specific customer order (autonomous activities). The latter can be planned and conducted independently of a specific customer to create and maintain the service potential of the service provider. In the opening case, this relates to the recruitment of staff at the florist and the delivery service provider, the creation and maintenance of the various IT systems of Interflora, the procurement and maintenance of a delivery van, and as a rule, the procurement of the flowers (unless a customer places an unusual order for which a florist needs to procure specific flowers) (Fließ, 2004).

As a next step, we follow Fließ in looking at the service blueprint in an international context. From the point of view of the blueprint, the international division of labor can take three forms: the duplication of service processes, vertical division of labor, or horizontal division of labor. *Duplication* means that all parts of a service process, from the customer request to the fulfillment of the request, are conducted in each country where the firm serves customers. This can be found in professional services such as auditing, management consulting, or advertising, but also in hotels or banks. In the case of a *vertical division of labor*, a part of the service process, including customer-induced and customer-independent activities, is transferred abroad. In contrast, another part remains in the home country. This is displayed by a vertical cut through the blueprint, signaling a temporal division. For example, the process may start in the home country and continue in the host country. This is the case in flower delivery, where the receiving of the order happens in the home country, while the putting together of the bouquet and its delivery occurs in the host country of the receiving customer. The service can be provided abroad by the firm itself or by third parties contracted for that purpose. For example, in

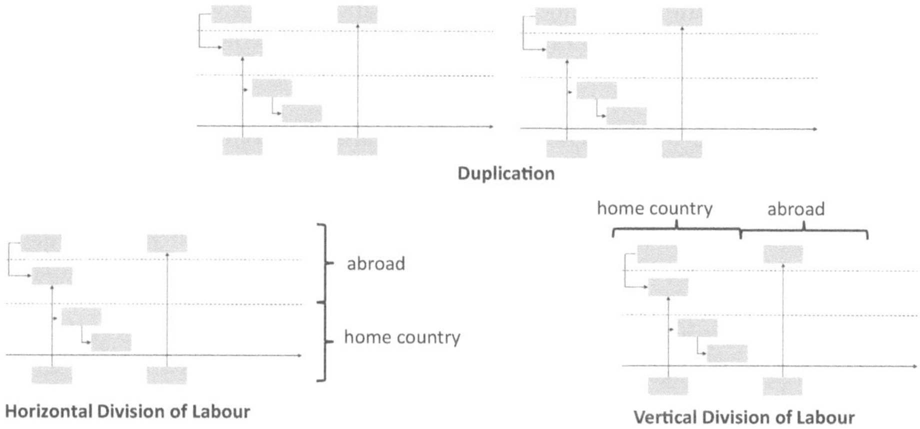


**Fig. 15.2** Options of the international division of labor in the service blueprint, source: (Fließ, 2004, p. 194) (permission obtained)

tourism, the booking of a trip may happen in a local travel agency in the home country, the reception of the guest might happen by an incoming agency in the travel destination, as well as the actual service provision by a local hotel and tour operator. In the case of a *horizontal division of labor*, the separation between home and abroad occurs along one of the lines of the blueprint. For example, activities in interaction with the customer (above the line of visibility) might occur abroad, while the service provider might conduct all other activities at home. Likewise, the firm can provide the entire customer-induced part of the process abroad while it conducts independent activities below the line of order penetration in another location. For example, in fast food chains, independent activities like procuring ingredients are frequently done centrally. A key reason for a horizontal division of the blueprint is the need for local responsiveness, as outlined in ► Chap. 8. Culture, language, differing customer needs, and legal requirements may necessitate front-office activities to be localized, while the service provider can centralize back-office tasks to achieve economies of scale (Fließ, 2004). Figure 15.2 shows these options graphically.

## Management of International Service Projects

Providing services to customers often takes the shape of projects, and in service MNEs, they are primarily international. We will first address the relevance of international project management (PM) for service firms and then go through the most critical aspects of international project management (IPM), focusing on the specific international aspects of PM. It will not be a complete treatment of project management but will focus instead on selected aspects that are particularly noteworthy regarding international projects. Though highly relevant in international projects, cross-cultural communication and collaboration in virtual teams will be omitted as they will be treated in ▶ Chap. 18, dedicated to these themes.

## The Importance of International Project Management for Service Firms

Whether an audit firm conducts a global audit, an engineering firm constructs a cross-border railway, an advertising agency creates a global advertising campaign, or a management consulting firm advises a client on a global corporate restructuring—many services, especially business services, are conducted as projects. In these projects, there is a defined start and end date, and the firm delivers a defined service package to the customer. This is especially true for professional service firms (PSFs) (Greenwood et al., 2010; Klimkeit, 2013). Some scholars even label PSFs as project-based organizations, where delivering revenue-generating services to clients (almost) exclusively takes the shape of projects (Sydow et al., 2004; Whitley, 2006). In all the examples above, they cross borders in one of the four modes of cross-border service supply introduced in ▶ Chap. 3. Frequently, they will be provided by mode 4, the presence of natural persons, as in the case of management consultants or engineers traveling abroad for the project's duration. Also, offices of architects based in a home country where they have their expertise and reputation would travel abroad temporarily for a construction project (Boussebaa & Morgan, 2015). In other cases, service projects are conducted by mode 3, establishing a commercial presence. This would typically be the case for the audit firm, which would involve staff from its foreign offices in all those countries where the client has subsidiaries. In some cases, mode 1, cross-border trade, can also be an option for international service projects, drawing on information and communication technology, for example, for globally distributed software development projects (Drechsler & Breth, 2019). This became more prevalent during the COVID-19 pandemic due to social distancing and international travel restrictions. To some extent, the global advertising campaign could be conducted by mode 1. However, more typically, advertising agencies would rely on their international network of member agencies present in the countries where they want to launch the campaign (mode 3) to make it relevant to local audiences. Sometimes, a combination of modes can be observed, for example, where the temporary presence of project managers and experts from other countries complements local staff. The remainder of this chapter will mostly assume modes 3 and 4 for the international delivery of projects, to some extent, mode 1.



## Characteristics and Success Factors of International Service Projects

Now, what are projects exactly? *Projects* are different from the ongoing routine operations of a company.

**Project**

A *project* is a temporary organization to which resources are assigned to deliver a beneficial change. (Turner, 2016, p. 1).

**Characteristics of Projects** So, a project aims at achieving a new state. While there are many different types of projects, they have specific characteristics in common, which differentiate them from ongoing operations. In particular, they are unique and limited (Köster, 2010, p. 3):

- *Limited*: Projects are limited in several ways. They are temporary, typically having a defined start and end date. The scope is limited, requiring the project to deliver a defined output, whether tangible, like a building, or intangible, like a higher level of staff skills. The financial and human resources available to the project are clearly circumscribed.
- *Unique*: Projects are unique because they are nonroutine activities. Each project may have different objectives, be conducted in a different context, geographic location, for a different customer, or in different organizational units. Even the same type of service provided to different customers will face different circumstances each time.

**Project Management** To achieve the projects' objectives, projects must be managed carefully. They require *project management*.

**Project Management**

*Project management* is the application of processes, methods, skills, knowledge, and experience to achieve specific project objectives according to the project acceptance criteria within agreed parameters" (APM, 2019)

**Difference to Domestic Projects** Now, how are international projects different from domestic projects? Most obviously, they involve locations and people in multiple countries. According to several authors, they also involve several different organizations or organizational units (Binder, 2007, p. 1; Köster, 2010, p. 14; Rea & Lientz, 2002, p. 3). We believe this can also frequently apply to domestic projects and is not a distinctive characteristic of international projects. However, if we focus on different subsidiaries of the firm and the overall much larger number of organizations and units (e.g., suppliers, customers, and subsidiaries) involved, we agree. Taken together, we can say that the scope of international projects in terms of the number of international locations, subsidiaries, and other organizations or organizational units is greater than that of domestic projects. Other things being equal, this implies a greater complexity than domestic projects (Köster, 2010, p. 14). Projects have stakeholders. They are groups of people affected by the projects in one way or another and therefore have expectations of what the project should do and how it should do it. They can involve

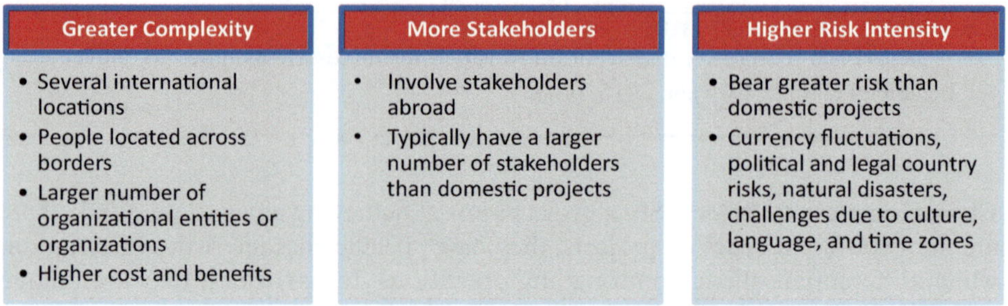


**Fig. 15.3** Main characteristics of international projects, own diagram

project team members, customers (internal and external), subcontractors, and many more. Due to their international character, international projects have more stakeholders spread across several countries (Köster, 2010, p. 15). Due to the complex international environment, international projects bear a higher risk than domestic projects. Currency fluctuations, political and legal country risks, natural disasters, and challenges due to culture, language, and time zones make international projects riskier (Köster, 2010, p. 15; Rea & Lientz, 2002, pp. 8–9). Figure 15.3 summarizes the key distinguishing characteristics of international projects.

Due to their characteristics, international projects often encounter challenges such as sudden changes due to the many parties involved or the complex external environment. So, it is not rare to see international projects fail (Rea & Lientz, 2002, pp. 13–14). Now, what can be done to increase the likelihood of successfully conducting international projects? What are the critical success factors?

**Critical Success Factors** Köster found several factors critical to the success of international projects: The projects' goals must be clear, and the team must be committed to them. Smooth communication needs to be established with a common language and intercultural communication skills. The supporting infrastructure in terms of suitable information and communication systems needs to be implemented. The project team needs adequate capabilities, including more interpersonal skills than in domestic projects. The project manager needs to consider the context sufficiently and deal with cultural, infrastructure, and jurisdiction differences. The right balance between a consistent, common methodology and flexibility is required. There is a need for flexibility in the dynamic environment of international projects, but also cohesion in the global team needs to be created with a common PM methodology. A supportive project culture needs to be established with open-mindedness, responsiveness, flexibility, and respect (Köster, 2010, pp. 20–22). In an empirical study among project managers of global projects, Fossum et al. (2019) found that selection and training to ensure sufficient skills of project staff correlate with the success of global projects in terms of project efficiency.

## Defining International Projects

**Managing Scope** First, a new project needs to be defined. This involves especially defining the project's scope: what is included and what is out of scope and therefore excluded. This is especially important in international projects due to their complexity, diversity, and risk and the many stakeholders who attempt to influence the project in their interest. It is good practice to have a written scope statement that clearly defines the project's scope before it starts. This is then signed off by the project owner, the project manager, and important stakeholders ("scope acceptance"), so the project manager can always refer to it in case discussions around the project's scope come up later. This is especially important because of the *scope creep* that can occur, particularly in international projects. Scope creep refers to a situation where the project's scope is gradually extended beyond its original extent. The project's resources frequently remain in line with the original scope, leading to challenges. In international projects, not all requirements may be known at the beginning, and at the same time, the complex environment may change, requiring changes to the project's scope. However, there is a difference between (uncontrolled) scope creep and controlled scope changes. The latter is controlled by scope change management each time stakeholders suggest a change to the scope. Changes are documented and signed off, and resources are adapted accordingly, as needed (Köster, 2010, pp. 65–66).

**Managing Stakeholders** As mentioned above, international projects involve diverse stakeholders in various countries. So, in the context of defining the scope, it is also essential to identify them, their relation to the project, and how to respond to them, so they support the project and do not work to derail it. In international projects, stakeholders as diverse as the following may be relevant: the company's board, which might be multicultural; shareholders; business units across the global firm that are involved or affected; affected subsidiaries; project staff across several countries; international external customers; the actual users of the project's outcome; subcontractors and international cooperation partners; providers of finance; regulators in all countries; media in all countries; and local communities in all locations. A typical process for managing stakeholders can look like the following:

- Identify the stakeholders of the project.
- Determine their interest in the project.
- Understand the stakeholders' influence on the project.
- Manage the response of the project to the stakeholders to leverage support and turn skeptical stakeholders into supporters.

In international projects, it is not easy for a project manager to identify all relevant stakeholders across the various countries involved. Therefore, it is helpful to involve team members and representatives from all relevant countries to help with the stakeholder mapping (Köster, 2010, pp. 74–76). To stimulate thinking about

**Fig. 15.4** Steps in project stakeholder management, own diagram, based on content from (Köster, 2010, pp. 74–76)

who are relevant stakeholders, the following questions can be helpful (Binder, 2007, p. 82):

- Who will use the outcome of the project?
- Who else will benefit from the project?
- Who will provide resources for the project?
- Who will have to adapt their practices due to the project?
- Who might be disturbed during the implementation of the project?
- Who might lobby against the project?

Figure 15.4 summarizes the main steps in project stakeholder management.

Aarseth et al. (2013) found in a survey of 550 project managers of global projects that managing external stakeholders such as local governments and authorities and local businesses such as suppliers is the primary organizational challenge on international projects. Based on interviews, they suggest the following elements of organizational support:

- Establish a local support office in locations where the firm plans a longer-term presence that would include staff from corporate communications and human resources (HR).
- Expatriates need to be prepared for global projects in terms of local culture and practices.
- The globalization strategy of the firm needs to include a global project strategy that includes guidelines on how to deal with local stakeholders.

15

## Managing Risk in International Projects

Since international projects typically involve high risks due to their internal and external complexity, as outlined above, it is particularly important to manage project risk carefully. Some risks can be anticipated. They can include inflation rates in countries where the project takes place, a high level of corruption, changes in tax rates, or opposition against the project by environmental action groups. For each of these, the likelihood of occurrence can be estimated, and the project manager can plan for them. Other risks cannot be anticipated. Natural disasters, political upheavals, or pandemics like COVID-19 are examples of such uncertainties. To be more resilient against uncertainties, the firm can design the project structure and contracts in a manner that reduces the impact of these uncertainties. The project

**Fig. 15.5** Different attitudes to risk, own diagram, based on content from (Köster, 2010, p. 100)

structure should be designed in such a way that it facilitates a continuing interaction with the various stakeholders. If project team members are sensitized, this allows them to identify emerging risks in the project's context. For example, a US-based technology company established a "change control board" in its projects where project managers can identify changing ideas of stakeholders, especially customers, that might constitute an emerging risk for the project. Regarding contracts, firms need to choose a suitable form of contract for the types of risks on the project. Furthermore, a clause requiring the customer to mention any emerging risk promptly allows discussing a response before risks harm the project (Köster, 2010, 98–99, 120–122).

**Cultural Attitudes to Risk** In international projects, project management is impacted by culture as well. Since ► Chap. 18 deals with culture in detail, we will only address it briefly here. The most obvious cultural difference that impacts how project staff deals with risks is that, in some cultures, people avoid risk as much as possible. In contrast, in other cultures, people are much more comfortable with embracing risk (see Fig. 15.5). In risk-avoiding cultures, such as Germany, Japan, or Korea, project managers attempt to identify risks in planning and put contingency procedures in place for dealing with them if they occur. In other cultures, like India, the United State, and the UK, where people tend to feel more comfortable with risk, they tend to put less effort into planning for risk and perceive risks as something that can be turned into an opportunity (Köster, 2010, p. 100).

Risks that can be anticipated need to be planned for and managed. Typical elements of project risk management include identifying risks, analyzing and prioritizing risks, planning for risks, and monitoring the project for risks. Many service MNEs require including an analysis of potential risks in the project proposal (Köster, 2010, pp. 102–103). Due to the scope of this book, we will only address risk planning: What to do about the various risks that project managers have identified, analyzed, and prioritized?

**Risk Planning** There are several *risk response strategies*: Risk avoidance, mitigation, transfer, pooling, and acceptance. With adequate planning, it may be possible to *avoid* risk. For example, in large international infrastructure projects, there may be a delay in payment by the client. To avoid this, a letter of credit from a bank involved in the transaction can be obtained. When the service provider submits all required documentation of the service delivered to the bank, the bank will release the agreed payment. However, it is not always possible to avoid risk. Risk *mitigation* is about reducing the impact of a risk if it occurs. For example, the firm can mitigate adverse movements in currency exchange rates by various instruments for hedging against currency fluctuations. Sometimes, risk can be *pooled* by entering a consortium, a joint venture, or a strategic alliance to share the risk. Firms frequently do this for large construction projects or the development of innovative, high-risk products. When a risk is *transferred*, it can still occur, but the responsibility for managing it resides now with someone else. This is regularly the case when the firm takes out insurance to transfer the risk to the insurance company. If the risk occurs, the insurance pays for it. However, the insurance may require a significant insurance premium. Finally, the project manager may *accept* some risks, especially if they are manageable and other strategies are either unavailable or too expensive (Köster, 2010, pp. 113–115).

**Corruption as a Risk in International Projects** In international projects, corruption is a particularly high risk in many countries. Transparency International (TI), an international nonprofit organization that works to fight corruption, defines corruption as "The abuse of entrusted power for private gain" (Transparency International, 2022). It can include corporations bribing public officials to obtain public contracts or public servants demanding money or other favors in return for services they should be providing for free. As the TI Corruption Perceptions Index demonstrates, corruption is widespread in many countries, especially in Africa, Asia, Latin America, and Eastern Europe (Transparency International, 2021). In addition, cultural differences factor into how corruption and bribery are dealt with. Project managers must be sensitive and watch out for anything unusual in international projects (Köster, 2010, pp. 117–118).

## Planning International Projects

After a project is decided upon in the initiation phase, the project manager needs to plan it. Many projects run into difficulties due to inadequate planning. Planning addresses the uncertainty surrounding projects and creates a structure. Due to the complexity of international projects, planning is especially difficult. The plan of an international project can never be complete due to too many changes. It needs the flexibility to respond to many different situations. So, it must be structured such that it can be changed at the detail level while higher levels remain unchanged (Rea & Lientz, 2002, pp. 79–80). Nevertheless, it is helpful to have a plan as a starting point (Köster, 2010, p. 128). Due to the scope of this book, we can only address some selected aspects of planning specific to international projects. We will address the impact of culture on planning and specifics of scheduling and resourcing international projects.



**Cultural Impact on Planning** The planning of international projects is impacted by a whole range of cultural differences between the various countries involved. Kathrin Köster identified seven cultural differences affecting planning. We outline three of them here as particularly relevant (see ◘ Fig. 15.6 for a summary). Some cultures, labeled "theoretical," put much effort into planning in much detail, while other cultures ("pragmatic") encourage a learning-by-doing approach and spend

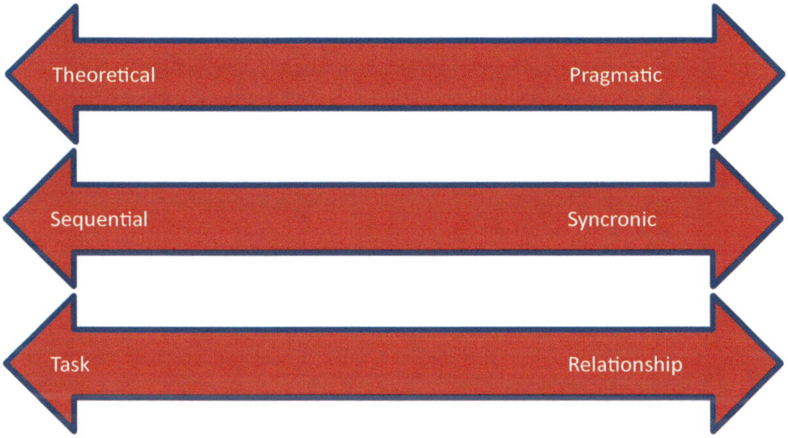


**Fig. 15.6** Cultural impact on planning, own diagram, based on content from (Köster, 2010, pp. 129–130)

less time on planning. As will be explained in more detail in ► Chap. 18, different cultures have different concepts of time. In cultures with a sequential concept of time, people see time as linear and estimate time, cost, and resources, while in cultures with a synchronic understanding of time, planning less strictly assigns activities one after the other in predetermined time slots. Some cultures emphasize completing all tasks on time, scope, and quality, so detailed work breakdown structures are created. In other cultures, at least as much, if not more, emphasis is placed on relationships than on tasks. So, project managers from such cultures would rather use the planning phase for networking to build strong relationships for the project than detailed planning (Köster, 2010, pp. 129–130). However, as we will also outline in ► Chap. 18, one should not blame each different approach to PM on national cultural differences. Individual attitudes, preferences, corporate and functional cultures, and different circumstances in the countries involved also play a role. In countries with less developed infrastructure, like India, or with frequent natural disasters, like the Philippines, people tend to take a more pragmatic attitude to planning and have become used to flexibly adapting while implementing projects.

**Scheduling of International Projects** A key element of project planning is scheduling. Project managers consider the time each activity takes and how the various activities are sequenced to determine the overall time the project will take to complete. Project managers widely use Gantt charts for this purpose. On international projects, specific circumstances need to be considered that impact scheduling: There is an increased risk that team members will be pulled off the project for local work according to local priorities. So, Lientz and Rea suggest discussing this with team members when planning, asking them to indicate what other work will run in parallel so that the project manager can consider this in scheduling (Rea & Lientz, 2002, p. 92). Köster (2010, pp. 139–141) suggests several other things to consider when scheduling international projects:

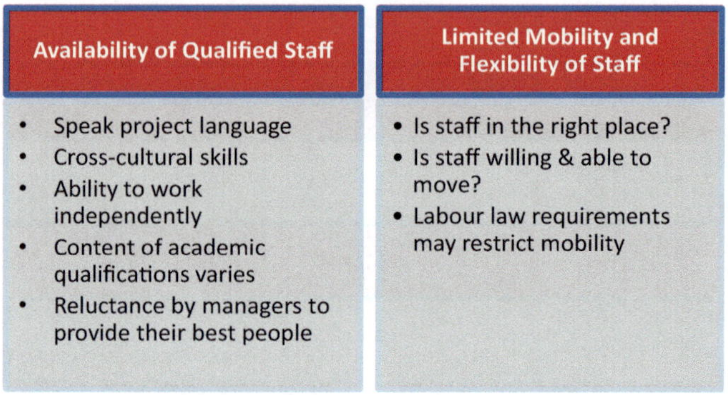


**Fig. 15.7** Issues in resourcing international projects, own diagram, based on content from (Köster, 2010, p. 145) and (Rea & Lientz, 2002, pp. 61–68)

- *Extra time for coordination, communication, and training*: A meeting with the project sponsor may take several days since, in relationship-oriented countries, project managers take much time to deal with stakeholders; more training for team members may be required.
- *Additional time for local adaptations*: Legal, customer, and other local requirements may make adaptations to processes or services necessary.
- *Extra time for team building*: Team building may take three times more than for domestic teams.
- *Consideration of additional public holidays and auspicious days*: Diverse teams face many local public holidays; in countries like China and India, astrology can be significant, so some days are seen as bad for starting a new project.

**Resourcing International Projects** Next, project managers must add resources to the schedules. The project manager needs to ensure that sufficient people are staffed on the project to carry out the tasks that are being planned. Finding the right team members for international projects is more complex than for domestic ones. The project may conflict with local priorities. Local managers may be reluctant to provide their best people for the project. Project staff needs the right language skills and cross-cultural communication skills. They need to be able to work semi-autonomously. Ideally, they have experience with international projects (Rea & Lientz, 2002, pp. 61–68). The fact that someone has a particular degree does not necessarily mean he or she has the proper knowledge for a project, as the content of academic degrees may vary significantly between countries. Limitations to the mobility of qualified staff can also be a challenge. A qualified employee may be identified but unwilling to move to the location where his or her input is needed. Labor law regulations can further restrict the mobility of staff. In many European countries, firms cannot order staff to relocate, and in the European Union, relocation can entail some bureaucracy (Köster, 2010, p. 145). Figure 15.7 summarizes these issues.

## Organizing International Projects

Once project managers have completed planning, the question is which organizational structure to use for the international project team to be most effective and efficient. There are several options (Binder, 2007, pp. 131–135):

- *Centralized project management*: In this structure, all team members worldwide report to the central project manager, making the project team a globally distributed virtual team. With this structure, suitable resources worldwide can be included in the project. However, it requires a mature project manager and methodology. This can be a suitable structure when the size of the team is relatively small, or the coordination is of low complexity; when the dispersion of team members is high; when team members are experienced; and when other forms are not applicable, for example, if no local coordinators are available.
- *Distributed project management with local coordinators*: In this case, the team is divided into local colocated teams, each with its local coordinator. This reduces the need for communication over distance. Local coordinators meet regularly with the project manager. However, finding the right resources in each location might be challenging, and expatriates might need to be used to fill gaps. This structure is particularly suitable when each location can develop a complete component of the outcome or when cultural or geographic proximity to the final customer is essential. Overall, Binder recommends it for most global projects.
- *Distributed project management with functional coordinators*: In this arrangement, there are coordinators, each focusing on a functional area and coordinating a globally distributed functional subteam. It is recommended when the complexity or size of work packages requires various groups of specialized, knowledgeable people in different locations; when the company allocates people to projects by knowledge, not location; when competencies are distributed across multiple locations, and work packages are grouped functionally; and when the project team must include members close to customers or important stakeholders. Most team meetings are virtual. It requires that team members have a good understanding of the global project management methodology.

As an example of the third form, think of a project to integrate two multinational enterprises undergoing a merger. Subteams might each focus on integrating one function, such as marketing, HR, or IT. Each functional coordinator would coordinate the integration of one function across the two legacy companies and across countries.

**Team Size as an Issue on International Projects** International project teams tend to get quite large. This is to represent the various countries and departments involved and have all the required skills and knowledge on the team. However, research found that large teams of 10 and more people are less effective than smaller teams. This applies to all dimensions of teamwork, such as communication, coordination, cohesion, mutual support, effort, and balance of contributions,

**Fig. 15.8** Cultural impact on project organization, own diagram, based on content from (Köster, 2010, pp. 168–169)

as Martin Hoegl found in an analysis of 58 software development projects, confirming similar earlier evidence. The author suggests four ways of keeping project teams small while at the same time ensuring sufficient knowledge and capacity for the successful completion of the project (Hoegl, 2005):

- *Create a multiteam project*: Project managers should divide larger projects into several smaller subprojects, assigned to separate teams rather than one large one (see the distributed structuring options above).
- *Core team* versus *extended team*: Project managers should only include the necessary experts in the core team; others take the role of advisory members, representing their organizational unit.
- *Define team-external contributions*: Project managers should outsource specific contributions with little need for ongoing interaction with the team to team external people.
- *Project phase-specific team members*: Project managers should keep team members on the project team only during phases in which they are needed.

**Culture and Project Organization** Organizational structures provide frames for orientation. They show team members how they fit in the organization, to whom they report, and, as the case may be, who reports to them. So, an organization also meets a need for belonging and esteem, and these needs may vary between cultures. Several cultural differences impact project organization. We will highlight only one here—the differences between hierarchy and equality (see Fig. 15.8). As we will outline in ► Chap. 18 in more detail, some cultures emphasize hierarchy much more than others. Project team members from hierarchical cultures prefer clear pyramid-like hierarchies and centralized decision-making. In contrast, members from more equality oriented cultures prefer a flatter, leaner organizational structure and expect more decentralized decisions (Köster, 2010, pp. 168–169).

**Responsibility in International Projects** Once the project structure has been designed and the tasks have been defined and scheduled, tasks need to be assigned to people or teams responsible for carrying them out in line with the project plan. A frequently used tool is a responsibility matrix, also called RASIC or RACI matrix (Meredith & Shafer, 2022, p. 212). It shows who is (R)esponsible for actually performing a task, needs to (A)pprove it at the management level, (S)upports it, needs to be (I)nformed, or (C)onsulted. See Fig. 15.9 for an example of a RACI matrix. On international project teams, however, responsibility charts can encounter challenges. They have been developed in Western PM practice and rest

| | | Responsibility | | | | | |
|---|---|---|---|---|---|---|---|
| | | Project Office | | | | Field Oper. | |
| **Activity** | **Task** | **Project Manager** | **Contract Admin.** | **Project Eng.** | **Industrial Eng.** | **Field Manager** | |
| Determine need | A1 | A | | C | R | | |
| | A2 | I | A | R | C | | |
| Solicit quotations | B1 | A | I | R | | C | |
| Write apprprop. request | C1 | I | R | A | C | | |
| | C2 | | C | A | R | | |
| | C3 | C | I | R | | I | |
| "<br>"<br>" | "<br>"<br>" | | | | | | |

Legend: R: Responsible, C: Consult, I: Inform, A: Accountable

**Fig. 15.9** Example of a RACI matrix, source: (Meredith & Shafer, 2022, p. 212), permission obtained

on certain Western cultural assumptions not necessarily shared by team members from non-Western cultures: individualism, task orientation, achievement orientation, and a sequential concept of time. Typically, project managers assign responsibilities in RACI matrices to individuals. In more collectivist cultures, people may feel uncomfortable seeing their name assigned as an individual responsible for carrying out a task until a specified timeline. In these cases, it can be helpful to assign tasks to small teams instead. The team would then decide who within the team would carry out which task (Köster, 2010, p. 182).

**The Organizational Context for Projects in Professional Service Firms** In projects with subteams distributed across a firm's international subsidiaries, collaboration can be challenging. The organizational context of the MNE is not always supportive of international collaboration. Priorities and interests of subteams may often differ from those of the central team. Especially professional service firms (PSFs) such as audit or law firms are traditionally networks of national member firms with a high degree of autonomy. Successfully delivering projects for multinational clients across borders is not straightforward. In globally integrated service MNEs, the organizational context can provide essential mechanisms such as authority, policies, procedures, and systems that enable international collaboration. See the following case study that explores the impact of organizational context on international project team collaboration in an audit firm.

## Organizational Context and International Projects in an Audit Firm

A large global audit firm established a regional headquarters that took over ownership of the previously independent member firms in Europe. The new headquarters integrated them into a transnational organization. The cross-border structural integration strengthened the authority of the global project leader over team members across Europe. Policies and procedures were made more consistent and formalized. The firm integrated systems for project staffing, financial project administration, and performance management. But also, the integration strengthened informal mechanisms for collaboration, such as cross-border networking, and the existing culture of collaboration. However, the formal structural integration did not by itself facilitate cross-border collaboration. It provided resources and mechanisms, but they were only drawn upon due to two factors. For one, international client projects required cross-border collaboration as there was interdependency between subteams. So, collaboration was necessary. Moreover, team members had an interest in the project's success. So, collaboration was desired. While the international structural integration facilitated collaboration, the international collaboration worked well even before the integration due to the necessity and willingness of collaboration. In the absence of formal mechanisms, project teams were drawing on informal mechanisms such as international networks, a culture of collaboration, and the informal authority of charismatic project leaders.

Business trip, International project leaders draw on their international network built on business trips, image by Joshua Woroniecki from Pixabay

Source: (Klimkeit, 2013)

## Implementing and Controlling International Projects

Once the previously outlined steps have set the stage, projects get implemented. The implementation will vary broadly, depending on the project's subject matter. From a project management perspective, monitoring and controlling the project is critical. Monitoring means tracing the project's progress against the goals set out in the initiation and planning phase. This is complemented by controlling, that is, verifying progress by evidence (Köster, 2010, p. 190).

**Cultural Impact on Monitoring Projects** Like other phases of IPM, monitoring is impacted by the different cultures involved in a project. We will focus on one factor here: task-oriented versus relationship-oriented cultures. We encountered this difference in the planning phase, so it is unsurprising that it also plays a role in monitoring and controlling project plan implementation. While team members from task-oriented cultures tend to deal well with classic methods of monitoring projects, a project manager from a task-oriented culture may run into difficulties with subteams in more relationship-oriented cultures (see ◘ Fig. 15.10). Without being personally present, it may be challenging to ensure project team members implement tasks as agreed. Ensuring speedy implementation of project tasks remotely by email or phone may not be met with success. Team members may interpret the lack of personal presence by the project manager as a lack of importance for the task at hand. In countries like Brazil, India, or China, project team members may feel neglected and not put in their best effort toward the project. Moreover, issues in implementation might not be detected promptly as team members may be reluctant to report issues, as they can see this as damaging the relationship with the project manager. As a consequence, the project manager may find out too late that the task completion is not on track (Köster, 2010, p. 194).

Due to their complexity, monitoring international projects means considering more indicators than domestic projects. Lim and Mohamed (1999) provide the following example that illustrates this nicely: In Petaling Jaya, in the conurbation of Kuala Lumpur, the capital of Malaysia, a local property developer planned a 1 million square meter shopping mall. Instead of being completed in 12 months as agreed, the contractor took 15 months and claimed a cost of RM146 million—46 million above the agreed RM100 million. This led to a long contractual dispute. The developer and the contractor have suffered losses and considered the project failed. However, the shopping mall has opened and proved very popular with tenants and shoppers. From the point of view of users, it is a great success.

◘ **Fig. 15.10** Cultural impact on project monitoring, own diagram, based on content from (Köster, 2010, p. 193)

| Completion | Satisfaction |
|---|---|
| Time | Convenience |
| Cost | Location |
| Quality | Prestige |
| Performance | Parking |
| Safety | Cost |

◘ **Fig. 15.11** Examples of critical success factors for international projects, own diagram, based on the shopping mall example from (Lim & Mohamed, 1999)

This contradicts the usual project goals measured in PM, such as time and cost. What this shows is that various stakeholders of a project may have very different criteria for success. Therefore, Lim and Mohamed suggest considering two sets of criteria for project success: *project completion* and *stakeholder satisfaction*. Due to the complexity of the stakeholder situation of international projects, this distinction is very relevant in our context. ◘ Figure 15.11, drawing on the shopping mall example of Lim and Mohamed, illustrates examples of success criteria of completion and (stakeholder) satisfaction.

## Learning from International Projects

International projects are ideal forums for developing new knowledge, and indeed, studies show that knowledge is created on international projects and shared throughout MNEs (Adenfelt, 2010). The characteristics of international projects lend themselves to creating knowledge that can then be shared with other members of the MNE beyond the individual project. As international projects are time-bound, complex, diverse, and risky, they provide many opportunities for learning that can be valuable for the MNE, especially for other similar projects (Köster, 2010, p. 307). Think of a management consulting firm that regularly conducts restructuring projects for clients. On the one hand, the client and their situation will vary on each project, thereby enabling learning new knowledge. On the other hand, what has been learned about restructuring on one specific client project, the solutions developed for the client, a successful procedure for managing the project, and what has been learned about the client, its industry, and country environment can be valuable for projects to be conducted later for similar clients with similar problems. Therefore, since the 1990s, multinational PSFs, especially in management consulting and advisory, have developed knowledge management systems to avoid reinventing the wheel and instead leverage knowledge gained on projects for other projects beyond the team members of an individual project. In practice, however, sharing knowledge from projects within the firm encounters many challenges. Frequently, wheels do get reinvented, and mistakes are repeated. Given the scope of this book and chapter, we cannot go into the details of knowledge management. Instead, we will focus on the specifics of learning from international projects, their challenges, and enablers.

**The Cultural Embeddedness of Learning** How knowledge is created and shared and how learning occurs is embedded in culture. In some cultures, seniority plays an important role, so primarily the knowledge of senior members of society would be considered valuable. Younger people would be reluctant to share their knowledge, especially if it contradicts the prevailing knowledge of older generations. Cultural attitudes like this can become barriers to sharing knowledge on international projects. For example, in a development aid project on erosion-control measures in cotton farming in Mali, it was found that, in some villages, farmers refused to apply measures to control soil erosion. An investigation found that the farmers who had been trained as multipliers in their villages were young, and the older farmers did not listen to them (personal conversation). On international teams, sharing knowledge, which essentially requires communication, means cross-cultural communication (Köster, 2010, pp. 313–314). In Chap. 18, we will outline a process of cross-cultural communication that can enhance understanding and, by extension, the sharing of knowledge from international projects.

**Intercultural Communication Barriers to Learning From Projects** Despite the high degree of suitability of international projects for learning, there are many barriers to learning from international projects. We will focus on the barriers Taylor and Osland (2012) identified regarding intercultural communication. They distinguish between factors that are related to the sender, someone who has knowledge to share, and the receiver, with whom the sender wants to share knowledge:

**Sender-Related Factors**

- *Marginality of the sender*: Marginal people reside on the periphery. They have fewer opportunities to be heard because they are not a member of a dominant coalition. In MNEs, people outside of the home country of the MNE are marginal. Others may frequently see their knowledge as less valuable or relevant. This holds especially in smaller subsidiaries in developing countries.
- *Stereotypes concerning the sender*: Stereotypes affect the sender's ability to be heard. If headquarters do not expect to hear solid, innovative ideas from certain nationalities, it may not pay attention, and vice versa. For example, a Japanese subsidiary may be so convinced of US individualism that they discard any recipes for effective teamwork from their US colleagues.
- *Communication style differences*: Different cultural styles of communication can hamper knowledge sharing. An example is the more direct Western communication style versus a more indirect style common in China. Westerners used to direct and explicit communication may find it difficult to see that knowledge transfer occurs when the Chinese communication style is relatively implicit and indirect.
- *Linguistic ability*: A lack of linguistic ability in a corporate language hampers knowledge transfer. The research found that people restrict communication to those who speak their language well, even when they may not be the most knowledgeable.

**Receiver-Related Factors**

- *[Lack of] Cosmopolitanism*: Cosmopolitanism refers to openness to the external environment. If a receiver at headquarters is not interested in the external environment, he or she will likely ignore incoming information. A whole organizational unit may be uninterested in knowledge generated elsewhere and miss potentially valuable input.
- *Satisficing*: People stop learning language and cultural understanding when it seems "good enough" to get on. Managers of MNEs that do not experience negative business results abroad may feel satisfied with their existing foreign language skills and cultural knowledge. For example, imagine a US technical manager in China who came to China when there were few highly qualified engineers. Fifteen years later, he may not realize their skills and knowledge have become much more sophisticated, and the information environment around him has changed.

Besides, the *characteristics of international projects* can make sharing of learning beyond the individual project challenging. They are often fragmented into geographic and functional subprojects, and knowledge management systems may be restricted to a local unit. Project evaluation may focus on narrow standard project management topics and not consider the broader learning from the project. Frequently, project staff operates under strong time pressure. Documenting learning from the project is often not a priority, especially when the next project is already about to commence (Köster, 2010, p. 315).

**Fostering Learning From International Projects** Given the many challenges of learning from international projects, how can learning from projects be fostered? Many things could be mentioned here, but due to the scope of this book, we will focus on three interrelated suggestions by Schindler and Eppler and add a few observations from our research. Schindler and Eppler's (2003) recommendations can be summarized as institutionalizing the debriefing from projects:

- *From single review to continuous project learning*: It is recommended not to wait until the end of a project to gather experiences but to do it continuously throughout the project. This is more relevant, positively impacting motivation and leading to a higher quality of insights gathered.
- *New project roles and tasks*: It is recommended to have a dedicated *debriefer* who facilitates the debriefing process. Besides, this person adds context information to the recorded insights. Research indicates that an independent project outsider is best positioned for this role.
- *Institutionalizing the lessons learned process*: Learning from the project should be integrated into the PM methodology as a standard practice. All project guidelines should enforce project learning as a core element of the project phase model, and project goals should include knowledge-related goals. Project team members need to be educated about its importance. Project managers need to lead by example. Like this, project team members no longer see learning as something "extra" appended to a project but as an element of how they conduct projects.

Based on findings by Klimkeit (2005), we would add that taking the right *approach to sharing knowledge from projects* is essential to motivate this activity. Collecting learning from projects is frequently associated with written documentation of lessons learned and project deliverables in electronic repositories. This is called the *codification* approach to knowledge management. This contrasts with the *personalization* approach that consists of person-to-person sharing of knowledge, whether on an informal, as-needed basis, or in a more structured way in specific meetings dedicated to sharing learning from projects (Hansen et al., 1999). Both theoretical consideration and practical experience indicate that the personalization approach seems much more motivating for staff. When they can share their knowledge in a direct, synchronous conversation with those who receive the knowledge shared, they get immediate positive feedback in the sense that they are perceived as someone holding valuable knowledge. Sharing knowledge verbally in a personal conversation is typically perceived as more motivating than sharing in a written format, such as typing it into a knowledge management system. Besides, as compared to the knowledge shared through a codified approach, when knowledgeable project staff shares knowledge personally, one can ascertain that the context in which it was gained is provided and the receiver applies it in the appropriate context. For example, this can mean the same type of project for a client with the same characteristics. Complementary, the codification approach can be used for some key frequently required pieces of knowledge for which repeated personalized sharing would be inefficient (Klimkeit, 2005).

## Managing Ongoing (Nonproject) International Service Delivery

While arguably most international business services take the form of projects, this does not apply to all. Other services are provided on a more ongoing basis. Think of IT service firms providing ongoing network administration support to their clients, call centers that manage all customer requests from their clients' customers, business travel agencies handling all travel needs of their clients, facility management service firms, contract logistics service providers, and any other services that the firm has outsourced to a third-party provider. Contracts typically run for several years and are frequently renewed for further years. During this time, any agreed services are provided on an ongoing basis.

You will remember how we introduced the service blueprint as a tool to design the delivery of services and how this can be used specifically for international services. Once a firm has designed a service, it will deliver it continuously. The globally coordinated delivery of services is most prominent in IT services, on which most literature focuses. So, this will also be the focus of this section. Initially, IT service providers offshored parts of their delivery to low-cost locations like India. Increasingly, customers required a global delivery of IT services worldwide, also addressing local differences such as language. So, service providers set up *Global Delivery Networks* (GDNs). These consist of a set of centers in various locations worldwide that provide coordinated services to customers globally. While some centers will be in typical offshoring locations, others will be in developed countries where customers are located (onshore) or nearby lower-cost locations, such as Eastern Europe (nearshoring). Not relying on just one location reduces risk and increases flexibility, as centers can shift work between locations. However, it increases complexity and the need for coordination. Such networks for *global IT service delivery* draw on expertise worldwide and benefit from local language skills, cultural understanding, and knowledge (Zelt et al., 2013).

**Global IT Service Delivery**

*Global [IT service] delivery* refers to a model for delivering IT services where the services provider may provide services from either onshore or offshore locations to customers who are globally located (Diao & Northcutt, 2011, p. 690)

Customers agree with the service provider on the services, such as managing servers, networks, applications, and business processes. The required service level, such as response times, is written down in *Service Level Agreements* (SLAs). A key challenge for the service provider is to have an appropriate staffing level to ensure that it can meet the SLAs while keeping costs down to remain profitable. The interaction between customers and service providers typically happens via a *Service Request Management System*. The system routes any request coming in from the customer to the appropriate team based on attributes such as customer, problem, and time of arrival. Routing by arrival times enables a "*follow the sun*" model, where teams are assigned tasks based on time zones to ensure requests are dealt with promptly (Diao & Northcutt, 2011).

Coordinating such a global service delivery can be challenging due to interdependencies between distributed work processes, conflicts of interest between distributed subteams, technologies with localized standards, and uncertainties due to geographically and organizationally distributed information. Firms can address the issue of interdependencies with workflow or business process models. Regarding the technology issue, one can introduce globally standardized formalisms for providing service. IBM's Application Assembly Optimization (AAO) approach is an example; other companies use similar models. A key element of these is the *work packet*, a self-contained unit of work with all the information necessary to carry out the work and defined predecessors and successors. Besides standardization, this takes advantage of modularity. IBM decomposes large service tasks into smaller work packets that can be combined into larger work packets. Such work packets can also be reassigned or delegated to other service providers without a global impact (Varshney & Oppenheim, 2011).



Despite standardization, uncertainty in global service delivery remains. There are mainly three reasons for this:

- *The business environment*: For example, unpredictable changes in market conditions or new technology developments may occur.

- *Communication problems*: Due to ambiguities in communication protocols and the fact that workers may not describe work in identical ways, work packets may be interpreted incorrectly.
- *Errors in the work done*: For example, software is prone to have bugs.

In situations with much uncertainty, like the above, having a very flexible organization can be helpful, with shifting project teams and decentralized networks of relatively autonomous teams (Varshney & Oppenheim, 2011).

For managing global service delivery, especially in IT services, global standards like ITIL and ISO 9000 have been developed. Service providers must define their high-level processes in line with such industry standards. However, the actual work done daily happens at a much lower level. For example, the change management process for dealing with change requests regulates what is done by staff delivering services. However, the typical system administrator deals more with procedures for provisioning a new database or the specific work instructions for fixing a particular problem when installing a particular software. The diverse nature of global environments in which global service delivery happens and the diversity of customers' IT environments poses challenges for the desirable standardization to drive efficiency. Some level of customization is required for the specific needs of customers. So, it is helpful to think of the processes in global service delivery in terms of three levels: high-level processes standardized at the industry level, procedures standardized at the level of the service provider, and work instructions determined at the level of local teams who work on daily service delivery for customers (see ◘ Fig. 15.12). The lower the level, the more descriptions of processes ("process assets") there are to address diverse local contexts, the more users these process descriptions have, and the more decentralized the governance of the level of the process tends to be. For example, at IBM, company-level processes for IT service delivery have been standardized and continuously improved for many years globally. At lower levels, process descriptions have been managed in diverse formats in local repositories. Then, IBM created a single business process management system to bring all of those into one system, create transparency, and enable some

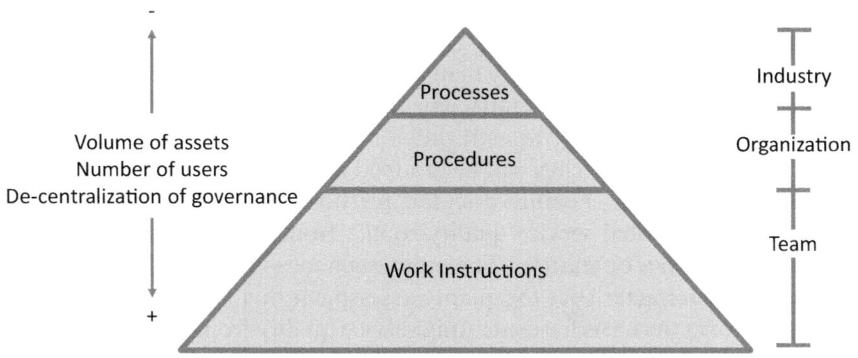


◘ **Fig. 15.12** Process levels in global service delivery, source: (Buco et al., 2011, p. 233), permission obtained

level of standardization where possible. Less variability in processes can lead to improved reliability, attainment of service levels, and reduced costs. It can also reduce human errors and facilitate training staff and subcontractors (Buco et al., 2011).

## Measuring and Ensuring Service Quality in International Services

Customer satisfaction is essential for service firms. Customers that are satisfied with a service can become loyal and regular customers. Keeping a customer as a repeat customer costs much less than acquiring a new one. Typically, the longer a customer relationship is, the more profitable a customer becomes for the business over time (Klimkeit et al., 2021). Studies found that *service quality* impacts customer satisfaction as well as the reputation of the firm, the willingness of customers to recommend the service to others, a positive attitude of customers, and the relationship with the customer.

**Service Quality**

*Service quality* [is] the discrepancy between consumers' perceptions of services offered by a particular firm and their expectations about firms offering such services (Parasuraman et al., 1988, p. 14)

So, when a service meets or exceeds customers' expectations, service quality as perceived by customers is high. A study by Sun and Pang has provided strong evidence that service quality is essential for the competitiveness of global service firms. Service quality is especially relevant in complex and dynamic environments, as is typical for the global environments of many service firms (Sun & Pang, 2017).

## Measuring Service Quality



So, service firms must set up quality management oriented toward customer preferences. A key element of quality management is to measure service quality to enable managers to manage quality. Several different methods have been developed for measuring service quality. They can be grouped into feature-oriented methods and event-oriented methods. Feature-oriented methods assume that the individual assessment of the global service quality results from the interaction of different quality characteristics or features. Therefore, such measurement approaches establish catalogs of characteristics for quality assessment that are as comprehensive as possible and form the basis for evaluating service quality from the customer's point of view. Among the methods of feature-oriented quality measurement are multiattributive and decompositional methods, but also the willingness-to-pay approach.

In the event-oriented methods, perceived service quality is inferred by naming and evaluating relevant customer contact situations during service creation. The approach is based on customer experiences perceived as particularly positive or negative. The event-oriented methods generally lead to qualitative statements, which firms must process further with the help of content analyses. Among the best-known measurement methods of this type are the critical incident technique and praise and complaint analysis (Benkenstein & Zielke, 2004).

Service firms most frequently use feature-oriented methods since they are easy to handle. However, in an international context, they tend to be less suitable. The importance of features varies between countries as quality evaluation is culture-dependent. Even adapted versions can be difficult, as words can have different meanings in different languages. Some expressions cannot be translated as there is no equivalency for them. Rating scales can also differ between countries. For example, a Japanese rating a feature as "very good" might mean the same as a Norwegian rating it as "quite good." Event-based methods, on the other hand, seem highly suitable in the international context. The culture-dependent importance of quality characteristics is considered through the account of the experience. The customer mentions the characteristics important to him or her. However, the translation of the customer accounts can exhibit the same problems. Both methods have advantages and disadvantages. So, a choice needs to be made based on the situation. The question of how much the quality measurement method should be standardized depends on the firm's strategy. If the firm pursues a global strategy, measurement should be largely standardized, while for a multidomestic strategy, a locally adapted measurement is more appropriate. For example, in tourism, the fact that guests come from various countries, have different expectations of quality, and exhibit different behaviors in case of negative quality makes a standardized approach unsuitable in most cases (Benkenstein & Zielke, 2004).

## Culture and Service Quality Management

As briefly mentioned above, culture has an impact on perceived service quality. Several aspects play a role. Customers from different cultures may have different service experiences and therefore derive different satisfaction levels with the service encounter. This is partly because customers from different cultures have different expectations of good service. Depending on how well service providers can adapt to these expectations, the experience with the same service will differ. Therefore, the success of the service encounter depends partially on the ability of service providers to adjust to the cultural expectations of the customer. Service employees may, for example, adapt their communication with the customer, such as tone of voice, facial expression, and vocabulary. Further, culture may influence service evaluations as customers prefer to interact with a service staff similar to themselves. So, customers with different backgrounds may perceive a service differently. In a study of restaurants, Lorenz et al. found that the adjustment of the service encounter related to higher customer satisfaction, fewer complaints, and higher intentions to patronize the operation again. However, it is not enough for service staff to learn the stereotypical cultural behaviors of guests from various cultures. Employees must be sensitive to cultural nuances (Lorenz et al., 2017). As the authors of the study state:

> Insensitive overt adaptations on the part of the service provider might end up veering toward the offensive, increasing the likelihood of a negative service encounter rather than preventing it (Lorenz et al., 2017, p. 489).

This is consistent with a finding of a case study by Kraak and Holmqvist (2017) that in British pubs, outside of the UK, guests perceived staff's use of the English language positively only if they saw it as authentic. That is why the pubs in their study employed mainly native speakers.

In an interesting case study of customer expectations of Western and Asian guests in Hong Kong hotels, Zhang et al. (2015) found that satisfaction, perceived value, and hotel attribute evaluations are significantly higher for Western than Asian travelers. The reason is that service-oriented Asian cultures foster higher expectations of service quality. Especially travelers from Japan, a country known for a high service orientation, rated the hotel service in Hong Kong most differently from those from the UK, Australia, and Canada. In the Asian cultures in the study, where hierarchy is emphasized, service employees perceived to have a low status are expected to provide particularly attentive service (Zhang et al., 2015). However, Liu et al. (2001) found that this does not mean that Asian guests complain more. On the contrary, while ratings may be worse due to cultural reasons, the tendency to actively complain about service is lower.

## Service Excellence in International Services

We stated above that customer satisfaction can lead to loyal customers who become repeat customers. However, today, the relationship between customer satisfaction and loyalty is weakening. Customers are willing to switch to other service providers faster, especially due to the convenient availability of information on alternative providers via the Internet. Simply satisfying customer expectations ceases to be a differentiator since many service providers are able to do so. Sometimes, customer loyalty may be purely calculative—for example, because of low prices—and there is no deeper emotional bond between customers and the provider. Therefore, service providers are increasingly adopting an orientation toward not just satisfying but *delighting* their customers (Klimkeit et al., 2021).

15

**Customer Delight**

[...] *Customer delight* can be understood as an intensely felt pleasure of a customer resulting from expectations being exceeded in a surprising way (Gouthier, 2013, p. 8, translated from the German language)

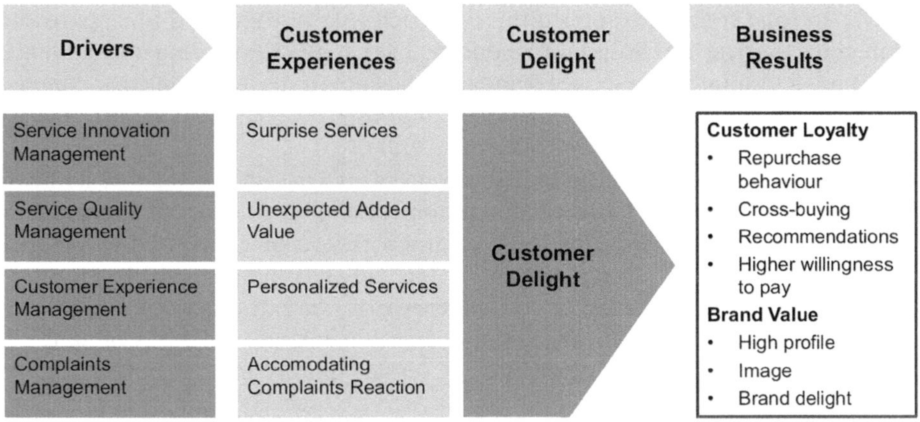


**Fig. 15.13** Model of Service Excellence, adapted from Gouthier (2013): 20, source: (Klimkeit et al., 2021, p. 2) (permission obtained)

How can service providers achieve customer delight? By providing *service excellence*. Service excellence does not just mean providing excellent service. Service excellence is a specific management system that allows companies to not only satisfy customers but also delight them to an appropriate extent (Gouthier, 2013). Several models of service excellence have been proposed (Gouthier et al., 2012). Johnston suggests the following elements: delivering on the service promise given to the customers, providing a personal touch, going the extra mile, and resolving problems well (Johnston, 2004). To facilitate the implementation of service excellence, a standard was developed in Germany (DIN Deutsches Institut für Normung e.V., 2011) that formed the basis for a European standard (Comité Européen de Normalisation, 2016) that was, in turn, the basis for the global standard ISO 23592:2021, published in June 2021 (ISO, 2021). In a book outlining the original standard, Gouthier (2013) describes the following four processes as drivers of a positive customer experience: service innovation management leading to innovative services, service quality management driving exceptionally competent service adding value, customer experience management leading to personalized service and positive surprises for customers, and complaints management implying accommodating responses to complaints. These positive experiences create service excellence, leading to customer loyalty (see Fig. 15.13).

To continuously improve service quality, also customer delight needs to be measured. Since customer delight is not just a higher level of customer satisfaction, a specific approach is required for measuring customer delight and service excellence. Such an approach has been outlined in the context of the standard mentioned above. The measurement approach consists of four steps (DIN Deutsches Institut für Normung e.V., 2011):

- Measurement alignment toward service excellence drivers
- Design of the measurement
- Realization of the measurement
- Evaluation and implementation of measurement findings

Maier Tolic et al. have applied this approach to a case study of Singapore and Malaysia's tourism and hospitality industry. They suggest extending it by adding a first step: determining the service standard a business aims for. Firms that contend with customer satisfaction do not need an additional measurement aligned to drivers of service excellence (Maier Tolic et al., 2021).

However, service excellence and the concept of customer delight at its heart have also been criticized. Critics claim customer delight can wear off as customers get used to extra services. This leads to an escalation of extra services that are increasingly costly and do not pay off in the end (Dixon et al., 2010). Gouthier (2013) responds that there are often inexpensive or free extra service elements that delight customers, such as the friendliness, engagement, and reliability of staff.

However, given that the perception of service quality is often subjective, the question is to what extent a concept such as service excellence can be applied universally. The fact that there is now a global ISO standard for service excellence suggests a part of our answer: Yes, this concept can be globally standardized at the level of the building blocks necessary to provide service excellence. However, the specific details of implementing such a standard will vary across service operations in different countries. For example, what exactly providing an accommodating response to a customer complaint means in practice for a specific complaint will vary from country to country, service industry to service industry, and service provider to service provider (Tang et al., 2021).

The closing case study on Singapore Airlines provides an example of global service quality management.

## Managing Customer Participation in International Services

You may remember that in ▶ Chap. 1, we briefly outlined the customer's role in providing services as a distinctive characteristic of services. In some form, the customer is present in a service encounter, physically or virtually, and needs to play a role. Whether explaining wishes to a hairdresser, providing information to a tax consultant, or physically playing an active role in a touristic activity, customers, to some extent, become coproducers of the service. While customer participation can also pose difficulties in a domestic environment, managing customer participation can be even more challenging in the international provision of services.



### Levels of Customer Participation

The level of customer participation can vary. In some cases, mostly just the presence of the customer is required. Think of air transportation, a stay in a motel, or a meal in a restaurant in consumer services. Sometimes, the customer only needs to provide access to goods or facilities to the service provider, especially in business services such as office cleaning. These services are relatively standardized, and firms provide them independently of individual customer purchases. For example, an airline operates a flight independently of the arrival of one specific individual passenger. These require a low level of customer participation. Other services need a medium or moderate level of participation. In order to create the service, the service provider needs some form of input from the customer. This can be information as in the above case of the tax consultant, an advertising agency in business services, or a haircut in consumer services. The input can also be of a more material form, such as in goods provided by a company to a freight forwarder in business services. While these inputs are needed, the service firm still provides the service itself. To some extent, the customer's inputs lead to the service's customization. Think of the haircut as an example. The haircut also illustrates that in these kinds of services, a service provider only performs the service once a customer purchases it. In services with a high level of customer participation, the customer becomes a cocreator of the service. Think of personal training in a gym in consumer services or an executive management seminar in business services. The customer's participation actively guides the customized service. Without the customer's purchase and participation, the service cannot be provided. The customer's inputs cocreate the outcome of the service. For example, without active participation, the customer of personal training in a gym will not achieve the desired outcome (Zeithaml & Bitner, 2003, p. 353). See ◘ Fig. 15.14 for a summary.

**Self-Service** Increasingly, service providers are asking the customer to increase participation by self-service for tasks previously provided by the service firm. Think of self-check-in at airlines as an example. From the firm's point of view, this lowers cost and increases productivity and competitiveness as it allows an adaptation to customer needs. The customer benefits from lower prices, faster service, flexibility,

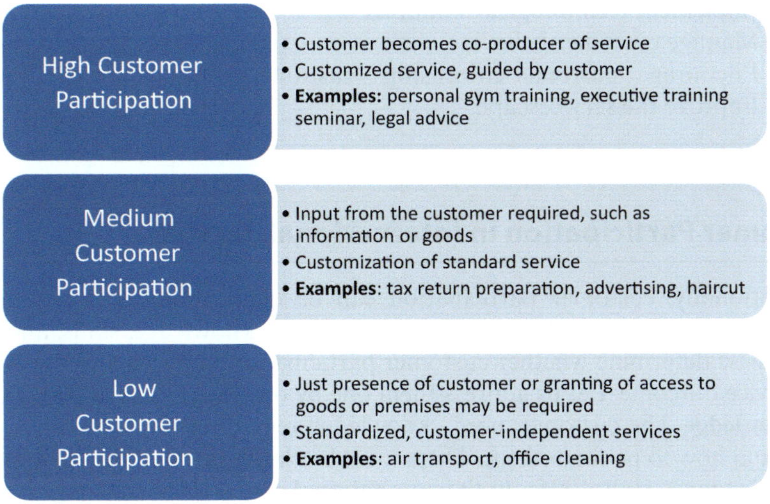


◘ **Fig. 15.14** Levels of customer participation, own diagram, mainly based on content from (Zeithaml & Bitner, 2003, p. 353) and (Lucht & Amshoff, 2009, p. 91)

and adaptation to his or her needs (Scherer et al., 2009). Self-service in restaurants tends to be cheaper and faster than waiting for a server to take orders and deliver the food. Self-check-in typically allows choosing the seats on an airplane.

## Preventing Customer Failure

Since customers play a vital role in the provision of services, a failure to play their role adequately can lead to a poor service experience for the customer and frustrate the service provider at the same time. In a study of service failures and customer performance in many service industries, Tax et al. (2006) identified four root causes of customer failure:

- *People*: Several attributes of customers, such as lack of skills and poor attitude and effort, and the failure to communicate important information to the service provider, can cause failure.
- *Processes*: Also, complex processes and a lack of information on procedures by service providers can lead to customer failure.
- *Servicescapes*: The physical environment, including signs, layout, and ambiance of a service operation, can impact a customer's mood, attitude, and behavior.
- *Technology*: Technology that is not well-designed, functional, and accessible can increase the likelihood of customer failure.

Tax et al. (2006) suggest the following steps to prevent customer failure:

1. Collect diagnostic data on customer failure points.
2. Identify root causes of customer failure (see the list above as guidance).
3. Establish preventive solutions, including five categories:
   (a) Redesign processes.
   (b) Implement technological solutions.
   (c) Manage customer behavior.
   (d) Encourage "customer citizenship" (customers supporting each other).
   (e) Improve the servicescape.



## Customer Participation in International Services

Internationally, customer participation can be challenging as it requires three things that customers may not possess everywhere: knowledge, skills, and willingness. These determine whether customer participation happens and the quality of the service outcome. Let us address them one by one (Scherer et al., 2009).

**Knowledge** The customer needs knowledge regarding the company, customer tasks, and how to perform them. There must be clarity on what the customer needs to do (Lengnick-Hall, 1996). In the international context, the challenge is that customers may have different expectations of the service and, therefore, of their own role in it. So, they may have to deviate from the roles they are used to playing as customers (Donthu & Yoo, 1998; Mattila, 1999). This requires communication with the customer to highlight their expected role and contribution so that the customer can understand them without prior knowledge. For example, a bank needs to explain which information it requires from the customer for a financial investment without technical jargon. Roles, contributions, and limits of customer participation should be communicated consistently and intelligibly (Lengnick-Hall, 1996).

**Skills** Besides knowing what to contribute, the customer must also be able to provide the required contribution. This requires physical, intellectual, emotional, and social skills. A passenger on a train who needs to carry his or her luggage would need physical skills. A customer of a tax consultant, as mentioned above, would need the intellectual skills to provide the required information. Customers need emotional and social skills to behave appropriately toward the service staff. The specific skills required will depend on the service firm. The customer needs skills consistent with the service firm's requirements to participate actively in service creation (Lengnick-Hall, 1996). It might be necessary to educate the customer accordingly.

**Willingness**: The customer must also be motivated to participate in the service creation. Research shows this is essential for integrating the customer into the service process (Lengnick-Hall, 1996). As we have outlined above, cross-cultural service research shows that customer expectations of service vary between cultures (Lorenz et al., 2017; Zhang et al., 2015). This applies equally to expectations of their own contribution (Donthu & Yoo, 1998; Mattila, 1999). As mentioned above, in Asian cultures, customers frequently expect the status difference between customer and service provider to be maintained (Zhang et al., 2015). In Western cultures, customers may often see themselves as partners in the service provision instead. So the customer's participation in the service creation is perceived differently depending on culture (Mattila, 1999).

## ? Review Questions

1. Explain the service blueprint and the options for designing cross-border service delivery while drawing to the blueprint.
2. Describe the specific challenges of managing cross-border projects and critical success factors.
3. Why is scope creep more likely on international projects?
4. Why is managing risk of specific importance and a challenge on international projects?
5. What needs to be considered when scheduling and resourcing international projects?
6. Outline the options for organizing international projects.
7. How is the monitoring of international projects impacted by culture?
8. Why can sharing knowledge from international projects be challenging?
9. Describe challenges and approaches to the ongoing international service delivery.
10. Explain approaches to measuring and managing quality in international service delivery.
11. How do you see the critique of the concept of service excellence?
12. What challenges do service firms encounter when managing the participation of customers in international service delivery?

## Closing Case: Singapore Airlines: Cost-Effective Service Excellence

On October 11, 2018, Singapore Airlines relaunched the world's longest commercial flight, a nonstop flight from the airline's hub at Changi Airport, Singapore, to Newark, just outside New York, being in the air for 18 h and 45 min. The airline had previously offered this flight until 2013, when it temporarily discontinued it for commercial reasons. The new flight uses the new Airbus A350–900 ULR and various comfort upgrades, such as having only premium classes and an upgraded food menu and entertainment offerings. This longest flight is just the latest of the many superlatives and firsts that the Singaporean airline has brought to the world of aviation.

Singapore Airlines (SIA), launched in 1972, has received many accolades for its service quality. By 2010, it had won the Condé Nast Traveler award 21 out of 22 times and three times the Skytrax award over a decade. It is currently rated as one of only 11 five-star airlines by Skytrax. In 2006, *Fortune* magazine ranked it as one of the 20 most admirable companies in the world. At the same time, it is one of the most cost-effective and profitable airlines in the world. SIA's fleet is young (74 months average instead of 160 months common in the industry). This means fewer delays and cancellations due to technical failures, and customers prefer new planes. SIA is frequently the first airline to offer new developments to customers, such as on-demand entertainment systems. The airline is said to offer the most extensive drink menu, the most comfortable seats, and the largest number of cabin crew on a flight. The firm spends 40% on training, 30% on process improvement, and 30% on innovation. Standardization is combined with customization to delight customers. SIA personalizes the customer experience by using its customer relationship management (CRM) system's information on birthdays and preferences. The staff addresses frequent flyers by name, knowing their favorite drinks and magazines. SIA trains staff to attend to small things to delight customers, such as providing vegetarian food even if a guest has not prebooked it. Standardization means that employees know their job so well that it frees mental

Singapore Airlines, image by Mr_Worker from Pixabay

space for sensing customer needs and responding creatively.

Since service quality depends on frontline employees who interact with customers, SIA invests heavily in human resource management (HRM). It starts with stringent selection and recruitment procedures. In selecting staff, SIA looks at many criteria, conducting three rounds of interviews and various tests (including testing how the SIA uniform suits them and attending a tea party). SIA is seen as an attractive employer. From 16,000 applications for cabin crew positions per year, the airline selects only 500–600. SIA attracts first-class university graduates who work hard. The airline makes extensive investments in the training and retraining of staff. It conducts an intensive four-month training course, the longest and most intensive in the industry. These courses include etiquette, cultural sensitivity, conversation, gourmet food, and wine appreciation. Staff learns to interact with people from different countries in different ways. For example, they learn to communicate at eye level with travelers instead of talking down to them. SIA conducts job rotations for a deeper understanding of other departments. This is based on SIA's SOAR ("service over and above the rest") philosophy. The respective training program draws on scenarios of real-life experiences, often delivered by senior crew members, which makes it credible. Building high-performance service delivery teams is another HRM priority. This aims to create "esprit de corps" among cabin crew. Cabin crew teams are created and fly together as much as possible to build camaraderie. Frontline staff is empowered to make decisions to control quality. This includes that staff also get precise information about the boundaries of their authority. For example, they can raise the baggage allowance of a traveler from 20 kg to 25 kg or 50 kg if they feel this is right and justifiable. The staff gets motivated through comprehensive reward and recognition schemes. Depending on performance, rewards can include interesting job content, share options, and variable pay. These are highly aligned with desired behaviors. International accolades received by the airline, like "best airline," "best cabin crew service," and "Asia's most admired company" also motivate staff further.

SIA's customer service is symbolized by the iconic "Singapore Girl," the archetypical flight attendant clad in the famous *sarong kebaya*. She embodies qualities such as femininity, grace, warmth, and a gentle demeanor. At the same time, SIA controls costs strictly and communicates this to the staff at every opportunity. The rule is that everything that touches the customer must be premium, while there is rigorous cost control for what is behind the scenes. SIA's cost structure is even lower than that of many European low-cost airlines.

**Questions**

1. How would you measure the service quality of SIA?
2. How does culture factor in managing service quality at SIA?
3. What challenges do you see for cabin crew adapting service to travelers?
4. How does SIA provide service excellence?
5. Drawing on the SIA case, what is your opinion on whether service excellence can be applied universally?

Sources: (Chong, 2007; Economist, 2018; Heracleous & Wirtz, 2010; Skytrax, 2022; Wirtz et al., 2008)

**Summary**

This chapter

- Defined the service blueprint as "Service blueprints map customer, employee, and service-system interactions. They show the full customer journey from service initiation to final delivery of the desired benefit" and explained its elements.
- Explained how a service blueprint can be used to design the international delivery of services.
- Defined projects as "An endeavor in which human, material and financial resources are organized in a novel way to undertake a unique scope of work, of given specifications, within constraints of cost and time, so as to achieve beneficial change defined by quantitative and qualitative objectives" and characterized them as limited and unique.
- Defined project management as "The application of processes, methods, skills, knowledge, and experience to achieve specific project objectives according to the project acceptance criteria within agreed parameters."
- Outlined characteristics and critical success factors of international projects.
- Explained international aspects of the project management cycle: defining international projects, managing risk, planning, organizing, implementing, and controlling international projects, and learning from international projects.
- Outlined the ongoing international delivery of services, focusing on IT services, defining global IT service delivery as "A model for delivering IT services where the services provider may provide services from either onshore or offshore locations to customers who are globally located."
- Defined service quality as the "discrepancy between consumers' perceptions of services offered by a particular firm and their expectations about firms offering such services," ways of managing it, and the impact of culture on perceived service quality.
- Defined customer delight as "Intensely felt pleasure of a customer resulting from expectations being exceeded in a surprising way" and outlined service excellence as a concept for achieving customer delight.
- Outlined customer participation in services and three things required of customers that can pose challenges in the international context: knowledge, skills, and willingness.




## References


Aarseth, W., Rolstadås, A., & Andersen, B. (2013). Managing organizational challenges in global projects. *International Journal of Managing Projects in Business, 7*(1), 103–132.

Adenfelt, M. (2010). Exploring the performance of transnational projects: Shared knowledge, coordination and communication. *International Journal of Project Management, 28*(6), 529–538.

Association for Project Management APM. (2019). *What is project management? Definition from APM body of knowledge 7th edition*. Retrieved from https://www.apm.org.uk/resources/what-is-project-management/

Benkenstein, M., & Zielke, K. (2004). Qualitätsmessung und Qualitätsmanagement international tätiger Dienstleistungsunternehmen: dargestellt am Beispiel touristischer Dienstleistungen. In

M. A. Gardini & H. D. Dahlhoff (Eds.), *Management internationaler Dienstleistungen: Kontext—Konzepte—Erfahrungen* (1st ed., pp. 241–262). Gabler.

Binder, J. C. (2007). *Global project management: Communication, collaboration and management across borders*. Gower Publishing, Ltd.

Boussebaa, M., & Morgan, G. (2015). Internationalization of professional service firms. In L. Empson, D. Muzio, J. Broschak, & B. Hinings (Eds.), *The Oxford handbook of professional service firms* (pp. 71–91). Oxford University Press.

Buco, M., Jamjoom, H., Parsons, T., & Schorno, S. (2011). Managing process assets in a global IT service delivery environment. In M. Z. Muehlen & J. Su (Eds.), *Business process management workshops* (pp. 232–237). Springer.

Chong, M. (2007). The role of internal communication and training in infusing corporate values and delivering brand promise: Singapore Airlines' experience. *Corporate Reputation Review, 10*(3), 201–212.

Comité Européen de Normalisation. (2016). *Service excellence—Creating outstanding customer experiences through service excellence (CEN/TS 16880:2016-04-01)*. Beuth.

Diao, Y., & Northcutt, D. (2011). Modeling a complex global service delivery system. In IEEE (Ed.), *Proceedings of the 2011 winter simulation conference (WSC)* (pp. 690–702).

DIN Deutsches Institut für Normung e.V. (2011). *Erzielung von Kundenbegeisterung durch Service Excellence (DIN SPEC 77224)*. Beuth.

Dixon, M., Freeman, K., & Toman, N. (2010). Stop trying to delight your customers. *Harvard Business Rev*, (7/8), 116–122.

Donthu, N., & Yoo, B. (1998). Cultural influences on service quality expectations. *Journal of Service Research, 1*(2), 178–186.

Drechsler, A., & Breth, S. (2019). How to go global: A transformative process model for the transition towards globally distributed software development projects. *International Journal of Project Management, 37*(8), 941–955.

Economist. (2018, October 11). Singapore Airlines launches the world's longest flight, 2018.

Fleurop-Interflora. (n.d.). *About us*. Retrieved from https://fleurop.com/en/about-us

Fließ, S. (2004). Länderübergreifende Organisation von Dienstleistungsprozessen. In M. A. Gardini & H. D. Dahlhoff (Eds.), *Management internationaler Dienstleistungen: Kontext—Konzepte—Erfahrungen* (1st ed., pp. 185–214). Gabler.

Fließ, S., & Kleinaltenkamp, M. (2004). Blueprinting the service company: Managing service processes efficiently. *Journal of Business Research, 57*(4), 392–404.

Fossum, K. R., Binder, J. C., Madsen, T. K., Aarseth, W., & Andersen, B. (2019). Success factors in global project management: A study of practices in organizational support and the effects on cost and schedule. *International Journal of Managing Projects in Business, 13*(1), 128–152.

Gouthier, M. (2013). *Kundenbegeisterung durch Service Excellence: Erläuterungen zur DIN SPEC 77224 und Best-Practices*. Beuth.

Gouthier, M., Giese, A., & Bartl, C. (2012). Service excellence models: A critical discussion and comparison. *Managing Service Quality: An International Journal, 22*(5), 447–464.

Greenwood, R., Morris, T., Fairclough, S., & Boussebaa, M. (2010). The organizational design of transnational professional service firms. *Organizational Dynamics, 39*(2), 173–183.

Hansen, M. T., Nohria, N., & Tierney, T. (1999). What's your strategy for managing knowledge? *Harvard Business Review, 77*(2), 106–116.

Heracleous, L., & Wirtz, J. (2010). Singapore Airlines' balancing act. *Harvard Business Review, 88*(7/8), 145–149.

Hoegl, M. (2005). Smaller teams–better teamwork: How to keep project teams small. *Business Horizons, 48*(3), 209–214.

ISO. (2021). *ISO 23592:2021 Service excellence: Principles and model*. Retrieved from https://www.iso.org/standard/76358.html

Johnston, R. (2004). Towards a better understanding of service excellence. *Managing Service Quality: An International Journal, 14*(2/3), 129–133.

Kingman-Brundage, J. (1991). Technology, design and service quality. *International Journal of Service Industry Management, 2*(3), 47–59.

Klimkeit, D. (2005). Networks, forms of exchange and motivations: Insights from social anthropology for the issue of knowledge sharing. In K.-D. Althoff, A. Dengel, R. Bergmann, M. Nick, & T. Roth-Berghofer (Eds.), *Professional knowledge management: Third biennial conference, WM 2005, Kaiserslautern, Germany, April 10–13, 2005,* Revised Selected Papers. Springer.

Klimkeit, D. (2013). Organizational context and collaboration on international projects: The case of a professional service firm. *International Journal of Project Management, 31*(3), 366–377.

Klimkeit, D., Tang, C. M., & Thirumaran, K. (2021). Introduction: Service excellence in Asian tourism and hospitality. In K. Thirumaran, D. Klimkeit, & C. M. Tang (Eds.), *Service excellence in tourism and hospitality* (pp. 1–7). Springer.

Köster, K. (2010). International Project Management. Sage Publications.

Kraak, J. M., & Holmqvist, J. (2017). The authentic service employee: Service employees' language use for authentic service experiences. *Journal of Business Research, 72*, 199–209.

Lengnick-Hall, C. A. (1996). Customer contributions to quality: A different view of the customer-oriented firm. *Academy of Management Review, 21*(3), 791–824.

Lim, C. S., & Mohamed, M. Z. (1999). Criteria of project success: An exploratory re-examination. *International Journal of Project Management, 17*(4), 243–248.

Liu, B. S.-C., Furrer, O., & Sudharshan, D. (2001). The relationships between culture and behavioral intentions toward services. *Journal of Service Research, 4*(2), 118–129.

Lorenz, M. P., Ramsey, J. R., Tariq, A., & Morrell, D. L. (2017). Service excellence in the light of cultural diversity: The impact of metacognitive cultural intelligence. *Journal of Service Theory and Practice, 27*, 475–495.

Lucht, T., & Amshoff, B. (2009). Die Internationalisierung der Geschäftstätigkeit der ACONSITE AG: Kundenintegration, Konfiguration und Koordination bei einer international tätigen Unternehmensberatung. In D. Holtbrügge, H. H. Holzmüller, & F. Wangenheim (Eds.), *Management internationaler Dienstleistungen mit 3K: Konfiguration—Koordination - Kundenintegration* (pp. 81–110). Gabler.

Maier Tolic, G., Klimkeit, D., & Dingeldey, A. (2021). Measuring customer delight in tourism and hospitality operations: Findings from Singapore and Malaysia. In K. Thirumaran, D. Klimkeit, & C. M. Tang (Eds.), *Service excellence in tourism and hospitality: Insights from Asia* (pp. 57–71). Springer International Publishing.

Mattila, A. S. (1999). The role of culture in the service evaluation process. *Journal of Service Research, 1*(3), 250–261.

Meredith, J. R., & Shafer, S. M. (2022). *Project management: A strategic managerial approach* (11th ed.). Wiley.

Parasuraman, A., Zeithaml, V. A., & Berry, L. (1988). SERVQUAL: A multiple-item scale for measuring consumer perceptions of service quality. *Journal of Retailing, 64*(1), 12–40.

Rea, K., & Lientz, B. (2002). *International project management*. Routledge.

Scherer, A., Zimmer, M., & von Wangenheim, F. (2009). Kundenintegration bei internationalen Dienstleistungen: Theoretische Einordnung, Motive und Herausforderungen. In D. Holtbrügge, H. H. Holzmüller, & F. Wangenheim (Eds.), *Management internationaler Dienstleistungen mit 3K: Konfiguration—Koordination—Kundenintegration* (pp. 57–80). Gabler.

15

Schindler, M., & Eppler, M. J. (2003). Harvesting project knowledge: A review of project learning methods and success factors. *International Journal of Project Management, 21*(3), 219–228.

Shostack, G. L. (1982). How to design a service. *European Journal of Marketing, 16*(1), 49–63.

Shostack, G. L. (1984). Designing services that deliver. *Harvard Business Review, 62*(1), 133–139.

Skytrax. (2022). *Singapore Airlines*. Retrieved from https://skytraxratings.com/airlines/singapore-airlines-rating

Sun, W., & Pang, J. (2017). Service quality and global competitiveness: Evidence from global service firms. *Journal of Service Theory and Practice, 27*(6), 1058–1080.

Sydow, J., Lindkvist, L., & DeFillippi, R. (2004). Project-based organizations, embeddedness and repositories of knowledge: Editorial. *Organization Studies, 25*(9), 1475–1489.

Tang, C. M., Klimkeit, D., & Thirumaran, K. (2021). Conclusion: The future of service excellence in Asia. In *Service excellence in tourism and hospitality* (pp. 217–220). Springer.

Taylor, S., & Osland, J. S. (2012). The impact of intercultural communication on global organizational learning. In M. Easterby-Smith & M. A. Lyles (Eds.), Handbook of organizational learning and knowledge management (pp. 579–604). John Wiley & Sons, Inc.

Tax, S. S., Colgate, M., & Bowen, D. E. (2006). How to prevent your customers from failing. *MIT Sloan Management Review, 47*(3), 30–38.

Transparency International. (2021). *Corruption perceptions index 2021*. Retrieved from https://www.transparency.org/en/cpi/2021

Transparency International. (2022). *What is corruption?* Retrieved from https://www.transparency.org/en/what-is-corruption.

Turner, J. R. (2016). A handbook for project management practitioners. In J. R. Turner (Ed.), *Gower handbook of project management* (4th ed., pp. 1–19). Routledge.

Varshney, L. R., & Oppenheim, D. V. (2011). Coordinating global service delivery in the presence of uncertainty. In R. Verma (Chair), *Proceedings of the 12th international research symposium on service excellence in management (QUIS12)*.

Whitley, R. (2006). Project-based firms: New organizational form or variations on a theme? *Industrial and Corporate Change, 15*(1), 77–99.

Wirtz, J., Heracleous, L., & Pangarkar, N. (2008). Managing human resources for service excellence and cost effectiveness at Singapore airlines. *Managing Service Quality: An International Journal, 18*(1), 4–19.

Zeithaml, V. A., & Bitner, M. J. (2003). *Services marketing: Integrating customer focus across the firm* (3rd ed.). McGraw-Hill Irwin.

Zelt, S., Uebernickel, F., & Brenner, W. (2013). Managing global IT delivery networks: A literature review from the supplier's perspective. In IEEE (Ed.), *46th Hawaii international conference on system sciences* (pp. 294–303).

Zhang, Z., Li, H., & Law, R. (2015). Differences and similarities in perceptions of hotel experience: The role of national cultures. *Journal of Travel & Tourism Marketing, 32*(sup1), S2–S14.

## Further Reading

Gouthier, M., Giese, A., & Bartl, C. (2012). Service excellence models: A critical discussion and comparison. *Managing Service Quality: An International Journal, 22*(5), 447–464 provides an outline of models of service excellence.

Köster, K. (2010). *International project management*. Sage Publications provides an excellent overview of international project management.

# Global Financial Management

## Contents




D. Klimkeit et al., *International Management in Service Firms*, Classroom Companion: Business,
https://doi.org/10.1007/978-3-031-50345-0_16

**Learning Outcomes**

After completing this chapter, you should be able to:

- Outline different ways to manage foreign exchange exposures
- Understand why MNEs in countries with illiquid and segmented capital markets can reduce their cost of capital by financing in more liquid and developed markets
- Comprehend international capital budgeting from different perspectives
- Evaluate different cash management systems and examine how they affect the cost of cash of an MNE
- Master the nature of transfer pricing and outline different methods to estimate the arm's length price

## Introduction

The first section of this chapter introduces typical approaches to managing transactions and operating exposures faced by multinational service firms. Compared to MNEs selling goods, service firms generally need less time to provide service and collect customer payments. As a result, their transaction exposure is minor, and their foreign exchange risk management focuses more on operating exposure. The second section introduces the cost of capital and illustrates the benefits of reducing the cost of capital for MNEs to raise capital in more liquid and advanced markets. The third section demonstrates the complexities of multinational capital budgeting using two approaches—from the parent firm's and foreign subsidiary's perspectives—for a hypothetical MNE. Subsequently, the fourth section focuses on the cash management of MNEs and shows different cash management systems. In particular, the benefits of a centralized cash management system are highlighted. The last section explains transfer pricing and summarizes the OECD Guidelines to obtain the arm's length price of the transaction between related companies. We conclude this chapter with a case on Google.

Clock money growth, image by Nattanan Kanchanaprat from Pixabay

**Opening Case: How Does A. P. Moller-Maersk Group Manage Foreign Exchange Exposure?**

Let us start with Maersk, the company we met with in the closing case of ► Chap. 5. As a global company providing ocean and inland freight transportation and associated services, Maersk's financial performance is subject to uncertainties related to bunker fuel prices and freight rates affected by foreign exchange rates. Maersk's currency risk relates to the fact that while income from Ocean activities is denominated mainly in US dollar (USD), the related expenses are incurred in both USD and a wide range of other currencies such as euro (EUR), Danish krone (DKK), Hong Kong dollar (HKD), Singapore dollar (SGD), and Canadian dollar (CAD). USD is also the primary financing currency because it is the currency of Maersk's net income.

The company's sensitivity to an increase in the USD exchange rate of 10% against all other significant currencies to which Maersk was exposed in 2021 is estimated to have the following impact:

| (in millions of USD) | | |
|---|---|---|
| **Currency sensitivity for financial instruments** | **Profit before tax** | **Equity before tax** |
| EUR | −108 | −141 |
| CNY | −88 | −88 |
| Other | −179 | −259 |
| **Total** | **−375** | **−488** |

For instance, when the euro appreciates 10% against the US dollar, Maersk's euro profit will become USD −108 million before tax. The primary purpose of hedging Maersk's currency risk is to hedge the USD value of its net cash flow and reduce fluctuations in its profit. Maersk uses various financial derivatives to hedge these risks, including forwards, options, and cross-currency swaps. The critical aspects of the currency hedging policy are:

- Net cash flows in significant currencies other than USD are hedged using a layered model with a 12-month horizon.
- Significant capital commitments or divestments in currencies other than USD are hedged.
- Most non-USD debt is hedged, depending on the asset-liability match and the currency of the generated cash flow.

Currency derivatives hedge future revenue, operating costs, and investments/divestments and are recognized on an ongoing basis in the income statement and the cost of property, plant, and equipment, respectively. The volume of use of currency derivatives to hedge operating cash flows and investments in foreign currencies in 2021 is shown below (values in millions):

| Main currencies hedged | Nominal amount of derivative |
|---|---|
| EUR | 876 |
| DKK | 282 |
| HKD | 179 |
| Other currencies | 849 |

Sources: (Maersk, 2022)

**Questions**

1. Why does Maersk need to hedge foreign exchange risk?
2. What tools have been used by Maersk to hedge its foreign exchange exposure?

16

## Management of Foreign Exchange Exposure

In ► Chap. 5, we classify the exposures of multinational service firms to exchange rates into transaction exposure, operating exposure, and translation exposure. Transaction exposure is the sensitivity of the domestic currency values of a firm's contractual cash flows (e.g., accounts receivable or payable) denominated in foreign currencies to unexpected changes in exchange rates. Operating exposure gauges how the present value of a firm changes with unexpected exchange rate shocks. It is a much broader concept than transaction exposure since it focuses on a company's future operating cash flows and is affected by various strategies of the firm and its competitors. Finally, translation exposure measures the extent to which changes in exchange rates affect an MNE's consolidated financial statements. In the opening case, Maersk faces a vast amount of foreign exchange risk because of the mismatch of currencies in its income and expenses. An expected change in the value of the US dollar causes a considerable variation in Maersk's cash flows and profits. Therefore, the firm needs to hedge the foreign exchange risk to reduce its cash flow volatilities and thus enhance the firm value. This chapter introduces strategies to manage different types of foreign exchange exposures.

## Management of Transaction Exposures

It is helpful to utilize a specific business situation where a firm faces transaction exposure to illustrate the control of transaction exposure. For example, suppose that Singapore Airlines signed a contract today to import aircraft spare parts from Airbus and was billed €five million payable in one year. The current interest rate and foreign exchange rates are as below:

- The Singapore interest rate: 3.50% per annum
- The interest rate in the euro area: 1.25% per annum
- The spot exchange rate: S$1.40/€
- The 1-year forward exchange rate: S$1.45/€

When Singapore Airlines makes the payment in one year, it must convert the Singapore dollar to euro. However, the actual exchange rate between the two currencies is unknown now. Therefore, Singapore Airlines does not know the exact purchase cost in Singapore dollars and faces transaction exposure. If the euro appreciates a lot in the year, Singapore Airlines would need more Singapore dollars to pay €five million. Fortunately, there are various techniques and strategies for Singapore Airlines to manage this transaction exposure.

### Strategy 1: Money Market Hedge

A money market hedge uses borrowing or lending transactions in the domestic and foreign money markets to lock in the home currency value of a foreign currency transaction. Its basic principle is the Interest Rate Parity theory, which states that the interest rate differential between two countries determines the differential between the forward and spot exchange rates (Aliber, 1973, p. 1451). Generally, a firm can reduce the foreign exchange risk of payables (receivables) by lending (borrowing) in foreign currency. For example, to eliminate the exchange exposure of foreign purchases, Singapore Airlines could convert Singapore dollars to euros now and then lend euros for one year. On the maturity date of the euro investment, which should also be the payment date of the bill, Singapore Airlines would use the proceeds from the euro investment to pay off its euro bill. The initial amount of the

**Table 16.1** Cash flows of a money market hedge, own table

| Transaction | Cash flow at present | Cash flow at maturity |
|---|---|---|
| 1. Buy euro spot with Singapore dollar | €4,938,271.60 | |
| | –S$6,913,580.25 | |
| 2. Lend euro | –€4,938,271.60 | €5,000,000.00 |
| 3. Pay the euro bill | | –€5,000,000.00 |
| Net cash flow | –S$ 6,913,580.25 | 0.00 |

Singapore dollar for this money market hedge depends on the current exchange rate and the euro's interest rate.

Table 16.1 exhibits the cash flows of the money market hedging strategy Singapore Airlines may adopt. Since the firm wants to use the euro investment to pay off €five million in one year, the future value of the euro investment must be an exact €five million. Based on the interest rate of the euro, Singapore Airlines needs to invest €five million/(1 + 1.25%) = €4,938,271.60 now. The equivalent amount in Singapore dollars is €4,938,271.60 × S$1.40/€ = S$6,913,580.25. One year later, ignoring the transaction cost, the sum of the euro principal (€4,938,271.60) and interest (€4,938,271.60 × 1.25% = €61,728.40) exactly offsets the bill of €five million. Because all the information (i.e., interest rates and exchange rates) is known now, the uncertainty of this money market hedge is almost zero. Table 16.1 also shows that the net cash flow is zero at maturity, indicating that this hedging is complete. Regardless of the actual exchange rate one year later, the Singapore dollar purchase cost is always S$6,913,580.25. With the current interest rate in Singapore, it is equivalent to S$6,913,580.25 × (1 + 3.5%) = S$7,155,555.56 one year later when the euro bill is due.

### Strategy 2: Forward Market Hedge

A forward market hedge in this context involves using foreign currency forward contracts to minimize transaction exposure. As explained in ► Chap. 5, a foreign currency forward contract is a formal agreement between two parties to exchange currencies at a future date at a pre-determined exchange rate. The party that agrees to buy the underlying currency is said to take a long position, while the party selling the currency takes a short position. Each currency forward contract has at least four main components: (1) the underlying currency, (2) the expiration or maturity date when the underlying currency is delivered and the deliverer is paid, (3) the size of the contract showing the specific amount of the underlying currency to be bought and sold, and (4) the forward exchange rate that will be used in the transaction on the expiration date. The value of currency forwards depends on the difference between the spot and the forward exchange rates on the expiration date. Figure 16.1 illustrates the payoff diagram of a currency forward contract to the long and short parties.

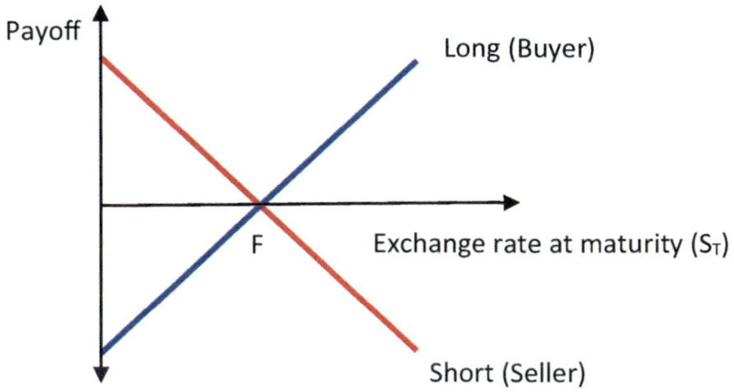


**Fig. 16.1** Payoff diagram of a currency forward contract, own diagram

In the diagram, the horizontal axis, $S_{T,}$ represents the spot exchange rate at maturity, and F is the forward exchange rate determined when the forward contract is signed. The vertical axis is the payoff in the monetary amount of the forward contract. The blue line shows the profit of the forward contract to the long party, which is increasing with the spot exchange rate at maturity, $S_T$. Ignoring possible transaction costs, the long party has a positive payoff at maturity if $S_T > F$, since she can buy the underlying currency at the pre-determined lower exchanger rate, F. On the other hand, if $S_T < F$, she will suffer a loss from the forward contract because she needs to pay a higher exchange rate to buy the currency. The payoff of the forward contract to the short party, represented in the red line, is exactly opposite to that of the long party. The short party gains when $S_T < F$ since she can sell the currency at a higher price and loses otherwise. When $S_T = F$, both the long and short parties have a zero payoff from the forward contract. In summary, a forward transaction is a zero-sum game in which one party's gain is equivalent to the other party's loss. Put differently, a forward contract has the following properties:

- The value of the contact to the long party: $S_T - F$
- The value of the contact to the short party: $F - S_T$

Generally speaking, one should take a long (short) position in the forward contract if one intends to hedge the exposure of accounts payable (receivable) in that currency.

Now let us revisit the example of Singapore Airlines. To conduct a forward market hedge for the account payable of €five million, Singapore Airlines can take a long position in a forward contract with a bank to buy €five million using Singapore dollars in one year at the current 1-year forward rate of S$1.45/€. In theory, there is no upfront fee for forwards, although, in practice, banks may require an initial deposit (e.g., 5% of the notional amount of the forward contract) to be paid upfront to reduce the default risk. Ignoring such fees, Singapore Airlines needs to pay the bank S$7,250,000 and get €five million in return at the agreed date, which is then used to pay its euro bill. The Singapore dollar cost is fixed regardless of the future exchange rate.

Notably, the goal of a forward market hedge is to reduce uncertainty, not to maximize profit. By locking in the future exchange rate, Singapore Airlines can

**Table 16.2** Singapore dollar costs of the €five million under an unhedged position versus a forward hedge, own table

| Spot exchange rate at maturity ($S_T$) | Singapore dollar cost of the €five million | | Gain/loss from hedge |
|---|---|---|---|
| | Unhedged position | Forward Hedge | |
| S$1.35/€ | S$6,750,000 | S$7,250,000 | –S$500,000 |
| S$1.40/€ | S$7,000,000 | S$7,250,001 | –S$250,000 |
| S$1.45/€ | S$7,250,000 | S$7,250,002 | 0 |
| S$1.50/€ | S$7,500,000 | S$7,250,003 | S$250,000 |
| S$1.55/€ | S$7,750,000 | S$7,250,004 | S$500,000 |

completely remove the foreign exchange exposure associated with its account payable. However, it may also pay more Singapore dollars for this euro bill compared to the cost without the forward hedge. Table 16.2 lists the Singapore dollar costs of the €five million of the two strategies, no hedge versus a forward hedge, at several possible exchange rates one year later. The forward hedge is advantageous to Singapore Airlines only if the spot exchange rate one year later is above the current 1-year forward rate. When the alternative (i.e., $S_T <$ S$1.45/€) happens, the unhedged strategy is preferred since the actual Singapore dollar cost of the euro bill is lower.

The above analysis is essentially ex-post since the future spot exchange rate is unknown beforehand. Therefore, the financial manager of Singapore Airlines needs to decide whether to hedge before the payment is due. This decision depends on what future exchange rate the financial manager expects. If she believes it to be lower than S$1.45/€, she will choose not to hedge. On the other hand, if she expects a future exchange rate much higher than S$1.45/€, she will prefer a forward hedge.

## Strategy 3: Options Market Hedge

**Options**

In the financial market, options are financial contracts that give the holder or the buyer the right, but not the obligation, to buy or sell a given quantity of an underlying asset at a pre-determined price—known as the strike price—at some time in the future.

16

There are two basic types of options: call options, which give the holder/buyer the right to *buy* the underlying asset at the strike price, and put options, which provide the holder/buyer the right to *sell* the underlying asset at the strike price. Investors in the options market can either have long or short positions. Those who take a long position to buy options are called holders, and those who take a short position to sell options are termed writers. Holders have the right but not the obligation to trade, and their decision depends on the difference between the spot price of the underlying asset and the strike price. Holders need to pay the price, termed as pre-

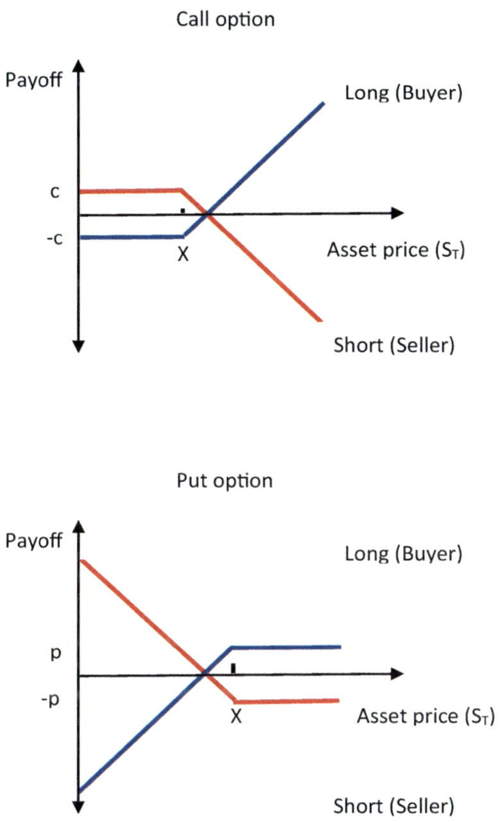


**Fig. 16.2** Payoff diagram of currency options, own diagram

mium, beforehand to buy the right from the writers of options. Therefore, the writer must trade with the holder if the holder decides to exercise her options. Alternatively, if the holder does not exercise her options, the writer collects the option premium but does not need to do anything. Options can also be classified into different styles. American options are option contracts that can be exercised any time before expiry, while European options can only be exercised at expiry.

Figure 16.2 illustrates the payoff patterns of European options. The option premium is represented by c for the call option and p for the put option. X is the strike price, and $S_T$ is the underlying asset's price at maturity. For the call option, the holder will exercise the option and use X to buy the underlying asset at expiry only if the asset's price is above the exercise price, that is, $S_T > X$. In this case, her gross profit is $S_T - X$, and her net profit is $S_T - X - c$. When $S_T \leq X$, she will not exercise the call option, and her gross and net profits are 0 and $-c$, respectively. On the other hand, the writer of the call option who sells the option to the holder collects the call premium c when $S_T \leq X$, and her profit is $X - S_T + c$ when the holder decides to exercise the option (i.e., $S_T > X$). When $S_T$ equals the sum of X and c, the writer and holder of the call option have a zero net profit. For the put option, the

**Table 16.3** Net profits of the holder and writer of options, own table

| Scenarios | Call option | | Put option | |
|---|---|---|---|---|
| | Holder | Writer | Holder | Writer |
| The spot price at maturity is above the strike price ($S_T > X$) | $S_T - X - c$ | $X - S_T + c$ | $-p$ | p |
| The spot price at maturity equals the strike price ($S_T = X$) | $-c$ | c | $-p$ | p |
| The spot price at maturity is below the strike price ($S_T < X$) | $-c$ | c | $X - S_T - p$ | $S_T - X + p$ |

holder will exercise the option and use X to sell the underlying asset at expiry only if the asset's price is below the exercise price, $S_T < X$. In this case, her gross profit is $X - S_{T,}$ and her net profit is $X - S_T - p$. When $S_T$ increases above X, she will not exercise the put option, and her gross and net profits are 0 and −p, respectively. On the other hand, the writer of the put option who sells the option to the holder collects the put premium p when $S_T \geq X$, and her profit is $S_T - X + p$ when the holder decides to exercise the option (i.e., $S_T < X$). When $S_T = X - c$, the writer and holder of the put option have a zero net profit. Table 16.3 summarizes these profits. American options have the same payoff pattern, except that the spot price of the underlying asset at days before or at maturity, $S_t$ ($t \leq T$), is compared to the exercise price X. Like the forward contract, options are also a zero-sum game: one party's gain is equivalent to the other party's loss, so the net change in wealth or benefit is zero.

Currency options are options with foreign currencies as the underlying asset. They are one of the most popular tools for corporations, individuals, or financial institutions to hedge against adverse movements in exchange rates. Before 1982, all currency options were over-the-counter contracts written by international banks, investment banks, and brokerage houses. These options are tailored to the buyer's specific needs, such as the amount of the underlying currency, the maturity length, and the exercise price (Feldman, 1985). Nowadays, many currency options are traded on organized exchanges such as the Chicago Mercantile Exchange (CME). Exchange-traded options are standardized in terms of contract size and maturity length. Usually, they are for more actively traded currencies such as the US dollar, the euro, the British pound, the Japanese yen, and the Swiss franc.



Hedging foreign exchange risk with options requires choosing between calls and puts on the currency of interest. The choice depends on the current foreign exchange exposure. For example, suppose one needs to pay (receive) some foreign currency in the future. In that case, one must choose a call (put) option on that currency because one can use the gain from the appreciation (depreciation) of the currency in the options market to offset the loss in the current transaction exposure. Since the Singapore dollar is not an actively traded currency, Singapore Airlines may need to find options on the euro and Singapore dollar in the over-the-

**Table 16.4** Quotations of options on the euro and Singapore dollar (S$/€), own table

| Strike price | Calls | Puts |
|---|---|---|
| *Contract size: €100,000* | | |
| 1.35 | 0.035 | 0.001 |
| 1.36 | 0.032 | 0.003 |
| 1.37 | 0.030 | 0.009 |
| 1.38 | 0.026 | 0.011 |
| 1.39 | 0.021 | 0.014 |
| 1.40 | 0.019 | 0.016 |
| 1.41 | 0.016 | 0.020 |
| 1.42 | 0.013 | 0.024 |
| 1.43 | 0.010 | 0.028 |
| 1.44 | 0.008 | 0.030 |
| 1.45 | 0.004 | 0.037 |

counter market. Let us assume the following information on one-year options is available for Singapore Airlines (Table 16.4):

The table lists the option premiums, quoted in units of Singapore dollars per euro, for calls and puts with different strike prices. All these options have a one-year maturity and are in European style. Each contract covers €100,000. The call premium increases with the strike price while the put premium decreases, as indicated in Fig. 16.2. Since Singapore Airlines wants to use options to hedge its existing account payable, it needs to choose call options on the euro. However, given that there are 11 call options available, which one should the firm choose? The choice depends on the future exchange rate Singapore Airlines expects to be in one year. For illustration purposes, we conjecture that the expected future exchange rate is the same as the current spot rate, S$1.40/€. To conduct the options market hedge, Singapore Airlines needs to long or buy 50 (=€5,000,000/100,000) call options and pay 0.019 × 100,000 × 50 = S$95,000 to the seller (writer) of the options. By doing this, the firm obtains the right to buy €5,000,000 at the strike price of S$1.40/€ one year from now. At maturity, whether to exercise these call options depends on the exchange rate between the two currencies. If the spot exchange rate at maturity is lower than S$1.40/€, Singapore Airlines will not exercise the call options but use Singapore dollars to buy the euro at the lower spot rate. For instance, with the spot rate of S$1.37/€ at maturity and a cost of capital of 4.5% per annum, the total cost is 1.37 × 5,000,000 + 95,000 × (1 + 4.5%) = S$6,949,275.00 at the maturity date. On the other hand, when the spot exchange rate at maturity is higher than S$1.40/€, Singapore Airlines will exercise the call options and use the fixed strike price to purchase the euro. As an example, assuming the future spot rate is S$1.43/€, the total cost to buy €5,000,000 is 1.40 × 5,000,000 + 95,000 × (1 + 4.5%) = S$7,099,275.00. This is the maximum cost Singapore Airlines needs to pay, and it remains the same for all future exchange rates above S$1.40/€. Compared to the unhedged strategy, which costs 1.43 × 5,000,000 = S$7,150,000.0 0, the options market hedging strategy saves S$50,725.00 for Singapore Airlines. The higher the future exchange rate, the more significant the benefits of the option hedging strategy over the unhedged strategy. When the exchange rate at maturity equals the strike price of the call options, Singapore Airlines is indifferent about exercising the options or not—its net profits under the two decisions are the same.

Now let us compare the three hedging strategies. The first two strategies obliterate uncertainties about the euro bill. Still, the money market hedge dominates the forward market hedge since the former leads to lower costs in the Singapore dollar for the euro bill. Further, the options market hedge is preferred to the money market hedge because it has an even lower cost in the Singapore dollar. Secondly, it provides a unique benefit to Singapore Airlines—it controls the downside risk while retaining the upside potential. Of course, these conclusions are drawn based on the current market information, including the interest rates, the spot exchange rate, the forward rate, and the option premiums. With different values of these inputs, we may have different conclusions regarding which hedging strategy is the most preferred.

So far, the discussions have been concerning hedging the foreign exchange exposures of the account payable of Singapore Airlines. However, if the firm has an account receivable of €five million in one year, it must take opposite positions in the three hedging strategies. ◘ Table 16.5 presents each strategy's specific steps and outcomes based on the current market information. In this case, the forward market hedge is the most preferred since it assures the largest amount of Singapore dollar proceeds from the account receivable of €five million. But, again, these values and conclusions are based only on the current market information. In the case of Maersk, forwards and options are the common tools utilized to hedge its foreign exchange exposures.

## Management of Operating Exposures



As illustrated in ► Chap. 5, operating exposure is a much broader concept than transaction exposure because the former measures the sensitivity of a firm's cash flows, profits, and value to unexpected shocks in future exchange rates. A firm's operating exposure is determined by both the structure of the market in which the firm sources its inputs and sells its service or products and the firm's ability to mitigate the impact of exchange rate changes by adjusting its markets, product mix, and sourcing (Eun et al., 2020, p. 249). While techniques for managing transaction exposure are well established, approaches to managing operating exposure are less developed. Because operating exposure is associated with a stream of transactions rather than individual transactions, the time horizon for hedging

**Table 16.5** A summary of Singapore Airline's hedging strategies for an account receivable of €five million, own table

| Strategy | Transactions | Outcomes |
|---|---|---|
| Money market hedge | 1. Borrow €4,938,272, convert to S$6,913,580, and invest in Singapore now | Receive S$6,913,580 now or S$7,155,556 in one year, regardless of the future spot exchange rate |
| | 2. In one year, collect €5,000,000 from the client to pay off the euro loan | |
| Forward market hedge | 1. Sell €5,000,000 forward for Singapore dollars now | Receive S$7,250,000 in one year, regardless of the future spot exchange rate |
| | 2. In one year, receive €5,000,000 from the client and deliver it to the short party of the forward contract | |
| Options market hedge | 1. Buy a put option on €5,000,000 with a strike price of S$1.40/€ and pay a premium of S$80,000 now | Receive at least S$7,000,000 in one year, regardless of the future spot exchange rate. Singapore Airlines controls the downside risk while keeping the upside potential |
| | 2. In one year, decide whether to exercise the put option based on the prevailing spot exchange rate | |

operating exposure extends beyond that provided by conventional hedging instruments. Consequently, managing operating exposure cannot be relegated to the firm's treasury department only. Instead, it is strategic and raises organizational issues (Grant & Soenen, 2004, p. 54).

Managing operating exposure is to stabilize cash flows in fluctuating exchange rates. The crucial part of managing operating exposure at the strategic level is for management to recognize a disequilibrium in parity conditions should it occur and be prepositioned to react most appropriately. Management can achieve this if it adopts an international diversification strategy for operating and financing bases. Diversifying operations means spreading sources and sales across many different currencies. International service firms can establish a flexible global sourcing policy to access low-cost inputs and sources. For instance, Japan Airlines is known to heavily hire foreign crews to stay competitive and profitable on international routes when the yen is very strong. Service firms can also diversify the markets for their services as much as possible to mitigate operating exposure. However, diversified operations have their pros and cons. The benefit is that firms are less sensitive to unexpected shocks in the exchange rate, while the shortcoming is that international diversification is costly and sometimes requires significant investments. Another challenge is how to discern between temporary and more permanent changes in exchange rates. If the changes are short term, diversifying operations may create issues such as excess capacity and diseconomies of scale. Diversifying the financing base means diversifying a firm's financing sources to exploit temporary deviations from parity conditions, such as the international Fisher effect. Suppose interest rate differentials do not equal the expected changes in exchange rates. In that case, firms can source capital from the currency with a lower interest rate and thus reduce their overall cost of capital. However, these opportunities are not equally available for all firms. A firm must be well known in the international investment community to be able to switch financing sources more efficiently.

Additionally, MNEs can manage operating exposures by adopting proactive operating and financing policies. Eiteman et al. (2016, pp. 361–369) list some commonly used proactive policies, as explained below.

**Risk-sharing contracts**; Risk-sharing is a contractual agreement between a buyer and a seller who agreed to "share" or "split" large currency movement impacts on payments between them. It benefits two firms from different countries interested in a long-term relationship based on the quality and reliability of services or products. Considering Singapore Airlines and Airbus, if the transactions between the two firms are frequent year by year, they can utilize risk-sharing contracts to mitigate the unfavorable impact of exchange rate fluctuations. For instance, they could agree that all purchases by Singapore Airlines will be made in the euro at the spot exchange rate on the invoice date as long as it is between S$1.35/€ and S$1.45/€. If the exchange rate is between these values on the payment dates, Singapore Airlines agrees to accept whatever transaction exposure exists. If, however, the exchange rate is outside this range on the payment date, the two firms will share the difference equally. Let us assume that Singapore Airlines has an account payable of €2,000,000 for June, and the spot rate on the invoice date is S$1.50/€. With the risk-sharing agreement, Singapore Airlines' payment would be

$$€2,000,000 \times \left[ S\$1.45/€ + \frac{(S\$1.50/€ - S\$1.45/€)}{2} \right] = €2,000,000 \times S\$1.475/€$$
$$= S\$2,950,000$$

The payment without the risk-sharing agreement would be €2,000,000 × S$1.50/€ = S$3,000,000. Therefore, this risk-sharing agreement saves Singapore Airlines S$3 ,000,000 – S$2,950,000 = S$50,000. However, this cost savings is at the expense of Airbus because it receives S$2,950,000 only, equivalent to €1,966,666.67 at the spot rate of S$1.50/€. On the other hand, if the exchange rate on the invoice date is S$1.30/€, the risk-sharing contract will benefit Airbus at the cost of Singapore Airlines. Thus, both firms incur expenses and benefits from exchange rate movements outside the specified band.

16

**Leading and lagging**: Leading and lagging refers to the flexible timing of payments on international business agreements to take advantage of anticipated exchange rate changes. With these agreements, firms may accelerate or delay payments to a foreign firm until the exchange rate is more favorable. For example, suppose Firm A has some foreign-currency accounts payable to Firm B, and the two firms have agreed on the leading and lagging payments. Firm A prefers to pay sooner if it expects the domestic currency to depreciate and later if it is predicted to appreciate. The rule reverses for foreign-currency-denominated accounts receivable. We can easily see that these agreements are zero-sum games—if it benefits your company, it hurts your counterparties. Therefore, they are more viable for firms intending to maintain a long-term cooperative relationship.

**Reinvoicing centers**: A reinvoicing center is a subsidiary or separate division of an MNE that deals with intra-company transactions in different currencies at one location. Setting up reinvoicing centers aims to streamline and centralize multi-currency transactions, thus mitigating exchange rate exposure for the company. They bill and pay all invoices in the currency of the originating country and then re-invoice the affiliate branches in their local currency. Take a UK-based ABC company with US and Canadian subsidiaries as an example. The US subsidiary owes the Canadian subsidiary outstanding debt denominated in the Canadian dollar. Meanwhile, the UK arm of the company just received payment in Canadian dollars and now owes an unrelated debt in US dollars. Without a reinvoicing center, each company subsidiary has to engage in its foreign exchange transaction; thus, all are subject to foreign exchange exposures. However, a reinvoicing center can reduce its exposures by having each division transact in its local currency with the center. Consequently, all the exchange rate risk is in the hands of the invoicing center. The reinvoicing center benefits the whole company since the concentrated risk management at the center allows for more specialized personnel and better price quotes from banks. Moreover, it improves the company's efficiency by avoiding duplication in hedging efforts across different parts—only the net foreign exchange exposure needs to be hedged. However, the disadvantages are the high setup cost, more complex bookkeeping, changed organization structure, and increased legal costs.

**Natural hedging**: A natural hedge refers to a strategy that reduces financial risks in the regular operation of a company by investing in different assets and financial instruments with negative correlations among them. Compared to usual hedging involving derivatives, natural hedging does not require sophisticated financial instruments. Suppose a company wants to offset an anticipated frequent long-term exposure to a foreign currency. In that case, it can achieve this by matching its foreign currency outflows (inflows) with foreign currency inflows (outflows). ◘ Figure 16.3 illustrates how a German firm can employ such a strategy to hedge operating exposure from its continuing US sales. To keep its competitiveness in the US market, the German company invoices all sales in US dollars, resulting in a continuous receipt of US dollars month after month. The German firm can acquire part of its debt capital in the US dollar market to reduce the continual foreign exchange exposure. By doing this, it can use the relatively predictable US dollar cash inflows from sales to service the principal and interest payments of the US dollar debt and hence become cash flow matched. Put differently, the German company has hedged an operational cash inflow by creating a financial cash outflow, and thus it is currency risk neutral. Additionally, instead of using financial cash outflow in the US dollar, the German company may also seek out potential suppliers in the United States and create accounts payable in US dollars, which can be paid using the continuing accounts receivable in US dollars. Alternatively, the German company can pay its foreign suppliers with US dollars, a currency-switching strategy.

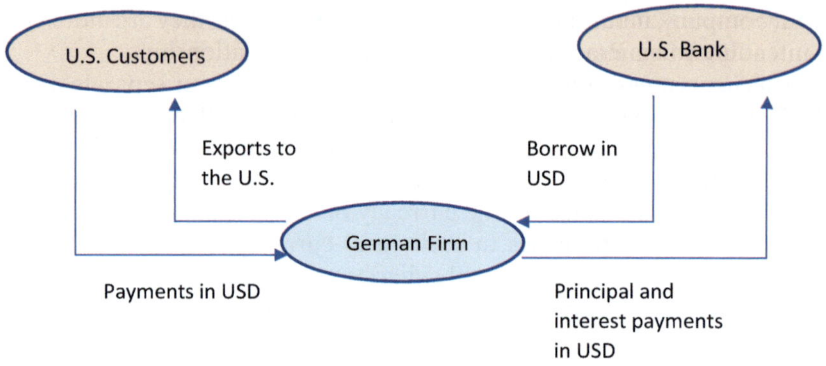


**Fig. 16.3** A natural hedge of a German firm, own diagram

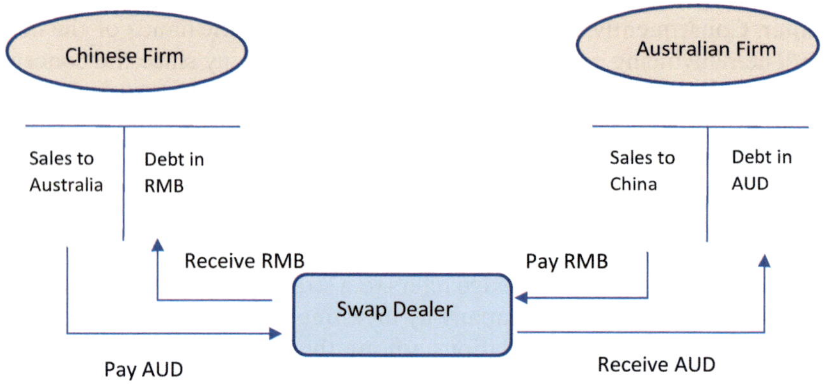


**Fig. 16.4** Currency swaps between a Chinese firm and an Australian firm, own diagram

**Cross-Currency Swaps**. As a popular financial hedging tool, a currency swap allows a firm to convert its debt in domestic currency to one in foreign currency. In a currency swap, a firm and a swap dealer, which acts as a middleman in setting up the swap agreement, agree to exchange an equivalent amount of two different currencies for a specified period. Typically, multinational firms borrow funds locally because they are well known there. If, however, they export or provide services abroad, their cash inflows are in foreign currencies. Currency swaps enable firms to pay foreign currencies and receive local currencies to service their local debt. Figure 16.4 presents such a working process. In this figure, a Chinese firm borrows Chinese yuan regularly in China, provides services in Australia, and earns Australian dollars. On the other hand, an Australian firm borrows from its domestic market and sells goods and services in China. The Chinese firm could pay Australian dollars and receive yuan through a swap dealer, which effectively converts its yuan-denominated debt service to Australian dollar debt service without borrowing Australian dollars. Simultaneously, the Australian firm enters a currency swap in the opposite direction—paying yuan and receiving Australian dollars. As the middleman, the swap dealer arranges for the desired swap's currency, amount, and timing. Practically, the initiating firm views the dealer as its counterparty and does not know who is on the other side of the swap arrangement. As the opening case indicates, Maersk also uses cross-currency swaps to manage its foreign exchange risk.

## Management of Translation Exposures

Translation exposure gauges the effect of an exchange rate change on a firm's financial statements. It arises as the financial accounting statements of foreign affiliates are translated into the currency of the parent firm. The finance literature generally suggests not to worry about this type of exposure and thus not to hedge it (Butler, 2016, pp. 295–296). The first reason is that translation gains or losses tend to be unrealized and have a little direct impact on firms' actual cash flows, which suggests that hedging translation exposure creates little shareholder value. Second, translation gains (losses) can be poor estimators of real changes in firm value, implying that managing translation exposure is inefficient in reducing the share price exposure. However, some empirical studies find evidence against these theoretical predictions. For instance, using questionnaire data from 101 public firms in Sweden, Hagelin (2003) finds that 33% of firms hedge their translation exposure, among which 74% use currency derivatives for the translation exposure hedge (p. 57). He also finds that firms with more significant percentages of revenues denominated in foreign currency (foreign revenues) are more likely to use currency derivatives to hedge translation exposure (p. 65), which is intuitively correct. In addition to currency forwards, options, and swaps detailed earlier, currency derivatives also include currency futures, which are essentially the same as currency forwards but are standardized in terms of the amount of currency and the maturity date. Because of this standardization, currency futures are traded on organized exchanges and have minimal counterparty risk, which is the probability that the other party in a transaction may default on the contractual obligations. How to utilize these currency derivatives to hedge translation exposure depends on the expectation of the future exchange rate. For instance, if a US-based firm with a subsidiary in the United Kingdom expects the pound to depreciate in the coming year, it may take a short position in forwards or futures or buy put options on the pound.

So far, we have discussed techniques to hedge or manage foreign exchange exposure. However, a more fundamental question for the management of multinational firms to consider is whether to hedge foreign exchange exposure. Hedging exposure is not cost-free. Instead, it attracts a lot of organizational and financial resources. Hence, it is imperative to know whether hedging adds value to firms. Theoretical research provides several rationales for the benefits of hedging. The first one is that hedging can increase firm value by reducing the volatility of future cash flows and the expected costs of financial distress and lowering the expected cost of taxes (Smith & Stulz, 1985, pp. 392–399). Second, Froot et al. (1993) suggest that failure to hedge foreign exchange exposure would force companies to forego viable investment opportunities due to uncertainties in their expected cash flows, termed as "the underinvestment issue," especially when external financing is costly (p. 1637). On the other hand, there have been arguments against hedging foreign exchange exposure. For instance, instead of increasing the expected cash flows of a firm, currency risk management typically consumes some of the company's resources and hence reduces cash flows. The impact of hedging exposure on firm value is a combination of the reduction of cash flow (which by itself lowers value) and the reduction in variance (which by itself increases value). Moreover, Copeland and Joshi (1996) argue that anticipating the consequences of hedging is difficult since so many other economic factors change when foreign exchange rates change (p. 66). Consequently, hedging activity risks being wasteful to the firm's shareholders and may increase exposure. The management of MNEs needs to understand the pros and cons of hedging foreign exchange exposures before they conduct such hedges.

## Hedging in Service Firms

It is also notable that international service firms may have different hedging choices than manufacturing firms due to their unique business model. Manufacturing firms need raw materials and resources from suppliers to produce tangible goods. It usually takes time for them to get payment from customers, which creates a lot of accounts payable and receivable. Service firms provide intangible output and do not hold inventory. They also do not require a physical production site. Therefore, other things being equal, service firms tend to have a lower level of foreign exchange exposure than manufacturing firms.

However, this does not mean that international service firms do not need to worry about foreign exchange exposure or take actions to hedge it. Some service firms still face foreign exchange exposure to some extent. For example, telecommunication providers buy a lot of equipment worldwide for their mobile towers and landlines. Similarly, web hosting firms like Google or Amazon purchase servers for their huge data centers, and logistics service providers have a large number of lorries and warehouses. Some service firms may also have significant accounts receivable denominated in foreign currencies to engage their international clients. Therefore, hedging foreign exchange exposure remains necessary for multinational service firms.



## The Global Cost of Capital

When sourcing capital, MNEs face an essential question: shall they do it locally or internationally? Of course, the decision depends on the characteristics of the domestic capital market (e.g., liquidity, segmentation). However, it should achieve the purpose of minimizing the cost of capital and maximizing the availability of capital. To explicitly answer this question, we need to understand the cost of capital and international portfolio theory before examining the costs and benefits of raising capital in the global market.

**Cost of Capital**

Cost of capital is the expected return of a company on a specific investment to make it worth the expenditure of resources. Put differently, the capital cost determines the return rate required to persuade investors to invest in the company.

Since most companies adopt a mixture of equity and debt financing, the cost of capital of a company can be calculated by the weighted average cost of equity and debt capital sources (WACC) as follows (Miles & Ezzell, 1980, pp. 726–727):

$$k_{\text{WACC}} = k_e \frac{E}{V} + k_d (1-t) \frac{D}{V}$$

where $k_{\text{WACC}}$ = weighted average after-tax cost of capital, $k_e$ = risk-adjusted cost of equity, $k_d$ = before-tax cost of debt, $E$ = market value of equity, $D$ = market value of debt, $V$ = market value of securities ($E + D$), $t$ = marginal tax rate.

## Cost of Debt

Companies can acquire debt through bank loans or instruments such as notes or bonds. Estimating the cost of debt requires a forecast of market interest rates, the proportions of various kinds of debt the firm expects to use, and the corporate income tax rate in the next few years. Empirically, the before-tax cost of debt, $k_d$, is calculated as the average interest costs of different debt components weighted by their market values. Then $k_d$ is adjusted for corporate income taxes to obtain the after-tax cost of debt since interests are tax deductible.

Suppose a firm issues debt denominated in foreign currencies. In that case, its effective cost of debt equals the after-tax cost of repaying the principal and interest in the firm's local currency, which includes the nominal cost of principal and interest in foreign currencies, adjusted for foreign exchange gains or losses. For example, a UK-based firm borrows US\$5,000,000 for one year at 6% interest. However, during the one year, the US dollar appreciates from an initial rate of £0.85/US\$ to £0.90/US\$. Therefore, to get the cost of the debt in pounds, we need to first calculate the pound proceeds of the initial borrowing at the spot rate of £0.85/US\$:

$$\text{US\$}5{,}000{,}000 \times \frac{£0.85}{\text{US\$}} = £4{,}250{,}000$$

At the end of the one year, the UK firm must repay the principal of US\$5,000,000 plus the 6% interest, that is,

$$US\$5{,}000{,}000 \times (1+6\%) = US\$5{,}300{,}000$$

At the spot rate of £0.90/US$ at the end of the one year, the UK firm must pay

$$US\$5{,}300{,}000 \times \frac{£0.90}{US\$} = £4{,}770{,}000$$

Therefore, the actual cost of the debt in pounds is not the nominal 6% paid in US dollars, but 12.24%:

$$\frac{£4{,}770{,}000}{£4{,}250{,}000} - 1 \approx 12.24\%$$

## Cost of Equity

Unlike the cost of debt, whose estimation is relatively straightforward, the cost of equity is hard to measure. For firms whose equity trades in a purely domestic market, the most conventional way to estimate the cost of equity is based on the capital asset pricing model (CAPM), developed in the early 1960s by William Sharpe, Jack Treynor, John Lintner, and Jan Mossin. This model indicates that a firm's cost of equity has two components: a risk-free interest rate and a firm-specific component that depends on the risk of the company and the performance of the market portfolio:

$$k_e = k_{rf} + \beta_i \left(k_m - k_{rf}\right)$$

where $k_{rf}$ = interest rate on risk-free bonds, $k_m$ = expected return rate on the well-diversified market portfolio of stocks, $\beta_i$ = measure of systematic risk for the specific firm *i*.

The key indication of CAPM is that a firm's cost of equity is determined by its systematic risk measured by beta ($\beta_i$), which gauges how the firm's stock returns vary with the market in which its stock is traded. All else equal, the higher the beta, the higher the firm's equity cost. Despite that many studies (e.g., Bhandari, 1988, p. 514; Fama & French, 1992, p. 434) have shown a low cross-sectional correlation between beta and expected stock returns, CAPM remains a widely accepted and used method of estimating the cost of equity.



Despite that CAPM assumes investors hold a fully diversified "world" portfolio, applications of CAPM usually focus on the home market portfolio. In global markets, a firm's equity beta depends on how the stock contributes to the volatility of the world market portfolio, not the home market portfolio. For MNEs with access to global capital markets, using the traditional CAPM will overstate the cost of capital because risks not diversifiable within a national economy can be diversified by holding a global portfolio. Thus, to reflect the reality of a globally determined cost of capital, all companies with access to global markets should consider using an international CAPM (ICAPM) that views a company as part of the global portfolio of stocks (Stulz, 1999, p. 12). In other words, for MNEs whose equity trades in the global market, ICAPM is employed to estimate their cost of equity capital:

$$k_e^{\text{global}} = k_{rf}^g + \beta_i^g \left(k_m^g - k_{rf}^g\right)$$

$k_{rf}^g$ is the risk-free rate in the global market, which may be similar to that in the domestic market. However, the expected international market return in the coming periods, $k_m^g$, is different from the expected return in the domestic market. The firm's beta, $\beta_i^g$, will change significantly compared to the domestic equivalent, $\beta_i$, since it now reflects the return comovement with a greater and more diversified global portfolio.

Stulz (1995, pp. 18–20) uses Nestle to illustrate how the estimated cost of capital for MNEs in small countries is different using local and global CAPM. For the local CAPM, using monthly return data from January 1990 to May 1993, Nestle's beta with respect to the Financial Times Swiss Index, a proxy of domestic market return in Switzerland, is 0.885. Its local beta is high, as expected, because Nestle represents a substantial fraction of the Swiss market capitalization. With a risk-free rate of 3.3% measured by the Swiss bond index yield and a local market return of 10.2% measured by the Swiss market portfolio, both are in Swiss francs, the estimated cost of equity capital of Nestle is 3.3% + 0.885 × (10.2% – 3.3%) = 9.41 %. On the other hand, let us suppose that the Swiss market is internationally integrated and that the world indices are good proxies for the global market portfolio of the global CAPM. The beta of Nestle with respect to the global market portfolio, proxied by the Financial Times Global index in the Swiss franc, is estimated to be 0.585. It is lower than the beta in the local CAPM because now Nestle contributes less significantly to the global market capitalization. With the same values of the risk-free rate and market return in the global market, the estimated cost of equity capital using the global CAPM is 3.3% + 0.585 × (10.2% – 3.3%) = 7.34%. Of course, one would not expect the risk-free rate and market return to be precisely the same in the global market as in the domestic market. With a return of 13.7% on the Financial Times Global index in the Swiss franc, for example, and assuming the risk-free rate remains at 3.3%, the estimated cost of capital under the global CAPM becomes 3.3% + 0.585 × (13.7% – 3.3%) = 9.38%. Multinational service firms can conduct a similar analysis.

## Accessing Global Capital

As mentioned previously, a firm's equity cost is the return potential investors require to invest in the firm's equity. Their investment decision depends on the firm's risk and their current investment portfolios. According to the portfolio theory, the total risk of a portfolio can be decomposed into systematic risk (the market), measured by beta, and unsystematic or idiosyncratic risk (the individual securities). Within a domestic portfolio, increasing the number of securities reduces

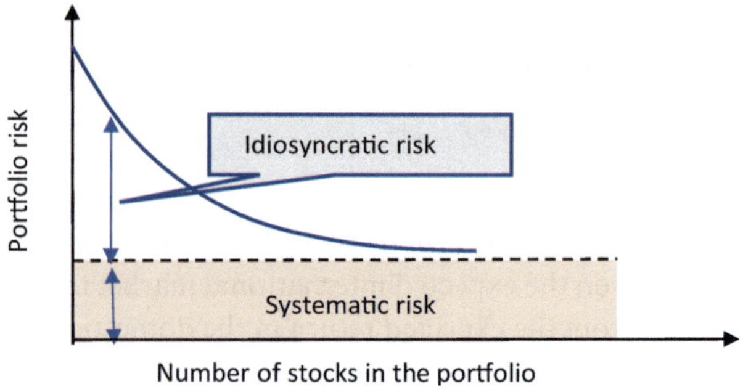


**Fig. 16.5** Systematic risk, idiosyncratic risk, and number of stocks in a portfolio, own diagram

the idiosyncratic risk component but leaves the systematic risk component unchanged—a benefit of diversification. Internationally, adding foreign securities helps reduce the systematic risk of global investors' portfolios and thus lowers its beta—a benefit of international diversification. This benefit occurs because the returns on foreign securities are not perfectly correlated with those of existing securities in the portfolio. Figure 16.5 displays this relationship between the number of stocks in a portfolio and the two types of risks. In addition, adding foreign securities could reduce the foreign exchange risk of international investors' portfolios because now they are tapping into a larger pool of investments in different countries. These global diversification benefits induce investors to demand foreign securities; thus, the firm issuing the security can raise capital at a lower cost.

In addition to the lower cost of capital required by diversified international investors, access to global capital brings additional benefits to multinational firms. The first benefit is improved market liquidity. As explained in ► Chap. 5, liquidity gauges how easily and fast transactions are completed without impacting the price of securities. The finance literature (Amihud & Mendelson, 1986, p. 480; Amihud et al., 2015, p. 351) suggests that the cost of equity capital decreases with market liquidity. More recently, Feng et al. (2022, pp. 11–13) calculated the average monthly stock liquidity in 43 markets from 1990 to 2021. They measure liquidity using three proxies: share turnover to gauge trading activity, Amihud's (2002, p. 34) illiquidity ratio to estimate a trade's price impact, and the number of zero-return days proposed by Lesmond et al. (1999, pp. 1116–1120). Their results, shown in Table 16.6, show a clear dispersion in liquidity across different markets. But on average, emerging markets are generally less liquid, with a lower share turnover, a bigger price impact of trading, and a larger proportion of trading days with a zero return, than developed markets. Therefore, MNEs, especially those from less liquid markets, can improve the market liquidity of their securities and thus lower the overall cost of capital by raising funds in the more liquid euromarkets (money, bond, and equity) and selling security issues abroad.

The second additional benefit of accessing global capital is circumventing financial market imperfections such as market segmentation. Segmentation arises when investors cannot move the money from one market to another, caused mainly by government constraints, institutional practices, and investor percep-

**Table 16.6** Average stock liquidity in 43 markets, source: Feng et al. (2022)

| Market | Turnover | Amihud | % of zero-return days |
|---|---|---|---|
| Argentina | 0.010 | 0.127 | 0.243 |
| Brazil | 0.119 | 0.189 | 0.186 |
| Chile | 0.008 | 0.183 | 0.317 |
| China | 0.168 | 0.002 | 0.141 |
| Cyprus | 0.007 | 2.039 | 0.379 |
| Egypt | 0.023 | 0.257 | 0.242 |
| Greece | 0.028 | 0.404 | 0.177 |
| India | 0.013 | 4.471 | 0.238 |
| Indonesia | 0.021 | 0.610 | 0.355 |
| Malaysia | 0.025 | 0.093 | 0.258 |
| Mexico | 0.020 | 0.249 | 0.279 |
| Pakistan | 0.076 | 1.254 | 0.297 |
| Peru | 0.010 | 0.477 | 0.492 |
| Philippines | 0.012 | 0.438 | 0.333 |
| Poland | 0.023 | 0.279 | 0.182 |
| South Africa | 0.030 | 0.159 | 0.226 |
| South Korea | 0.133 | 0.039 | 0.156 |
| Sri Lanka | 0.013 | 2.062 | 0.407 |
| Taiwan | 0.103 | 0.003 | 0.169 |
| Thailand | 0.057 | 0.145 | 0.246 |
| Turkey | 0.105 | 0.043 | 0.184 |
| Australia | 0.052 | 0.181 | 0.211 |
| Austria | 0.022 | 0.177 | 0.234 |
| Belgium | 0.022 | 0.091 | 0.138 |
| Canada | 0.042 | 0.094 | 0.166 |
| Denmark | 0.034 | 0.050 | 0.222 |
| Finland | 0.037 | 0.504 | 0.192 |
| France | 0.032 | 0.079 | 0.149 |
| Germany | 0.025 | 0.104 | 0.153 |
| Hong Kong | 0.040 | 0.053 | 0.203 |

(continued)

**Table 16.6** (continued)

| Market | Turnover | Amihud | % of zero-return days |
|---|---|---|---|
| Israel | 0.021 | 0.590 | 0.236 |
| Italy | 0.059 | 0.078 | 0.126 |
| Japan | 0.058 | 0.007 | 0.145 |
| Netherlands | 0.070 | 0.023 | 0.108 |
| New Zealand | 0.020 | 0.134 | 0.273 |
| Norway | 0.051 | 0.093 | 0.222 |
| Portugal | 0.025 | 0.382 | 0.243 |
| Singapore | 0.035 | 0.090 | 0.240 |
| Spain | 0.044 | 0.054 | 0.148 |
| Sweden | 0.054 | 0.038 | 0.163 |
| Switzerland | 0.053 | 0.010 | 0.132 |
| United Kingdom | 0.068 | 0.014 | 0.153 |
| United States | 0.111 | 0.002 | 0.080 |
| **Emerging** | 0.048 | 0.644 | 0.262 |
| **Developed** | 0.044 | 0.130 | 0.179 |
| **Global** | 0.046 | 0.381 | 0.220 |

Notes: "Turnover" is the monthly share trading volume divided by shares outstanding. "Amihud" is the average ratio of the absolute value of daily stock return in percentage to daily trading volume in thousands of US dollars. "% of zero-return days" is the proportion of trading days with a zero stock return in a month. The sample period is from January 1990 to December 2021



tions. Before 1980, national capital markets were small, inactive, and segmented, with domestic investors holding most of the local shares. Numerous barriers, such as high taxation, high transaction costs, and explicit restrictions on foreign ownership, capital mobility, and foreign exchange transactions, caused many firms to face high capital costs. Some of these barriers were removed after the market reforms of deregulation and liberalization that began in developed economies in the 1970s and emerging economies in the late 1980s. During the 1990s, restrictions on cross-border portfolio investment were gradually eased under pressure from the Organization for Economic Cooperation and Development (OECD), a consortium of most of the world's industrialized countries. Despite some solid arguments for capital market liberalization (e.g., new capital source and more risk sharing), the sizeable foreign portfolio flows during the 1990s were considered by some regulators a cause of market crises such as the 1994 Mexican crisis and the 1997 Asian financial crisis. Till now, barriers to some national capital markets still exist. For instance, in China, domestic households are restricted from investing abroad, and foreign investors are restricted from accessing Chinese financial markets.

While capital controls may help maintain financial stability during times of stress, the finance literature suggests that they tend to increase domestic firms' capital costs. Stulz (1999, p. 12) shows that for companies that are large and visible enough to attract global investors, having an international shareholder base means having a lower cost of capital and hence a greater equity value for two main reasons. First, because equity risks are shared among more investors with different portfolio exposures, and thus a different "appetite" for bearing certain risks, equity market risk premiums should decline for all companies in countries with access to global markets. Second, when firms in countries with less-developed capital markets raise capital in countries (e.g., the United States and the United Kingdom) with highly developed markets, they get lower-cost capital and aspects of the prevailing corporate governance systems in those markets. Therefore, raising capital overseas for companies in less-developed markets means that more sophisticated investors, armed with more advanced technologies, will monitor their performance and management. This increases investor confidence in the future performance of those companies and hence improves the terms on which they raise capital. Using a sample of 126 firms from 32 developed and emerging markets with different historical records and liberalization circumstances, Errunza & Miller (2000, pp. 588–590) found that market liberalizations decrease the cost of equity capital. For example, sample firms experienced a significant decline of 42% in the cost of capital due to their shares being listed in the United States through American Depository Receipts (ADRs). More recently, Hillier and Loncan (2019) studied the effect of stock market integration on the cost of capital and investment, using Brazil as a case study. They find that integration, as proxied by foreign ownership, positively impacts the financing side by reducing firms' cost of capital (p. 189).

To summarize this section, MNEs resident in countries with illiquid and segmented capital markets can reduce their cost of capital by financing in more liquid and developed markets, primarily because diversified international investors require a lower return on their investments in the firms. Additionally, improved market liquidity (i.e., bonds and stocks are easier to trade with lower transaction costs) and corporate governance (i.e., investors feel more confident about firms' operations and information) are two other factors contributing to the cost of capital reduction. A firm pursuing this goal must design a financing strategy that will attract international investors and choose different paths (equity or bond issues, as explained in ► Chap. 5) to access global markets and minimize the overall cost of capital. On the other hand, the firm should also be aware of the risks and costs of raising capital in the global market, including foreign exchange risk, political risk, and more rigid disclosure requirements.

## Multinational Capital Budgeting

The goal of the financial manager is to maximize shareholder wealth, which is created when the firm makes an investment whose return outweighs costs in a present value sense. Therefore, the financial manager must select good capital projects that will increase the firm's overall profitability. These decisions determine the firm's competitive position and ultimate long-term survival. For MNEs, the process of making such decisions is termed multinational capital budgeting, which is the process a business undertakes to evaluate potential major projects or investments in foreign markets. It evaluates prospective foreign investment alternatives such as acquiring capital assets or a foreign company and commits long-term funds, i.e., capital expenditures, to preferred projects. As such long-term commitments usually involve large amounts of money, careful planning is required to determine which capital assets to acquire.

Budget, image by Steve Buissinne from Pixabay

## Capital Budgeting Process

**Capital Budgeting**

Capital budgeting is the process of identifying, analyzing, and selecting investment projects whose returns (cash flows) are expected to extend beyond one year. It is a continuous process and is carried out by different functional areas of management, such as production, marketing, engineering, financial management, and so on. (Goel, 2015, p. 12)

Multinational capital budgeting adopts the same theoretical framework as domestic capital budgeting, whose basic steps are outlined in ◘ Fig. 16.6. However, global service firms considering foreign investment opportunities face more complex problems and challenges than firms considering domestic investments. Foreign projects have unique foreign exchange and political risks under different tax regulations. Moreover, two other factors contribute to the complexity of multinational capital budgeting. The first factor is the cash flows of these firms. Cash flows of the parent firm, which often depend on the form of financing, must be distinguished from those of foreign projects or subsidiaries since they contribute to the firm value differently. Moreover, one must realize that cash flows generated by new investments in one foreign subsidiary may be taken away from another, resulting in

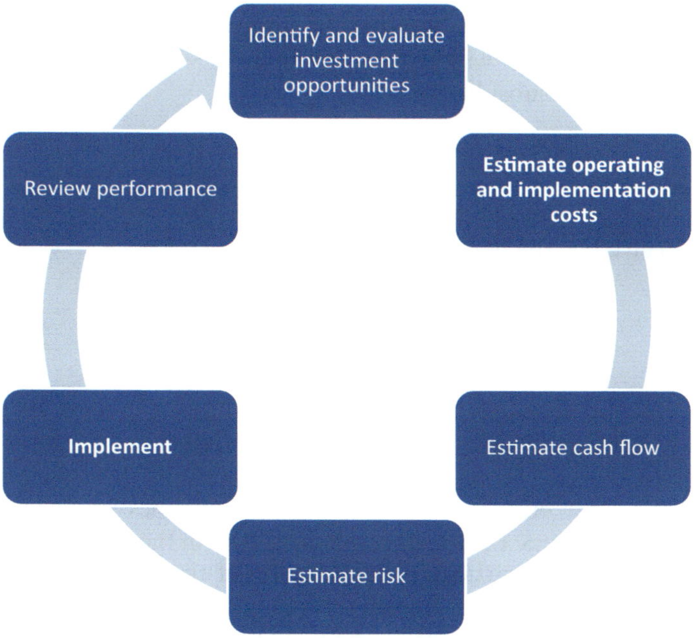


◘ **Fig. 16.6** Steps of domestic capital budgeting, own diagram

a zero value of the investments to the parent firm. Second, inflation rates in different countries lead to different discount rates employed to calculate the present values of new projects in these countries. With unexpected changes in foreign exchange rates, these factors will affect the cash flows and, thus, the parent firm's competitive position over time. All these unfamiliar complexities must be quantified as modifications to either expected cash flows or the discount rate. In this process, theoretical deduction and common sense may be required to reduce arbitrariness.

## Different Perspectives of Multinational Capital Budgeting

Understanding the perspective taken in multinational capital budgeting matters is also helpful. Should the capital budgeting for an international project be conducted from the viewpoint of the subsidiary that will administer the project or from the parent that will finance the project? The outcomes can vary with the perspective taken because the net after-tax cash inflows to the parent firm can differ significantly from those to the subsidiary. Let us use an example of a new project funded by a France-based parent firm and administered by its subsidiary in Malaysia. The new project in Malaysia is expected to generate an annual cash inflow of RM50 million. With a corporate tax rate of 24% in Malaysia, the after-tax cash flows to the Malay subsidiary is

$$\text{RM}\,50,000,000 \times (1 - 24\%) = \text{RM}\,38,000,000$$

The Malay subsidiary needs to remit the cash flows to the parent firm and pays withholding taxes. With a withholding tax rate of 3%, the after-tax cash flows remitted by the Malay subsidiary is

$$\text{RM}\,38,000,000 \times (1 - 3\%) = \text{RM}\,36,860,000$$

If the exchange rate between the euro and the Malaysian ringgit is RM4.71/€, the cash flows received by the parent is

$$\frac{\text{RM}\,36,860,000}{\text{RM}4.71/€} = €7,825,902.34$$

16

These cash flows are summarized in ◘ Fig. 16.7. The cash flows to the parent firm are subject to more taxes and foreign exchange risks than those to the foreign subsidiary.

Admittedly, other business stakeholders are sometimes involved in a "joint" capital budgeting process. For instance, medical staff in the healthcare sector plays a dominant role, so they participate in all aspects of the capital budgeting process (Mukherjee et al., 2016, p. 68). But more generally, which perspective should the financial manager of an MNE take? There are arguments for each stand. On the one hand, proponents of the parent firm perspective argue that cash flows to the

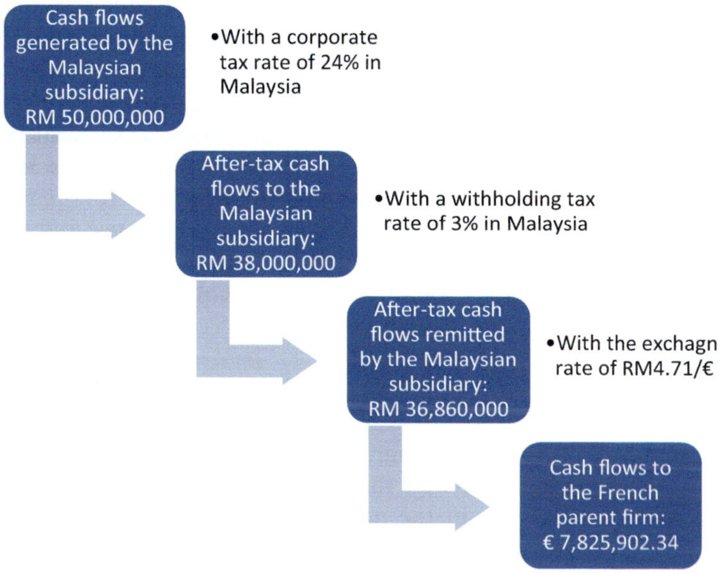


**Fig. 16.7** Cash flows to the parent and the foreign subsidiary, own diagram

parent firm are ultimately the basis for dividends to stockholders, reinvestments, debt repayment, and many other purposes that affect the stakeholders of the whole firm. Therefore, any project that can create a positive net present value for the parent should enhance the firm's value. On the other hand, proponents of the subsidiary perspective point out that the parent perspective violates a cardinal concept of capital budgeting, namely, that financial cash flows (cash to fund a project) should not be mixed with operating cash flows (cash generated by a company's main business activities). Most of a foreign subsidiary's cash flows to the parent are financial rather than operating. Moreover, evaluating a project from the perspective of the foreign subsidiary serves several valuable purposes. For instance, one can easily compare the performance of the new project with that of a competing project or a benchmark investment (e.g., yields of government bonds with the same maturity of the new project) in the same host country if both are measured in local returns. Therefore, MNEs should invest in the new foreign project only if they can earn a risk-adjusted return greater than locally based competitors can make on the same project. In practice, MNEs are found to evaluate foreign projects from both the parent and the subsidiary viewpoint. Szpiro & Dimnik (1996, pp. 61–66) reported on a field study of capital budgeting and strategy in 23 multinational firms. The analysis classifies multinational capital budgeting processes into three schemes: centralized, where top management makes all important strategic capital budgeting decisions while operating managers implement projects selected by top management; decentralized, where operating managers identify and initiate projects that are approved by top management based upon projected financial performance; and integrated, which has elements of both decentralized and centralized capital budgeting. The findings suggest that around half of the 23 firms chose a centralized scheme, and quite a few selected the decentralized approach.

To understand the complexities of multinational capital budgeting, let us use a hypothetical firm called LGlobal as an illustrative case. LGlobal is a US-based global service firm with subsidiaries in many countries, including India. It is now seeking foreign direct investment in India due to the long-term growth prospects in this market. Therefore, the first step in evaluating LGlobal's potential new investment in India is to construct a set of pro forma financial statements for this new project. Toward this end, let us further assume the following:

- The purchasing power parity (PPP) holds for the Indian rupee and the US dollar exchange rate for the life of the project so that the future exchange rate is determined by expected inflation rates in the two countries:

$$S_{t+1} = S_t \times \frac{1 + i_{INR}}{1 + i_{USD}}$$

  where $S_t$ is the current spot exchange rate between the Indian rupee and the US dollar, $S_{t+1}$ is the future exchange rate one year later, and $i_{INR}$ and $i_{USD}$ refer to the expected inflation rate in the next year in India and the United States, respectively. We further assume that the US and Indian inflation rates are 3% and 6% per annum, respectively.
- The initial capital investment for the new project is INR20 billion. With a year 0 average exchange rate of INR81.65/USD, the cost will constitute an investment of USD 244,947,948.56.
- The massive investment is financed with 50% equity, all from LGlobal, and 50% debt, whose 75% comes from LGlobal and 25% from an Indian bank. The US dollar-based weighted average cost of capital of LGlobal is estimated to be 10%, and the WACC for the project itself on a local Indian level in rupee terms is estimated to be 25%. The loan arranged by the Indian bank is an eight-year loan in rupee at 28% annual interest, fully amortizing, and the interest payments are entirely tax deductible. The parent firm provides most of the debt, with a yearly interest rate of 10% and a five-year maturity denominated in the US dollar. Assuming the PPP holds, the dollar loan will have an effective interest expense in rupee terms of 13.20% before taxes, which is determined by the internal rate of return of repaying the dollar loan in full in rupee.
- The total revenue of the new project is INR50 billion in year 1. It is expected to grow at 20% in the following 2 years and an inflation rate of 6% over the last 2 years. License fees are 2% of total revenue. Total costs and expenses (including license fees) are INR45 billion in year 1, increasing at the Indian inflation rate of 6% over time.
- Assume there is no depreciation or amortization. Then, for simplicity, changes in net working capital (NWC, the difference between current assets and current liabilities) are zero in years 1–5.
- The corporate tax rate is 25% in India. Tax credits resulting from current-period losses are carried forward toward next year's tax liabilities. Dividends are distributed at a 30% rate if net profit is positive and 0 otherwise.

**◘** Table 16.7 illustrates the cash flows (interest and principal) related to various loans and the corresponding foreign exchange gains or losses (i.e., the difference between the actual payment based on the spot exchange rate and the scheduled payment based on the initial exchange rate in year 0) over the next 5 years. The cash flows of the Indian local loan are straightforward, with a principal of INR20,000 × 0.5 × 0.25 = INR2,500 million, an interest rate of 28%, and a period of 8 years. The loan by LGlobal to the Indian subsidiary is denominated in US dollars, so it must be repaid in US dollars, not rupee. When the loan agreement is signed, the spot exchange rate is INR81.65/USD, the rate used to calculate the "scheduled" repaying of principal and interest in rupee. However, the rupee is expected to depreciate in

**◘ Table 16.7** LGlobal Indian's debt service schedules and foreign exchange gains/losses, own table

| **Exchange rate (INR/USD)** | **81.65** | **84.03** | **86.48** | **88.99** | **91.59** | **94.25** |
|---|---|---|---|---|---|---|
| Project year | 0 | 1 | 2 | 3 | 4 | 5 |
| *Indian local loan at 28% for 8 years (millions of INR)* | | | | | | |
| Loan principal | 2500.00 | | | | | |
| Interest payment | | (700.00) | (668.42) | (627.99) | (576.24) | (510.01) |
| Principal payment | | (112.80) | (144.38) | (184.81) | (236.56) | (302.79) |
| Total payment | | (812.80) | (812.80) | (812.80) | (812.80) | (812.80) |
| *LGlobal loan at 10% for 5 years (millions of USD)* | | | | | | |
| Loan principal | 91.86 | | | | | |
| Interest payment | | (9.19) | (7.68) | (6.03) | (4.21) | (2.20) |
| Principal payment | | (15.05) | (16.55) | (18.21) | (20.03) | (22.03) |
| Total payment | | (24.23) | (24.23) | (24.23) | (24.23) | (24.23) |
| *LGlobal loan converted to rupee at scheduled and actual spot rates (millions of INR)* | | | | | | |
| *Scheduled at INR81.65/USD* | | | | | | |
| Interest payment | | (750.00) | (627.15) | (492.02) | (343.37) | (179.86) |
| Principal payment | | (1228.48) | (1351.33) | (1486.46) | (1635.11) | (1798.62) |
| Total payment | | (1978.48) | (1978.48) | (1978.48) | (1978.48) | (1978.48) |
| *Actual (at spot rate)* | | | | | | |
| Interest payment | | (771.84) | (664.22) | (536.28) | (385.16) | (207.63) |
| Principal payment | | (1264.26) | (1431.19) | (1620.17) | (1834.09) | (2076.26) |
| Total payment | | (2036.11) | (2095.41) | (2156.44) | (2219.25) | (2283.89) |

(continued)

■ **Table 16.7** (continued)

| **Exchange rate (INR/USD)** | **81.65** | **84.03** | **86.48** | **88.99** | **91.59** | **94.25** |
|---|---|---|---|---|---|---|
| Project year | 0 | 1 | 2 | 3 | 4 | 5 |
| *Cash flows in INR on LGlobal loan (millions of INR)* | | | | | | |
| Total actual cash flows | 7500 | (2036.11) | (2095.41) | (2156.44) | (2219.25) | (2283.89) |
| Internal rate of return (IRR) of cash flows | **13.20%** | | | | | |
| *Foreign exchange gains (losses) on LGlobal loan (millions of INR)* | | | | | | |
| Foreign exchange gains (losses) on interest | | (21.84) | (37.07) | (44.26) | (41.79) | (27.76) |
| Foreign exchange gains (losses) on principal | | (35.78) | (79.86) | (133.70) | (198.98) | (277.64) |
| Total foreign exchange losses on debt | | (57.63) | (116.93) | (177.96) | (240.77) | (305.41) |

line with purchasing power parity. Consequently, the "actual" exchange rates exceed INR81.65/USD when the LGlobal loan is repaid, leading to losses in foreign exchange. These foreign exchange losses are recognized on the income statement of the Indian subsidiary, as shown in ■ Table 16.8. The simplified pro forma income statement suggests that the new Indian subsidiary operation of LGlobal is expected to have a positive accounting profit in its third year and more profits after that. In the first 2 years, the earnings before taxes (EBT) in millions of rupees are −1007.63 and −182.5, respectively. In year 3, the Indian subsidiary has an EBT of INR845.53 million, but it does not need to pay corporate tax (because of the tax credit) or distribute dividends. In years 4 and 5, the after-tax net income is INR 920.10 million and INR 1060.12 million, respectively, and 30% is allocated to equity holders.



**Capital budget from the foreign subsidiary's perspective**: ■ Table 16.9 shows the capital budget from the viewpoint of the Indian subsidiary. It is based on the free cash flow (FCF), which is calculated by summing earnings before interest and taxes (EBIT), depreciation and amortization, recalculated taxes, changes in net working capital (NWC), and capital investment. Here, EBIT, not EBT, is used because the capital budget produces cash flows that will be discounted to present value with a discount rate, which includes the cost of debt (i.e., interest). Interest should not be subtracted twice. Related to this, we need to recalculate taxes based on EBIT. Depreciation, if any, should be added back to get the net operating cash flow, and changes in NWC need to be subtracted from the net operating cash flow

**Table 16.8** Simplified pro forma income statement of LGlobal's Indian project, in millions of rupee, own table

| Exchange rate (INR/USD) | 81.65 | 84.03 | 86.48 | 88.99 | 91.59 | 94.25 |
|---|---|---|---|---|---|---|
| Project year | 0 | 1 | 2 | 3 | 4 | 5 |
| Total revenue | | 5000.00 | 6000.00 | 7200.00 | 7632.00 | 8089.92 |
| Total costs and expenses | | 4500.00 | 4770.00 | 5056.20 | 5359.57 | 5681.15 |
| Earnings before interest and taxes (EBIT) | | 500.00 | 1230.00 | 2143.80 | 2272.43 | 2408.77 |
| Less interest on LGlobal debt | | (750.00) | (627.15) | (492.02) | (343.37) | (179.86) |
| Less foreign exchange losses on debt | | (57.63) | (116.93) | (177.96) | (240.77) | (305.41) |
| Less interest on local debt | | (700.00) | (668.42) | (627.99) | (576.24) | (510.01) |
| Earnings before taxes (EBT) | | (1007.63) | (182.50) | 845.83 | 1112.04 | 1413.50 |
| Less income tax (25%) | | – | – | – | (191.94) | (353.37) |
| Net income | | (1007.63) | (182.50) | 845.83 | 920.10 | 1060.12 |
| Net income (millions of USD) | | (11.99) | (2.11) | 9.50 | 10.05 | 11.25 |
| Return on sales | | −20.15% | −3.04% | 11.75% | 12.06% | 13.10% |
| Dividends distributed (30%) | | – | – | 253.75 | 276.03 | 318.04 |
| Retained | | (1007.63) | (182.50) | 592.08 | 644.07 | 742.09 |

in calculating FCF. Note that both depreciation and changes in NWC are assumed to be zero in this example for simplicity.

The terminal value of the project is the continuing value of the project in the years after year 5, which is the last year of the pro forma financial analysis. It is the present value of all future FCFs that the asset is expected to yield. To get this value, we calculate the present value of a perpetual net operating cash flow (NOCF) generated in year 5 with the WACC of the Indian subsidiary and a growth rate of zero:

$$\text{Terminal value} = \frac{\text{NOCF}_5(1+g)}{k_{\text{WACC}} - g} = \frac{1806.58(1+0)}{0.25-0} = \text{INR } 7226.32 \text{million}$$

The results of the capital budget from the subsidiary's perspective show a negative net present value (NPV) of −INR11,702.71 million and an internal rate of return (IRR) of only 8.37%, which is much lower than the 25% cost of capital of the sub-

**Table 16.9** Capital budget from the Indian subsidiary's perspective, in millions of rupee, own table

| **Exchange rate (INR/USD)** | **81.65** | **84.03** | **86.48** | **88.99** | **91.59** | **94.25** |
|---|---|---|---|---|---|---|
| Project year | 0 | 1 | 2 | 3 | 4 | 5 |
| EBIT | | 500.00 | 1230.00 | 2143.80 | 2272.43 | 2408.77 |
| Less recalculated taxes at 25% | | (125.00) | (307.50) | (535.95) | (568.11) | (602.19) |
| Net operating cash flow | | 375.00 | 922.50 | 1607.85 | 1704.32 | 1806.58 |
| Initial investment | (20,000.00) | | | | | |
| Terminal value | | | | | | 7226.32 |
| Free cash flow (FCF) | (20,000.00) | 375.00 | 922.50 | 1607.85 | 1704.32 | 9032.90 |
| Net present value (NPV) at 25% | (11,702.71) | | | | | |
| Internal rate of return (IRR) | 8.37% | | | | | |

sidiary. These are the returns the project would yield to a local Indian investor in rupee. Therefore, the project is not acceptable from this viewpoint.

**Capital budget from the parent firm's perspective**: As mentioned earlier, the capital budget from the viewpoint of the parent firm focuses on cash inflows and outflows, denominated in the currency of the parent-resident country, associated with the investment over the life of the foreign project. The cash flows should be after tax and discounted at the parent firm's reasonable capital cost. In the case of LGlobal, it needs to consider three types of cash inflows: dividends, license fees, and debt services. These cash inflows should be adjusted for any withholding taxes imposed by the Indian government and converted to US dollars. Assuming the Indian withholding tax rates of 20%, 10%, and 5% for dividends, license fees, and interest payments, respectively, we obtain the USD-denominated net dividends, net license fees, and net interest payments remitted, which are then combined to get the total earnings for the Indian project over the next 5 years, as shown in Table 16.10. The terminal value is calculated based on the present value of a perpetual net operating cash flow (NOCF) in year 5 with the WACC of LGlobal plus a foreign investment premium of 5% and a growth rate of zero:



$$\text{Terminal value} = \frac{\text{NOCF}_5(1+g)}{k_{\text{WACC}} - g} = \frac{28.37(1+0)}{0.10+0.05-0} = \text{USD189.10million}$$

**Table 16.10** LGlobal India's remittance of income to parent company, in millions of rupee and US dollar, own table

| **Exchange rate (INR/USD)** | **81.65** | **84.03** | **86.48** | **88.99** | **91.59** | **94.25** |
|---|---|---|---|---|---|---|
| Project year | 0 | 1 | 2 | 3 | 4 | 5 |
| *Dividend remittance* | | | | | | |
| Dividend paid (INR) | | – | – | 253.75 | 276.03 | 318.04 |
| Less Indian withholding taxes at 20% | | – | – | (50.75) | (55.21) | (63.61) |
| Net dividend remitted (INR) | | – | – | 203.00 | 220.83 | 254.43 |
| Net dividend remitted (USD) | | – | – | 2.28 | 2.41 | 2.70 |
| *License fees remittance* | | | | | | |
| License fees remitted (INR) | | 100.00 | 120.00 | 144.00 | 152.64 | 161.80 |
| Less Indian withholding taxes at 10% | | (10.00) | (12.00) | (14.40) | (15.26) | (16.18) |
| Net license fees remitted (INR) | | 90.00 | 108.00 | 129.60 | 137.38 | 145.62 |
| Net license fees remitted (USD) | | 1.07 | 1.25 | 1.46 | 1.50 | 1.54 |
| *Debt service remittance* | | | | | | |
| Promised interest paid (USD) | | 9.19 | 7.68 | 6.03 | 4.21 | 2.20 |
| Less Indian withholding taxes at 5% | | (0.46) | (0.38) | (0.30) | (0.21) | (0.11) |
| Net interest remitted (USD) | | 8.73 | 7.30 | 5.72 | 4.00 | 2.09 |
| Principal payments remitted (USD) | | 15.05 | 16.55 | 18.21 | 20.03 | 22.03 |
| Total principal and interest remitted (USD) | | 23.77 | 23.85 | 23.93 | 24.02 | 24.12 |
| *Capital Budget: Parent viewpoint (millions of US dollar)* | | | | | | |
| Dividends | | 0 | 0 | 2.28 | 2.41 | 2.70 |
| License fees | | 1.07 | 1.25 | 1.46 | 1.50 | 1.54 |
| Debt service | | 23.77 | 23.85 | 23.93 | 24.02 | 24.12 |
| Total earnings | | 24.84 | 25.10 | 27.67 | 27.93 | 28.37 |
| Initial investment | (214.33) | | | | | |
| Terminal value | | | | | | 189.10 |
| Free cash flow (FCF) | (214.33) | 24.84 | 25.10 | 27.67 | 27.93 | 217.47 |

(continued)

**Table 16.10** (continued)

| Exchange rate (INR/USD) | 81.65 | 84.03 | 86.48 | 88.99 | 91.59 | 94.25 |
|---|---|---|---|---|---|---|
| Project year | 0 | 1 | 2 | 3 | 4 | 5 |
| Net present value (NPV) at 15% | (27.36) | | | | | |
| Internal rate of return (IRR) | 10.49% | | | | | |

With an initial investment of USD244,947,948.56 × (0.5 + 0.5 × 0.75) = USD214.33 million, the Indian project has an NPV of −USD27.36 million, with an IRR of 10.49%. Although the IRR is slightly higher than the one obtained from the perspective of the Indian subsidiary (8.37%) and is roughly the same as the cost of capital of LGlobal (10%), it remains lower than the sum of LGlobal's WACC and the foreign investment premium, which is required for LGlobal to invest in foreign countries. Therefore, our analysis indicates the Indian project is an unsuitable investment from the parent's perspective.

Our conclusions about the Indian project from both the subsidiary and the parent viewpoints are drawn based on a set of "most likely" assumptions related to factors such as inflation and exchange rates. It is not difficult to understand how sensitive the NPV and IRR are to these assumptions. Therefore, it is common to conduct a sensitivity analysis to test how the NPV and IRR of a foreign project are sensitive to methodology and risks, such as political and foreign exchange risks, by simulating what would happen to earnings and NPV under a variety of "what if "scenarios. For the methodology part, one may ask how the NPV would change if a different model is used to estimate the terminal value. For the sensitivity analysis on risks, what if India imposes controls on paying dividends and interest to LGlobal? What if the Indian rupee appreciates instead of depreciating against the US dollar over the next 5 years? When a foreign project is analyzed from the parent's perspective, the additional risk stemming from its foreign location can be measured by adjusting the discount rates or the cash flows. Sometimes, experience and intuition are required in this adjustment process. On the other hand, we must recognize that multifaceted budgeting for an international business is becoming more commonplace. With the world becoming more uncertain, financial managers of MNEs need to be ready to revise and adjust these budgetary elements and plans to help better steer and correct the course of the business.



## Global Cash Management

**Cash Management**

Cash management refers to a firm's investment in transaction balances to cover scheduled fund outflows during the cash budgeting period and the funds tied up in precautionary cash balance.

Cash is the primary asset companies use to pay their obligations regularly. Cash inflows and outflows of companies must be prudently managed to meet their payment obligations, plan for future payments, and maintain adequate business stability. Cash management is at the core of financial and treasury management. Effective cash management reduces the risk of loss, streamlines processes, and facilitates better decision-making, allowing businesses to manage and scale their operations more effectively.

## Complexities of Global Cash Management

Global cash management utilizes cash effectively worldwide through unified management of all cash the corporate group maintains. Many cash management techniques are the same for multinational companies and domestic ones. For instance, both should keep a cash reserve, source funds at the lowest cost, and place excess funds at the greatest return. However, compared to companies with domestic operations only, MNEs must consider the cost of foreign exchange transactions in their cash management because they regularly deal with many different currencies. More formally, MNEs need to decide whether the cash management function should be centralized, possibly at corporate headquarters, or handled locally by each subsidiary.

It is helpful to utilize a cash problem faced by the hypothetical US multinational firm, LGlobal, to illustrate the difference between a centralized and a decentralized cash management system. In this case, we assume LGlobal has three sales affiliates in Germany, India, and Japan. In its cash budget for the next week, LGlobal prepares a payment matrix outlining all expected inter-affiliate cash receipts and disbursements of LGlobal as well as the receipts from and disbursements to external parties with which LGlobal does business. ◘ Table 16.11 pres-

◘ **Table 16.11** The matrix of cash receipts and disbursements for LGlobal, in thousands of US dollars, own table

| Receipts | Disbursements | | | | | | |
|---|---|---|---|---|---|---|---|
| | United States | Germany | India | Japan | Total internal | External | Total receipts |
| United States | – | 20 | 45 | 60 | 125 | 110 | 235 |
| Germany | 15 | – | 30 | 40 | 85 | 130 | 215 |
| India | 30 | 35 | – | 25 | 90 | 170 | 260 |
| Japan | 40 | 50 | 15 | – | 105 | 125 | 230 |
| Total internal | 85 | 105 | 90 | 125 | 405 | – | – |
| External | 100 | 125 | 145 | 115 | – | – | 485 |
| Total disbursements | 185 | 230 | 235 | 240 | – | 535 | 1425 |

ents the details of this matrix. The values in the table are denominated in thousands of US dollars, which is the reporting currency of LGlobal. The functional currency of each foreign affiliate is the local currency, however. We can see from this table that the US parent expects to receive the euro equivalent of US$20,000 from its German affiliate, the rupee equivalent of US$45,000 from its Indian affiliate, and the yen equivalent of US$60,000 from its Japan affiliate, a total of US$125,000 from inter-affiliate transactions. In addition, the parent expects to receive US$110,000 from external parties, so its total receipts are expected to be US$235,000 in the coming week. As for disbursements, the US parent expects to make payments of US$15,000 to its German affiliate, US$30,000 to its Indian affiliate, US$40,000 to its Japan affiliate, and US$100,000 to its external parties, a total of US$185,000. The cash flows of the three affiliates can be understood analogously. To summarize, the equivalent of US$405,000 is expected to flow among the US parent and the three foreign affiliates, but these transactions will not lead to any increase in the cash of the whole firm because they are essentially taking money out of one pocket of the corporate group and putting it into another. On the other hand, LGlobal expects to receive the equivalent of US$535,000 from the external parties and to pay US$485,000 externally, leading to an increase of US$50,000 in cash during the week.

## Various Global Cash Management Systems

Let us now consider different cash management systems and examine how they might affect the cost of cash of an MNE.

1. No netting systems: In this case, cash is managed at the local subsidiary level. For LGlobal, ◘ Table 16.11 indicates 12 foreign exchange transactions among the parent and the three foreign affiliates. ◘ Figure 16.8 diagrams these transactions. The equivalent of US$405,000 in fund flows among the parent and affiliates represents a needless use of administrative time in arranging the trades and a waste of corporate funds in making the transactions. In practice, the cost of transferring funds, which includes transaction expenses and the opportunity cost of funds tied up in inter-affiliate float, ranges from 0.25 to 1.5%. Assuming the cost to be 0.5%, the cost for transferring US$405,000 is US$2025 for the week.
2. Bilateral netting system: In this system, each pair of affiliates determines the net amount due between them, and only the net amount is transferred. Thus, the 12 foreign exchange transactions of LGlobal can be reduced by half through this netting system. As an example, the US parent and the German affiliate would net the US$20,000 and the US$15,000 to be received from one another, resulting in only one payment of US$5000 from the German affiliate to the parent. ◘ Figure 16.9 illustrates the results of bilateral netting among the LGlobal parent and affiliates. It indicates that a total of US$65,000 flows among the parent and the affiliates in six transactions. The bilateral netting system eliminates the equivalent of US$340,000 in foreign exchange transactions. At 0.5%, the

16

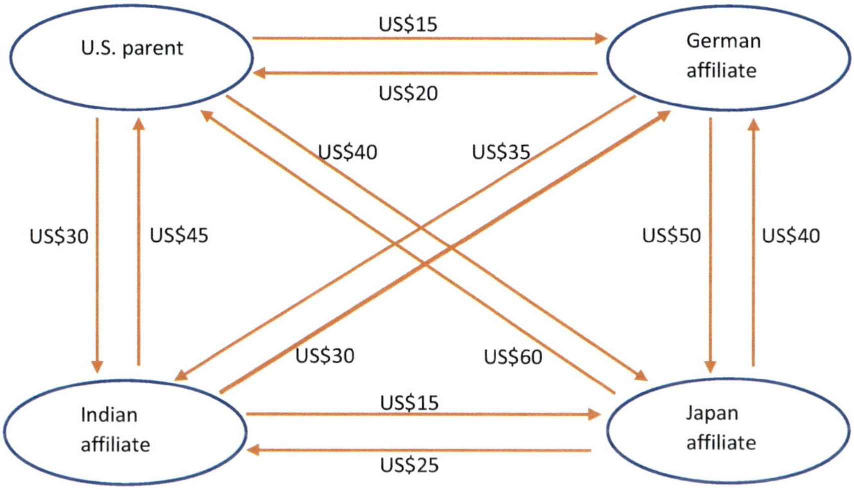


**Fig. 16.8** LGlobal's inter-affiliate foreign exchange transactions without netting, in thousands of US dollars, own diagram

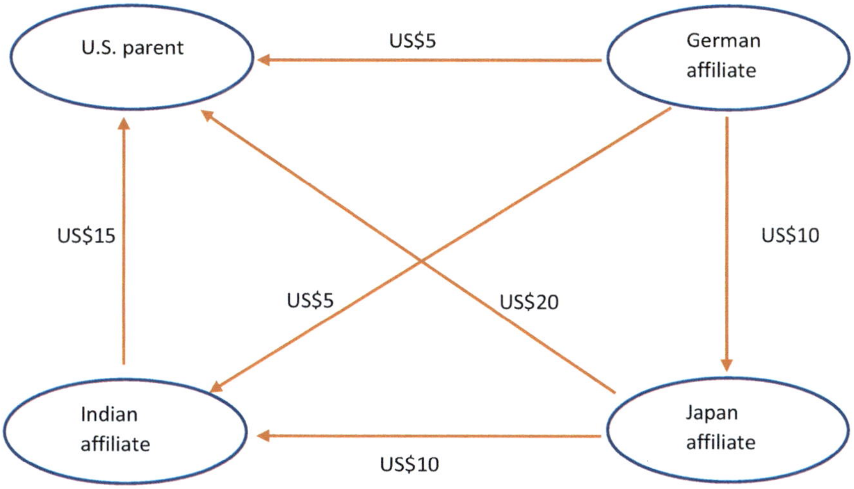


**Fig. 16.9** LGlobal's inter-affiliate foreign exchange transactions with a bilateral netting system, thousands of US dollars, own diagram

cost of netting inter-affiliate foreign exchange transactions becomes US$325, a savings of US$1700 over a non-netting system.

3. Multilateral netting system: A multilateral netting system can further reduce the cost of foreign exchange transactions. In this system, each affiliate nets all its inter-affiliate receipts against all its disbursements and then transfers if it is a net payer or receives if it is a net receiver. As shown in Table 16.11, total inter affiliate receipts will always equal total inter-affiliate disbursements. Thus,

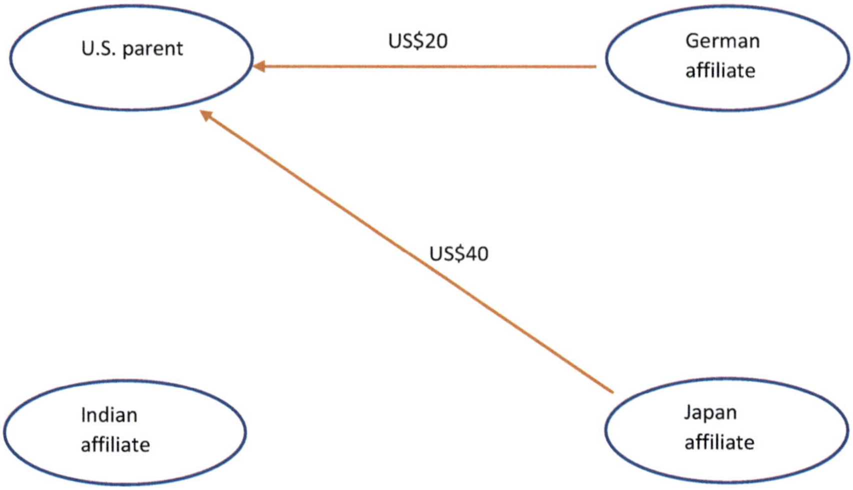


**Fig. 16.10** LGlobal's inter-affiliate foreign exchange transactions with a multilateral netting system, in thousands of US dollars, own diagram

under a multilateral netting system, the net funds to be received by the affiliates will always equal the net disbursements made by the affiliates. The results of LGlobal's foreign exchange transactions with a multilateral netting system are shown in Fig. 16.10. The Indian affiliate receives US$10,000 from the Japan affiliate and US5,000 from the German affiliate but needs to pay the parent US$15,000, so its net receipts equal zero. On the other hand, the German affiliate needs to pay the Indian affiliate US$5000, the Japanese affiliate US$10,000, and the parent firm US$5000, so it is a net payer of US$20,000. The Japanese affiliate is also a net payer with a total payment of US$40,000. Thus, only two foreign exchange transactions are necessary under a multilateral netting system. At 0.5%, the cost of transferring funds is US$300, a further savings of US$25 over a bilateral netting system. Furthermore, since the number and the volume of foreign exchange transactions significantly reduce, the multinational firm faces lower foreign exchange rate risk under this netting system.

While a multilateral netting system reduces the risk and cost of foreign exchange transactions of a multinational firm, it still requires an administrative structure in which a netting center manager overviews the inter-affiliate cash flows, estimates the amount of net payments, and determines which affiliate to make payments or receive funds. Moreover, rather than having a central cash manager, multinational firms adopting the multilateral netting system have a local cash manager in each affiliate responsible for investing excess cash and borrowing when there is a temporary cash shortage.



4. Centralized cash depository: The administrative costs of foreign exchange transactions can be further reduced through a centralized cash depository, through which all inter-affiliate payments will flow. Figure 16.11 presents LGlobal's inter-affiliate foreign exchange transactions with a central depository, a modified multilateral netting system diagram. The German and Japanese

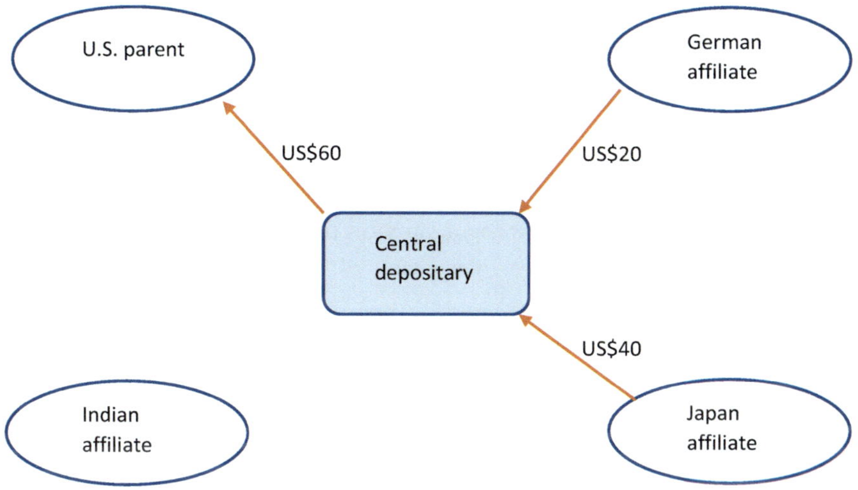


**Fig. 16.11** LGlobal's inter-affiliate foreign exchange transactions with a centralized cash depository, in thousands of US dollars, own diagram

affiliates remit the equivalent of US$20,000 and US$40,000, respectively, to the central depository, which then transfers US$60,000 to the US parent. One might question the rationale of setting up the central depository as it appears that the foreign exchange transaction has doubled from US$60,000 under the multilateral netting system (Fig. 16.10) to US$120,000 with such a central depository. However, this is not necessarily the case. The central depository can instruct the German and the Japanese affiliates to transfer the funds in their local currencies to the depository, which then converts these currencies to the US dollar and remits them to the US parent.

So far, we have illustrated LGlobal's inter-affiliate foreign exchange transactions under different netting systems. However, the primary benefit of having a centralized cash depository derives from the affiliates' business transactions with external parties. As shown in Table 16.11, the parent firm expects to receive US$110,000 but to pay US$100,000 externally, resulting in net receipts of US$10,000 at the end of the week. Analogously, the German, Indian, and Japanese affiliates expect net receipts of US$5000, US$25,000, and US$10,000, respectively. In total, US$50,000 of net receipts are expected from LGlobal. Figure 16.12 diagrams these flows to the central depository. With such a central depository, excess cash is remitted to the central cash pool, and the principal cash manager arranges to cover money shortages, a method termed "cash pooling." One benefit of this arrangement is that the central cash manager has a global view of the MNE's overall cash positions, because of which she will know the best borrowing and investing rates. Consequently, such a centralized system facilitates funds mobilization: Systemwide cash excesses are invested at the highest rates, and cash shortages are covered by borrowing at the lowest rates. Without a centralized depository, one affiliate may borrow locally at an unfavorable rate while another invests locally at a disadvantageous rate.

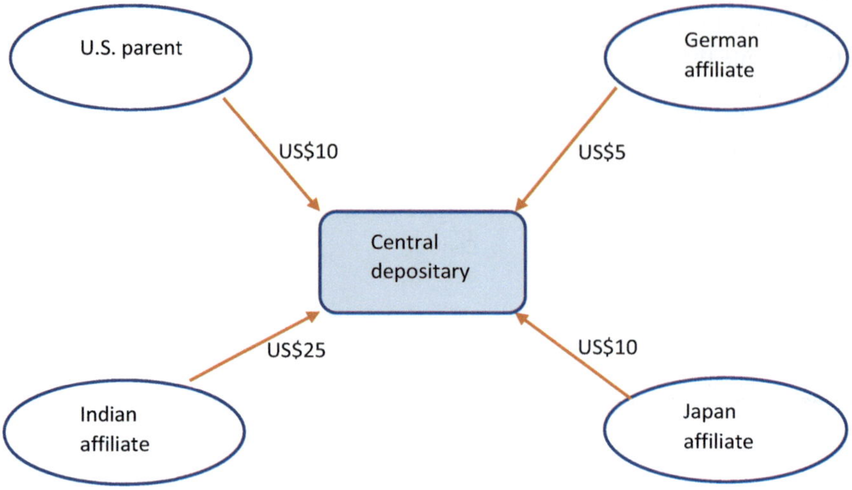


**Fig. 16.12** Flows of LGlobal's net cash receipts from transactions with external parties with a centralized depository, in thousands of US dollars, own diagram

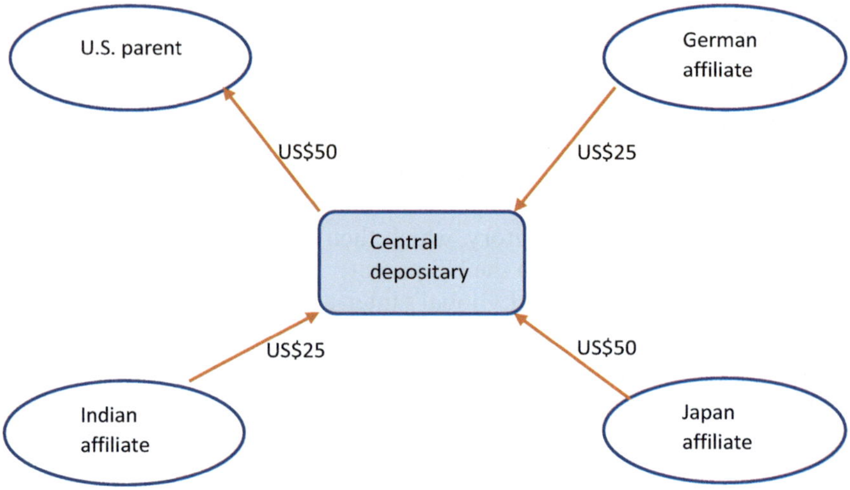


**Fig. 16.13** Net cash flows of LGlobal affiliates through centralized depository after netting multilateral netting payments and net payments from external transactions, in thousands of US dollars, own diagram



It is not difficult to see that cash management efficiency can be further improved by bilaterally netting the inter-affiliate cash flows with the external ones and only letting the net sums go through the central depository. Figure 16.13 shows these netting flows. For inter-affiliate transactions, the parent expects to receive US$60,000 from the central depository next week (Fig. 16.11). Meanwhile, it expects to transfer US$10,000 to the central depository (Fig. 16.12). Collectively, the central depository will remit

US$50,000 to the parent firm. With the same logic, the central depository expects to receive US$25,000, US$25,000, and US$50,000 from the German, Indian, and Japanese affiliates, respectively. In total, the central depository receives US$100,000 and disburses US$50,000, for an expected net increase in cash of US$50,000 for the week. Put differently, instead of two separate sets of cash flows totaling US$60,000 from the multilateral netting system and US$50,000 from transactions with external parties, only one set of cash flows occurs after the netting. Although the total amount does not change in this case, the number of foreign exchange transactions is reduced. When affiliates have net payments to external parties, the amount of cash flows after the netting in the one set of cash flows is lower than that in the two separate sets of cash flows.

Another significant benefit of a centralized cash depository is that it can significantly reduce the whole firm's investment in precautionary cash balances without reducing its ability to cover unforeseen expenses. To understand this point, let us assume that the parent firm and the affiliates of LGlobal have to make all its planned payments to external parties before they receive any cash from other external parties. Take the Japan affiliate as an example. It will have to pay the equivalent of US$115,000 to external parties before it receives any of the expected US$125,000. Thus, the Japan affiliate will need a transaction balance of US$115,000 to cover unexpected transactions. Additionally, LGlobal needs to keep a prudent cash balance to cover incidental transactions during the cash budget period, and the safety desirability of the firm determines its size. The larger the precautionary cash balance, the less the risk of financial embarrassment. We assume that the cash needs of each affiliate are normally distributed and independent. If LGlobal follows a more conservative strategy, it may keep three standard deviations of cash needs in addition to the cash needed to cover the expected transactions for the planning period. ◘ Table 16.12

**◘ Table 16.12** Transaction and precautionary cash balances of LGlobal under different cash management systems, in US dollar, own table

| **Affiliate** | **Expected transactions** | **Standard deviation of cash needs** | **Expected transactions and precautionary balance** |
|---|---|---|---|
| *Panel A: Under a decentralized cash management system* | | | |
| United States | 100,000 | 50,000 | 250,000 |
| Germany | 125,000 | 65,000 | 320,000 |
| India | 145,000 | 80,000 | 385,000 |
| Japan | 115,000 | 55,000 | 280,000 |
| **Total** | 485,000 | – | 1,235,000 |
| *Panel B: Under a centralized cash management system* | | | |
| **Total** | 485,000.00 | 127,082.65 | 866,247.95 |

shows these cash needs for LGlobal parent and affiliates. The expected transactions and precautionary balance in the next week are the sum of expected transactions and three times the standard deviation of cash needs. Each affiliate holds its transaction balance and precautionary cash under a decentralized cash management system, as shown in Panel A. Thus, the whole firm's total transaction balance and precautionary cash are US$1,235,000. However, the amount of cash the multinational firm holds is considered a portfolio under a centralized cash management system. While each affiliate holds cash to cover its expected transactions, a central cash manager at the central cash depository holds the precautionary cash balances, whose standard deviation depends on the standard deviations of affiliate-level cash needs. In the case of LGlobal, the standard deviation of cash needs held by the central cash manager is

$$\sqrt{50,000^2 + 65,000^2 + 80,000^2 + 55,000^2} = \text{US\$127,082.65}$$

Thus, only thrice of US$127,082.65 (=US$381,247.95) is held for preventive purposes by LGlobal's central cash manager. Under the centralized cash management system, US$866,247.95 is needed to cover expected transactions and precautionary balances. The precautionary cash balance under the decentralized cash management system is reduced almost by half (i.e., from US$750,000 to US$381,247.95). Instead of standing by for preventive purposes, the cash can be invested in more profitable projects.

Motivated by the above-mentioned benefits of a centralized cash management system, academia and practitioners advocate a trend toward centralizing global cash management. For instance, Polak (2009, p. 109) suggests that centralizing treasury activities allows corporations to achieve higher efficiency, greater transparency, and access to real-time information across a broad geographical area and many entities. In reality, however, few MNEs operate with a fully centralized cash management setup. Instead, most of them work with some degree of centralized structure. Using interview data with 20 treasury experts in European multinational companies, Bartsch (2019) finds a distinction between strategic and operational aspects of cash management. Although the majority supported centralization, there is no "one cash management perspective." In particular, many interviewees thought that just because one does something from a central hub does not make it better.



In an environment with constant change and development, the degree of centralization is often affected by many factors, such as legal and tax implications, access to financial markets, technological infrastructure, staff training, and corporate culture. Among these factors, technology is considered a driver and enabler of centralization. In recent years, cloud-based cash and treasury management technologies have been developed and become popular in improving organizational flexibility, cash management processes, and security. Additionally, cash management solutions have become more accessible for businesses of all sizes. There are many affordable options from different vendors to integrate and optimize other cash management functions of an MNE. However, implementing the new cash management solutions may require cooperation and alignment between various departments of the firm.

## Transfer Pricing

**Transfer Price**

"The transfer price is the internal value placed on a raw material, good, or service as it moves from one related organizational entity to another within a consolidated corporate group." (Cravens, 1997, p. 128)

Transfer pricing is conducted for various reasons, ranging from economic (e.g., efficiency in resource allocation), functional (e.g., divisionalization of the organization into profit centers responsible for both revenues and costs), organizational (e.g., enhancing integration and differentiation within divisionalized organizations), to strategic (e.g., influence by and on accounting mechanisms) necessity (Kumar et al., 2021, p. 275).

However, transfer pricing can be subject to unethical exploitation. MNEs often use transfer pricing to allocate pre-tax profits among various subsidiaries to reduce the parent company's overall tax burden. As a simple and extreme example, a UK-based multinational firm has subsidiaries in Japan and Bermuda. It costs the firm £1,000,000 to render a specific service in the United Kingdom. It then sells that service to the Bermuda affiliate for £1,000,000, leaving no profits in the United Kingdom. The Bermuda affiliate immediately sells that service to the Japanese affiliate for £2000,000, leaving £1,000,000 profit in Bermuda. That Japanese affiliate sells the service at the actual market price of £2000,000 to its clients, leaving no profits in Japan. Bermuda is a well-known tax haven due to its low corporate tax rate, while the tax rates in the United Kingdom and Japan are much higher. Through transfer pricing, the UK-based firm does not need to pay taxes in the United Kingdom or Japan. Instead, it moves the taxable profit to Bermuda and pays lower taxes.

A body of work has documented profit-shifting behavior by MNEs. For example, according to Tørsløv et al. (Tørsløv et al., 2023, p. 1499), around 36% of multinational profits—profits booked by firms outside of their headquarters' country—are shifted to tax havens globally, and US multinationals shift twice as much profit as other multinationals relative to the size of their foreign earnings.

## Transfer Pricing Guidelines

The profit-shifting behaviors of MNEs have attracted the attention of economists and policymakers. In 2015, the Organisation for Economic Co-operation and Development (OECD) and the G20 launched the Inclusive Framework on Base

Erosion and Profit Shifting (BEPS), aiming at curbing tax avoidance possibilities stemming from mismatches between different countries' tax systems. According to the framework, the basis of transfer pricing is the arm's length principle which states that the price agreed in a transaction between two related parties must be the same as the price agreed in a comparable transaction between two independent parties. With the objective of avoiding tax erosion, this principle is agreed upon by all member countries of the OECD. It provides a single international standard of tax computation, enabling various governments to collect their share of taxes and creating enough provisions for MNEs to avoid double taxation. OECD's BEPS Actions 8–10 address transfer pricing guidance to ensure that transfer pricing outcomes are better aligned with the value creation of the MNE group[1]:

- Action 8—Intangibles: It addresses transfer pricing issues relating to controlled transactions involving intangibles, which are mobile and often hard to value. Misallocation of the profits generated by valuable intangibles has heavily contributed to base erosion and profit shifting.
- Action 9—Risks and capital: It considers the contractual allocation of risks and the resulting allocation of profits to these risks, which may not correspond with the activities actually carried out. It also addresses the level of returns to funding provided by a capital-rich MNE group member, where those returns do not correspond to the level of activity undertaken by the funding company.
- Action 10—High-risk transactions: It focuses on other high-risk areas, including the scope for addressing profit allocations resulting from controlled transactions which are not commercially rational, the scope for targeting the use of transfer pricing methods in a way leading to diverting profits from the most economically significant activities of the MNE group, and the use of a specific type of payments between members of the MNE group (e.g., management fees and head office expenses) to erode the tax base in the absence of alignment with the value-creation.

On 11 February 2020, the OECD released its final report with transfer pricing guidance on financial transactions. It is follow-up guidance concerning BEPS Action 4 (Limiting base erosion involving interest deductions and other financial payments) and Actions 8–10.[2] It aims to clarify the arm's length principle application and provides a detailed guideline for the accurate delineation analysis of financial transactions. Essential items discussed in the report include:

- Intra-group lenders without functional substance: Companies should evaluate whether they have any profit from intra-group lending in countries that do not have the people functions needed to manage and control the financial risks. Such a lender would be entitled to no more than a risk-free return, and the remainder would be allocable to the party exercising control over the investment risk.



1 More details about the OECD's Base Erosion and Profit Shifting (BEPS) Actions 8–10 can be found from ► https://www.oecd.org/tax/beps/beps-actions/actions8-10/.

2 The report is available at ► https://www.oecd.org/tax/beps/transfer-pricing-guidance-on-financial-transactions-inclusive-framework-on-beps-actions-4-8-10.pdf.

- Precise delineation of guaranteed loans: Companies should evaluate whether any loans were made to a group company that could only borrow due to a guarantee by another group company and could not have raised the funds on its own. Such a transaction can be delineated as a loan to the guarantor followed by a capital contribution from the guarantor to the borrower.
- Actual delineation of the terms of funding: The report emphasizes the importance of the true delineation of the transaction. Companies should evaluate all the terms of their intra-group funding and consider how to document that the terms and conditions—not merely the interest rate—are at arm's length.
- Cash pools: Generally, a cash pool leader performs no more than a coordination or agency function. Accordingly, her remuneration as a service provider will typically be similarly limited, although it acknowledges that cash pool leaders with more functionality can exist. Any company with material income in a cash pool leader should be prepared to substantiate that allocation of income based on the performance of control functions over credit, liquidity, and other risks by employees of the cash pool leader.
- Credit rating: The report provides extensive guidance about determining the stand-alone rating of group companies and considering the benefit of a group membership. Companies should consider their group's policies for determining credit ratings of subsidiaries in light of the report and particularly consider the group's view on willingness and ability to support troubled group companies.

On 20 January 2022, the OECD consolidated all transfer pricing guidance into one single publication and released the 2022 edition of the OECD Transfer Pricing Guidelines for Multinational Enterprises and Tax Administrations, which represents the international consensus on the valuation, for income tax purposes, of cross-border transactions between associated enterprises.

## A Simple Transfer Pricing Example

Unlike transactions between unrelated parties, transactions between related companies are less directly affected by market forces (i.e., supply and demand) due to corporate synergies, economies of scale, or tax planning. When analyzing these transactions, one needs to evaluate the agreed price of services rendered, the profit margin, and the risks assumed from both an economic and a legal point of view to verify whether the related parties comply with the arm's length principle. While a complete understanding of the methodology is out of our scope in this chapter, let us use a loan agreement between Company ABC and its foreign subsidiary Company XYZ as an example to illustrate how to apply the arm's length principle to detect transfer pricing and recharacterize it. Company ABC provides USD 10 billion to Company XYZ in the form of a revolving credit facility (RCF) arrangement, a flexible financing tool allowing the borrower to repay the loan or take it out again during an allotted period. The RCF has a maturity of 5 years and an interest rate of 5% per annum. After 4 years, Company XYZ uses up to USD 8 billion of the RCF, paying off most of the balance and monitoring how much available credit remains. However, an amount of USD 4 billion continues to be a loan under the RCF due to an inability to repay the RCF. A year later, the RCF reaches the maturity date and is subsequently renewed, with a maturity of 5 years and a maximum amount of USD 5 billion. At the beginning of the sixth year, the amount drawn under the RCF becomes USD 4.5 billion. In this example, the RCF between the two related companies might not be aligned with the arm's length principle and thus lead to a dispute with tax authorities for at least three reasons. First, the actual tenor of the RCF is 10 years instead of 5 years since it is renewed at the end of the fifth year. Second, the interest rate should be adjusted and increased following the maturity extension. Third, the loan is never fully repaid because the amounts borrowed under the RCF never go below USD 4 billion.

## Transfer Pricing Methods

As summarized by Rossing et al. (2017, pp. 8–11), MNEs can choose between the five methods suggested by the OECD to determine an arm's length transfer price:

1. Comparable uncontrolled price (CUP) method: This method identifies the market price in a similar market transaction and applies this market price to the intra-group transaction. The CUP can refer to either an internal market price, which is available when an MNE group company sells the same service to an external customer or a group company, or an external market price, which refers to the price observed in a comparable transaction between two companies not related to the MNE group. As an example of the internal CUP method, a US-based car rental company can rely on the licensing fee it charges an independent third party that uses its branding to determine how much to charge its Mexican subsidiary for using its brand name and logo. If, however, the US-based company has no relationships with third parties and thus has no similar internal transactions to use, it can apply the external CUP method by identifying comparable transactions between two unrelated companies, that is, a price close to the market price of the licensing fee in this case.
2. Resale price (RP) method: This method uses the price charged by an MNE re-seller (i.e., distributor) to an independent customer unrelated to the MNE and subtracts a comparable market-based gross margin. The difference between the market price and a market-based gross margin is considered an arm's length transfer price. For instance, the distributor provides the service to an independent customer with a unit price of USD 10,000 and an average gross margin of 20%. Then the 20% is applied as an arm's length gross margin for the MNE distributor. Finally, the transfer price per unit is set at USD 8000 to ensure the correct application of the RP method. The RP method aims to ensure that the intra-group re-seller earns a gross margin similar to that of independent market players based on the comparability factors. It is suggested by the OECD Guidelines when MNEs cannot find internal or external CUPs.
3. Cost plus (CP) method: Unlike the RP method, which focuses on the resale price of the distributor, the CP method focuses on the manufacturer as a tested

party, takes the manufacturer's cost of goods sold, and adds an appropriate markup based on the markup in comparable transactions between independent parties. The markup can be the one applied by the MNE manufacturer when selling products to an independent party or the one used by an independent manufacturer. Service firms can use this method to determine the transfer price of shared services provided by a shared service center for their subsidiaries in other countries. The OECD Guidelines suggest the CP method when MNEs cannot find internal or external CUPs.

4. Transactional net margin (TNM) method: When none of the abovementioned methods is available, the MNE can choose the TNM method, which works similarly to the CP and RP methods but examines net margins earned in comparable market transactions rather than gross margins. The TNM method is typically applied to the MNE that does not own intangibles because it is relatively easy to obtain data from comparable independent companies performing similar routine functions. A key element for applying the TNM method is selecting a net profit indicator that may consider items such as sales, costs, or assets as denominators. Another important aspect is the availability of segmented financial information that effectively identifies revenues, costs, and operational expenses associated with the transaction to be tested. For example, France-based Company A has provided service to its wholly-owned subsidiary outside France for EUR 5000,000 with a net profit margin of 10%. Thus, the direct and indirect costs amount to EUR 4,500,000. The net profit margin for a comparable transaction between Company A and an independent company is 20%. Applying the TNM method, the arm's length price of the price of service provided to Company A's foreign subsidiary is EUR 4,500,000/(1–20%) = EUR 5,625,000, and the net profit is EUR 5,625,000 – EUR 4,500,000/(1–20%) = EUR 1,125,000.
5. Profit-split (PS) method: This method examines the total net profit generated from the intra-group transaction without referencing comparable market conditions. It is considered relevant when both parties in the intra-group transaction own intangibles and are engaged in complex intra-group transactions. The total profit is split between the two related companies based on what independent parties would likely have expected to realize from engaging in a similar transaction, considering the functions performed, risks assumed, and assets owned by each party of the intra-group transaction. For example, consider a software company with a sales affiliate working with its research and development (R&D) affiliate to bring new software to market. The R&D affiliate bears the costs and risks of launching the new software. The two related parties must determine the correct profit split terms to include in their agreement. Based on their relative investments and risks, they can evaluate the contributions made by both parties for R&D, marketing, and other necessary expenses and then split the net profit based on the relative contributions. For example, suppose the two parties invested a total of USD100 million in bringing the new software to market, and the R&D affiliate contributed USD75 million. In that case, the R&D affiliate will make 75% of future profits, and the sales affiliate will collect the remaining 25%.

## Comparability Analysis

The most critical aspect of applying the arm's length principle to an intra-group transaction is undertaking a "comparability analysis." In this analysis, one must (1) identify the commercial or financial relations between the related parties and the conditions and economically relevant circumstances attaching to those relations to delineate the intercompany transaction accurately; and (2) compare the conditions and the economically relevant circumstances of the accurately delineated intercompany transaction with those of comparable transactions between independent enterprises (Russo & Dekker, 2021, p. 30). The goal of the comparability analysis is to obtain the "real" price of an intra-group transaction that is in line with the actual contribution of the associated enterprises to the creation of value.

An essential part of the comparability analysis involves applying the transfer pricing methods, also known as comparability factors, and assessing the availability of market data in the context of the relevant transfer pricing methods. The comparability analysis consists of four core steps in the practical process, as shown in ◘ Fig. 16.14. The first step is identifying the specific intra-group transactions to be analyzed and the particular group companies involved. Usually, analysts (e.g., internal controllers, tax staff, and external transfer pricing consultants) usually illustrate the transactions, and the related parties provide an overview for further analyses. In the second step, they need to perform an analysis (in particular, a functional analysis) of the controlled transactions under investigation. The analysis is usually undertaken by the MNE's tax function in collaboration with external transfer pricing specialists by interviewing key employees of business functions and reviewing formal contracts guiding the intra-group trade. The analysis outcomes show the tasks performed, the risk assumed, and the assets each company owns regarding the intra-group transactions. The third critical step is to identify

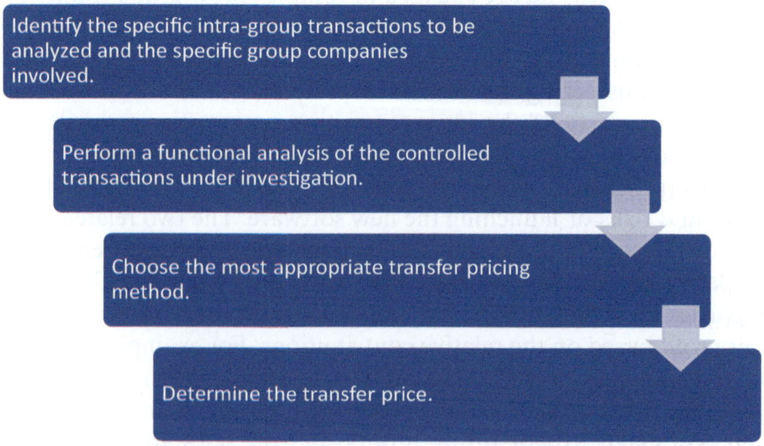


◘ **Fig. 16.14** Core steps of a comparability analysis, own diagram

the most appropriate transfer pricing method based on the availability of comparable market data. The CUP method is most preferred among the five transfer pricing methods mentioned above, assuming the necessary data are available. Otherwise, the methods focusing on gross margins (i.e., the RP and the CP methods) are recommended by the OECD Guidelines, followed by the TNM approach, which focuses on net profit margins. The PS method is recommended if none of the above techniques is appropriate due to a lack of data. Finally, the transfer price is determined in the fourth step based on the specific transfer pricing method chosen in the previous step.

## Challenges and Changes

Despite the OECD Guidelines, recent political and public concerns about tax avoidance of MNEs have stimulated critiques of current rules and debates about proposals for change. In addition, the financial crisis is considered a turning point after which the regulatory environment for large businesses became more intensely scrutinized and entered the public imagination (Anesa et al., 2019, p. 17; Picciotto, 2022, pp. 647–648). In this context, Rogers and Oats (2022) examine how the common understanding of the arm's length principle has developed and changed by conducting a qualitative study on the work of senior transfer pricing tax professionals in the United Kingdom and the United States over 10 years starting from 2006. Their analysis focuses on the response of elite transfer pricing professionals to one specific aspect of transfer pricing, the mechanism for allocating taxable profits between countries, and tries to understand transfer pricing as a field of practice. Specifically, they ask two questions: First, how has the common understanding and knowledge of the arm's length principle developed? And second, how have senior transfer pricing professionals' views of the principle changed? An overlapping group of interviewees was asked the same questions during the two rounds of interviews, one in 2006/2007 and the other in 2016/2017. They found that the arm's length principle was considered the preeminent mechanism for allocating taxable profits between the countries where MNEs operate in the first round of interviews. However, from the second interview, which followed significant disruption impacting the transfer pricing field, they found that the principle was no longer held in such high regard, and potential alternative approaches were possible. They also found that these senior professionals were sensitive to field disruptors and displayed adaptability. They were willing to recognize and discuss non-taxation in addition to double taxation and to consider alternative approaches to allocating combined profits of MNEs to each taxing jurisdiction (pp. 94–100).

Meanwhile, many countries have implemented regulations that strengthen information reporting to curb profit shifting. Some studies evaluate the effectiveness of these regulations. For instance, Bustos et al. (2022) examine the effect of the transfer-pricing regulations introduced by Chile in 2011. These regulations expanded information reporting requirements on international transfers by multinationals, changed legislation to make it easier for the tax authority to enforce transfer-pricing rules, and increased resources devoted to enforcing these rules by the tax authority. Their results suggest that the reform did not significantly reduce profit shifting. The propensity of MNEs to make tax-motivated payments to their foreign affiliates for intellectual property, interests, or services did not change after the reform (pp. 36–37).

On the other hand, ongoing tax reforms may substantially affect MNEs' motives to shift profit through transfer pricing. For example, in October 2021, with the leadership of the OECD, 136 countries and jurisdictions agreed to implement a minimum corporate income tax of 15% from 2023 (OECD, n.d.). Such an agreement would extensively remove incentives for countries to offer rates lower than 15% if well implemented, and hence, it will demotivate MNEs from shifting profits across national borders.

## Review Questions

1. What is a money market hedge? How to utilize it to reduce the foreign exchange exposure related to an account payable?
2. The cruise industry suffered major financial losses due to the Covid-19 travel restrictions. Suppose a UK-based cruise vacation company has reacted by restructuring its fleet, removing less efficient ships throughout the whole fleet. The company signed a contract in June 2023 to sell one cruise ship to a US buyer at a price of US$ 750 million and is expected to receive the payment in June 30, 2024. When the contract was signed, the exchange rate was 1 Pound = 1.25 US dollars. Identify the foreign exchange exposure faced by the UK firm and illustrate how a forward contract can be used to hedge this exposure.
3. How can currency options be used to manage transaction exposure?
4. Compare the three strategies introduced in this chapter in hedging transaction exposure.
5. Do you agree that managing operating exposure is more challenging than managing translation exposure? Please explain why.
6. Briefly discuss four proactive strategies to reduce operating exposure.
7. Discuss why some firms hedge foreign exchange exposure while others do not.
8. An MNE has $12 billion of market value in equity and $8 billion in debt. Its tax rate is 20%, cost of equity is 10%, and its cost of debt is 5%. Please calculate the firm's cost of capital using WACC.
9. Why will using the traditional CAPM overstate the cost of capital of MNEs with access to global capital markets? How should one estimate their cost of equity?
10. Firm A is located in a small and emerging market. Its market capitalization is relatively large in the local market. With a risk-free rate of 3%, a return of 10% on the local market portfolio and a beta of 1.2, please estimate Firm A's cost of equity using CAPM. If the company has access to the global equity market, which model should be used to estimate its cost of equity? How will the new model change its equity cost estimation?

11. What are the benefits of MNEs from illiquid and segmented markets raising capital in liquid and advanced markets?
12. What is multinational capital budgeting? How is it different from domestic capital budgeting?
13. Briefly outline the multinational capital budgeting process from the perspectives of the parent firm and the foreign subsidiary. Which viewpoint do you think the financial manager of an MNE should take?
14. What is global cash management? Briefly describe some cash management systems.
15. What are the benefits of using a centralized cash depository to manage cash?
16. Use an example to illustrate transfer pricing.
17. What is the arm's length principle? Please summarize the OECD Guidelines on how to apply this principle in transfer pricing.
18. What are the five methods suggested by the OECD to determine an arm's length transfer price? Please give an order to these methods based on the OECD instructions.
19. Show how to conduct a comparability analysis in transfer pricing.
20. Discuss the current challenges faced by governments and MNEs in transfer pricing.

## Closing Case: How Did Google Utilize Transfer Pricing for Tax Avoidance?

As a giant multinational service firm providing many products and services, Google has 87 subsidiaries across over 35 jurisdictions. Google has been under the spotlight in the past two decades partly because of its tax affairs.

The heart of Google's international operations is located in central Dublin, Ireland. In 2009, the Dublin subsidiary, which employs nearly 2000 people and sells advertising throughout Europe, the Middle East, and Africa, was credited with 88% of the search juggernaut's $12.5 billion sales abroad. However, most of the profits went to the tax haven of Bermuda, where there's no corporate income tax at all, through a convoluted route known as the "Double Irish" and the "Dutch Sandwich." The strategy works as follows. When a company in Europe, the Middle East, or Africa purchases a search ad through Google, it sends the money to Google Ireland. Although the Irish government taxes corporate profits at 12.5%, Google mostly escapes that tax because its earnings do not stay in the Dublin office. In fact, this office reported a pretax profit of less than 1% of revenues in 2008. So instead, Google transferred these profits to the Netherlands because (1) Irish law makes it difficult for Google to send the money directly to Bermuda without incurring a significant tax hit; (2) Ireland does not tax certain payments to companies in other European Union states; and (3) Dutch tax laws are generous about sending money to Bermuda. As a result, Google's subsidiary in the Netherlands is just a shell without employees but passes

Tax avoidance, image by photosforyou from Pixabay

on about 99.8% of what it collects to Bermuda. Essentially, Google's Bermuda subsidiary is an Irish company, hence the "Double Irish" nickname.

Google Ireland licenses its search and advertising technology from Google, headquartered in the United States. The Irish subsidiary is supposed to pay an "arm's length" price (i.e., the same amount an unrelated company would pay) for the rights. Yet because licensing fees from the Irish subsidiary generate income taxed at as high as 35% in the United States, Google has the incentive to set the licensing price as low as possible. As a result, the transfer pricing allows Google to attribute its overseas profits to its Irish operations instead of the United States, where Google developed most of its technology.

These strategies have saved Google billions of dollars and significantly boosted its overall earnings. Its rate from 2007 to 2009 was only 2.4%, much lower than the tax rate of other giant technology companies in the United States (e.g., Apple, Oracle, Microsoft, and IBM), ranging from 4.5 to 25.8% during the same period. Notably, all these arrangements are legal. Google is not alone. According to company spokesman Jane Penner, "Google's practices are very similar to those at countless other global companies operating across a wide range of industries".

**Questions**

1. What is transfer pricing?
2. Do you think Google's practice is appropriate?
3. What are the consequences of corporate tax avoidance through transfer pricing?
4. What are the possible ways to curb tax erosion via transfer pricing?

Sources: (Drucker, 2010; SEC, n.d.)

16

**Summary**

This chapter

- Introduced three strategies to manage transaction exposure:
  - Money market hedge
  - Forward market hedge
  - Options market hedge
- Outlined different proactive strategies adopted to reduce operating exposure:
  - Risk-sharing contracts
  - Leading and lagging
  - Reinvoicing centers
  - Matching currency cash flows
- Illustrated how to estimate the cost of debt and equity for a multinational firm and explained why a firm from an illiquid and segmented market can reduce its cost of capital by raising capital in advanced markets:
  - Diversified international investors
  - Improved market liquidity
  - Better corporate governance
- Showed how multinational capital budgeting differs from domestic capital budgeting and used a hypothetical firm to illustrate global capital budgeting from two perspectives:
  - The foreign subsidiary's perspective
  - The parent firm's perspective
- Discussed different cash management systems and examined how they affect the cost of cash of an MNE:
  - No netting systems
  - Bilateral netting system
  - Multilateral netting system
  - Centralized cash depository
- Introduced transfer pricing and the OECD's Guidelines on how to estimate the arm's length price of transactions between related parties:
  - Comparable uncontrolled price method
  - Resale price method
  - Cost plus method
  - Transactional net margin method
  - Profit-split method

## References

Aliber, R. Z. (1973). The Interest rate parity theorem: A reinterpretation. *Journal of Political Economy, 81*, 1451–1459.

Amihud, Y. (2002). Illiquidity and stock returns: Cross-section and time-series effects. *Journal of Financial Markets, 5*, 31–56.

Amihud, Y., Hameed, A., Kang, W., & Zhang, H. (2015). The illiquidity premium: International evidence. *Journal of Financial Economics, 117*, 350–368.

Amihud, Y., & Mendelson, H. (1986). Asset pricing and the bid-ask spread. *Journal of Financial Economics, 17*, 223–249.

Anesa, M., Gillespie, N., Spee, A. P., & Sadiq, K. (2019). The legitimation of corporate tax minimization. *Accounting, Organizations and Society, 75*, 17–39.
Bartsch, C. (2019, September 10). *Factors to consider when centralising cash management*. Retrieved from The Global Treasurer: https://www.theglobaltreasurer.com/2019/09/10/factors-to-consider-when-centralising-cash-management/.
Bhandari, L. C. (1988). Debt/equity ratio and expected common stock returns: Empirical evidence. *Journal of Finance, 43*, 507–528.
Bustos, S., Pomeranz, D., Serrato, J. C., Vila-Belda, J., & Zucman, G. (2022). *The race between tax enforcement and tax planning: Evidence from a natural experiment in Chile*. Working paper.
Butler, K. C. (2016). *Multinational finance: Evaluating the opportunities, costs, and risks of multinational operations*. Wiley.
Copeland, T., & Joshi, Y. (1996). Why derivatives don't reduce FX risk. *The McKinsey Quarterly, 1*, 66–79.
Cravens, K. S. (1997). Examining the role of transfer pricing as a strategy for multinational firms. *International Business Review, 6*, 127–145.
Drucker, J. (2010, October 22). *'Dutch Sandwich' saves Google billions in taxes*. Retrieved from NBC News https://www.nbcnews.com/id/wbna39784907.
Eiteman, D. K., Stonehill, A., & Moffett, M. (2016). *Multinatonal business finance*. Pearson.
Errunza, V. R., & Miller, D. P. (2000). Market segmentation and the cost of capital in international equity market. *Journal of Financial and Quantitative Analysis, 35*, 577–600.
Eun, C. S., Resnick, B. G., & Chuluun, T. (2020). Foreign exchange exposure and management. In C. S. Eun, B. G. Resnick, & T. Chuluun (Eds.) *International financial management* (p. 249).
Fama, E. F., & French, K. R. (1992). The cross-section of expected stock returns. *Journal of Finance, 47*, 427–465.
Feldman, R. A. (1985). *Foreign currency options: Reducing exchange risks: An innovative approach.* Retrieved from IMF eLIBRARY https://www.elibrary.imf.org/view/journals/022/0022/004/article-A009-en.xml.
Feng, F. Y., Kang, W., & Zhang, H. (2022). *Liquidity shocks and the negative premium of liquidity volatility around the world*. Working paper.
Froot, K. A., Scharfstein, D. S., & Stein, J. C. (1993). Risk management: Coordinating corporate investment and financing policies. *Journal of Finance, 48*, 1629–1658.
Goel, S. (2015). *Capital budgeting*. Business Expert Press.
Grant, R., & Soenen, L. (2004). Strategic management of operating exposure. *European Management Journal, 22*, 53–62.
Hagelin, N. (2003). Why firms hedge with currency derivatives: an examination of transaction and translation exposure. *Applied Financial Economics, 13*, 55–69.
Hillier, D., & Loncan, T. (2019). Stock market integration, cost of equity capital, and corporate investment: Evidence from Brazil. *European Financial Management, 25*, 181–206.
Kumar, S., Pandey, N., Lim, W., Chatterjee, A., & Pandey, N. (2021). What do we know about transfer pricing? Insights from bibliometric analysis. *Journal of Business Research, 134*, 275–287.
Lesmond, D. A., Ogden, J. P., & Trzcinka, C. A. (1999). A new estimate of transaction costs. *Review of Financial Studies, 12*, 1113–1141.
Maersk. (2022, February 9). *Annual report 2021*. Retrieved from https://investor.maersk.com/news-releases/news-release-details/annual-report-2021.
Miles, J. A., & Ezzell, J. R. (1980). The weighted average cost of capital, perfect capital markets, and project life: A clarification. *Journal of Financial and Quantitative Analysis, 15*, 719–730.
Mukherjee, T., Al Rahahleh, N., & Lane, W. (2016). The capital budgeting process of healthcare organizations: A review of surveys. *Journal of Healthcare Management, 61*, 58–76.
OECD. (n.d.). *International community strikes a ground-breaking tax deal for the digital age*. Retrieved from https://www.oecd.org/tax/international-community-strikes-a-ground-breaking-tax-deal-for-the-digital-age.htm.
Picciotto, S. (2022). Technocracy in the era of Twitter: Between intergovernmentalism and supranational technocratic politics in global tax governance. *Regulation and Governance, 16*, 634–652.
Polak, P. (2009). "The centre holds"—from the decentralised treasury towards fully centralised cash and treasury management. *Journal of Corporate Treasury Management, 3*, 109–112.

Rogers, H., & Oats, L. (2022). Transfer pricing: Changing views in changing times. *Accounting Forum, 46*, 83–107.

Rossing, C. P., Cools, M., & Rohde, C. (2017). International transfer pricing in multinational enterprises. *Journal of Accounting Education, 39*, 55–67.

Russo, A., & Dekker, A. (2021). Chapter 2: Accurate delineation of intra-group financial transactions. In A. Bakker, & S. Kale (Eds.) T*ransfer pricing and intra-group financing: The entangled worlds of financial markets and transfer pricing*. 2nd revised edition (p. 30). IBFD Publications.

SEC. (n.d.). *List of subsidiaries of registrant Google Inc. A Delaware Corporation*. Retrieved from https://www.sec.gov/Archives/edgar/data/1288776/000119312508032690/dex2101.htm.

Smith, C. W., & Stulz, R. M. (1985). The determinants of firms' hedging policies. *Journal of Financial and Quantitative Analysis, 20*, 391–405.

Stulz, R. M. (1995). the cost of capital in internationally integrated markets: The case of nestle. *European Financial Management, 1*, 11–22.

Stulz, R. M. (1999). Globalization, corporate finance, and the cost of capital. *Journal of Applied Corporate Finance, 34*, 8–25.

Szpiro, D. A., & Dimnik, T. (1996). Capital budgeting in multinational organizations: Exploring the strategic context. *Managerial Finance, 22*, 58–74.

Tørsløv, T. R., Wier, L. S., & Zucman, G. (2023). The missing profits of nations. *Review of Economic Studies, 90*, 1499–1534.

## Further Reading

Madura, J. (2021). *International financial management*. Cengage. This book builds on the fundamental principles of corporate finance to provide timely information and an understanding of managerial topics in a global environment necessary to prosper in international business. Chapters 11 and 12 detail how to manage various foreign exchange exposures. Chapter 14 provides an overview of the multinational capital budgeting process and identifies the helpful information used in the process.

Pizzutilo, F. (2014). Rethinking multinational enterprises' capital budgeting in the globalized new millennium. *Journal of Finance and Economics, 2*, 58–59. This short article outlines the complexities of capital budgeting for foreign direct investments. Interested readers are recommended to read all articles published in the Journal of Finance and Economics special issue in 2014 (Volume 2 Issue 3) to understand the complexities of multinational capital budgeting in the modern globalized financial and economic markets. These studies addressed some challenging tasks related to foreign direct investments and developed models to handle the intricacy associated with non-domestic business.

## References

# Global Management of Human Resources

## Contents




D. Klimkeit et al., *International Management in Service Firms*, Classroom Companion: Business,
https://doi.org/10.1007/978-3-031-50345-0_17

**Learning Outcomes**

After completing this chapter, you should be able to:

- Explain the context in which international human resource management in multinational service firms takes place
- Outline various international workforce planning approaches
- Explain the specifics of selecting staff for international assignments
- Describe what to consider when transferring and repatriating staff for international assignments
- Outline how to conduct performance management of staff internationally
- Explain approaches for the compensation of a global workforce

## Introduction

Many Service MNEs (multinational enterprises) send managers abroad to a foreign subsidiary, to fill a management position temporarily, manage a project, or provide a development opportunity for a junior manager. Such managers need to be selected, prepared, and cared for while they are on secondment and return home. However, even without seconding staff abroad, a globally spread workforce poses challenges to human resource (HR) management. The firm must decide how to staff its subsidiaries, compensate a global workforce, and manage staff performance. Each time, HR managers must decide how much to standardize and adapt their approaches to workforce management locally. Professional service firms have specific requirements for global HR management. This chapter will provide an overview of how HR managers in Service MNEs address these challenges.

Buenos Aires (Image by Julian Zapata from Pixabay)

17

### Opening Case: Hiring a Team in Buenos Aires

When Thomas arrived at Buenos Aires (BA) airport in early July, coming from Frankfurt, Germany, reception in Argentina was cold in the literal sense: It was winter and quite chilly in the morning. The first thing Thomas had to buy was a scarf. Arriving in the office the following Monday, the reception was much warmer by his Argentinian colleagues who invited him to lunch. Thomas was seconded to BA for 3 months by AdviseCo, a major global management advisory firm. The purpose was to assess if the shared service center his company recently established in BA was a suitable location to set up a new team for his internal service function "Service" and then possibly launch the team's recruiting.

Until Thomas' secondment, Service only used a shared service center in India. The rationale for having a team in BA was that a BA team could support the whole American continent during regular working hours and benefit from Spanish language skills in addition to English. In India, some team members had to work at night to support member firms of AdviseCo in the American time zones.

The Human Resource (HR) team in BA was a helpful contact for Thomas' assessment. They helped procure a work permit for Thomas and had it extended after the first 6 weeks in BA. From global team leaders of Service contemplating hiring team members in BA, Thomas obtained job descriptions of possible positions that might be filled in BA. He passed them on to the HR team in BA, who scanned the local labor market for these positions. The outcome was positive: The HR team was optimistic about filling these positions quickly. This was the most crucial outcome of Thomas' assessment. Setting up the team would not have been possible without finding people with the required profile for the intended positions.

Besides, Thomas learned about salary levels for the intended positions, labor law regulations in Argentina, HR policies of the shared service center in BA, and local logistics for the potential new team. To his surprise, HR informed him that it is common for students in Argentina to work full-time and study in the evenings and on weekends. Many employees in the shared service center are students, and if Service excluded the option of hiring students, it might be more complex and take longer to recruit staff for the planned team. Thomas was puzzled and discussed the matter with the global team leaders, who said that the policy of Service usually was to hire graduates or even experienced employees with several years of experience after graduation. From a functional leader in the shared service center, Thomas learned that employees of that team could work from home one day a week as it was a common practice in the industry in Argentina. AdviseCo would be at a competitive disadvantage in the labor market if it did not offer this option. Thomas found that salary levels in BA were significantly lower than in countries like the United States. However, the high inflation rate of 25% then was a concern. HR routinely increased salaries by 15% at one point in the year and by another 10% at another point to compensate for the inflation. Since the peso lost value against the dollar simultaneously, the salary increases from the dollar perspective were less than 25% but still had to be monitored closely. Thomas also learned from HR that many benefits were offered to staff by the Argentinian member firm, such as gym membership, a newspaper subscription, and vouchers for shopping, to remain competitive in the labor market where such benefits were common. Further, employees got the day off work on their birthday and could transfer their acquired extent of annual leave from a previous employer to AdviseCo. This was because employees started with a few annual leave days, which grew longer as they stayed with the firm.

However, to stabilize the peso exchange rate to the US dollar, the Argentinian government at the time imposed some restrictions. Instead of imported laptops, locally produced ones needed to be used. Expatriate managers had to be paid in pesos, and converting the salary payment into dollars was complicated. However, as Service did not plan to second expatriate managers to manage the team in BA, this was not a relevant issue. Besides the positive signals on the labor market availability for the intended positions, another thing was decisive for Thomas' positive report on his assessment of the BA center: The center leadership allowed teams to follow a staff augmentation model. This means that staff in the center could be hired and managed by a manager located elsewhere and therefore be members of a global virtual team. As Service was organized in global virtual teams, this approach fit perfectly with Service's policy. Like this, future staff in BA could feel like an integral part of a global team rather than be isolated in BA.

Just before Service's global leader gave the green light for setting up the team in BA, an issue came up that almost derailed the launch of the recruiting: A manager of AdviseCo from the United States who was on a business trip to BA got robbed in the street. This led some managers to raise concerns about safety in BA and whether setting up a team in that location was a good idea. A conference call with the manager showed, however, that he did not see this as a showstopper and that, to the contrary, he had many positive things to say about the staff in BA. He reported that they spoke good and easy-to-understand English, were well-qualified, and took the initiative and responsibility rather than just doing what they were told.

So, recruiting for a team of initially 12 positions was launched, and the predictions of the HR team were proven right. Within 2 months, all 12 positions were filled with well-qualified staff. The HR team conducted a first screening of applications and pre-selected suitable ones. Then, HR invited applicants to a video conference room in the center in BA, where HR managers facilitated a job interview with a global team leader who joined the interview by videoconferencing. For some positions, applicants had to pass a test set up at a computer in the center, and following a second interview, they were hired. In the meantime, Thomas ensured that the reporting lines for each new staff were clear, that the team could sit together in a suitable part of the open plan office, got the required IT equipment, and participated in Service's global performance management (PM) process. Additionally, Thomas and the involved global team leaders organized a two-day onboarding event for the team, parts of which were delivered in BA and parts of it by managers who joined the event virtually by videoconferencing. Once the team was up and running, the global team leaders were happy with the staff they had hired in BA and expanded the team.

**Questions**

1. Which factors facilitated the team setup in BA, which made them challenging?
2. How would you deal with the situation that excluding students as employees might make recruiting more difficult?
3. What challenges do you foresee in managing and assessing the performance of staff in this team?

Sources: Based on own field study

## The Context of International Human Resource Management in Service MNEs

As mentioned in previous chapters, human resource management (HRM) is particularly important in service firms. In this section, we first outline the importance of HRM in service firms and the need for local adaptation of HRM in service firms. Then, we explain the context in which international human resource management (IHRM) occurs.

### International Human Resource Management in Service MNEs

Services are people-based businesses. The critical resource for most services is the employees of the firm rather than capital goods. How the front-office staff interacts with the customer has a crucial impact on the evaluation of service quality by the customer. So, a service firm needs to ensure it hires suitable people who are well-trained and motivated. The front-office staff must be trained in customer interaction skills such as empathy and assurance (Galperin & Lituchy, 2014). The importance of effective HRM for service quality has been established empirically. Different service industries require different skill sets, so HRM practices must be adapted. Take the Ritz Carlton Hotel Company as an example. Mark DeCocini, the Regional Vice President Asia-Pacific of Ritz Carlton Hotel Company, holds that customer satisfaction comes from employee satisfaction. The latter, in turn, derives from three principles: selection of the right employees using innovative channels, provision of effective on-the-job training, and encouragement of employee engagement and active participation (Zheng, 2009).

In knowledge-intensive service firms such as professional service firms (PSFs), HRM is especially essential. PSFs derive their competitive advantage from their human resources. Senior staff leaving the firm may mean losing essential competencies and client relationships. The business of PSFs draws on their human resources to develop innovative solutions for their clients. So PSFs need to attract and retain the best talent. The firm needs to provide employees with ways of developing professionally and keep them motivated (Kaiser et al., 2015; Sokolov & Zavyalova, 2022).

HRM practices are based on values that differ between countries. Many HRM practices commonly used in service firms, such as human resources development, have been developed in a Western context and may not transfer to different cultural contexts. For example, Galperin and Lituchy, investigating HRM in service firms across cultures, found different learning styles in different cultures. In collectivist cultures, people see learning as a collective experience. In Senegal, it was found to be the most effective learning style to conduct learning in discussions with others when participants shared observations. So, training and development interventions in groups are preferred (Galperin & Lituchy, 2014). Zheng studied HRM practices in service firms in six countries in Asia and found significant differences in practices and employee outcomes of these practices, such as service quality and employee retention. The study also found that in Asia, informal HRM practices seem to work well. In particular, for employees that have been recruited via informal networks, staff turnover is lower. She concludes that "HR practices are very much contextualized, influenced by the country-specific variables, such as cultural and institutional settings" (Zheng, 2009, p. 493). On the other hand, many Service MNEs have built cross-border teams that follow consistent global professional practices, and firms are seconding managers across borders. Increasingly, Service MNEs build a global cadre of international managers who can be deployed in any country where they are needed and who have a more global identity (Sparrow et al., 2013).

## The Context of International Human Resource Management

Before defining IHRM, let us first define *Human Resource Management* (HRM).

**Human Resource Management (HRM)**

*HRM* refers to those activities undertaken by an organization to effectively utilize its human resources (HR) (Dowling et al., 2017, p. 2).

**Dimensions of IHRM**: These activities of HRM include things like HR planning, staffing, performance management, training and development, and compensation and benefits. In MNEs that must manage a global workforce across their various operations in the world, further considerations come into play. Drawing on a model by Morgan (1986), Dowling et al. (2017, p. 3) find that in IHRM, two further dimensions have to be considered besides the *activities of (domestic) HRM* listed above:

- *The categories of countries involved*: the parent country, where an MNE has its headquarters (HQ); various host countries, where subsidiaries are located; and other countries that might be a source of employees
- *The categories of international employees*: host country nationals (HCNs) that are nationals of a country where a subsidiary is located; parent country nationals (PCNs) from the parent country of the MNE that might be seconded to a subsidiary; and third country nationals (TCNs) from other countries that might be employed in a subsidiary as well



For example, a German MNE may employ French citizens in its subsidiary in France (HCNs), send German citizens (PCNs) to its subsidiary in China, and second some of its employees from Mexico on an assignment in its subsidiary in Colombia (TCNs).

**International Human Resource Management (IHRM)**

We define the field of *IHRM* broadly to cover all issues related to the management of people in an international context (Stahl et al., 2012, p. 1).

**Settings of IHRM:** In MNEs, IHRM takes place in specific settings, in particular at headquarters and in the various subsidiaries (Tarique et al., 2022, pp. 23–25):

- *Headquarters of an MNE*: This setting involves HR professionals working at the headquarters of an MNE. From their central perspective, they develop HRM practices and coordinate their global deployment across subsidiaries. They manage international secondments of employees. They play a strategic role in managing the global workforce of the MNE.
- *Subsidiaries of an MNE*: This setting involves HR professionals working in their home country in a subsidiary of a foreign-owned MNE. They need to implement global HRM practices in their subsidiary, though they are often developed by HR professionals at headquarters who lack an understanding of local practices.

Increasingly, *domestic firms* also face issues of IHRM. Many employees of a domestic firm may have a different national background and, even if they have citizenship of the country, may display many traits of their parent country's culture. Even domestic firms may thus have quite a multicultural workforce. The firm may have to hire staff from abroad to fill positions that locals cannot fill. So even in a domestic firm, HR professionals often need to develop international HR skills.

**Global Standardization:** As outlined above, strong arguments exist for locally adapting HRM practices to a country's specific context. At the same time, there are undeniable benefits from globally standardizing HRM practices in an MNE. So, HRM faces the same dilemma of addressing *global integration/standardization* and *local responsiveness* that we introduced in ► Chap. 8. Dowling et al. characterize the aim of global standardization of HRM practices as:

> to reach [...] consistency, transparency, and alignment of a geographically fragmented workforce around common principles and objectives (Dowling et al., 2017, p. 48).

More specifically, the arguments for *global standardization* in IHRM are (Bloom et al., 2003):

- Generate a perception of equal treatment among managers who operate across borders and encounter the same HRM practices everywhere.
- Create a shared understanding of expectations the firm has of employees.
- Facilitate the administration of a global workforce through consistent global systems.

Imagine a PSF that initially has separate performance management systems in each country. A manager in the United States with a staff member in France cannot post his performance assessment in the French system but must send it by email to a local manager in France, who enters it into the French system. Once a global performance system is introduced, the manager can directly enter his assessment in the global system, and the employee in France can also find it there and comment on it if she likes.

Such global standardization of IHRM practices can primarily be found in MNEs with very international business operations across borders. These firms tend to apply such standard practices mainly to managers who work at international boundaries, such as HQ managers with a global role or managers who have been seconded to a subsidiary.

**Local Responsiveness:** Regarding *local responsiveness*, Dowling et al. summarize: "The aim of realizing local responsiveness is to respect local cultural values, traditions, legislation or other institutional constraints such as government policy and/or education systems regarding HRM and work practices" (Dowling et al., 2017, p. 48). Remember the example of 360° feedback from ▶ Chap. 8: Many Western firms implemented this method of performance feedback, which includes that employees also provide feedback to their bosses. Organizations attempting to implement it in China came across challenges due to the Confucianist idea that leaders and subordinates have an assigned position in society. Out of respect for authority, few employees dare to give feedback upward (Liu, 2012). Different cultural and institutional environments across countries drive local responsiveness in IHRM. We outlined some examples of such cultural differences, their impact on HRM practices, and their effectiveness above. In addition, the institutional environment has an effect. This includes the education system and industrial relations between organized labor and employers. For example, in Germany, the dual vocational training system that combines theoretical learning in vocational schools with practical experience from working in companies is very established. A similar number of young people enter dual vocational training as those seeking higher education (Authoring Group Educational Reporting, 2016). This system is held in high regard in Germany, while it does not exist in many other countries. MNEs recruiting and selecting staff need to consider these differences. Remember from the opening case how in Argentina, it is common for students to work full-time and study in the evening and on weekends. This makes it common for employers to hire students for entry positions for which, in other countries, the firm would hire graduates. When MNEs exclude this option, it will reduce the labor pool from which to hire for positions such as in the shared service center in Buenos Aires. Employment law varies considerably between countries. MNEs must consider this in every country where they have operations; otherwise, they face legal risks (Florkowski, 2006). For example, in most countries, employment is protected by a contract, while the United States has a system of employment at will. In most countries, termination is not permitted due to health, pregnancy, maternity, or characteristics such as disability, age, or gender. Termination is mostly only allowed under certain conditions, requiring a specified notice period. Most countries also require financial compensation for terminated staff (Tarique et al., 2022, p. 166).



**Effects of the Institutional Context:** We can identify different effects of the institutional context on IHRM practices (Dowling et al., 2017, pp. 51–52):

- *Country-of-origin effect* or *home-country effect*: MNEs are shaped much by institutions in their country of origin and therefore tend to export HRM practices to their subsidiaries.
- *Host-country effect*: The host country's institutional environment influences a subsidiary's HRM practices. For example, in Germany, MNEs must consider collective wage agreements when determining pay levels.

The resulting HRM practices in foreign subsidiaries of MNEs are typically a blend reflecting both the country-of-origin effect from headquarters and the host-country effect of their host country. To some extent, all subsidiaries of a US MNE will display practices deriving from the US institutional environment and practices and adaptations stemming from the respective host country environment.

## Planning the Workforce for Global Markets

MNEs must have the right people at the right place wherever they have operations in the world. The objective of *global workforce planning* is:

» to estimate employment needs of the MNE and to develop plans for meeting those needs (Tarique et al., 2022, p. 214).

The term *workforce* refers to the employees of the MNE, while the term *labor force* refers to the labor market, the pool of potential employees in a location. The size of the labor force from which a subsidiary can recruit staff varies by factors such as the unemployment rate, the participation rate of women and men in the labor market, or the number of people with the required formal education. An MNE must either find staff in the locations where it operates or relocate staff from somewhere else. Ideally, HR professionals get a chance to estimate the availability of qualified talent in a location before the MNE decides to set up a new operation in that location (Tarique et al., 2022, p. 214). Remember how in the opening case, Thomas had the local HR professionals assess the availability of the job profiles that team leaders were contemplating filling in BA before deciding to set up the new team in the shared service center. The positive outcome of that assessment was a critical factor in the favorable decision, and, indeed, recruiting went fast and successfully.

## Factors That Impact International Workforce Planning

Several factors impact international workforce planning. We will focus on the following three (Tarique et al., 2022, pp. 215–219):

**Population Characteristics:** In many developed countries, the aging population creates challenges in the labor market as more people retire than young people enter the labor force. In developing and emerging markets, on the contrary, the labor force is much younger but may often lack the skills required for positions in MNEs. In countries like Germany, Japan, and the United States, a large percentage

**Table 17.1** Required data about the local labor force

| Required data about the local labor force |
|---|
| Participation levels (No. of people of working age who work or look for work) |
| Unemployment rate; mobility |
| Levels and quality of education (e.g. No. of graduates per year, subjects) |
| Technical skills and experience (e.g. No. of similar jobs in other firms ► for experienced hires) |
| Language skills |
| Source: Partly drawing on content from Tarique et al. (2022, p. 215) |

of the population is over 60, while in India, South Africa, and Mexico, the percentage is much lower. The participation of men and women in the labor force also impacts the labor pool from which MNEs can hire. The *labor force participation rate* is calculated as the labor force divided by the total working-age population (OECD, 2023). This significantly impacts the size of the labor force and varies much from country to country. Both governments and companies in countries with labor shortages are contemplating solutions such as attracting more migrant workers, extending the working age, or using robots to fill vacant positions.

**Emigration and Immigration:** We have seen in recent years an unprecedented level of migration, partly voluntary to seek work abroad, partly involuntary, driven by warfare or political circumstances (World Economic Forum, 2020). This movement impacts the size of the labor force both in the emigration and immigration countries. Due to the free labor movement in the European Union (EU), many people from Eastern European countries like Poland or Romania migrated to other EU countries to work. More recently, due to the war in Ukraine, many Ukrainians who fled to other European countries, such as Poland, Germany, or the Netherlands, are entering the workforce in their host countries (Economist, 2023).

**Technology and Job Exporting:** Due to the development of information and communication technology, MNEs broaden their horizon when looking for suitable talent. For many positions, staff no longer need to be in a particular location as distributed virtual teams become more common. This allows companies from developed countries to "export jobs" to emerging economies where qualified staff is available in sufficient numbers but at a lower cost.

Table 17.1 summarizes critical data required for assessing the labor force in a location. In more developed countries, such data may be available from government agencies. However, in less developed countries, the availability and accuracy of such data can be challenging. International organizations such as the International Labor Organization (ILO) and the Organization for Economic Cooperation and Development (OECD) are generally reliable sources. A local chamber of commerce in the host country or consulting firms can be additional sources of information (Tarique et al., 2022, p. 215).

The opening case on the shared service center in Buenos Aires can be seen in the context of job exporting as Service took advantage of the sufficient availability of qualified staff in an emerging market at a relatively low cost. This was one factor facilitating the team's setup in BA. Good English skills, in addition to Spanish, were another facilitating factor. The fact that many potential employees in the labor force are students was an initial challenge, the same as the temporarily assumed high crime rate in BA and government restrictions on imports of equipment such as laptops.

## Staffing Approaches

As outlined above, MNEs can draw on three categories of staff when staffing their international operations: host country nationals (HCNs) that are nationals of a country where a subsidiary is located; parent country nationals (PCNs) from the parent country of the MNE that might be seconded to a subsidiary; and third country nationals (TCNs) from other countries that might be employed in a subsidiary as well. There are several different staffing approaches in which the MNE relies mainly on one or the other of these categories of employees. They are drawing on the work of Perlmutter, who describes different attitudes of managers of MNEs (Heenan & Perlmutter, 1979; Perlmutter, 1969): the Ethnocentric, Polycentric, Geocentric, and Regiocentric approaches. Applied to staffing, the approaches can be characterized as follows (Dowling et al., 2017, pp. 109–112):

**Ethnocentric Approach:** Headquarters makes strategic decisions on subsidiary staffing. PCNs hold key positions in subsidiaries. The reasoning is that subsidiaries lack adequately qualified HCNs. Headquarters management wants to ensure good communication with their subsidiaries and ensure control of the subsidiary. The belief is that this is best ensured by seconding PCNs to take critical positions in subsidiaries (Zeira, 1976). The approach has several drawbacks. It reduces development opportunities for HCNs, which can be demotivating and lead to increased turnover. PCNs will often take time to adapt to a country environment and may make decisions that are inadequate in the local context. PCNs frequently earn higher salaries than HCNs.

**Polycentric Approach:** Headquarters allows subsidiaries some autonomy in making decisions. Subsidiaries are primarily managed by HCNs, while the secondment of PCNs is rare. The reasoning for this approach is that it avoids the adaptation problems of PCNs. HCNs know the local culture and language. This can avoid challenges in countries where filling positions with foreign managers is seen critically. Sometimes, legislation in a country may require HCNs for management positions. HCNs are typically cheaper than PCNs. Contrary to PCNs, who are primarily assigned temporarily only, HCNs tend to remain in the firm longer, providing continuity. The flip side is that the relationship with headquarters tends to be weaker as HCNs may pursue local priorities, and communication problems may arise with headquarters. For both PCNs and HCNs, development opportunities outside their home country are limited.

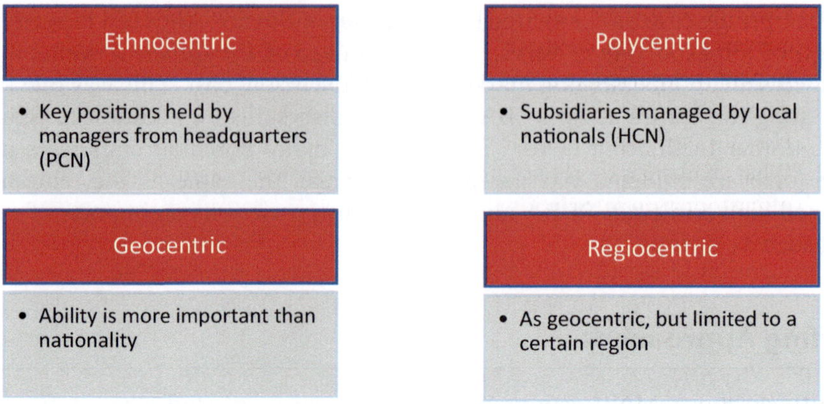


**Fig. 17.1** Staffing approaches. (Own diagram based on content from Dowling et al., 2017, pp. 109–112)

**Geocentric Approach:** Headquarters takes a global perspective. For staffing, ability is seen as more important than nationality. So, staffing of a subsidiary can involve any employee category, including TCNs from third countries. The rationale is to develop an international group of global managers that can be employed anywhere in the MNE. This avoids the problem of the polycentric approach that subsidiaries take on a life of their own that may be at odds with global priorities. It supports global cooperation within the MNE. However, as in the ethnocentric approach, some governments—and some HCNs—may resent employing PCNs or TCNs. If a subsidiary employs many non-nationals, much administration obtaining visas and work permits is needed. It is also an expensive option with relatively high salaries plus costs for relocation and training.

**Regiocentric Approach:** Headquarters allows managers some autonomy within their region. Besides with many HCNs, subsidiaries may be staffed with managers from other operations within the same region. A subsidiary in Asia may receive managers from other subsidiaries in Asia. The rationale is to facilitate interaction within the region and with PCNs deployed to a regional headquarters. Compared to the Ethnocentric or Geocentric approach, the approach enables more responsiveness to local conditions. Conversely, interaction and cooperation are restricted to regions, and full global integration is not achieved. Qualified managers from a subsidiary can move to regional headquarters, but secondment to global headquarters is rare.



**Selecting a Staffing Approach:** Fig. 17.1 provides an overview of the four approaches. Now, how do MNEs select a staffing approach for a subsidiary? Dowling et al. summarize the various factors identified in research into four categories of determinants: context specificities, company specificities, local unit specificities, and IHRM practices (Dowling et al., 2017, pp. 113–114):

- *Context specificities*: There may be significant cultural and institutional differences between an MNE's parent country and a subsidiary's host country, which impacts staffing approaches primarily due to the parent-country and host-country effects outlined above. Also, differences in staffing approaches between industries have been observed.

- *Company specificities*: Each company tends to have a preferred approach to staffing based on its strategy, organizational structure and culture, previous international experience, and corporate governance. For example, some MNEs leave their subsidiaries more local autonomy than others, which affects staffing approaches.
- *Local unit specificities*: How the subsidiary has been established, whether by greenfield investment or acquisition, plays a role. Acquired firms tend to have more HCNs than greenfield operations. If a subsidiary's strategic role and importance to the MNE are high, headquarters may want to take more control by seconding PCNs. We would add the maturity of local management as a factor. If the current local management in the subsidiary has little management experience, headquarters are more likely to second PCNs or TCNs to fill leadership positions.
- *IHRM practices*: HRM practices like selection, training and development, and career management, including expatriation, have an essential effect on enabling the selected staffing approach.

**Staffing of Emerging Markets in Professional Service Firms:** Services firms, especially professional service firms (PSFs), frequently encounter difficulties finding enough qualified and experienced employees to staff their offices in emerging markets. These often exhibit strong growth coupled with a scarcity of such employees over whom competition exists between PSFs (Suseno & Pinnington, 2017). While many service firms would generally favor a polycentric approach to ensure culturally appropriate service to customers, the local context can make it challenging to find enough suitable HCNs.

## International Assignments and Repatriation

Many service firms send employees abroad, whether for a short time on a project basis or an extended period, to fill a position in a subsidiary for which a PCN or TCN is better suited than available HCNs. This is particularly the case for large international professional service firms (PSFs) such as management consulting firms, law firms, or audit firms, which have a project-based business and frequently require staffing projects across borders. Furthermore, longer-term assignments in subsidiaries are important in PSFs to transfer know-how or to provide learning opportunities for junior managers (Suseno & Pinnington, 2017). Employees seconded on an assignment abroad by their employer are called *expatriates* or *international assignees*.

## Reasons for International Assignments

There are several different reasons why companies generally and service firms in particular second employees abroad (Suseno & Pinnington, 2017):

- *Staffing of projects or positions*: Large PSFs have an international business with many international projects. To staff projects with the best available talent for specific fields of expertise, the staff is transferred across borders to work on a project such as an IT implementation or advising on a merger or acquisition. Additionally, for permanent positions in a subsidiary abroad, there may not be suitable HCNs, so PCNs or TCNs are seconded abroad for a certain number of years.
- *Transferring knowledge and practices*: When a subsidiary is set up, MNEs send experienced managers to transfer know-how, skills, and practices to enable the subsidiary to succeed. In knowledge-intensive service firms, such as PSFs, this knowledge transfer is essential for the successful operation of the subsidiary.
- *Providing learning opportunities*: Frequently, firms see a secondment abroad as an opportunity for junior managers to learn and develop their skills and, thereby, their careers. Given the importance of continuous learning in knowledge-intensive service firms such as PSFs, this is a crucial reason for secondments in these firms.

Often, companies pursue not just one of the above aims but a combination of several (Sparrow et al., 2016, p. 138). A study by Tungli and Peiperl among 136 MNEs from the United States, the United Kingdom, Germany, and Japan found differences in the primary motivation. In German MNEs, providing learning opportunities (developing international management skills) was the main reason. In Japanese and UK MNEs, the main reason was to transfer knowledge and practices (set up a new operation). US MNEs conduct secondments primarily for staffing (to fill a skill gap) (Tungli & Peiperl, 2009).

**Challenges in PSF:** PSFs, such as law firms, encounter two opposing challenges regarding secondments. To provide professional services such as legal advice, firms require highly skilled staff that spends extended periods in a given jurisdiction. In some cases, however, there may be more international work than competent lawyers willing to move to another country as they prefer to stay in their home country. In other cases, there may not be enough international work for high-performing lawyers who intend to relocate abroad as part of their personal and career development (Suseno & Pinnington, 2017).

## Types of International Assignments



Different types of international assignments can be distinguished by their length. The length of assignments is, in turn, driven by the purpose and nature of the assignment. Put simply, two types of assignments are in use (Tahvanainen et al., 2005):

- *Short-term assignments*: They last up to 6 or 12 months. Typically, they are used to lead a project or conduct troubleshooting. They may also be used to facilitate the learning of junior managers who gain international experience or to manage a specific operation on a short-term basis. Selection and preparation are mostly informal, and the family does not accompany the assignee.

- *Traditional assignments*: It is also called long-term assignments. The primary purpose is to fill a position in the operation receiving the assignee. Besides, transferring knowledge, skills, and practices to develop the organization, such as a subsidiary, is often pursued. Selection and preparation are more formal, such as providing cross-cultural training, and the assignee's family accompanies him or her.

## Failure of International Assignees

Frequently, international assignees are not successful in their assignments and return home prematurely. This is called *expatriate failure*.

**Expatriate Failure**

The term *expatriate failure* has been defined as the premature return of an expatriate (that is, a return home before the period of assignment is completed) (Dowling et al., 2017, p. 125).

However, even assignees who remain until the planned end of the assignment may adapt poorly and be less effective than was intended, which can also cause damage to the firm. Furthermore, sometimes former assignees leave within 2 years after their return from the assignment, which leads to a loss of valuable employees. So there are reasons for a broader definition of expatriate failure, including insufficient effectiveness and problems upon repatriation (Dowling et al., 2017, pp. 125–126).

A study conducted in 2009 found that, on average, 6.3% of assignees from Germany, Japan, the UK, and the United States are considered failures in terms of premature return. However, there are some differences by home country of MNEs. In 9.4% of German companies, more than 10% of assignees failed; in the UK, this failure of more than 10% of assignees occurred in 6.6% of companies; in Japan, in 5.6% of companies; and in the United States, in 13.7% of companies in the study. This is a significant improvement for the United States since, in an earlier study in 1982, in 76% of US companies, more than 10% of assignees failed. The authors of the study see this as a sign that the selection and preparation of assignees in US MNEs seem to have improved (Tungli & Peiperl, 2009).

**Cost of Assignee Failure:** Failure of international assignees leads to high costs for the company. The assignee's performance suffers from an inability to adapt, which is detrimental to the subsidiary, and customer relationships may be damaged. The assignee may experience a loss of self-esteem and self-confidence (Mendenhall & Oddou, 1985).

**Reasons for Assignee Failure:** Several studies have investigated the reasons for failure. The most crucial factor found is the inability of the assignee and the family to adjust to the new environment. Often preparatory training is only provided to the assignee, not the family members. While the assignee is involved in social networks at work, the spouse is left alone to cope with the new location and develop relationships. Further reasons include mistakes in the selection of assignees, the assignee's personality or lack of maturity, inability to deal with the often larger responsibility during the assignment, insufficient preparation on culture and language, and insufficient support for the assignee by the company during the assignment (Tarique et al., 2022, p. 251).

## Selection of International Assignees

As the list of reasons for assignee failure has shown, mistakes in the selection of assignees are a key reason for failure. Frequently in case of failure, it turns out that the person selected has not been a good choice for the international assignment. So, what can companies do to increase the chances of a successful international assignment? It starts with a thorough analysis of the requirements of the position. Besides the technical and managerial requirements, the extent of the required interaction with nationals of the assignment country needs to be understood. Second, requirements stemming from the country of assignment need to be understood. This includes culture, society, language, and other relevant factors, such as the standard of living. Drawing on this information, candidates are evaluated (Tarique et al., 2022, p. 242).

**Selection Criteria for International Assignees:** The practice of global firms and research show important selection criteria to include the following ones (Tarique et al., 2022, pp. 243–247) (also see ◘ Fig. 17.2):

- *Job suitability*: Most firms select assignees primarily based on their ability to perform the job, filling a need in the subsidiary. Experience has shown that other criteria are at least as important.
- *Cultural adaptability*: Assignees need to be able to adapt to the new environment. The foreign culture must be accepted while completing the tasks. Assignees need to be psychologically positioned to live in a different culture and adjust to different working styles, patterns of interaction, and the general environment.
- *Personal characteristics*: Research found that assignees who adjust well share several personal characteristics. Besides others, openness to experience was one of the most essential characteristics. Assignees who are open to experience correctly interpret the foreign culture, have less rigid views, and accept the foreign culture.
- *Desire for foreign assignment*: The desire of the assignee and family for the assignment is essential for the willingness to adjust to the new environment.
- *Local language ability*: Research found that the ability to speak the host country's local language is associated with the assignment's success.
- *International experience*: Studies have shown that the amount of previous international exposure of the assignee significantly improves cultural adjustment. Various types of previous exposure can factor into this, such as previous international assignments, study abroad, or visits to other countries.

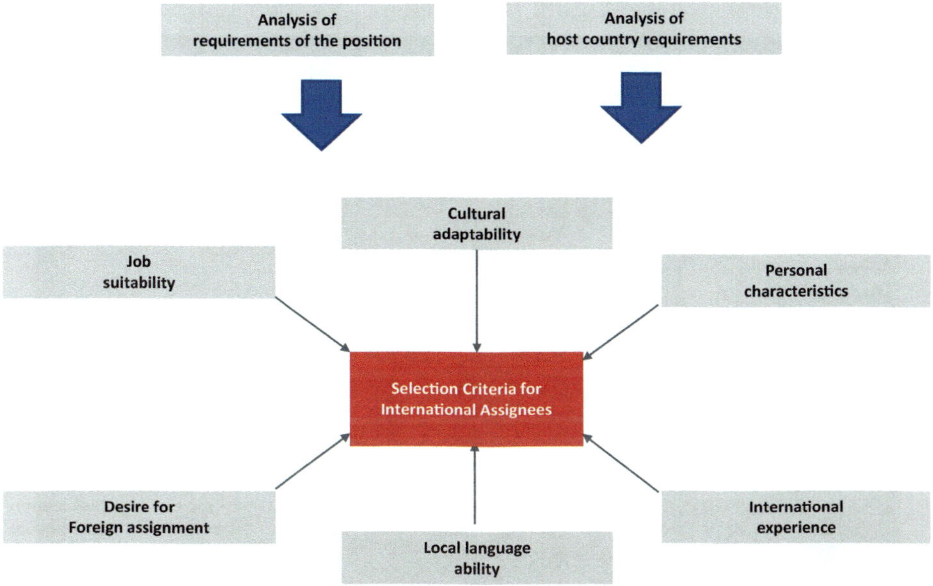


**Fig. 17.2** Selection criteria for international assignees. (Own diagram based on content from Tarique et al., 2022, pp. 243–247)

The short case below shows an example from a law firm where the selection of assignees has not been conducted according to the criteria above.

**Selection of International Assignees in an Australian Law Firm**

In an Australian law firm, it was common practice to send employees who did not fit in well with the organizational culture and were considered difficult to work with to an office abroad. However, this only shifted the problem abroad. As one lawyer explains:

> In the past we've often sent quite cantankerous irascible people up there who have ended up sort of alienating most of the people in the firms they've been sent to or whatever, because they were the difficult ones in Australia. So you thought well they can go to Jakarta for a while and surprise, surprise there's a revolt in the office over there, because they're the ones who aren't patient or prepared to spend the time with solicitors there, explaining and training (Suseno & Pinnington, 2017, p. 216).

Sydney harbor, Australia. (Image by Patty Jansen from Pixabay)

Source: Based on Suseno and Pinnington (2017)

## Training and Preparation of International Assignees

Besides selecting the right people, preparing the assignee for the secondment is essential to mitigate the risk of international assignee failure. Various types of training play a particular role in preparing the assignee for the host country environment. Even though cross-cultural training has shown to be effective, Deresky (2017, pp. 386–389) reports that most US companies do not provide such training to prepare their assignees. She explains the lower failure rates of assignees from Japanese companies to a large extent by the better assignee training and preparation programs. This includes that Japanese assignees are allowed more time to adjust once they arrive in the host country. NEC Corporation, for example, operates a permanent training boot camp for international assignees offering extensive training exercises. In addition to training the assignee, the family is also prepared for the secondment (Deresky, 2017, pp. 386–389). Besides cross-cultural training, training in the host country's language and familiarity with everyday life in the host country are necessary (Mendenhall & Oddou, 1985).

17

International assignee training can be broadly categorized into *pre-departure training* and *in-country training*. Most training takes place before the departure of the assignee. This includes cross-cultural training, which we will explain in detail in ► Chap. 18 and not elaborate on here. However, the impact of on-the-job training after arrival in the host country can be greater as skills such as dealing with cultural differences can be experienced directly in an actual situation. Specifically, for total immersion in the new culture, it has been suggested to place the assignee family with a host family for some time (Ronen, 1989). A preliminary visit to the host country by the assignee and spouse can be very helpful in getting a feel for the country. Firms should conduct this in a way relevant to the assignment and not as a touristic trip. It allows better-informed preparation. Following the visit, the assignee might decide not to go on the assignment. However, this would be less expensive than a failure later during the assignment. A survey found that three-quarters of MNEs offer such a visit to their designated international assignees (Dowling et al., 2017, pp. 179–180).

## Assignee Training and Preparation in Service Firms

In service firms, training and preparation of international assignees is essential, especially if the assignee will be in contact with customers. This is because a customer's interaction with the service staff forms a significant part of the service quality perceived by the customer. Service staff must show attitudes such as responsiveness, assurance, reliability, and empathy to ensure a quality customer experience. National cultures can, however, impact how customers expect and evaluate a service. Therefore, preparation for appropriate behavior in line with the host country culture is particularly vital for assignees of service firms: how to reassure customers and demonstrate reliability and empathy in the host culture. In addition, training and development activities provided by service firms need to consider the cultural background of the international assignees receiving them. As we mentioned at the beginning of this chapter, group-based training is more effective in collectivist cultures than individual learning experiences (Galperin & Lituchy, 2014). In an empirical study of HRM in service firms in six Asian countries, Zheng (2009) found that skill development across managerial, teamwork, and interpersonal skills strongly impacted service delivery and harmonious relationships between employer, employee, and customers.

## Repatriating International Assignees

When the assignment is completed, the assignee—if not seconded to another host country—returns home. This is called *repatriation*.

**Repatriation**

[...] the expatriation process also includes *repatriation*: the activity of bringing the expatriate back to the home country (Dowling et al., 2017, p. 189).

As you will remember from our discussion of international assignee failure, frequently, assignees leave the company within 1–2 years upon repatriation. Previously many saw repatriation as straightforward and underestimated the challenges. Today, scholars and practitioners broadly recognize that repatriation could be associated with losing valuable experience and other problems requiring active management. Companies are increasingly making efforts to facilitate the return of assignees and better use their experiences gained abroad (Harvey & Novicevic, 2006). The following short case highlights the challenges of repatriation of dual-career couples, where both the assignee and his or her spouse have been pursuing a career before the assignment.

**Repatriation of Dual-Career Couples from the United States and Europe**

A study among 14 dual-career couples from the United States, Finland, Poland, and Belgium identified challenges some of these couples encountered upon repatriation from an international assignment.

Some repatriates had the impression that their careers had not progressed during the assignment as people in their parent company had forgotten about them. As a Belgian repatriate returning from Russia explains:

> The international assignment has not influenced my career too much because when you come back you feel like a small fish dropped in a big ocean. People didn't see you around for a few years, so they basically forgot you. [...] When you go back to your working life in your home country ... then comes the frustration part because you no longer have the freedom at work and you go back to the bigger structure (with less autonomy) (Kierner & Suutari, 2018, p. 889).

In some cases, the spouse of the assignee was not able to work during the assignment and faced challenges getting back into the labor market upon repatriation, as the spouse of a US assignee returning from Finland points out:

> I did not have a job to repatriate to. ... Currently, I am working on my resume in order to start looking for a job. It seems it is going to be a challenge. ... I lost contact with the job market here. Now I have to rebuild, and it seems to take some time (Kierner & Suutari, 2018, p. 889).

Being abroad in a different culture for several years has changed couples. Seen from their new perspective, some of them perceive some cultural aspects of their home country critically, making it less attractive to return home, as a Finnish repatriate returning from China explains:

> Finland is really a very closed society and it is not all that positive. ... Finally, you get used to that again, but there is the whole process that you have to go through and adapt yourself to this new environment (Kierner & Suutari, 2018, p. 889).

Furthermore, the social connections of assignees have suffered during their time abroad, as a Belgian assignee returning from Russia points out:

School children; Changing schools can be challenging for children of repatriates. (Image by Eric Musiat from Pixabay)

> You have not seen these people for few years so it takes some time to reestablish your credibility, get to know them again, and to re-form connections (Kierner & Suutari, 2018, p. 889).

In some cases, repatriation also required a difficult readjustment of children to a school back home, as the spouse of a Polish assignee returning from Finland explains:

> There was only a problem with my daughter's school. Kids bond with the place, and it was a bit painful for my daughter to change school. After a few months in public school we ended by changing to an international school (Kierner & Suutari, 2018, pp. 889–890).

Source: Kierner and Suutari (2018)

## Factors in Repatriation Challenges

As shown above, repatriation frequently does not go as expected (Paik et al., 2002). Here are factors that have been found to impact the readjustment of international assignees to their home country (Dowling et al., 2017, pp. 193–198):

- *Career anxiety*: Frequently, assignees do not get a guaranteed job upon return. They also fear that executives in their home country may forget about them once they are on assignment abroad. This anxiety is increased by a lack of information about their post-assignment job. In the home country, changes such as restructuring, mergers, or acquisitions that frequently involve a reduction in the labor force increase anxiety further.
- *Work adjustment*: Sometimes, before the assignment, the candidate may receive the suggestion that an international assignment is essential for career progression. Returning home, the assignee may find that this progress does not materialize. Instead, colleagues who remained at home have been promoted. The position offered upon return often does not reflect the new experience gained abroad. Responsibility may be less than in the position held during or before the assignment.
- *Family adjustment*: During the assignment, the assignee and family may have a too-rosy memory of life back home. Coming back, they are struck by reality. On the assignment, the assignee's position provided an elite lifestyle, while back home, they return to a less high-profile life. This is frequently exacerbated when the income has been reduced in the position back home.
- *Effect on partner's career*: Often, the partner of an assignee does not obtain a work permit. In cases where the partner has been working before the assignment, the extended period without a job can make it difficult to enter the workforce again.

**A Process for Successful Repatriation:** To address the various challenges of repatriation, the following process has been suggested (Dowling et al., 2017, pp. 190–191; Tarique et al., 2022, p. 263):

- *Before the assignment*: Career planning for the assignee should begin before the assignment so that the assignee has a suitable position earmarked that leverages the experience gained. Some companies appoint a sponsor or mentor for the assignee in the home country who looks after job opportunities for the post-assignment period.
- *During the assignment*: Regular communication between the company back home and the assignee should be maintained to keep the assignee updated on any relevant new developments. Several companies offer the opportunity to travel back home to maintain relationships with colleagues and supervisors and enhance visibility. Many firms even insist that the assignee takes home leave rather than travel to third countries. Contact with the mentor should continue throughout. Many things may have changed back home during the assignment, and the assignee and family must come to terms with them. Companies should prepare the assignee for the return.

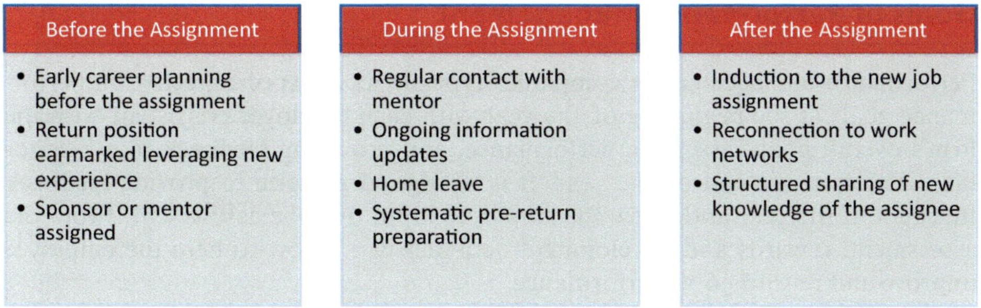


**Fig. 17.3** A suggested repatriation process. (Own diagram based on content from Tarique et al., 2022, pp. 263–264, and Dowling et al., 2017, pp. 190–191)

- *After the assignment*: The company needs to provide an induction to the new job assignment, ensure logistics such as an assigned office space, and facilitate reconnecting the assignee to the social network in the firm. Further, the company needs to organize structured ways of benefitting from the knowledge the assignee gained from the assignment.

See Fig. 17.3 for a summary of the suggested process.

## International Performance Management

Service firms, especially knowledge-intensive firms such as PSFs, rely on the knowledge and skills of their staff to create outputs that are valuable to their customers or clients. So, managing human capital is crucial for ensuring the firm's high performance (Swart et al., 2015). More generally, employees need to be competent and engaged so the firm can attain its objectives. MNEs hence pay much attention to the performance of their staff. This highlights measuring the employees' performance to drive the firm's performance. Many MNEs, therefore, conduct international employee performance management (IPM). In MNEs, *employee performance management* becomes more complex. Various cultural factors must be considered regarding the process and its acceptability for employees worldwide (Tarique et al., 2022, pp. 365–366).

**International Employee Performance Management**

An *International employee performance management* system is "an intervention of an MNE for the purpose of managing the performance of its global workforce so that performance (at the individual, team and organizational level) contributes to the attainment of strategic global objectives and results in overall desired performance of the MNE" (Tarique et al., 2022, p. 367).

## Goals of Performance Management

Performance management in companies typically consists of agreeing on performance goals at the beginning of the year with each employee consistent with the firm's overall goals, assessing performance, and providing feedback in a face-to-face session at the end of the year. It is also good practice to provide feedback throughout the year and allow the employee input into the assessment. From the assessment, rewards and development activities can follow to help the employee improve and reward good performance.

So, IPM pursues two distinct goals (Tarique et al., 2022, p. 368):

- *Evaluation goals*: IPM aims to provide feedback to employees on their performance. Based on this performance appraisal, firms can decide on rewards and promotions. High-potential employees are identified, while employees with inadequate performance can be given a signal that they need to improve.
- *Development goals*: IPM also aims to support employees in their development, primarily to address areas where performance needs improvement. Suitable development activities such as training can be identified, which is also intended to enhance the motivation and commitment of the employee.

## Performance Management in PSFs

Performance management is an essential issue in PSFs that depend on their professional staff's engagement and motivation. Improving performance management in PSFs, such as law firms, both domestically and internationally, can significantly contribute to job satisfaction. Traditionally, performance appraisal in PSFs such as law firms focused on whether professionals have generated new client contracts and how many billable hours they have made. Over time, performance management has become more formalized and evaluated a broader set of criteria, such as people management and teamwork. Regarding consequences of performance appraisal, some PSFs apply the traditional "lock-step" system, whereby all employees at a given level receive the same payment. Since this may demotivate the high performers, other PSFs apply a merit-based system where pay depends more on individual performance (Suseno & Pinnington, 2017).

## Global Standardization vs. Local Adaption of International Performance Management



You will remember how we discussed the benefits of global standardization and local adaptation of HR practices at the beginning of this chapter. In IPM, this tension is particularly acute since IPM connects the goal setting and appraisal of employees at the local level with the overall goals of the global firm (Vance, 2006). IPM practices are much impacted by a country's local cultural and institutional context. Consider the example of Germany. The institution of worker co-

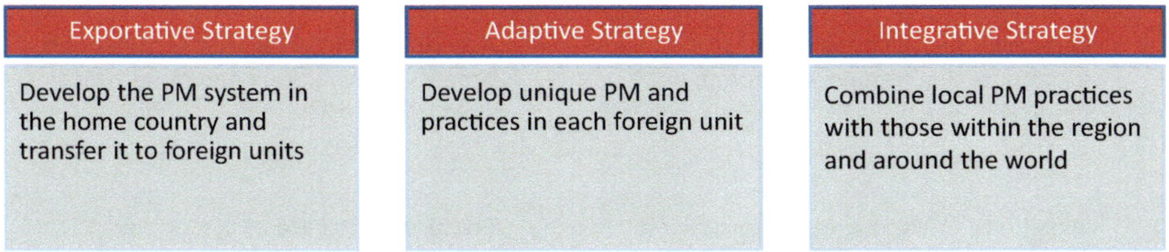


**Fig. 17.4** Strategic options for international performance management. (Own diagram based on content from Tarique et al., 2022, p. 371)

determination, enshrined in the concept of the social market economy, including strong works councils, implies much input from employees in a process like IPM. The vocational training system strengthens this by creating well-educated workers with a recognized professional certification. German long-term orientation means that IPM is oriented more toward long-term development goals than short-term performance-based remuneration (Dickmann, 2003).

At the same time, the headquarters of many MNEs tend to deploy IPM systems developed in the parent country across the world. As many MNEs are based in Western countries, this means attempting to implement a system based on Western performance management (PM) concepts. Several valid arguments favor such an approach: achieving global integration and consistency of the MNE, fairness, and control. Consistent systems also facilitate international assignments (Tarique et al., 2022, p. 370). Likewise, managing a global virtual team with employees spread across several countries is rendered easier. Remember the example of the PSF that introduced a global performance management system, greatly facilitating the manager in the United States to give performance feedback to the employee in France in one global system.

**Strategic Options for IPM:** How should MNEs deal with this tension? MNEs have three strategic options for IPM (Tarique et al., 2022, p. 371): an exportative, adaptive, or integrative strategy (see Fig. 17.4):

- *Exportative strategy*: developing PM practices in the home country of the MNE and transferring them to subsidiaries abroad, largely unadjusted
- *Adaptive strategy*: developing customized PM practices in each subsidiary
- *Integrative strategy*: combining locally developed practices with practices from the home country and other countries within the region of the subsidiary

**Factors for an Effective IPM System:** For the implementation of an effective IPM system, it is helpful to consider the following factors (Tarique et al., 2022, p. 373):

- *Relevance*: The evaluation process and criteria must be relevant to the job being evaluated. Reviewers need to have a good understanding of what the job requires in different subsidiaries.
- *Acceptability*: The process and criteria must be acceptable to the reviewer and especially to the person whose performance is evaluated (ratee). Fairness requires evaluating only such criteria under the control of the ratee and that local context conditions are considered. The process must be such that the ratee

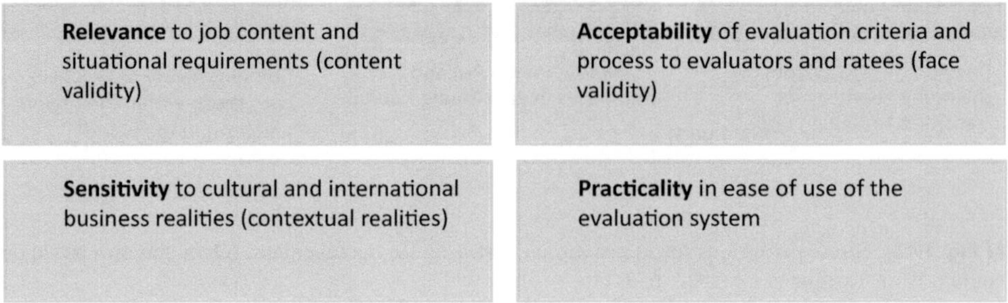


**Fig. 17.5** Factors for an effective IPM system. (Own diagram based on content from Tarique et al., 2022, p. 373)

finds it fair and accurate. The evaluator must show the ratee how to improve and ensure that the ratee is given, for example, required training.
- *Sensitivity*: Local business realities and culture need to be taken into consideration. Local conditions can make a good performance in a job more or less challenging to achieve.
- *Practicality*: The PM system should be straightforward; otherwise, people may not use it. Alternatively, it may only be used superficially, which does not generate the value expected from such a system.

Figure 17.5 summarizes these factors.

## Appraisal of HCN Employees by Foreign Managers

The challenges of administering a global IPM system are compounded by situations where the evaluator is of a different national background from the ratee. This can be a PCN (or TCN) international assignee who supervises local staff in a subsidiary or a manager in a global virtual team who resides in a different country from the ratee. Torbiörn (1985) conducted an interesting analysis of the role of HCNs and displayed it graphically (see Fig. 17.6). An HCN performs a role conceptualized in the MNE's parent country, which is geographically and culturally distant. The concept of the role crosses a cultural boundary and is performed in a different context from where it was conceived. In the local subsidiary, local stakeholders, such as customers, managers, or government authorities who are geographically and culturally close, may expect HCNs to play roles different from that defined by the parent company. Both the global concept and local expectations impact the actual role behavior of the HCN.

Consider a situation where an HCN in the Philippines reports to a manager in the United States, the parent country of the MNE, who conducts the performance evaluation. The US manager is far away culturally and geographically, while local managers who sit on the same floor of the same building and are culturally close express certain expectations regarding the role. It may be difficult for the HCN not

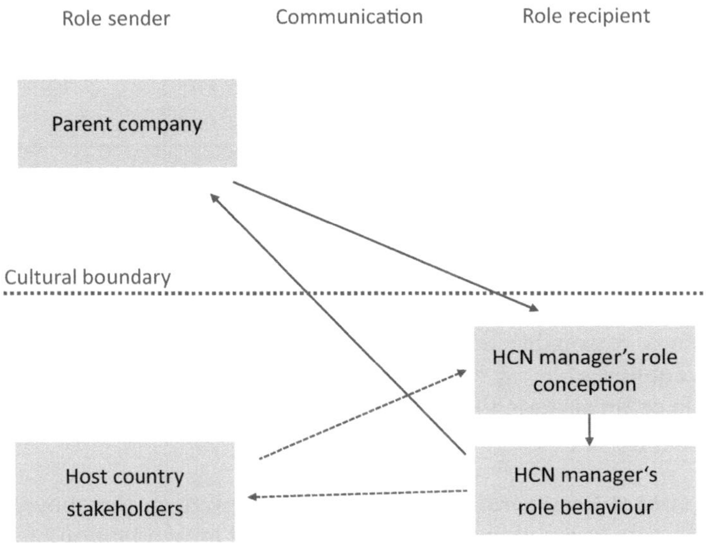


**Fig. 17.6** Factors in HCN role behavior. (Source: Torbiörn, 1985, p. 61; permission obtained)

to consider the local stakeholders' expectations. So, in performing the role, the HCN will behave partly in a way that does not align with the US manager's expectations. The outcome of the evaluation given by the US manager may not be as good as expected by the HCN.

These challenges can also occur for staff in the new team in BA in the opening case study, who will be supervised by managers of different nationalities based in other countries, such as in the United States or Europe.

## International Compensation and Benefits

How they are rewarded, that is, what amount of compensation, which benefits they receive, and how these are determined matters a lot to employees. It impacts the attraction, retention, and motivation of employees as well as profitability. At the same time, labor cost tends to be the company's biggest cost block in service firms. So, designing an adequate compensation system is an essential task for a service firm.

In MNEs with a global workforce, the task is even more complex. There are widely different costs of living (Mercer, 2022), competitive levels of reward, and benefits. This is compounded by different taxation levels that impact the net income and globally mobile employees as international assignees (Festing & Tekieli, 2018). When dealing with global compensation and benefits, one can distinguish between compensation for international assignees and *global remuneration*. Since each of the two are complex, we will focus on global remuneration here.

**Global Remuneration**

*Global remuneration* deals with the compensation and benefit structure of all employees of an MNE in various locations/subsidiaries around the world (Tarique et al., 2022, p. 320).

**Aims of Global Compensation and Benefits:** The main aims of a global compensation and benefits system include (Tarique et al., 2022, p. 320):
- Attract and retain talent in all locations of the MNE
- Facilitate the transfer between the various locations of the MNE
- Maintain a reasonable relationship between compensation of employees in various countries
- Maintain compensation that is competitive in the local labor market while minimizing costs

**Factors in Global Remuneration:** As can be recognized in the above outline, the general tension between global standardization and local adaption of HRM practices in MNEs also applies to international compensation and benefits. Therefore, global remuneration considers two factors:
- An overall philosophy of how the MNE compensates its employees
- The external context in the various countries, such as established local practices, taxation systems, and laws regulating compensation

Typically, the overall compensation strategy is standardized in line with the company's strategic objectives, while the specific compensation and benefits practices are adapted to address requirements from the local context (Tarique et al., 2022, p. 321).

## International Compensation

**Issues in International Compensation:** When designing the remuneration strategy for the firm, global HR needs to address several issues (Tarique et al., 2022, pp. 321–322):
- *Comparability*: HR must identify comparable positions across countries. For example, there may be positions with the term "manager" in the title in various countries that may not be comparable.
- *National and organizational cultures*: Some cultures are performance-oriented, and variable compensation based on performance is common practice, while in others, compensation traditionally depends on the number of years with the company. Additionally, how much people avoid uncertainty drives if and how much performance-oriented pay is accepted in relation to fixed pay.
- *Salary–benefits ratio*: Each country has traditions regarding how much overall compensation consists of salary versus benefits. This is due to culture as well as government regulation.

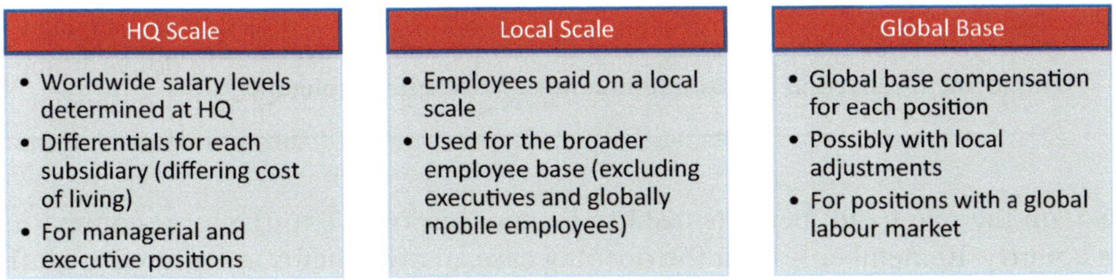


**Fig. 17.7** International compensation options. (Based on content from Tarique et al., 2022, p. 3216)

**Options for International Compensation:** Given these complexities, what can a global compensation system of an MNE look like? Several different options are in use in practice (Tarique et al., 2022, p. 326):

- *Headquarters scale*: Salary levels across the world are determined at headquarters, applying some differentiation to account for differing cost of living. This is usually applied to executive and managerial positions only.
- *Local scale*: Employees are paid on a local scale, in line with local norms for compensation. MNEs usually use this for employees below the managerial level in a country.
- *Global base*: HR develops a global base for each position, maybe with some differentiation for subsidiaries. This implies that more or less the same compensation is paid for a given position across the world. This is usually used for specific categories of positions only. MNEs apply this for positions for which there is a global labor market, such as software engineers.

In practice, HCNs at the top levels are frequently compensated according to the headquarters scale, while the remaining staff is paid according to the local scale. Figure 17.7 summarizes the options.

## International Benefits

In addition to the salary, companies provide *benefits*. Examples include vacation days and leaves on special occasions, corporate pensions, healthcare and other insurance, and stock options. Benefits vary significantly between countries. This is due to different government regulations and employees' expectations. A benefit such as healthcare insurance provided voluntarily in one country may be mandated in another and provided by the government in a third country. The concept of lifetime employment in Japan, which can also be considered a benefit, is rooted in Japanese culture. Further factors that explain international differences in benefits provided include a country's wealth, demographic structure, history, and industry mix (Hempel, 1998).

**Benefit**

A *benefit* will be taken to be any form of non-pecuniary payment or right that is employment related in a substantial number of countries (Hempel, 1998, p. 278).

So, on the one hand, benefits need to be very responsive to the local context in a country. Remember how in the opening case, many benefits are offered to staff by the Argentinian member firm, such as gym membership, a newspaper subscription, leaves on birthdays, and vouchers for shopping. This is to remain competitive in the labor market, where such benefits are common. At the same time, there are advantages for an MNE to have some level of global consistency: Benefits are one way in which MNEs can display and strengthen one corporate culture across their operations worldwide. This can be done, for example, by providing benefits consistently that are seen as characteristic of this company. Consistency will also facilitate the transfer of employees across borders (Hempel, 1998).

**Qualitative Parity:** To achieve some level of "qualitative parity" between employees in the various operations of the firm worldwide while being flexible to local circumstances, it has been suggested that MNEs provide something from each of the following categories of benefits (Tarique et al., 2022, p. 336):

- *Core benefits*: benefits that the company wants to provide to every employee worldwide
- *Required benefits*: benefits required by law in a country
- *Recommended benefits*: benefits provided when cost allows it
- *Optional benefits*: benefits provided when it is a common practice in a country

These options are summarized in ◘ Fig. 17.8.

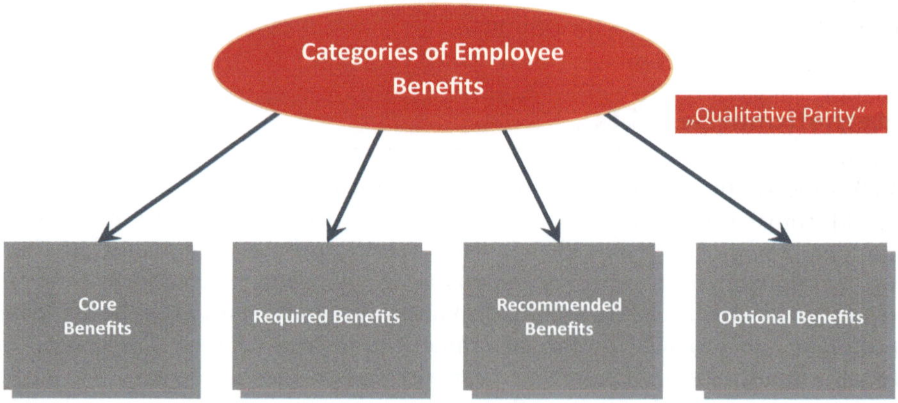


17

◘ **Fig. 17.8** Categories of (international) employee benefits. (Own diagram based on content from Tarique et al., 2022, p. 336)

## Review Questions

1. Why is human resource management particularly important for service firms?
2. How is IHRM different from HRM?
3. What are some key arguments favoring global standardization versus local adaptation of HRM practices?
4. Explain the two factors that impact the HRM practices in subsidiaries of an MNE.
5. Outline the four staffing approaches for MNEs.
6. What are the different reasons for seconding international assignees?
7. Why do international assignees frequently fail in their roles, and what can companies do to reduce the risk of failure?
8. Outline the primary criteria used in the selection of international assignees.
9. Why can the repatriation of international assignees be challenging?
10. Outline the two goals of employee performance management.
11. What are the different options for MNEs to deal with standardization vs. adaptation of employee performance management?
12. Explain the four factors that should be considered in implementing an effective international performance management system, drawing on the example of a company you are familiar with.
13. What particular challenges can the appraisal of HCNs by foreign managers encounter?
14. What are the main aims of a global compensation and benefits system?
15. Outline the main options for a global compensation system.
16. Explain the concept of "qualitative parity" for the benefits an MNE provides globally.
17. Discuss the frequent practice that HCNs at the top levels in a subsidiary are compensated according to the headquarters scale while the remaining staff is paid according to the local scale.

## Closing Case: The Role of Corporate HR in Talent Management at BankCo

BankCo is a large international banking and financial services company headquartered in the UK. The firm has over 150,000 employees and operations in more than 40 countries. Most employees work in retail banking. Other businesses consist of investment banking, wealth management, and payment networks. The firm operates across Europe, the United States, the Middle East, and Asia.

BankCo's HR department has defined the HR business partner's role as the primary contact for the firm's divisions regarding HR. While in some countries, this role is very effective, in others, it does not work well. BankCo makes it a point that global talent management processes are implemented consistently across the various operations worldwide. Some aspects of it can be adapted locally, though, as an HR manager outlines:

» There are some things that are absolutely non-negotiable—this is the way you're going to do them, this is

City of London. (Image by Kai Pilger from Pixabay)

> the process, this is the documentation and you can't veer from that. Then there's something in the middle where there's some framework you need to work this activity around ... but how you do that is entirely up to you (Sparrow et al., 2013, p. 1785).

One of the non-negotiable things is the branding of the global talent management process and the terminology used in its context. In implementing talent management policies from headquarters, BankCo encounters challenges at the country level due to culture, as an HR manager explains:

> I think you can have a world class talent management process, but [there is a national] culture that sits within the capability of your line managers to work within those processes (Sparrow et al., 2013, p. 1786).

BankCo's global group HR attempts to manage the behavior of line managers in the countries that implement talent management in line with the values of the global process.

Complementing the local HR business partner roles, dedicated roles for global talent management were created in each business division of the firm. This highlights the importance of talent management at the level of the divisions. This role aims to drive consistency in talent management. This was not easy to achieve, though, as one divisional HR manager admits:

> [the purpose of the role is] to ensure that there is one consistent approach. At the moment there are lots of different interpretations [of talent management processes] (Sparrow et al., 2013, p. 1787).

To drive consistency in talent management, the divisional talent management professionals built relationships with local HR personnel, especially the HR business partners. The new role was coordinated by global group HR, but the implementation still varied much between divisions, as illustrated by a divisional HR manager:

> [Group] do a really good job of facilitating, but you can use it as much as you want [or not] as well (Sparrow et al., 2013, p. 1787).

BankCo had internationalized rapidly. Due to one acquisition, BankCo expanded from 20,000 employees, mainly based in the UK, to 40,000 people in 53 countries. This initially drove a need for a centralized approach to achieve integration. While BankCo developed the process centrally, there remained many variations in implementation in practice. For example, an essential element used in the process—the performance-potential matrix—was used in different ways due to different local business contexts. While in most parts of BankCo, it was used as an elite process, one national affiliate used it in a more egalitarian way. The leadership model underlying the definition and measurement of potential was globally provided. The application of the matrix varied, such as the level of transparency regarding talent status attributed, the design of career paths for employees, the usage of coaching, and how the process was linked to rewards.

The global financial crisis significantly impacted global talent management at BankCo. The bank adopted a more decentralized holding structure, so talent management became less globally integrated. BankCo developed a new talent strategy for each business. A global perspective was no longer always seen as desirable, as outlined by a divisional HR manager:

> This is really hard to do, because the issues facing each of the businesses are so different (Sparrow et al., 2013, p. 1790).

**Questions**

1. How does BankCo solve the tension between global standardization and local adaptation of HRM practices?
2. How and why might other service firms find different solutions?

Sources: Based on content from Sparrow et al. (2013)

**Summary**

This chapter:

- Defined international human resource management as "all issues related to the management of people in an international context"
- Outlined the context of international human resource management in service firms: primarily headquarters and subsidiaries of MNEs
- Explained that local HR practices in MNEs are impacted by both a country-of-origin and host-country effects
- Described approaches to international workforce planning—the ethnocentric, polycentric, geocentric, and regiocentric approaches—and how MNEs choose a suitable approach

- Explained reasons for using international assignments and types of assignments, and discussed the failure of international assignees and their preparation
- Outlined selection criteria for candidates for international assignments: job suitability, cultural adaptability, personal characteristics, desire for the assignment, language ability, and international experience
- Defined repatriation as "the activity of bringing the expatriate back to the home country," and addressed challenges encountered in repatriation and ways of dealing with them
- Explained how to conduct international employee performance management, defined as "an intervention of an MNE for the purpose of managing the performance of its global workforce"
- Described goals of international performance management as evaluation and development goals and outlined different strategies
- Outlined how MNEs deal with the compensation and benefits for their global workforce, different options for global compensation, and an approach for determining adequate benefits, defined as "any form of non-pecuniary payment or right that is employment related in a substantial number of countries"

## References


Authoring Group Educational Reporting. (2016). *Education in Germany 2016: An indicator-based report including an analysis of education and migration.* Retrieved from https://www.bildungsbericht.de/en/archive/the-national-report-on-education-2016/NationalReportonEducation2016.pdf.

Bloom, M., Milkovich, G. T., & Mitra, A. (2003). International compensation: Learning from how managers respond to variations in local host contexts. *The International Journal of Human Resource Management, 14*(8), 1350–1367.

Deresky, H. (2017). *International management: Managing across borders and cultures* (9th ed.). Pearson Education.

Dickmann, M. (2003). Implementing German HRM abroad: Desired, feasible, successful? *The International Journal of Human Resource Management, 14*(2), 265–283.

Dowling, P. J., Festing, M., & Engle, A. D. (2017). *International human resource management* (7th ed.). Cengage Learning EMEA.

Economist. (2023, February 22). The desparate uncertainty of Ukrainian refugees.

Festing, M., & Tekieli, M. (2018). Global reward management. In *The Routledge companion to reward management* (pp. 209–221). Routledge.

Florkowski, G. W. (2006). *Managing global legal systems: International employment regulation and competitive advantage.* Routledge.

Galperin, B. L., & Lituchy, T. R. (2014). Human resource development in service firms across cultures. *Human Resource Development Review, 13*(3), 336–368.

Harvey, M., & Novicevic, M. M. (2006). The evolution from repatriation of managers in MNEs to 'patriation' in global organizations. In G. K. Stahl & I. Björkman (Eds.), *Handbook of research in international human resource management* (pp. 323–343). Edward Elgar.

Heenan, D. A., & Perlmutter, H. V. (1979). *Multinational organization development.* Addison-Wesley.

Hempel, P. S. (1998). Designing multinational benefits programs: The role of national culture. *Journal of World Business, 33*(3), 277–294.

Kaiser, S., Kozica, A., Swart, J., & Werr, A. (2015). Human resource management in professional service firms: Learning from a framework for research and practice. *German Journal of Human Resource Management, 29*(2), 77–101.

Kierner, A., & Suutari, V. (2018). Repatriation of international dual-career couples. *Thunderbird International Business Review, 60*(6), 885–895.
Liu, X. (2012). Culture and quality assurance approach: A case study of 360-degree feedback in China. *Proceedings of 2012 international conference on management innovation and public policy* (pp. 1812–1815).
Mendenhall, M., & Oddou, G. (1985). The dimensions of expatriate acculturation: A review. *Academy of Management Review, 10*(1), 39–47.
Mercer. (2022). *Cost of living city ranking*. Retrieved from https://www.mercer.com/our-thinking/career/cost-of-living.html.
Morgan, P. V. (1986). International human resource management: Fact or fiction. *Personnel Administrator, 31*(9), 43–47.
OECD. (2023). *Labor force participation rate*. Retrieved from https://data.oecd.org/emp/labour-force-participation-rate.htm.
Paik, Y., Segaud, B., & Malinowski, C. (2002). How to improve repatriation management: Are motivations and expectations congruent between the company and expatriates? *International Journal of Manpower, 23*(7), 635–648.
Perlmutter, H. (1969). The tortuous evolution of the multinational corporation. *Columbia Journal of World Business, 4*(1), 9–18.
Ronen, S. (1989). Training the international assignee. In I. L. Goldstein (Ed.), *Training and development in organizations* (pp. 417–453). Jossey-Bass.
Sokolov, D., & Zavyalova, E. (2022). Trendsetters of HRM: A systematic review of how professional service firms manage people. *Personnel Review, 51*(2), 564–583.
Sparrow, P., Brewster, C., & Chung, C. (2016). *Globalizing human resource management*. Routledge.
Sparrow, P., Farndale, E., & Scullion, H. (2013). An empirical study of the role of the corporate HR function in global talent management in professional and financial service firms in the global financial crisis. *The International Journal of Human Resource Management, 24*(9), 1777–1798.
Stahl, G. K., Björkman, I., & Morris, S. (2012). *Handbook of research in international human resource management* (2nd ed.). Edward Elgar.
Suseno, Y., & Pinnington, A. H. (2017). The war for talent: Human capital challenges for professional service firms. *Asia Pacific Business Review, 23*(2), 205–229.
Swart, J., Hansen, N. K., & Kinnie, N. (2015). Strategic human resource management and performance management in professional service firms. In L. Empson, D. Muzio, J. Broschak, & B. Hinings (Eds.), *The Oxford handbook of professional service firms* (pp. 476–501). Oxford University Press.
Tahvanainen, M., Welch, D., & Worm, V. (2005). Implications of short-term international assignments. *European Management Journal, 23*(6), 663–673.
Tarique, I., Briscoe, D. R., & Schuler, R. S. (2022). International human resource management. In *Policies and practices for multinational enterprises* (6th ed.). Routledge.
Torbiörn, I. (1985). The structure of managerial roles in cross-cultural settings. *International Studies of Management and Organization, 15*(1), 52–74.
Tungli, Z., & Peiperl, M. (2009). Expatriate practices in German, Japanese, UK, and US multinational companies: A comparative survey of changes. *Human Resource Management, 48*(1), 153–171.
Vance, C. M. (2006). Strategic upstream and downstream considerations for effective global performance management. *International Journal of Cross Cultural Management, 6*(1), 37–56.
World Economic Forum. (2020). *Global migration, by the numbers: Who migrates, where they go and why*. Retrieved from https://www.weforum.org/agenda/2020/01/iom-global-migration-report-international-migrants-2020/.
Zeira, Y. (1976). Management development in ethnocentric multinational corporations. *California Management Review, 18*(4), 34–42.
Zheng, C. (2009). Keeping talents for advancing service firms in Asia. *Journal of Service Management, 20*(5), 482–502.

## Further Reading

Dowling, P. J., Festing, M., & Engle, A. D. (2017). *International human resource management* (7th ed.). Cengage Learning EMEA and Tarique, I., Briscoe, D. R., & Schuler, R. S. (2022). International human resource management: Policies and practices for multinational enterprises, 6th ed. Routledge provide a good overview of IHRM.

Galperin, B. L., & Lituchy, T. R. (2014). Human resource development in service firms across cultures. *Human Resource Development Review, 13*(3), 336–368 outline IHRM in service firms focusing on learning and development.

# Managing Services Across Cultures and Distributed Virtual Teams

## Contents




D. Klimkeit et al., *International Management in Service Firms*, Classroom Companion: Business,
https://doi.org/10.1007/978-3-031-50345-0_18

**Learning Outcomes**

After completing this chapter, you should be able to:

- Explain the concept of culture and its role in managing international services
- Outline the value dimensions of Hofstede, Hall and Hall, and Trompenaars and Hampden-Turner
- Critically reflect the role of culture in international management
- Outline the impact of culture on leadership and the motivation of international staff
- Describe a process for culturally sensitive communication
- Outline different types of cross-cultural training
- Explain the opportunities and challenges of distributed virtual teams
- Outline practices for making virtual teams successful

## Introduction

Due to the globalization of the service sector, many service firms today face a cross-cultural situation, both inside and outside of the firm: subsidiaries in many countries, a multicultural workforce, and cross-cultural encounters with customers and other stakeholders. This chapter will first address understanding and then dealing with cultural differences to collaborate successfully across cultural boundaries. At the same time, many Service MNEs (multinational enterprises) have created distributed virtual teams (DVTs) that belong together organizationally but are spread across geographic locations. The COVID-19 (Coronavirus Disease-2019) pandemic has reinforced this as many employees shifted to working from home. So, this chapter will also provide guidance on achieving successful collaboration in distributed virtual teams.

Signature of M&A Contract. (Image by Edar from Pixabay)

## Opening Case: Three International Mergers and Acquisitions

An Italian technology manufacturing firm (ItalTechCo) acquired a US technology manufacturing firm (USTechCo). Generally, the acquisition has not been very conflictual. However, in several instances, the Chief Executive Officer (CEO) of USTechCo distributed information on what had been discussed between the two CEOs and the department heads in an early phase to lower levels of management. This caused tensions with the Italian CEO, who considered the information confidential and would have preferred it not to be distributed. At ItalTechCo, managers saw information as power and distributed it only "drop by drop, little by little" (Italian consultant). They saw providing more information as sometimes rather creating more confusion than being helpful. At USTechCo, there is a much more participative approach, extending the integration much faster to lower levels of management. The American CEO wanted to make everybody committed and take everybody on board. This cultural difference is also visible in the office layout of the two firms. At ItalTechCo, one must pass a tunnel and a door at the end, requiring a special badge to enter the CEO's office. At USTechCo, the CEO sits in an open-plan office with everybody else. There is also a second cultural difference involved. As the Italian consultant hired to facilitate the integration pointed out, people in the US firm tend to be more used to and less afraid of changes in the workplace and are also changing jobs more often than their Italian counterparts. In the Italian firm, the information about upcoming changes, such as integration or restructuring, created more anxiety among employees, inducing the Italian CEO to act more cautiously. An institutional difference is also involved, making the CEO careful about which information to distribute at which point. As the consultant points out:

> In Italy, if you say 'we'll undergo a carve-out and then a restructuring,' then you have the workers councils, then you have the unions… (Italian consultant).

In another instance, managers of the US firm were more empowered to make decisions in the integration teams. In contrast, managers of the Italian firm always had to refer to their boss for a decision, which slowed down the team's progress and led to complaints from the US managers.

In an acquisition of a wood manufacturing firm (WoodCoTarget) by another firm (WoodCoAcquiror) in the same industry in Europe, the integration in the finance department went badly, mainly because of inappropriate communication by WoodCoAcquiror leadership in the pre-combination phase, so the plan was revised. While the key issues were not cultural, cultural differences did play a role in some instances. WoodCoAcquiror was a publicly listed company, whereas WoodCoTarget was a private entrepreneurial business. At

WoodCoTarget, people from the Controlling department used to go and visit production regularly to try to understand what was going on and explain the monthly results. Controllers at WoodCoTarget were used to talk to people in production and, along the way, learn how production is doing. WoodCoAcquiror's Controlling department was much more shareholder-driven and focused on aggregating figures. There was no personal contact with production. Controlling only sent emails, like,

> We need these figures until this date.

This led to strong frustration and loss of interest in the integration among WoodCoTarget controllers and respective comments:

> Everything happens via email nowadays. They do not talk to us personally anymore.

> In the old days, we concentrated on production, now only figures count.

This led to a loss of motivation:

> Who is interested in what we are doing, anyway? I will only wait for instructions from WoodCoAcquiror now.

A private equity firm has merged three manufacturing firms it owned in its portfolio of firms, which were in the same industry: One Swedish-headquartered (SwedeManCo), one UK-based (UKManCo), and one with headquarters in the United States (USManCo). A consultant has advised on the integration. Several conflicts occurred. While there were several causes, culture was crucial in one case. In the teams managing the integration, participants of the three firms wanted to and could go at different speeds. The main difference was between the Americans and the Swedes. Members of SwedeManCo had a culture of dialogue and consultation, which upset USManCo members who wanted to move faster. Managers struck compromises, and the consultant explained each other's working methods. However, some members of USManCo were pushing too far and were removed from the integration management team. They were told,

> You are going to frustrate yourself to death if you try to do this [push for faster decisions] (consultant).

In one instance, the new CEO named executives and expected them to make decisions themselves, which irritated some as they were used to the CEO making all the significant decisions.

**Questions**

1. How would you label the various cultural differences that occurred in these transactions?
2. What could have been done to prevent or mitigate the challenges?

Sources: Based on own field studies

## The Role of Culture in Managing International Services

Managers of service firms with international activities are constantly facing situations where differences in cultural values, beliefs, or observable behaviors play a role. Think of a manager seconded to a subsidiary who needs to manage local staff with different expectations of leadership and who require other forms of motivation than the leader may be used to. The same situation can occur without being seconded if the team is a geographically distributed virtual team (DVT) where the manager leads employees based in other countries. Even at home, the workforce may be culturally diverse, hailing from various cultural backgrounds. When managers establish new business relationships with customers, suppliers, or alliance partners from other countries, culture impacts how best to establish the connection. For example, how do you introduce yourself, and how do you establish credibility? Do you get down to business immediately or start by building a relationship? This is especially relevant when a meeting is about selling a service to a new customer abroad: How do you convince a potential customer to buy your service in that culture? When making decisions in an MNE (multinational enterprise), there are various culturally accepted ways of arriving at a decision: by consensus, by a top-down decision of a leader? Especially in human resource management, culture is very relevant. Culture factors into how to best select and recruit employees, how to train and develop them, how to manage their performance, and how to compensate employees.

Specifically in service firms, culture plays a vital role in coordination and integration since, frequently, coordination by socialization is more appropriate than by more formal mechanisms, as outlined in ► Chap. 9. This is especially true when the service is customized and cannot be standardized and formalized. Developing a service culture shared across the whole firm can become a crucial competitive requirement in service firms where customer contact is essential (Grönroos, 2015, pp. 446–448). In services, many quality characteristics, as perceived by customers, are culturally shaped (e.g., reliability, responsiveness, empathy, politeness, helpfulness). Behavior of service staff that is considered culturally inappropriate has implications on the service quality perceived by customers. What complicates matters is that in service industries like tourism and hospitality, a range of diverse cultures of guests and hosts comes into play. So, service firms with international contacts must sensitize their employees to cultural differences. Sometimes, cultural specifics are at the center of customer demand, as in the example of Italian food, which for many customers symbolizes Italian culture and perhaps conjures memories of a vacation in Italy. At the same time, internationally mobile customers expect the same quality in every location, for instance, from hotel chains or restaurant chains. So service firms must develop a robust corporate culture that transcends geographic boundaries while remaining sensitive to local cultural differences where required (Gardini, 2004, pp. 22–26).

## Understanding Culture

How can *culture* be defined? Cultural anthropology is the academic discipline of culture. So, it makes sense to look to anthropology for a definition of culture. Unfortunately, many management scholars have drawn on concepts from anthropologists Kluckhohn and Strodtbeck from the 1950s (Schneider et al., 2014, p. 29). Like other academic disciplines, anthropology has moved on in the 70 years since the 1950s, so we draw on a more recent definition from anthropologists Peoples and Bailey instead.

**Culture**

*Culture* is the *shared, socially learned knowledge* and *patterns of behavior* characteristic of some group of people (Peoples & Bailey, 2018, p. 23, emphases except "culture" in original text).

This definition contains several essential aspects that require further explanation.

**Shared:** Culture is shared in a group of people in such a way that they can communicate and interact with each other without needing to explain their behavior and without many misunderstandings most of the time. Sharing a culture is not a straightforward matter, however. Culture can be shared at various levels. We tend to think of cultures in terms of national cultures that exist in one nation-state, such as "French culture" or "German culture." However, in practice, nation-state and culture frequently do not match. While in countries like Japan and South Korea, culture might be relatively homogenous, if you think of countries like India or China, but also Belgium, Switzerland, or South Africa, several different cultures can be found within the borders of a nation-state. In many countries in Europe today, many migrants are present that originate from quite different cultural backgrounds. So, the term "some group of people" is deliberately imprecise. Depending on our intention, we can use a very broad definition of "some group of people," as in "Western Culture" or "Asian culture." Other cultures found on some Pacific islands can consist of only a few hundred people. In addition, what is often referred to as "subcultures" can be found within nation-states, such as corporate cultures, occupational cultures, rural vs. urban subcultures, or the LGBTQ (Lesbian, Gay, Bisexual, Transgender, and Queer) community as a subculture within a nation-state (Peoples & Bailey, 2018, pp. 23–24).

**Socially Learned:** The members of one generation learn culture from the previous generation. With some changes, they will transmit it to the following generation. Anthropologists label this as *enculturation*, a process by which children learn a culture from those surrounding them as they grow up. This has an important implication: Culture is not transmitted biologically or genetically. A child is perfectly able to learn the culture of any society it grows up in, independently of the culture of its biological parents. Culture is socially learned because that learning does not happen on an individual level by trial and error. Instead, it is a social process that includes mechanisms such as intentional instruction by parents and others and observation and imitation of the behavior of others. This spares us from the adverse effect of, for example, eating things that damage our health. Through social learning, humanity can benefit from the previous experience of others. Innovations can spread, and knowledge accumulates. At the same time, people can change ideas more quickly if external conditions change than if cultural knowledge was inscribed into their genes (Peoples & Bailey, 2018, pp. 25–26).

**Cultural Knowledge:** Cultural knowledge benefits human societies: It allows us to behave in a way that most of the time avoids misunderstandings and having to explain what we are doing. It leads most people to behave in a way considered meaningful and acceptable by others most of the time. It avoids unnecessarily upsetting others. Cultural knowledge directs behavior so people can survive and adapt to their environment. Now, what does cultural knowledge comprise? There are many elements, but in line with Peoples and Bailey, we will outline five that can be considered as particularly important (Peoples & Bailey, 2018, pp. 30–33):

- *Norms*: Norms are shared ideas about how people are supposed to behave in certain situations. For example, how should one behave appropriately as a guest at a wedding or as a student in the classroom?
- *Values*: Values are beliefs in society about the desirable way of life. Values are very central to a culture. They impact the goals we pursue and affect individual motivations and reasons for why we do what we do. Values provide standards that people believe must be upheld. Consider civil rights in Western democratic societies or ideas about expected work ethics. In practice, however, people do not always act in line with values for various reasons.
- *Symbols*: Symbols are things that represent or call to mind something else. They are arbitrary in the sense that there is no inherent need to interpret a symbol in a particular way. Symbols are conventional, which means that they only carry a particular meaning because most people in a society agree that they do. Think of the meaning of a red or green traffic light. Symbols can include things like gestures, a way of walking, styles of dress, or facial expressions that a member of a culture would find difficult to explain.
- *Classifications of Reality*: Classifications of reality are how the members of a culture divide the world into categories of things or people. While phenomena have many differences and similarities, a culture recognizes only some as relevant. This can relate to natural things, such as which plants and animals are considered edible, and to the social world, like how a culture classifies people into categories.
- *Worldviews*: Worldviews are the way people interpret reality. This includes how they see themselves in relation to the world in which they live. Worldviews deal with the grand philosophical questions of human life, such as the meaning of human existence, notions of good and evil, and what supernatural powers are like. They also address the relationship of human beings to nature: Are we masters of nature, or should we strive to live in harmony with nature?

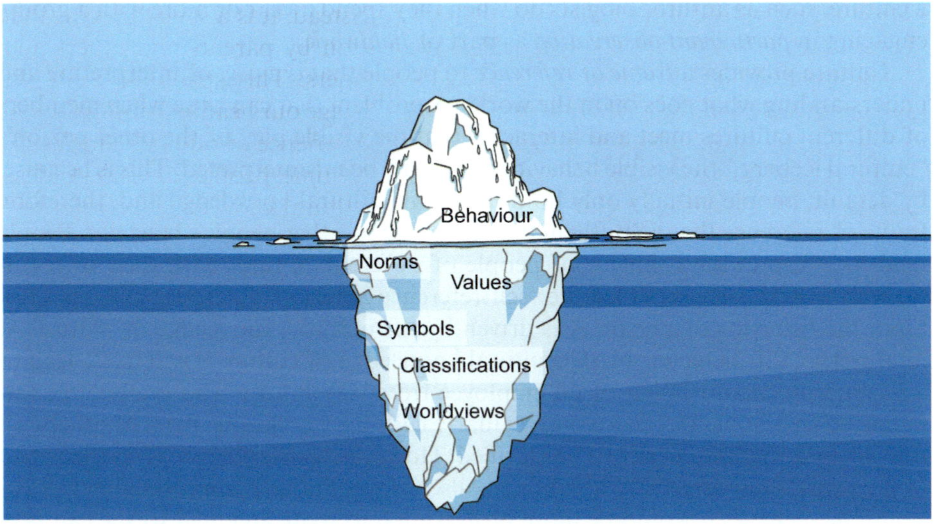


**Fig. 18.1** Culture as an iceberg. (Own diagram using iceberg drawing from Mote Oo Education from Pixabay)

**Patterns of Behavior:** Finally, within a culture, we can observe some regular patterns of behavior that are more or less common to members of that culture and may differ from patterns of behavior found in other cultures. Having said so, members of a culture differ in their behavior in many ways. There are several reasons for this: People have different social identities, such as gender, wealth, or occupation. Behavior varies with the context or situation. A woman may behave quite differently toward her husband, children, or employees. Individuals are unique in many ways. Finally, cultural expectations of desired behavior may be ambiguous, leading to differences in behavior. Nevertheless, one can observe some regularity in the behavior of members of one cultural group (Peoples & Bailey, 2018, p. 29).

Inspired by Hall (1976), comparing culture to an iceberg has become common. We adopt the general idea of Hall's concept without the details and include the elements of culture derived from Peoples and Bailey in our version of the culture iceberg (see Fig. 18.1). As is well known about icebergs, what is visible is only a small part. In contrast, the biggest part of the iceberg is hidden below the water's surface. This also applies to culture. Only the patterns of behavior are directly observable as we see how people dress, what they say, as well as their body language. To understand a culture, however, we must look beyond the surface of patterns of behavior. As outlined above, the various elements of cultural knowledge impact the patterns of behavior. This is most obvious for the norms of appropriate behavior and the values that drive the goals people pursue in their life. These, especially the norms, are still more or less accessible by asking people what behavior they see as appropriate and what they value in life and see as important. The other elements tend to be more challenging to elicit as members of a culture hold them more unconsciously and see them as taken for granted (this partly also applies to the values). They require a more prolonged process of interaction with members of a culture, such as anthropologists do when they spend a year or more with a group, engaging in *participant observation* as part of *fieldwork*.

Culture provides a *frame of reference* to people that is a way of interpreting and understanding what goes on in the world. A problem that can arise when members of different cultures meet and interact is that the visible part of the other person's "cultural iceberg," the visible behavior, can easily be misinterpreted. This is because, by default, people initially only hold their own cultural knowledge and, therefore, frame of reference that helps them to make sense of other people's behavior. People tend to interpret the behavior of people of different cultures with their own cultural knowledge. This is called the "self-reference criterion" (Deresky, 2017, p. 112). Since the behavior of person A is driven by the cultural knowledge of culture A, interpreting this behavior by the cultural knowledge of culture B will likely lead to a misinterpretation. Think of an employee from one culture who prefers to communicate by phone. He, therefore, regularly calls up a colleague from another culture when something needs to be clarified. However, that colleague feels disturbed in her work and perceives the phone calls as impolite and unprofessional intrusions. She believes it would be more professional to write an email so she can take time to consider the request and answer when she has time to do so. On the contrary, the requester might consider emails impersonal and see it as more professional to discuss things in a direct phone conversation that allows immediate feedback and expresses appreciation for the colleague by engaging in a direct phone conversation with her.

**Cultural Spheres of Influence:** As mentioned above, while most people think of culture in terms of national cultures, culture also exists in many other groups of people. Understanding this is facilitated by the definition of culture from Peoples and Bailey we use here. Schneider and colleagues have outlined these various contexts in which groups of people share a culture nicely as *cultural spheres of influence,* as all these spheres of culture impact people's behavior. Certainly, national cultures significantly influence people's worldviews, classifications of reality, and other elements of cultural knowledge. However, corporate cultures can be equally strong. This is why Geert Hofstede, in his seminal study we outline below, chose to conduct all of his initial surveys at IBM, which was said to have a particularly strong corporate culture. When two companies merge, the differences between corporate cultures become apparent. We mentioned above the cultural differences that exist between regions within a country. Everyone who has ever worked in a company for some time will notice that within the company, different departments like Human Resource (HR), Information Technology (IT), and Marketing each have their own unique culture with their norms, values, and symbols. Connected to these are professional cultures that cut across companies. IT people of one company may find it easier to connect and communicate with IT people of another company than with HR or Marketing people within their own company. Industries also develop their specific cultural knowledge. The culture of the automotive industry is quite different from that of the banking or advertising industries. This should make it evident that one cannot easily predict the behavior of a given person working in a particular position in a particular firm by referencing that person's national culture alone. It is not clear that national culture will always impact behavior more strongly

**Fig. 18.2** Cultural spheres of influence. (Based on content from Schneider et al., 2014, pp. 64–83)

than other spheres of culture (Schneider et al., 2014, pp. 64–83). Maybe a punk in Tokyo has more in common with a punk in Berlin than with a banker in Tokyo. See Fig. 18.2 for a display of the major cultural spheres of influence.

## Approaches for Analyzing Cultural Differences

Given the complexity of culture, the question is how to approach cultural differences: How to understand the major differences one is likely to face when dealing with members of other cultures in a work-related setting. Scholars have developed approaches for analyzing cultural differences that simplify the complexity by highlighting key differences that one can observe between cultures. These are typically based on values. Given the vital role of values as an element of cultural knowledge generally and their impact on goals and motivations and, therefore, behavior, there is a logic in doing so. Nevertheless, given the many other elements of cultural knowledge, we need to be aware of the limitation of focusing on values only. Moreover, as outlined above, people do not always behave according to the values of their culture for various reasons.

Before outlining some major approaches, let us say a few words about stereotyping. The problem with cultural stereotypes is that they make us expect every member of a culture to think the same way, feel the same way, and behave the same way, which is obviously not the case. Especially stereotyping can lead us not to be open to revising our stereotype when we encounter members of a culture that do not fit the stereotype. Instead, it can be helpful to think of models of culture as providing something like a normal curve. This has a hypothetical cultural mean for a given cultural group with variation around it. So, we can find some Brazilians more reserved than the average Chinese and some Chinese more expressive of their emotions than the average Brazilian. However, most Brazilians are more expressive than most Chinese (Schneider et al., 2014, p. 19).

## Hofstede's Value Dimensions

Geert Hofstede conducted the first major cross-cultural study in management in the late 1960s and early 1970s. It comprised a survey of 116,000 IBM employees in 40 countries. Hofstede chose IBM due to what was seen as a strong corporate culture, so he assumed that any cultural variation must be due to national cultural differences. Hofstede asked respondents for their preferences regarding management style and work environment. The original study identified four "value orientations" outlined below (Schneider et al., 2014, p. 42).

**Power Distance:** There are differences in power in any society. The question is how people deal with them: Are they emphasized or downplayed? At work, this becomes most obvious by comparing whether a boss would accept being criticized by his staff if they believe the boss is wrong. Further, would employees dare to criticize the boss or be reluctant to do so? Answers to these questions refer to the level of *power distance* in a society.

**Power Distance**

*Power distance* refers to "the extent to which the less powerful members of institutions and organizations within a country expect and accept that power is distributed unequally" (Hofstede et al., 2010, p. 61).

In high-power-distance countries, people see superiors and subordinates as essentially unequal. In these cultures, subordinates expect superiors to tell them what to do. Visible signs like dress codes, large offices, titles, and other status symbols demonstrate power distance. In low-power-distance countries, both sides see themselves as essentially equal. For example, everyone, including top management, would use the same canteen. People see hierarchies as just differences in roles that can be changed. Subordinates would expect the boss to consult them before making a final decision. Superiors are respected for their experience and knowledge, not just for their position. Hofstede found high power distance for most countries in Asia, Latin America, Arabic countries, Eastern Europe, and Africa and low power distance for Israel, Nordic countries, Baltic countries, German-speaking countries, the United States, the UK, and the Netherlands (Hofstede et al., 2010, pp. 54–74). Remember how in the opening cases, it was apparent in various ways how the Italian firm ItalTechCo had a higher power distance than the American firm USTechCo. In the third opening case, the US-Firm USManCo had a higher power distance than the Swedish firm SwedeManCo.

**Individualism vs. Collectivism:** In some societies—labeled *collectivist*—the interest of the group or the collective, whether the family, the team, or the department, is emphasized over the individual's interest. In other societies—labeled *individualist*—people are classified by their individual characteristics, not by their membership in a group. They are seen to stand by themselves as individual beings.

**Individualism and Collectivism**

*Individualism* relates to "societies in which ties between individuals are loose: everyone is expected to look after him- or herself and his or her immediate family." *Collectivism* pertains to "societies in which people from birth onward are integrated into strong, cohesive in-groups, which throughout people's lifetime continue to protect them in exchange for unquestioning loyalty" (Hofstede et al., 2010, p. 92).

In organizations, individualism implies that employees do not feel firmly attached to the organization and strive for a sense of personal accomplishment. Collectivism emphasizes the belonging of the individual to the organization. Good working conditions are valued. In Japan, people might perceive a company like a family, and companies traditionally reward loyalty to the company with life-long employment. In individualistic societies, people see the relationship with the company as more calculative and transactional (Hofstede et al., 2010, pp. 89–120).

**Masculinity vs. Femininity:** In many societies, there are clear ideas of how men and women are to behave: People expect men to be assertive, competitive, and tough. Women are supposed to be more concerned with taking care of home and family and be modest and gentle. In other societies, role expectations of men and women are not so clearly different. Rather, modesty, tenderness, and quality of life are generally valued, regardless of gender. Hofstede explains this as the difference between *masculinity* and *femininity*.

**Masculinity and Femininity**

Hofstede calls a society *masculine* "when emotional gender roles are clearly distinct: men are supposed to be assertive, tough, and focused on material success, whereas women are supposed to be more modest, tender, and concerned with the quality of life." Hofstede calls a society *feminine* "when emotional gender roles overlap: both men and women are supposed to be modest, tender, and concerned with the quality of life" (Hofstede et al., 2010, p. 140).

At work, in masculine societies, management is aggressive, and rewards are based on performance. Employees seek material rewards and promotions. People live in order to work. The share of women in the workplace is lower. In feminine societies, management is more consensus-oriented. People work in order to live. Employees seek good working relationships with superiors and colleagues. The share of women in the workplace is higher (Hofstede et al., 2010, pp. 136–170). The more consensus-oriented decision-making in the Swedish firm SwedeManCo compared to USManCo in the opening cases can also be seen in the context of higher feminism in the SwedeManCo.

**Uncertainty Avoidance:** As humans, we cannot predict the future. Not knowing what will happen can cause anxiety. However, the feeling of anxiety caused by uncertainty is subjective and impacted by culture. Given the same uncertain situation, people in one culture may perceive more unease than people in another culture. Therefore, in some cultures, *uncertainty is avoided* more strongly than in others, where people feel more at ease when faced with uncertainty.

**Uncertainty Avoidance**

*Uncertainty avoidance* is defined as "the extent to which the members of a culture feel threatened by ambiguous or unknown situations" (Hofstede et al., 2010, p. 191).

In countries with high uncertainty avoidance, people attempt to establish clear rules that increase predictability and reduce uncertainty to mitigate the feeling of stress caused by uncertainty. At work, people change jobs less frequently and seek formalization and clear rules and procedures. In low uncertainty avoidance societies, people change jobs more frequently, there are fewer rules in place, and more improvisation occurs (Hofstede et al., 2010, pp. 189–217). Remember how in the opening cases, it became apparent that the Italian firm ItalTechCo had a higher uncertainty avoidance than the American firm USTechCo.

**Long-Term Orientation:** When conducting the Chinese Values Survey, Hofstede identified a fifth dimension—long-term orientation. He found that in Asian countries like China, emphasis was placed on learning, self-discipline, and investment into the future of the business, while leisure time and immediate rewards were not in focus. These societies were labeled *as long-term oriented.* This contrasted with other societies, which focused more on short-term performance and rewards—called short-term-oriented societies.

**Long-Term Orientation**

*Long-term orientation* refers to "the fostering of virtues oriented toward future rewards—in particular, perseverance and thrift" (Hofstede et al., 2010, p. 239).



In business, long-term orientation fosters persistence and frugality, which leads to savings that can be invested in the business's long-term success. In short-term-oriented countries, businesses focus on the bottom line and expect profits on a monthly or quarterly basis (Hofstede et al., 2010, pp. 236–244).

Chinese shop; Chinese family businesses are often long-term oriented. (Image by Neale Bacon from Pixabay)

While the Hofstede study has been very influential, it has also received much criticism. We can only briefly summarize this here. As mentioned above, some criticize Hofstede for not distinguishing between values and actual behavior, which may differ. Hofstede essentially takes countries as units of analysis, not considering intracultural variation in societies like Belgium. Hofstede conducted his study in only one company—IBM. However, the staff selected by IBM may not be typical representatives of their country's culture. Hofstede conducted the original study, providing the bulk of his data, between 1967 and 1973. Many things have changed in the world since, such as the move away from communism in Central and Eastern Europe (Dowling et al., 2017, pp. 32–33). The later GLOBE (Global Leadership and Organizational Behavior Effectiveness) study addressed several of the shortcomings of the Hofstede model (Javidan et al., 2006). This study has its limitations as well, though (Graen, 2006), and most of the GLOBE dimensions are similar to Hofstede, so we will not present it here. We will address the GLOBE study in the context of motivation and leadership instead.

## Hall and Hall's Value Dimensions

Hall and Hall are anthropologists that have also been influential in cross-cultural studies in management. The dimensions of culture that they identified are based on interviews and observations in business environments. We will outline two dimensions that have been particularly influential in cross-cultural studies.

**High and Low Context:** When communicating, depending on the person we talk to, the situation, and our cultural background, we provide more or less information about the context of the message we want to convey in addition to the message itself. This is to enable the recipient to understand our message. The amount of context information that people provide varies between cultures. In high-context cultures, people provide little context explicitly with the message, and even the message itself can be brief and subtle. This is because, in these cultures, people will have spent much time socializing with their counterparts, thereby developing extensive shared understandings and knowledge about each other. So, a message does not need much explicit context. This differs in low-context cultures, where colleagues or business partners will have spent much less time socializing and therefore need more explicit context with a message to understand it. Communication needs to be more explicit and comprehensive. Most of the information is in what people say explicitly, while in high-context cultures, the message's recipient knows most information already. In high-context cultures, communication is more indirect, relying on facial expressions and voice intonation, while in low-context cultures, it is more direct and explicit. Japanese, Arabs, and Mediterranean Europeans are seen as having a high-context culture, while Americans, Swiss, Germans, and other Northern Europeans are seen as having a low-context culture (Hall & Hall, 1990, pp. 6–9).

**Monochromic and Polychromic Time:** Culture also impacts how people deal with time. In some—monochromic—cultures, people focus on one thing at a time. Time is divided into segments along a straight line that are scheduled one after the other. People do not like to be interrupted and expect others to be on time for appointments, and the meeting will not run over schedule. In other cultures—labeled polychronic—time is seen as several things running parallel. People can do several things at the same time. Meetings can be rescheduled at short notice to meet someone important. If someone is on the way to a scheduled meeting and meets someone important along the way, it is seen as essential to "give time" to that person, even if it means arriving late. Members of Latin cultures would rather be late at the next meeting than abruptly finish their current meeting before its "natural" ending. As people can do several things simultaneously, the expectation would be that those who are already present at the next meeting could use the time while they wait to do something else. Checking something on the smartphone while talking to someone would be common, while it would be considered rude by a member of a monochromic culture. Germans, Swiss, and Americans are considered members of monochromic cultures, while Southern Europeans and Latin Americans are considered to have a polychromic culture (Hall & Hall, 1990, pp. 13–21).



## Trompenaars and Hampden-Turner's Value Dimensions

Trompenaars and Hampden-Turner conducted surveys of employees of various levels and businesses on cultural values, focusing on the relationship between people. By 2012, they had conducted 80,000 surveys in over 100 countries. While their model does not have a solid academic foundation, it is frequently used in management training to describe behavioral differences between cultures and provide guidance for cross-cultural interaction (Dowling et al., 2017, pp. 35–36). We will outline three of their seven cultural dimensions that we perceive as valuable additions to the previously outlined models.

**Universalist vs. Particularist:** Human beings tend to always judge other people's behavior as good or bad. As you can imagine by now, culture impacts our judgment. In some cultures, people believe that what is good and bad can be defined and always applies, regardless of the person. These are called *universalistic* cultures. The ideal is to treat everyone the same way, regardless of relationship or position. Exceptions should not be made. In *particularistic* cultures, what is judged as right or wrong also depends on the relationship with the person in question. People see family and friends as more important than universal rules. People should consider individual circumstances. At work, a universalist attempts to have consistent, universal rules to treat everyone fairly. A particularist would create networks and understanding of specific cases. People seek fairness by treating all cases based on their specific merits. The authors summarize the difference nicely by stating how particularists and universalists see each other:

> » A Universalist says about particularists: "They cannot be trusted, they will always help their friends," while a particularist says about universalists: "They cannot be trusted, they would not even help a friend" (Trompenaars & Hampden-Turner, 2012, p. 44).

Trompenaars and Hampden-Turner find that US Americans, Canadians, Germans, Swiss, and Norwegians are universalistic, while Argentina, Mexico, Tanzania, Saudi Arabia, India, and Thailand are particularistic cultures (Trompenaars & Hampden-Turner, 2012, pp. 41–63).

**Affective vs. Neutral:** In interaction with others, people develop emotions. Cultures differ, however, in the extent to which showing emotions is seen as appropriate. In *affective* cultures, people show emotions openly through body language, gestures, facial expressions, and voice. In *neutral* cultures, on the contrary, people are expected to keep their emotions under control. Therefore, at work, in neutral cultures, expressive behavior is seen as a lack of control over one's feelings. Showing a "poker face" is the norm. In affective cultures, however, such a cool and detached attitude would appear as negative and dislike. Finland, Germany, China, and Ethiopia are seen as neutral, while Brazil, Italy, Saudi Arabia, and Pakistan are very affective (Trompenaars & Hampden-Turner, 2012, pp. 87–99).

**Achievement vs. Ascription:** Above, we addressed how much emphasis society places on status differentials and hierarchy (power distance). Another question regarding status differentials is what the basis of those differentials is? On which basis does a society award higher status to certain people than others? Some societies award status mainly on what that individual has achieved personally. They are *achievement-oriented.* Other societies award status mainly based on a person's age, gender, family background and social connections, ethnic group, educational institutions, or profession. Status in these societies is *ascribed.* This can be summarized as status based on what someone does vs. what someone is. In business, in achievement-oriented cultures, respect for a manager derives from the manager's knowledge and performance. Performance-based remuneration is common. In ascription-oriented cultures, respect for a manager is based on criteria like seniority. Performance-related remuneration tends to be less effective. The United States, Canada, Germany, Norway, and Australia are seen as achievement-oriented, while status is based on ascription in Argentina, Turkey, Saudi Arabia, Nigeria, and India (Trompenaars & Hampden-Turner, 2012, pp. 125–145).

From an academic perspective, the Trompenaars and Hampden-Turner model is problematic. They do not provide an explicit explanation for the origin of their dimensions. They use some aspects of previous studies without justification while leaving out other aspects. The authors have not demonstrated the validity and reliability of their dimensions (Dowling et al., 2017, p. 36). However, they do describe differences that one can perceive in practice and therefore have practical relevance.

## A Critical Reflection on Models of Culture

We believe it is imperative to add a critical reflection to the presentation of the cross-cultural models outlined above. While each can be criticized for various reasons, here we will address the overall limitations of such models. This concerns how they should be used. If used correctly, they can be helpful as a tool for understanding cultural differences. In business practice, one can observe the differences these models address. However, they should be used as a starting point only and not as the ultimate truth about a country's culture.

**Treat Cultures as Homogeneous:** You will remember how we outlined multiple spheres of culture, such as national, regional, corporate, and others. However, the cross-cultural models we outlined focus only on the national level. By using them in an unthinking manner, we may be led to assume national cultures as homogenous and forget about the many other spheres and subcultures that will exist in any culture. In practice, it will often be challenging to disentangle the effect of various spheres of culture, such as in an international merger where two corporate cultures and two national cultures come together. Likewise, studies might lead us to assume that differences between cultures will be more significant than within cultures. Growing evidence shows that cultural differences within nations can be more significant than differences between national cultures (Schneider et al., 2014, p. 4). Gerhart found, for example, that only 23% of the variance in the GLOBE study is due to country differences (Gerhart, 2009). Instead, cross-cultural studies might make us assume everyone within a culture is the same (Brannen, 1999).

**Disregard Other Factors Impacting Behavior:** Similarly, cross-cultural models may make us believe that people's behavior is driven by their culture alone. As we outlined above, when explaining the role of patterns of behavior in the definition of culture we use, however, several further factors impact the behavior of people: social identities, the context of a situation, and the individuality of people (Peoples & Bailey, 2018, p. 29). As Nardon and Steers remind us, culture does not occur in a vacuum but in a specific context. What behavior should we expect from a Saudi manager working for a French firm in Brazil? Moreover, what if, on top of this, he tries to adapt to our culture? So managers should focus on the specifics of a situation, not just the national culture of a counterpart (Nardon & Steers, 2014, pp. 138–139). According to Nardon and Steers, at least three context factors impact international encounters between managers: the cultural context, the organizational context, and the situational context. They provide the example of Japanese managers of Kia in the United States: They find very different subcultures in their operations in Southern California and Georgia. The same applies when they deal with Marketing or Finance, suppliers or car dealers, and individuals with different roles and personal characteristics. Airlines like TAM and AeroMexico reject their national cultures' tendency to disregard punctuality and establish clear global behavioral guidelines, e.g., to ensure the punctuality of airplanes. Regarding the situation, the structural situation of the manager (rank, department), the geographic location where interaction takes place, and the nature of the interaction between the individuals involved, including individual characteristics and process of interaction (in person, virtually), all play a role. Think of whether a meeting between an Indian and a French lady takes place in India or France or online or a third country, whether they are colleagues, or one is a service provider while the other is a customer. Remember how in the opening case of the merger between SwedeManCo, UKManCo, and USManCo, culture only played a conspicuous role in one of the several conflicts. Remember how in the opening case of ItalTechCo and USTechCo, besides uncertainty avoidance, there were also institutional reasons, e.g., the more substantial role of trade unions in Italy, which was a reason for the more cautious spreading of information by the Italian CEO. The difference in communication style between WoodCoTarget and WoodCoAcquiror in the opening case cannot be attributed clearly to one of the value dimensions outlined but constitute rather corporate cultural differences.

**Little Understanding of Change:** Cross-cultural models may convey the impression that culture is more or less stable. Research found, however, a more differentiated perspective on this. While cultures change only slowly most of the time, in many societies, at least partly, trends away from traditional norms toward more individualistic, liberal, and hedonistic norms have been observed, something labeled *cultural convergence*. Some significant environmental changes can also lead to faster changes in culture (Leung et al., 2005). Think of the cultural changes that the global COVID-19 (Coronavirus Disease-2019) pandemic will have precipitated. In many companies where working from home has not been an option traditionally, even after the acute phase of the pandemic, many firms continue to offer this as an option for some days of the week. The more casual dress code that came about from home office work seems to be, to some extent, at least retained in some workplaces as employees return to the office. The boost for tools for online conferences leads to less business travel for short meetings that managers instead hold online, even when the situation and regulations would allow business travel again. International connections increase, laws and regulations are harmonized in regional blocs such as the European Union, and migration increases cultural diversity. However, in management studies, there is controversy around how much cultural convergence takes place. John Child found that convergence can be observed at the macro level, relating to organizational structures, processes, technologies, and management concepts. Regarding the micro level, relating to cultural knowledge and patterns of behavior, still, much divergence can be found (Child, 1981). In other words: The fact that across the world, people use iPhones, wear Western-brand jeans, and drink Coca-Cola does not mean that necessarily norms, values, and worldviews will converge the same way. The growing Islamic extremism across several countries worldwide can well be interpreted as a backlash against "Westernization" or cultural convergence.

**Difference Between Values and Practices:** As outlined above, the fact that people hold specific values does not necessarily mean they will always act according to them. This is true for a range of reasons. We have mentioned some of them above: social identities, situational context, and individual differences between people. In addition, behavior expectations from different cultural spheres may clash (Schneider et al., 2014, p. 63), as in the case of Latin American airlines mentioned above. Faced with such clashes, individuals must make choices about how to behave, making their behavior less predictable. Finally, what people say drives their behavior may not be what really drives it. Scholars call this the difference between "espoused theory" (how people explain their behavior) and "theory in use" (what really drives behavior) (Schneider et al., 2014, p. 29). Cross-cultural models typically describe the *espoused values*, which may not coincide with those people follow in practice. This is why the scholars who developed the GLOBE model distinguish values and practices and criticize Hofstede for not making that distinction (Javidan et al., 2006).

To conclude, while cross-cultural models can help to understand cultural differences that one is likely to encounter in cross-cultural interactions, one should use them only as a starting point, not as definitive statements about cultures. These models should be used with an open mind, willing to modify the understanding of a culture they convey. We believe the definition of culture we use here sensitizes us to several of the abovementioned complexities. ◘ Figure 18.3 summarizes the key

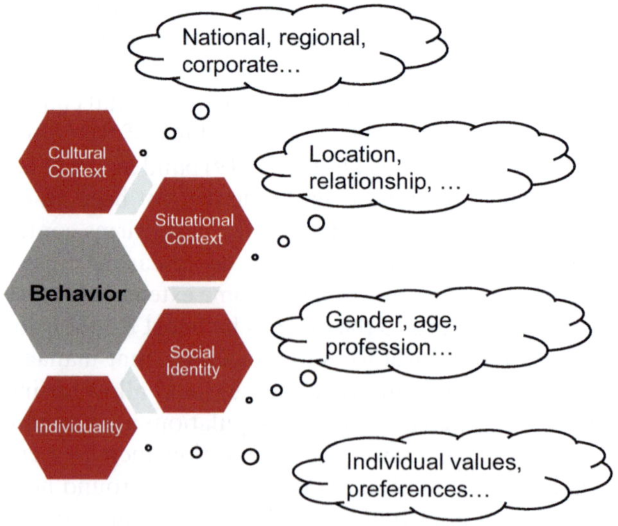


◘ **Fig. 18.3** Culture and behavior. (Own diagram)

18

influences on behavior that we see: the cultural context (in several spheres), the situational context, social identities, and individuality.

## The Impact of Culture on Leadership and Motivation

We will now focus on one context in business where cultural differences play an essential role: leadership. To be a good leader means being able to sustain the motivation of employees. What motivates people and how they can be motivated is influenced by culture. The role of a leader and expectations of good leadership behavior also vary from culture to culture.

Gelade and colleagues have investigated the role of employees' satisfaction with specific job characteristics on their commitment to the company. They surveyed 50,000 workers of one company in 29 countries and found clear relationships between Hofstede's masculinity and individualism value dimensions and job satisfaction and commitment of employees. Commitment is the mental connection of an employee to his or her company that makes it less likely for the employee to leave the company (Gelade et al., 2008).

- The higher individualism is (e.g., the United States), the more employees value their autonomy, opportunities for personal advancement, and work–life balance.
- The higher collectivism is (e.g., China and Singapore), the more motivated employees are when their jobs fully use their skills, and the company provides them with good working conditions, fringe benefits, and training.
- The higher masculinity is (e.g., Japan, Mexico), the more motivated employees are with opportunities for high pay, personal accomplishment, and job advancement.
- The higher femininity is (e.g., Denmark, Sweden), factors relating to employees' relationships with managers and coworkers encourage more employee commitment.

When trying to understand what motivates people, we need to understand what goals people pursue, their needs, values, and expectations. The role that work plays for people and how it can contribute toward fulfilling goals and needs varies between cultures. For most people, work is about earning a living to finance accommodation, food, and other things. However, often work means more to people than income. They derive from it status, a sense of achievement, social contacts, and other things. A study on the meaning of work for people across eight different countries conducted by George England and others found that while income plays an essential role in all countries in the study, it played a far more significant role than any other factor in Japan. In the Netherlands, the relative importance of the various factors, including interest in the job, contacts with others, and a way to serve society, was much more evenly distributed (Deresky, 2017, pp. 440–441). Deresky reports on problems Japanese car maker Mazda encountered in its plant in Michigan, United States. While in Japan, rewards take the form of plaques, applause, and management attention, American workers expected a more material reward. Japanese workers, on the contrary, feel insulted by material rewards as they see them as implying that they would only work hard to achieve those rewards (Deresky, 2017, p. 442).

However, in line with our arguments above, we must not make the mistake of explaining differences in motivation by culture alone. A study by Furnham and colleagues found, for example, a correlation between work motivations and the level of economic development. Survey participants in European countries have attributed lower importance to competitiveness, money, and savings than non-Europeans. In the Middle and Far East, on the contrary, participants have shown the highest level of competitiveness and acquisitiveness of money (Furnham et al., 1994).

What constitutes effective leadership varies from culture to culture. People in various cultures have different expectations of the characteristics of a leader. For example, in Italy and France, leaders are in high regard for their political power and social prominence; in Latin America, people see an appreciation for art as important; in Germany, people admire a broad general knowledge, while in the United States, an informal private lifestyle of leaders would not surprise people (Deresky, 2017, p. 454).

We mentioned the GLOBE project before, the Global Leadership and Organizational Behavior Effectiveness research project. As the name suggests, the effectiveness of leadership in different cultures is in focus. The research found that some leadership behaviors are accepted everywhere, such as being a good team builder, communicator, and trustworthy. Other expectations of leaders vary between cultures. For example, in the Philippines, charismatic leadership behavior, characterized as visionary and inspiring, is considered particularly important for effective leadership. Brazilians see especially team-oriented behavior, such as being diplomatic and integrative, as crucial for a leader's effectiveness. Canadians estimate a participative style, encouraging staff to take responsibility, as essential. In Nigeria, humane behavior, being compassionate toward staff, is perceived among the most critical behaviors of effective leadership (Den Hartog et al., 1999). Overall, researchers of the GLOBE project concluded that such leaders are most successful who meet the expectations of those reporting to them and do not violate cultural norms (Dorfman et al., 2012).

## Communication Across Cultures

Now, given the impact of culture on communication and collaboration, how can communication in multicultural settings be conducted successfully, avoiding misunderstandings and conflict? Communication is critical in cross-cultural collaboration. It can build a bridge between people of different cultures and resolve conflict and misunderstanding if conducted appropriately. It is helpful to apply a model of cross-cultural communication. In the following, we will essentially follow a model outlined by Deresky (2017, pp. 150–174).

Generally, communication consists of several elements:

- The sender has a message in mind that he or she wants to transmit to the receiver.
- The sender encodes this message by putting it in symbols like words, body language, material things, or—today, in electronic communication—emoticons.
- The sender uses a medium to convey a message, whether personal communication, telephone, email, video conferencing, instant messenger, or other.
- The receiver decodes the message, that is, attempts to understand from the symbols used what the sender wants to say, what the intended message is.
- Typically, the receiver sends back a response of some sort from which the sender gains hints as to whether the receiver has understood the message as intended.

All these elements are infused with culture, from the codes used to encode the message to the preferred medium to decode the message and the response given. The decoding of the message and interpretation is often selective, focusing on specific aspects of the message while de-emphasizing others. This is because the sender and receiver live in their own world of meaning, partly determined by their different cultures, the relationship between sender and receiver, its history, and their expectations. You will remember what we said about how culture provides a frame of reference. The sender encodes the message based on his frame of reference, while the receiver interprets it based on her own culture. So the cultural frame of reference of the receiver infuses the decoding of the message, which can lead to a different understanding of the message than was intended by the sender (Deresky, 2017, pp. 150–151). While Deresky sees this potential undermining of communication by culture as "noise," we agree with Abramson and Moran that culture should not be seen as noise but rather as "a key ingredient within the practice of communication" (Abramson & Moran, 2018, p. 48). Nevertheless, the different cultural frames of reference of sender and receiver impact a process called *attribution*.

**Attribution**

*Attribution* is the process by which people look for an explanation of another person's behavior (Deresky, 2017, p. 151).

Especially in cross-cultural communication, we may often be puzzled by what someone says or does as it falls outside the norms we are used to. When trying to make sense of it, we attribute intentions to the sender, and this attribution may be negative (e.g., "he tries to fool me," "he wants to make himself important," "he has no clue and tries to hide it"), which can undermine the communication.

Deresky (2017, pp. 174–175) suggests the following five-step process for effective cross-cultural communication:

**Developing Cultural Sensitivity:** The sender should attempt to get to know the receiver and encode the message in a way the receiver can understand. This requires an awareness of one's own culture and how it impacts communication. Further, the various determinants of behavior we mentioned above need to be understood: What is the cultural context (national, corporate, and other spheres of culture)? What is the situation in which communication takes place? What is the relationship between the sender and the receiver? What is their social identity? What behavior is the person used to? What will be the receiver's expectations? We would say it makes a difference in which country the encounter takes place or if it is online; what the hierarchical relationship is; whether one is the customer and the other the service provider; whether the receiver has previously been exposed to one's own culture. Developing this cultural sensitivity would have been helpful in the opening cases to prevent the problems that arose to some extent.

**Careful Encoding:** The sender, when encoding the message, should use symbols that the receiver will likely understand based on the receiver's frame of reference. The sender should avoid colloquial language or local cultural references not necessarily understood outside of one's home country. Speaking clearly and slowly and avoiding complicated language can help.

**Selective Transmission:** Choosing the suitable communication medium appropriate to the content and situation is essential. For example, video conferencing provides more hints for decoding the message correctly than email. This can be important for building relationships or for resolving conflict. This will be elaborated more in a later section of this chapter. Finding out the common communication media in the organization of the receiver is helpful (remember the WoodCoAcquiror and WoodCoTarget opening case). Likewise, knowing if the receiver's culture is high-context or low-context allows the sender to encode appropriately.

**Careful Decoding and Feedback:** The receiver must also be aware of the cultural and situational context, like the sender, to help appropriately decode the message. What helps, in addition, is giving feedback that helps the sender to know if the message has been understood correctly by the receiver. For example, the receiver may summarize what she understood in her own words. Empathetic listening is also a helpful practice: trying to understand not just the words of the sender but the emotions and feelings behind the words. As the saying goes, trying to put oneself into the other person's shoes can be particularly helpful in cross-cultural communication.

**Follow-Up Actions:** To build and maintain trust in a cross-cultural situation, following up on what has been agreed upon is crucial. Not acting on what has been agreed upon when the other side expects action is also sending a message—a negative one. This will also be expanded on later. Unfortunately, cultural differences can also affect a mutual understanding of what has been agreed upon and how binding, for example, a verbal agreement is.



## Corporate Practices for Facilitating Global Collaboration

To conclude this part of the chapter, we will address what companies are doing to facilitate cross-cultural communication and collaboration. In many MNEs, top management has recognized the challenges and opportunities of cultural diversity for effective collaboration and communication across borders. One way of dealing with this is to establish a robust corporate culture that transcends national cultures. Another is to offer cross-cultural training.

## Building a Strong Corporate Culture

You remember how Hofstede chose IBM for his study because the company was known for having a strong corporate culture across all its locations. Also, you will remember how especially for service firms, establishing a strong corporate culture across the firm can be essential to guide employees as a means of coordination and integration by socialization. To the extent that the firm establishes strong values that employees across the global firm uphold, this can go some way toward facilitating cross-cultural communication and collaboration in the face of cultural diversity. Companies can do several things to build a robust corporate culture. When recruiting and selecting new staff, recruiters can consider compatibility with the desired corporate culture. When promoting staff into management positions, managers can make demonstrated behaviors in line with the desired corporate culture a criterion for who gets promoted. The desired values of the firm can be written down and communicated to employees at every opportunity. Socialization can be undertaken for new employees, whether by formal training addressing the firm's values or more informally by advice from supervisors and colleagues. In this context, executives and managers must "walk the talk" and behave according to the desired values to act as role models (C. W. L. Hill, 2021, pp. 425–429).

## Cross-cultural Training

Many MNEs provide dedicated cross-cultural training to employees. This applies particularly to expatriates seconded to a subsidiary abroad to take on a temporary management role. In other cases, employees in a global role who interact with colleagues from around the world daily as part of their regular work also receive cross-cultural training. Regarding preparing expatriates for a secondment abroad, we can distinguish between pre-departure and in-country training. In the latter case, the expatriate learns on the job, frequently facilitated by other expatriates who may be assigned as a "buddy" or by the predecessor in the role. In the following, we will outline various training forms mainly used pre-departure.

**Didactic Training:** Didactic training, also called the "university model" (Bhawuk & Brislin, 2000, p. 168), consists of providing factual information about a host country, its history, geography, religion, culture, business, and practical living conditions. It uses PowerPoint slides, photos, and videos to teach key elements of a culture and other information. While it is still popular, by itself, it fosters passive rather than active learning and remains theoretical. It does not train actual behavior or address the more emotional and psychological aspects of cross-cultural communication (Bhawuk & Brislin, 2000; Littrell & Salas, 2005).

**Attribution Training:** You will remember what we said about the mechanism of attribution. Attribution training focuses directly on developing an expatriate's ability to attribute the behavior of people in the host country in the same way as the locals would. It helps to take the host country culture's point of view to explain observed behavior (Littrell & Salas, 2005).

**Culture Awareness Training:** Above, we said that for cross-cultural communication, it is crucial to become aware of one's own culture and how it drives frames of reference, attributions, and behavior. Cultural awareness training raises awareness of one's own culture to enhance the understanding of how it contrasts with a foreign culture (Littrell & Salas, 2005).

**Behavior Modification Training:** Behavior modification training imparts to international assignees very directly appropriate habitual behavior considered appropriate in a host culture. Behavior like greeting (handshake, bowing, kissing) is demonstrated and then repeated many times by the person taking the training. Depending on the home and host culture's customs, forms of greeting may initially feel uncomfortable, especially if kissing or a handshake implies bodily contact, which is uncommon in the home country. Because it is expensive, companies do not use it much, but studies show its effectiveness in combination with other types of training (Bhawuk & Brislin, 2000; Littrell & Salas, 2005).

**Culture Assimilators:** Culture assimilators present typical scenarios or "critical incidents" that international assignees will likely encounter in the host country. Trainers offer several different options for responding in such a situation, and the expatriate is to choose which one he or she believes is the culturally appropriate response. The trainer then presents the most appropriate behavior and gives feedback on the participant's choice. Culture assimilators are also available for self-guided learning. Research has shown assimilators to be effective. However, not all have been rigorously developed and tested; some are dated and require an update (Bhawuk & Brislin, 2000).

**Experiential Exercises:** Experiential exercises were developed in response to the didactic training to provide participants with more active involvement. Trainers divide participants into two groups that represent two hypothetical cultures. They get each a briefing on typical behaviors, and trainers ask them to interact with each other. This provides an "aha" effect that raises awareness of cultural differences generally and intends to involve participants emotionally. However, it creates an artificial situation and requires a combination with other forms of training to be helpful. Often, it is used at the start of cross-cultural training, followed by other forms (Bhawuk & Brislin, 2000).

**Culture General Assimilators:** Different from methods that focus on preparing participants for one particular culture, the culture general assimilator addresses topics that are relevant in cross-cultural communication generally. They include dealing with intense feelings in cross-cultural situations, such as anxiety, ambiguity, prejudices, and ethnocentrism. The assimilator helps understand cultural differences in areas like work, time and space, roles, and hierarchies. Trainers address relevant psychological processes such as categorization and attribution. They present one hundred critical incidents that cover the themes mentioned above. Research has found support for the effectiveness of the culture general assimilator (Bhawuk & Brislin, 2000).

Overall, research shows a positive impact of cross-cultural training. It positively affects the adjustment of expatriates to the host culture, which enhances performance and reduces the premature return of expatriates due to difficulties of adaptation. Littrell and Salas recommend customizing cross-cultural training to the participants' needs. The rigor of the training should be tailored to the difficulty of the destination (Littrell & Salas, 2005). In the opening cases, cross-cultural training would have helped prevent conflict to some extent.

## Collaborating Successfully in Globally Distributed Virtual Teams (DVTs)

Due to the COVID-19 pandemic, distributed virtual teams (DVTs) have become very common across the world. However, DVTs are by no means a new phenomenon. Since Internet technology in the 1990s greatly facilitated communication and collaboration across geographic locations, DVTs have been commonplace in MNEs. Especially in multinational professional service firms (PSFs) such as audit firms, consulting firms, or advertising networks, DVTs have long been a way of conducting projects for international customers that require services to be provided across many countries worldwide. This chapter will define DVTs, outline their business case and challenges, and then explain how collaboration in DVTs can be successful.

### Definition and Characteristics of DVTs

**Distributed Virtual Teams**

*[Distributed] Virtual teams* are work arrangements where team members are geographically dispersed, have limited face-to-face contact and work interdependently through the use of electronic communication media to achieve common goals (Dulebohn & Hoch, 2017, p. 569).

So, specific characteristics make DVTs unique and different from traditional presence teams (App, 2013, pp. 28–29):

- They are distributed across geographic locations
- Communication frequently happens in English
- Frequently the team spans different time zones
- Few, if any, meetings happen in presence
- Communication happens mostly via media such as email, phone, chat, or video conference
- Different cultures are involved
- Team members require additional skills

While most of the abovementioned characteristics are self-explanatory, the additional skill requirements will be outlined later in this section.

## Opportunities and Challenges in DVTs

**Opportunities in DVTs:** Now, given that DVTs may not be the most obvious or natural way of organizing a team, why do companies use DVTs? There are several reasons. By setting up a virtual team, companies can draw on the most suitable available talent across the world. There are well-educated and experienced people in many countries of the world. A DVT avoids all the challenges of immigration and mobility of talent that would be required by bringing people together in one location while at the same time not being limited to the available talent in just one location. This can also enhance the motivation of staff who can work in the location that is the center of their lives and enhance the attractiveness of the firm as an employer. Further, research found that the diversity that a DVT typically implies can benefit the team as it brings diverse experience. The multiple perspectives taken by team members can improve the problem-solving capability of the team (Siebdrat et al., 2009). MNEs from high-cost locations can lower costs by including team members from lower-salary countries (Jarvenpaa & Leidner, 1999). By having team members distributed across time zones, work can be passed on from members in one time zone to members in another to allow the team to work effectively around the clock. This is used, for example, for IT-related work such as software development and testing. DVTs also reduce the need for travel and its cost (Dulebohn & Hoch, 2017). Klimkeit (2019) also confirms several of these benefits for Global Business Services (GBS) organizations that maintain DVTs across several shared service centers (SSCs) worldwide. For example, in one company, flexibility was enhanced by shifting work from one part of a team in Asia to another in Europe when the workload in the Asian team was high. In the same company, work around the clock was used at the end of each quarter to include all last-minute entries in the closing of the accounting books. Regarding the motivation of employees, being part of a global team was seen as a significant motivation for employees in a DVT setting (Klimkeit, 2019).

**Challenges in DVTs:** At the same time, as you may imagine, the characteristics of DVTs can pose many challenges. The distributed and virtual character can create various communication difficulties. Media like instant messaging or email do not convey the same number of cues as face-to-face communication, which can lead to misunderstandings. Differences in time zone, culture, and lack of proficiency in the English language exacerbate this. Building trust can be more difficult when face-to-face contact is not possible. Reaching an agreement between team members can be more complicated than in traditional teams due to cultural and other differences. Accommodating different time zones to enable synchronous communication by phone or video conference can be challenging if regular working times have little overlap. Clarifying issues relating to tasks can be challenging given time zones, communication media, language, and cultural differences (Siebdrat et al., 2009). Teamwork problems, such as ambiguity around the role of team members, low individual commitment, work overload, and social loafing (people putting in less effort on a task when working in a group), can be aggravated in DVTs' virtual and distributed settings. This can also impact the perception of service levels by customers who may perceive a lack of consistency, permanence, and reliability (Jarvenpaa & Leidner, 1999). Studies found that DVTs have higher levels of conflict than presence teams (Lin et al., 2008). Team members in DVTs may feel isolated, and team leaders may face challenges monitoring and managing the team (Dulebohn & Hoch, 2017). The high volume of emails common in many DVTs can negatively affect performance. The diversity of DVTs can have mixed effects on the team's performance (Marlow et al., 2017).

## Making DVTs Succeed: Leadership

Given the many challenges that DVTs face, the question is what leadership can do to prevent or mitigate the challenges and achieve successful teamwork. First, we outline what leading a virtual team implies and then address some general good practices for effective collaboration and communication in virtual teams.

**Selecting the Right Team Members:** As mentioned above, working on a DVT requires specific skills. So, the first task of a DVT leader is to select team members who possess those skills or train selected members in the required skills. In a virtual team, teamwork skills are essential to overcome the challenges of the characteristics of DVTs. This includes establishing a basis for everyone to contribute their diverse capabilities and providing mutual support. Further, due to the dispersed nature of DVTs, team members need the skill for self-leadership. They need to be able to work independently without much direction and oversight by a team leader. The leader of a DVT is not always able to detect and address problems, so team members must be able to deal with many problems that arise themselves (Siebdrat et al., 2009). Members of DVTs need the ability to control their emotions, be open to new challenges, and be able to tolerate the ambiguity that the situation of DVTs often entails. They need cultural intelligence to deal with the cross-cultural situation. Experience in working in a DVT is beneficial (Ivanaj & Bozon, 2016, pp. 82–83).

**Motivating Across Distance:** To keep team members motivated and engaged, leaders of DVTs must make sure that team members benefit personally from their engagement in the DTV. Malhotra and colleagues recommend starting each virtual team meeting with the recognition of successes. This can include a virtual reward ceremony and a virtual party to celebrate success. Frequently, team members work part-time on the DVT and have other ongoing tasks in a more traditional setting where they report to a local manager. Malhotra et al. further recommend informing team members' managers about their excellent work, for example, via an executive who would praise the employees following a briefing received (Malhotra et al., 2007). We would add, though, that the specific form of praise needs to be sensitive to what is appropriate in the culture of the employees and their managers. Fosslien and West-Duffy recommend sending team members physical packages with handwritten notes or cake that are particularly appreciated in a work environment where everything else is virtual (Fosslien & West-Duffy, 2019).

**Make Remote Employees Feel Connected:** To address the challenge that DVT team members may feel isolated, leaders must take action to counter this perception. To ensure every team member feels included, leaders should wait with making decisions until everyone across the various time zones has had a chance to provide their opinion. Social media firm Buffer sets up so-called "pair calls" every week where two randomly paired virtual employees get 30 minutes to get to know each other and discuss hobbies and other non-work topics. Likewise, employees share some impressions of their lives on Instagram stories (Fosslien & West-Duffy, 2019).

**Goal Setting and Controlling Performance:** Besides the softer elements of leadership outlined above, the "harder" aspects require attention: setting goals and controlling performance. Herrmann and colleagues suggest that *management by objectives* is particularly useful in virtual teams. Rather than managing employees' tasks closely, managers agree on precise goals with team members, and they have much freedom in how exactly to achieve them. This allows remote team members more autonomy within a defined corridor, which lends itself to a virtual setting. It can increase team members' motivation but requires a low need for control of the leader. Controlling the performance of DVT team members carries specific requirements as well. What does feedback from team members like "project is running fine" really mean in practice? Sensing this is more difficult in a virtual setting. Controlling performance requires the leader to have a repertoire from calm restraint to more tightly timed follow-up in challenging circumstances, depending on the situation. Either way, communication by leaders needs to be more explicit than in presence teams (Herrmann et al., 2012, 41–42;159–160).

## Making DVTs Succeed: Good Practices

**Building Trust:** Building trust is vital for any team collaboration, but in virtual teams, it can be more challenging to build trust. Ways in which presence teams build trust, such as by repeatedly socializing face-to-face, are not available. So other ways need to be used. Team members have trust in a team when they believe that other team members will be honest, make good-faith efforts to honor commitments, and will not take advantage of one if they have the opportunity to do so. Jarvenpaa and Leidner found in their study of virtual teams several communication behaviors and actions by team members that facilitated building and maintaining trust in virtual teams (Jarvenpaa & Leidner, 1999): Early on, social communication around hobbies, weekend activities, and similar help create trust. In the long run, however, it is insufficient for maintaining trust by itself. Likewise, openly expressing enthusiasm at the outset helped to establish trust. Communicating intensively at the beginning to resolve any uncertainties regarding the tasks of the team helped to build trust the same way as initiatives by team members who made suggestions and volunteered to take on tasks. To maintain trust in the long run, other behaviors have proven critical. Predictable communication, like setting the right expectations about how regularly messages would be sent and informing about planned absences, helps maintain trust. The same applies to swift responses to messages. In teams with high trust, leaders who have proven to have skills relevant to the role and maintained a positive tone throughout have emerged. Successful virtual teams initially set rules for collaboration but then moved on to focus on getting the tasks at hand done. Finally, teams maintained trust by remaining calm despite turbulence. See ◘ Fig. 18.4 for a summary. Malhotra et al. summarize the

| Building Trust Initially | Maintaining Trust |
|---|---|
| • Regular exchange of personal information<br>• Show enthusiasm for joint achievement of goals<br>• Clarify technical problems at the start<br>• Achieve joint understanding of tasks<br>• Show initiative | • Regular communication<br>• Quick response to questions<br>• Equitable leader<br>• Establish rules<br>• Maintain calmness in difficult situations |

**Fig. 18.4** Building trust in virtual teams. (Based on content from Jarvenpaa & Leidner, 1999)

above findings by stating that trust in DVTs is more based on action than goodwill. This requires that team members make intentions and actions explicit (Malhotra et al., 2007). A certain leap of faith may occur at the beginning of a DVT's collaboration. Because team members assume that leaders have selected the right people to be on the team, the team may establish *swift trust*. However, this remains fragile and needs to be replaced by forms of trust that are more based on trustworthy action, as outlined above (N. S. Hill & Bartol, 2018, pp. 115–117).

**Appropriate Use of Media:** Since virtual teams crucially depend on media to communicate and collaborate, making appropriate use of them is essential. Experience shows that many mistakes can be made in media use, leading to misunderstanding, conflict, and, consequently, ineffective collaboration. Daft et al. (1987) developed a model for when to use which medium, which is still helpful even though the specific media available today have evolved since the original study. Their model rests on the concept of *media richness*.

**Media Richness**

Media can be characterized as high or low in "*richness*" based on their capacity to facilitate shared meaning [...] A rich medium facilitates insight and rapid understanding (Daft et al., 1987, p. 358).

According to Daft et al., media richness consists of four elements:

- Feedback: Instant feedback allows asking questions
- Multiple cues: Voice inflection, body gestures, words, and graphic symbols may be part of the message
- Language variety: One can convey a range of meanings with language symbols
- Personal focus: One can tailor messages to the frame of reference, needs, and current situation of the receiver

Considering these criteria, natural language in face-to-face communication has the highest media richness, allowing immediate feedback, multiple cues, language variety, and a personal focus. Unaddressed documents like flyers have the lowest media

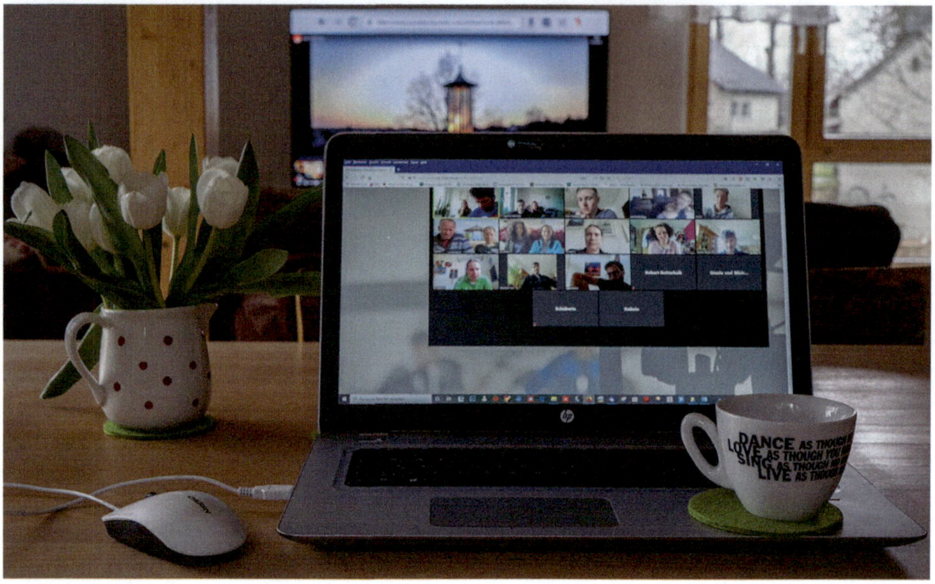

Video conferencing; Virtual teams often connect via video conferencing. (Image by AS_Appendorf from Pixabay)

richness. So, should we always use natural language, as it has the highest media richness? No. For one, in virtual teams, that is not possible. And then Daft et al. hold that different situations demand different levels of media richness. Ideally, team members choose the medium with the right level of media richness for the situation. There are communication situations with a high level of ambiguity. In these situations, there are multiple and conflicting interpretations of a situation. Managers are unsure which questions to ask, and no objective data are readily available to provide the answer. Ambiguity is high when managers' frames of reference differ, for example, in a cross-cultural situation. Managers must establish shared meaning before mutual understanding can occur. According to Daft et al., situations of high ambiguity demand media with high richness. Managers would ideally meet face-to-face to discuss and develop a shared understanding of the situation and decide what to do next. Using media with low richness would oversimplify the situation, and essential cues for understanding would be lost. Face-to-face meetings would overcomplicate the situation where there is low ambiguity, the problem is well understood and precise, and managers need to communicate quantified data. Scheduling a personal meeting would waste time when a short, written message is enough to transfer such information quickly (Daft et al., 1987). So, on virtual teams, lean, text-based tools like email or bulletin boards should be used when a manager wants to push routine information like plans in one direction. More interactive tools like web conferencing are more appropriate for more complex tasks like bringing diverse perspectives together. Contentious interpersonal issues like telling team members they have not done their job correctly or resolving conflicts demand a richer medium. Sometimes, face-to-face meetings may be necessary, even for virtual teams (N. S. Hill & Bartol, 2018).

**Dealing with Conflict:** Teamwork can always lead to situations of conflict. Due to the characteristics of DVTs, conflict is particularly likely. This is due to the use of media, the late discovery of conflicts, cultural differences, and the lack of informal conflict resolution available to presence teams (Herrmann et al., 2012, pp. 176–186). To maintain the effectiveness of the DVT, the leader must take action to prevent conflict and deal with it if it occurs. Liao (2017) distinguishes three types of conflict in DVTs:

- Relationship: due to interpersonal differences between team members
- Task: due to different opinions regarding the tasks of the team
- Process: due to differences in how members go about team tasks

Relationship-related conflict occurs more likely in DVTs because team members are more likely to attribute questionable behaviors or team processes to personal factors rather than the situation. This emphasizes the importance for leaders of DVTs to engage in relationship building in the team. Besides virtual parties, leaders can consider some face-to-face meetings where possible. To prevent task-related conflict, leaders can organize regular web conferences where team members update the status of their tasks and uncertainty regarding tasks can be resolved. Hybrid teams, where some team members are co-located while others connect virtually, are particularly prone to conflict. Such situations carry the risk that the leader forms in-groups with members he or she can meet personally, thereby creating two levels of team membership. Leaders of DVTs must be particularly diligent about such situations to avoid the remote members feeling like second-class citizens (Liao, 2017). Teams can prevent task- and process-related conflict by taking enough time at the start to clarify work routines, such as who needs to provide or fetch which information at which point, which media to use when and how, and clarify which information is confidential and how to deal with it. Herrmann et al. (2012, pp. 186–193) also make practical suggestions for when conflicts occur in DVTs:

- Leaders should intercept conflict early on, for example, by making a phone call when they have not heard from a team member for some time.
- Team members should use rich media for conflict resolution when a conflict escalates.
- Teams should confine conflict resolution to those immediately involved.
- Putting others in cc: in emails relating to a conflict should be avoided.

**Socialization Mechanisms:** Klimkeit (2019) conducted a study into collaboration in DVTs in Global Business Services (GBS) organizations comprising several shared service centers (SSCs) spread across continents. For example, an accounting team might have sub-teams in SSCs in Argentina, Poland, and Malaysia collaborating in various ways. Klimkeit found that companies can only realize the potential of bringing the various SSCs into one GBS organization when applying specific socialization mechanisms. See ◘ Fig. 18.5 for an overview of the mechanisms.

| Mechanism | Explanation |
|---|---|
| **Standardization of Skills** | |
| Knowledge Sharing | Sharing of knowledge between locations, often in the context of conference calls, but also spontaneously by individuals in case of questions; internal trainings by peers. |
| **Standardization of Norms** | |
| Creating a Global Team Identity and Culture | By structural integration of the centers in the GBS model, a joint identity is formed; activities for creating a joint culture. |
| **Mutual Adjustment** | |
| Use of Rich Media | By use of video conferencing software in distributed teams, accoustic and visual impressions are combined for a deeper connection. |
| Personal Meetings | In spite of modern communication tools, occasional personal meetings between team leaders and their distributed team reinforce the connection. |
| Networking | In bilateral and multilateral, formal and informal ways, networking creates valuable contacts for collaboration between locations. |
| Liaison Roles | Dedicated roles are created at staff level, where staff of several locations jointly work on internal topics. |

**Fig. 18.5** Socialization mechanisms for facilitating collaboration in DVTs. (Source: Klimkeit, 2019, p. 32; permission obtained)

Some of them, such as the use of rich media, personal meetings, and networking, support what was already said above. Others have not been addressed in the other studies. We will highlight some of them here. To facilitate collaboration in DVTs, ensuring a consistent knowledge base across the team members is beneficial. This also enables the high level of autonomy required of DVT team members. If all have a high level of knowledge, they can work more independently. The SSCs in the study achieved this by *sharing knowledge* between the DVT's various locations, often in regular conference calls and spontaneously. Further, SSCs organized internal training where employees taught their colleagues as peers. *Creating a global team identity and culture* is also very helpful in ensuring collaboration in DVTs. Due to geographic distance, it is not evident that a joint team identity exists. Shared values and norms provide orientation for team members and facilitate collaboration. In the study, bringing their various SSCs into one joint GBS organization helped the firms build a collective identity of SSC teams across locations. DVTs undertook several activities to generate a shared culture. For example, one company launched a cross-location project to define a joint culture. Dedicated *liaison roles* can further contribute to collaboration in DVTs. These are defined roles at the staff level that have the task to connect the various distributed sub-teams. This complements contacts that often exist already at the management level. One company set up cross-location teams with one team member per location that worked on internal topics such as knowledge management, compliance, or IT.



## Review Questions

1. Outline why culture is particularly important for service firms.
2. Define and explain the concept of culture and its elements.
3. Which role do cultural frames of reference play in cross-cultural misunderstandings?

4. Discuss the implications of the fact that there are various spheres of culture.
5. Outline the value dimensions of Hofstede, Hall and Hall, and Trompenaars and Hampden-Turner.
6. Why can we not predict a person's behavior by knowing the respective culture?
7. Outline the impact of culture on how to motivate employees.
8. What do we learn from Project GLOBE about the impact of culture on effective leadership?
9. Explain the concept of attribution and its impact on cross-cultural communication.
10. Outline the process proposed by Deresky for mindful cross-cultural communication.
11. Explain the different types of cross-cultural training.
12. Define distributed virtual teams and describe their characteristics.
13. Outline opportunities and challenges of virtual teams.
14. Describe some practices for making virtual teams succeed.
15. Explain the concept of media richness and its impact on appropriate media use.

## Closing Case: Virtual Teams at Thomson Reuters

In 2008, Thomson Corporation, a Canadian information provider, acquired the British Reuters Group plc. Following the acquisition, Thomson Reuters (TR) implemented a new operating model across the Markets Division. TR is one of the leaders in the international professional information field, providing information to customers in areas like finance and risk, legal, and tax and accounting. At the time of the case study, TR employed more than 60,000 staff across more than 100 countries. Based on a global network, some dedicated local front-line team members dealt with clients. The initial organization still relied much on local managers. Each country unit controlled its budget.

After the acquisition of Reuters by Thomson, management decided to reshape the whole Sales and Client Service organization within the Markets Division. Major customers in investment banking, trading, and professional investors were globalizing their businesses. So, Thomson Reuters implemented a new operating model affecting 400 people worldwide. Sales and Client Service was split into four business segments plus four cross-segment channels, creating a matrix. One senior site manager was appointed per country for legal reasons but did not have staff reporting to him or her. The global team now had to manage global customers, requiring new skills. People who used to work locally now were engaged across several countries. New roles required new communication capabilities, relationship building, personal organization, and self-discipline skills due to virtual management. Now employees were working in a more multicultural environment. Therefore, Human Resources (HR) offered "Global Virtual Team" workshops to prepare staff for virtual work. TR conducted much tech-

Stock trading monitor. (Image by Lorenzo Cafaro from Pixabay)

nology investment. The firm had to invest in video conferencing, introducing the tool WebEx. TR provided mobile devices to staff, enabled work from home, and implemented a Customer Relationship Management (CRM) system. HR offered training on how to use these global communication technologies.

In some cases, the account manager was now in a different country than the client. Moreover, managers now had direct reports in other countries, which required more autonomy, responsibility, and trust. Managers started to travel to meet their team members personally and build relationships. However, staff from Latin countries like France and Italy struggled with virtual management as they preferred a more implicit communication style where personal face-to-face relationships played a role. Managing remote staff exerted pressure on the work–life balance of managers who had to travel more and took time to adapt to a new style of working across time zones. They felt they now had to be "accessible all time, everywhere." HR offered managers information on local culture and labor regulations and set up a "Cultural Wizard" website to help with cultural diversity. "Global Virtual Team Management" workshops were conducted. They addressed how to build relationships, maintain engagement, and manage the performance of remote staff. Managers received tips for effective online meetings. Training also highlighted the differences between traditional team management and virtual team management.

Guiding and motivating people in virtual teams turned out to be a real challenge. However, managers also discovered opportunities by accessing a broader talent pool beyond geographic considerations. Levels of English proficiency increased, and the possibility to contribute beyond personal boundaries was seen as fun, increasing staff satisfaction levels. Some smaller offices, such as in Luxemburg and Belgium, were closed, and people offered to move to other locations, which was not received well. The main difficulty was the combination of team member empowerment and managing difficult situations, which suggested closer managerial involvement. TR put processes in place for setting goals with staff and reviewing their achievement at year-end. The firm saw this as essential for virtual team success, but that was not enough for staff empowerment. Building trust was seen as most important, which required some stability in leadership and team, but the reality was different. Communicating more accurately and precisely as required in the virtual setting proved difficult for some managers. This should increase efficiency by having shorter online meetings and less travel, but it proved more difficult in practice. Team building and remote management remained much more difficult in the virtual world.

TR learned that virtual organization also implied cost: In theory, it should reduce travel, but there was always a requirement, for example, for meetings with team members expected to be uneasy. Finally, TR realized they had to revise the new operating model: The company gave back more autonomy to the local level. Nevertheless, TR saw diversity as a benefit of the new organization they did not want to miss anymore: It became a reality and increased creativity.

As Pierre Rosius, the HR manager, summarizes:

> Virtuality through remote management, dispersed teams, and virtual organization originally sounded like an answer to globalization. However [...] the virtual approach cannot fit to any situation without a prepared-on-purpose organization (Ivanaj & Bozon, 2016, p. 248).

**Questions**

1. How do the challenges encountered at Thomson Reuters relate to what we outlined about virtual teams above?
2. Could the challenges Thomson Reuters experienced have been avoided?
3. What is your assessment of the fact that the company partly reversed its new operating model?

Sources: Ivanaj and Bozon (2016, pp. 238–250)

**Summary**

This chapter:

- Explained the concept of culture, defined as "the *shared, socially learned knowledge* and *patterns of behavior* characteristic of some group of people," and its role in managing international services
- Outlined value dimensions of Hofstede (power distance, individualism, masculinity, uncertainty avoidance, and long-term orientation), Hall and Hall (high vs. low context, monochromous vs. polychromous time), and Trompenaars and Hampden-Turner (universalist vs. particularist, affective vs. neutral, and achievement vs. ascription)

- Critically reflected the role of culture in international management
- Outlined the impact of culture on leadership and motivation of international staff
- Described a process for culturally sensitive communication: developing cultural sensitivity, careful encoding, selective transmission, careful decoding and feedback, and follow-up actions
- Outlined different types of cross-cultural training: attribution training, culture awareness training, didactic training, behavior modification training, culture assimilators, experiential exercises, and culture general assimilators
- Explained characteristics, opportunities, and challenges of distributed virtual teams, defined as "work arrangements where team members are geographically dispersed, have limited face-to-face contact, and work interdependently through the use of electronic communication media to achieve common goals"
- Outlined practices for making virtual teams successful

## References

Abramson, N. R., & Moran, R. T. (2018). *Managing cultural differences: Global leadership for the 21st century* (10th ed.). Routledge.

App, S. (2013). *Virtuelle Teams*. Haufe-Lexware.

Bhawuk, D., & Brislin, R. (2000). Cross-cultural training: A review. *Applied Psychology, 49*(1), 162–191.

Brannen, M. Y. (1999). The many faces of cultural data. *AIB Newsletter* (first quarter), pp. 6–7.

Child, J. (1981). Culture, contingency and capitalism in the cross-national study of organizations. In L. Cummings & B. Shaw (Eds.), *Research in organizational behaviour* (Vol. 3). JAI Press.

Daft, R. L., Lengel, R. H., & Trevino, L. K. (1987). Message equivocality, media selection, and manager performance: Implications for information systems. *MIS Quarterly, 11*(3), 355–366.

Den Hartog, D. N., House, R. J., Hanges, P. J., Ruiz-Quintanilla, S. A., Dorfman, P. W., Abdalla, I. A., Adetoun, B. S., Aditya, R. N., Agourram, H., & Akande, A. (1999). Culture specific and cross-culturally generalizable implicit leadership theories: Are attributes of charismatic/transformational leadership universally endorsed? *The Leadership Quarterly, 10*(2), 219–256.

Deresky, H. (2017). *International management: Managing across borders and cultures* (9th ed.). Pearson Education.

Dorfman, P., Javidan, M., Hanges, P., Dastmalchian, A., & House, R. (2012). GLOBE: A twenty year journey into the intriguing world of culture and leadership. *Journal of World Business, 47*(4), 504–518.

Dowling, P. J., Festing, M., & Engle, A. D. (2017). *International human resource management* (7th ed.). Cengage Learning EMEA.

Dulebohn, J. H., & Hoch, J. E. (2017). Virtual teams in organizations. *Human Resource Management Review, 27*(4), 569–574.

Fosslien, L., & West-Duffy, M. (2019). How to create belonging for remote workers *MIT Sloan Management Review*.

Furnham, A., Kirkcaldy, B. D., & Lynn, R. (1994). National attitudes to competitiveness, money, and work among young people: First, second, and third world differences. *Human Relations, 47*(1), 119–132.

Gardini, M. A. (2004). Internationalisierung von Dienstleistungen: Reflexionen zur Multikulturalität internationaler Dienstleistungskontexte. In M. A. Gardini & H. D. Dahlhoff (Eds.), *Management internationaler Dienstleistungen: Kontext—Konzepte—Erfahrungen* (1st ed., pp. 11–36). Gabler.

Gelade, G. A., Dobson, P., & Auer, K. (2008). Individualism, masculinity, and the sources of organizational commitment. *Journal of Cross-Cultural Psychology, 39*(5), 599–617.

18

Gerhart, B. (2009). How much does national culture constrain organizational culture? *Management and Organization Review, 5*(2), 241–259.
Graen, G. B. (2006). In the eye of the beholder: Cross-cultural lesson in leadership from project GLOBE: A response viewed from the third culture bonding (TCB) model of cross-cultural leadership. *Academy of Management Perspectives, 20*(4), 95–101.
Grönroos, C. (2015). *Service management and marketing: Managing the service profit logic* (4th ed.). Wiley.
Hall, E. T. (1976). *Beyond culture*. Anchor Books.
Hall, E. T., & Hall, M. R. (1990). *Understanding cultural differences: Germans, French, and Americans*. Intercultural Press.
Herrmann, D., Hüneke, K., & Rohrberg, A. (2012). *Führung auf Distanz: mit virtuellen Teams zum Erfolg* (2nd ed.). Springer Gabler.
Hill, C. W. L. (2021). *International business: Competing in the global marketplace* (13th ed.). McGraw-Hill Education.
Hill, N. S., & Bartol, K. M. (2018). Five ways to improve communication in virtual teams. *MIT Sloan Management Review (Fall 2018)*.
Hofstede, G., Hofstede, J. G., & Minkov, M. (2010). *Cultures and organizations: Software of the mind* (3rd ed.). McGraw Hill.
Ivanaj, S., & Bozon, C. (2016). *Managing virtual teams*. Edward Elgar Publishing.
Jarvenpaa, S. L., & Leidner, D. E. (1999). Communication and trust in global virtual teams. *Organization Science, 10*(6), 791–815.
Javidan, M., House, R. J., Dorfman, P. W., Hanges, P. J., & Sully de Luque, M. (2006). Conceptualizing and measuring cultures and their consequences: A comparative review of GLOBE's and Hofstede's approaches. *Journal of International Business Studies, 37*(6), 897–914.
Klimkeit, D. (2019). Global business services. *Intelligent Sourcing (Summer 2019)*, pp. 26–37.
Leung, K., Bhagat, R. S., Buchan, N. R., Erez, M., & Gibson, C. B. (2005). Culture and international business: Recent advances and their implications for future research. *Journal of International Business Studies, 36*(4), 357–378.
Liao, C. (2017). Leadership in virtual teams: A multilevel perspective. *Human Resource Management Review, 27*(4), 648–659.
Lin, C., Standing, C., & Liu, Y.-C. (2008). A model to develop effective virtual teams. *Decision Support Systems, 45*(4), 1031–1045.
Littrell, L. N., & Salas, E. (2005). A review of cross-cultural training: Best practices, guidelines, and research needs. *Human Resource Development Review, 4*(3), 305–334.
Malhotra, A., Majchrzak, A., & Rosen, B. (2007). Leading virtual teams. *Academy of Management Perspectives, 21*(1), 60–70.
Marlow, S. L., Lacerenza, C. N., & Salas, E. (2017). Communication in virtual teams: A conceptual framework and research agenda. *Human Resource Management Review, 27*(4), 575–589.
Nardon, L., & Steers, R. M. (2014). Managing cross-cultural encounters. *Organizational Dynamics, 2*(43), 138–145.
Peoples, J., & Bailey, G. (2018). *Humanity: An introduction to cultural anthropology*. Cengage Learning.
Schneider, S. C., Barsoux, J.-L., & Stahl, G. K. (2014). *Managing across cultures* (3rd ed.). Pearson.
Siebdrat, F., Hoegl, M., & Ernst, H. (2009). How to manage virtual teams. *MIT Sloan Management Review, 50*(4), 63–68.
Trompenaars, F., & Hampden-Turner, C. (2012). *Riding the waves of culture: Understanding diversity in global business* (3rd ed.). McGraw Hill.

## Further Reading

Ivanaj, S., & Bozon, C. (2016). *Managing virtual teams*. Edward Elgar. Publishing is a comprehensive guide to managing virtual teams.

Schneider, S. C., Barsoux, J.-L., & Stahl, G. K. (2014). *Managing across cultures* (3rd ed.). Pearson provides an excellent introduction to cross-cultural management.

# Correction to: Global Service Delivery and Project Management

**Correction to:**
**Chapter 15 in: D. Klimkeit et al., *International Management in Service Firms*, Classroom Companion: Business, https://doi.org/10.1007/978-3-031-50345-0_15**

This book was inadvertently published with an incorrect placement of Figures 15.10 and 15.11 and a Photo 15.2. It has been corrected in this version.

The updated version of this chapter can be found at
https://doi.org/10.1007/978-3-031-50345-0_15


D. Klimkeit et al., *International Management in Service Firms*, Classroom Companion: Business, https://doi.org/10.1007/978-3-031-50345-0_19

# Supplementary Information




D. Klimkeit et al., *International Management in Service Firms*, Classroom Companion: Business,
https://doi.org/10.1007/978-3-031-50345-0

# Index

## O



## P



## R



## S



## T



## V

GPSR Compliance

*The European Union's (EU) General Product Safety Regulation (GPSR) is a set of rules that requires consumer products to be safe and our obligations to ensure this.*

*If you have any concerns about our products, you can contact us on ProductSafety@springernature.com*

In case Publisher is established outside the EU, the EU authorized representative is:

Springer Nature Customer Service Center GmbH
Europaplatz 3
69115 Heidelberg, Germany

**Batch number: 10732064**

Printed by Printforce, the Netherlands